People and Computers XIX – The Bigger Picture

SIMON FRASER UNIVERSITY
W.A.C. BENNETT LIBRARY

Tom McEwan, Jan Gulliksen
and David Benyon (Eds)

People and Computers XIX – The Bigger Picture

Proceedings of HCI 2005

 Springer

Tom McEwan, MSc, PgCert, MBCS, CITP, Ceng, ILTM, SEDA-accredited teacher in HE
School of Computing, Napier University, Edinburgh, UK

Jan Gulliksen, MSc, PhD
Department of Information Technology/HCI, Uppsala University, Uppsala, Sweden

David Benyon, BSc, MSc, PhD
School of Computing, Napier University, Edinburgh, UK

Typeset by *Winder.*

British Library Cataloguing in Publication Data
A catalogue record for this book is available from the British Library

ISBN-10: 1-84628-192-X   Printed on acid-free paper
ISBN-13: 978-1-84628-192-1

Printed in the United Kingdom by Athenaeum Press Ltd., Gateshead

9 8 7 6 5 4 3 2 1

Springer Science+Business Media
springeronline.com

Contents

Closing Keynote of HCI2005: The Bigger Picture

Preface: The Bigger Picture

Human–Computer Interaction was once a narrowly focused discipline — the study of the interaction *between* human and computer — one of a new breed of multi-disciplines with its roots in ergonomics, cognitive psychology and so on. No-one thinks like that now. At the very least, the discipline concerns the interaction of humans *through* computers, with the technology put in its rightful place: a mediating artefact, between human and human, and between human and information, and between systems of activities undertaken by groups of humans in their cultural context. In this preface we summarize the content and structure of this volume, in the context of the conference and our keynote speakers.

We present here the bigger picture of HCI, a communal self-portrait of a multi-discipline that is now "all grown up" and making its way in the world. The relative youth and identity of HCI is a recurring theme. Mayes [1991] describes a discipline now past infancy, Shneiderman [2003] wonders whether HCI was child, adolescent or adult, Preece et al. [2002] sees Interaction Design as a discipline beyond HCI. It's twenty years since the first British HCI conference at the University of East Anglia. This is the 19th People and Computers volume. With two joint conferences (INTERACT'90 and INTERACT'99) this is our 21st birthday. We believe that that HCI has the "keys of door", is graduating from college and finding a role in industry and society. It makes all sorts of partnerships, some ill-advised and temporary (though perhaps exciting and memorable), some enduring (but perhaps a little less exciting).

This volume is snapshot of the best of current HCI. This is no longer just British HCI: the majority of the accepted papers are from overseas, with thirteen other countries represented here. (The Nordic nations are particularly present, a consequence of a conscious decision to involve the NordiCHI community in running this conference. This has been a delightful partnership — and many of its natives see Scotland as a Nordic nation anyway!).

Herein are the finest of over three hundred submissions for HCI2005: The Bigger Picture. This is substantially higher than in recent years, and left your editors and the programme committee with a considerable dilemma. Ninety-two 'full-paper' submissions were each subject to an average of four reviews by carefully matched experts from the formidable list of reviewers on Page xv. We are delighted to thank reviewers publicly for their huge contribution. The reviews were of a very high standard, often running to several pages of thoughtful appraisal and almost all were completed within a tight deadline. The reviews were then meta-reviewed by members of the programme committee, who prepared a detailed analysis for discussion. Conferences cannot run without an army of unpaid reviewers and committee members, and it is they that you, and we, must thank for this volume. Collectively our reviewers rated sixty-two full papers worthy of publication and the programme committee had a hard time cutting these back to the thirty we have space for here. We'd also like to thank unsuccessful submitters and offer them every encouragement in their work.

Past editors have wrestled with the challenge of straitjacketing papers into themes, and usually by the time of the conference we find little correlation between these themes and the conference session structure. In our call for papers, we mentioned a need to play around with the initials of HCI and so (very loosely) partition this volume into three sections — an 'H', a 'C' and an 'I', reflecting three levels of focus and three tracks running through the conference plan. Of course, most of these papers could validly appear in any of the three tracks, so we'd like you to view this structure in the context of the life's work of our eminent and legendary keynote — Ted Nelson, of the Oxford Internet Institute (who makes the final presentation of the opening day of the conference): this volume is a non-linear narrative best enjoyed in a hypermedia form (hence the accompanying CD-ROM and the post-it notes for your own annotation). Production schedules mean that our keynotes' papers generally appear in Volume 2 of the proceedings, this year published in http://eWiC.bcs.org, the emerging digital library of the British Computing Society, and Ted's own paper will appear there.

We start, as we should, with the 'H', with the human aspects and actions at the human scale. Fernaeus & Tholander (Sweden) discuss collaborative design using tangible interaction for children, while Read (UK) continues the child-centred theme, exposing usability flaws in digital ink for Tablet PCs, while identifying new opportunities for this emerging technology. Mohamedally et al. (UK) also report on the use of Tablet PCs, as well as the need for developers to use technology to mediate users' needs, describing tools that both permit lo-fi prototyping and allow designers to elicit knowledge from this process. This theme of listening continues with Strøm (Denmark), in the first of two contributions, who compares two other ways for software developers to listen to users' voices: stories and scenarios. We need smarter ways to engage with users and capture information efficiently for future use by developers and designers. At a more formal level of listening, Lumsden et al. (Canada) present a much-needed guide to using online questionnaires.

Of course, increasingly, users don't want to, or can't, articulate their needs, and design for ambient intelligence is a recurring theme in the conference this year. In this vein, Clerckx et al. (Belgium) take a step towards defining an integrated design environment for context-sensitive user interfaces, while Lonsdale et al. (UK) also look at awareness of location in a museum gallery space. Haywood & Cairns (UK) look at interaction in museums too, focusing on engagement and learning for children. Similarly, Mirel et al. (USA) help us understand complex, hard-to-elicit, needs, in this case of experts and how they use online models to carry out knowledge work and advise and create policy in e-government. Wong et al. (UK) also address our need for a much deeper understanding of usability in the public sector with a case study on the fitness for purpose of a public information kiosk for those most at risk in society. Some of these issues resurface in Renaud's (UK) study of visuo-biometric authentication for older users (which hopefully all of us eventually become).

Centring on the human, means focusing on one part of our bigger picture at a time. Shifting focus and attention, and zooming out and considering the whole display are amongst the research areas in which the conference opening keynote, Dr Mary Czerwinski of Microsoft has a formidable track record. There is no-one more appropriate to launch our theme of the Bigger Picture, and her paper will also appear in eWiC.

Our 'C' might stand for canvas, composition or context, but perhaps culture is a more encompassing theme. The challenge for systems designers is to create solutions that continue to work across cultures. We can learn much about this by considering HCI's own various cultures and the different between theory and practice. From the other end of the earth, Plimmer (New Zealand) has a timely reflection on HCI's place amongst other disciplines, and in particular within a small country, and in the preparation of learners for practice. Bark et al. (Norway/Sweden) identify the techniques that Nordic HCI practitioners actually use, and how useful they find each. Smith et al. (UK/Sweden/Ireland) continue the global flavour, and reflect on the evolutionary state of HCI in India and the partnerships that foster development. Chen et al. (USA) literally track HCI's own evolution and relationships within itself, with a citation analysis of a selection of HCI channels. Social network analysis is also intrinsic to Bonhard & Sasse (UK) with an HCI approach to the design of recommender systems, while Riegelsberger et al. (UK) continue this search for expertise, examining the relative richness of different interaction media and how this affects the degree of trust in advisers' expertise.

Three papers, linked by the theme of cultural dimensions, complete this section. Emotion and values are central to Dormann's (Canada) analysis of Web design, and she detects the position along Hofstede's MAS dimension of homepages in different countries. Strøm's (Denmark) second contribution compares interaction design decisions made in a low-income traditional country and in a high-income developed one, and identifies how to take different cultures' views of privacy and honesty into account. Ford & Kotzé (South Africa) concludes this section by finding limitations in cultural dimensions and identifies additional variables to take into account.

"What does the 'I' stand for anyway?" was a (very) early morning question from Dan Diaper at HCI2004, and a stimulus to our hermeneutic approach to the letters H, C and I. Certainly the answer includes Industry Day, the central day of the conference. At the time of writing we are just appearing on the operational horizons of senior industrialists, so cannot name our industrial keynotes here, but the strong formal industrial representation at British HCI conferences is an enduring and effective part of our tradition. Here, 'I' represents our home territory: interface, interactivity, interaction - aspects which other information technologists defer to us. Perhaps we take this for granted and forget that interface is where we often have the opportunity to hook stakeholders and keep their attention. It's the pixel level of our Bigger Picture. Every interface component has subtle shades of differentiation from previous elements, but the choice of the correct one provides the subtlety and shade required in analysis.

We start our rational disassembly of the senses (apologies to Rimbaud), with the haptic, and Raisamo et al. (Finland) contrasting detection thresholds for mouse and trackball, depending on the variation in either frequency or magnitude of feedback vibration, finding mouse and magnitude to be the most effective combination. We zoom in on the big picture with Jetter et al. (Germany) who extend existing table visualizations by introducing HyperGrid. The navigation of interaction space continues with Hansen et al. (Denmark) and MIXIS, turning a mobile phone with camera into a 3D navigation device. We then look at the interface's effect on the user: Awan & Stevens (UK) contrast the effects of static and animated diagrams in learners accurately assessing their acquired knowledge; Jacucci et al. (UK) find, in children's use of a tangible interface in video authoring, opportunities to exploit constraints to achieve creative outcomes. Juvina & Van Oostendorp (Netherlands) contrast the visual and auditory modalities for navigation support and find gender differences. Tzanidou et al. (UK), delve deeper into the visual in an analysis of web navigation and what this should mean for web design and e-commerce. Savage & Cockburn (New Zealand) report improved performance and reduced subjective workload with speed-dependent automatic zooming, while Hürst et al.'s (Germany) elastic audio slider provides intelligible audio feedback. Frauenberger et al. (UK/Austria) also focus on auditory interfaces, but use this to demonstrate mode-independent patterns of navigation.

As editors, we are especially pleased to welcome the final paper in this volume, the keynote address with which Professor Alistair Sutcliffe will close our conference. This is the first keynote that we have been able to include in volume 1 for several years and a testament to his organization and close involvement with the British HCI Group. This paper leads our community forward from this conference to face the grand challenges of the future.

This is the first return to Scotland for the conference this century, and the first since the Scottish parliament was restored. It coincides with a time when the contributions of the Edinburgh Enlightenment are widely re-evaluated. This period, roughly 1730-1780, coincided with enlightenments in other countries, but Edinburgh has a unique identity that still matters to HCI. This was a time when Scotland was free from the constraints of both church and crown, and before transportation, and then communication, enabled easy control from London. David Hume, Adam Smith and many others had space and time to think and could call upon the resources of four Scottish universities, as they formulated concepts fundamental to the modern world: economics, social sciences, affective components of technology and society. They were free to take a less orthodox view of the industrial revolution and to see the bigger picture of society — that people have a passion to achieve objectives, using whatever technology is at hand, and do so in a rich context of community, laws and division of labour.

The religious police of the time certainly found these ideas heretical, yet were unable to prevent a growing social desire for tolerance and an acceptance of the right not to conform to accepted wisdom. We hope our conference will share this mindset. Fundamentalist 'doctrines' have impeded the success of too many information and communication technology (ICT) systems but it's just as bad to simply identify a failure to apply HCI knowledge. As HCI comes into maturity, pointing out what's wrong is no longer enough, we need to take responsibility for creating the climate for solutions to emerge. Each of this conference's three sub-themes are relevant: a deeper understanding of how the human body interacts with technology; taking a wide enough picture of the overall context and recognising the role of cultural factors in certain combinations of situations and people; at the character-level of our bigger picture — where actions and activities take place on a human scale, individually or in groups, and where technology offers part of the solution not the problem.

Tom McEwan, Jan Gulliksen & David Benyon

June 2005

References

Mayes, T. [1991], Preface, *in* D. Diaper & N. Hammond (eds.), *People and Computers VI: Usability Now! (Proceedings of HCI'91)*, Cambridge University Press, pp.1–2.

Preece, J., Rogers, Y. & Sharp, H. (eds.) [2002], *Interaction Design: Beyond Human–Computer Interaction*, John Wiley & Sons.

Shneiderman, B. [2003], Foreword, *in* J. A. Jacko & A. Sears (eds.), *The Human–Computer Interaction Handbook: Fundamentals Evolving Technologies and Emerging Applications*, Lawrence Erlbaum Associates.

The Committee

Conference Chair	Tom McEwan *Napier University Edinburgh, UK*
Technical Chairs	David Benyon *Napier University Edinburgh, UK*
	Jan Gulliksen *Uppsala University, Sweden*
Webmaster	Marc Fabri *Leeds Metropolitan University, UK*
Short Papers	Olav Bertelsen *University of Aarhus, Denmark*
	Nick Bryan-Kinns *Queen Mary, University of London, UK*
Industry Day	Catriona Campbell *The Usability Company, UK*
	Lynne Coventry *NCR, UK*
Tutorials	Shaun Lawson *University of Lincoln, UK*
	Lars Oestreicher *Uppsala University, Sweden*
Workshops	Paul Cairns *University College London, UK*
	Peter Wild *University of Bath, UK*
Interactive Experiences	Morten Borup Harning *Open Business Innovation, Denmark*
	Adrian Williamson *Graham Technology plc, UK*
Doctoral Consortium	Ann Blandford *University College London, UK*
	Paul Curzon *Queen Mary, University of London, UK*
	Shailey Minocha *Open University, UK*
Posters	Lynne Baillie *Telecommunications Research Center, Austria*
	Marianne Graves-Petersen *University of Aarhus, Denmark*
Laboratory &	Andy Dearden *Sheffield Hallam University, UK*
Organisational Overviews	Dimitris Rigas *University of Bradford, UK*
Panels	Willem-Paul Brinkman *Brunel University, UK*
	Helen Sharp *Open University, UK*
HCI Educators Workshop	Janet Read *University of Central Lancashire, UK*
Treasurer	Sandra Cairncross *Napier University Edinburgh, UK*
Social Programme	Lachlan MacKinnon *University of Abertay Dundee, UK*
Publicity	Euan Dempster *University of Abertay Dundee, UK*
Exhibition Manager	Stephen Brockbank *Solas, UK*
Student Volunteers	Greg LePlatre *Napier University Edinburgh, UK*
Technical Support Manager	Brian Davison *Napier University Edinburgh, UK*
Conference Fringe	Dave Roberts *IBM United Kingdom Ltd, UK*
	Jane Morrison *Consultant, UK*
British HCI Group	Fintan Culwin *London South Bank University, UK*
Liaison Officer	
Previous Conference Chair	Janet Finlay *Leeds Metropolitan University, UK*

The Reviewers

Seffah Ahmed	*Concordia University, Canada*
Liz Allgar	*Leeds Metropolitan University, UK*
Ghassan Al-Qaimari	*University of Wollongong in Dubai, United Arab Emirates*
Francoise Anceaux	*University Valenciennes / CNRS-LAMIH-PERCOTEC, France*
Tue Haste Andersen	*University of Copenhagen, Denmark*
Mattias Arvola	*Linköpings Universitet, Sweden*
Chris Baber	*University of Birmingham, UK*
Lynne Baillie	*Forschungszentrum Telekommunikation Wien (FTW), Austria*
Sandrine Balbo	*University of Melbourne, Australia*
Gordon Baxter	*University of York, UK*
Russell Beale	*University of Birmingham, UK*
Roman Bednarik	*University of Joensuu, Finland*
Olav W Bertelsen	*University of Aarhus, Denmark*
Richard Boardman	*Google, USA*
Inger Boivie	*Uppsala University, Sweden*
Agnieszka Bojko	*User Centric Inc, USA*
Chris Bowerman	*University of Sunderland, UK*
Fiona Bremner	*General Dynamics Canada, Canada*
Stephen Brewster	*University of Glasgow, UK*
Willem-Paul Brinkman	*Brunel University, UK*
Nick Bryan-Kinns	*Queen Mary, University of London, UK*
Sandra Cairncross	*Napier University Edinburgh, UK*
Paul Cairns	*University College London, UK*
Luigina Ciolfi	*University of Limerick, Eire*
Gilbert Cockton	*University of Sunderland, UK*
Karin Coninx	*Limburgs Universitair Centrum, Belgium*
Jane-Lisa Coughlan	*Brunel University, UK*
Lynne Coventry	*NCR, UK*
Fintan Culwin	*London South Bank University, UK*
Daniel Cunliffe	*University of Glamorgan, UK*
Paul Curzon	*Queen Mary, University of London, UK*
Oscar de Bruijn	*University of Manchester, UK*
Andy Dearden	*Sheffield Hallam University, UK*
Euan Dempster	*Heriot-Watt University, UK*
Meghan Deutscher	*University of British Columbia, Canada*
Jean-Marc Dubois	*Université Victor Segalen Bordeaux 2, France*
Lynne Dunckley	*Thames Valley University, UK*

Mark Dunlop	*University of Strathclyde, UK*
Alistair Edwards	*University of York, UK*
Maximilian Eibl	*Technical University Chemnitz, Germany*
David England	*Liverpool John Moores University, UK*
Paul Englefield	*IBM United Kingdom Limited, UK*
Sue Fenley	*Reading University, UK*
Bob Fields	*Middlesex University, UK*
Sally Fincher	*University of Kent, UK*
Peter Fröhlich	*Forschungszentrum Telekommunikation Wien (FTW), Austria*
Peter Gardner	*University of Leeds, UK*
Claude Ghaoui	*Liverpool John Moores University, UK*
Gautam Ghosh	*Norway*
Joy Goodman	*University of Cambridge, UK*
Jan Gulliksen	*Uppsala University, Sweden*
Morten Borup Harning	*Dialogical ApS, Denmark*
Bo Helgeson	*Blekinge Institute of Technology, Sweden*
Elliott Hey	*IBM United Kingdom Ltd, UK*
Hans-Juergen Hoffmann	*Darmstadt University of Technology, Germany*
Kate Hone	*Brunel University, UK*
Kasper Hornbaek	*University of Copenhagen, Denmark*
Baden Hughes	*University of Melbourne, Australia*
Poika Isokoski	*University of Tampere, Finland*
Judith Jeffcoate	*University of Buckingham, UK*
Julius Jillbert	*Hasanuddin University, Indonesia*
Timo Jokela	*University of Oulu, Finland*
Matt Jones	*University of Waikato, New Zealand*
Charalampos Karagiannidis	*University of the Aegean, Greece*
Rene Keller	*University of Cambridge, UK*
Elizabeth Kemp	*Massey University, New Zealand*
Pekka Ketola	*Nokia Multimedia, Finalnd*
Alistair Kilgour	*Open University, UK*
Palle Klante	*OFFIS, Germany*
Paula Kotzé	*University of South Africa, South Africa*
Edward Lank	*San Francisco State University, USA*
Marta Lárusdóttir	*Reykjavik University, Iceland*
Effie Lai-Chong Law	*ETH Zürich, Switzerland*
Shaun Lawson	*University of Lincoln, UK*
Linda Little	*Northumbria University, UK*
Jo Lumsden	*National Research Council of Canada, Canada*
Catriona Macaulay	*Dundee University, UK*

Stuart MacFarlane	*University of Central Lancashire, UK*
Lachlan MacKinnon	*Heriot-Watt University, UK*
Robert Macredie	*Brunel University, UK*
Thomas Mandl	*Universität Hildesheim, Germany*
Phebe Mann	*Open University, UK*
Masood Masoodian	*University of Waikato, New Zealand*
Dr Rachel McCrindle	*University of Reading, UK*
Tom McEwan	*Napier University Edinburgh, UK*
David McGookin	*University of Glasgow, UK*
John Meech	*Human Factors Europe Ltd, UK*
Shailey Minocha	*Open University, UK*
Sunila Modi	*University of Westminster , UK*
David Moore	*Leeds Metropolitan University, UK*
David Morse	*Open University, UK*
Ali Asghar Nazari Shirehjini	*Fraunhofer-IGD, Germany*
Stuart Neil	*University of Wales Institute Cardiff, UK*
Nina Reeves	*University of Gloucestershire, UK*
Lars Oestreicher	*Uppsala University, Sweden*
Claire Paddison	*IBM United Kingdom Ltd, UK*
Volker Paelke	*University of Hannover, Germany*
Rodolfo Pinto da Luz	*Universidade Federal de Santa Catarina, Brazil*
Margit Pohl	*University of Technology Vienna, Austria*
Simon Polovina	*Sheffield Hallam University, UK*
Helen Purchase	*Glasgow University, UK*
Roope Raisamo	*University of Tampere, Finland*
Chris Raymaekers	*Hasselt University, Belgium*
Janet Read	*University of Central Lancashire, UK*
Irla Bocianoski Rebelo	*Federal University of Santa Catarina, Brazil*
Karen Renaud	*Glasgow University, UK*
Tony Renshaw	*Leeds Metropolitan University, UK*
Dimitris Rigas	*University of Bradford, UK*
Dave Roberts	*IBM United Kingdom Ltd, UK*
Tony Rose	*Cancer Research UK, UK*
Ian Ruthven	*University of Strathclyde, UK*
Eunice Ratna Sari	*TRANSLATE-EASY, Indonesia*
Robert Schumacher	*User Centric, Inc, USA*
Helen Sharp	*Open University / City University, UK*
Bhiru Shelat	*System Concepts, UK*
Sule Simsek	*University Of Missouri-Rolla, USA*
Frances Slack	*Sheffield Hallam University, UK*
Andy Sloane	*University of Wolverhampton, UK*

Georg Strøm   *University of Copenhagen, Denmark*
Desney Tan   *Microsoft Research, USA*
Anthony Tang   *University of British Columbia, Canada*
Adi Tedjasaputra   *TRANSLATE-EASY, Indonesia*
Phil Turner   *Napier University Edinburgh, UK*
Susan Turner   *Napier University Edinburgh, UK*
Katerina Tzanidou   *Open University, UK*
Mark Upton   *EDS, UK*
Colin C Venters   *University of Manchester, UK*
Robert Ward   *University of Huddersfield, UK*
Peter Wild   *University of Bath, UK*
Adrian Williamson   *Graham Technology, UK*
Michael Wilson   *CCLRC, UK*
William Wong   *Middlesex University, UK*
Panayiotis Zaphiris *City University, UK*

H — HCI at the Human Scale

II — HCI at the Human Scale

"Looking At the Computer but Doing It On Land": Children's Interactions in a Tangible Programming Space

Ylva Fernaeus & Jakob Tholander

Department of Computer and Systems Sciences, Stockholm University, Forum 100, 164 40 Kista, Sweden
Email: *ylva@dsv.su.se, jakobth@dsv.su.se*

We present a tangible programming space designed for children's collaborative construction of screen-based interactive systems. The design is based on three goals for interaction and activity: supporting co-located collaborative activity, screen-based execution, and what we call behaviour-based programming. Further, we analyse the interactions within a group of 10 year olds who used the system to create a live fantasy world together. The results show how the tangible resources shaped the activity of programming so that bodily actions and positioning became prominent. This is conceptualized through the notion of embodied programming, which highlights how programming activity must be understood through its interlinking to external resources and context.

Keywords: tangible interaction, physical programming, children and programming, interaction design and children, embodied interaction

1 Introduction

In designing interactive systems for children a significant challenge is to address ways of efficiently integrating technology with children's social, cultural and physical circumstances. One way of addressing these issue is by designing systems that allow for increased bodily and social engagement around technology [Crook 1997]. In HCI in general, the notion of 'embodied interaction' has been proposed as a theoretical foundation for understanding how these aspects may be further taken into account in design [Dourish 2001]. This notion is largely based on studies of activity and social interaction, where the concept of embodiment in meaning making practices has increasingly been emphasized [Goodwin 2000; Heath & Hindmarsh 2000]. Especially, this has been the case in ethnomethodological studies, where focus is on what people actually 'do' when interacting with computational artefacts [e.g. Suchman 1987; Heath & Luff 2000]. In such studies, 'embodiment' is used to refer to how bodily actions, such as gesture, gaze and physical positioning, in a significant sense play a part in meaning making and social interaction with technology. A basic assumption of such work is that representational forms are resources that structure people's actions and thereby shape the content of the activity that they engage in, and that activity changes along with changes of representations.

In HCI, the concept of embodiment is used also to describe tangible user interfaces (TUI). In Ullmer & Ishii's [1997] original conceptualization of TUIs, embodiment refer to how interface elements may take the form of physical objects, and hence work simultaneously as devices for input and output of computational processes. Lately, this notion has been further elaborated and relaxed, to refer to the degree of physical coupling between input and output devices [Fishkin 2004].

Hence, the concept of embodiment has at least two usages in HCI. One use is theoretically based in studies of social action and has been used to describe aspects of people's interaction with technology. The other is to describe more straightforwardly how tangible user interfaces are physically manifested.

In this paper, we are concerned with embodiment in the context of children's interaction when using new tools for building with computational media. This means that focus is on how children's everyday practices, as well as physical resources, may be incorporated into the activity of *programming*, which traditionally has been regarded as occurring mostly 'inside the machine' or, 'in one's head' [Norman 1993]. We conceptualize this through the notion of 'embodied programming', exemplified by a tangible programming space designed to allow for collaborative programming actions by a group of children in informal and playful settings.

The paper starts by laying out the goals for interaction that the system is based upon and a brief overview of the design activities out of which it emerged. Next is a short description of the programming space as it was finally implemented. Thereafter we present an analysis of the interactions within a group of 10-year olds while using the system to build an interactive fantasy world together. Finally, we discuss our results with respect to spaces for co-located interaction designed for children.

2   Designing for Children's Collaborative Dynamic Systems Construction

Particular for the screen-based, computational media is that it allows for creation of dynamic and interactive systems such as games, simulations and animated fantasy worlds. Systems such as these are parts of children's culture, and the ability to express oneself in this particular media is often referred to as an important literacy skill in contemporary culture [di Sessa 2000; Fernaeus et al. 2004; Snyder 2002]. Moreover, being able to create own dynamic systems, such as games, is something that many children would like to do. Yet, getting children to engage productively with the computational media has proven difficult to achieve in realistic school settings, as well as in more informal after-school clubs.

In studies involving children who build things on the computer, children are often encouraged to work in small groups [e.g. Kafai & Ching 2001; Suzuki & Kato 2002]. However, the resources that they have at hand are normally designed with the individual user in mind, rather than addressing the specific requirements of successful collaboration. In the analysis of children's interaction around computers, studies have shown that in collaborative settings children often spend considerable efforts in working around these circumstances [Crook 1997].

In our design work we aim to support the kind of interaction and sharing that is characteristic of children's everyday play activities, for instance when building and creating with materials such as sand, clay and Lego bricks. Important properties of such settings are that they allow for action and interaction to be performed concurrently, and that physical manipulation may be conducted jointly as well as individually. This relation between individual and collective activity for successful collaboration around technology has been emphasized for instance by Kaptelinin & Cole [2002]. Moreover, in their everyday play activities children continuously invent and reinvent the rules of the activity, and also reinterpret the meanings of the artefacts with which they play [Vygotsky 1976].

In the development of interactive systems for children, a current trend is to develop novel technologies that afford social and collaborative activity [Druin 1999]. In new interfaces for programming, these aspects are addressed through tools that support networked [Tisue & Wilensky 2004], as well as bodily and tangible forms of interaction [Suzuki & Kato 1995; Eisenberg et al. 2002; Montemayor et al. 2002; Wyeth & Purchase 2003; McNerny 2004]. With tangible programming tools, users are able to collaboratively make programs by manipulating physical objects that represent functions, objects and relations in the program.

We contribute to this research by presenting a shared physical programming space for children's collaborative and co-located creation of games, simulations and interactive fantasy worlds. The system is based on three basic goals for interaction and activity:

To support co-located collaborative activity. The system aims to support children to collaboratively engage in a shared endeavour of co-constructing interactive systems. To get this to happen, children need support in developing a common sense of ownership of what they are building, and also that the situation provides a rich supply of external resources, to which access is not constrained by physical limitations. Instead, rules and constraints in the activity should to a larger extent be defined through social participation in the group.

To allow for building of systems that run on a screen. We aim to support children's co-construction of screen-based systems, since it allows for a larger range of computational expressions than possible in tangible media. Other approaches to tangible programming are to use screen-based interfaces to control tangible constructions (e.g. Lego Mindstorms), or to use tangible objects to program other physical devices [McNerny 2004], or to simply let the arrangement of tangible objects control the behaviour of the objects themselves [Wyeth & Purchase 2003].

To support behaviour-based programming. In behaviour-based programming, programs are constructed by manipulating and reconfiguring elements that each represents parts of the behaviour of an object, for instance how it should move, or how it should act upon collision with other objects. This allows children to build systems that are rich in dynamic and interactive properties without having to engage too much with the details of the underlying code-syntax and algorithms.

These three goals for interaction have emerged both through our theoretical commitments in viewing cognition as an embodied phenomenon as well as through our work with groups of children using visual programming tools in ordinary PC-settings. Central in this work has been design for and studies of children:

1. Making programs by combining and reconfiguring readily prepared *behaviour objects* to create the functionality in their systems [Tholander et al. 2002].

2. Debugging and performance of existing programs using *collaborative role-play* activities away from the computer [Fernaeus & Tholander 2003].

Below is a short description of these two activities.

2.1 Staging Programming Activities with Children

Our previous work has shown that building programs through combining and reconfiguring readily prepared behaviour objects is appropriate for the targeted age groups to be able to practically realize the systems they want to build. To make use of pre-built pieces of existing programming code, and to combine these to create more complex behaviours of objects in interactive applications is used in many programming environments. However, most programming systems for children use rule-based models of programming, for example StageCast Creator [Smith & Cypher 1999; Smith et al. 2001] and Agentsheets [Repenning & Perrone 2001]. We have explored behaviour-based programming by letting children build systems in ToonTalk [Hoyles et al. 2002] and with paper-based programming prototypes [Fernaeus & Tholander 2003]. The behaviours can be attached to anything on screen, for instance a home drawn picture or a photograph of a clay figure created in school. The ability to have simple ways of controlling these pictures, for instance to make them jump with the arrow keys, is often more in line with what the children want to pursue with the programming activities than to engage with the lower levels of rule-based programming.

An important part of this work has been to develop libraries of different kinds of behaviours and to package them as sets of running examples called Anima Gadgets (for game programming) and Animal Gadgets (for making eco systems simulations). The selection of predefined behaviours can be tailored for a range of different activities such as programming of games, dynamic simulations, or fantasy worlds. The expressiveness of the programming material then depends more on what pre-built behaviours that have been prepared and how these can be combined and reconfigured, than on the properties of the underlying programming language [Tholander et al. 2002].

2.2 Collaborative Role-play Activities

An important part of our activities with children has been collaborative simulated execution of games away from the computer. These activities have turned out to be fun and sociable way of supporting children in externalizing their ideas and collaboratively think about behaviours, relations and interactions between objects in the system.

In these activities a group of children collaboratively act out the functionality of a system that they are currently developing on the computer, as a way of discussing, test running, and debugging its functionality. The activities are modelled after the set of behaviours available in the programming environment, and all the materials used in the activity, such as behaviour cards and pictures, correspond to the resources that the children have available when programming on the computer.

When conducting such an activity, clay figures or large paper elements representing objects in the computational system are arranged on an area such as the floor or a table serving as the background. One or several persons are assigned the role of users, and the rest get assigned the responsibility for the execution of one or a small set of programming rules in the system, for instance that of removing an object from a game if it collides with another object. The system is played by iteratively and collaboratively evaluating all the rules/behaviours in the system. In each iteration the children perform their actions if the conditions for their behaviours are fulfilled. The activities normally start out from games and systems running on the computer, and during such activities, the systems are often 'reprogrammed' in several variations.

3 Design of the Programming Space

The basic concept for the tangible programming space is to allow for behaviour-based programming in a social setting, similar to that of the role-play activities described above. Our design process has involved explorations and user-studies of low-fidelity prototypes made with paper and clay as well as hands-on explorations of various resources for actually implementing the tangible system. This differs in many ways from participatory design approaches that have become dominant in research concerning interaction design and children [Druin & Fast 2002]. Instead, our approach to user involvement is to stage activities aiming to engage children in productively using technology. Based on analysis of such activities we further develop and refine our designs.

The system takes the shape of a physical space, (see Figure 1) equipped with a number of tangible resources laid out on a surface on the floor. The tangible resources are used to manipulate the looks and the behaviour of visual objects displayed on a screen projected on a wall. Figure 1 shows the physical setup of the system, consisting of:

1. A large white plastic mat with 14×14 wirelessly identifiable position tags underneath.

2. A set of plastic programming cards.

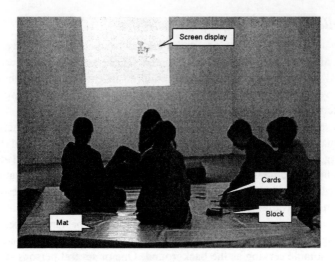

Figure 1: The setup of the programming space.

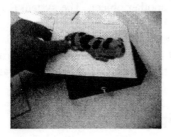 

Figure 2: Programming cards: Picture and behaviour cards placed on the creator blocks on top of the mat.

3. Several tangible creator blocks that are wirelessly connected to the software on the computer.

4. A visual display showing the system that is being built.

The system includes a construction mode and an execution mode. In the construction mode, three types of basic actions can be performed: New objects (pictures) can be added to the display, behaviours can be added to existing objects on the display, and existing objects can be deleted. It is also possible to load and to save existing game configurations. In execution mode the objects on the screen start acting according to the behaviours that have been attached with them.

The *creator blocks* connect the physical system with its virtual representation. When users interact with the system, they add objects and behaviours to the on-the screen representation by simply placing cards on top of the creator blocks (see Figure 2). A rectangle moves on the screen in correspondence to how the creator block is moved on the mat. The position of the creator blocks and the id of the cards

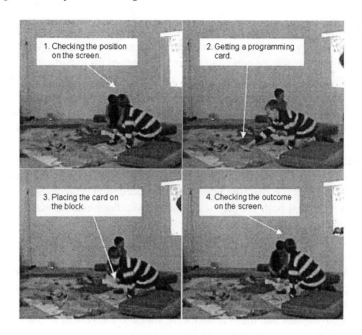

Figure 3: Typical steps taken when adding things to the display.

placed on them are wirelessly communicated to the software running on the host computer.

There are two kinds of *programming cards*: pictures and behaviour cards. Picture cards are used to place new objects at specific locations on the screen, while the behaviour cards are used to specify the functionality of objects that have already been added. To add a new picture at a specific location, a picture card is placed on top of the creator block. Behaviours are added to existing objects by first make sure the creator block is at a position where there is an object and then putting a *behaviour card* on top of it (see Figure 3). Behaviour cards consist of a set of behaviours for movement, collisions, user interaction, and for making objects belong to specific groups.

Control cards are cards for controlling the system, such as running, stopping and saving a game or simulation. When placing an empty card on top of a reader, the current game setup is logically saved onto that card. Once this card is read again by a reader, the game stored 'on' the card is displayed on the screen.

4 Children's Interaction in the Programming Space

This section presents an analysis of a group of children interacting within the programming space. The study involved five 10-year-old children who worked for three two-hour sessions building an interactive world together. The study was set-up to provide input on the design following our principles of staging productive activities with children. This has turned out to be a good way of understanding and analysing design issues in settings where children become familiar with the technology, thereby attempting to avoid potential novelty effects. All the children came from the same school class and voluntarily signed up to participate during the autumn break. The study took place in an art gallery, and ended with a public event where the group presented their work to friends, family and others.

When introducing the technology to the children, we explained that it could be used for a number of different scenarios such as making of games, simulations of food webs, and to make illustrations of other school oriented issues. After this introduction, the children were intentionally left to work mostly on their own. The role of the researchers was to make sure that the technology worked properly and to generally support the children whenever they needed assistance. The only given restrictions were that both the physical space on the floor and the screen should be part of what they created. A significant part of the work took place at the table where the children created characters, objects, and surfaces in modelling clay, cloth and plastic. The children built a world on top of the mat using the different materials they had at hand. A photo of the world was added as a background image for the visual display. The children also sketched out the central elements of the narrative on a whiteboard where one of them acted as script and lead the discussion. Photos of the physical objects that they created were added to the system so that the pictures were associated to corresponding new picture cards.

The behaviour cards used in the study consisted of a small set of simple behaviours for movement, colours and collisions. The colour cards were used to logically group objects into different 'teams', as a way of specifying types of objects and how those would interact with other types of objects. These worked together with the collision behaviours for 'eating', e.g. adding the 'eat green' behaviour to an object would make another object with the colour green to disappear upon collision. There was also a 'wall'-behaviour, which made objects impossible to pass by other objects.

The project that the children finally ended up with took the form of an interactive story that they named 'Desert City'. The story was set in a desert landscape with a jungle, sand dunes, a cave, an oasis, and a city surrounded by a wall. The plot of the story was that a baby Bedouin was chased by the evil Dracula who lived in a cave in the jungle. The baby was living inside the city and was guarded by its parents and other friendly people. There was only one place to enter the city through the city wall. In the jungle there were palm trees with coconuts and oranges that the people in the jungle lived on. There were also threats towards Dracula such as a leopard and a poisonous snake. Figure 4 shows the invitation that the children wrote to describe their project to the visitors of the exhibition. On the invitation they also included a screen-shot of the system.

5 Interaction Resources in Design and Programming

Two digital video cameras were used to film the entire workshop. We analysed the video material using Interaction Analysis [Jordan & Henderson 1995] in which talk, interaction, and artefacts are focused upon. In the analysis of the children's activities with and around the system we investigated their use of the different interactive

Come to Kista+Konst and play
at 1–3 pm on Saturday 13th of November
Desert City is almost like a game made by Carl, Ivan, Nawar, Niki, and Sebastian.
In forth grade in Eriksbergsskolan.
You will get to see a game present on both computer and on the floor.
Ylva and Jakob and company have helped us build this game world.
We have worked with fabrics, modelling clay, a mat on the floor and computer thingamajigs. We look at the computer but we do it on land.

Figure 4: Children's description and a screen-shot of the Desert City when playing.

resources they had at hand. Issues that we found particularly prominent in their interactions were: first, the physicality of the programming cards, second, their use of the virtual and physical space for sharing and coordination of actions, and three, how they blended social rules of play with construction of computational rules.

5.1   The Physicality of Programming Resources

The children made use of the programming cards in a range of different ways throughout the activity. The most obvious use was of course to program the objects and characters to be included in the system. However, the children also extensively incorporated their cards in a number of additional ways. For instance, when discussing and negotiating alternative designs of objects and of the physical space where the city was laid out, they often used the cards to demonstrate their ideas to each other. This could include the behaviours they wanted to use for a particular idea, or how they saw relations between different objects in their imagined city. For instance, in Figure 5, the girl is demonstrating to her friend how the two cards she is holding should be related in the game. Hence, the tangible forms of representation of the programming objects afforded a range of actions that were of a rather different kind than mere programming actions. Thereby, in thinking and negotiating about the design of the system, the cards were a primary resource.

A related finding concerns the relation between design decisions regarding the story and the actions required to actually implement these in the system. Through the ways the children used the cards throughout the activity, the boundaries

Figure 5: "This one is protected by this one" — demonstrating ideas by using programming cards.

between design, programming and implementation of objects became blurred. The fact that the cards were involved in brainstorming, negotiations, and discussions about the design, blurred the distinction between actually programming the system and designing it. In several cases when no creator block was available the children instead made design decisions and then collected the cards needed for the implementation in a stack that they placed on the mat. Thereby, all the necessary decisions regarding the design as well as programming of the objects had already been taken, even though the actual implementation of the objects still remained. The action of placing the cards on the creator blocks were often a mere practicality while the important work were conducted elsewhere. This stands in contrast to programming with tools such as Stagecast Creator and ToonTalk where the particular actions involved in implementing a system often plays a more significant role in the activity [e.g. Rader et al. 1997].

5.2 Shared Spaces for Joint Activity

Another resource for interaction that the children used throughout the workshop was their bodies and how they were physically positioned on the mat. The fact that the programming space was laid out as carpet on the floor that several children could sit around, and even walk on, significantly influenced the sense making practice that the children engaged in. The physicality of the programming space allowed the children to socially interact in ways that are hard to see when programming in traditional desktop settings. The snapshots in Figure 6 are taken from a sequence where three parallel activities had been going on for some time. In this example, one of the children stands up and walks over to the other side of the mat. By physically relocating himself, he also partly contributed to shifting the focus of the conversation and allowed for him to take part in another aspect of the fantasy world under construction.

An observation related to the previous one regards how the children organized themselves throughout the activity. Repeatedly, they divided into 'subgroups' (consisting of one or more children) that performed parallel activities. However, these were not conducted in isolation from each other but extensively involved

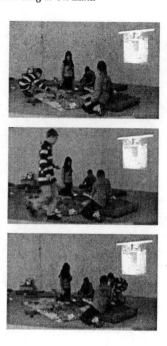

Figure 6: Moving from the 'desert' to the 'city wall'.

Figure 7: All looking at the shared space (left) leading one of the boys to hand over a card to his friend (right).

interactions across the different subgroups. An important trigger to these interactions was the possibility of actually seeing the actions performed by the others on the mat. Moreover, also the projection on the wall worked as a shared space where the programming actions of the others became available. References to the projection often triggered interactions such as telling someone that a behaviour was missing, discussing the rules of the game they were building, or simply handing over a card that one assumed that someone needed (see Figure 7). Shifting between and referring to these two different shared interactive surfaces became central in the activity.

Another aspect important of our observations was the possibility of working individually as well as collectively. With a setting that does not allow for parallel

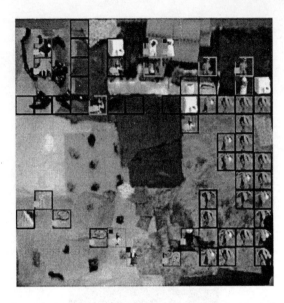

Figure 8: Screen-shot of the display when in programming mode.

activities, it becomes difficult to distinguish the individual from the collective. The ability to make this distinction could be seen for instance in referring to parts of the system as 'ones own'. We believe that this was used by the children both for developing a sense of personal ownership, and also to get the sense of being a part in a shared endeavour.

5.3   Negotiation of Social Rules

Already a few minutes into the first session when still just exploring the technology, the children divided into groups and agreed upon rules for the activity that each group had to follow. These included how many characters each team could construct, what behaviours they were allowed to use, and what colours their characters were allowed to have. The rules for the activity were stated as "You get three players, and we get three players" which they continuously monitored as indicated by statements like "He is cheating". The rules of the activity were also continuously refined as suggested by "Okay let's have five players instead" when somebody added more than the agreed upon number of characters. Hence, these social rules that the children created involved many aspects beyond the joint creation of a shared fantasy world.

Figure 8 shows how the screen display of the final version of the Desert City looked when in programming mode. All the characters and objects in the system have been assigned a colour by the children (displayed as a surrounding square). This assignment of colours follows a strict system of rules that the children came up with on their own. 'Good' characters and objects have been assigned the colour 'green', evil ones were given the colour 'red', and 'blue' was used for things considered as 'food' in their fantasy world. Black was the colour used for walls.

The coloured squares on top of the characters represent different movement and collision behaviours. Throughout the activity, while constructing the game and before executing a different version they checked that the characters and behaviour did not break these rules that they had set up for the activity.

By creating social rules for how they should jointly interact with and around the system they made the interaction with the system highly collaborative. The social rules also enhanced the activity to go beyond that of only using the system.

This allowed them to involve social elements of play into the construction activity itself. For instance, at several instances, the children hid cards from each other so that it would not be possible for the others to add a particular behaviour to some of 'their' characters. By hiding a card, the children could actually hide a piece of programming code from their friends, which is an action that would be quite peculiar to support in a desktop application. However, this was not an immediate design choice on our behalf. Instead, the possibility of such actions arises as a consequence of giving the programming code a physical manifestation in the form of plastic cards. This contributed to the possibility for the children to define and negotiate their own social rules for how the activity should be conducted, which was important in creating the social grounds needed for achieving a truly collaborative activity.

6 Concluding Remarks

In this paper, we have used the notion of 'embodied programming' to emphasize the importance of investigating and understanding new possibilities for action and social interaction that physical and tangible forms of computation may afford. We have presented a tangible programming space that allows groups of children to collaboratively create dynamic systems to run on a computer screen. The design is based on three basic goals for interaction and activity, all based on our experiences from working with children building systems in traditional PC settings. These goals were:

1. Supporting co-located collaboration.

2. To allow for screen-based execution.

3. To allow for what we call behaviour-based programming.

By investigating how children actually 'do' programming when interacting in the space, a number of important elements were found that relate to key aspects for research in physical and tangible interfaces. In this case, this regards the involvement of bodily actions and social practices into the activity, which structured the character of the activity to become essentially different from similar tasks conducted in a traditional PC setting. We have been given particular emphasis to three aspects that we found important to the collaborative aspects of the activity: *the tangible resources, the physical surfaces and shared spaces, and the involvement of social rules.*

The restricted and computationally active area on the floor together with the screen projection worked as a shared place around which the children could orient their actions. This, together with the physicality of the programming cards provided a richer set of resources for giving account of one's actions to others, which is often difficult in virtual collaborative workspaces [Heath & Hindmarsh 2000]. Hence these were central resources for achieving a sense of sharing and collaboration throughout the activity.

Moreover, the physical properties of the design allowed children to create a highly personal interactive fantasy world. They extensively incorporated elements from their social play practices into the activity of constructing a system together, by blending rules of play with rules constructed in the computational system. Game construction thus became a sub-element of the larger activity where virtual, physical and social aspects played a part. The social setting in combination with the tangible properties of the system provided possibility for children to engage in a collaborative activity that would be difficult to achieve in a traditional PC setup.

The particular focus of this paper has been on interaction related to the activity of programming. However, our results have implications for the design of technologies for co-located collaborative interaction in a more general sense as well. Through the interaction and construction available with tangible interfaces with this kind of properties we can provide possibilities for children to build their own bridges between physical and virtual objects through playful collaborative activity. Our work has illustrated how children's everyday play practices can be a valuable resource when designing systems for collaboration.

Acknowledgement

We would like to thank Christopher Balanikas, Martin Jonsson and Johan Mattsson for helping us to implement and stabilize the different components of the programming space, and also Ulla West for inviting us to perform the study at the Kista+Konst art gallery, and also for assisting us in our work throughout the study.

References

Crook, C. [1997], Children as Computer Users: the Case of Collaborative Learning, *Computers & Education* **30**(3-4), 237–47.

di Sessa, A. [2000], *Changing Minds: Computers, Learning, and Literacy*, MIT Press.

Dourish, P. [2001], *Where the Action Is: The Foundations of Embodied Interaction*, MIT Press.

Druin, A. (ed.) [1999], *The Design of Children's Technology*, Morgan-Kaufmann.

Druin, A. & Fast, C. [2002], The Child as Learner, Critic, Inventor and Technology Design Partner: An Analysis of Three Years of Swedish Student Journals, *The International Journal for Technology and Design Education* **12**(3), 189–213.

Eisenberg, M., Eisenberg, A., Gross, M., Kaowthumrong, K., Lee, N. & Lovett, W. [2002], Computationally-enhanced Construction Kits for Children: Prototype and Principle, *in* G. Stahl (ed.), *Proceedings of International Conference of the Learning Sciences*, Lawrence Erlbaum Associates, pp.79–85.

Fernaeus, Y., Aderklou, C. & Tholander, J. [2004], Computational Literacy at Work, Children's Interaction with Computational Media, *in* D. Kinshuk, G. Sampson & P. Isaías (eds.), *Proceedings of IADIS International Conference Cognition and Exploratory Learning in Digital Age (CELDA 2004)*, IADIS Press, pp.181–8.

Fernaeus, Y. & Tholander, J. [2003], Collaborative Computation on the Floor, *in* B. Wasson, R. Baggetun, U. Hoppe & S. Ludvigsen (eds.), *Proceedings of Computer Support for Collaborative Learning CSCL2003*, InterMedia, pp.65–7.

Fishkin, K. P. [2004], A Taxonomy for and Analysis of Tangible Interfaces, *Personal and Ubiquitous Computing* **8**(5), 347–358.

Goodwin, C. [2000], Action and Embodiment within Situated Human Interaction, *Journal of Pragmatics* **32**(10), 1489–522.

Heath, C. & Hindmarsh, J. [2000], Embodied Reference: A Study of Deixis in Workplace Interaction, *Journal of Pragmatics* **32**(10), 1855–78.

Heath, C. & Luff, P. [2000], *Technology in Action*, Cambridge University Press.

Hoyles, C., Noss, R. & Adamson, R. [2002], Rethinking the Microworld Idea, *Journal of Educational Computing Research* **27**(1), 29–53.

Jordan, B. & Henderson, A. [1995], Interaction Analysis: Foundation and Practice, *Journal of Learning Science* **4**(1), 39–103.

Kafai, Y. & Ching, C. C. [2001], Affordances of Collaborative Software Design Planning for Elementay Student's Science Talk, *Journal of Learning Science* **10**(3), 323–63.

Kaptelinin, V. & Cole, M. [2002], Individual and Collective Activities in Educational Computer Game Playing, *in* T. D. Koschmann, R. Hall & N. Miyake (eds.), *CSCL 2: Carrying Forward the Conversation*, Computers, Cognition & Work, Lawrence Erlbaum Associates, pp.303–16.

McNerny, T. S. [2004], From turtles to Tangible Programming Bricks: Explorations in Physical Language Design, *Personal and Ubiquitous Computing* **8**(5), 326–37.

Montemayor, J., Druin, A., Farber, A., Simms, S., Churaman, W. & D'Amour, A. [2002], Physical Programming: Designing Tools for Children to Create Physical Interactive Environments, *in* D. Wixon (ed.), *Proceedings of SIGCHI Conference on Human Factors in Computing Systems: Changing our World, Changing Ourselves (CHI'02)*, *CHI Letters* **4**(1), ACM Press, pp.299–306.

Norman, D. A. [1993], Cognition in the Head and in the World: An Introduction to the Special Issue on Situated Action, *Cognitive Science* **17**(1), 1–6.

Rader, C., Brand, C. & Lewis, C. [1997], Degrees of Comprehension: Children's Understanding of a Visual Programming Environment, *in* S. Pemberton (ed.), *Proceedings of the SIGCHI Conference on Human Factors in Computing Systems (CHI'97)*, ACM Press, pp.351–8.

Repenning, A. & Perrone, C. [2001], Programming by Analogous Examples, *in* H. Lieberman (ed.), *Your Wish Is My Command: Programming by Example*, Morgan-Kaufmann, pp.351–70.

Smith, D. C., Cypher, A. & Tesler, L. [2001], Novice Programming Comes of Age, *in* H. Lieberman (ed.), *Your Wish Is My Command: Programming by Example*, Morgan-Kaufmann, pp.7–20.

Smith, D. C. & Cypher, A. [1999], Making Programming Easier for Children, *in* Druin [1999], pp.202–21.

Snyder, I. [2002], *Silicon Literacies: Communication, Innovation and Education in the Digital Age*, Routledge.

Suchman, L. A. [1987], *Plans and Situated Actions — The Problem of Human–Machine Communication*, Cambridge University Press.

Suzuki, H. & Kato, H. [1995], Interaction-level Support for Collaborative Learning: AlgoBlock — An Open Programming Language, *in* J. L. Schnase & E. L. Cunnius (eds.), *Proceedings of Computer Supported Collaborative Learning CSCL 1995*, Lawrence Erlbaum Associates, pp.349–55.

Suzuki, H. & Kato, H. [2002], Identity Formation/Transformation as a Process of Collaborative Learning of Programming Using AlgoArena, *in* T. D. Koschmann, R. Hall & N. Miyake (eds.), *CSCL 2: Carrying Forward the Conversation*, Computers, Cognition & Work, Lawrence Erlbaum Associates, pp.275–96.

Tholander, J., Kahn, K. & Jansson, C.-G. [2002], Real Programming of an Adventure Game by an 8-year-old, *in* P. Bell, R. Stevens & T. Satwicz (eds.), *Keeping Learning Complex: Proceedings of Fifth Second International Conference on the Learning Sciences (ICLS 2002)*, Lawrence Erlbaum Associates. Available at http://www.dsv.su.se/research/kids/pdf/RealProgInICLSTemplate.pdf (last accessed 2006-06-11).

Tisue, S. & Wilensky, U. [2004], NetLogo: A Simple Environment for Modeling Complexity, *in Proceedings of International Conference on Complex Systems*. Proceedings not yet published but paper avaialble at http://ccl.northwestern.edu/papers/netlogo-iccs2004.pdf (last accessed 2005-05-31).

Ullmer, B. & Ishii, H. [1997], Tangible Bits: Towards Seemless Interfaces Between People, Bits and Atoms, *in* S. Pemberton (ed.), *Proceedings of the SIGCHI Conference on Human Factors in Computing Systems (CHI'97)*, ACM Press, pp.234–41.

Vygotsky, L. S. [1976], Play and its Role in the Mental Development of the Child, *in* J. S. Bruner, A. Jolly & K. Sylva (eds.), *Play: Its Role in Development and Evolution*, Penguin, pp.461–3.

Wyeth, P. & Purchase, H. C. [2003], Using Developmental Theories to Inform the Design of Technology for Children, *in* S. MacFarlane, T. Nicol, J. Read & L. Snape (eds.), *Proceedings of Interaction Design and Children*, ACM Press, pp.93–100.

The Usability of Digital Ink Technologies for Children and Teenagers

Janet C Read

Child Computer Interaction Group, University of Central Lancashire, Preston PR1 2HE, UK

Tel: *+44 1727 893285*

Fax: *+44 1772 894913*

Email: *jcread@uclan.ac.uk*

URL: *http://www.chici.org*

This paper describes an empirical study that considered the usability of digital pens, Tablet PCs, and laptop PCs for handwritten text input by young users. The study was carried out in two parts, firstly with young children aged 7 and 8, and then with older children aged 12 and 13. The study found that digital pens were particularly well suited to older children and that the both sets of children were able to use the Tablet PC without too many errors. Digital ink technologies are often evaluated by the calculation of recognition rates and this paper exposes some of the flaws in the process of estimating recognition rates from activities involving the copying of text. With particular reference to the personalization of text, possibilities for the use of digital ink for the task of writing are explored and a new interaction, digital doodling, is presented.

Keywords: teenagers, children, usability, empirical study, digital pens, Tablet PC, handwriting recognition, digital doodles, evaluation.

1 Introduction

In the book Human–Computer Interaction in the New Millennium, John Carroll describes HCI as:

> The study and practice of usability. It is about understanding and creating software and other technology that people will want to use, will be able to use and will find effective when used. [Carroll 2002]

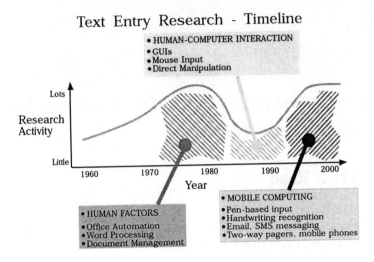

Figure 1: Text entry timeline [MacKenzie & Soukoreff 2002b].

This aligns closely with the three requirements for product success that are proposed by Dix et al. [2003], these being for products to be used (attractive, engaging, fun), usable (easy to use), and useful (accomplish what is required).

These 'permanent' definitions of HCI effectively dictate the landscape upon which HCI is painted. The detail within the HCI community changes over time with different aspects of interaction gaining favour and momentum at the expense of others. Pattern languages, Web interaction, task analysis, and mobile technology are all examples of issues that have drifted in and out of favour over the years.

The study of the usability of text input methods and specifically the effectiveness of different text entry methods is one area of research that has moved in and out of fashion. The timeline in Figure 1 shows how changes in interest in this area have primarily resulted from the arrival of new technologies [MacKenzie & Soukoreff 2002b].

The growth in sales of pen-based systems and the improved functionality of handwriting recognition are both important developments with respect to text entry research. When text is captured using a stylus on a Tablet PC or by the use of a digital pen, a new method for interaction is available. The handwritten text can be manipulated and stored without recognition or can be converted into ASCII text using handwriting recognition software.

The people that interact with technology have also changed over time. Over the last 20 years, the user population has expanded to include a wide range of people including children, older people and people with sensory and motor disabilities. Children are an interesting user group, they represent the only user group that is ageing in a positive way, their acquisition of skills and knowledge is rapid and their motivation for using computers is very different from the work place adult user.

Figure 2: Roles of children in interactive product development [Druin 2002].

The investigation of children and their impact at different stages of product development as shown in Figure 2 has resulted in the emergence of a new discipline, Child Computer Interaction (CCI) [Read 2005]. This discipline takes its roots from a few early pioneers Frye & Soloway [1987], Solomon [1978], and Kafai [1990] and owes much of its current impetus to the design work by Druin [1999] and the vision of Bekker et al. [2002] in instigating a dedicated conference series.

1.1 Motivation for the Research

Twenty years ago it was highly unusual for a child to be doing text input at a machine but nowadays children spend a considerable time at the computer, inputting short and lengthier text via a range of different applications ranging from the search bar in Google, through the chat interface of MSN to the familiar Microsoft Word word processing package. It is common for children to be expected to word-process schoolwork, often creating the first draft using pen and paper and then typing up the final version for assessment or display.

For adult users, prolonged keyboard use is known to cause muscle ailments, stress injuries, and eyestrain [Thelen 1996]. Children are using the same technologies as adults with little regard for any long-term effects of computer text input by children, whether that is at a keyboard, on a mobile phone keypad, or by some other method. The effect of prolonged computer use on the eyesight and posture of children was known in the early nineties with Palmer [1993] reporting vision problems and Weikart [1995] detailing muscle disorders. More subtle affects, such as the impact of computer text creation on the language and understanding of children have been less well explored. The creation of text using digital pen and ink technologies may reduce some of these problems.

1.2 The Research Study

The work described in this paper is an exploration of the usability of three pen based digital ink text input methods for children. It begins with an overview of text entry and then goes on to explore some alternative text entry technologies including descriptions of handwriting with a stylus on a Tablet PC, handwriting with a graphics tablet and pen on a standard PC, and handwriting with a digital pen on digital paper. The paper then provides an overview of the methods that are commonly used for the evaluation of text input technologies.

An empirical study is then presented that explores the usability of the three digital ink technologies with two distinct user groups; one was a group of seven and eight year old children, the other a group of twelve and thirteen year old children.

The paper concludes with a discussion of the results, and a discussion of some emerging issues.

2   Computer Text Input for Children

There are good reasons for encouraging children to engage in computer text input. Writing text in emails, for instance is known to help children understand the notion of writing for an audience [Garvey 2002] and is also seen to be liberating as emails can be *'written in any style'* and *'allow children to explore their inner voice'* [Turrell 1999]. Written work produced at a computer can be made to look good, thus motivating poor writers [Day 1994], and computers allow the representation of ideas in dynamic forms, provide improved feedback to pupils, and allow information to be easily altered [Moseley et al. 1999].

Traditionally, text is input to a computer using an alphabetic keyboard. These keyboards can be arranged in different ways with the most common presentation being the QWERTY keyboard that lays the characters out in the same way as the early typewriters. The action of using a keyboard for text entry is occasionally referred to as keyboarding, but as the term keyboarding also refers to the mastery and use of electronic organs, in this paper, the action of entering text, is described as typing.

The process of typing can be broken into five phases, these are, character recognition, storage, motor activity, keystroke and feedback [Cooper 1983]. Character recognition is when the typist recognizes the letter on the keyboard, storage is the process by which the typist is able to be reading ahead (possibly four to eight characters at a time for experienced adults), the motor activity is the movement of the fingers to the keys, the keystroke is the pressure needed to press the key and the feedback is essential for error detection and correction (this could be omitted or could be made to happen later, for example with blind users who may have the text read back to them at a later time).

It is possible to become quite skilled at the alphabetic keyboard; but many people, and particularly children, find typing difficult [Norman & Fisher 1982]. The layout of the keyboard makes high demands on short-term memory and poor motor control can also limit keyboard efficiency as children may 'miss' the appropriate key, hold it down for too long, or fail to press it sufficiently.

2.1   Alternatives to the Keyboard

The most commonly found alternatives to the alphabetic keyboard are the reduced keyboards (as seen on mobile phones) and the recognition technologies of speech and handwriting. Text entry at a mobile phone is a specialist area of research and is not explored here in any detail; readers are directed to the work by MacKenzie & Soukoreff [2002b] for a full treatment of this area.

The two recognition technologies are essentially quite similar; the user communicates by speaking or writing and this is captured by the hardware and then digitized. The digitized speech or writing is then converted into ASCII (or similar) representation by the application of recognition algorithms, sound, word or character matching, and in some instances, the application of language models. These recognition processes are error prone both at the point of capture and at the point of recognition [Plamondon & Srihari 2000]. Speech recognition is problematic for children as their speech is immature and young children are often unable to read the training text that is needed to individualize (train) the recognition algorithms. Work by the author has established that speech recognition without training is highly error prone with children [Read et al. 2001].

Handwriting recognition software is reasonably robust and can be used without individualization; earlier work by the authors has established that there is scope for its use with child users [Read et al. 2004]. To use handwriting recognition for text input there is a need for technology that can support the capture of the written text and software to carry out the recognition.

2.2 The Usability of Digital Ink Technologies

The effectiveness or usefulness of handwriting recognition interfaces is generally measured by determining the accuracy of the recognition process. This is only relevant if the handwritten text is to be converted into ASCII text before use. If no conversion is intended, the accuracy of the recognition algorithms is irrelevant. Research studies tend to report recognition error rates that are generally derived from information about what the user wrote and what the recognizer subsequently output. There is very little research that takes a holistic view of recognition-based systems. The value of the system to the user, and the effort saved by the user is seldom reported [Hartley et al. 2003; Huckvale 1994].

The accuracy of the recognition process for text entry is typically measured by apportioning a percentage score to text after it has been through the recognition process. Metrics that are used for this have been derived from those used for the accuracy of keyboard input, and accuracy (or error rate) scores are generated by comparing a string of presented text (input) (PT) with a string of transcribed text (output) (TT) [Frankish et al. 1995; MacKenzie & Chang 1999; Tappert et al. 1990]. The two strings are compared and the 'errors' in the transcribed text are classified as insertions (I), deletions (D) or substitutions (S). These are then totalled and used to calculate the Character Error Rate (CER):

$$CER = (S + I + D)/N$$

where N is the total number of characters in the presented text.

To calculate the errors, the two phrases are aligned by the use of a minimum string distance (MSD) algorithm that generates a set of optimal alignments (those which result in the least error rate) between the two text strings [MacKenzie & Soukoreff 2002a]. An example is shown here:

```
PT = The cat jumped over the moon
TT = Then cat jumpd over he moon
```

The MSD in this case is 3 and there is one optimal alignment which is:

```
PT = The- cat jumped over the moon
TT = Then cat jump-d over -he moon
```

Once the optimal alignments are generated, it is possible to identify the individual errors by inspecting the two text strings. In this example there is an insertion after The (shown by a dash in the PT), a deletion after jump (shown by a dash in the TT and a deletion after over (also seen in the TT) resulting in an error rate of 3/23 or 13%. As these alignments, and the resulting error rates, can be generated automatically the character error rate metric is an attractive choice for researchers [MacKenzie & Soukoreff 2002a].

Reported error rates for pen-based input devices vary according to the type of writing that is supported; a study by MacKenzie & Chang [1999] tested error rates with 32 subjects copying words of discrete characters onto a tablet, using a constrained grid and reported error rates of between 7% and 13%. Frankish et al. [1995] reported error rates for free form text (natural text) that averaged 13%, and fell to 9% when only lower case letters were used.

The efficiency of text input is normally measured in characters per second or words per minute, and user opinions are obtained by asking the users for their views or by observing them as they use the technology.

3 Empirical Study

The study that is described here compared three methods for text input using digital ink technologies. The three methods were handwriting with a stylus on a Tablet PC, handwriting with a graphics tablet and pen on a standard PC, and handwriting with a digital pen on digital paper.

The focus in the study was on the usefulness of the technologies with the assumption that the writing created on them would be required later in some ASCII form; therefore, recognition rates were important. It was hoped that the study would identify whether or not the technologies were useful, whether or not children of both ages could use the technologies and also to find out how recognition rates improved between the Tablet PC and the Wacom tablet and laptop presentation.

The study was carried out over two sessions. The first session involved 15 children aged seven and eight; the second session was for a group of 25 twelve and thirteen year old children. The organization of both sessions was identical; the description that follows applies therefore to both groups of participants.

3.1 Apparatus

The apparatus that was used varied for the two sessions. In the session with the younger children, the children used either a Tablet PC (as shown in Figure 3) or a Digital Pen (as shown in Figure 4), hereafter referred to as the primary technologies. In the session with the older children, the children were also directed to one of these two technologies but were subsequently given the opportunity to use a Laptop PC with graphics tablet (referred to later as the secondary technology). This option was not offered to the younger age group as the author had used this extensively with that age group and was aware of the usability and the expected recognition rates for this product. The decision to not offer it to the younger children was also taken with the intention of improving the efficiency of the experiment given that children took quite a long time doing the experimental tasks.

Figure 3: Child using the Tablet PC.

Figure 4: Child using the digital pen.

The Tablet PC that was used was a Toshiba Portege and this was used with Calligrapher handwriting recognition.

The digital pen that was used was a Logitech USB pen and this was used with the digital paper notebook that was supplied with the pen. The writing appeared on the notebook, just as if it had been written with a biro.

The writing from the digital pen was uploaded to a laptop once it was written and it was recognized by the software that was supplied with the MyScript software that supported the pen application.

The standard PC was a Hi Grade Notino laptop with a Wacom graphics tablet attached at the USB port. The children wrote on the graphics tablet and their writing was displayed on the laptop screen. The writing was not visible on the graphics tablet. The recognition software that was used was the Calligrapher software, which was the same as that used in the tablet application.

3.2 Procedure

The experiments took place on a single day in a laboratory setting at the University. The younger children carried out the work in the morning, the older children in the afternoon. The children that took part in the experiments came from two local schools and were convenience samples in as much as they were from classes that the schools had chosen to bring to the experiment following a request from the researcher.

Awful   Not very good   Good   Really good   Brilliant

Figure 5: Smileyometer used to rate the Applications.

The children entered the room in small groups and were brought to a table where the researcher allocated them to one of the two primary technologies. Before the children used the technologies, they were given an explanation of how they worked and were also told what the purpose of the study was.

As the children completed each application, they rated their experience using a Smileyometer [Read et al. 2002] — see Figure 5.

3.3   Design

This was an exploratory study, designed to establish how usable the technologies were, whether or not the children would use them (given a choice) and what recognition rates could be expected for these technologies.

3.3.1   Design of the Text Phrases

The children were presented with a single A4 sheet of text phrases for copying into the technology. These phrases had been taken from the text phrases published by MacKenzie & Soukoreff [2003], and were selected on the basis of their word familiarity for the younger children and for easy spellings. Both groups saw the same phrases. The phrases were displayed in a size 16 comic sans serif font with five phrases on each side of the paper. The phrases that were presented on the first side of the paper were:

> My watch fell in the water
> Time to go shopping
> You must be getting old
> The world is a stage
> Do not say anything

The phrases that were on the rear of the paper were:

> Are you talking to me
> You are very smart
> All work and no play
> Did you have a good time
> Play it again Sam

The order of the presentation of the first five phrases and of the second five phrases was different for each event; this meant that although the phrases followed one another in sequence, the first phrase that was written differed across the technologies and across the children. For instance, My watch fell in the water appeared either 1st, 2nd, 3rd, 4th or 5th. The researcher ensured that the presentation

	Young Children	Older Children
Number	8	11
Average	0.181	0.072
SD	0.125	0.082

Table 1: The error rates for the digital pens.

---

of these phrase sets was arranged to minimize the effect of learning on the recorded recognition rates and to provide a reliable set of results.

3.3.2 Design of the Interfaces

The three technologies were presented in different ways. The digital pens were placed on a table and the children wrote with them into the digital paper notebooks that had been provided with the pens. These were A4 size, spiral bound and presented in a portrait layout.

The Tablet PC was used with an experimental interface that was identical to the one on the laptop PC. This interface gave the children a space to write and when they were ready it displayed the results of the recognition process to them. They then cleared the interface and wrote their next phrases.

At the end of the session, the digital ink from the pens was uploaded to the computer and recognized by the Logitech notes software. The writing on the Tablet PC and the laptop was recognized using calligrapher software. Both types of recognition software utilized a standard dictionary.

3.3.3 Design of the Evaluation Sheet

An evaluation sheet was presented to the children after they had used the technologies. This required the children to give a rating for each of the technologies that they used.

3.4 Analysis

There were two analysis processes. The text that was generated from the recognition activities was aligned to the text that was copied by using an MSD algorithm, and a character error rate was derived as explained in Section 2.2.

The ratings from the children with respect to the technologies were given numerical scores from 1 (awful) to 5 (brilliant).

3.5 Results

Not all the children wrote all write all ten phrases at each technology, but all completed the first five phrases. Because of this, the numerical results that are presented here only represent the error rates from these first five phrases. Optimally, these represent 88 characters; some children wrote less than 88 characters as they missed out letters or words, and some added letters or words to end up with more than 88 characters. The error rates were all measured against 88 characters; the implication of this is discussed later in the paper. Table 1 shows the error rate statistics for first five phrases written on the digital pens.

	Tablet PC		Wacom and Laptop
	Young Children	Older Children	Older Children
Number	7	12	10
Average	0.170	0.156	0.193
SD	0.118	0.113	0.139

Table 2: Error rates for the Tablet PC and the Wacom Tablet.

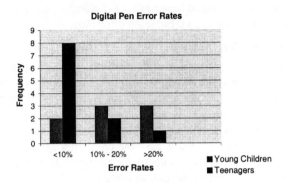

Figure 6: Error rate distribution for digital pens.

The error rates for the first five phrases on the Tablet PCs (used by both sets of children) and the first five phrases on the Wacom and laptop (used only by the older children) are presented in Table 2 — Error Rates for the Tablet PC and the Wacom Tablet.

There is a significant difference ($t_{17} = 2.41$, $p < 0.05$, two-tailed) between the results for the younger children and the older children in the error rates for the digital pens. Summary data from their writing is shown in Figure 6 where it can be seen that for many of the older children, error rates were very low; in fact, three children produced work that resulted in no recognition errors.

There was not a significant difference for the error rates between the two user groups when the Tablet PC was being used (distribution shown in Figure 7), but for the older children, the results between the Tablet PC and the Digital Pens were significantly different, $t_{21} = 2.17$, $p < 0.05$, two tailed).

The average preference scores for each technology are shown in Table 3.

The results for the digital pens are particularly interesting as there is a significant difference ($p < 0.05$) between the recognition rates for the younger and the older children. As shown in Figure 6, very few of the younger children had well recognized writing. For one of the younger children, a portion of writing was not captured even though it was clearly seen in the notebook. The reason for this was not discovered but it may be that the way the child held the pen interfered with its operation.

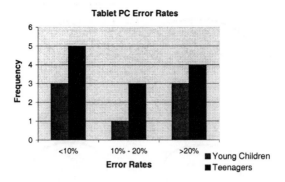

Figure 7: Error rate distribution for Tablet PC.

	Digital Pen	Tablet PC	Laptop PC
Young Children	4.182	4.429	N/A
Older Children	3.733	4.273	3.417

Table 3: Average preference scores for each technology.

It is interesting to note that there is not a significant difference between the writing at the tablet for the younger and older children, neither was there any significant difference between the tablet and the Wacom for the older children. The Tablet PC was generally preferred by the children, but the digital pen also gained a high score for user choice, especially from the younger children (who had had relative success with that technology).

4   Findings from the Work

The findings from the work are considered in three sections; the first looks at the usefulness of the technologies, the second at how usable the technologies were and the third explores whether or not the children would use them.

4.1   How Useful was the Technology? Recognition Rates Revisited

The major determinant of usefulness in this study was the recognition accuracy of the process. The accuracy rates seemed quite high in some instances (older children using the digital pens for example) and even with the tablet technologies the recognition rates are reasonable when compared to other similar studies [Read et al. 2003]. It may be that with real use (i.e. composed text), these recognition rates would be higher; in the studies reported here, the children copied phrases rather than composed their own words and in Read et al. [2004] it was shown that copied text resulted in more errors than composed text.

The reason for there being a difference between copied and composed text is partially explained as follows. Figure 8 shows the four text strings, IT, WT, PT and TT, that are present in a recognition process.

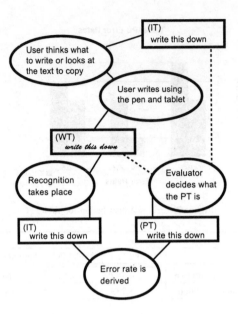

Figure 8: The text strings in a system.

Type of error	Number of instances
Wrote in text speak	3
Spellings incorrect	5
Missed words	2
Substituted words	1

Table 4: Reasons for variance in intended and written text.

The first string (IT) is the 'intended text' and this may have been presented to the users for subsequent copying or may be thought text that exists only in the users head. This text is then written by the user to create a second text string that is the written text (WT).

When the user is composing text (rather than copying), this written text is inspected and interpreted for use as the presented text (PT). When text has been copied, the intended text is generally, but not always, used as the presented text (PT). In the example shown in Figure 8, it can be seen that the user intended to write write this down but in fact did not write the e in write and so using the intended text as the presented text (as was done in this experiment reported here) will result in a worse recognition rate (1 substitution, 1 deletion) being recorded than perhaps should have been (1 substitution).

To determine the size of the effect of using the intended text as the presented text, the writing that the children did using the digital pens was investigated for those cases when the intended and the written text varied. This investigation included a

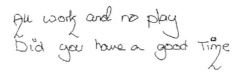

Figure 9: Writing displaying personalization.

look at the second five phrases (not included in the summary data in the results). The reasons for the intended and written text being different are summarized in Figure 4.

The child that wrote in text speak used r u talking 2 me instead of are you talking to me (this resulted in three instances of text speak and one spelling, which it could be argued was also a text speak!). This would result in an almost 33% error rate even before a single character was recognized. Incorrect spellings and substituted words can have varying effects on recognition rates depending on the distance from the intended text. Missed words are generally small words and their impact is often small; in this study words that were missed were both unimportant words, an a and an is.

4.2   How Usable was the Technology? Errors Examined

All the children were able to quickly use the technologies presented to them and the technologies were all suitable for the task. There were a couple of instances where the child needed some assistance, three of the younger children needed to be shown how to write on the Tablet PC and four of the older children needed help with the Wacom tablet but this they provided for each other as a number of these children had used Wacom tablets and pens in their artwork at school.

With the digital pens, aside from the problem with the pen not capturing the digital ink, the most common error was with children starting too near the top of the page. This caused poor (or absent) recognition of the first phrase and happened with three of the children (all in the younger group). One boy wrote all his phrases with the book upside down and these were subsequently not recognized at all by the software — his results were not included in the summary in Table 1.

All three technologies supported the children's individuality as they allowed for different writing styles, but in some instances, this reduced recognition. Figure 9 shows an example from one girls writing that clearly shows how she embellished her writing with irregular descenders and circles in place of dots. Remarkably, this writing was recognized quite well, probably due to the fact that the embellishments were added as she wrote; children that added embellishments after they had written created more problems for the recognition process.

It is clear when looking at the writing in this form (as shown in Figure 9) that children, (and in this small experiment, this was notably the older girls) see their writing as both individual and as an artistic product, seven of the girls in the study wrote with embellishments. The conversion of this writing into ASCII text seems to be almost an act of vandalism and so the possibilities for manipulation of digital ink, especially for this user group, are worth further exploration.

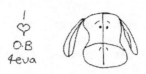

Figure 10: Digital doodling.

4.3   Would the Technology be Used? Digital Doodles

The high ratings that the children gave to the technologies suggest that were they available to children in schools these digital ink tools might be used. For users with high levels of discretion (and children are such a user group) technology is only adopted if it makes things easier, faster, or more fun than the present alternative. One particular aspect that was seen in the work of this study was the interplay between art and writing, especially with the older children, and this cannot be easily enabled in a QWERTY writing environment.

Pen and paper provides a very creative medium that children explore from an early age. When they are very young, they use drawings to express ideas and convey meaning but as age, they draw less and write more [Kress 1997]. During the teenage years it is common for children to add art forms to their writing and to their writing artefacts (books etc.) in the form of doodles. In a small investigation of the prevalence of doodles among older children, the researcher found that over 85% of children of this age added doodles to over 50% of their standard pen outputs. These doodle behaviours are enabled by digital ink; an example from the work of this study can be seen in Figure 10 which shows how one child added her own symbols to her writing.

It is perhaps unsurprising that digital doodling might happen with pen technologies, as the nature of the pen is very different from the nature of the keyboard. Pens are used for both art and writing whereas the keyboard is simply a text creation tool. Microsoft have recently acknowledge this by providing a pen writing space to their recent MSN chat application.

The older children saw the potential in the technology; one child remarked that she could write letters in secret using the digital pen, destroying the paper version, but keeping the digital version safe in the technology, another suggested that the pen could double as a mobile phone and be used to store everything! One challenge for digital ink recognition technology is to be able to discriminate between doodles and writing so that only the writing is recognized. In the study described here, the recognition software that was supplied with the digital pens coped well with doodles but the software on the Tablet PC tried to recognize the drawings (and failed!).

5   Further Work

These results indicate that children can use both the novel technologies of digital pens and tablet PCs. The results show that when children copy text into these technologies, recognition rates of around 80% can be expected for most children, but these may be higher for composed rather than copied text. The results for the younger children using Tablet PCs (average error rate 17%) compare favourably with the results reported for children using Wacom tablets and PCs (average error rate 34%) [Read et al. 2004] and suggest that there is a measurable improvement when the problem of separation between writing surface and screen is removed.

The children using the technologies in this study were all enthusiastic and the older children were keen to offer suggestions for the possibilities for the technology use in the classroom. The involvement of older children in the envisioning and testing of future technologies is an area that is worth further investigation. Observing the author writing this paper using a QWERTY keyboard, one teenager remarked *'just think, in about ten years time someone will invent ink and say ' Hey that's a good idea you can use it with paper and stuff'*.

The author intends to carry out further work with digital text and digital doodling for older children. This work will focus on personalization of text, both presented as digital ink and as ASCII representations.

Other work will determine the recognition rates that might be possible for composed text and a longitudinal study of the usability of digital pens.

Acknowledgements

The author wishes to acknowledge the co-operation and assistance of the pupils and teachers from English Martyrs Junior school and Archbishop Temple High school.

References

Bekker, M. M., Markopoulos, P. & Kersten-Tsikalkina, M. [2002], *Interaction Design and Children*, Shaker Publishing.

Carroll, J. M. [2002], *Human–Computer Interaction in the New Millenium*, Addison–Wesley.

Cooper, W. E. (ed.) [1983], *Cognitive Aspects of Skilled Typewriting*, Springer-Verlag.

Day, J. [1994], Is Good Looking Writing Good Writing?, *in* C. Singleton (ed.), *Computers and Dyslexia: Educational Applications of New Technology*, Dyslexia Computer Resource Centre, University of Hull, pp.26–36.

Dix, A., Finlay, J., Abowd, G. D. & Beale, R. [2003], *Human–Computer Interaction*, third edition, Prentice–Hall.

Druin, A. [2002], The Role of Children in the Design of New Technology, *Behaviour & Information Technology* **21**(1), 1–25.

Druin, A. (ed.) [1999], *The Design of Children's Technology*, Morgan-Kaufmann.

Frankish, C., Hull, R. & Morgan, P. [1995], Recognition Accuracy and User Acceptance of Pen Interfaces, *in* I. Katz, R. Mack, L. Marks, M. B. Rosson & J. Nielsen (eds.), *Proceedings of the SIGCHI Conference on Human Factors in Computing Systems (CHI'95)*, ACM Press, pp.503–10.

Frye, D. & Soloway, E. [1987], Interface Design: A Neglected Issue In Educational Software, *in* J. M. Carroll & P. P. Tanner (eds.), *Proceedings of SIGCHI/GI Conference on Human Factors in Computing Systems and Graphics Interface (CHI+GI'87)*, ACM Press, pp.93–7.

Garvey, J. [2002], Authenticity, Modelling and Style: Writing and ICT, *in* M. Williams (ed.), *Unlocking Writing*, David Fulton Publishers, pp.77–91.

Hartley, J., Sotto, E. & Pennebaker, J. [2003], Speaking versus Typing: A Case-study of the Effects of Using Voice — Recognition Software on Academic Correspondence, *British Journal of Educational Technology* **34**(1), 5–16.

Huckvale, M. [1994], Purpose: The Missing Link in Speech and Handwriting Recognition, Paper presented at the AISB Workshop on Computational Linguistics for Speech and Handwriting Recognition. http://http://www.phon.ucl.ac.uk/home/mark/papers/spwrite.htm (last accessed 2005-06-07).

Kafai, Y. B. (ed.) [1990], *From Barbie to Mortal Kombat, Gender and Computer Games*, MIT Press.

Kress, G. [1997], *Before Writing — Rethinking the Paths to Literacy*, Routledge.

MacKenzie, I. S. & Chang, L. [1999], A Performance Comparison of Two Handwriting Recognizers, *Interacting with Computers* **11**(3), 283–97.

MacKenzie, I. S. & Soukoreff, R. W. [2002a], A Character-level Error Analysis for Evaluating Text Entry Methods, *in* O. W. Bertelsen, S. Bødker & K. Kuuti (eds.), *Proceedings of NordiCHI 2002*, ACM Press, pp.241–4.

MacKenzie, I. S. & Soukoreff, R. W. [2002b], Text Entry for Mobile Computing: Models and Methods, Theory and Practice, *Human–Computer Interaction* **17**(2), 147–98.

MacKenzie, I. S. & Soukoreff, R. W. [2003], Phrase Sets for Evaluating Text Entry Techniques, *in* G. Cockton, P. Korhonen, E. Bergman, S. Björk, P. Collings, A. Dey, S. Draper, J. Gulliksen, T. Keinonen, J. Lazar, A. Lund, R. Molich, K. Nakakoji, L. Nigay, R. Oliveira Prates, J. Rieman & C. Snyder (eds.), *CHI'03 Extended Abstracts of the Conference on Human Factors in Computing Systems*, ACM Press, pp.754–5.

Moseley, D., Higgins, S., Bramald, R., Hardman, F., Miller, J., Mroz, M., Tse, H., Newton, D., Thompson, I., Williamson, J., Halligan, J. & Bramald, P. [1999], Ways forward with ICT: Effective Pedagogy using Information and Communication Technology for Literacy and Numeracy in Primary Schools, Technical Report, Newcastle University.

Norman, D. A. & Fisher, D. [1982], Why Alphabetic Keyboards Are Not Easy To Use: Keyboard Layout Doesn't Much Matter, *Human Factors* **24**(5), 509–15.

Palmer, S. [1993], Does Computer Use Put Children's Vision at Risk?, *Journal of Research and Development in Education* **26**(2), 59–65.

Plamondon, R. & Srihari, S. N. [2000], On-line and Off-line Handwriting Recognition: A Comprehensive Survey, *IEEE Transactions on Pattern Analysis and Machine Intelligence* **22**(1), 63–84.

Read, J. C. [2005], The ABC of CCI, *Interfaces* **62**, 8–9.

Read, J. C., MacFarlane, S. J. & Casey, C. [2001], Measuring the Usability of Text Input Methods for Children, *in* A. Blandford, J. Vanderdonckt & P. Gray (eds.), *People and Computers XV: Interaction without Frontiers (Joint Proceedings of HCI2001 and IHM2001)*, Springer-Verlag, pp.559–72.

Read, J. C., MacFarlane, S. J. & Casey, C. [2003], A Comparison of Two On-line Handwriting Recognition Methods for Unconstrained Text Entry by Children, *in* P. Gray, P. Johnson & E. O'Neill (eds.), *Proceedings of HCI'03: Volume 2*, Research Press International for British Computer Society, pp.29–32.

Read, J. C., MacFarlane, S. J. & Horton, M. [2004], The Usability of Handwriting Recognition for Writing in the Primary Classroom, *in* S. Fincher, P. Markopoulos, D. Moore & R. Ruddle (eds.), *People and Computers XVIII: Designing for Life (Proceedings of HCI'04)*, Springer, pp.135–50.

Read, J., MacFarlane, S. & Casey, C. [2002], Endurability, Engagement and Expectations: Measuring Children's Fun, *in* M. M. Bekker, P. Markopoulos & M. Kersten-Tsikalkina (eds.), *Interaction Design and Children*, Shaker Publishing, pp.189–98.

Solomon, C. [1978], Teaching Young Children to Program in a LOGO Turtle Computer Culture, *ACM SIGCUE Outlook* **12**(3), 20–9.

Tappert, C. C., Suen, C. Y. & Wakahara, T. [1990], The State of the Art in On-line Handwriting Recognition, *IEEE Transactions on Pattern Analysis and Machine Intelligence* **12**(8), 787–808.

Thelen, E. [1996], Motor Development, *American Psychologist* **51**(11), 1134–52.

Turrell, G. [1999], Email — Punching Holes in Classroom Walls, *in* R. Selwyn & R. Dick (eds.), *MAPE Focus on Communications*, MAPE Publications, pp.Section C, 1.

Weikart, P. S. [1995], Purposeful Movement: Have We Overlooked the Base?, *Early Childhood Connections: The Journal for Music and Movement-based Learning* **1**(4), 6–15.

PROTEUS: Artefact-driven Constructionist Assessment within Tablet PC-based Low-fidelity Prototyping

Dean Mohamedally, Panayiotis Zaphiris & Helen Petrie

Centre for HCI Design, City University London, Northampton Square, London EC1V 0HB, UK

Email: *{cp496,zaphiri,hlpetri}@soi.city.ac.uk*

Low-fidelity prototyping is a widely used HCI knowledge elicitation technique. However, empirical evaluation methods for low-fidelity prototyping have remained relatively static even with the development and use of software prototyping tools. In this paper, we describe a framework based on constructionism theory to model design artefacts as measurable constructs within low-fidelity prototypes. This provides a novel approach to acquiring further cognitive user metrics within software based low-fidelity prototyping in the HCI domain. We describe two mobile software tools, PROTEUS and PROTEUS EVALUATOR, developed for the Tablet PC platform, which use our framework to aid our understanding of prototypes during their temporal construction. Results of using the tools in two scenario experiments are reported, each conducted with 40 HCI postgraduate students.

Keywords: low-fidelity prototyping, constructionism, knowledge elicitation, Tablet PC software, HCI software tools.

1 Introduction

Knowledge elicitation methods in HCI are a critical function to the success of requirements and design gathering stages [Maiden et al. 1995], usability testing and user evaluation stages of software development [Zaphiris & Kurniawan 2001]. Examples of this start with initial questionnaire feedback, requirements task walkthroughs, interviews techniques, and focus group debates. It can rapidly scale upwards to more complex psychometric and design and evaluation processes such as various fidelities of prototype construction, direct and indirect observation practices for monitoring user actions and response time comparisons, and methods for eliciting mental categorization models e.g. in distinguishing expert and non-expert technology usage patterns.

A wide variety of tested and proven experimental user-based techniques exist for practitioners [Burge 2001] to utilize. However, as HCI specialists will know from experience, knowledge acquisition and analysis of data from traditional user-based methods is time consuming and usually requires experts in their respective fields. As Kidd [1987] defined, knowledge acquisition of experts involves the following processes:

1. Deploying a technique to elicit data from the expert users.

2. Interpreting verbal data and infer the underlying knowledge and reasoning of the users.

3. Utilising this interpretation to construct a model or language that exemplifies the user's knowledge and performance.

4. Interpreting further data by an iteratively evolving model until the knowledge domains are complete.

5. The principle focus for the knowledge acquisition team should be in constructing models, in domain definition, or problem identification and problem analysis.

For HCI practitioners working as part of development teams whereby their results can lead to significant changes in design, it is important to define and incur the highest quality of empirical data captured.

By adopting digital processes, analysis of such data can be enhanced with software tools that incur faster data acquisition and processing times than humanly possible, along with large data storage and retrieval capabilities. Digital tools can therefore raise the quality of user centred knowledge elicitation and analysis. In this paper we present an approach to acquiring further cognitive user metrics within low fidelity prototyping in the HCI domain, through the use of software tools.

This paper continues as follows; in Section 2 we briefly describe low-fidelity prototyping and current software tools that are widely used. Section 3 presents a background to existing constructionist methodology, for the reader to grasp the dynamics of how constructionism links to design artefacts. As part of our framework, constructionist metrics and event patterns over the timeline history of prototyping construction are also proposed. In Section 4 we describe the iterative design and development of our tools to facilitate our framework. Section 5 outlines our experiment scenarios to validate our framework. Section 6 goes on to describe the findings of our scenario tests in order to validate our framework. Section 7 discusses our participatory design (PD) sessions to evaluate and improve our software tools, for use by HCI practitioners and educators, and finally Section 8 concludes our work with suggestions for future research in this area.

2   Low-Fidelity Prototyping

The practice of low-fidelity prototyping in HCI uses simple materials and equipment to create a paper-based simulation of views to an interface or system with the aim of exploring early user requirements and visualizing layout, accessibility and potential aesthetic approval of design ideas.

Over the years, strategies and uses of prototyping methods [Hardgrave & Wilson 1994] have grown to become a key asset in the HCI toolkit. With traditional paper and pen based approaches, it is common to denote features of a user interface with visual artefacts metaphorically described on paper, e.g. menu bars with triangles on either end, or rectangular buttons for actions. If it is being constructed with movable separate pieces of paper these artefacts allow members of a prototyping team to interact with it and easily reach a consensus on the effectiveness of position, size and purpose. It is also common to label features and visual artefacts, with annotation descriptions of their purposes and links to other artefacts.

There are numerous software painting and drawing programs available such as Windows Paint, Macromedia Flash, Adobe Illustrator, Microsoft Visio and PowerPoint, and the GIMP, to name a few in no order of preference. These artistic and diagrammatic tools can be utilized for low-fidelity prototyping and sketching of user interface designs. Recently, more HCI practitioner-orientated low-fidelity prototyping tools have been developed, including software from the GUIR team at Berkeley [Walker et al. 2002] which has produced Denim and Silk to facilitate prototyping of early stage website design. Denim allows low fidelity prototype sketches of website designs to be 'run' associated with hyperlink navigation to other prototype sketches akin to storyboarding. Also their Suede system [Klemmer et al. 2000] is a powerful speech based Wizard of Oz Prototyping tool based on speech dictation interfaces.

3   Constructionism in User-Centred HCI

3.1   *Constructionist based Artefacts Modelling*

Constructivist learning theory [Piaget 1973; Vygotsky 1978] argues that knowledge is not just transmitted, but is constructed. Thus we refer to the construction of new knowledge by learners themselves with sensory information and the behaviour of self-constructed knowledge that is built up through experience [Jonassen 1994].

This theory branched in the form of constructionism. Constructionism [Papert 1991; Resnick 1996] in the HCI-applicable sense is an epistemological view concerned with the reinforcement of existing user knowledge and creation of new knowledge. This is critically achieved through the use of tangible artefacts and metaphors that users can affiliate with from their sensory information and their past experience and intuitions.

Several knowledge elicitation techniques in HCI can be argued to elicit user-centred data through the use of tangible artefacts. Low-fidelity prototyping is noted, by use of paper materials and sketching individual artefacts. In addition; card sorting, affinity diagramming, brain storming and perhaps others are also constructionist. They reinforce and create new user-centred knowledge domains through iterations

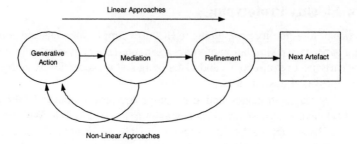

Figure 1: Linear and Non-linear approaches in artefact-driven construction.

of activity, consensus and refinement of tangible and metaphorically identifiable artefacts e.g. cards and physical objects.

These new knowledge domains are created by the users themselves constructing visibly representative artefacts during the knowledge elicitation activity. They may use what they create to further define new artefacts or redefine existing ones, and so forth. This chaining effect has already been described previously as part of the principles within Activity Theory [Leont'ev 1978; Vygotsky 1978].

In simplest terminology, 'activity' is defined as "the engagement of a subject towards a certain goal or objective" [Luria 1981; Ryder 1998]. Vygotsky contributed to Activity Theory by describing activity mediated through artefacts. In general, artefacts are both a set of constructed initial activities but they can also be a product of an activity, and can be modified throughout the timeline of an activity.

As Bertelsen [2000] denotes "Using Star's [1989] terminology, design artefacts are boundary objects because they adapt to different situations of application and at the same time maintain identity, thereby mediating divergent needs and viewpoints." Bannon & Bødker [1991] describe this format of mediation as a critical part to understanding artefacts and distinguishing them from each other. Béguin & Rabardel [2000] similarly uses this idea of mediation to explain the artefacts within the cycle of construction as a combined result of generative activity, mediation and refinement stages.

3.2 Constructionist Metrics

Here we describe an internal cognitive design cycle that demonstrates how a single artefact is created from several key stages (Figure 1):

1. Decisions (Generative Activity and first innovation).

2. Mediation (Backtracking, pausing for reflection).

3. Refinement (Assessment and innovation, leading to modifications).

Upon refinement several artefacts can become reinforced by further Decision stages, leading to subsequent branching of Mediation and Refinement within (recursive constructions). Decision making as an activity can thus branch into 3 dimensions:

Name	Type	Value	Explanation
Ta	total time	shorter time	confident but lacking mediation or in a hurry
Tb	total time	longer time	strong mediation but not necessarily confident (could be indecisive)
Aa	addition	lots, in a short time	strong confidence, instinct and implies using personal domains of knowledge
Ab	addition	few, in a short time	not confident at task, relies on mediation
Ac	addition	lots, in a long time	strong confidence, attention to detail (methodological approach)
Ad	addition	few, in a long time	not confident at task, doesn't rely on mediation
Ma	modifications	few, in a short time	strong confidence, weak mediation (possibly pre-final refinement)
Mb	modifications	lots, in a short time	mediation and refinement stages, either indecisive or debating, strong output on agreement consensus
Da	deletions	few	confident in output
Db	deletions	lots	either non-confident, or understanding/ expertise is being corrected under mediation
AM	additions and modifier pair	lots	atomic expertise — strong sense of refinement /perfectionist
MD	modifiers and deletion pair	lots	suggests mediation and resolution towards positive refinement stage
AD	additions and deletion pair	lots	either non-confident, or understanding/ expertise is being corrected under mediation

Table 1: Proposed event patterns within an internal design construct.

- Addition (First Set).

- Modification (Mutate or Get and Set).

- Removal (Delete).

In addition to these, a fourth variable exists, a 'Mediation Point' which we can describe as a point in time when a generative activity (Decision) halts for an arbitrary period (like a rest), and then continues onwards in the timeline with mediation and refinement either leading on to a new artefacts construction or to modification of the existing. This mediation point is important to us to distinguish sums of artefacts from a single artefact in a construct. For example, sketching a prototype view of a DVD movie menu interface may show one artefact collection as a navigation block which has icons, labels and a button style; a mediation point will separate this as one artefact before the user has considered a next artefact to be created e.g. a background menu image.

Thus several events within a generative activity can become measurable either on their own or as clusters. In Table 1 we describe several possible event patterns as part of our framework to describe artefact driven constructionism within the temporal view of generative activities.

4 Design and Development of Framework Tools

There is a depth of user knowledge beyond which paper based methods can acquire that software tools can assist with. Existing desktop tools provide assistance to this. However in addition, mobile devices e.g. PDAs and Tablet PCs are already becoming "part of the HCI practitioner's toolkit" — expensive toys yes, but they are slowly becoming more prevalent for multiple serious uses by HCI practitioners and educators, especially when on-demand and on-site activities require it. Therefore our approach is from the ground up designed to augment them with the techniques in software using state of the art capabilities, and enabling such techniques to be effectively taken to client-side location domains, store and process client-side HCI data efficiently.

We designed and developed two software tools with the aim of:

1. providing as close a simulacra as possible to the existing practical methodology of low fidelity prototyping in software; and

2. provide a technique for electronically automating the evaluation of our framework with the software solution provided in (1).

4.1 Software Development Platform

As a visually rich representation of low fidelity prototyping, the form of digital inking meant the need for a visually rich and high resolution interface, with strong mimicking of the existing interaction level with novel advantages in being able to maintain portability for on-site uses; a key advantage in updating current-day HCI knowledge elicitation methods given the nature of wireless networking and mobile computing options. The Tablet PC platform from Microsoft was specifically chosen as the mobile platform to host our framework in the form of the PROTEUS tool (*PROT*otyping *E*nvironment for *U*ser-interface *S*tudies), with a second tool, PROTEUS EVALUATOR, to assist in the analysing of artefact creation over time within PROTEUS based low fidelity designs.

The Microsoft Tablet PC Software Development Kit (SDK) with Visual Studio.Net 2003 provides rich API libraries to developing for new pen interactivity models, post normal laptop usability patterns. As a hybrid mobile device between PDA and PC, a Tablet PC's inking facilities in particular feature well with pressure sensitivity in onscreen pen motion, pen gestures for user metaphor based event firing and real-time recognition of handwriting on visual user interface components.

4.2 Expert Iterative Design

Participatory design (PD) sessions with 4 HCI practitioners were conducted for the development of the software tools, firstly with a pre-understanding survey to elicit requirements and request for features by priority. After debate it was clearly understood and agreed that standard paper and software approaches are great for eliciting basic informal requirements. However, it was also understood that being

Figure 2: Expert prototyping design session of the PROTEUS tool.

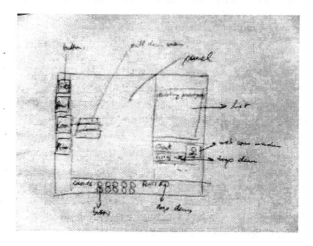

Figure 3: Example low fidelity paper prototype of the PROTEUS user interface.

able to visualize a design as changes over time and seeing decisions through the constructionism model as artefacts would reveal user knowledge and cognitive abilities that are not otherwise easily and conveniently acquired directly.

The practitioners were introduced to the concept of Tablet PC-based pen gesturing actions and onscreen handwriting recognition as a potential interface to the tool. They were also introduced to the notion of temporal analysis capturing key design artefacts being created, as per requirements of our framework. Using these requirements attributes, low fidelity paper prototypes were then created by the practitioners to elicit potential user interface designs (Figures 2 & 3) which aided us with consistency of options, navigation of incorporated tools, and investigate potential routes for minimizing user actions.

The interaction model mimics the physically tangible model of paper based prototyping as close as possible; e.g. pen sensitive drawing/selecting/erasing (pen

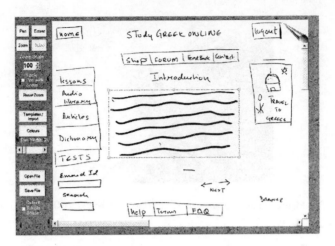

Figure 4: PROTEUS with a low fidelity prototype of a website design scenario.

down with depth for drawing), auto-selecting connected elements (pen double click motion), picking up and moving visual elements (pen drag motion on selected elements), and quick erasing (pen eraser button).

These digital pen actions have the added advantage of providing a resource of data for digitally logging all motions and actions, and record-keeping of the artefact formation in progress, as well as being fast and convenient for using a pen in a one-handed mobile or stationed environment. It also enables us to calculate in software arbitrary mediation point delays between artefacts, originally set at a default of 10 seconds. Thus after 10 seconds of inactive use, further constructs are considered to be a new artefact, mediation or a refinement.

The uses of this interaction model were explored further in individual interviews with the practitioners to gain solely their personal opinions and feature requests. This enabled us to inquire additional requirements which were agreed during a follow-up focus group session as well as (after consensus of the four HCI experts) removing and minimizing less used and potentially obstructive features. Post evaluations of the tools were conducted with design practitioners through a number of post-questionnaires which found that the users were happy for the tools to be deployed in HCI scenarios.

PROTEUS version 1.0 (Figure 4) simulates the actions of a low-fidelity paper prototype being constructed with the addition of all user events being recorded, including every pen stroke and user interface choice via SDK GUID calls. Using this data it constructs temporal roll-back views of the prototypes creation so that every action of manipulation of the virtual paper prototype can be evaluated at a later date to elicit potential weaknesses or strengths at prior stages of the prototype design process.

The time indexed ink-encoded GIF file output (serialized from the Tablet PC SDK) can be shared with others and imported into existing designs as prototype

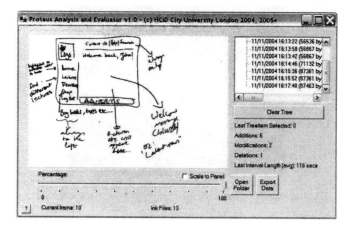

Figure 5: PROTEUS EVALUATOR Tool analyses prototype artefacts over time.

element templates. This is in addition to applying now standard ink manipulation and interaction modifiers such as selection, scaling and moving of ink strokes and collections of strokes, applying transparency, and colouring to highlight and distinguish artefacts, and page zooming for refining ink details. Ink-encoded GIFs, which are serialized by the Tablet PC SDK, retain their added editable information including their time stamps, even though they can be read by any graphical image editor and Web-browser supporting the standard GIF file format. This makes them very useful for sharing prototypes quickly with others but also in maintaining the integrity of editable features with PROTEUS users.

All activity in the form of decisions are tracked and can be rolled back to prior times, e.g. to compare what users activities occurred in the decision making of a group of artefacts at different temporal instances via the PROTEUS EVALUATOR tool. This allows the practitioner to review the mediation point stages such as those leading to mediation and refinement facilitation (Figure 5). This interactive reviewing method was requested as a feature for use with on-site experiment sessions, by allowing a practitioner to inquire further details in post interviews and focus groups with participants, allowing them to visually refer to any point of the original design timeline with the history of actions re-playable. Examples of this include erasing off parts to an artefact or moving artefacts around.

A pre-test questionnaire and walkthrough trials were conducted with the HCI experts to:

- Present them with our Tablet PC tools and enable them to the digital inking methods in their experimental practices.

- Evaluate their understanding of the tools.

- Engage them in contributing ideas for enhancing the scope on any further requirements for use in their field operations.

Figure 6: PROTEUS on a Tablet PC in use during the student scenarios.

Throughout these expert trials they could raise any points of interest or complaints. Finally a post-test Quality of User Interface Satisfaction questionnaire (QUIS) Chin et al. [1988] was given to collect information about their general impressions about the tools and any modifications they thought were necessary. From the data collected, a number of key user interface issues such as menu options, accommodating appropriate pen-sized interface actions, interface terminology, button styles and integrated help requirements were modified into subsequent builds.

5   Experimental Scenario Testing

In order to better understand the application of constructionist assessment in prototyping, it was decided that scenario testing of the tools and the framework would be undertaken with 40 postgraduate MSc participants recruited from an Advanced HCI class module. This would enable us to compare the constructionist framework of artefacts analysis with an existing expert HCI marking methodology.

The participants were invited to utilize the PROTEUS tool in two scenarios for the design cycle of an online language learning website, and a novel interface to a train ticket machine. Working in groups of 5–7, they utilized 4 Tablet PCs (1GHz+, each with 512Mb RAM running Windows Tablet PC 2005) in turns in a classroom location. Whilst one half of the class used the well-established paper format for one scenario, the same scenario was being completed with the software tools by the other half of the class.

At the second scenario, the students switched methods from paper to software and vice versa (Figure 6). Each scenario was given 20 minutes to complete the task. Upon completion of their prototypes, the different groups were shown the others solutions to demonstrate the variety of prototyping ideas that groups can give using low fidelity prototyping in practice.

For HCI lecturers, practitioners and researchers, the methodologies for evaluating practical paper and software based forms of low fidelity prototyping are fairly similar in acquiring key user requirements, eliciting more of the conceptual basis and creativity of ideas than precision in style.   Understanding the user's

	Low-Fidelity Prototyping Expert Assessment Criteria
1	Use of colours and variety of pens to distinguish elements
2	Demonstrating a sense of proportions and scale
3	Use of simple shapes to denote complex objects
4	Representation consistency in reuse of shapes and colours
5	Use of contextual language, annotation and terminologies
6	Ease of 3rd party understanding of the users' representations
7	Aesthetics awareness and use of layout, usability design
8	Ideas and innovation presented to the domain proposed
9	Context of design and accessibility to domain proposed
10	Overall quality of effort

Table 2: Our department's low fidelity prototyping expert assessment criteria.

mental models also gives us useful data centring on the usage of appropriate design metaphors and the achieving key tasks for functionality. Table 2 shows our department's expert assessment criteria as used to evaluate paper prototype courseworks from an Advanced HCI MSc class.

These expert criteria can only determine metrics of user mental models with a final prototype design view and does not elicit qualitative measures that may have been significant within the duration of the prototype's timeline. Hence, it is this data which can be compared with that of our framework, which can give additional qualitative measures over the temporal construction of the prototype design.

6 Scenario Results

Expert marking evaluations of the prototypes were conducted with two HCI practitioners marking the software based views, and a different two HCI practitioners marking the paper views, such that bias of software against paper expert comparisons could be avoided.

No statistical significance was found between the expert quality marks of paper version prototypes to the expert quality marks of software version prototypes ($t_{11} = 1.68, p > 0.05$). This indicates that using the Tablet PC software was not a negative influence on the practical methodology of low fidelity prototyping. However, a second t-test of Scenario 2's outputs alone (software vs. paper) demonstrates $t_5 = 3.13, p < 0.013$. This indicates the software method was preferred than the paper method and this may show that the effectiveness of using such digital tools is potentially dependent on the scenario of use. As shown in Figure 7 mean marks for the second scenario (ticket machine interface) were higher than those of the first scenario (language learning website), with inferences to using more creative scenario ideas. We suspect the variety of pen options in the software aided in eliciting this higher creativity quality.

To evaluate the constructionist data, our PROTEUS EVALUATOR tool generates Excel compatible spreadsheets directly from the time encoding of events that occurred within the creation of the ink-encoded GIF files from the software sessions.

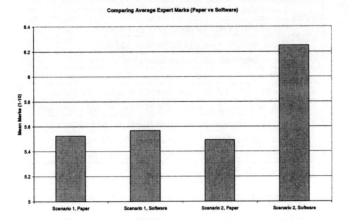

Figure 7: Paper vs. Software expert marking for the two scenarios.

This allows us to compare electronically generated results of the software based prototypes in terms of artefact-driven confidence vs. the independent expert markers evaluations; Figure 8 shows some of the automated results of artefact-driven constructs assessment vs. expert HCI marking. The expert marks were awarded out of 100% based on the assessment criteria defined in Table 2.

The use of the PROTEUS EVALUATOR tool to analyse the constructions of artefacts within the users PROTEUS based prototype designs determined several key points in our experiments:

- Confident groups spent less time in refinement stages.

- Low values of generative activities obviously imply either non-enthusiasm or inability to construct confident and positive design artefacts.

- The average interval time between mediation points involving modifications has been found to be considerably shorter than additions and deletions, we suspect due to mediation (reflecting on choices made) and refinement (assessing possible outcomes) giving a clearer idea of what to manipulate.

- Successive generative activities indicate sources of innovation.

Weaker teams in terms of expert marking criteria measured longer decision-mediation-refinement cycles before considering creating new artefacts.

7   Users Evaluation of the Tool

After the scenario testing, a full scale post questionnaire based on the User Satisfaction QUIS [Chin et al. 1988] questionnaire was filled by the 40 student participants. This QUIS is based on a 0 to 9 Likert scale for a variety of categories, as shown in Figure 9. Subsequently, an ease-of-use post questionnaire based on the

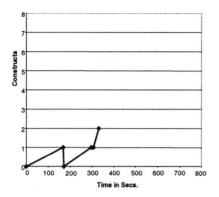

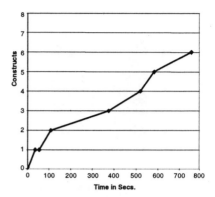

(a) Scenario 1, Team 2: experts awarded 46%; software detected 5 mediation points, over a short time period, with little mediation/ refinement time in between.

(b) Scenario 1, Team 5: experts awarded 61%; 7 mediation points detected in software, with long periods of generative activity indicating thoughtful team consensus.

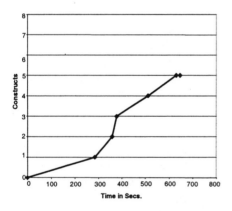

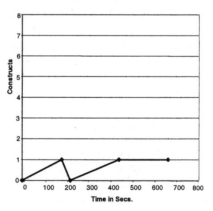

(c) Scenario 2, Team 1: experts awarded 70%; 6 mediation points detected, with little mediation time in between rapid generative activity, possibly indicating confidence in design.

(d) Scenario 2, Team 5; experts awarded 52%, 4 mediation points detected, little generative activity but long mediation, an indecisive team.

Figure 8: Artefact constructs detected with PROTEUS EVALUATOR vs. Expert marking.

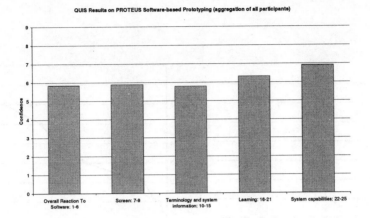

Figure 9: QUIS results on user interface satisfaction.

CSUQ questionnaire Lewis1995 was conducted with additional questions to indicate personal preferences between software and paper methods.

In both of QUIS and CSUQ questionnaires, the PROTEUS tool was rated above average in all questionnaire categories. A mean of 82% of the users stated that they found the tool was comparable, if not better than the existing paper practice. 69% of users felt that the tool gave them new capabilities in the sense they only expected these features within a mouse-desktop paint/diagrammatic program and not within the natural feel of a pen-based direct inking tool. 89% of participants felt that the tools and software options provided covered the interaction level sufficiently to facilitate productive low-fidelity prototyping in the HCI context.

8   Conclusions and Further Work

We have provided an example of our framework for electronically evaluating otherwise complex user confidence and capability issues from observing the construction of artefacts in prototyping, as an additional measure to existing low fidelity evaluation. Our contributions are as follows:

- We have constructed a specific HCI software solution, PROTEUS, which enables the major functional requirements of low fidelity prototyping to be captured via a mobile device, in the form of a Tablet PC; this enables on-site elicitation and digital recording and sharing of prototypes.

- We have developed a second tool, PROTEUS EVALUATOR, to assist in analysing design artefacts and constructionist data in the timeline of PROTEUS designs. This has led to the exploration of using the artefact-driven constructionist theory to create a working model of artefact driven assessment metrics. This forms a research opportunity for mapping potential cognitive decision making characteristics within the temporal creation of user knowledge elicitation.

- Finally we have conducted two scenario driven experiments using our framework with PROTEUS, and compared data with expert formal assessment guidelines, to demonstrate links with the existing methodology.

For HCI practitioners and educators, existing paper based prototyping methods are obviously quick, cheap and practical if the space and materials are available. Low-fidelity ideas are captured efficiently this way. However, their outputs are not effectively recorded on paper in a consistent and shareable form, and intermediate decisions made are not easily recorded on paper (e.g. how they arrived at particular artefacts that are consistently used metaphorically in their design and what potential decisions did they make along the way), nor is the final output completely indicative of the personal confidence, initiative and capability of the user(s) involved. Automating the collection of this data in readily usable formats is seen as a beneficial capability. For the advancement of practical HCI methodology there is an advantage especially so for HCI educators to be realized here with such tools.

We would like to see this work expanded further and applied to other scenarios. In particular we intend to continue to map further cognitive measures within artefacts, e.g. expanding on the clustering of multiple constructionist event types (Table 2). We believe similar techniques can be applied to other knowledge elicitation methods such as affinity diagramming and card sorting which also use constructionist ideals.

References

Bannon, L. & Bødker, S. [1991], Beyond the Interface: Encountering Artifacts in Use, *in* J. M. Carroll (ed.), *Designing Interaction: Psychology at the Human–Computer Interface*, Cambridge University Press, pp.227–53.

Bertelsen, O. W. [2000], Design Artefacts — Towards a Design-orientated Epistemology, *Scandinavian Journal of Information Systems* **12**(1-2), 15–27.

Burge, J. E. [2001], Knowledge Elicitation Tool Classification, PhD thesis, Worcester Polytechnic Institute, USA.

Béguin, P. & Rabardel, P. [2000], Designing for Instrument Mediated Activity, *Scandinavian Journal of Information Systems* **12**(1-2), 173–90. Special Issue: Information Technology in Human Activity.

Chin, J. P., Diehl, V. A. & Norman, K. L. [1988], Development of an Instrument Measuring User Satisfaction of the Human–Computer Interface, *in* J. J. O'Hare (ed.), *Proceedings of the SIGCHI Conference on Human Factors in Computing Systems (CHI'88)*, ACM Press, pp.213–8.

Hardgrave, B. C. & Wilson, R. L. [1994], An Investigation of Guidelines for Selecting a Prototyping Strategy, *Journal of Systems Management* **45**(4), 28–35.

Jonassen, D. H. [1994], Thinking Technology: Towards a Constructivist Design Model, *Educational Technology* **3**(4), 34–7.

Kidd, A. [1987], Knowledge Acquisition: An Introductory Framework, *in* A. Kidd (ed.), *Knowledge Acquisition for Expert Systems: A Practical Handbook*, Plenum Press, pp.1–15.

Klemmer, S. R., Sinha, A. K., Chen, J., Landay, J. A., Aboobaker, N. & Wang, A. [2000], SUEDE: A Wizard of Oz Prototyping Tool for Speech User Interfaces, *in* M. Ackerman & K. Edwards (eds.), *Proceedings of the 13th Annual ACM Symposium on User Interface Software and Technology, UIST'00, CHI Letters* **2**(2), ACM Press, pp.1–10.

Leont'ev, A. N. [1978], *Activity, Consciousness and Personality*, Prentice–Hall.

Luria, A. R. [1981], *Language and Cognition*, John Wiley & Sons.

Maiden, N. A. M., Mistry, P. & Sutcliffe, A. G. [1995], How People Categorise Requirements for Reuse: A Natural Approach, *in* P. Zave & M. D. Harrison (eds.), *Proceedings of the 2nd IEEE International Symposium on Requirements Engineering (RE'95)*, IEEE Computer Society Press, pp.148–57.

Papert, S. [1991], Situating Constructionism, *in* I. Harel & S. Papert (eds.), *Constructionism*, Ablex, pp.1–12.

Piaget, J. [1973], *To Understand is to Invent*, Grossman.

Resnick, M. [1996], Distributed Constructionism, *in* D. C. Edelson & E. A. Domeshek (eds.), *Proceedings of the Second International Conference on the Learning Sciences (ICLS-96)*, Association for the Advancement of Computing in Education. http://llk.media.mit.edu/papers/archive/Distrib-Construc.html (last accessed 2005-06-06).

Ryder, M. [1998], Spinning Webs of Significance: Considering Anonymous Communities in Activity Systems, *in* M. Hedegaard & S. Chaiklin (eds.), *Proceedings of the Fourth Congress of the International Society for Cultural Research and Activity Theory: Activity Theory and Cultural Historical Approaches to Social Practice*. http://carbon.cudenver.edu/~mryder/iscrat_99.html (retrieved 2004-10-06).

Star, S. L. [1989], The Structure of Ill-structured Solutions: Boundary Objects and Heterogeneous Distributed Problem Solving, *in* L. Grasser & M. Huhns (eds.), *Distributed Artificial Intelligence*, Pitman, pp.37–54.

Vygotsky, L. S. [1978], *Mind In Society: The Development of Higher Psychological Processes*, Harvard University Press. Edited by Michael Cole, Vera John-Steiner, Sylvia Scribner, Ellen Souberman.

Walker, M., Takayama, L. & Landay, J. A. [2002], High-fidelity or Low-fidelity, Paper or Computer Medium?, *in Proceedings of the Human Factors and Ergonomics Society 46th Annual Meeting*, Human Factors and Ergonomics Society, pp.661– 5.

Zaphiris, P. & Kurniawan, S. H. [2001], User-centered Web-based Information Architecture for Senior Citizens, *in* N. Avouris & N. Fakotakis (eds.), *Proceedings of Panhellenic Conference with International Participation on HCI: Advances in Human–Computer Interaction*, Typorama, pp.293–8.

The Reader Creates a Personal Meaning: A Comparative Study of Scenarios and Human-centred Stories

Georg Strøm

DIKU, University of Copenhagen, Universitetsparken 1,
DK-2100 Copenhagen O, Denmark
Email: *georg@diku.dk*

Different types of written textual descriptions are often used in interaction design. This paper describes an empirical study of how conventional scenarios and stories with emotional and dramatic elements may contribute to software developers' understanding of interfaces, of contexts and situations of use. The results show first, that software developers create a personal understanding of written descriptions by combining parts of them with their personal experiences. Second, that both scenarios and stories improve their understanding of technical information. Third, that stories with emotions and dramatic elements improve their understanding of contexts and situations of use substantially more than conventional scenarios. Fourth, that software developers may find it comparatively easy to write stories with emotional and dramatic elements.

Keywords: stories, human-centred stories, scenarios, software development, emotions, requirements, conceptual design.

1 Written Texts are an Important Medium in Industrial Software Development

In most cases it is not possible for software developers to be in continuous contact with users or customers who can describe their situations of use and what they need. In addition most software development is so complex that it is necessary in advance to describe and agree on what is going to be developed. My own experience indicates that mainly is done through the use of written verbal descriptions; in particular in the first phases of a software project where major decisions are taken. Written verbal descriptions are used to communicate the context of use and requirements from customers, usability or marketing people to the software developers, and they are used to communicate the suggested goals of the development back to customers and users.

Rosson & Carroll [2002] describe how conventional scenarios can be used in software development and Hertzum [2003] and Nielsen [2004] describe empirically and in details how scenarios can be used and improve the communication during software development. However, it is almost impossible from such studies to determine whether descriptions with different characteristics, for instance scenarios with deeper and better descriptions of the motivations of the users, may be more useful. In particular when preceding events in a project and the status and position of the writer influence how and when a written description is used in a development project.

Another problem is that each of the present studies focus on the use of just one textual genre. Within a specific genre it is only possible to express a certain range of thoughts and emotions. Because of these limitations, it is recommendable to use a range of genres in industrial software development. It is therefore necessary to do comparative studies that can reveal which genres that are most suitable for specific purposes.

Scenarios is one of the genres that can be used to describe the interaction with and context of use of an interface. Some proponents of scenarios indicate that scenarios and stories are almost synonymous [Erickson 1995; Rosson & Carroll 2002] but an empirical study of actual scenarios reveal that scenarios are a much more restricted genre than stories in general. Conventional scenarios are driven by the interface, their plots focus on demonstrating different functions in it, their descriptions of the characters are superficial compared to stories in fiction literature, and they describe no serious conflicts [Strom 2003b]. Some scenarios consist only of lists of seemingly unrelated events, they are not narrative or proper stories at all, as defined by White [1981].

In contrast, a fiction short story normally includes at least one serious conflict, the emotions of the characters in it are shown through dialogue and through specific descriptions of their actions, and the plot is driven by the characters' efforts to succeed in conflicts or to overcome obstacles [Knight 1985]. In contrast to conventional scenarios, such stories tend to involve and engage the emotions of the reader.

Clausen [2000] argues that stories using methods from fiction writing are better than technical descriptions when system developers shall communicate with users, and he found that they could be written and used by computer science students in software design projects. Stories similar to fiction writing can in particular be used to describe how people use a computer system [Clausen 2000]; they are Human-centred, in contrast to scenarios that primarily are driven by the interface [Strom 2003a].

The following is an introduction from a conventional scenario:

> Marissa was not satisfied with her class today on gravitation and planetary motion. She is not certain whether smaller planets always move faster, or how a larger or denser sun would alter the possibilities for solar systems. [Rosson & Carroll 2002]

The introduction describes clearly what the designers want to include in the interface. In contrast, there is nothing about the motivations of the main character: Nothing that indicates why she wants to learn more about the topic, why she will use the interface described in the scenario to learn more, or how she will use it to get more information. In contrast, a human-centred story may describe a user of a similar interface like this:

When Marissa was small she used to watch television with her older brother and ask him "Why don't the moon fall down?" or "What would happen if we lived on the sun?" She is now in high school. She is interested in astrophysics, but she is afraid to be considered a brainy girl and to become unpopular. (This is inspired by Carl Sagan [1985, 1996].)

The quotes or pieces of dialogue show the emotions and thoughts of the main character, such that it is possible to become engaged in the conflict she is caught in and to imagine why and how she will use a Web-based interface to get in contact with other students who share her interests.

It is necessary to distinguish between fiction and the use of methods from fiction writing. It is possible to describe a real, non-fiction, situation of use by using dialogue and other methods from fiction writing, and to show how the emotions and motivations of the participants drive the events. In contrast, even though a requirement specification is written without any methods from fiction writing, and even when it is based on careful studies of users and their needs, it is normally a work of fiction: It describes something that does not exist, and that indeed may never come into existence.

In addition to scenarios or other types of stories it is necessary to use technical descriptions of the functions and interfaces of the software to be produced. Such descriptions can give a more complete and compact information, and they can be organized more systematically, which make them easier to use as references.

I will therefore investigate how conventional scenarios and human-centred stories affect how software developers perceive situations of use and technical information when they are read together with technical descriptions, and I will try to identify some aspects that affect the perception.

2 Method

In 2003 and 2004 I taught courses in the use of different textual descriptions in software development to computer science students. The first study was done during these courses (the participation was voluntary). It consisted of an analysis of 30 conventional scenarios and 28 human-centred stories written in the course.

The participants appeared to have above average technical writing skills, but none of them had any previous fiction writing training or skills. Even though they were not selected in a manner that favoured readers of fiction literature, 18 out of 26 participants replied that they had read fiction literature within the last two months.

During the course each participant wrote first a scenario and then a human-centred story describing a situation when an application for processing digital images were used. The participants were given identical written instructions for the writing of the scenario and the human-centred story.

As part of the course I did an evaluation of the human-centred stories. It was based on what I had learned in a creative writing course where I had participated in the evaluation of about fifty stories and on what might be considered the goal of fiction writing: That the characters and dialogues in the story are believable, that words and rhythms of the language are consistent through the story, that there is an apparently plausible plot that progress through the story until it reaches a conclusion, and that all these elements contribute to a consistent reader experience. (This definition is based on the work by Knight [1985] and Sharples [1999].)

When the courses were completed, I counted the number of new ideas that were mentioned in the scenarios and human-centred stories. I defined a new idea as a function or a usage problem where the solution was obvious, and where the usage problem or function was not mentioned in the written instructions for the assignments.

The second study was conducted in 2003–2004. Eight software developers with a programming or computer science background and five with an engineering background participated in the study. Even though they were not selected in a manner that favoured readers of fiction literature, seven of the 13 participants told that they had read fiction literature within the last two months.

The participants told that they had spent from half an hour to three hours on reading the texts. They had on average spent about four minutes reading each page. There was no relation between the types of texts they had read and the time they had spent reading them.

The texts were assigned randomly to the participants; the scenarios and human-centred stories were not mixed because the participants' opinions about one type of text then might influence their evaluation of another:

- Three of the participants read only technical descriptions of four different applications.

- Five read both technical descriptions and conventional scenarios that described the same four applications.

- Five read technical descriptions together with human-centred stories that described the same four applications.

The texts described applications of the following types: Project management software, PDA based time-registration for social assistants, a call-centre system and a mobile phone with built-in camera.

I had written the technical descriptions myself and used them in an earlier study [Strom 2003a]. They were based on applications I were familiar with and similar to good technical descriptions I had seen when working in private companies.

I had also written the human-centred stories and used them in the earlier study [Strom 2003a]. Some of them had been evaluated in the creative writing course in which I participated, and based on the feedback I had received they can be described as of an almost publishable standard.

The scenarios were based on the human-centred stories. That was done in order to ensure that they described exactly the same events as the human-centred stories. (Otherwise it would be almost impossible to make a valid comparison). They were similar to good scenarios from private companies and public sources that I had evaluated in an earlier study [Strom 2003b].

In conclusion, the technical descriptions, stories and scenarios were of a uniform quality, with only minor defects, but not of an outstanding or superior quality.

The technical descriptions equalled on average 4 typewritten pages. That is similar to a technical summary but smaller than a normal design specification. The scenarios each had a length on about 1 page, which is slightly more than most scenarios I have seen, whereas the human-centred stories had an average length on about 4 pages, which is close to the normal minimal length of fiction short stories [Knight 1985]. (It is difficult to engage the reader and resolve a conflict in a story that is much shorter.)

In the second study I used a combination of quantitative and qualitative methods with a concurrent triangulation strategy [Creswell 2003]. This means that I combined qualitative and quantitative methods in the same study, and that I collected the qualitative and quantitative information at the same time. I did that in order to capture as much information as possible within the time spent with each participant.

I conducted semi-structured interviews with standardized questions that made it possible to make quantitative comparisons between the replies of the participants. For each application the interviews included the following groups of questions:

1. Open questions where the participants were asked to describe how each described application supported one specific function, which benefits the application offered and possible problems during its use.

2. Two questions about the usability or usefulness of the application. The participants were asked to select a value on a 1–5 scale that included a verbal description of each value, and encouraged to argue for their choice.

3. One question about how good an impression the technical description gave of how the application would function during actual use, and one question about the credibility of the scenario or story (for those participants who had read one of those). The participants were asked to rate the texts on a 1–5 scale that included a verbal description of each value, and encouraged to argue for their choices.

The interviews were recorded and transcribed. In order to identify the multitude of different aspects that might occur in the interpretation of a written text, it was necessary to extract qualitative information. Using principles based on Kvale [1997] I identified recurrent themes in the transcripts, collected and evaluated the parts in different interviews that might be related to each theme, interpreted the parts and in some cases selected a single or a few quotes to illustrate it.

In order to do a reliable comparison between scenarios and stories, it was necessary to extract additional quantitative information from the interviews. The descriptions of how each application supported one specific function (from the first group of questions) were ranked from the one that gave the most correct information and most precisely expressed information about the function, to the one that gave the least correct and least precise information. The ranking was used instead of a grading according to preset criteria, because such a grading could not reliably take into account any correct information that was not expected when the grading was made, or how precisely the information was described in the reply.

The quantitative results from the questions in the second and third groups could be directly tabulated. The number of different aspects in the participants' interpretation of the texts, for instance the number of misunderstandings made, was determined by first making a set of definitions of the different aspects, and then by using these to identify their occurrences in transcripts of the interviews. I calculated both normal averages and weighted averages where the different backgrounds of the participants were taken into account (the difference was minimal), and I identified statistical significant differences by testing in the normal distribution.

The quantitative and qualitative results were finally triangulated. This means that they were compared and that the conclusions were based on a combination of them.

3   Computer Science Students are Capable of using Methods from Fiction Writing

It is almost impossible to find a fiction writer who can fit into a development team, who knows interaction design and who quickly can acquire the required domain knowledge. It is therefore only feasible to use human-centred stories in software development, if they can be written by people who already participate in and know about such projects.

The first study shows that computer science students after a single lesson in fiction writing could write human-centred stories, in some cases of an almost publishable standard. They were capable of writing realistic dialogue, they described convincing characters, and they were capable of writing a consistent language that fitted the style and the topics of their stories.   The largest problem was that a significant proportion of the stories included dramatic plots with infidelity, serious crime or other events that moved the focus away from the interaction with the interface.   However, when the students were made aware of that problem, it was fairly easy for them to solve.

4   Writing Human-centred Stories Create New Ideas

When designing interfaces it is often difficult to identify new needs and to invent features that fulfil them.   Therefore it is valuable if the writing of human-centred stories can facilitate both.

The first study shows that the human-centred stories compared to the scenarios described substantially more new ideas for the interface. The writing of a scenario resulted on average in 1.5 new ideas, whereas the writing of a story on average resulted in 2.1 new ideas ($p = 0.05$). In addition, when the lower number of stories is taken into account, the writing of stories resulted in 60% more different ideas.

There were only a few cases where the same participant had included the same idea in a scenario and a story. This indicates that the writing of the stories and the ideas generated during it were independent of the writing of the scenarios.

In contrast to the scenarios, the stories described the characters' emotional relations to the use of different functions, for instance that they could express anger through the use of a function or hesitate before deleting an item. These relations cannot be explored through conventional scenarios, and they are important when designing an emotionally satisfying interface.

When a scenario is driven by the interface, it is easy to exclude anything that is difficult to implement or not already part of the interface. In contrast, when a story describes a situation where a user has a realistic need of accomplishing a specific result, the writer is almost forced to describe how it can be done. In order to progress with the story, he or she must invent something that overcomes the problems.

5 The Reader Creates His or Her Own Personal Understanding of the Topics of the Texts

Successful software development requires that the developers understand what they are supposed to develop. This requires that their understanding of the written descriptions their work is based on is consistent with the understanding of the people who have written and approved them.

The second study revealed large differences in how the same text was understood; in some cases the understanding contradicted parts of the text. This was not because the participants did not understand the words of the texts. It was because each participant created his or her personal understanding by combining parts of the text with his or her personal experiences. When doing that the participant often discarded parts of the text that did not fit his or her personal experiences.

One of the participants had earlier worked at a help-desk, and he had read a description of a general system for a call-centre (as with the other excerpts from interviews, this is translated by the author from Danish):

Q: What are the advantages of the call-centre system?

A: You get registered what comes in. You can see what each person is doing, if any tasks are hanging, if there is something that does not get solved.

The participant creates a situation of use based on his own experiences, even though it does not fit parts of the text. The interview continues:

Q: How is it possible for the same operator to handle calls to different companies?

A: He shall give a customer number or something like that. And the number will indicate whether it is company A, B and C.

This fits the help-desk experienced by the participant, but not the call-centre described in the text. The text describes how the company is identified automatically based on the number that is called, and how the system then provides the operator with the necessary information to handle the call. The text does not mention any customer number. Later in the interview the same participant is asked:

Q: What are the consequences of operators being warned before angry calls ...?
[Calls from a number where a previous caller has been abusive.]

A: It depends on the number of calls. A call-centre as TDC [Danish Telecom] with thousands of calls, there the customers are impersonal. The centre I thought about had maybe fifty customers that you knew and who came back.

The present situation, the question that is asked, changes the understanding that the participant has created. Instead of talking about a help-desk and a small call-centre, he is now talking about a large general call-centre. The new understanding is confirmed in the following:

Q: What are the consequences for the operator, when he or she shall play different roles, for instance ... handle calls to a travel agency or a complaint because of a missing newspaper.

A: I have all the time thought about a specific IT-system. But it is right, as you say, that they might as well handle travel agencies, car reservations or others. So it requires a large flexibility ... it is different worlds ... they will probably feel stressed.

The participant has now totally changed the understanding he has created of the topics of the text and the situation of use.

The errors in the understanding are not consequences of an insufficient or superficial reading of the texts. They appeared in particular to occur when participants actively thought about the text and made an effort to create an understanding of it. This indicates that reading can be almost as active a process as writing, and that the participants create their personal understandings based on:

- Parts of the texts; their understanding may contradict other parts of it.

- Parts of their knowledge and personal experiences that best fit the text.

- Aspects of the situations in which they create their own understanding.

The process is similar to the blending of different objects that is described by Fauconnier & Turner [2002]. It seems that the reader places impressions or mental images generated by parts of the text on top of different personal experiences, accepting these that fit together and discarding those that do not. The process is similar to a design-process as described by Boden [1990] and to Schachter's [1996] description of how memories are re-created when recalled, and it appears to be a common aspect of human thinking.

The results show only eight cases (out of more than 150 comments) where a participant expressed that he or she was conscious about the personal experiences that were used to create an understanding and how they influenced his or her interpretation of the text. One said (about the project management application):

> I have been brainwashed with Microsoft Project, so it is possible it
> is the basis [of my evaluation].

There were no cases among the more than 150 comments where a participant mentioned alternative or multiple interpretations of the same piece of text. It was as if the participants in each moment felt compelled to choose only one interpretation.

6 Readers Create an Evaluation of the Usability

It is not uncommon that readers try to evaluate the usability or other aspects of the use of an interface based on a description of it. It is of course important that the evaluation is as reliable as possible. In addition it is important that the basis of it is known: Otherwise it is difficult to determine how reliable it is.

None of the participants in the second study evaluated the interface and possible problems by going through the description in a systematic manner. Some commented on general aspects as this reader of a human-centred story:

> ... because it must be so flexible, it must also be complex ... when you have learned it, it is easy, but it takes time to learn and get used to ...

Some based their evaluation on the manner in which the interaction was described, as this reader who concluded that the software was difficult to use, because the story gave an extended description of the operation:

> The text indicates it is not that easy. There are many things, many menus to navigate. You shall skim different places, then go back in another menu and maybe enter something.

Other participants created an evaluation of the usability by blending the description with a known interface as in this example:

> ... [Sending multimedia messages] appears to be very easy. Like writing an SMS or an e-mail. I know it, because I have a heavy Nokia — 9210 — which can transmit such stuff.

Some participants evaluated the usability by blending the described interface with a specific user, as this reader of a technical description:

> It is possible that a social helper who lack routine need time to become familiar with it ... social helpers have different educations, some can use it directly, others are — PC-imbeciles.

None of the participants evaluated the usability by blending the description with a specific situation of use; none of them considered how the usability was dependent on the situation of use.

When the participants were asked about other issues than usability, they sometimes blended the description with a specific situation of use, as with this reader of a scenario who blended it with his personal experiences when asked how useful a project management tool was for the software developers:

> ... project management tools are for project managers, not developers. For developers it is not important that the figures are right. You do not ask the project manager to make changes in your editor. You are doing two different tasks.

	Read only technical description	Read also scenarios	Read also human-centred stories
Referred explicitly to the technical description	**0.7**	**1.6**	1.6
Misunderstandings	2.3	2.2	**0.0**
Referred to an imaginary user or situation of use	2.2	2.2	**0.7**
Referred to an existing user	2.7	0.6	1.0
Referred to own experiences	1.0	0.8	0.5
Referred to known interface	1.7	1.6	1.0

Table 1: Different aspects in the interpretation of the texts: Averages for each group of participants. Statistically significant differences (p = 0.05) are highlighted.

The blendings were often critical towards the texts, and the contents of the texts were questioned as shown by this reader who compared a technical description and a human-centred story:

It is described in the story as if it is very difficult, but in the specification it appears that he uses only two or three menus, and it appears to be logical with the information he shall enter.

Another said:

This is a sunshine story. But in real life, people make mistakes.

7 Both Conventional Scenarios and Human-centred Stories Improve the Understanding of Technical Information

The participants in the second study were asked to describe how each application supported one specific function. The replies were ranked with 1 as the best and 13 as the lowest ranking, and the results showed a substantially better understanding when the participants read a scenario or a story together with a technical description: average rankings of 7.0 and 5.6 vs. 10.8 ($p = 0.05$ between technical descriptions only and technical descriptions read together with scenarios).

The results also show that those who had read a scenario or a story substantially more often during the interview referred to the technical description (it appears they were more aware of its contents): On average 1.6 times (for scenarios and stories), vs. 0.7 times ($p = 0.05$ between technical descriptions only and technical descriptions with scenarios). See Table 1.

It was not possible to identify any relation between the time each participant reported to have spent reading the texts and his or her understanding of them.

An earlier study [Strom 2003a] shows that stories read without technical descriptions does not give a better understanding than technical descriptions. It appears that it is the combination of technical descriptions and scenarios or stories that gives a better understanding.

8 Human-centred Stories give a Better Understanding of a Situation of Use

When decision makers shall decide whether a feature shall be included in the requirements, and when the software developers shall decide how it shall be implemented, it is important that they understand its purpose and the expected situations of use. In addition, it is likely that the designers are more motivated and take more care if they are aware of when and how a feature shall be used.

The second study shows that reading of human-centred stories substantially reduced the number of misunderstandings of the situation of use, both compared to when only a technical text was read, and when a technical text was read together with a conventional scenario. There were no misunderstandings among the readers of stories, whereas the participants in the two other groups on average had 2.2 misunderstandings ($p = 0.05$ between scenarios and stories). See Table 1. (Misunderstandings are here defined as personal understandings that contradict at least one part of the text.)

It is possible that readers of stories use the descriptions of the emotions and motivations of the participants as an additional reference that helps them to understand how the interface is used. They blend their understanding of the interaction with an interface with the descriptions of the users' emotions and motivations and their own knowledge about human motivations and emotions.

Some misunderstandings can be attributed to a lack of background information in the scenarios. One participant concluded that a young man in one of the scenarios was paedophile. The scenario mentioned that he took a picture of two girls, but did not mention that they were approximately his own age. (The interpretation was made even though the following part of the scenario made it unlikely that he was a paedophile.)

Other misunderstandings can be attributed to the fact that readers of only technical texts or of scenarios substantially more often indicated that they made their own story with imaginary users or situations of use and used it to create their personal understanding ($p = 0.05$ between scenarios and stories). See Table 1. The following is from a participant who had read a technical description of how a social helper used a PDA:

> ... this means, if Mrs Jensen for some reason is not at home, what shall I do then? You may get the services recorded, I can imagine that you have a handful of standard services, and that you put a mark in the proper box.

If the developers do not have any personal experience with the domain, their personal stories may have little to do with the actual users or situations of use. In addition, when different members of a project group base their understanding of the users and context of use on personal stories that are not known by other members of the group, it may easily lead to misunderstandings.

Participants who had only read technical descriptions referred substantially more often to how they expected that an existing user would use the interface. See Table 1. In some cases themselves; in other cases people they had met:

> Some of the call-centre workers I have met have been of such a type
> that this could not work.

There were no significant differences between how often readers only of
technical descriptions, of scenarios and of human-centred stories referred to their
personal experiences. See Table 1. It is possible that the personal experiences are so
vivid and strong that their use when creating an understanding is not affected by the
reading of a single scenario or story.

The second study shows that scenarios contribute to the understanding of the
interaction with an interface and the situation of use, but that human-centred stories
can contribute substantially more.

9 Software Developers want Emotions and Dramatic Elements in the Stories

A number of participants in the second study made precise comments about how the
texts were written. They clearly noticed the style and other characteristics of the
texts they read.

Both readers of scenarios and human-centred stories expressed most often that
they wanted stories with more dramatic elements (compared to that they wanted
stories with less): On average 1.9 times vs. 0.7 times ($p = 0.05$). They expressed that
stories with emotions and dramatic elements seemed more real:

> When you make some drama when you tell, it makes you believe
> that this product exists and is in use.

An analysis of the comments shows that the participants wanted emotions and
dramatic elements, but that they reacted when the dramatic elements were so strong
that they moved focus away from the use of the interface.

Scenarios and human-centred stories were rated as equally credible: 2.2 vs. 2.3
on a 1–5 scale. This indicates that stories with emotions, conflicts and dramatic
elements, and even with humour, are not regarded as less serious than scenarios
without such elements.

10 Discussion

Every evaluation of a story and probably also of a non-fiction article include some
subjective elements. However, even when that is taken into account the results of
the first study demonstrates that computer science students are capable of writing
human-centred stories that may be used in software development.

In the first study there have been a training effect from the beginning of the
course to the writing of scenarios. However, the scenarios and stories were both
written later in the course, reducing the training effect between them. The results
also show that even though the stories were written after the scenarios, they were not
based on them.

The results indicate that it is common that computer science students and
software developers in Denmark read fiction literature. However, that may not be
the case in other countries. Computer science students and software developers in

other countries may be less familiar with fiction literature and therefore find it more difficult to read and write stories with methods from fiction writing.

The technical descriptions, scenarios and stories used in the second study were of a similar good quality, they were not outstanding, and they had only minor defects that did not affect the results. Comments made by the participants indicate that this is in agreement with their evaluations of the texts.

The human-centred stories were substantially longer than the scenarios used in the study. However, both scenarios and stories described the same events, it is normally easier to get an overview through a shorter text, and comments I have received to descriptions of interactions in other stories indicate that longer conventional scenarios may be tedious and difficult to read. This suggests that the benefits of human-centred stories shown in the second study are in spite of them being longer than the scenarios; the benefits must be attributed to how the stories include conflicts and show motivations, emotions and settings of the events.

The comparison was made between technical descriptions alone, scenarios read together with technical descriptions and human-centred stories read together with technical descriptions. These are probably the most common situations in software development; it is unlikely that software developers only will be given a scenario or a story without some sort of structured technical description.

The qualitative and quantitative results were extracted from the transcripts in a consistent manner; the quantitative and qualitative results and the theoretical model lead to the same conclusion, which confirm the reliability of the results.

However, the study probably underestimates the amount of misunderstandings and reading problems that may occur in actual software development.

The technical descriptions were substantially shorter than many used in system development (on average 4 pages, whereas texts on more than 30 pages are common in industrial software development). It was therefore easier for the participants to get an overview of each technical description. It is also likely that most of those who volunteered to participate had above average reading skills, and that they read the texts more carefully because they knew they would be asked questions about them.

It shall be taken into account that the scenarios were based on the human-centred stories, so the actions described in them were plausible given the emotions and motivations of the characters. If scenarios are written without such a realistic background, it is more likely that their plots are perceived as implausible [Strom 2003b]. This means that the reported differences between scenarios and human-centred stories probably are smaller than what can be expected when scenarios without such a realistic background are used.

The participants in the second study had not contributed to the writing of the texts used in the study. If, as in the development project described by Nielsen [2004], the developers had spend time discussing what the contents of the scenarios or stories should be and participated in the writing, it is possible that the advantages of human-centred stories as compared to conventional scenarios would be smaller. As long as the participants remember the background and motivations of the characters from their discussions, they can imagine their emotions in specific situations and may therefore need only brief descriptions of the specific events to support their memory.

11 Conclusion

The two studies give a valid and reliable description of how scenarios and human-centred stories (stories that are driven by the emotions and motivations of the characters in them) may contribute to software developers understanding of interfaces and the contexts they are used in.

The results of the first study demonstrate that computer science students can learn to write human-centred stories of a quality that is sufficient for use in industrial software development, in particular if they attend one of the numerous short courses in fiction writing (or creative writing).

Compared to the writing of conventional scenarios, the writing of human-centred stories generated substantially more new ideas for the interface. They gave a more realistic description of the situation experienced by the user, and the built-in conflicts stimulated the identification of new needs and functions.

The second study demonstrates that reading is an active process; the reader does not absorb the contents of a text, but creates his or her own understanding based on his or her personal experiences together with parts of the text. This means that the reader's understanding may contradict other major parts of the text. This has nothing to do with a lack of comprehension or reading skills; in contrast, it appears to be an essential part of reading, and it is a process that is similar to and almost as creative as the process of writing.

One particular problem is that readers tend to select the first understanding that fits part of a text. They may avoid some mistakes by accepting that different understandings of a text are possible and by discussing them openly.

The reader uses his or her personal experiences and imagination to create what cannot be found in the text. The reader may imagine situations where an interface is used, and based on them create an understanding of the interface and how it is used. In addition, it appears that the reader often is unaware of how he or she uses personal experiences to create an understanding, and it is likely that other persons do not know the specific experiences that the reader uses to create his or her understanding.

This may lead to misunderstandings in software development. In order to ensure that the members of a development group have a similar understanding of an interface and the possible situations of use, it is therefore advisable that they take time to discuss what they have read, and to share the experiences and stories they have imagined and used to create their understanding of what they have read.

The participants created understandings of the usability and of other aspects of an interface by blending the description of the interface with their own experiences, for instance with an interface of the same type. They assumed for instance that a described mobile phone in general was as easy or difficult to use as other mobile phones they had encountered. In daily life that is an effective and sensible method: It gives a good indication of whether an interface can be used by a particular user or in a particular situation of use.

However, this method may be misleading if the goal is to evaluate the usability of an interface compared to other interfaces of the same type or to identify specific problems in it. In such cases it is important that the readers are aware of and discuss which examples of interfaces they use as comparison and which differences they notice.

Compared to a technical description, a combination of technical descriptions and scenarios or human-centred stories gave a better understanding of the structure of a system and the specific elements in the interface. This confirms the value of scenarios in software development.

The results indicate that the use of human-centred stories gave a better understanding of situations of use, both compared to technical descriptions alone and to technical descriptions combined with conventional scenarios. It appears that the readers use the emotions and motivations in the human-centred stories as an additional reference when they create their understanding of the situation of use. That will probably also be the case for users and other stakeholders. It is therefore likely that their understanding also will benefit from the emotions and background described in the stories.

Stories with emotions and dramatic elements are more readable, making it more likely that they actually are read (not only by software developers, but probably also by user representatives and other stakeholders). In addition, software developers in general prefer stories with emotions and dramatic elements. However, they complained if the events in the story were so dramatic that focus moved away from the interaction with the interface. This means that stories that are based on everyday problems or conflicts are the most useful and acceptable in software development.

Acknowledgements

Thanks to the participants for their time and effort, to Jesper Hermann, University of Copenhagen, for his comments and to the reviewers for their comments.

References

Boden, M. A. [1990], *The Creative Mind: Myths and Mechanisms*, Weidenfeld and Nicolson.

Clausen, H. [2000], *Informationsteknologiens menneskelige grundlag*, Teknisk Forlag A/S.

Creswell, J. W. [2003], *Research Design, Qualitative, Quantitative and Mixed Methods Approaches*, Sage Publications.

Erickson, T. [1995], Notes on Design Practice: Stories and Prototypes as Catalysts for Communication, *in* J. M. Carroll (ed.), *Scenario-Based Design: Envisioning Work and Technology in System Development*, John Wiley & Sons, pp.37–57.

Fauconnier, G. & Turner, M. [2002], *The Way We Think: Conceptual Blending and the Minds Hidden Complexity*, Basic Books.

Hertzum, M. [2003], Making Use of Scenarios: A Field Study of Conceptual Design, *International Journal of Human–Computer Studies* **58**(2), 215–39.

Knight, D. [1985], *Creating Short Fiction*, Digest Books.

Kvale, S. [1997], *InterView*, Hans Reitzels Forlag.

Nielsen, L. [2004], Engaging Personas and Narrative Scenarios, PhD thesis, School of informatics, Copenhagen Business School.

Rosson, M. B. & Carroll, J. M. [2002], *Usability engineering: Scenario-based Development of Human–Computer Interaction*, Morgan-Kaufmann.

Sagan, C. [1985], *Contact*, Simon and Schuster.

Sagan, C. [1996], *The Demon-haunted World*, Random House.

Schachter, D. L. [1996], *Searching for Memory, the Brain the Mind and the Past*, Basic Books.

Sharples, M. [1999], *How We Write*, Routledge.

Strom, G. [2003a], Perception of Human-centered Stories and Technical Descriptions when Analyzing and Negotiating Requirements, *in* M. Rauterberg, M. Menozzi & J. Weeson (eds.), *Human–Computer Interaction — INTERACT '03: Proceedings of the Ninth IFIP Conference on Human–Computer Interaction*, IOS Press, pp.912–5.

Strom, G. [2003b], Using Creative Writing for developing Realistic Scenarios, *in* C. Stephanidis & J. Jacko (eds.), *Human–Computer Interaction, Theory and Practice. Proceedings of Human–Computer Interaction International 2003*, Lawrence Erlbaum Associates, pp.15–6.

White, H. [1981], The Value of Narrativity in the Representation of Reality, *in* W. J. T. Mitchell (ed.), *On Narrative*, University of Chicago Press, pp.1–24.

What Difference Do Guidelines Make? An Observational Study of Online-questionnaire Design Guidelines Put to Practical Use

Jo Lumsden, Scott Flinn, Michelle Anderson & Wendy Morgan

National Research Council of Canada, IIT e-Business, 46 Dineen Drive, Fredericton, New Brunswick E3B 9W4, Canada

Tel: *+1 506 444 0544*

Fax: *+1 506 444 6114*

Email: *{jo.lumsden, scott.flinn}@nrc-cnrc.gc.ca*

As a new medium for questionnaire delivery, the Internet has the potential to revolutionize the survey process. Online-questionnaires can provide many capabilities not found in traditional paper-based questionnaires. Despite this, and the introduction of a plethora of tools to support online-questionnaire creation, current electronic survey design typically replicates the look-and-feel of paper-based questionnaires, thus failing to harness the full power of the electronic delivery medium. A recent environmental scan of online-questionnaire design tools found that little, if any, support is incorporated within these tools to guide questionnaire designers according to best-practice [Lumsden & Morgan 2005]. This paper briefly introduces a comprehensive set of guidelines for the design of online-questionnaires. Drawn from relevant disparate sources, all the guidelines incorporated within the set are proven in their own right; as an *initial* assessment of the value of the *set of guidelines* as a practical reference guide, we undertook an informal study to observe the effect of introducing the guidelines into the design process for a complex online-questionnaire. The paper discusses the qualitative findings — which are encouraging for the role of the guidelines in the 'bigger picture' of online survey delivery across many domains such as e-government, e-business, and e-health — of this case study.

Keywords: online-questionnaire, design guidelines, evaluative case study.

1 Introduction

As a new medium for questionnaire delivery, the Internet has the potential to revolutionize the survey process. Online (Web-based) questionnaires provide several advantages over traditional survey methods in terms of cost, speed, appearance, flexibility, functionality, and usability [Bandilla et al. 2003; Dillman 2000; Kwak & Radler 2002]. Online-questionnaires can provide many capabilities not found in traditional paper-based questionnaires: they can include pop-up instructions and error messages; they can incorporate links; and it is possible to encode difficult skip patterns making such patterns virtually invisible to respondents. Despite this, and the emergence of numerous tools to support online-questionnaire creation, current electronic survey design typically replicates the look-and-feel of paper-based questionnaires, thus failing to harness the full power of the electronic survey medium. A recent environmental scan of online-questionnaire design tools found that little, if any, support is incorporated within these tools to guide questionnaire design according to best-practice [Lumsden & Morgan 2005]. This paper briefly introduces a comprehensive set of guidelines for the design of online-questionnaires. It then focuses on an informal observational study that has been conducted as an *initial* assessment of the value of the set of guidelines as a practical reference guide during online-questionnaire design.

2 Background

Online-questionnaires are often criticized in terms of their vulnerability to the four standard survey error types: namely, coverage, non-response, sampling, and measurement errors. Although, like all survey errors, coverage error ("the result of not allowing all members of the survey population to have an equal or nonzero chance of being sampled for participation in a survey" [Dillman 2000, p.9]) also affects traditional survey methods, it is currently exacerbated in online-questionnaires as a result of the digital divide. That said, many developed countries have reported substantial increases in computer and Internet access and/or are targeting this as part of their immediate infrastructure development [OECD 2001]. Indicating that familiarity with information technologies is increasing, these trends suggest that coverage error will rapidly diminish to an acceptable level (for the developed world at least) in the near future, and positively reinforce the advantages of online-questionnaires.

Non-response errors occur when individuals fail to respond to the invitation to participate in a survey or abandon a questionnaire before completing it. Given today's societal trend towards self-administration [Dillman 2000] the former is inevitable, irrespective of delivery mechanism. Conversely, non-response as a result of questionnaire abandonment *can* be relatively easily addressed [Dillman 2000]. For example, by incorporating a range of features into the design of an online-questionnaire, it is possible to support respondents' estimation of the length of a questionnaire — and to provide respondents with context sensitive assistance during the response process — and thereby reduce abandonment while eliciting feelings of accomplishment [Crawford et al. 2001].

For online-questionnaires, sampling error ("the result of attempting to survey only some, and not all, of the units of the survey population" [Dillman 2000, p.9]) can arise when all but a small portion of the anticipated respondent set is alienated (and so fails to respond) as a result of, for example, disregard for varying connection speeds, bandwidth limitations, browser configurations, monitors, hardware, and user requirements during the questionnaire design process. Similarly, measurement errors ("the result of poor question wording or questions being presented in such a way that inaccurate or uninterpretable answers are obtained" [Dillman 2000, p.11]) will lead to respondents becoming confused and frustrated.

Sampling, measurement, and non-response errors are likely to occur when an online-questionnaire is poorly designed (note that coverage errors, on the other hand, are orthogonal to good-questionnaire design; mixed-mode delivery is suggested as a means to combat these errors). Individuals will answer questions incorrectly, abandon questionnaires, and may ultimately refuse to participate in future surveys; thus, the benefit of online-questionnaire delivery will be not fully realized. To prevent errors of this kind, and their consequences, it is extremely important that practical, comprehensive guidelines exist for the design of online-questionnaires. Many design guidelines exist for paper-based questionnaire design [e.g. American Statistical Association 1999; Belson 1981; Brewer 2001; Fink 1995; Jackson 1988; Lindgaard 1994; Oppenheim 1992; Taylor-Powell 1998] but the same is not true for the design of online-questionnaires [Dillman 2000; Norman et al. 2003; Schonlau et al. 2001]. The guidelines introduced in this paper, and their subsequent study, help address this discrepancy.

3 Comprehensive Design Guidelines

In essence, an online-questionnaire combines questionnaire-based survey functionality with that of a webpage/site. As such, the design of an online-questionnaire should incorporate principles from both contributing fields. Hence, in order to derive a comprehensive set of guidelines for the design of online-questionnaires, we performed an environmental scan of existing guidelines for paper-based questionnaire design [e.g. American Statistical Association 1999; Belson 1981; CASRO 1998; Fink 1995; Jackson 1988; Lindgaard 1994; Oppenheim 1992; Taylor-Powell 1998] and website design, paying particular attention to issues of accessibility and usability [e.g. Badre 2002; Brewer 2001; Coyne & Nielsen 2001, 2002; Hinton 1998; Kothari & Basak 2002; Lynch & Horton 1997; National Cancer Institute 2002; National Institute on Aging & National Library of Medicine 2001; Stover et al. 2002; Stover & Nielsen 2002; W3C 1999]. Additionally, we reviewed the scarce existing provision of online-questionnaire design guidelines [Dillman 2000; Norman et al. 2003; Schonlau et al. 2001]. Principal amongst the latter is the work of Dillman [2000]: expanding on his successful *Total Design Method* for mail and telephone surveys [Dillman 1978], Dillman introduced, as part of his *Tailored Design Method* [Dillman 2000], fourteen additional guidelines specifically aimed at directing the design of online-questionnaires. Albeit seminal, Dillman's guidelines do not incorporate much of the relevant guidance uncovered as part of our environmental scan. We therefore propose — after collating, filtering, and

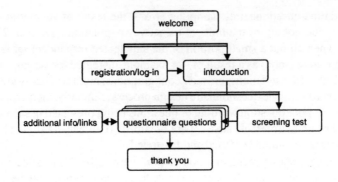

Figure 1: Organizational structure of online-questionnaires (arrows show progression, a double-barred arrow indicating choice in the structure).

General Organization	Formatting	Question Type & Phrasing	General Technical Issues
Welcome Page	Text	General Guidance	Privacy & Protection
Registration/: Login Page	Colour	Sensitive Questions	Computer Literacy
Introduction Page	Graphics	Attitude Statements	Automation
Screening Test Page	Flash	Phraseology	Platforms & Browsers
Questionnaire Questions	Tables & Frames	Types of Question	Devices
Additional Info/Links	Feedback	Open-Ended	Assistive Technology
Thank You	Miscellaneous	Closed-Ended	
Layout	Response Formats	Rank-Order	
Frames	Matrix Questions	Categorical/Nominal	
Forms & Fields	Drop-Down Boxes	Magnitude Estimate	
Navigation	Radio Buttons	Ordinal	
Buttons	Check Boxes	Likert Scale	
Links		Skip	
Site Maps			
Scrolling			

Table 1: Organization of the guidelines, showing topics covered.

integrating the disparate guidelines — a comprehensive set of guidelines for online-questionnaire design that are more encompassing than Dillman's. Approximately 33% of the resulting set of guidelines stem directly from paper-based questionnaire design guidelines; the remainder (67%) are derived from webpage design guidelines as they apply to questionnaire design. This paper will only highlight the key elements of the guidelines; the full set of guidelines is available on request.

3.1 Overview of the Guidelines

Although the guidelines provide minimal support for other aspects of the design process for online-questionnaires, their main focus is on the design and implementation stages associated with online-questionnaire creation. They describe the general organizational structure that should be adopted by the majority of online-

There are a number of issues of importance when designing the textual content of an online-questionnaire:

a. Fonts used should be readable and familiar, and text should be presented in mixed case or standard sentence formatting; upper case (or all capitals) should only be used for emphasis;

b. Sentences should not exceed 20 words, and should be presented with no more than 75 characters per line. If elderly respondents are anticipated, then this limit should be reduced to between 50 and 65 characters per line. Paragraphs should not exceed 5 sentences in length;

c. Technical instructions (those being instructions related to the basic technical operation of the website delivering the questionnaire) should be written in such a way that non-technical people can understand them;

d. Ensure that questions are easily distinguishable, in terms of formatting, from instructions and answers;

e. For each question type, be consistent in terms of the visual appearance of all instances of that type and the associated instructions concerning how they are to be answered. In particular, keep the relative position of the question and answer consistent throughout the questionnaire. Where different types of questions are to be included in the same questionnaire, each question type should have a unique visual appearance;

f. When designing for access by users with disabilities and the elderly, employ a minimum of size 12pt font and ensure that the font colour contrasts significantly with the background colouring. Text should be discernible even without the use of colour. It is advisable to test font colours and size with a screen magnifier to ensure usability prior to release;

g. If targeting an elderly audience, provide a text-sizing option on each page, use bold face but avoid italics, and left-justify text. It is also advisable to increase the spacing between lines of text for ease of reading by this respondent group;

h. Make sure that text is read (by screen readers) in a logical order. Specifically, set the tab order on the pages. This is especially true for actual questions in the questionnaire — think carefully about the order in which a visually impaired user will hear the elements of a question, including the instructions and response options.

Table 2: An excerpt from the online-questionnaire design guidelines.

questionnaires (see Figure 1) and then progressively refine the guidance according to the issues shown in Table 1.

Since it is not possible to include the comprehensive set of guidelines in this paper, excerpts are shown in Tables 2 & 3 to provide a 'flavour' for the guidelines as a whole; the guidance in Table 2 relates to the formatting of text in online-questionnaires whilst that in Table 3 relates to the layout of form and field components commonly used to construct online-questionnaires.

When reading the examples, it is important to note that none of the guidelines are particularly innovative in their own right; each has been drawn from the aforementioned sources covered by the environmental scan. What *is* novel, however, is the fact that applicable guidelines from these disparate sources have been collated into a unified set which is presented methodically as a comprehensive, practical guide to online-questionnaire design; webpage design concepts such as visual design

Layout:: Forms and Fields: By their very nature, questionnaires include elements common to forms — that is, layout and the use of fields for data entry. Users with disabilities can find forms and fields problematic, and so it is important that the following guidelines — which are relevant across all respondent groups — be taken into consideration when laying out these elements of a questionnaire:

a. Locate field labels close to their associated fields so that respondents can easily make the association; this also prevents labels becoming lost when a screen is magnified by users with visual impairment.

b. A 'submit' (or similar) button should always be located adjacent to the last field on any given page so that it is easily identified by respondents at the point at which they have completed the question responses; this is again especially important for users of assistive technology since it goes some way to ensuring that such a button will not be overlooked when the screen is magnified.

c. The tab order for key based navigation around the fields in a questionnaire should be logical and reflect the visual appearance as far as is possible.

d. Fields are most easily read if stacked in a vertical column and any instructions pertaining to a given field should appear before and not after the field if it is to be understood by users of assistive technology.

Table 3: Another excerpt from the online-questionnaire design guidelines.

principles have been integrated with the large body of knowledge on paper-based questionnaire design principles to provide practical support for designers of online-questionnaires.

4 An Observational Study

Having established the set of guidelines, we set up an informal study to observe the extent of the influence of the guidelines on the design of an online-questionnaire. This is the first in a series of planned evaluations to determine the effect of applying the guidelines to online-questionnaire design, and in turn, the effectiveness of the set of guidelines as a practical support measure during the design process.

4.1 The Observational Procedure

A contract software developer was hired to create an online-questionnaire for the purpose of surveying public awareness of security issues when using the Internet. We established the following process by which we could observe the use of the guidelines when applied to this real, substantial online-questionnaire development project.

The software developer (henceforth referred to as M) employed to develop the electronic survey had no previous experience of questionnaire development (paper-based or electronic). We specifically selected a developer without prior experience since we did not want previous exposure to online-questionnaire design to influence the design process under observation. M did, however, have extensive experience with website design. We felt that a developer with this profile may be representative of many of the users of the online-questionnaire design and delivery tools on the market and/or of the typical developers of online-surveys within business environs.

M was provided with a plain text list of the 29 questions (including response sets where applicable) that were to be incorporated in the survey; no indication was given as to the question type/style nor to layout. For our purposes, we did not want to assess M's ability to appropriately phrase the survey questions; instead, experts in questionnaire design and the domain being studied formulated the questions and response options independently of this observational study.

As a 'warm up' exercise, M was asked to develop a first prototype of the online-questionnaire. M was not provided with any advice on questionnaire design at this point. The aim of this exercise was simply to familiarize M with the technology and protocols of the organization as well as the survey questions; the resulting prototype was effectively a 'throw away' prototype and as such is not the focus of this discussion.

After the 'warm up' exercise, M was furnished with a set of guidelines for the development of *paper-based* questionnaires. These were drawn from the same sources for paper-based questionnaire design as were used to generate the comprehensive set of guidelines discussed in the previous section. M was then asked to design and develop an online-questionnaire with reference to the guidelines for paper-based questionnaire design. A screen shot of part of the resulting online-questionnaire (known hereafter as Q1) is shown in Figure 2.

Finally, upon completion of Q1, M was provided with the complete, comprehensive set of guidelines for the design of online-questionnaires (of which the paper-based design guidelines formed a subset). M was asked to design and develop another online-questionnaire with reference to the complete set of guidelines. A screen shot of part of the resulting online-questionnaire (known hereafter as Q2) is shown in Figure 2. During each of the above design and development exercises, M was asked to maintain a log of design issues and their resolution relative to the guidelines available at the time.

Although one might argue that learning had a significant effect on the final design of Q2, and to a certain extent this will be true, we had no option but to deliver the guidelines in this order. Since the paper-based guidelines are a subset of the comprehensive guidelines, we could not have isolated the influence of the paper-based guidelines had the comprehensive set been used by M prior to the paper-based set. Additionally, we essentially wanted to use the observed experience with the paper-based guidelines as a 'control' against which to compare the effect of the comprehensive set of design guidelines; we felt that it would have been an unfair comparison to have simply compared the 'warm up' version of the online-questionnaire to Q2 — the paper-based guidelines are readily available to questionnaire designers and so their use as a 'control' was considered more realistic for this study.

Once both versions of the online-questionnaire were fully tested, the survey was made publicly available online. All respondents were required to complete an identical click-through consent form; thereafter, in an alternating pattern, respondents were presented with either Q1 or Q2 — for example, if respondent x was allocated Q1, then respondent $x + 1$ was allocated Q2. Using this allocation, each questionnaire had an equal exposure rate; no respondent was aware of the

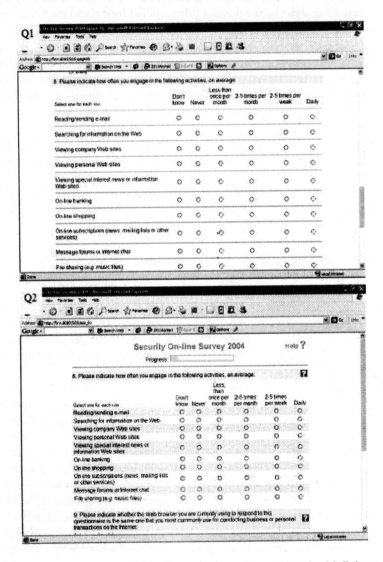

Figure 2: Screen shot of question 8 from both versions of the online-questionnaire, labelled accordingly.

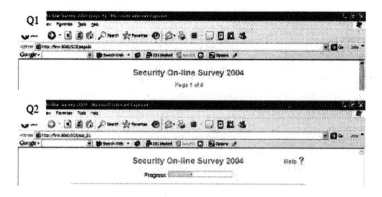

Figure 3: Progress indicators from both versions of the online-questionnaire, labelled accordingly.

existence of the alternative version of the questionnaire. For the purpose of the actual survey being conducted, the wording and type of each question was identical across both Q1 and Q2; what differed between Q1 and Q2 were the aesthetics, structure, provision of help, and level of automation.

4.2 Comparing the Two Designs

Consider the difference in aesthetics and structure between Q1 and Q2. Q1 comprised 4 long scrolling pages; in Q2, the questionnaire was split up into a maximum of 15 pages (depending on skip question responses) with, as far as possible, minimal need for scrolling. Q2 made more use of block shading to enhance the readability of the questionnaire and to differentiate between questions, instructions, and response options. Questions within Q1 were typically quite condensed within each page — each page had a 'cluttered' feel; in Q2 more use was made of white space between questions to enhance readability. Conversely, as shown in Figure 2, response options in matrix questions were brought into closer proximity in Q2 to support easier visual association between radio buttons and response labels and ensure that response labels were never widowed, as a result of scrolling, from the radio buttons.

It is in the scope of help and level of automation that the two versions of the questionnaire differ the most. Although Q1 does provide some indication of progression through the questionnaire, given the extent of questions per scrolling page of the questionnaire, the scale provides for only a very high level judgement of progress. In contrast, Q2 uses a progress indicator which, given the lesser extent of questions on each page, is better able to support a more accurate assessment of progress. Both indicators are shown in Figure 3.

The online-questionnaire included four skip questions. Q1 provided written instruction to the respondents to direct them to the next applicable question, as determined by their response to the skip question (see Figure 4). In contrast, all skip questions (and thereby patterns) were encoded within Q2 such that the cognitive load associated with skip patterns was removed entirely from the respondents who were subsequently wholly unaware that they were following skip patterns (see Figure 4).

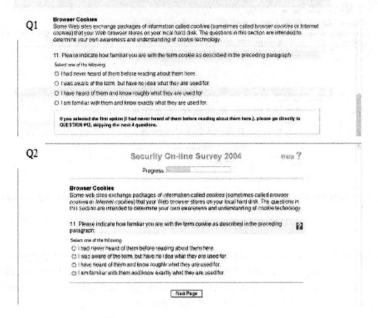

Figure 4: A skip question from both versions of the online-questionnaire, labelled accordingly.

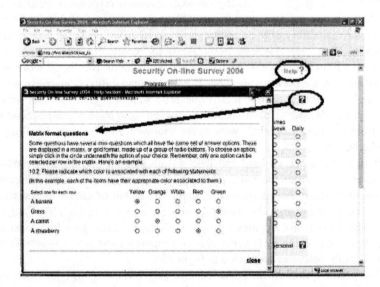

Figure 5: Help facility in Q2 — clicking on the help links in a page brings up context-sensitive help to assist respondents in the mechanics of responding.

Finally, Q2 included a pop-up help facility which was entirely absent from Q1. At the top of each page, a link to a pop-up help screen was always available (see Figure 5) and provided help about the mechanics associated with answering all of the question types in the questionnaire; adjacent to each *question* there was also a 'help' link which provided context sensitive help relative to the mechanics of that particular question type — Figure 5 shows an example of help for a matrix style question.

As can be seen, there were a number of substantial differences between the two versions of the questionnaire in terms of general aesthetics, structure, automation, and help. While the guidelines for paper-based questionnaire design that were applied to Q1 prompted effective question formatting (this was the focus of most entries in M's log for Q1), it was the comprehensive set of guidelines for online-questionnaire design that appeared to prompt M to make substantial changes to the aforementioned aspects of Q2. On the basis of our observations, it would seem that without the comprehensive set of guidelines, M's design was restricted to following the traditional paper-based model — the comprehensive guidelines seemed to encourage M to 'think out of the box' — or more laterally — and embrace the functionality available in the electronic delivery mechanism (a process which did not seem to happen 'intuitively' without prompting from the guidelines). They also appeared to encourage M to give considerable thought to each functional design decision (e.g. tabular presentation and the accessibility issues associated with such presentation) since extensive discussion of rationale concerning such decisions formed the basis of most comments in M's log for Q2. Anecdotally, M seemed to appreciate the support of the guidelines — as indicated in the following quotation taken from a post-development interview:

> "By using Web-based guidelines, it encompasses the practicality of paper-based guidelines as well as guidance for a Web medium [...] the advantages of having such guidelines are countless. [...] The guidelines offered solutions for problems I hadn't even considered [...] The [comprehensive set of] guidelines improve[d] the questionnaire."

4.3 Comparing the Responses to the Two Designs

In terms of functionality and look-and-feel, the comprehensive set of guidelines appears to have had a substantial influence on the design of the questionnaire (based on a qualitative comparison of Q1 and Q2). We therefore decided to look for qualitative differences in the 'responses' returned for the two versions of the questionnaire. That is, we wanted to see what, if any, impact the above noted differences in functionality and look-and-feel had on the manner in which the respondents completed the two versions of the questionnaire; we were not concerned with the semantics of their responses. It is important to reiterate that both Q1 and Q2 asked exactly the same questions and presented the response options to these questions using the same question style; thus, any differences between the quality and/or quantity of responses between Q1 and Q2 can essentially be attributable to the differences discussed in Section 4.2.

A total of 236 questionnaires were completed: Q1 achieved a completion rate of 64.6% which was only slightly less than the 65.7% rate attained by Q2. There was no significant difference in the average time taken to complete each version of the questionnaire.

Based on the hypothesis that Q2, as a result of its aesthetic and functional enhancement, would be 'easier to use' and therefore less frustrating, we anticipated that respondents using Q2 would complete more of the open-ended questions than respondents using Q1; that is, Q2 respondents would be more inclined to invest the necessary additional effort required to complete this type of question. This was not found to be the case and, in fact, there was no real difference in the average length of such responses between the two versions of the questionnaire. That said, albeit not statistically significant, 14.5% of Q1 respondents left questions unanswered (not counting open-ended questions or those which should have been left unanswered by virtue of applicable skip patterns) whereas this figure was only 10.1% for Q2. This would suggest that the aesthetics and functionality of Q2 were more conducive to supplying a response to questions.

For all matrix style questions, we assessed the extent to which respondents relied on neutral responses and/or exhibited response set behaviour. There was no significant difference between Q1 and Q2 in this regard.

Perhaps the two most interesting findings concern respondents' handling of skip questions/patterns and abandonment behaviour. Consider, first, skip questions. Obviously, skip questions and their associated patterns were completely automated in Q2, and thereby hidden from the respondents. As such, it was impossible for respondents to Q2 to waste effort answering questions that should have been skipped. In contrast, Q1 required respondents to comprehend written skip patterns and manually skip the applicable questions. Consequently, 11.6% of respondents who should have skipped at least one question, answered questions that they should have skipped. On average, these respondents answered 85% of the questions that they should have skipped (ranging from a minimum of 25% to a maximum of 100% of such questions). Naturally, this represents a significant waste of respondents' time and effort and is likely to lead to irreparable levels of frustration. It highlights the benefit of automating this aspect of online-questionnaire delivery.

Approximately 35% of respondents who started the survey failed to complete it; this figure was essentially the same for both Q1 and Q2. We hypothesized that, as a result of its enhanced functionality and aesthetics, Q2 would hold the attention of such respondents for considerably longer than Q1; that is, respondents would complete more of Q2 before abandoning it than Q1. To test this hypothesis, for each of the respondents who abandoned the survey part way through, we calculated (taking into account skip patterns) the last possible question that they *could* have seen on the basis of the last webpage requested. For ethical reasons, we could not record the precise questions which respondents *actually* answered since they had abandoned the survey and so we too had to abandon their partial results; the only data we could ethically access was the series of webpage request patterns from the server log. From this, we calculated the extent of completion for each respondent as a percentage of the total possible given their path thus far. On average, respondents who abandoned Q1 completed 32.4% of the questionnaire before giving up; in contrast, respondents to Q2 went significantly further (on average 42.4%) before abandoning the survey ($t_{122} = 1.82$, $p = 0.035$). Had we been able to assess the precise question at which the respondents abandoned their versions of the survey, we feel that the difference in extent of completion would have been even more pronounced; each of the four pages in Q1 contain considerably more questions than the fifteen pages in Q2 and so in essence our calculations were potentially giving the respondents to Q1 a large benefit of doubt — it was highly unlikely that respondents were on the last question of a page when they abandoned the survey. Given the importance, yet associated difficulty, of achieving high response rates for questionnaire-based surveys, this finding is important; it would suggest that there is demonstrated potential for the set of comprehensive design guidelines to assist online-questionnaire designers to develop questionnaires which encourage respondents to persevere with a questionnaire.

4.4 Discussion

On the basis of the aesthetic and functional disparity between the two versions of our questionnaire, we had (somewhat naïvely perhaps) anticipated finding more significant differences in terms of quality and quantity of responses between Q1 and Q2. With hindsight, however, we feel this study has helped raise interesting questions concerning what constitutes success in this domain. How can two (or more) designs for the same online-questionnaire be fairly and effectively compared and evaluated? What are the dimensions of a successful and effective online-questionnaire? To what extent can these dimensions be addressed through the online medium as opposed to simply being a facet of questionnaire topic, question wording, scale choice etc.?

That said, the results outlined in the previous section suggest that application of the comprehensive set of guidelines to the design process for an online-survey may be extremely beneficial in tackling two of the most complex issues associated with questionnaire-based surveys: respondent perseverance and handling of skip patterns. In this regard, we feel that our study has yielded positive results.

5 Conclusions

Albeit this was an *initial* observation of the merit of the guidelines for online-questionnaire design, we feel that some interesting and valuable findings have come to light. It would appear that the guidelines encourage more lateral thinking in terms of online-questionnaire design while, at the same time, promoting careful consideration of design issues that effect accessibility and thereby usability. This is reflected in the aesthetic and functional differences between Q2 and Q1.

It would have been advantageous to have been able to 'tag' a post-questionnaire questionnaire to the online-survey in order to elicit information about respondents' subjective impressions of their allocated questionnaires. However, we felt this would have been too much on top of what was already a complex questionnaire and would ultimately have been detrimental to the survey itself. The extent of progress prior to abandoning the online-survey is therefore our only insight into respondents' subjective assessment of their allocated questionnaire: the results suggest that the comprehensive set of guidelines for online-questionnaire design has the potential to improve subjective reaction to surveys delivered online.

Finally, as mentioned in Section 2, online-questionnaires have the potential to reduce non-response errors as a result of questionnaire abandonment but only when appropriate measures are incorporated within the design of online-questionnaires. The significant improvement in extent of completion prior to abandonment for Q2 indicates that the comprehensive set of guidelines has demonstrated potential for combating this error type for online-questionnaires.

We feel that the observed qualitative results of this study are encouraging for the further development of the guidelines, for the development of mechanisms for their inclusion in the design process for online-questionnaires, and ultimately for their role in the 'bigger picture' that is online survey delivery across many domains such as e-government, e-business, and e-health.

References

American Statistical Association [1999], American Statistical Association Series: What is a Survey?, http://www.amstat.org/sections/srms/brochures/designquest.pdf (retrieved 2003-06-07).

Badre, A. N. [2002], *Shaping Web Usability: Interaction Design in Context*, Pearson Education.

Bandilla, W., Bosnjak, M. & Altdorfer, P. [2003], Self Administration Effects? A Comparison of Web-Based and Traditional Written Self-Administered Surveys Using the ISSP Environment Module, *Social Science Computing Review* 21(2), 235–43.

Belson, W. A. [1981], *The Design and Understanding of Survey Questions*, Gower Publishing.

Brewer, J. [2001], How People with Disabilities Use the Web, W3C Working Draft, W3C. See http://www.w3.org/WAI/EO/Drafts/PWD-Use-Web/ for current and previous versions.

CASRO [1998], Guidelines for Survey Research Quality, http://www.casro.org/guidelines.cfm (retrieved 2003-06-07). Council of American Survey Research Organization.

Coyne, K. P. & Nielsen, J. [2001], Beyond ALT Text: Making the Web Easy to Use for Users with Disabilities, Technical Report, Nielsen Norman Group.

Coyne, K. P. & Nielsen, J. [2002], Web Usability for Senior Citizens, Technical Report, Nielsen Norman Group.

Crawford, S. D., Couper, M. P. & Lamias, M. J. [2001], Web Surveys: Perceptions of Burden, *Social Science Computing Review* 19(2), 146–62.

Dillman, D. A. [1978], *Mail and Telephone Surveys: The Total Design Method*, John Wiley & Sons.

Dillman, D. A. [2000], *Mail and Internet Surveys: The Tailored Design Method*, second edition, John Wiley & Sons.

Fink, A. [1995], *How to Ask Survey Questions*, Sage Publications.

Hinton, S. M. [1998], From Home Page to Home Site: Effective Web Resource Discovery at the ANU, *in* H. Ashman & P. Thistlewaite (eds.), *Proceedings of the Seventh International World Wide Web Conference (WWW7)*, Vol. **30**(1–7) of *Computer Networks and ISDN Systems*, Elsevier Science, pp.309–16. See also http://www7.scu.edu.au/.

Jackson, W. [1988], *Research Methods: Rules for Survey Design and Analysis*, Prentice–Hall.

Kothari, R. & Basak, J. [2002], Perceptually Automated Evaluation of Web Page Layouts, *in Paper Presented in an Alternative Track of the Eleventh International World Wide Web Conference (WWW2002)*. http://www2002.org/CDROM/alternate/688/index.html.

Kwak, N. & Radler, B. [2002], A Comparison Between Mail and Web Surveys: Response Pattern, Respondent Profile and Data Quality, *Journal of Official Statistics* **18**(2), 257–74.

Lindgaard, G. [1994], *Usability Testing and System Evaluation: A Guide for Designing Useful Computer Systems*, Chapman & Hall.

Lumsden, J. & Morgan, W. [2005], Online Questionnaire Design: Establishing Guidelines and Evaluating Existing Support, *in* M. Khosrow-Pour (ed.), *Managing Modern Organizations with Information Technology: Proceedings of the 16th Information Resources Management Association International Conference (IRMA 2005)*, IRM Press, pp.407–10.

Lynch, P. J. & Horton, S. [1997], *Web Style Guide*, Yale University Press. See also http://www.webstyleguide.com/.

National Cancer Institute [2002], National Cancer Institute's Research Based Web Design & Usability Guidelines, http://usability.gov/guidelines/index.html (retrieved 2003-06-10).

National Institute on Aging & National Library of Medicine [2001], Making Your Web Site Senior Friendly, http://www.nlm.nih.gov/pubs/checklist.pdf (retrieved 2003-06-19).

Norman, K. L., Lee, S., Moore, P., Murry, G. C., Rivadeneira, W., Smith, B. K. & Verdines, P. [2003], Online Survey Design Guide, http://lap.umd.edu/survey_design/tools.html (retrieved 2003-06-17).

OECD [2001], Bridging the "Digital Divide": Issues and Policies in OECD Countries, http://www.oecd.org/dataoecd/10/0/27128723.pdf (retrieved 2003-06-03).

Oppenheim, A. N. [1992], *Questionnaire Design, Interviewing and Attitude Measurement*, Pinter Publishers.

Schonlau, M., Fricker, R. D. & Elliott, M. N. [2001], Conducting Research via E-mail and the Web, http://www.rand.org/publications/MR/MR1480/ (retrieved 2003-06-16).

Stover, A., Coyne, K. P. & Nielsen, J. [2002], Designing Usable Site Maps for Websites, Technical Report, Nielsen Norman Group.

Stover, A. & Nielsen, J. [2002], Accessibility and Usability of Flash for Users with Disabilities, Technical Report, Nielsen Norman Group.

Taylor-Powell, E. [1998], Questionnaire Design: Asking Questions with a Purpose, Technical Report G3658-2, University of Wisconsin.

W3C [1999], Web Content Accessibility Guidelines 1.0, http://www.w3.org/TR/1999/WAI-WEBCONTENT-19990505 (retrieved 2003-06-08).

Designing Interactive Systems in Context: From Prototype to Deployment

Tim Clerckx, Kris Luyten & Karin Coninx

Limburgs Universitair Centrum — Expertise Centre for Digital Media Universitaire Campus, B-3590 Diepenbeek, Belgium
Email: *{tim.clerckx, kris.luyten, karin.coninx}@luc.ac.be*
URL: *http://www.edm.luc.ac.be*

The possibility of communicating with the (in) direct environment using other devices and observing that same environment allow us to develop ambient intelligent applications which have knowledge of the environment and of the use of these applications. Despite the support for software development for this kind of application, some gaps still exist, making the creation of consistent, usable user interfaces more difficult. This paper discusses a technique that can be integrated into existing models and architectures and that supports the interface designer in making consistent context-sensitive user interfaces. We present an architecture and methodology that allows context information to be used at two different levels — dialogue and interdialogue levels — and ensures that the consistency of the interface is always maintained in the event of context changes during use of the software.

Keywords: user interface design, context aware user interface, model-based user interface development.

1 Introduction

The spread of the ISTAG[1] Ambient Intelligence scenarios has clarified future technological needs and developments. These scenarios indicate what the industry is looking for and how new technologies are applied, in which the user is the focal point. Although various components of these scenarios are still pipe dreams, the technology for other components is now ready to be applied to the situations discussed.

---

[1] Information Societies Technologies Advisory Group, http://www.cordis.lu/ist/istag.htm.

In order to familiarize the reader with our objectives, we introduce the following brief scenario, based on the test case envisaged in Schmidt et al. [1999]. A mobile telephone can react appropriately to various situations: in the example, use is made of light and heat sensors in combination with the buttons on the device. Thus, the interface will show the information differently in strong light (the telephone is 'visible') than in low-intensity light (the telephone is hidden in the bag). The telephone can thus assume, if there is no light and a higher temperature, that the mobile is buried in the inside pocket. By integrating context information with the design of the user interface, as proposed in this paper, the designer can for example easily ensure that, if the light is weak and the temperature is low, the dialogues contain less information, which can be shown larger because this may be desirable in that situation.

Unlike the experiment described in Schmidt et al. [1999], the emphasis here is not on context gathering by abstraction of the sensors, but on making context information applicable in the user interface. In this paper, context in the software engineering process and, more specifically, in User Interface engineering, is integrated into model-based user interface development.

Applications interrogate their environment using sensors and by communicating with other applications in their environment. For instance, an application builds up the context from all the data gathered. We concentrate not on the way in which context is gathered and combined, but on how the context information data can be used during both design and use of the user interface. Context can be defined in various ways [Dey et al. 2001; Coutaz & Rey 2002; Schmidt et al. 1999]. According to Dey, context is only relevant if it influences the user's task: A system is context-aware if it uses context to provide relevant information and/or services to the user, where relevancy depends on the user's task. This is why attention should be devoted, at the design stage, to the link between the tasks of the user on the one hand and to the type of context influencing these user tasks on the other hand. Here, we use the following definition, based on Dey's definition of a context-sensitive system [Dey et al. 2001] and with the focus on sensing the environment in order to pursue uniformity and clarity in this work: Context is the information gathered from the environment which can influence the tasks the user wants to, can or may perform.

Despite extensive research concerning the acquisition, integration and interpretation of context information in software applications, as far as we know no other initiatives exist which integrate context at all stages of the design and use of the interface. In this context, we introduce DynaMo-AID, part of the Dygimes [Coninx et al. 2003] framework. DynaMo-AID is both a user interface design process and a runtime architecture which makes use of extensions of conventional models such as task, dialogue, presentation and application models, in order to support the design of context-aware applications. The Dygimes framework provides support for combining and further processing these different models. Thus, the framework contains a renderer that converts a high-level device-independent XML description into a concrete user interface, a module for combining these XML descriptions with a task model and an algorithm that can calculate a dialogue model from the temporal relationships in the task model [Luyten et al. 2003].

DynaMo-AID was introduced in Clerckx et al. [2004a] where the models to design the user interface were discussed. Clerckx et al. [2004b] elaborates on the context-sensitive task model which is used in the design process. This paper describes how context can be applied in the design and creation of the user interface with the emphasis on the runtime architecture and the support for prototyping. The implementation is entirely written in Java so as to make it available on as many platforms as possible. The rest of this paper will discuss this in more detail. The following section gives a summary of related work, so that this work can be positioned within existing research. We then show that our approach can be regarded as complementary to various other initiatives. In the subsequent sections, we show how context can be taken into account in the design phase of the user interface. One way this is supported is to automatically generate prototype user interfaces enabling the genuine look and feel of the context-aware interface to be experienced at an early stage of interface design. Following the discussion of current achievements, future work is discussed and appropriate conclusions drawn.

2 Related Work

Writing software that can adapt to the context of use is an important component of present-day applications. Support for these types of application is still a major topic for research. The Context Toolkit [Salber et al. 1999; Dey & Abowd 2004, 2000] is probably the best known way of abstracting context and making it 'generally' usable. A clear division of components that embed, aggregate and interpret context information is envisaged. A method is proposed in Dey et al. [2001] to give end users the opportunity to develop context-aware applications. However, less emphasis is placed on the effects and use of context on and in the user interface; instead they are targeting software engineers for the development of context aware applications.

An abstraction of context is useful for processing the data from sensors in a generic way in an application. The use of sensors is the ideal way to obtain information from the immediate physical environment. Thus, we see that procuring and interpreting the right information from the sensors can be dependent on the application that is built [Schmidt et al. 1999]. A thorough survey of context sensing systems and their use in an interactive system is given in Schmidt [2002]. In contrast to what Schmidt proposes in his work, we concentrate less on the hardware component and more on the software component: conventional user interfaces that are influenced by context changes. Despite the increasing penetration of computer systems into physical objects, it is also still important to provide current devices (PDA, mobile phone, Tablet PC, ...) with context-sensitive user interfaces, see Hinckley et al. [2000], Schmidt et al. [1999].

Contextors by Coutaz & Rey [2002] are geared more towards the user. In addition to an encapsulation of context information, similar to the encapsulation envisaged in the Context Toolkit, the user and interaction with the user are given more consideration. By defining a software model (a variation of the Arch model [Coutaz 1994]), consideration is explicitly given to the influence that context changes can have on the dialogue with the user.

Henricksen & Indulska [2004] approaches context less from the point of view of the sensors, but their work shows an integration of context into the software

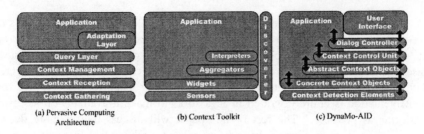

(a) Pervasive Computing
Architecture

(b) Context Toolkit

(c) DynaMo-AID

Figure 1: Comparison of three architectures for context-aware applications.

engineering methodology. This is a necessary evolution in order to maintain the consistency and relevancy of the software models when building context-sensitive applications. However, so far this is not related to software development environments that abstract context, such as the context toolkit or contextors.

Winograd [2001] distinguishes between three models for context management:

Widget-based: Widgets encapsulate the device drivers at a more abstract level. Interaction with these entities takes place by sending messages to the widget and interpreting messages from the widget.

Networked services: In this case, a service to which applications can be linked presents context information.

Blackboard approach: Here, context information is held at a central point and applications can sign in to be notified if they want to make use of this information.

A modern approach is to combine these three models into a hybrid model. One can argument that a widget-based approach implies a very close connection between devices and the direct dialogue with the user. An established infrastructure approach of networked services is the context fabric [Hong & Landay 2004]. In this infrastructure, devices can query an infrastructure and register for events in order to make use of context information. Communication between the devices and the infrastructure is supported with an XML-based Context Specification Language.

The approach we present here involves a more strict division and context will only indirectly influence dialogue with the user. As a result of the strictly layered structure in the model presented below, at the lowest levels it is possible to work with both networked services (Web services, for example) and via the blackboard approach (achieving a socket connection with a context server). In the following section, we will examine more closely how the model here complements the existing context management models rather than trying to replace them.

3   Context Architectures

Figure 1 shows the comparison between two architectures and our own architecture, which are suitable for gathering and processing context information from context-sensitive applications.

The first architecture (Figure 1a), described in Henricksen & Indulska [2004], fits into a software engineering framework for context sensitive pervasive computing. Here, the abstraction for the context manager is already placed at the level of context gathering. The context manager interprets information from the context-gathering layer, which is translated by the context reception layer and acts as a distributed database for the application, which can relay queries to this context manager. This architecture takes no account of the effects on the user interface: a software engineering process that uses it will not provide explicit support to the influence of context changes in the user interface.

The Context Toolkit [Dey & Abowd 2004; Salber et al. 1999; Dey & Abowd 2000] (Figure 1b) is an object-oriented architecture that allows the application to approach the context information at different abstraction levels. This is not therefore a strictly layered structure, as is the case in Pervasive Computing Architecture. The application layer can access both directly objects that only encapsulate sensors as well as objects that abstract context information instead, such as objects that aggregate or even interpret context information. The Context Toolkit contains context widgets for sensor encapsulation, interpreters to interpret context data, aggregators to merge several types of context widget and a discoverer to search out services in the environment.

Figure 1c shows our approach. Here, the raw context information with respect to the application and the user interface are dealt with separately. The user interface can only be influenced by the context by communicating events and associated data (may or may not be abstract information about the detected context change) to a superior layer. If a layer receives an event from a lower layer, it will interpret the associated information and decide whether the context change is significant enough to pass on the interpreted information to the next layer up. Significant means a defined threshold has been exceeded or a value change has taken place invoking a change. The user interface can thus only be updated by the dialogue controller which will first have been notified by the Context Control Unit, which has in turn picked up an event from an abstract context object and so forth. In this way, the user interface designer can confine her/himself to modelling of the user interface at an abstract level, and how this is liable to context. This implies no account needs to be taken of how context information is available in the application.

By contrast, the application can make use of the different levels of context information. Thus, the programmer still has the freedom to include concrete context information for her/his application. In this way, we attempt to combine the various approaches of the first and second architectures for the application of context information to the user interface and the application respectively.

As a result of the difference in approach to the use of context information between application and user interface and the distinction between application and user interface, this architecture lends itself to integration in a human computer interaction (HCI) framework. Note that in our approach the user interface can only be changed via the dialogue controller, which makes use of models (task, dialogue and environment models). This protects consistency with the presentation defined by the designer, with the result that the usability available to the user when generating the user interface from the models is ensured.

4 Designing Context-Sensitive Applications

Before we explain the design phase, it is necessary to say how we structure context information. Several approaches are already available for modelling and using context in applications. Coutaz & Rey [2002] define the contextor as a software abstraction of context data which interprets sensor-based or aggregated information. In this way, several contextors can be merged to form a logical component.

The Context Toolkit [Dey & Abowd 2004] includes abstract widgets for:

- Encapsulating raw context details and abstracting implementation details.

- The re-use of context widgets for various applications.

In our approach, we choose to deal with these two goals at two abstraction levels. On the one hand, low-level widgets can separate raw context/sensor data from further interpretation. On the other hand, high-level widgets are easy to use and re-use for user interface designers and applications.

We define:

A Concrete Context Object (CCO) is an object that encapsulates a type of context (such as low-level sensors).

An Abstract Context Object (ACO) is an object that can be queried about the status of the context information.

An ACO uses at least one CCO. At runtime the number of CCOs can change depending on the services available at that time. The function of the ACO can be compared to the interpreter in the Context Toolkit. However, the ACO entirely encapsulates all sensor data and is the only link between user interface designer and context information. As a result, the user interface designer is only confronted with abstract context information.

Our architecture lends itself to split the implementation of an application into the implementation of three independent parts: the user interface, the context objects and the application core. Contracts exist between these parts that make it possible to envisage communication between these entities.

User Interface: The user interface designer concentrates on modelling the user interface using a model-based approach. Communication between user interface and application is provided by linking application tasks in the task model with methods available for the user interface in the application core. In order to integrate context information, the user interface designer can select from abstract context objects.

Context Objects: The context objects can be separately implemented, for example by engineers for the encapsulation of hardware components (CCOs) and by AI specialists for the interpretation (ACOs) of raw context information.

Application Core: The application core can be implemented by software engineers and can make use of all artefacts supplied by the Context Object section. This contrasts with the user interface, which can only be influenced by context changes via the dialogue controller.

User interface designers do not always have a programming background. For this reason, we decided to design the user interface in a more abstract way than purely writing code. Several approaches already exist, which deal with user interface design using the model-based approach [Mori et al. 2003; Puerta 1997; Coninx et al. 2003] in order to design user interfaces for various types of context.

The first step in the user interface design process is to draw up the task model. Since a traditional task model can only model static user interfaces, we expanded the ConcurTaskTrees (CTT) notation [Clerckx et al. 2004b]. The CTT notation [Paternò 1999] provides a graphical syntax, a hierarchic structure and a way of establishing temporal relationships between various (sub) tasks. A very important advantage of the CTT formalism is the generation of Enabled Task Sets (ETS) out of the specification. Paternò [1999] defines an ETS as: *a set of tasks that are logically enabled to start their performance during the same period of time.* We use the set of ETSs that can be identified in the task specification as a basis for the different dialogues the user interface will need to complete its tasks.

We adapted this notation such that context information can be explicitly taken into account in the task specification. In order to achieve a concrete user interface, it is assumed that the designer adds abstract user interface components to the task model. This information is platform-independent so that the rendering backend can ultimately use this information to construct a concrete user interface for various platforms.

The next step consists of completing the dialogue model. In order to support the designer, the statuses and transitions between the various individual dialogues are automatically generated, so as to simplify the work of the designer. The tool includes an algorithm to calculate the different dialogues and transitions between dialogues from the task specification [Luyten et al. 2003]. Afterwards, the designer can always adjust these transitions: she/he can add or remove transitions according to the results of a previous testing stage or the designers experience for example. This way the user interface designer can manipulate transitions that would be triggered by context changes. The designer thus has control over the influence of context on the usability of the user interface. More information about the design of the specific models can be found in Clerckx et al. [2004a] and Clerckx et al. [2004b].

5 Prototyping the User Interface

Figure 2 shows the DynaMo-AID Design tool; a complete set-up with custom sensors is shown in Figure 3. The set-up in Figure 3 consists of a Printed Circuit Board (PCB) with a temperature and light sensor and some push-buttons, a laptop connected to this PCB on which the CCOs are located which encapsulate the sensors on the PCB and a PC with our prototyping tool, where the ACOs are directly connected to the laptop. Note that context information, user interface models and prototypes are integrated in the same environment. If we go back to our case study from the introduction, we can use the sensors to derive information from the environment of the mobile telephone [Schmidt et al. 1999]. Suppose we want to distinguish between 3 possible statuses for the mobile telephone: in the hand (temperature and pressure increase), lying on the table (standard light intensity, temperature and pressure) and hidden (fall in light

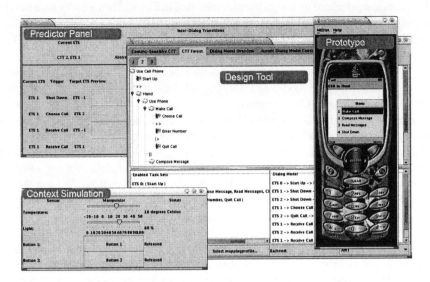

Figure 2: DynaMo-AID Design Tool (first version).

Figure 3: Hardware setup.

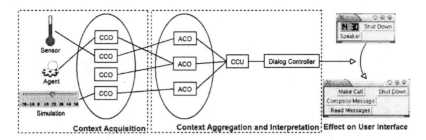

Figure 4: An overview of the different types of context input, and how they communicate with the user interface.

intensity). If the mobile telephone is in the user's hand, the user can perform normal tasks, such as composing and reading text messages, telephoning, etc. If the mobile telephone is placed on the table, a clock will appear and interaction with the device is possible via a microphone and a loudspeaker.

In order to design the user interface, the designer first has to draw up a task model, using a notation which allows it to describe tasks for various types of context. Thus, the designer must specify which tasks are possible if the mobile telephone is in the user's hand, if it is lying on the table or if it is hidden. A separate, complete dialogue model will then be calculated automatically for these three types of context and presented to the designer. The designer her/himself can then indicate between which statuses transitions are possible under the influence of context changes (we will call these interdialogue transitions, see next section). The designer can thus decide, for example, only to make a transition from telephone in the hand to telephone on the table or telephone hidden if the user interface is in the main menu status. This avoids the user interface adjusting if this is not desirable. If the user is entering a text message and she/he puts the mobile telephone down on the table, he/she would not always be pleased if the user interface suddenly adjusted itself. In this way, the designer keeps usability under control. ACOs are linked to these transitions to make it clear what has to be taken into account in order to make the transition. An example of an ACO is the mobile-in-hand object. This object can indicate whether the telephone is in the user's hand, using the CCO for the temperature sensor and the CCO for the push-button.

Figure 4 shows that use of CCOs can mean that several types of sensor are possible. This is shown in the left part of the figure and will be further explained in this paragraph. The middle part shows the context aggregation and interpretation components. The right part shows that the dialogue controller changes the state of the user interface prototype caused by a context change. Due to the separation of these parts the context acquisition can happen in several ways. Firstly, the typical hardware sensors, as in our hardware set-up. Furthermore, the tool also provides support for working not only with hardware sensors, but also for linking the CCOs to a software-like simulation panel, where the designer can simulate context situations by adjusting manipulators on the panel so that the CCOs are controlled by them. In this way,

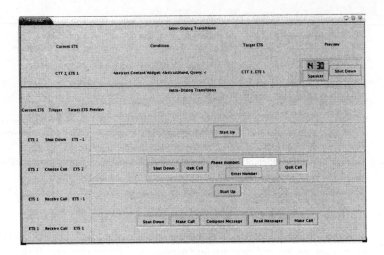

Figure 5: The Dialog Predictor panel.

the designer can rapidly test his prototype without the hardware implementation (encapsulation) having to be achieved and the work can easily be linked to genuine sensors by replacing the CCOs. Another possibility is to operate a software agent via the CCO, which autonomously generates data and, in this way, enables the user interface to be tested by simulation. This method is also known as the 'Wizard of Oz' method: hardware can be simulated in our design tool without the need for the actual hardware, similar to that which is provided in the Papier Mâché toolkit [Klemmer et al. 2004].

One of the major possibilities of the DynaMo-AID Design tool is the prediction of possible changes in the User Interface following termination of a task, the implementation of a user action or a context change. Figure 5 shows the Dialogue Predictor panel: it shows the tasks from the task model that are currently valid (left), which transitions are possible to other tasks (centre) and how these tasks will then be visualized (right). The combination of these different factors (task model, dialogue model, context information and user actions) takes place in real-time. The design tool generates a prototype user interface which it derives from the tasks in the task specification. The specific presentation of a gathering of tasks is generated from a device-independent XML-based user interface description which the designer can attach to the tasks. These user interface descriptions are described in more detail in Clerckx et al. [2004a] and are beyond the scope of this paper.

6   The DynaMo-AID Runtime Architecture

6.1   Smooth Migration from Design to Deployment

The runtime architecture is intended to provide a smooth transition between the design and deployment of the context-sensitive user interface. This is ensured by abstracting the context information, which means that both genuine information

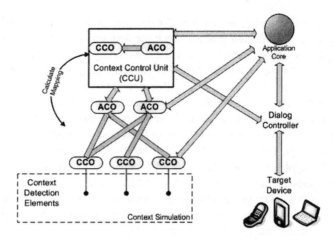

Figure 6: The DynaMo-AID runtime architecture.

from sensors and simulators can be used in the design phase. Simulators can be both agent-based (Concrete Context Objects which autonomously simulate data) or directly dictated by the designer. The latter is very valuable during design of the user interface. These user interfaces therefore have a strong link with the information provided from the immediate environment in all phases of their creation (design, testing and deployment). Figure 6 gives a summary of the DynaMo-AID runtime architecture.

6.2   Context-driven Dialogues

Three major components can be detected here in Figure 6:

The application core: is the heart of the application and consists of the application running on the device, together with any services made available during the application runtime.

The dialogue controller: controls communication between user interface, abstract context information and the application core. The dialogue controller possesses information about the user's tasks and how these can be influenced by the context.

The CCU: encapsulates context information at such an abstract level that it only tells the dialogue controller that the context change that has taken place is significant enough to adjust the status of the user interface.

The dialogue controller has a dynamic dialogue model and a dynamic task model at its disposal in order to decide when the user interface has to be updated. These dynamic models are extended versions of traditional models, but adjusted so that account can be taken of the current context, if this influences the tasks the user can, wants to or may perform. For the task model, we use the decision nodes notation from earlier work [Clerckx et al. 2004b]. This dynamic task model produces information during the design process about the dialogue model and a tool ensures that, during design of the dialogue model, the consistency with the previously defined tasks, which may or may not be liable to context changes, is guaranteed. The dynamic dialogue model consists of possible statuses of the user interface, such as in a traditional State Transition Network [Parnas 1969]. The difference is in the transitions that can occur. Here, we make a distinction between intra-dialogue and inter-dialogue transitions. An intra-dialogue transition is a transition between two statuses which is performed if the task described for the transition is performed by the user or the application. An inter-dialogue transition, by contrast, is a transition between two possible statuses of the user interface, but can only be performed if a context change has taken place which fulfils the conditions defined by the designer for the transition. Both types of transitions are made explicit to the designer in the tool by means of the Dialogue Predictor panel (Figure 5).

From the time the application is launched, the status of the user interface and the application can be changed by three actors: the user, the application and the CCU. Firstly, the CCU will detect the current context, supplied by the abstract interaction objects and the dialogue controller will be notified of the status in which the user interface will have to be launched. From then on, the user interface can be changed by the three actors. The user interacts with his device and can thus manipulate the user interface. The presentation renderer on the target device thus communicates events to the dialogue controller and this can then decide whether the status of the user interface needs to be changed or whether information about the user's action should be relayed to the application core. The application can also influence the user interface, for example, showing the results of a query if the application has finished processing the query. On the other hand, a service which becomes available for the application, for example upon entry to a WiFi hotspot, can influence the user's tasks and the dialogue controller will have to take this into account.

The last actor on the list is the CCU. The following section explains how this actor reacts to context changes, detected by abstract context objects, and how context information reaches the CCU.

6.3   Context Sensing and Processing

As previously mentioned, we distinguish between abstract and concrete context objects (ACOs and CCOs). The aim of this is to make available a number of high-level widgets to the application and the user, without the latter having to know how all this has been implemented and so that the underlying implementation and sensors used can be changed. This additional distinction also offers the possibility of being able to change the sensors used during the runtime of the application, depending on the services available now and in the future. The CCU does after all ensure that mapping takes place from ACO to CCOs each time new services become available or when services disappear. In the first instance, this can easily be implemented by subdividing the CCOs into various categories. The ACOs then indicate to the CCU the categories of CCOs from which they can use context information.

Making a distinction between ACOs and CCOs also means that these can be programmed separately and therefore by other people with a different background.

CCOs can for example be made by hardware specialists who can program close to the device driver, while ACOs can be programmed by specialists in Artificial Intelligence so as to have the context interpreted in an intelligent way.

The task of the CCU can be divided into three sub-tasks:

- Recalculating the mapping of ACOs on CCOs: a service can be a supplier of context information. If this is the case, the CCU can make use of this and treat the service as a CCO and link to ACOs which can make use of this context information.

- Detecting context changes: if a context change takes place in an ACO, the CCU will look at the dialogue model in order to decide whether the context change has a direct influence, so that an interdialogue transition has to be implemented.

- Invoking an interdialogue transition: the CCU sends an event to the dialogue controller and tells it that a context change has taken place and that the interdialogue transition has to be implemented (as can be seen on the right-side of Figure 4).

The section discussing context architectures has already stated that, from the point of view of the user interface, use is made of a strictly layered structure. By building in these abstraction levels, changing the user interface under the influence of context changes remains fully controlled. After all, context changes can only have an effect on the user interface in the statuses and for the context indicated by the user interface designer in the design phase. This layered structure does however imply some additional complexities. For instance, when passing on information to an adjacent layer, an interpretable artefact always has to be given as well. In order to transmit information between hardware sensors and CCOs, little has to be established conventionally since implementation of the CCOs usually has to take place ad hoc because this will be highly specific code. ACOs combine CCOs and contain code for interpreting groups of CCOs. If it is evident from this interpreted information that a context change has taken place, this is notified to the CCU. If a transition then exists in the dialogue model to follow up this context change, the dialogue controller will be notified to invoke the appropriate transition.

7 Future Work

Despite the improved harmonization of the activities of the hardware engineer (building sensors), the application programmer and the interface designer, a reliable link with a traditional software engineering process is missing, which could lead to complete integration. One possibility in this respect is to integrate the Model-Driven Architecture[2] more fully with the various interface models already used in this context.

Another important area of application, to which we will devote more attention in the future, is interfaces for disabled people. Here, it is of the utmost importance

---

[2]hhtp://www.omg.org/mda/

for the interface always to react appropriately and predictably to changes in the environment. Predictability is guaranteed by the model-based approach, which clearly indicates which tasks the interface has to fulfil. The possibilities offered by the interface are thus clearly demarcated and the influence of context on the interface is determined at the design stage. Nevertheless, the solution we propose here also offers the possibility of dealing with new situations (for example, a remote software service that fails) without this having to be explicitly modelled.

8 Conclusion

We believe the work presented here is only one step towards a fully integrated development environment to develop context-sensitive user interface design. Various models from model-based user interface development (task, dialogue and presentation model) are combined with potential dynamic context changes in the design phase of the interface. As far as we know, this is currently the only approach to involve context information in this way in the design process of an interactive system. However, more work is required in order to achieve an environment that can make highly complex interfaces.

We have demonstrated in this paper how existing context management systems can be expanded to take the interaction section into account as well. By abstracting the context to the dialogue layer of the interface, we can explicitly take into account context changes during design of the interfaces. Moreover, the abstraction layer here ensures that context can be simulated and a working prototype can therefore easily be created in a laboratory setting. We expect this to increase the usability of the final interface since it is possible to perform user testing early in the design process.

Acknowledgements

Part of the research at EDM is funded by EFRO (European Fund for Regional Development), the Flemish Government and the Flemish Interdisciplinary institute for Broadband technology (IBBT). The CoDAMoS (Context-Driven Adaptation of Mobile Services) project IWT 030320 is directly funded by the IWT (Flemish subsidy organization).

References

Clerckx, T., Luyten, K., & Coninx, K. [2004a], DynaMo-AID: A Design Process and a Runtime Architecture for Dynamic Model-based User Interface Development, *in* R. Bastide, P. Palanque & J. Roth (eds.), *Proceedings of the 9th IFIP Working Conference on Engineering for Human–Computer Interaction Jointly with the 11th International Workshop on Design, Specification and Verification of Interactive Systems (EHCI-DSVIS 2004)*, Vol. 3425 of *Lecture Notes in Computer Science*, Springer. In press.

Clerckx, T., Luyten, K. & Coninx, K. [2004b], Generating Context-sensitive Multiple Device Interfaces from Design, *in* L. Jacob & J. Vanderdonckt (eds.), *Proceedings of the 9th ACM International Conference on Intelligent User Interface jointly with the 5th International Conference on Computer-Aided Design of User Interfaces (IUI-CADUI 2004)*, ACM Press, pp.288–301.

Coninx, K., Luyten, K., Vandervelpen, C., van den Bergh, J. & Creemers, B. [2003], Dygimes: Dynamically Generating Interfaces for Mobile Computing Devices and Embedded Systems, *in* L. Chittaro (ed.), *Human–Computer Interaction with Mobile Devices and Services: Proceedings of the 5th International Symposium on Mobile Human–Computer Interaction (Mobile HCI 2003)*, Vol. 2795 of *Lecture Notes in Computer Science*, Springer-Verlag, pp.256–70.

Coutaz, J. [1994], Software Architecture Modeling for User Interfaces, *in* J. J. Marciniak (ed.), *Encyclopedia of Software Engineering*, John Wiley & Sons, pp.38–49.

Coutaz, J. & Rey, G. [2002], Foundations for a Theory of Contextors, *in* C. Kolski & J. Vanderdonckt (eds.), *Proceedings of the 4th International Workshop on Computer-aided Design of User Interfaces (CADUI 2002)*, Vol. 3, Kluwer Academic Publishers, pp.13–33. Invited talk.

Dey, A. K. & Abowd, G. D. [2000], The Context Toolkit: Aiding the Development of Context-aware Applications, Paper presented at the Workshop on Software Engineering for Wearable and Pervasive Computing. http://www.cc.gatech.edu/fce/contexttoolkit/pubs/SEWPC00.pdf (last accessed 2005-06-07).

Dey, A. K. & Abowd, G. D. [2004], Support for the Adaptation and Interfaces to Context, *in* A. Seffah & H. Javahery (eds.), *Multiple User Interfaces, Cross-Platform Applications and Context-Aware Interfaces*, John Wiley & Sons, pp.261–96.

Dey, A. K., Salber, D. & Abowd, G. D. [2001], A Conceptual Framework and a Toolkit for Supporting the Rapid Prototyping of Context-aware Applications, *Human–Computer Interaction* 16(2-4), 97–166.

Henricksen, K. & Indulska, J. [2004], A Software Engineering Framework for Context-aware Pervasive Computing, *in* A. Tripathi et al.(eds.), *Proceedings of the Second IEEE International Conference on Pervasive Computing and Communications (PerCom'04)*, IEEE Computer Society Press, pp.77–86.

Hinckley, K., Pierce, J., Sinclair, M. & Horvitz, E. [2000], Sensing Techniques for Mobile Interaction, *in* M. Ackerman & K. Edwards (eds.), *Proceedings of the 13th Annual ACM Symposium on User Interface Software and Technology, UIST'00, CHI Letters* 2(2), ACM Press, pp.91–100.

Hong, J. & Landay, J. A. [2004], Context Fabric: Infrastructure Support for Context-Awareness, http://guir.cs.berkeley.edu/projects/confab/. GUIR: Berkeley Group for User Interface Research.

Klemmer, S. R., Li, J., Lin, J. & Landay, J. A. [2004], Papier-Mâché: Toolkit Support for Tangible Input, *in* E. Dykstra-Erickson & M. Tscheligi (eds.), *Proceedings of SIGCHI Conference on Human Factors in Computing Systems (CHI'04)*, ACM Press, pp.399–406.

Luyten, K., Clerckx, T., Coninx, K. & Vanderdonckt, J. [2003], Derivation of a Dialog Model from a Task Model by Activity Chain Extraction, *in* J. Jorge, N. Jardim Nunes & J. Falcão e Cunha (eds.), *Interactive Systems. Design, Specification, and Verification: Proceedings of the 10th International Workshop, DSV-IS 2003*, Vol. 2844 of *Lecture Notes in Computer Science*, Springer-Verlag, pp.191–205.

Mori, G., Paternò, F. & Santoro, C. [2003], Tool Support for Designing Nomadic Applications, *in* D. Leake, L. Johnson & E. Andre (eds.), *Proceedings of the 8th ACM International Conference on Intelligent User Interface (IUI 2003)*, ACM Press, pp.141–8.

Parnas, D. L. [1969], On the Use of Transition Diagrams in the Design of a User Interface for an Interactive Computer System, *in Proceedings of the 1969 24th National Conference*, ACM Press, pp.379–85.

Paternò, F. [1999], *Model-Based Design and Evaluation of Interactive Applications*, Springer-Verlag.

Puerta, A. [1997], A Model-Based Interface Development Environment, *IEEE Software* **14**(4), 40–7.

Salber, D., Dey, A. K. & Abowd, G. D. [1999], The Context Toolkit: Aiding the Development of Context-enabled Applications, *in* M. G. Williams & M. W. Altom (eds.), *Proceedings of the SIGCHI Conference on Human Factors in Computing Systems: The CHI is the Limit (CHI'99)*, ACM Press, pp.434–41.

Schmidt, A. [2002], Ubiquitous Computing — Computing in Context, PhD thesis, Lancaster University.

Schmidt, A., Aidoo, K. A., Takaluoma, A., Tuomela, U., van Laerhoven, K. & van de Velde, W. [1999], Advanced Interaction in Context, *in* H.-W. Gellersen (ed.), *Handheld and Ubiquitous Computing: Proceeding of the First International Symposium on Handheld and Ubiquitous Computing (HUC 1999)*, Vol. 1707 of *Lecture Notes in Computer Science*, Springer-Verlag, pp.89–101.

Winograd, T. [2001], Architectures for Context, *Human–Computer Interaction* **16**(2-4), 401–19.

Using Context Awareness to Enhance Visitor Engagement in a Gallery Space

Peter Lonsdale[†], Russell Beale[‡] & Will Byrne[†]

[†] *School of Engineering,* [‡] *School of Computer Science,*
University of Birmingham, Edgbaston, Birmingham B15 2TT, UK
Email: *{pxl, rxb, w.f.byrne}@cs.bham.ac.uk*

Context-awareness can greatly enhance the usability of mobile devices by making it possible for users to continue with other activities without having to pay too much attention to the device. At the same time context-aware applications can provide timely support for user activities by responding to changes in the user's state and acting accordingly. We describe our work on developing a generic context awareness architecture that is being deployed in a gallery space to enhance learner engagement with the gallery exhibits. Our system makes use of contextual information to determine what content should be displayed on the device. Users can also navigate this content by explicitly changing their context in the dimensions of physical location and dwell time. Visitors have the opportunity to physically interact with the abstract information layer that is overlaid on the gallery space. The system also actively encourages movement in the gallery by identifying links between paintings. We describe our architecture, implementation, and the design challenges faced in deploying this system within a gallery.

Keywords: context awareness, mobile learning, museum, mobile usability, PDAs, location awareness.

1 Introduction

Context awareness is a relatively nascent field of research that centres on the use of information pertaining to the user and their environment to drive the behaviour of a device or system (for reviews of context-awareness applications and research perspectives, see Chen & Kotz [2000] and Dourish [2004]. By taking account of contextual information, systems can be made easier to use, and can provide more appropriate responses, than if they respond passively to user requests. There is currently considerable interest in the use of context awareness to provide enhanced usability in this way, and in particular developers of mobile applications are looking to context awareness to provide solutions to the specific problems posed by the design limitations of mobile computing devices.

Context awareness is especially important for mobile devices because it allows us to overcome the usability problems associated with small, handheld devices [Sharples & Beale 2003], and also to make effective use of the user's physical and social surroundings to provide timely support to their activities. We can provide enhanced user support by using contextual information to drive mobile applications, and simultaneously we can exploit physical context as a means to interact with the application. For example, a user's location can drive delivery of content on a device, and at the same the user can utilize the system's sensitivity to their location as a navigation tool, selecting different items of content by altering their physical location.

1.1   *Context Awareness for Mobile Learning*

Mobile learning is too often conceived of as simply the mobile equivalent of e-learning. The assumption is that learning can be delivered through content displayed on mobile devices in the same way as it is displayed on other systems such as desktop PCs. However, the use of mobile computing devices is qualitatively different to the use of other computing devices, and we must take account of this when developing m-learning applications. We must also consider that a user with a mobile device is often much more influenced by their surroundings than a user of a desktop PC might be.

Mobile devices such as phones and PDAs are used in a huge variety of settings and environments, and we cannot rely on having the user's full attention. Mobile learning is not something that can be delivered, it is something that might happen, given the right combination of learner, surroundings, content, and activity. This serendipitous nature of mobile learning is further enforced by the very informal way in which people use things like mobile phones and PDAs. They are not setting out to learn something, they are often engaged in something else entirely, and we must make the best use we can of the devices they have to hand to support their activities [Rogers 2002]. We can do this using context awareness to ensure that the device is always ready with relevant information, but does not need to distract the user in order to achieve this readiness.

The EU IST Project MOBIlearn [Bormida et al. 2002] has focused on the development of a large scale platform for delivering learning content to learners with mobile devices, including mobile phones, Tablet PCs, and PDAs. As part of this work, the University of Birmingham has developed an architecture for context awareness that is currently being deployed at the Nottingham Castle Museum gallery to provide an enhanced and more engaging experience for visitors to the gallery. Our aims have been:

- To provide timely support to the user.

- To allow the user to maintain their attention on the world.

- To allow the user to inspect, understand, and alter the current context model for their own purposes.

1.2   Context Awareness for Museum and Galleries

Museums, galleries, and heritage sites seek to engage visitors in the artefacts they exhibit, as well as encourage participation in the learning space provided. The use of computer technologies in museums is not a new concept, and kiosk-based content presentation and interactive exhibits are a common sight. Mobile devices offer opportunities to provide technological means to engage visitors whilst they are situated within the gallery space itself. Moreover, the small size and portability of these devices means that we can seek to engage the user without distracting their attention from the exhibits they are trying to enjoy.

Context-aware mobile applications have been used effectively to deliver supporting information to tourists in the form of location-aware tourist guides, for example the CyberGuide project [Abowd et al. 1997]. Similarly, location-aware applications have been used to deliver content that is appropriate to a visitor's particular location within a gallery space — notable examples include Tate Modern's multimedia pilot study [Proctor & Burton 2003] and the CAERUS system [Naismith & Smith 2004].

Wearable and mobile computers have also been used to provide augmented experiences that go beyond basic location awareness. Baber et al. [2001] describe a system that combines location-dependent content delivery with profiling of visitor needs, to provide a visit tailored to individual requirements. Oppermann & Specht [1999] describe a system that uses contextual information as the basis for supporting the user but not distracting them, whilst MacColl et al. [2002] describe their experiences of combining context and virtual presence.

Location remains the primary feature of context that is exploited in most context-aware applications [Bristow et al. 2002; Chen & Kotz 2000; Dix et al. 2000; Selker & Burleson 2000]. To provide effective support for visitors to museums and galleries it is crucial to know where they are. Knowing what area a visitor is in means we can offer appropriate content and suggest possible activities. Knowing exactly which artefact a visitor is currently looking at means we can offer content and activities specifically for that artefact.

1.3   Uses of Context

A visit to a museum is not just a series of stops in front of artefacts. The experience has a beginning, a middle, and an end. It is a process. We have sought to address this by considering visitor movement within the gallery. We began by designing our system to use location and timing information to provide appropriate content to users with mobile devices in a gallery space. What became clear was that the delivery of content in this way allowed us to encourage visitors to interact with the artefacts in a different way. A review of the content supplied to us by the gallery indicated that many of the paintings on display shared interesting histories or were linked in some way that was never made visible to visitors. By flagging these connections to the visitors we are able to encourage greater movement between the paintings on display, beyond the basic linear path that most people follow in the gallery. This physical engagement with the learning space is an often neglected facet of learning.

In our preliminary trials of our prototype, we discovered that because the system relies on context to deliver content, changes in that context can be exploited by the user themselves to deliberately trigger content changes and hence move to another item of content when desired. In other words, context becomes not just a mechanism for the system to select content, but also a tool with which the user themselves can navigate the information space. These two aspects of context aware gallery exploration, *context as content selector* and *context as navigation tool*, have driven our subsequent development of a system to support visitors to the gallery. The concept is that an information space that is overlaid on the existing physical space of the gallery can be navigated through physical means, engendered by the implementation of a context-sensitive application. Mobile devices are hard to use, because they have small screens, and the user is usually trying to do something else at the same time as navigate the onscreen menus. By using physical movement as an interaction method, we can give people a new way to interact with the information space that we have overlaid onto the physical gallery space.

2   Context Awareness Architecture

Context aware applications typically involve the use of rulesets or some other kind of matching system to generate appropriate system *responses* (e.g. content display or option selection) from appropriate *stimuli* (e.g. changes in location, orientation, lighting levels, user input etc.). This approach requires the definition of fairly rigid rules (or their equivalent) and an exhaustive set of possible responses that the system can make. Our approach has been driven by the need to support the process of learners moving through a learning space, and hence our model and architecture for context awareness is much more process centred.

Another motivating factor in moving away from programmatically defined rules is the desire to support content developers and experience designers who wish to make use of context aware applications without wanting to engage in software development.

We have devised an architecture, described in detail in Beale & Lonsdale [2004], for context awareness that involves the definition (in textual form) of a set of software objects called context feature objects. Each of these context feature objects responds to a specific stimulus from actual context data, and responds by searching for matching metadata tags on the available content that the system can currently deliver. Any match results in the current score for that item of content or action being increased. When all available content and actions have been scored, those with higher scores are deemed to be of more relevance to the current context than those with lower scores. This scoring or ranking process occurs every time the context changes, e.g. whenever the user moves to another location.

The context awareness system is configured by specifying a set of context feature objects and link objects using a structured syntax that the system parses at runtime to generate actual software objects that perform the context awareness processing. In specifying context feature objects, it is necessary only to know the name of the metadata tag that is appropriate and the range of values that a context feature object should respond to. Links between context feature objects are similarly defined. In this way we have provided a non-programmatic interface to the context awareness system, and one that could easily be translated into even more usable tools such as a graphical user interface for the configuring of context aware applications.

Contextual data itself is assumed to be gathered by separate systems, and is input into the context awareness architecture in a generic fashion by specifying simply a name for the data and then supplying its value. Context feature objects that are able to respond to the type of information passed in will do so. In this way the context awareness architecture is only loosely coupled to the technical infrastructure which provides the actual context data, and different sources of context data may easily be substituted at any time. From a technical perspective, this functionality is further enhanced by the use of a Web services architecture to deploy the system. This means that communication with the context awareness architecture is easily achieved through standard protocols and data formats.

2.1 Conceptual Context Model

The easiest way to understand the contextual approach we have taken is through the metaphor of a movie. The movie itself has a main theme, and a variety of subplots and threads running through it. This is equivalent to the overall context. It is dynamic, changing over time and with the interactions of the participants, where history is important. A scene in the movie corresponds to a *context state*: a specific set of themes and characters are to the fore and have primary importance. A scene from the movie has these key characters in it, plus some props — this corresponds to what we call the *context substate*. Thus, as in a movie, the whole movie is needed for a full understanding, but a lot of information does exist in a single frame.

2.2 Context Feature Objects

Our software architecture comprises a set of software objects called context feature objects (CFOs) that correspond to real-world context features relating to the learner's setting, activity, device capabilities and so on to derive a context substate, as described above. Data can be acquired through either automated means (for example sensors or other software subsystems) or can be input directly by the user. This context substate is used to perform first exclusion of any unsuitable content (for example high-resolution webpages that cannot be displayed on a PDA) and then ranking of the remaining content to determine the best *n* options. This ranked set of options is then output to the content delivery subsystem.

2.2.1 Types of Context Features

Context feature objects are either *excluders* or *rankers*. Items of content that are deemed entirely inappropriate for the current context are excluded. That is to say they are removed from the list of recommended content and not subject to any further consideration — items that match a single exclusion criterion will not receive any further rankings and will not be recommended no matter how high a score they receive, and so exclusion is qualitatively different to simply receiving a low or zero ranking. Content remaining in the list after the exclusion process is then ranked according to how well it matches the current context. The ranking process simply increments the score of each item of content that has metadata matching the stimulus values of any particular context feature. The size of the increment depends on the *salience value* of the context feature doing the ranking. Individual CFOs can have their salience values changed so that they exert more influence on the ranking process.

A CFO has a set of possible values, and an indicator of which value is currently selected. It is also possible for CFOs to have multiple sets of possible values, with the current active set being determined by the current value of another linked context feature. Whilst this has no bearing on the recommendation process, it is important in terms of providing an inspectable model of the context state to the user, who can observe the influence of one context feature on another. For example, options relating to current activity can change depending on the user's current location.

2.2.2   Linked Context Features

Each context feature object responds to only one metadata tag and performs either an exclusion or ranking function. To achieve more complex filtering of content, CFOs can be linked together so that their function can depend on the state of other context feature objects. Link objects are used to send either the *values* of context features or the *time* they have held that value to other context features. Criteria on that link determine whether action should be taken.

For example, we might have a context feature that responds directly to input from a sensor network specifying the location of the user. Another context feature infers the level of interest of the user by taking input from a link that acts on the *time* the location feature has had its current value. A user dwelling in one place for a longer period implies a higher level of interest in that location. A third context feature may respond to user input that can over-ride the inferred level of interest — this uses a link object that acts on the *value* input by the user. Conflicts between links and context features are resolved using salience values which specify the relative importance of each. These salience values are at present specified by the designer(s) of the context-aware experience, but more automated methods of conflict resolution could be employed in future iterations.

2.3   Output

The ordered list of ranked items of content is passed to delivery subsystems for use in determining exactly what content should be made available to the user. In this way, the context-awareness sub-system has no way of specifying exactly what is made available — the system is intended only to make recommendations to the system and to the user. This method of recommendation is preferred so that should the system make a mistake, and make inappropriate recommendations, its output does not override selections made elsewhere in the system (for example, the user might specify a particular page of content and then not want that item to be replaced by another).

It should be clearly understood that the recommendations made are not only done on content — recommendations can also determine new navigational strategies through the virtual or real space. We are not concerned with only filtering content, but in the more general question of providing appropriate support, which may be reordering information, offering it in a different order, or directing the user to another part of the physical space — which will in turn affect the context system.

3 In the Gallery

We have deployed our context awareness architecture in the gallery space at Nottingham Castle. Our intention is to provide visitors to the gallery with an enhanced experience through the utilization of contextual information to drive the behaviour of their mobile device. Content and options displayed on the screen will be tailored according to the user's current context, and users are also able to make explicit use of the context sensitivity to drive the behaviour of the device themselves.

3.1 Designing the Experience

We have consulted with the curators at Nottingham Castle Museum to ensure that our system will deliver appropriate support to visitors in the gallery space. Several issues arose during our consultation, of which two are immediately relevant to the design of the context aware visitor experience:

Lack of focused attention: visitors will usually enter the gallery space via one door, move through the space in a linear way, and then exit without really paying much attention to what they see on the way.

Deadspots: certain artefacts within the gallery are often overlooked by visitors, for a variety of reasons; positioning, lighting, or other factors.

We wanted initially to use our context awareness system to attempt to overcome these issues, and thus provide a more engaging experience for the visitors whilst at the same time addressing these areas that concern the gallery staff.

A crucial part of the design centres on the fact that visitors move through a physical space. This movement was determined to be the primary context feature for our system to use. In addition, movement itself is not constrained to two or even three dimensions — visitors' movements can be described also in terms of the fourth dimension, time. The particular path a visitor takes through the gallery, the time they spend at individual paintings, and whether or not they retrace their steps can all be used to drive a context aware application. Our system has been set-up to deliver appropriate content using the following principles:

- *Which painting is the user currently closest to?* This is determined from our positioning system as described below. The system is able to provide accurate data about which painting the user is currently closest to.

- *How long has the user been in their current position?* An increased dwell time at a specific painting is assumed to indicate a higher level of interest in that painting.

- *Has the user been in this position before?* If the user has been to a painting before, the content they viewed on their previous visit can be used to determine the appropriate level of content to display this time. Previous content can also be offered for review.

As well as using context awareness to determine what the device does, we are also exploring the use of context awareness as a means to physically engage the learner in the learning space, and to encourage movement within that space.

3.1.1   Encouraging Movement Within the Space

Mobile devices are often deployed in museums and similar locations as a means to deliver content or provide some other element of interactivity to the exhibits. But delivering content means that we are in danger of replacing hands on interaction with 'heads down one-way transmission of information' [Hsi 2003]. Instead, what we can do is to use the device and the content it can display to cause the visitor to see the artefacts in a different way, and to expose the links between paintings that were not visible without the use of the technology to point them out.

This functionality has been implemented through structuring the audio content provided by the device to highlight links with other paintings in the gallery space. Users are expected to navigate to the other paintings without additional assistance, which is in part the reason we have seen the use of the context sensitivity as a navigation tool.

3.1.2   Enabling Navigation through Physical Movement

We have observed that users wanted to navigate the information space by physically changing their context so that they were effectively driving the system through physical actions. Our application already supported this through being sensitive to context changes, but to further enhance usability in this area we have explored the use of salient contextual information on the user interface so that users can monitor the state of the context system and determine whether they have achieved the state they are aiming for. In this case, it became necessary to indicate to the user the exact location the device was currently registering for them, whether it thought they were moving or stationary, and how long it thought they had been in that location.

3.2   Deploying the Experience

To provide the functionality described above within our context awareness architecture, it is necessary to define two context feature objects to monitor Painting and Interest. The Painting CFOs responds directly to which painting is closest to the user, and scores all items of content that are relevant to that painting. The Interest CFOs also responds indirectly to location. A Link is defined between Painting and Interest which specifies a number of possible values for Interest, depending on the time that Painting has held its current value. The longer that Painting holds its value, the higher the value of Interest.

If a visitor retraces their steps, the context architecture is able to determine the last known value of Interest, by consulting an internal database that stores sets of values of the CFOs. Using Painting as the search key for this database, the context system can determine what level of interest was reached last time the visitor was at this painting.

The functionality described here could be achieved using a far less involved set of rules. However, our implementation offers a high degree of flexibility and also the chance for non-programmers to easily create context aware experiences without having to worry about the specifics of the code behind the system. The gallery experience is just one example of a relatively simple application that can be deployed using our architecture. The architecture itself is designed to be flexible and extensible, to allow for much greater complexity than was used for these initial gallery trials.

We are using a bespoke ultrasound tracking system to determine the location of users as they move around the gallery space. This system has been developed at the University of Birmingham as part of another project [Cross et al. 2002], and has been successfully adapted to provide input to our context awareness system.

The ultrasound system comprises a set of transmitters placed at known points on the walls of the gallery, and a receiver which connects to a PocketPC device. The receiver is able to triangulate its position from the signals received from the fixed transmitters.

4 Results of User Trials

From December 2004 to April 2005, we conducted user trials of our context aware system at Nottingham Castle Museum gallery. At time of writing, our results are at a preliminary stage, and we have not yet analysed data gathered from our questionnaires or audio/video recordings.

All participants were visitors to the Nottingham Castle Gallery who were approached and asked if they wished to take part in our study. All were given a brief introduction to the system and its aims. All participants (except the control condition) were asked to complete a pre- and post-task questionnaire so that we could assess what they had learned from their visit.

We gather data from several sources for our trials:

- Pre- and post-task questionnaire data, to determine what visitors have learned from their visit.

- Video recordings: of visitors' movements in the gallery.

- Audio recordings: of visitors' conversations whilst using the system.

- System logs: of content delivered, movement between paintings, options selected on the PDA.

We used an independent measures experimental design to determine the impact of the use of our handheld guide (experimental condition) in comparison with traditional guide materials (baseline condition: a printed booklet) and no provision of guide materials at all (control condition).

Preliminary results are drawn from informal observations taken by the experimenters during the trials. We found that visitors using the paper guide tended to follow a more 'rigid' pattern of movement around the gallery, visiting paintings in a specific order, then stopping to consult the guide book. In contrast, visitors with the PDA were more likely to move around the gallery according to what interested them, after scanning the room for paintings that caught their eye. It seemed that because the handheld guide had no inherent structure, this structure was not imposed on the visitors' behaviour.

A number of specific problems were observed when people were using the system. People quickly developed high expectations of the system based on previous experience, often remarking on paintings that did not offer the same depth of content as the others. Content availability was apparent from the screen display, but this seemed non-intuitive for many users. Even the basic system was perceived as overly complex by many users, emphasising the need for content delivery systems such as this to remain as simple as possible. Despite perceiving the system as complex, most users seemed to find the system useful once they had discovered what it could provide.

However, few users made use of the content navigation options on the device, and were content to simply have content delivered in the order the system dictated.

5 Conclusions and Next Steps

The system described here has been deployed in Nottingham Castle Museum gallery and is currently undergoing user trials. Preliminary testing of our prototypes has indicated that are important research issues surrounding the use of context sensitive architectures both to drive applications and to provide alternative means of content navigation for users. The main challenges in this area are those of determining appropriate ways to represent these new metaphors for navigation to users, and creating usable interfaces within the constraints imposed by the design of mobile devices.

In particular, it seems that context-aware applications must be simultaneously *invisible* — in the sense that the user can use the system without being concerned with the details of how it is performing its task — and optionally highly *visible*, so that the user can inspect the state of the system, correct mistakes, and use the contextual information for their own purposes such as content navigation.

References

Abowd, G. D., Atkeson, C., Hong, J., Long, S., Kooper, R. & Pinkerton, M. [1997], Cyberguide: A Mobile Context-aware Tour Guide, *Wireless Networks* **3**(5), 421–33.

Baber, C., Bristow, H., Cheng, S., Hedley, A., Kuriyama, Y., Lien, M., Pollard, J. & Sorrell, P. [2001], Augmenting Museums and Art Galleries, *in* M. Hirose (ed.), *Human–Computer Interaction — INTERACT '01: Proceedings of the Eighth IFIP Conference on Human–Computer Interaction*, Vol. 1, IOS Press, pp.439–47.

Beale, R. & Lonsdale, P. [2004], Mobile Context Aware Systems: The Intelligence to Support Tasks and Effectively Utilise Resources, *in* S. Brewster & M. Dunlop (eds.), *Human–Computer Interaction — Mobile HCI 2004: Proceedings of the 5th International Symposium on Mobile Human–Computer Interaction*, Vol. 3160 of *Lecture Notes in Computer Science*, Springer-Verlag, pp.240–51.

Bormida, G. D., Lefrere, P., Vaccaro, R. & Sharples, M. [2002], The MOBILearn Project: Exploring New Ways to Use Mobile Environments and Devices to Meet the Needs of Learners, Working by Themselves and With Others, *in* S. Anastopoulou, M. Sharples & G. Vavoula (eds.), *Proceedings of the European Workshop on Mobile and Contextual Learning*, University of Birmingham, pp.51–2.

Bristow, H. W., Baber, C., Cross, J. & Wooley, S. [2002], Evaluating Contextual Information for Wearable Computing, *in Proceedings of the 6th International Symposium on Wearable Computers (ISWC 2002)*, IEEE Computer Society Press, pp.175–86.

Chen, G. & Kotz, D. [2000], A Survey of Context-aware Mobile Computing Research, Technical Report TR2000-381, Dartmouth College, USA.

Cross, J., Wooley, S., Baber, C. & Gaffney, V. [2002], Wearable Computing for Field Archeology, *in Proceedings of the 6th International Symposium on Wearable Computers (ISWC 2002)*, IEEE Computer Society Press, p.169.

Dix, A., Rodden, T., Davies, N., Trevor, J., Friday, A. & Palfreyman, K. [2000], Exploiting Space and Location as a Design Framework for Interactive Mobile Systems, *ACM Transactions on Computer–Human Interaction* 7(3), 285–321.

Dourish, P. [2004], What We Talk About When We Talk About Context, *Personal and Ubiquitous Computing* 8(1), 19–30.

Hsi, S. [2003], A Study of User Experiences Mediated by Nomadic Web Content in a Museum, *Journal of Computer-assisted Learning* 19(3), 308–19.

MacColl, I., Millard, D., Randell, C., Steed, A., Brown, B., Benford, S., Chalmers, M., Conroy, R., Dalton, N., Galani, A., Greenhalgh, C., Michaelides, D., Rodden, T., Taylor, I. & Weal, M. [2002], Shared Visiting in EQUATOR City, *in* C. Greenhalgh, E. Churchill & W. Broll (eds.), *Proceedings of the Fourth International Conference on Collaborative Virtual Environments (CVE 2002)*, ACM Press, pp.88–94.

Naismith, L. & Smith, P. [2004], Context-sensitive Information Delivery to Visitors in a Botanic Garden, *in Proceedings of ED-MEDIA: World Conference on Educational Multimedia, Hypermedia and Telecommunications*, Association for the Advancement of Computers in Education (AACE), pp.5525–5530.

Oppermann, R. & Specht, M. [1999], Adaptive Mobile Museum Guide for Information and Learning on Demand, *in* H.-J. Bullinger & J. Zieger (eds.), *Proceedings of the 8th International Conference on Human–Computer Interaction (HCI International '99)*, Lawrence Erlbaum Associates, pp.642–6.

Proctor, N. & Burton, J. [2003], Tate Modern Multimedia Tour Pilots 2002–2003, *in* J. Attewell & C. Savill-Smith (eds.), *Proceedings of the Second European Conference on Learning with Mobile Devices — MLEARN 2003*, Learning and Skills Development Agency (LSDA), p.545.

Rogers, T. [2002], Mobile Technologies for Informal Learning — a Theoretical Review of the Literature, *in* S. Anastopoulou, M. Sharples & G. Vavoula (eds.), *Proceedings of the European Workshop on Mobile and Contextual Learning*, University of Birmingham, pp.19–20.

Selker, T. & Burleson, W. [2000], Context-aware Design and Interaction in Computer Systems, *IBM System Journal* 39(3-4), 880–91.

Sharples, M. & Beale, R. [2003], A Technical Review of Mobile Computational Devices, *Journal of Computer-assisted Learning* 19(3), 392–5.

Engagement with an Interactive Museum Exhibit

Naomi Haywood & Paul Cairns

UCL Interaction Centre, 31–32 Alfred Place,
London WC1E 7DP, UK

Tel: *+44 20 7679 5208*

Fax: *+44 20 7679 5295*

Email: *Naomi.Haywood@web.de, p.cairns@ucl.ac.uk*

URL: *http://www.uclic.ucl.ac.uk/paul*

Learning and engagement have been recognised as very important in defining the effectiveness of interactive museum exhibits. However the relationship between these two notions is not fully understood. In particular, little is known about engagement with interactive exhibits and how it relates to learning. This paper describes a hypothesis seeking approach to find out how children engage with an interactive exhibit at the Science Museum. Engagement is found to be described in terms of the three categories: participation, narration and co-presence of others. These aspects of engagement can be seen to arise from specific aspects of the interaction design of the exhibit. Moreover, they also overlap with features required for a positive learning experience. These findings suggest many fruitful directions for future research in this area.

Keywords: immersion, interactive exhibit, narrative, learning, co-presence.

1 Introduction

Museums are a major source of public education outside of the formal schooling system in the UK [Teachernet 2004]. However, rather than competing with formal education, they provide a complementary resource for both formal and informal learning. For example, many museum visitors are groups of school pupils who visit the museum as part of their formal education. Further, many museum visitors are families, with parents aiming to allow their children to encounter areas of informal education that they may not otherwise encounter [Jensen 1994]. Museums also function as source of leisure and entertainment. Indeed, museums are one of the central provisions for entertainment which are widely accessible to the general public [Falk & Dierking 2000]. Thus, museums must aim to provide entertainment that is simultaneously informative and educational. Increasingly, museums look to interactive exhibits to fulfil this aim.

For the purposes of the current discussion, we take interactive exhibits to be exhibits that allow for interaction in some form other than mere visual perception. Frequently this interaction involves physical manipulation, such as visitors clicking buttons or flicking switches in response to specific questions or demands presented on screens. Interactivity therefore allows visitors to determine what the exhibit presents. For example, many interactive exhibits allow visitors to determine the order of presented information and whether they want to obtain more information concerning a specific area of interest [vom Lehn et al. 1999]. It must be noted, though, that not all exhibits that claim to be interactive would actual meet this criterion. Indeed, the recent "interactive exhibit" at the British Museum [2004] was a purely visual experience albeit some of it in 3D computer animation.

The general aim of these interactive exhibits is to allow for learning and entertainment. For the consideration of interactive exhibits, Falk & Dierking [2000] define learning broadly in terms of how users are able to comprehend the presented information. For example, a visitor may interact with an exhibit presenting images of the human heart, its functions and individual parts. If this visitor is subsequently able to note that the heart is a muscular organ which pumps blood around the blood vessels, then learning can be said to have occurred. Falk & Dierking also broadly define entertainment in terms of the exhibit being engaging. For example, if visitors spend time interacting with an exhibit without taking part in other activities, then this exhibit can be said to be engaging.

Recently, museums have made frequent use of interactive exhibits and generally consider their use to be successful in terms of learning and engagement [Gammon 2003]. However, the precise nature of how learning and engagement occur and how they may relate to each other remains uncertain. For example, it is possible that visitors spend long durations of time interacting with exhibits without reading the presented information. Therefore while the exhibit may be engaging, it may not encourage visitors to learn. Further, it is possible that visitors may learn from an interactive exhibit despite spending only a short duration of time interacting with it and simultaneously being involved in other activities.

The goal of museums is to produce successful exhibits and therefore to be able to reliably design exhibits for learning and engagement. Much research had been and is being done on investigating the educational effectiveness of museums. Indeed, this is the sole focus of the *Journal of Education in Museums*. However, though engagement has been identified as significant, it is not known how to design exhibits for engagement. In particular, we were unable to find a clear discussion of the role of interaction in making an exhibit engaging. In part at least, this seems to be because it is not really understood what engagement actually is [Brown & Cairns 2004].

The purpose, then, of this study is to develop hypotheses of what it means for an interactive exhibit to be engaging, how engagement as understood from the study may relate to learning and, where possible, what elements of the interaction could lead to engagement. The hypotheses found suggest avenues for future research. This hypothesis seeking approach is necessarily qualitative and we have developed a grounded theory [Strauss & Corbin 1998] in order to elicit and organise a conception of engagement based on first hand accounts of using an interactive exhibit. Though learning is important, it was probed for rather than measured as it was felt that an explicit measure of learning would interfere with the participants' experience or reporting of engagement. Instead, the relationship of the theory of engagement to learning is developed and explored in the discussion.

As is well known in HCI, the context of use can strongly influence specific interactions. Museums present quite specific contexts. As noted by Gammon [2003] individuals in museums frequently behave in a considerably different manner from when they are in other contexts. Moreover, vom Lehn et al. [1999] found that the learning experience of an individual was also determined by collaboration with others. For example, adults may point out key features to children, and visitors may observe each other interacting with exhibits. This suggests that any learning occurring by means of interactive exhibits is embedded in the social context.

For this reason, the study was conducted with a specific exhibit, the Energy Everywhere exhibit, in the Science Museum, London. Ten children were recruited to interact with the exhibit and then interviewed about their experiences. The grounded theory developed centred around three concepts of participation, narration and the co-presence of others. A key finding, which contrasts with vom Lehn et al.'s [1999] studies, is that co-presence is an important factor in the theory of engagement rather than collaboration which was considered important for learning. These concepts will be explained and demonstrated in the results section. The succeeding section discusses these concepts in terms of how interaction with the exhibit relates to engagement and learning and, therefore, possible lines of future research. The discussion will also be used to re-contextualize the theory within the existing literature.

2   Energy Everywhere

Before describing the methodology of the study, it is useful to briefly describe the actual exhibit studied. The exhibit is part of a permanent exhibition, *Energy — fuelling the future*, at the Science Museum in London. This exhibition was developed by Science Museum staff in collaboration with educators, scientists and consultants experienced in exhibition design. It opened in July 2004 and includes a total of six interactive exhibits, various information terminals and works of art relating to energy. The present research focuses on one specific exhibit, named Energy Everywhere. This exhibit is positioned at the entrance of the exhibition and is aimed at pupils of key stages two and three of the National Curriculum and families with children between seven to fourteen years old.

The exhibit is an animated film with a linear structure that starts when it detects the presence of a person in the vicinity of the exhibit. The person is invited to stand on a flashing yellow square in front of the screen and to clap their hands to start. This sets a sequence of animated scenes with sounds and a voice-over describing how energy is present in the scenes and how it is being transformed from one form to another. The graphics for the scenes are quite abstract where iconized forms such as trees and landscape are depicted but made up from words for the object itself. For example, the sun appears at the beginning and is drawn from many instances of the word 'energy.'

At three specific points in the sequence, the visitor is invited to interact with the exhibit by making gestures. The three gestures are: digging for coal; spinning your arms around to generate wind; and clapping hands to make lightning strike.

The exhibit also prompts the visitor if they do not do the appropriate actions, for instance, it may display and say "Clap louder" if the visitor does not clap loud enough for it to detect. Successfully completed actions are also acknowledged with "Well done!" both appearing on the screen and being spoken.

In all the exhibit takes around five minutes to complete the full sequence.

3   Method

In order to formulate hypotheses of engagement in an interactive exhibit we used a grounded theory approach [Strauss & Corbin 1998]. The basis for data gathering was interviews with museum visitors. Grounded theory allows for quite flexible interviewing that could be open to examining the specific concept of engagement but also exploring other concepts should they appear related to engagement in the minds of the interviewees. Also, grounded theory allows for an acceptable and rigorous working up of the interview data into a robust framework that could be used as the starting point for further studies.

The basic approach of the study was to have visitors use the Energy Everywhere exhibit and then to be interviewed afterwards about their experience. Due to the timing of the project and the Science Museum's development of the exhibit, the earlier interviews were performed with a prototype in a special evaluation room out of the context of the full exhibition. The later interviews were done based on the actual exhibit in the exhibition gallery when it had been installed. Potentially, the visitors using the prototype could have had an unrealistic experience but the theoretical sampling approach of grounded theory allowed the later interviews to fully explore the effect of the exhibition context on the overall experience. Additionally, there is the risk that, by knowing they were participants, the children might have engaged differently with the exhibits. In the prototype this was unavoidable but with the final exhibit, children were only approached once they had finished using the exhibit. As their experiences were integrated in the results with those of the earlier participants, it is hoped that any artificiality has been ameliorated.

The interested reader is invited to contact the authors for full details of the method, ethical clearance, consent and transcripts of the interviews.

3.1   Participants

Since research on learning suggests that there are age and sex differences in terms of how learning occurs [Richardson & Sheldon 1988] the present research aimed at recruiting a balance of girls and boys. Further, recruitment was based on ensuring that a wide range of ages within the target age group was considered.

The children were recruited from the visitors to the Science Museum. Both the children and their guardians were approached. The general purpose of the interview was explained to them and consent was obtained from both rather than just the guardian.

In total ten children participated, six interacted with the prototype and four interacted with the final exhibit. Of the six children who interacted with the prototype three were girls and three were boys. Their ages ranged from ten years to thirteen years. Of the four children who interacted with the final exhibit three were girls and one was a boy. Their ages ranged from nine years to twelve years. The age range does present a risk that engagement could be a significantly different experience particularly if individual differences are also taken into account. However, the grounded theory should bring out both the commonality and divergence of experience that could be attributed to age. As it happened, there was no evident simple relationship between age and the sense of engagement.

All children were native English speakers and went to schools in the UK. Further, all children took part in the research individually though under supervision from their accompanying guardian. That is, guardians were explicitly discouraged from using the exhibit themselves.

Ten children is a somewhat small sample but recruiting children in the main exhibit was problematic. It was felt that the children who took part should have completed using the exhibit as a sign of at least some degree of engagement. Unfortunately, not many children who used the exhibit did actually complete the full cycle of use.

Nonetheless, the grounded approach provides assurances that the description of engagement developed is at least faithful to the experience of the ten children who did take part. This is sufficient for the goals of the study to develop *some* notion of engagement that can be developed in future research. It should also be noted that the experiences of those children that did not complete the exhibit would make an equally fascinating study but it would be orthogonal to the goals of the current work.

3.2 Interviews

The grounded theory was constructed on the data gathered from semi-structured interviews focused around three key areas. Engagement clearly was a key area that the interviews tried to address. Initially, the questions on engagement were very exploratory. For example, children were asked to compare the experience with watching television or reading.

Learning was also included as a focus for the interviews because it clearly is intended to be an important aspect of the exhibit. However, no effort was made to rigorously measure learning as this could easily result in changing the experience of engagement. For example, if a visitor was pre-tested before using the exhibit, they might suppose that they would be post-tested and so alter their natural behaviour with the exhibit. Alternatively, it would seem unethical to spring a test on a child after using the exhibit but prior warning of the test could either put children off from participating in the study or again alter their approach to the exhibit. Thus, learning was probed but not measured. Even so, we found it was still possible to find quite concrete examples of learning.

Collaboration was also considered a key area for consideration as it had been identified by vom Lehn et al. [1999] as important for the success of museum exhibits. For example, questions specifically asked about how the children talked with others around them whilst using the exhibit.

Naturally, as the interviews progressed, it became clear that these key areas were different from what had been expected. Grounded theory recommends that interview schedules should change to adapt and fully expand the dimensions emerging from the data. Thus, final interviews changed the emphasis towards ideas that had emerged in earlier interviews. For instance, children were no longer asked to compare their experience with television or reading but instead asked to relate their experience to playing. Also, the notion of collaboration mutated into that of co-presence and children were asked more about what the presence of others meant rather than how they specifically interacted with others.

The interviews lasted between fifteen and twenty minutes. They were recorded with consent from the children and their guardians. Video recording was not used as it was felt that the interview data was the primary source. Indeed, the interviewer did attempt to note particular attitudes and facial expressions of the children as they used the exhibit but it was not possible to meaningfully interpret them for the aims of the study.

3.3 Analysis

The analysis of the data followed the usual grounded theory practice of analysing as interviews were done. Thus it was possible to adapt the interviews over the course of the study. Microanalysis and open coding were used extensively at the start of the interviews in order begin to define concepts, dimensions and categories in the data. Axial coding was also done as the data accumulated in order to bring out the relationships between the emerging concepts and to gain a holistic sense of the data.

As expected, once interviews were underway, common themes began to emerge. The later interviews, where they reiterated already identified concerns, were not fully coded. Instead, the focus of the coding was on the more novel areas, in particular, on the differences between the prototype and exhibit contexts. This approach concerning the analysis of interviews stands in accordance with suggestions by Glaser [1992] and Dick [2002] who propose that it is advantageous to consider key parts of interviews rather than coding entire interviews.

4   Results

The process of gathering, analysing and interpreting the results is inherently integrated in the grounded theory approach. This means that it is not easy to present how the central categories of the theory emerged. Instead, we present a (necessarily linear) account of the three categories, namely *participation*, *narration* and *co-presence of others*. These arose from the data as being the main distinct concepts that underpin the engagement of the children with the exhibit.

The categories are derived from the transcripts of the interviews but again it would be neither possible nor appropriate to present these in full. Therefore, important quotes from these transcripts are presented in order to provide examples of the obtained results.

4.1 Participation

For the present research participation is defined as a playful process during which information is made personal by children becoming part of the presented scenes. It emerged that children had a sense of participation while interacting with Energy Everywhere and that this sense is determined by the concepts of *simple graphics* and *power*.

Simple Graphics Participation in Energy Everywhere seems possible based on the simplicity of the presented graphics. The children seemed able to feel part of the presented screens and they indicated specifically that it was the graphics that encouraged this. Further, it emerged that children enjoy sensation. For example, one child noted:

"Everything was painted in words, that's so unreal [...] it made me think of different kinds of things I know [...] when moving around I felt like I could be part of these things [...] I liked it."

Further, when talking about the simplicity of the graphics, children frequently noted that this allowed them to play. Therefore it seems that children conceptualise their interaction with Energy Everywhere in terms of play. For example, one child noted:

"[The exhibit] was like a game, you play with it and because it's so simple you have to develop it further in your head."

Another child noted:

"The small words were like a puzzle to play with [...] I liked playing with it."

However, some children perceived the simple, iconic graphics as confusing and therefore felt detached from Energy Everywhere. Specifically, some children noted that the use of small words to form graphics made it difficult to simultaneously read the words and perceive the picture. It seems that this made it difficult for these children to participate in the learning experience presented by the exhibit. For example, one child noted:

"I didn't know whether to read the words or look at the whole picture first [...] That was confusing [...] and made it difficult to learn."

Power An important aspect of children's interaction with Energy Everywhere is their experience of power. In many instances children related their enjoyment of the exhibit and their participation in it to the power that it made them possess. The following dialogue expresses this point:

Child: "It was cool [...] I made energy [...] I forgot that other children can do that too [...] That's cool."
Researcher: "Did you also have power when you made wind?"
Child: "I had power because I made the wind [...] It's not real power because it's only a simulation [...]. That's cool."

When questioned if there were specific features of the exhibit or specific times during their interaction that they felt powerful, children noted times when they were able to directly interact with the exhibit. Specifically, many children noted that they felt powerful while pretending to dig up coal, moving their arms to make wind or clapping their hands to make lightning hit a tree. For example, one child noted:

> "It was when I made the lightning finally hit the tree and it exploded [...] That was when I felt like I had lots of power."

Importantly, children frequently related their experience of power to there being nothing between them and the screen. It seems that this allowed children to pretend that they were carrying out the activities in real life. For example, one child noted:

> "There was no mouse or anything [...] so it didn't feel like it was a computer. It's much more like really pretending you're digging."

4.2 *Narration*

Narration can be defined as the formation of stories and accounts of events. The present research indicates that for interactive exhibits narration is conceptualised in terms of *linear structure* and *fantasy*.

Linear Structure Children frequently referred to Energy Everywhere as a story in terms of it possessing a beginning, a middle and an end. It emerged that this perception of Energy Everywhere as a story possessing a linear structure shapes children's interaction with the exhibit. For example, one child noted:

> "[The exhibit] is like a story of how energy moves [...] in the beginning it shows how energy comes from under the ground, then it moves [...] in the end it shows how energy can become lightning [...] that shows you what you have to do."

The linear structure of Energy Experience also seems to have allowed children to learn the connectivity of the presented information by creating stories around this structure. The following dialogue is indicative of this suggestion:

> *Child*: "At first the energy is stored in the sun. This allows for coal to be created under the ground. Miners must then dig it up so that it can be used [...] Then coal can be burned and used by people, for example to heat houses in the old days [...] Energy moves around differently, depending on what kind it is."
> *Researcher*: "So the things you saw were connected?"
> *Child*: "Yes, they were connected by energy moving and the things that can happen to energy, like lightning and fire."
> *Researcher*: "Can you tell me how you know this?"
> *Child*: "It showed it on the screen [...] I connected things by looking at it."

However, in some cases children made incorrect causal inferences. These incorrect inferences mainly relate to perceived causal relationships between features of the presented information. In particular, some children's narratives expressed that the energy of some features presented on the screen leads to the movement of other features, which is not always correct. For example, one child's narrative includes the statement:

"The clouds in the air make energy for the waves to move."

When asked if there was anything about the exhibit that confused her, this child stated that there was not. Therefore it seems that children may make incorrect inferences without perceiving Energy Everywhere as confusing.

Fantasy It emerged that children's narratives are not based merely on following the linear structure provided by the exhibit, but rather that children's narratives frequently include fantasy. For example, one child created a story, in which she imagined herself flying over the presented landscape. Specifically, it emerged that in creating these narratives children frequently extend the presented information to include their own fantasies. For example, one child noted:

"The waves looked silly, like in a cartoon [...] not the real thing [...]
That was funny [...] and it made me feel like I was part of a cartoon
[...] I like that."

Another child noted:

"The trees made up of words made me think of children's books [...]
here trees move because of the wind [...] I make the wind."

Another fantasy seems to be triggered by the exhibit demanding that children pretend to dig up coal. Pretending to dig up coal necessitates the ability to fantasise that the action of moving ones arms resembles digging up coal. Children frequently noted that moving their arms seemed to make sense only when imagining what it is like to dig up coal in reality. Further, children frequently noted that after having imagined what it is like to dig up coal, they imagined the impact of other information presented. For example, one child noted:

"It [moving his arms in pretence of digging up coal] made sense only if
I imagined what it is really like [...] it must be hard for miners to dig
for so much coal [...] When I was swinging my arms to make wind I
thought of how strong wind can make trees fall [...] I imagined what it
is like for firemen to clear them off roads."

However, it must be noted that the information that made up these fantasies was not always correct. For example, one child stated:

"I was flapping my arms like a bird. I guess birds make wind in the air
by flapping their wings."

4.3   Co-presence of Others

The present research suggests that the co-presence of others, but not collaboration is an important feature of children's interaction with Energy Everywhere. This is surprising since questions concerning collaboration were an important feature of the initial interview guidelines. However, children did not mention collaboration from their own initiative and did not consider collaboration to be an important aspect of their experience when prompted by the researcher. This suggests that collaboration is not an important feature of children's conception of their learning experience in this exhibit. Therefore collaboration does not seem to be important in connecting learning and engagement. Instead it emerged that in order to adequately conceptualise children's experience with interactive exhibits it is essential to consider the co-presence of others. It seems that while there are no specific features within Energy Everywhere that allow for this co-presence of others, the exhibition as a whole does. This is expressed clearly by one child:

> "There was space for others to stand around [. . .] and I could see them when I looked."

It emerged that this category of co-presence of others is based on the concepts of *reassurance and feedback*, *distractions*, *attracting attention* and *communication*.

Reassurance and Feedback Children frequently noted that other visitors provided them with reassurance and feedback concerning their actions:

> "I wanted to know if I was doing it right, so I turned to my mum [. . .]
> She nodded and smiled so I knew I was doing it right."

Further, children frequently noted that the mere presence of others reassured them and provided them with feedback. It emerged that in many cases this reassurance and feedback is more important than reassurance and feedback provided by the exhibit. This is expressed in the following dialogue:

> *Child*: "Since there were so many people watching me, it must be interesting and I must be doing a good job."
> *Researcher*: "And the words 'Well done!' [presented on the screen], did they tell you that you were doing a good job?"
> *Child*: "Yes, but I wasn't so sure, it might always say that."

Distractions It emerged that the possibility of distractions caused by the co-presence of others allows children to increase their engagement with the learning experience. For example, one child noted:

> "There was so much noise and stuff happening [around the exhibit]. I had to just look at the screen and not look away so that I would not miss bits of what is being taught [. . .] That was like in the cinema when you can't see around you."

However, it also emerged that actual distractions seem to reduce the experience of engagement. For example, after another child walked between him and the screen one child noted:

"I turned to look at who was watching me and then didn't know what I had to do any more [...] It felt like it would be best to start again because I forgot what I had learnt."

These negative effects of distractions seem to relate not only to children's physical actions, but also to their creation of narratives and their experience of enjoyment. For example, after another child repeatedly clapped his hands, one child noted:

"The whole thing about what was happening to the energy seemed less real [...] and was not so much fun."

Attracting Attention Children frequently noted that their interaction with Energy Everywhere attracted the attention of other visitors. It emerged that some children enjoy this attention:

"Clapping my hands was really cool. It was noisy and many people turned to look at me."

Also, attracting the attention of others frequently motivates children to spend time with Energy Everywhere and examine it in more detail. For example, one child noted:

"I liked the sound and the pictures [...] another child watched me clap to start [...] that made me want to take a closer look."

Additionally, attracting the attention of others motivates children to perform actions correctly. For example:

"My friends were watching me so I didn't want to make any mistakes."

It emerged that the time, at which the attention of other visitors is attracted is important. For example, children frequently noted that attracting the attention of others by clapping their hands to initiate their interaction with Energy Everywhere encouraged them to continue this interaction. Further, it seems that attracting the attention of others early during their interaction allows children to gain reassurance and feedback concerning whether their actions are correct. This is expressed in the following dialogue:

Child: "I clapped my hands to start. This made my friend turn to look."
Researcher: "And how did it make you feel that your friend turned to look?"
Child: "Good [...] She must like the exhibit so I wanted to continue."

In contrast, during later stages of interaction attracting the attention of co-present individuals made children feel embarrassed. This could be due to the length of time spent interacting by that stage or possibly the gestures made. For example, one child noted:

"When I was spinning my arms my mother looked at me funnily [...] I felt stupid and would have preferred to stop."

Another child noted:

"It was a bit strange waving my arms in front of everyone [...] People were staring [...] I felt a bit silly and wanted to stop."

Communication It emerged that the co-presence of others is associated with children's desire to talk to others about their experience with Energy Everywhere. Further, it emerged that this desire to talk to others is related to a desire to learn. For example, one child noted:

"Seeing my friends [who were interacting with another exhibit] made me want to tell them what I learnt [...] I wanted to learn a lot so that I could tell them lots."

Moreover, children seemed to consider learning in terms of what they can later communicate to others. For example, one child noted:

"I like how I learn about energy moving [...] so that I can tell my friends how it changes."

For some children this learning seems to be important only if they are able to communicate this learning to others. This was expressed clearly by one child:

Child: "There were so many things to learn and do."
Researcher: "Can you give me an example of something you learnt and did?"
Child: "I learnt about the wind moving the sea, and clouds forming, and many other things."
Researcher: "Would you be able to explain what you have learnt to someone who doesn't know about energy?"
Child: "Yes, I think most of the things I saw and what I then did [...] I must be able to explain to others what I saw otherwise there is no use in learning things."

5 Implications for Engagement

In order to understand how interactive exhibits may lead to engagement, we discuss how the categories underpinning engagement arose from the interactive structure of the Energy Everywhere exhibit. Of course, these relationships are based only on the experience of the children who participated with this exhibit. The discussion is therefore couched in terms of areas for further exploration rather than definitive design guidelines for interactive exhibits.

Though no effort was made to formally measure learning in this study, it is worth drawing out the relationship between the theory developed here and existing theories of learning in children. In particular, engagement as described here is commensurate with supporting learning though whether it supports learning the right thing is another matter.

The following two subsections make the links from interaction to engagement and from engagement to learning. The discussions will also be used to contextualise the results in the existing literature related to this area.

5.1 From Interaction to Engagement

The basic interaction of the children with the Energy Everywhere exhibit is that they perform physical actions in order to both take part in the scenes presented and also to allow the sequence of scenes to progress. The present results suggest that these initial physical activities make sense to children only if they use fantasy to imagine how these activities are carried out in real life. This indicates that while performing initial actions children use fantasy to make sense of their actions. Fantasy seems to be an important feature of engagement since it is associated with enjoyment and allows individuals to step into their own imaginary world [Jones 1997]. Since children continued to make frequent use of fantasy, it is possible that the initial necessity to fantasise may encourage the use of fantasy throughout their interaction with Energy Everywhere. This suggests that this early physical interaction could be a useful feature of interaction to encourage engagement.

In addition to the association between fantasy and sense-making, fantasy also seems important by allowing children to become part of the presented scenes. For example, when moving their arms in the pretence of digging up coal some children perceive this in terms of "really" pretending to dig up coal rather than as part of their interaction with the exhibit. The children clearly make the distinction between really pretending and somehow 'humouring' the exhibit. Thus, to some extent, it is not just that the children have power through the immediacy of their interaction but that immediacy relates directly to their sense of fantasy. The two concepts work together to reinforce the feeling of engagement.

One of the more surprising concepts to emerge was the use of a narrative to also help make sense of the exhibit. The linear sequence of the exhibit contrasts with other sorts of interactive exhibits where children are free to select the information presented. This could be considered as a constraint and so reduce the possibility of engagement. Instead, it seems that the continuous use of fantasy is related to the linear structure of the exhibit. Specifically, it seems that children create narratives, which allow for the use of fantasy while still following the linear structure.

Interestingly, the narratives that the children create do not necessarily match with the narrative intended by the exhibit. This may be because the exhibit's narrative is not always clear and the children are having to fill in the gaps to continue making sense of the exhibit. This suggests that a more clearly defined narrative could actually reduce the engagement by removing the need for the children to fantasise. In any case, this result has theoretical implications since it suggests that the common notion that fantasy is largely free from external constraints (e.g. Piaget [1951] and Singer [1994]) may not hold true for fantasy occurring in interactive exhibits.

The simple graphics also seemed to have the drawback of disorienting some children. This disorientation seemed to be somewhat akin to the Stroop Effect [Stroop 1935] in that children could not choose whether to attend to the words or the pictures made from the words. The resulting confusion is likely to reduce engagement [Douglas & Hargadon 2000] and so perhaps these simple graphics may actually not be simple enough.

Though not related directly to the interactive element of the exhibit, the co-presence of others is a feature of the construction of the exhibit. The unmediated interaction requires space around which others can stand and this space is a clearly defined area which should be for the child using the exhibit. The co-presence then allowed for other possibilities that would support engagement with the exhibit.

Falk & Dierking [2000] discuss the importance of providing cues and encouragement for developing engagement. Though the exhibit does provide these things, the children seem wise to the possibly superficial nature of the encouragement. Fortunately, they are able to seek it from the people they do trust who are around them and watching them. The encouragement may be explicitly provided or implicitly, inferred from the interest and attentiveness of those watching.

The presence of others though was not always positive. As the exhibit progressed, the children were required to make some quite large movements that would possibly draw unnecessary attention to themselves and perhaps make them look "silly." It could be that this was due to the length of time for which the children had been the centre of attention. Initially, being attended to may have been motivating but over a longer period, it may be too much attention and the children become self-conscious. Alternatively, it could simply be that the children do no like making large and unusual movements. In either case, it seems exhibits need to balance the opportunity for being "in the spotlight" with the over-exposure that this might entail.

It is worth noting that both the positive and negative aspects of co-presence correspond with the findings of Brown & Cairns [2004] with engagement in games. There, engagement occurred when players were motivated to learn to play the game but full immersion would not occur unless the players were able to reduce self-awareness. Co-presence seems to be both motivating and heightening self-awareness and so is equivocal in its effect on engagement.

5.2   *From Engagement to Learning*

Narration is known to be an important element in learning. Plowman et al. [1999] studied multimedia learning environments such as CD-ROMS and proposed that narration is linked to learning by making the presented information personal. Similarly, Falk & Dierking [2000] proposed that the establishment of personal context leads to deeper learning by allowing individuals to attach meaning to the presented information.

Further, it seems that by means of narration children are able to consider events and actions from various perspectives, a process known as decentring. For example, decentring is evident when children consider the presented information from the perspective of a coal miner or a fireman clearing trees off roads. As noted by Piaget [1951] fantasy is important for decentring in terms of its relationship to the process of assimilation.

Vygotsky [1978] also considered fantasy to be important for general learning since it allows for the creation of novel cognitive structures. Vygotsky notes that fantasy is thus essential for the separation of meaning from origins and is based on changes occurring within the Zone of Proximal Development, that is, the difference between children's actual level of achievement and children's potential level of achievement. Vygotsky argues that, while fantasising, children are no longer constrained by their surroundings and are instead able to explore the limits of their own understanding.

Thus the features of the interaction that lead to narration are therefore supporting personalisation of the information and hence could lead to a good learning experience.

Co-presence can also be understood to be important for learning. The presence of others clearly motivated children, at least initially, and motivation has been identified as key to learning [Piaget & Inhelder 1969]. Moreover, the children also reported that doing well at the exhibit meant that they would be able to tell others about it. This is not only motivating but Gammon [2003] argues that an increased willingness to discuss information subsequent to interacting with an exhibit is an indicator of personal learning. Geier [2004] also notes that in many instances narration allows for first-person experiences to be communicated to others.

Thus co-presence of others not only motivates children but also gives them the opportunity to consider and actually communicate their experiences to others. However, the mere fact of co-presence contrasts with the importance of collaboration [Falk & Dierking 2000]. This research confirms that learning from exhibits is a social experience, though socialisation may not be so explicit as collaboration in order for learning to occur. Jackson & Fagan's [2000] notions concerning the importance of collaboration for enhancing the educational value of engagement may need to be extended to include the importance of the co-presence of others.

Of course, it should also be noted that the narratives that children created did not always correspond with what was being taught and that others around them could be a source of distraction and inhibition. This suggests that engagement can lead to positive learning experiences but that the focus of engagement needs to be considered carefully when designing the exhibit.

6 Conclusion

The grounded theory described here suggests that children's engagement with interactive exhibits can be understood in terms of three key categories: participation, narration and co-presence of others. These categories can be clearly related to some aspects of the exhibit design and so suggest fruitful areas for future research into the design of interactive exhibits and the nature of engagement with them. In particular, the theory suggests that it may be sufficient to design only for co-presence of others rather than collaboration in order to provide an engaging experience. Moreover, engagement with the exhibit does have parallels with what is needed for successful learning, and this was not previously known. Thus, this research provides many new questions whose answers could lead to the improved design of museum exhibits for engagement and learning.

Acknowledgements

Many thanks to the Science Museum for the extensive support provided and to all of the participants and their guardians who took time from their visits to talk to us. Thanks also to Sarah Faisal and Lidia Oshlyansky for their helpful comments on this paper and the anonymous referees for their substantial feedback.

References

British Museum [2004], Mummy: The Inside Story, http://www.thebritishmuseum.ac.uk/ mummy/ (last accessed 2005-02-07).

Brown, E. & Cairns, P. [2004], A Grounded Investigation of Game Immersion, *in* E. Dykstra-Erickson & M. Tscheligi (eds.), *CHI'04 Extended Abstracts of the Conference on Human Factors in Computing Systems*, ACM Press, pp.1297–1300.

Dick, B. [2002], Grounded Theory: A Thumbnail Sketch, http://www.scu.edu.au/schools/ gcm/ar/arp/grounded.html (retrieved 2004-03-01).

Douglas, Y. & Hargadon, A. B. [2000], The Pleasure Principle: Immersion, Engagement, and Flow, *in* F. M. Shipman, P. J. Nuernburg & D. L. Hicks (eds.), *Proceedings of the Eleventh ACM Conference on Hypertext and Hypermedia — Hypertext'00*, ACM Press, pp.153–60.

Falk, J. H. & Dierking, L. D. [2000], *Learning from Museums: Visitor Experiences and the Making of Meaning*, Altamira Press.

Gammon, B. [2003], Assessing Learning in Museum Environments. A Practical Guide for Museum Evaluators, http://www.ecsite-uk.net/about/reports/ indicators_learning_1103_gammon.pdf (retrieved 2004-03-10).

Geier, M. [2004], Role-playing in Educational Environments, http://www.cc.gatech.edu/ megak/7001/Roleplaying.html (retrieved 2004-07-10).

Glaser, B. [1992], *Basics of Grounded Theory Analysis: Emergence vs. Forcing*, Sociology Press.

Jackson, R. L. & Fagan, E. [2000], Collaboration and Learning within Immersive Virtual Reality, *in* E. Churchill & M. Reddy (eds.), *Proceedings of the Third International Conference on Collaborative Virtual Environments (CVE 2000)*, ACM Press, pp.83–92.

Jensen, N. [1994], Children's Perceptions of their Museum Experiences: A Contextual Perspective, *Children's Environments* 11(4), 300–24.

Jones, M. G. [1997], Learning to Play; Playing to Learn: Lessons Learned from Computer Games, http://www.gsu.edu/ wwwitr/docs/mjgames/ (retrieved 2004-07-22).

Piaget, J. [1951], *Play, Dreams and Imitation in Childhood*, Routledge and Kegan Paul.

Piaget, J. & Inhelder, B. (eds.) [1969], *The Psychology of the Child*, Basic Books.

Plowman, L., Luckin, R., Laurillard, D., Stratfold, M. & Taylor, J. [1999], Designing Multimedia for Learning: Narrative Guidance and Narrative Construction, *in* M. G. Williams & M. W. Altom (eds.), *Proceedings of the SIGCHI Conference on Human Factors in Computing Systems: The CHI is the Limit (CHI'99)*, ACM Press, pp.310–17.

Richardson, K. & Sheldon, S. [1988], *Cognitive Development to Adolescence*, Lawrence Erlbaum Associates.

Singer, J. L. [1994], Imaginative Play and Adaptive Development, *in* J. H. Goldstein (ed.), *Toys, Play and Child: How do these Aspects Inform Engagement and Learning?*, Cambridge University Press, pp.6–26.

Strauss, A. & Corbin, J. [1998], *Basics of Qualitative Research — Techniques and Procedures for Developing Grounded Theory*, second edition, Sage Publications.

Stroop, J. [1935], Studies of Interference in Serial Verbal Reactions, *Journal of Experimental Psychology: General* **18**, 643–62.

Teachernet [2004], Museums Moving with the Times, http://www.teachernet.gov.uk/teachingandlearning/resourcematerials/museums/ (last accessed 2005-02-07).

vom Lehn, D., Heath, C. & Hindmarsh, J. [1999], Discovering Science: Action and Interaction at the Exhibit-face, http://www.kcl.ac.uk/depsta/pse/mancen/witrg/pdf/vlehnDiscover.pdf (retrieved 2004-03-03).

Vygotsky, L. S. [1978], *Mind In Society: The Development of Higher Psychological Processes*, Harvard University Press. Edited by Michael Cole, Vera John-Steiner, Sylvia Scribner, Ellen Souberman.

User Needs in e-Government: Conducting Policy Analysis with Models-on-the-Web

Barbara Mirel, Mary Maher[†] & Jina Huh

*University of Michigan, 1075 Beal, Ann Arbor,
Michigan 48109, USA*

Tel: *+1 734 332 8969, +1 734 645 3664*

Fax: *+1 734 302 2408*

Email: *bmirel@umich.edu, jinah@umich.edu*

[†] *Economic Research Service, 1800 M Street NW,
Washington DC 20036-5831, USA*

Tel: *+1 202 694 5126*

Fax: *+1 202 694 5638*

Email: *memaher@ers.usda.gov*

Design conventions are emerging in e-government models-on-the-Web but they are not based on evidence of analysts' actual what-if analyses for purposes like policymaking. From field studies, we developed representations of policy analysts' actual work and compared them to the assumed goals and tasks built into existing online models, inferred through goal-based requirements methods. We found a large gap exists and argue that current online models are impoverished because they ignore expertise users bring to bear on their work.

Keywords: e-government, public policy, models, Web development, decision support systems, expertise, user models, usability, transparency.

1 Introduction

Increasingly, e-government simulations are available on the Web to support users in analysing and making decisions with federal data. For example, online economic models simulate commodity production, prices, and adoption of new technologies to help users forecast and assess economic and environmental impacts under various conditions, entered as what-if scenarios. These applications provide graphical user interfaces (GUIs) to powerful simulation models that analysts previously could only run in proprietary languages.

In these online simulations a common de facto design standard is emerging. Design conventions, usually beneficial for human-computer interactions, are troubling in this developing genre. Like all design standards, these embody assumptions about users' core activities, problem solving actions, and scope of model-based analysis. But these standards do not derive from systematic user experience analysis or usability testing. In fact, little if any evaluative evidence exists to show whether these quickly emerging design conventions actually fit people's demonstrated approaches to complex, what-if analyses. Therefore, the broad and open question that our study addresses is: Are current models-on-the-Web as they are now designed truly the right product for analysts' needs?

To answer this question we analyse how well the notion of users' work built into the designs of current models-on-the-Web fits the work that analysts actually do in context. We study users who are policy analysts, specifically specialists in agricultural economics who construct policy arguments for such questions as: "What incentives may prompt farmers to adopt effective strategies for managing risks from drought?" We find a large gap between policy advisers' actual work and the work envisioned by current applications. Basically, current applications represent and support an impoverished view of what-if analysis.

Our findings suggest that for more useful, fit-to-purpose online models, design thinking needs to change about the scope of users' work and the identities they bring to bear on it. Specifically, designers must recognize and design for the pragmatic and domain expertise that shapes policy analysts' goals, scope, and problem solving processes, including critical influences missing from models-on-the-Web today — the frameworks analysts apply and share with stakeholders about what constitutes legitimate and effective policy arguments.

To pursue this line of research, we face several challenges, for example how to capture and represent users' actual work in context when it is nonlinear and dynamic; and how to extract and represent models of work embodied in existing applications in ways that map to descriptions of users' contextual and goal-driven work. To address these challenges, we combine diverse methods that are similarly oriented to designing for goals and fitness to purpose.

2 Relevant Research

A top research priority in many digital government fields is to better support people in what-if analysis and decision-making [Cushing et al. 2003]. Yet few studies exist about the usability of models-on-the-Web, and we have found none that addresses the use of online models for policy analysis.

Given the scant human-computer interaction (HCI) and digital government research about models-on-the-Web, we draw on relevant studies from other fields to establish what is known so far about policy analysts' processes of what-if analysis and to uncover effective strategies for extracting built-in notions of users' goals and complex work from already existing applications.

As cognitive psychology and complex problem solving research suggests, policy analysts are experienced problem solvers who have subject matter expertise and domain-specific strategic knowledge [Zachary 1988]. They work within exacting time pressures and construct pragmatic arguments that have to convince stakeholders who have diverse interests, priorities, and perspectives. As research in cognitive psychology and complex problem solving shows, this group of users brings a distinct expertise to analysis that defines their inquiry approaches [Feltovich et al. 2004; Pannell 2004; Zeitz 1997; Feltovich et al. 1997; Johnson 1988; Zachary 1988]. The following expertise is relevant:

Experts play with system constraints and determine effects of possible actions and choices before ever making them. They focus more on strategies than procedures and choose moves based on their mental images of and visible cues about a model, its assumptions, and its interactions and dependencies among variables. They call up domain- and policy discourse-specific frameworks to define their problems and appropriate lines of argument, frameworks, for example, to argue that a model is credible for the situation at hand. In addition, expert analysts are distinctively skilled in discovering patterns in data displays and matching them to their own array of well-developed mental patterns for the outcomes that could occur in a situation in question.

In terms of fitting software support to these analysts' expert-based approaches to work, research in decision support systems emphasizes that for complex tasks, decisions, and fuzziness, analysts need support and guidance in information processing, process structuring, *and* communication/reporting [Zigura & Buckland 1998]. In addition, for the integrated human judgement and quantitative, statistical forecasts that this work involves, analysts require autonomy and support for the following judgements: Choosing an appropriate model for one's purposes; determining relevant and acceptable inputs for scenarios; arranging output for meaning; and adjusting statistical forecasts to account for special factors [Fildes et al. in press]. Control over these judgements gives analysts a sense of ownership of their work, and ownership has proven to be a prime determinant of effective solutions [Fildes et al. in press]. Yet user control has its limits. Certain aspects of a statistical model-on-the-Web must remain opaque to protect analysts from misapprehending the underlying complexity and making inaccurate inferences.

This review of relevant research about users is incomplete without an examination of how to turn these analysts' contextually-driven practices and needs into requirements that do not let situation, purpose, and stakeholders' influences fall through the cracks. Studies in requirements engineering shed light on this issue [Cockton 2000; Chung et al. 1999].

For example, 'problem frames' [Jackson 2000] re-orient requirements analysis to users' problems in the world as the driving force behind solutions. In this perspective, shared phenomena between actors in the problem space give rise to requirements For our study, this means that stakeholders' influences — for instance their expectations for arguments — must be built into the application.

Insights into how to generate such problem-sensitive requirements are found in studies on goal modelling and non-functional requirements. The reverse engineering approaches of goal-based requirements analysis methods (GBRAM) are most relevant to our project [Antón 1996; Hsi & Potts 2000]. These methods provide a means for inferring and describing goal-based requirements in terms of users' problems and purposes, thereby corresponding to user models drawn from analysts' actual goal-driven work. With this 'family resemblance', it becomes possible to compare the two sets of user models. We do so, and to assess the fit we apply evaluation categories found in model-misfit research by Blandford & Green [2002] and Sutcliffe et al. [2000].

3   Our Methodology

To develop user models of what-if analysis in context, we conducted field studies of 40 analysts from 10 organizations who are experienced using models in agricultural and ag-ecological decision-making. They included 17 policy analysts, 23 non-academic and academic research analysts, one business strategist, and three model programmers. Some policy analysts are also research analysts and wear different hats at different times. Interviews were semi-structured and asked about drawbacks and benefits of online models and about one or two sample modelling analysis that interviewees had done. Interviewees walked us through their processes, knowledge, challenges, critical incidents, and time constraints. We also observed three of these analysts as they used a model to analyse a policy issue of their choice.

From interview and observation data, we constructed policy analysts' workflows and analysed the functional roles of and motivations behind analysts' moves and strategies. We composed scenarios and developed visual 'mountainscape' representations of users' work, a suitable metaphor for complex exploratory inquiry [Mirel & Allmendinger 2004]. We abstracted policy analysts' patterns of inquiries and the phenomena they share with stakeholders that drive this work.

To identify the notion of users' work embodied in existing online models, we analysed five online simulations:

FAIR — see http://fairmodel.econ.yale.edu/main.htm
POLYSYS — see http://agpolicy.org/polysys.html
EPIC — see http://www.public.iastate.edu/ elvis/i_epic_description.html
DREAM — see http://www.ifpri.org/dream.htm
Crystal Ball — see http://www.decisoneering.com

These models are all similar in scope to our project and cited by interviewees as well known and widely respected. From these online models, we identified common design traits and extracted the notions of work built into them. We adaptively applied GBRAM to one of them and examined the application's structure and the functional relationships among fields and features. From results, we identified goals and concepts that are present and absent, central and peripheral in the application.

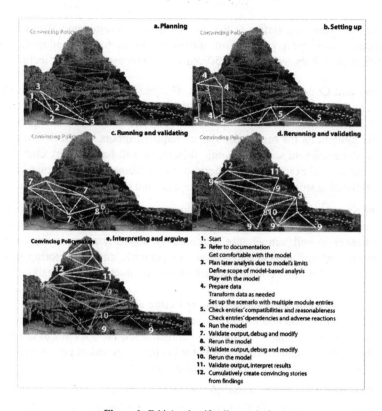

Figure 1: Fabio's what-if policy analysis.

We compared this extracted user model to our user representations from field study findings and assessed the fit between the two.

4   Results and Discussion

4.1   Field Study: Users' Model-based Analysis in Context

4.1.1   Scenario of Use

The following case is drawn from composite field study findings and informed by the modelling literature [Costantini et al. 2002]. In it, the analyst interacts with a model-on-the-Web that is better aligned to his needs than current applications really are. We number the analyst's inquiry processes and depict these numbers on the 'analytical mountainscapes' storyboarded in Figure 1. In the moutainscape, the analyst moves toward the goal of creating convincing arguments for policymakers — the mountaintop – and his paths take him in and out of an intricate cave, which is the underlying simulation model. He excavates the cave (model) to set up and run scenarios as well as to assure throughout analysis that his new knowledge and evolving arguments are valid and complete.

Fabio Cortini is a staffer at the FAO Drylands Development Working Group and needs to brief policymakers on optimal measures for combating the risk of desertification in Italy over the next 50 years. The process he follows includes:

Planning and Conceptualizing Analysis. ❶ Fabio chooses a simulation model that forecasts soil temperatures and moisture under various conditions. ❷ He refers to the documentation and assesses the model's methods for various estimates, its limitations for his needs, and its required inputs. He sees that to factor in some relevant socio-economic factors, he will have to look elsewhere. ❸ Later he will examine these other sources, combine them with conclusions and convincing stories from modelling results, and construct final arguments.

❸ Knowing the model's limits, Fabio can now define the scope of his model-based analysis. He intends to assess risks region-by-region by evaluating changes in soil temperature triggered by humidity changes, by comparing deep-level soil temperatures to air temperature, and by factoring in effects over time for other conditions such as crop production and irrigation.

Setting up and Running Simulations. ❹ Before he creates and runs his scenarios, Fabio plays with the model and conducts a dry run with some benchmark soils in Italy at a national and sub-national level. He does this to test whether the model is valid and acceptable for his purposes and to gain insight into its workings, causal logic, and probability methods.

❹ Satisfied by results from the dry run, Fabio now collects available input data for the model. ❹ He knows from reading the documentation that daily climatic input must be compatible with the model's risk estimates so he carries out some data transformations. ❹ He does the same with soil layer inputs. He spends hours preparing these data.

❺ When finished, Fabio begins entering the data as scenario inputs in the model-on-the-Web. To do so, he must move through many different tabbed screens, each consisting of several layers of entry screens. He starts by putting monthly means and daily statistics into the weather generator to produce daily climatic inputs. ❺ Next he enters reference crop data and pauses briefly because the application only allows one crop condition for all regions. In actuality, different regions often have distinct conditions for crop cultivation. Fabio explores the application to see if he might be able to work around this restriction but to no avail. Therefore, pressed for time, he enters the single condition and makes a mental note that he must qualify his arguments accordingly.

❺ Next, to enter the soil layer input, Fabio refers to outside sources for region-specific calibration options. Many of the options are time consuming, so Fabio just does basic recalibrations, planning to do others later if time permits. He finishes entering the soil inputs after traversing a series of layered screens. He is taxed by having to keep track of consistencies between his entries and by having to assure that in relation to each other they are all reasonable.

Analysing and Making Meaning. ➏ Finally entries are complete, and Fabio clicks 'Run' to generate outcomes. ➐ The results do not correspond to what he expects. To determine why not, he digs into the model and its processing methods. He also studies the documentation and his input spreadsheet. Finally, he finds that the Soil Taxonomy for soil moisture and temperature has to be modified. He does so which, due to dependencies, involves modifying the weather generator as well. ➑ He runs the scenario again.

➒ The output is still faulty. Now only the temperature variable is displayed in the second layer of soil. Pursuing a tedious but ultimately effective strategy, Fabio backtracks to earlier input screens and modifies certain soil depths, knowing that these entries should 'trick' the program into generating the right data for the second soil layer. These revisions involve moving through numerous prior screens, checking his new entries against previous ones, and assuring that he is only changing what is needed without adversely affecting other entries.

➓ Once more, he reruns the first scenario, and now the output looks good. ➓➊ He begins to manipulate results to find important patterns for arguments germane to desertification risks. He arranges and rearranges the data displays, filters out various factors, and, when he spots correlations and trends of interest, narrows in on relevant details. He jots down notes and moves on, ready to think about the next scenario. He needs to refresh his memory about the set of parameters he has entered so far and those needed next for his projected arguments. He goes back to look at his earlier work.

Ultimately, Fabio runs more than 80 scenarios, continuously needing to decide on the best combinations of factors to enter as input based on emerging insights and prior scenario choices. ➓➋ He constructs provisional arguments as he goes, and at certain points exports output to a different software package for more intensive analysis later.

At this point, after just a few scenario runs, what Fabio knows so far is that risks of desertification are low in most regions and that even differently calibrated soil traits show good water holding capacity. He is surprised, however, that humidity changes only partially affect soil moisture and that, contrary to Soil Taxonomy indications and field measurement projections, deeper level soil and air temperatures do not differ much. These contradictions trouble Fabio, and next he will begin to look into them more deeply.

4.1.2 Abstracting a User Model from Actual Work in Context

As Fabio's case shows, policy analysts recursively move through four broad exploratory processes: Planning and conceptualizing (see Figure 1a); setting up, running and rerunning simulations (Figure 1b, c and d); interpreting and making meaning from output (Figure 1e); and creating arguments and convincing stories (Figure 1e). Argumentation conventions drive all these processes but in our representations of users' work below we omit the actual composition of evolving arguments because details in our scenario do not extend that far.

Below, we represent users' work as application-level patterns of inquiry. Patterns include problems, goals, and questions — the very reasons *why* models-on-the-Web are created — and they include contextual conditions and constraints that affect the achievement of these goals. In Fabio's case, these latter forces are fairly similar across patterns so we describe them only once below. Following them, we describe the distinct parts of each pattern of inquiry.

4.1.3 The Following Contextual Conditions and Constraints Affect Analysis in all Three Patterns of Inquiry — Planning, Set up, and Interpretation

- Technical and modelling constraints: Pre-defined formats for input and output: pre-defined dependencies, logic, and allowed inputs, predefined interactivity to access information and analyse output.

- Inputs that may be allowed by modelling rules but that are practically unreasonable.

- A tension between model opacity and transparency: The need for some parts of a model to be opaque for accuracy but others to be transparent for user judgements.

- Socio-political constraints: Influences exerted by shared and expected conventions for convincing policy arguments, e.g. addressing diverse interests, perspectives, and priorities; discussing long and short term implications of recommended policies; presenting a convincing case against rejected alternatives; including qualifications due to model constraints; and addressing who gains and who loses.

- Cognitive constraints: Limits in cognitive capacity for processes of expert analysis.

- Time constraints.

Despite similar constraints across patterns of inquiry, patterns for planning, set up, and interpretation, each has distinct problems, goals, and questions. In these patterns, we present goals at a high level instead of more finely grained ones (e.g. accessing a schematic of an underlying model) because we aim to represent users' work in ways that do not foster a premature shift to mapping low level needs or actions to discrete, context-free features or feature fixes. (See Figure 2.)

4.1.4 Implications for Requirements

These goal- and problem-oriented patterns suggest that requirements for models-on-the-Web must account for the fact that policy analyses are never complete or valid unless they dynamically involve all these interlocked patterns. Moreover, goals relate to assuring the model's fit with argument purposes, not simply working the model. Toward these ends, requirements go beyond the obvious of assuring the ability to enter inputs and generate and save outputs. They must target users' needs to access the modelling information relevant to public debate, conventions of

	Planning and Conceptualizing
Problem	Is this the right model for my purposes?

Goals and Sub-goals	Get into a comfort zone with the model:
	    Recognize its limitations for my purposes and circumstances.
	    Prove the model is valid and apt for the integrity of my analysis.
	    Consult with model developers for adjustments as needed.
	Set a scope and questions for analysis that can be addressed by the model.
	Prepare data /other preconditions to fit model and analysis requirements.
	Validate my understanding by doing dry runs — mentally, actually, or both.

Questions	Is the model appropriate for my context and focus? How will model constraints qualify my arguments? Are data, elasticities and equations up to date?

	Setting up and Running Scenarios
Problem	What sets of scenarios will build a case for proposed policy choices?

Goals and Sub-goals	Conceptualize/vet a relevant set of scenarios for various lines of reasoning.
	Construct each scenario by choosing appropriate and necessary input:
	    Assure internal consistency and reasonable figures in entries
	    Guard against adverse interactions between parameters, other entries.
	    Remember what has been entered already and its effects next entries.
	    Make sure inputs reflect desired scenario and extend cumulative stories.
	Specify output displays that fit analysis needs.
	Validate, debug, modify, and re-run scenarios to assure analytical integrity.

Questions	What baselines and other parameters do I use? What interactions occur between changes/input I make? What input have I done already and does that affect what I enter next?

	Interpreting and Making Meaning
Problem	What arguments do scenario outcomes alone and cumulatively imply?

Goals and Sub-goals	Validate outcomes.
	Match patterns in outputs to mental model patterns for a given situation.
	    Manipulate layout and arrangements to facilitate interpretation.
	    Compare results.
	Progressively find and create a convincing story.
	Build this case by determining the next scenarios to run.
	At opportune times, export output to other software for in-depth analysis.

Questions	Are outcomes valid? What equations underlie output numbers or graphs? How much impact did the conditions I entered have and on what? How can I sort output to find patterns and relationships of interest?

Figure 2: Patterns of inquiry from a user's point of view.

policy arguments, and analytical integrity and to manage evolving knowledge and cumulative scenarios without overloading their cognitive capacity.

4.2   Notions of Users' Work Built Into Online Simulations

4.2.1   Common Designs in Models-on-the-Web

How well do the designs of current models-on-the-Web represent users' actual work in context? Our findings show that it is appropriate to generalize an answer to this question because designs across applications share similar traits. Models-on-the-Web commonly have tabbed modules that include fields for defining inputs, and they have pre-defined output screens. Designs also include a 'run' button, output screens — graphs, tables or both — and functionality for reading in data, defining formats for output, saving output, browsing datasets, and editing through toolbars and menus. They rarely allow users to directly manipulate results other than saving and exporting them. Designs offer information about input fields and model constraints through generic help and context-sensitive explanations.

4.2.2   Goal-based Requirements Analysis of one Model-on-the-Web

We analysed the Dynamic Research Evaluation for Management (DREAM) model, an application that lets users run scenarios with a multi-market, partial equilibrium model to project how the adoption of various new technologies may affect commodity prices, production, consumption, trade, and household income in one or many regions.

From this application, we abstracted its structure to identify where support for analysis is 'bloated' and where it is impoverished. Figure 3a depicts the nine modules DREAM presents in tabbed screens, and Figure 3b shows the inputs that screens within modules allow users to enter. As Figure 3 suggests, structurally the application is 'set up-centric', 'bloated' for set up goals and tasks. The predominant goals it supports coincide with what we defined earlier in the set up pattern of inquiry as 'Construct each scenario by choosing appropriate and necessary input' and 'Specify output displays that fit analysis needs'. Support for other goals, e.g. *vetting* a relevant *set* of scenarios or arranging data displays in output, is absent. Getting into a comfort zone with a model is peripheral.

4.2.3   Misuse of Information Objects

In order to achieve these other goals, DREAM expects users either to do the work in other software or to infer modelling logic and assumptions from visible modules that reflect input requirements and from generic information in documentation, online help and field-sensitive help. Clearly, as Fabio's scenario shows, planning and interpretation in analysis are neither separate activities nor can users complete them simply by amassing separate pieces of data or *information objects*. Rather they involve complex *problem-solving behaviours* and *purposes*. DREAM's 'information object' orientation diminishes users' problem solving and impoverishes analysts' capacity for expert judgement.

4.2.4   Misfit Between the Display and Users' Strategies

The need to get into a comfort zone with the model exemplifies DREAM's insufficiencies. In DREAM, the displayed sequence of tabbed modules approximates

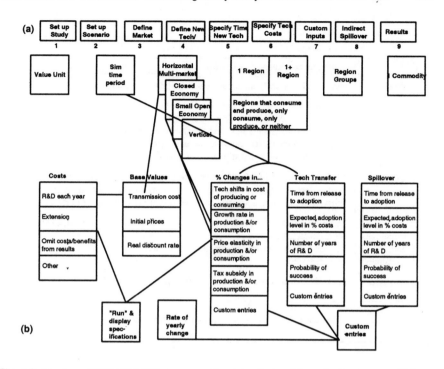

Figure 3: Structure of DREAM. (a) The sequence of modules displayed through tabbed screens. (b) Input fields for user entries, with links showing dependencies between entries.

the order users should follow to set up and run scenarios. But this order is not beneficial for getting into a comfort zone and understanding the 'guts' of the model's methodology. To explore the model, users need to start with the fourth and fifth tabs related to technology inputs. Unfortunately, nothing in the visible structure of DREAM signals this importance. Moreover, even when users go to these screens, context sensitive help for fields gives only generic definitions of discrete modelling factors; and users can only get cues about the roles of various variables and associated equations through error messages. Structurally missing in the application is any layering of guidance information for problem solving purposes. It is not just that 'set up-centricity' and dictionary-type help diminish ease of use. In terms of fitness-to-purpose, they actually dictate *against* the expert problem solving exploration and mentally projected moves and strategies that characterize analysts' work.

In terms of problems and goals, it appears that DREAM assumes the pattern of inquiry shown in Figure 4 which, as we detail in the next section, is impoverished compared to users' real world work.

DREAM also assumes a pattern for interpreting output but envisions it largely as a read-only activity, as discussed in the next section. The workflows built into DREAM's structures and functionality are shown in Figure 5.

	Setting up and Running Scenarios
Problem	How should I specify the inputs to set up and run this single scenario?

Goals and Sub-goals	Conceptualize scenarios for various lines of reasoning.
	Construct the scenario by choosing appropriate and necessary input
	    Assure dependencies and conditional relations across entries are met
	    Make sure inputs are complete and in the right form.
	Specify output displays that fit analysis needs.

Questions	What baselines do I use? What elasticities make sense for this set up? What values are feasible based on the modelling rules and assumptions? What input have I done already and does that affect what I enter next?
Conditions and Constraints	Technical constraints: Predefined formats for input and output; predefined dependencies, logic and allowed inputs; predefined interactivity. Tension between model opacity and transparency. Time pressures.
Obstacles addressed	Lack of ready access to information about parts of the model.

Figure 4: Pattern of inquiry from DREAM's point of view.

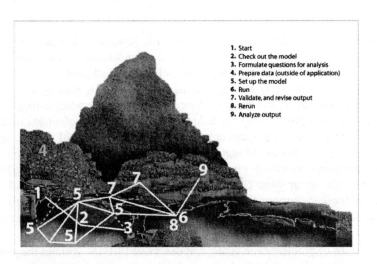

1. Start
2. Check out the model
3. Formulate questions for analysis
4. Prepare data (outside of application)
5. Set up the model
6. Run
7. Validate, and revise output
8. Rerun
9. Analyze output

Figure 5: User workflows embodied in the online simulation.

Note in Figure 5 that only one storyboard panel is needed to capture this workflow as opposed to the multiple panels in Figure 1. The workflow depicted in Figure 5 reflects DREAM's limited notion of setting up and running a scenario, particularly its lack of requirements for users to shape their analysis to stakeholders' influences and the goals of policy debates.

4.3   Comparing Actual and Built-in User Models

In comparing actual and built-in user models, we find that even in the seeming overlap in patterns for setting up and running a scenario, important differences occur. For set up, DREAM envisions activities tied primarily to the goal of choosing and entering *required* input. Users' judgements about appropriate input are peripheral. In addition, both Fabio's and DREAM's pattern of setting up and running scenarios involve the goal of conceptualizing relevant sets of scenarios but DREAM only supports it superficially. DREAM has a feature for listing the names of previously run scenarios but provides no information about the lines of reasoning behind them, something users need. Nor does it facilitate through cues, reminders or history features policy analysts' valued practice of mentally *vetting* possible *sets* of scenarios before ever running them to build a case for argument. Moreover, validating is peripheral. DREAM's tabs provide navigational capabilities for backtracking, debugging, modifying and re-running scenarios — a goal we saw Fabio pursue frequently. But the application does little to support this goal in any other way. Backtracking, therefore, is cognitively burdensome. Here as elsewhere the online simulation fails to conceive of and design for the complex process management that experts actually do in what-if analysis.

The online model is even more impoverished in its views of analysts' work in patterns for planning and interpreting. For example, recursively achieving the goal of getting into a comfort zone with the model — a goal that our study participants emphasize as the primary goal of model-based analysis — is thwarted by an online simulation that is overly-restrictive. Its functions and features keep large parts of the model opaque that must be transparent to users for effective analysis and argument. In addition, as mentioned earlier the online simulation assumes that interpretation of output is achieved as a view-only process, belying the interactive data manipulation that to experienced analysts is a non-negotiable process of making meaning from outcomes.

4.3.1   Evaluation

These comparisons coupled with strikingly obvious differences in the scope of work reflected in the paths depicted in Figures 1 & 5 show user model mismatches that exemplify what Sutcliffe et al. [2000] define as missing functionality, inadequate functionality, poor support, and missing feedback. We cannot overemphasize the fact that these issues reflect deep-seated flaws in understanding users' work, not in helping users work the program.

In Blandford & Green's [2002] terms, misconstrued notions of users' work lead to designs that users find too viscous, that is they give users too little control over exploring aspects of the model for argumentation purposes. Designs offer users too little progressive evaluation and too many hidden dependencies. They lack a closeness of mapping with the domain, especially conventions for what constitutes effective policy arguments; and they push users above and beyond the hard mental operations inherent in complex analysis by placing extra demands on cognitive resources for managing and monitoring cumulative scenarios and processing bit-sized pieces of information into meaning.

4.3.2   High Level Design Recommendations

Designs would be more useful if they better addressed the now unsupported core goals and tasks in users' expert-based approaches to what-if policy analysis. We recommend requirements and design choices that will maintain users' *integrated* approaches to planning, set up, interpretation, and argumentation. As the above comparison shows, what is missing from current online models are user-centred means for achieving the following goals with ample control and undue cognitive load- perhaps more in the form of guidance, cues, awareness, and information layering than operational procedures.   The lengthy unmet user goals below underscore how much is currently missing for coherent and complete policy analyses.

> Get into a comfort zone with the model:
>> Access information on-demand relevant to problem solving purposes.
>> Recognize the model's limitations for given purposes and circumstances.
>> Prove the model is valid and apt for analytical integrity.
>> Call up model information on-demand to set and appropriate inquiry scope.
>> Uncover modelling assumptions to see how arguments must be qualified.
> Prepare data and other preconditions to fit both the model and analysis goals.
> Mentally run and vet a relevant set of scenarios for various lines of reasoning without cognitive overload.
> Tie and track scenarios to arguments relevant to stakeholders and policy realities.
> Choose appropriate input:
>> Explore prior entries, data sources, and model constraints as needed.
>> Assure internal consistency and reasonable figures in entries.
>> Recursively call up model information, e.g. to guard against adverse interactions between parameters, other entries.
>> Remember what has been entered already and its effects on next entries.
>> Make sure inputs reflect the desired scenario and extend cumulative stories.
> Judge validity of output, debug, and modify, accessing relevant information for problem solving purposes:
>> See at a glance how modelling estimates and methods relate to the results.
>> See at a glance the relevant statistical measures behind the generated output.
> Manipulate output layout and arrangements to facilitate interpretation:
>> Compare results within and across scenarios.
>> Adjust statistical forecasts for special factors in output, input, or modelling.
>> Detect and manage errors, inaccuracies, faulty inferences/assumptions.
> Manage cumulative complexity in progressive inquiry/arguments, without cognitive overload
> Recall/monitor cumulative interpretations in relation to stakeholders priorities, perspectives, and argument conventions
> Assure cumulative interpretations adequately support argument conventions.
> Monitor inquiry progress to determine the next scenarios to run to build this case.

5   Conclusions and Future Work

Our research into actual vs. application-based notions of users' complex what-if analyses for policy purposes shows that in actuality, what-if analyses are conducted largely by experienced analysts who bring to bear their domain- and argument-specific strategies. Their purpose and scope of work are dictated by argumentation in their fields and the policy arena, not limited to successfully generating output from input. Their paths are exploratory, shaped by stakeholders' influences. Their patterns of inquiry are recursive and dynamic. Their analysis involves complex information processing, process management, and socially driven construction of evolving arguments and stories. They experience large cognitive demands that need to be offloaded, and they need guidance and ample freedom to assure they can take full advantage of the opportunity to mix their expert judgement with the computational power of modelling and statistical forecasting.

Models-on-the-Web take a simplified, impoverished view of what-if analysis. Online simulations superimpose the input-output process of modelling itself onto analysts' model-based problem solving. They assume the dominant activity in this work is to enter input and view output. Ignoring analysts' integrated flow of analysis, they expect users to go outside the application for other things. Within the application, analysts' needs for strategically relevant information are met only with generic definitions. Support for many of users' core goals and questions is at best peripheral, questions like: Why didn't this set of conditions have the effects I thought it would? Have I adequately addressed opponents' strongest argument yet?

Current designs for models-on-the-Web miss the mark about users' work partly because they do not envision or design for the identities that users bring to their work as experienced problem solvers. In this role, they expect to conduct integrated patterns of inquiry and to them apply their domain-specific knowledge, argument-specific reasoning, and expert judgement. Without substantively understanding these cognitive, socio-political identities and the analytical approaches they engender, designers cannot adequately negotiate the crucial tension between model opacity and transparency and arrive at requirements that get this balance right. Our user models from field study findings provide a first step in understanding these users, their work, and the gap between this work and what is assumed and built into current online simulations.

If designers continue to reproduce current designs for online models, we may have a generation of models-on-the-Web that impoverishes policy analysis. To improve usefulness, HCI specialists need to rethink current designs and the assumptions behind them. At present, we still know too little to determine what designs will look like for online models that are truly fit-to-purpose. We are currently looking into this question. Our future work will iteratively experiment with and user test prototypes and relate them to continued studies of users' needs and requirements in context.

References

Antón, A. I. [1996], Goal-based Requirements Analysis, *in* C. Shekaran & J. Siddiqi (eds.), *Proceedings of the 2nd IEEE International Conference on Requirements Engineering (ICRE'96)*, IEEE Computer Society Press, pp.136–44.

Blandford, A. & Green, T. [2002], From Tasks to Conceptual Structures: Misfit Analysis, http://www.uclic.ucl.ac.uk/annb/shortosmABTG.pdf (last accessed 2005-05-26).

Chung, L., Nixon, B. A., Yu, E. & Mylopoulos, J. [1999], *Nonfunctional Requirements in Action*, Vol. 5 of *The Kluwer International Series in Software Engineering*, Springer.

Cockton, G. [2000], L'Avenir de L'Interface — The Future of the Interface, http://www.cet.sunderland.ac.uk/ cs0gco/Avenir.doc (last accessed 2005-04-26).

Costantini, E. A. C., Castelli, F. & L'Abate, G. [2002], Using the EPIC Model to Estimate Soil Moisture and Temperature Regimes and to Assess Desertification Risk, *in* A. Faz, R. Ortiz & A. R. Mermut (eds.), *Sustainable Use and Management of Soils in Arid and Semiarid Regions*, Vol. II, Quaderna Editorial, pp.361–3.

Cushing, J., Beard-Tisdale, K., Bergen, K., Clark, J., Henebry, G., Landis, E., Maier, D., Schnase, J. & Stevenson, R. [2003], Research Agenda for Biodiversity and Ecosystem Informatics (BDEI), Final Report to the National Science Foundation (NSF) for the Research Agenda for Biodiversity and Ecosystem Informatics. Available at http://dgrc.org/dgo2004/disc/ posters/tuesposters/rp_cushing.pdf.

Feltovich, P., Hoffman, R., Woods, D. & Roesler, A. [2004], Keeping It Too Simple: How the Reductive Tendency Affects Cognitive Engineering, *IEEE Intelligent Systems* **19**(3), 90–4.

Feltovich, P., Spiro, R. & Coulson, R. [1997], Issues of Expert Flexibility in Contexts Characterized by Complexity and Change, *in* P. Feltovich, K. Ford & R. Hoffman (eds.), *Expertise in Context*, MIT Press, pp.125–46.

Fildes, R., Goodwin, P. & Lawrence, M. [in press], The Design Features of Forecasting Support Systems and Their Effectiveness, *Decision Support Systems* .

Hsi, I. & Potts, C. [2000], Studying the Evolution and Evaluation of Software Features, *in* N. Schneidewind, L. Briand & J. M. Voas (eds.), *Proceedings of the International Conference on Software Maintenance (ICSM'00)*, IEEECSP, pp.143–51.

Jackson, M. [2000], *Problem Frames: Analyzing and Structuring Software Development Problems*, Addison–Wesley.

Johnson, E. [1988], Expertise and Decision Under Uncertainty, *in* M. Chi, R. Glaser & M. Farr (eds.), *The Nature of Expertise*, Lawrence Erlbaum Associates, pp.209–28.

Mirel, B. & Allmendinger, L. [2004], Visualizing Complexity, *Informaton Design Journal* **12**(2), 141–51.

Pannell, D. [2004], Effectively Communicating Economics to Policy Makers, *The Australian Journal of Agricultural and Resource Economics* **48**(3), 535–55.

Sutcliffe, A., Ryan, M., Doubleday, A. & Springett, M. [2000], Model Mismatch Analysis, *Behaviour & Information Technology* **19**(1), 43–55.

Zachary, W. [1988], Decision Support Systems: Designing to Extend Cognitive Limits, *in* M. Helander (ed.), *Handbook of Human–Computer Interaction*, North-Holland, pp.997–1030.

Zeitz, C. [1997], Some Concrete Advantages of Abstraction: How Experts' Representations Facilitate Reasoning, *in* P. Feltovich, K. Ford & R. Hoffman (eds.), *Expertise in Context*, MIT Press, pp.43–65.

Zigura, I. & Buckland, B. [1998], A Theory of Task/Technology Fit and Group Support Systems Effectiveness, *MIS Quarterly* **22**(3), 313–33.

Fit for Purpose Evaluation: The Case of a Public Information Kiosk for the Socially Disadvantaged

B L William Wong, Suzette Keith & Mark Springett

Interaction Design Centre, Middlesex University, London N14 4YZ, UK

Email: *{w.wong, s.keith, m.springett}@mdx.ac.uk*

This paper describes and assesses the deployment of an integrated set of techniques collectively described as fit-for-purpose evaluation. It details the deployment of the approach in a pilot study of kiosk-based delivery for health and general Citizens Advice Bureau services. The study showed that the kiosk design appeared to address basic usability and accessibility needs, but the system had architectural problems that seriously impacted on its usability. These problems only came to light when a deeper analysis of clients' information seeking needs was factored in. This case study demonstrates the need for a multi-perspective approach to evaluation — fit for purpose — to facilitate not only identification but also deep diagnosis of usability problems. The paper concludes with lessons we have learnt about methodological issues and how one might orchestrate nine different user-centred techniques in order to understand why, as in this case, apparently well designed systems do not satisfy the needs of its target users.

Keywords: fit-for-purpose, evaluation, information seeking, kiosk, digital divide, socially disadvantaged.

1 Introduction

Can a usable-looking system — showing an attractive display, big salient buttons, clear navigation, and containing appropriate information — still result in usage failure and user rejection? A system can have 'good' navigation which satisfies criteria for consistency, familiar language and salience, but users may still be unable

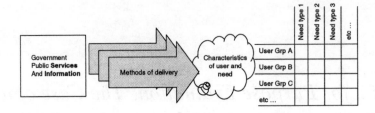

Figure 1: Compatibility between user characteristics and context, needs for information and methods of delivery.

to find the information they need, as we will see in this case study. Why do the target users still choose not to use the system in preference to a person-based information adviser? How can we improve the system so that more of the target users are likely to use it? These were some key issues we faced with when asked to assess the 'quality' of the Electronic Advice Project (EAP), a public information kiosk designed to provide health and social service information to the socially disadvantaged. The EAP prototype was jointly deployed by a local Citizen's Advice Bureau (CAB), a social services advice organization, and a local Primary Care Trust (PCT), the government primary health care provider in the UK, see Keith & Wong [2004].

In this paper we report on the above project as a case study that highlighted the need for an evaluation approach tracing user problems to deep conceptual mismatches as well as investigating interface level aspects of the design. In doing so we emphasize the importance of tracing deep causes or critical threads, a theme emphasized by Carroll et al. [1993], Blandford et al. [2004], Springett [1992] and others. We emphasize the distinction between the artefact component (language, visual aspects and manipulations at the interface) and the task component (task-mapping) described by Keenan et al. [1999]. This paper is also partly motivated by the need to accurately pinpoint errors in the design process that led to manifest problems and in turn set the agenda for changes both product and process improvements, see Hvannberg & Law [2003]. This approach we refer to as a fit for purpose evaluation. It involves an assessment of the goodness of fit between the targeted clients' needs and their ability to access the needed information contained in the kiosk. Figure 1 shows the need to determine the compatibility between purpose, user, context and delivery mechanism. It also shows how the same needs when shared by different user groups with different user characteristics, may require that government information and services be delivered by different methods.

Different user characteristics and context of use determine the groups they can belong to. The need of one group, say, recent refugee migrants, for mental health information, would be different for another group, say, unemployed youth having a need for mental health support. The unemployed youth group would, for example, be different in terms of literacy, and socio-cultural expectations. This suggests the need for different information delivery methods for the diversity is user groups. Furthermore, their problems are frequently not singular, but they instead experience

"... linked problems such as unemployment, poor skills, low incomes, poor housing, high crime environments, bad health and family breakdown" [Thompson 2000]. To complicate things further, the information that these users need are often distributed across many different government departmental 'silos', such as the websites of the Department of Health, Department of Work and Pensions, and council services, making the search for related and relevant information distributed across the silos a very challenging task.

While there are necessarily usability issues such as ease of use, efficiency, learnability, a fit for purpose evaluation is also concerned with access issues such as whether the clients of the CAB, who represent the socially disadvantaged members of the digital divide, were able to access and interpret the needed information obtained through a walk-up-and-use information kiosk deployed in a public place. In a comparative assessment of information access to a digital library project by people from a low income neighbourhood, Bishop [1999] highlighted that 'content must reflect needs and interests'. This research revealed 'the importance of a deeper analysis into the circumstances of use in order to determine what would make sense from the user's point of view'

The following sections will briefly describe some background, the EAP system, the methodology we adopted for the case study, the key findings and recommendations, and lessons we learnt about fit for purpose evaluations.

2 Background: The EAP Kiosk

The EAP kiosk was designed as a walk-up-and-use information kiosk that provided ready access to citizens' advice and health education information to a socially disadvantaged user community and to create a citizen 'advice presence' in health settings. It was part of a trial intended to find an innovative way of providing social, welfare, health and legal information which were thought to be often also required by sick people visiting government clinics, the notion of linked problems.

An important goal for the design is to encourage and empower people to take early action, and thus to reduce pressure on advice agencies caused by late presentation of critical problems. The desired consequence for the information agencies is that many problems would be resolved before becoming critical and with less need for intervention. Thus efforts by the CAB and other agencies could focus on the remaining 'most critical' problems and 'most needy' clients.

In order to achieve this objective the Kiosk was to be installed within the community where people congregate and at places that offered easy access and long opening hours, this includes for example One Stop Shops and Community Centres on local authority housing estates. The information terminal was developed as a Web portal with links to over 250 specially selected national websites covering health and advice information, and also a locally held database with links to local clubs and societies. The home page offers a welcome and links to browse information in four categories including the local database, health education, information on medical conditions and an advice service (Figure 2).

A touch screen interface was developed that supported exploration and browsing through what is initially a shallow 3 layer hierarchy of up to 30 websites.

Figure 2: Home page of the kiosk portal.

The other sites are accessed as further links from the top level websites, which can have a deep structure. In addition there was a database of local organizations and locally developed health education content.

The kiosk did not replicate information already available on the Web, but attempted to organize the information into relevant categories, and then presents the user with a one-stop Web portal to two broad types of information:

1. Health information such as how to quit smoking, sexually transmitted diseases, pregnancies and others.

2. Welfare and legal advice such as dealing with landlords, tax credits, citizen's rights, immigration policy, and disability support and other benefit information.

It was envisaged that this would reduce some of the time and effort spent by clinicians in addressing non-health issues such as socio-economic consequences of illness and disability, and benefits available to citizens.

3 Methodology

A fit for purpose study involves determining whether the purpose for which the system was commissioned translates into the physical design and implementation of the delivered system in meeting the needs of its target users. It uses a battery of complementary techniques to provide a multi-perspective approach to problem diagnosis. Its mission is to go beyond evaluation of the functional specifications of the system or interface level issues such as ease of use and learning, which while important, offers too narrow a scope for assessing whether the delivered system addresses the needs of the user group it was intended to serve.

In our case study, the fit for purpose evaluation involved a characterization of the CAB's clients and their information needs and how the EAP kiosk system delivers the information and services needed by the CAB's clients, who are largely socially disadvantaged groups of the local community [Keith et al. 2005].

In this study, nine techniques organized in two parts, were used, allowing us to triangulate the findings and to provide a broader perspective to gain insights into information access of the kiosk system by socially advantaged users who have low literacy and poor information search skills.

3.1 Part I Client Profiling

Our goal at this stage was to develop a description of the users of the CAB services, their problems, and their information needs. Due to strict client confidentiality requirements, a series of indirect analyses were conducted to identify and predict the information needs of the various client groups. We used the following techniques:

General Demographic Analysis. Using the 2001 UK Census data, a statistical analysis of the demographics of the population in the areas was conducted to provide a context from which to interpret the findings and client profiles.

Client Profile Analysis provides a demographic profile, e.g. ethnicity, age, sex, of the actual clients of the CAB. A statistical analysis was performed on the data contained in 74 Client Information Forms and associated Client Monitoring Forms, which recorded actual visits to the CAB during the two week period of 9-18 February 2004.

Problem Profile Analysis studied the reasons clients had for visiting or seeking assistance at the CAB. A statistical analysis was performed on the data from the same 74 Client Information, and Client Monitoring forms. The analysis created a profile of each client segment based on the group(s) of reasons for visiting the CAB. The problem profiles provide a way of relating the client profiles to the information clusters profile (discussed next) for each.

Information Profile Analysis identified the related clusters of information sought by the CAB clients during visits. For example, clients seeking assistance with Income Support were found to be also likely to seek information on Housing Benefits and Council Tax benefits.

3.2 Part II Information Delivery Assessment

This part of the study assessed the quality of the EAP kiosk in its ability to deliver the required information. The following assessment techniques were used:

Context Assessment. Three site visits were conducted at the Walk-in Centre where the EAP kiosk was deployed at the Edgware Community Hospital. The site visits included an observation of the use, the context of use, and the suitability of the location for the use.

Usage Profile Analysis. This was an analysis of nearly 36,000 webpages accessed by users of the kiosk over a three month period from 28 October 2003 to 2 February 2004. The usage profile reveals the kind of information that the kiosk users were using during that period.

Co-discovery Usability Evaluation [Kemp & van Gelderen 1996]. This method which employs pairs of people working co-operatively was used to examine the information content of the EAP. The four computer literate young adult males were selected as representative of the high usage users identified in the EAP log data, and also because they had the computer literacy skills necessary to overcome interface design issues identified by the expert evaluation. The setting described to the subjects was to simply walk up and use the system for 15 minutes. A joint debriefing session was held with all four participants to discuss the information found and the characteristics of preferred websites visited

Expert evaluation of the User Interface [Nielsen 1994]. This two-part assessment comprised:

1. An analytical analysis of the interface components.

2. An heuristic evaluation of the interface derived from broad principles of human computer interaction and applied to a sample of the EAP interface.

Cognitive Walkthrough [Wharton et al. 1994]. This assessment explored the way a user is expected to progress through an interaction sequence to achieve a goal and was applied to a sample from the EAP interface.

4 Results and Discussion

For brevity reasons, we will not report on the actual results themselves. Instead, the findings from each set of analyses will be integrated and we will highlight key ones. The first set of results integrates our findings from the general demographic analysis, the client profile analysis, the problem profile analysis, and the information profile analysis, to create a picture of who the clients of the CAB are and in particular the information they needed. The results of this integration are:

1. The Client-Information Profiles that describe the characteristics of each client group in terms of their problems and the types of information they are likely to seek.

2. The Abilities–Needs framework that describes the relationship between information skills and literacy, and the complexity of their information needs.

The second set of results summarizes the context assessment, usage profile analysis, co-discovery usability evaluation, expert evaluation and cognitive walkthrough. These findings are presented with the view of assessing the compatibility between the clients and their abilities, their context of use, their information needs based on their problems, and the delivery technology.

4.1 Who are the Clients and What Do They Need?

The EAP was intended to serve the socially disadvantaged user community in a local Borough. Its goal was that of promoting and providing ready access to citizens' advice and health education information in a non-threatening way.

Our analysis of the socio-demographic distributions of the client groups of the CAB showed a number of key characteristics: while the population in two of the wards studied showed large ethnic diversity (as many as 42 different ethnic groups), the main client groups are female British, 25–44 years old, Somali women, British men between 35–59 years old, and Ghanaian men and women. Two thirds of the clients are likely to lack adequate English language skills, be unemployed or have low incomes, and lack familiarity with computers.

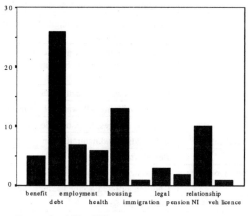

Reasons for visiting CAB

Figure 3: Frequency of reasons for visiting the CAB.

Such people were likely to have low literacy and information skills, see Bishop [1999]. Thus, they are likely to have problems with interpreting the information they find on the kiosk, and with knowing how to navigate the enormous site, as the CAB kiosk is a portal system that provides access to over 250 other related sites that are owned by different national organizations. We also expect them to have problems formulating their information seeking goals in order to find the information in the first place. For instance, many would arrive at the CAB seeking help because they are about to be evicted from their homes. Till that point in time, many were unable to articulate what is the real problem: Was it for help with housing benefits? income support? child support? council tax? or debt management? Such users can be expected to have difficulties with independent information seeking and will therefore require the assistance of, say, CAB advisers.

Our analysis of their reasons for calling at the CAB showed 43 different reasons which we had aggregated into three main problem categories of debt management, housing, relationship, and a further three less frequently cited reasons of seeking assistance about benefits, employment and health. Their frequency distribution is charted in Figure 3 and is summarized in Table 1.

1558 records from visits to the CAB between Oct–Dec 2003 were randomly sampled. Many of the records in the sampled set had to be transposed from repeating records in the original data set to single multiple response cases in the new sample. This resulted in a smaller sample set of 211 multiple response records, consisting of 59 variables each. Clusters were identified on the basis of frequency of occurrence in a variable, and whether that occurrence correlates with other occurrences in other variables. We identified nine groups, or clusters, of related information that different client groups needed. While imprecise, there were some agreement with CAB staff that they represented realistic groupings. Three example clusters are presented in Table 2.

Problem Category	Examples of Problems / Reasons cited
Benefits	General benefit inquiry, eligibility, and overpayment, consumer refunds
Debts	Disability Living Allowance, council tax, consumer tax, eviction, homelessness, housing, mortgage, possession, rent arrears, TV licences
Employment matters	Dismissal and threatened dismissals
Health	Disability Living Allowance, blue badge, incapacity
Housing	Benefits, charges, help, homelessness
Immigration and naturalization	Immigration and naturalization
Legal issues	Benefit fraud
Life assurance and pension issues	Life assurance and pension issues
Relationship issues	Children suffered accidents, bullying, child support, divorce
Vehicle licensing	Vehicle licensing

Table 1: Problem categories and examples of reasons within each category.

Cluster 1: The B02-B03-B13 Benefits Cluster.

Income Support (B02), Housing Benefits (B03) and Council Tax Benefits (B13). While other benefits also appear in this cluster, their presence is not strong, i.e. they do not occur as frequently as the identified variables. Thus, clients visiting the CAB seeking Income Support are also very likely to be seeking Housing Benefits as well as Council Tax Benefits.

Cluster 2: B07 Sickness Benefit Cluster.

This is not really a cluster, but a single strong variable. Clients are mainly seeking only the Sickness Benefit, and no other benefit.

Cluster 4: Debt Cluster.

It was interesting to observe that Debt issues appears to as three fairly independent clusters: Consumer Debt C00, Utilities Debt U00, and Housing Debt H00. The three debt groups are un-related. Clients with consumer or utilities debt do not appear to seek out advice or help in terms of benefits. They seem very focused on their debt problems. In this sample, consumer or utilities Debt have no correlations with housing issues, and only very remote associations with legal advice. Housing debt, which occurs less strongly than the other two, is very well correlated with the search for advice on Housing Benefits B03.

Table 2: Examples of problem clusters.

Cluster 1 Benefits Cluster is an example of a strong multi-factor cluster of inter-related problems, while Cluster 2 Sickness Benefit Cluster is a single variable cluster, and Cluster 4 Debt Cluster appears as a loose grouping of three factors.

Combining our results, we then created six Client-Information Profiles that described the characteristics of various client groups, the problems they are likely to have and the information they are likely to need. The Client-Information Profiles bring together the earlier analysis that describe the various client groups, e.g. Clients with Debt Problems, with the information cluster that supports the need for problem-related information, e.g. the Debt Information Cluster. It tells us who the clients are, and the information clusters they are likely to require. An example is presented in Table 3.

Clients with Debt Problems are likely to be:	... and are likely to seek information on:
White British, female, between 25–44 years' of age (one third of sample). Black African, female, between 18–44 years of age. (one third of sample). Female clients approaching the CAB with debt problems are more likely to be younger than male clients seeking assistance. Clients in the age group 35–44 are most likely to face debt problems (11/74 or 23.4%), while smaller proportions, 5/74 (6.7%), and 4/74 (5.4%) encountered debt problems in the 25–34, and the 45–59 age groups respectively. Debt does not appear to be a problem associated with the older clients.	The Debt information Cluster, with three fairly independent aspects of debt Consumer Debt C00 Utilities Debt U00 Housing Debt H00 (+ Housing Benefits B03) Clients with consumer or utilities debt do not appear to seek out advice or help in terms of benefits; and have no correlations with housing issues, and only very remote associations with legal advice. They seem very focused on their debt problems

Table 3: Client-Information Profile 1: Clients with Debt Problems.

		Information Needs		
		Don't know what they need to know	Simple needs	Complex needs
Ability: Literacy & Info Skills	High	e-brochure & kiosk ware (awareness, articulation)	Independent Web search e-brochure & kiosk ware (bite-size take-away)	Independent Web search. Adviser required.
	Low	e-brochure & kiosk ware (awareness, articulation)	e-brochure & kiosk ware (bite-size take-away)	Adviser required

Table 4: The Abilities–Needs Framework and example information delivery strategies.

Another key outcome from integrating the results in this study is the Abilities–Needs Framework. It is a two dimensional table that translates the insights gained from our analysis of the clients' socio-demographic profiles and into information literacy and needs terms with examples of how the needed information can be delivered. This framework can be used to reason about the type and level of assistance, or the information delivery method that would be better suited to the type of need and ability. This framework is presented in Table 4.

The ability dimension refers to the broad level of literacy: the ability to read and write, and the ability to seek information using a particular delivery mode, such as a paper directory, a computer database, or searching the World Wide Web. According to the Client Profiles reported earlier, many of the CAB's clients are likely to have low literacy and information skills, putting them at an immediate disadvantage when seeking information they need to help them solve some of the problems they face.

The information needs dimension describe very broadly the types of problems that clients seek help for. The Information Cluster profiles suggests that some problems can be dealt with by information that is specific and un-related. We have called such needs in this framework 'simple needs'. Referring to the Information Cluster analysis again, we see another set of information needs which are more extensive and are from different sources, e.g. health information and benefits information. We have referred to this as 'complex needs'. A final category we have included in this dimension is what we refer to as 'don't know what they need to know' category. Such clients may not be aware what their problem is although they know that they have a bad situation at hand.

The framework allows us to reason about the service delivery alternatives that are informed by the needs and abilities of the client groups. Referring to Table 4, there are three broad categories of service delivery alternatives:

1. **E-brochures and kiosk ware.** There are two aspects to this type of service delivery:

   - Bite-size take-away information.
   - Awareness and articulation.

   Bite-size take-away information are presentations of bundles of information in meaningful chunks that are to be defined by the problems that people are likely to visit the CAB for. The information is in small summarized chunks and would be adequate for users with simple needs, regardless of their ability. Awareness and articulation information could be created in alternative forms directed at helping people who do not know what their problems are to articulate their problems. This is one way of pushing information to user groups so as to advertise and educate users about the services and information available with the goal of helping people to become aware of their problems and to help them articulate their problems.

2. **Independent Web search.** This type of service delivery requires that the user has higher literacy and information search skills, i.e. they are able to formulate queries, read and understand the content, and use the links to expand their search. This group would probably benefit from normal access through a regular website, rather than being restricted in their search activities by a kiosk or portal. Such a delivery option will work only if the user has the literacy and information skills, and where their needs are either simple or less complex. However, it is likely that where the needs are complex, as in the need to appear in court, assistance from an adviser is more appropriate.

3. **Adviser required.** In this final service delivery alternative, due to the complex nature of the client's needs, or as mentioned earlier, the need to be represented in legal proceedings, it would be reasonable to expect that assistance from a person, such as a CAB adviser, would be needed. In such circumstances, the level of literacy or information skills would probably be inadequate in bringing together too many diverse issues (e.g. court room procedures, case preparation, contacts with other agencies).

4.2 Assessing Information Delivery

In this part of the study, the goal was to determine the compatibility of the kiosk to deliver the information and the meaning users needed, and the ability of the target client groups to find the information they need and to make sense of it. In this section we report on our assessment of the delivery methods defined previously.

Our evaluation of the project indicates that there are a number of well implemented aspects of the project, such as the large buttons of the touch screen make it quite obvious what areas of the display are interactive, and the navigation menu, while deep, is again clear how one might navigate the system. From our discussions with the designers of the project, the rationale behind many of the designs were considered sound and were thought to be taken in the interest of the client groups. There were however, a number of incompatibilities when the system is viewed in context of its intended use. These mis-matches include:

1. The suitability of the location at which the kiosk was deployed. The kiosk provides access to information that is often very personal and potentially embarrassing in nature. Walking up and using the kiosk in a public and open space is one form of announcing to all that one has a problem. This is one of the common problems of information kiosks. Also, in deploying the kiosk in an Accident and Emergency-type of walk-in centre where the primary purpose is to seek medical assistance, e.g. one might be in pain, it seems unlikely people would want to explore a very large information space such as the EAP kiosk. During our field visits, the kiosk was observed to be un-used or being played with by young children.

2. The target user groups are largely socially disadvantaged groups and are characterized by factors such as low levels of education, low income and language difficulties. These factors suggests that members of these groups are likely to have low literacy and low information skills. The required information content is often at a deeper level in the system and the information seeking process becomes very challenging. This is due to a number of factors, most of which are beyond the control of the CAB developers. These factors include:

   - The lack of support for a user to formulate search goals, e.g. one may need help at home with problems with a landlord. Is the help needed about housing benefits, legal advice, or debt?

   - The lack of consistency in navigation between the kiosk and sites owned by other national organizations that the kiosk links to.

   - The difficulty of the language used in the website e.g. 'officialese' vs. colloquial terms.

   - The complexity of the information in the site, e.g. conditions under which certain benefits apply; and ease with which one can then find help as many of the sites are national sites with little or no information about physical help available in the local areas.

Our co-discovery usability evaluation showed that reasonably skilled users can still get side-tracked by the presentation of many links and getting lost. While this is challenging enough for users with high literacy and information skills, these are often difficulties that are likely to cause the intended users to abandon their use of the kiosk. The deeper levels of the site, are incompatible with the abilities of the target user community.

3. The target user community need information that is relevant and easily accessible. Relevant information means the provision of direct answers to the problems faced by the user community. This information needs to be communicated in a quantity, form and level of difficulty that the target users are able to make sense of and work with. Easily accessible refers to how much effort is needed to locate the required information. The current hierarchical information architecture of the kiosk is incompatible with this need. It requires a significant effort to find desired information located across different branches, in different websites owned by different national organizations.

4. Awareness of what the kiosk does or does not have information about. As an information resource, it provides an entry point to a significant pool of useful information. The kiosk was promoted as a bright yellow kiosk in a public place with a periodic 'attractor' screen that says it is an information kiosk, but this does not do enough to motivate the user group to want to use it. It is not clear to the user group from the the attractor screen what the type of information it contains and the value it might have to their problems.

4.3 Design Recommendations

In addition to our findings, we also made a number of design recommendations in view of the incompatibilities and the better understanding we now have of the target user community. The more pertinent recommendations are presented next.

1. Information delivery strategy. The review of the system in the context of its use, raised the following question, "Should the EAP kiosk be part of an IT plan or part of the communications and service delivery strategy?". As one of the key intentions of this project is to communicate and to educate their client groups, it is recommended that the strategy needs to define how the different client groups identified in this study are reached. Some questions that should be addressed include: What role should the kiosk play in the overall strategy of reaching the clients? What information should the kiosk focus on providing?

2. Service delivery alternatives. The study developed an Abilities–Needs Framework for reasoning about information service delivery alternatives. The framework suggests that there are client groups who would require more assistance and information than could be gained from a short interactive session. Therefore, the kiosk should focus on the following roles:

   • Awareness and articulation.

   • Bite-size take-away information.

- Independent Web searching only if the system is deployed in a physical context that allows extended periods of use of the system with some degree of privacy.

This suggest that the kiosk should have two levels of information. The first level is for accessing information supporting roles 'a' and 'b'; and the second level is to support detailed Web access. The role of the adviser must continue to support clients with complex problems, regardless of levels of literacy and information skills.

3. Required information in take-away, printable bite-size chunks.   Current information is too detailed and too voluminous to digest at a kiosk. Instead, it needs to provide:

   - Customizable bites.   Much of the current content is more suitable for independent Web searches where users have higher literacy and information skills, and are likely to need time to search through links to find the necessary information. For such users, it would be helpful if the system supports the function of 'collecting' the information they require from the different but related sites they visit. This could be as simple as the provision of a notepad tool so that they only collect the relevant information, which they can print and take away with them.

   - Prepared bites. Information to support simple information needs such as listings of doctors in the locality, their addresses, opening hours, and so on, can be designed for printing.

4. Provide answers rather than links-of-links approach.   The information architecture of the system must provide answers quickly, i.e. with minimal search effort, and with information described in a manner that is compatible with the users understanding and description of the concepts relevant to the search. Accessing a page of further links will lead to more effortful searches and longer durations of searches.   The designs should be directed at an 'inverted pyramid' structure, that reveals relationships of the kind represented by the identified information clusters, giving answers to questions up front.

5. Problem-oriented information structure as additional navigation mechanism. The Client-Information Cluster Profiles define 'natural groupings' of related and easily navigable clusters and components. This navigation structure offers the means of enabling access to across-silo information.   For example, if information about benefits are likely to be sought in the cluster Income Support (B02), Housing Benefits (B03), Council Tax Benefits (B13), the content design should present the relevant information collectively in one location, rather than having the user seek the information in different organizational silos.   As a further example, all relevant guidelines, procedures, or forms, for instance, could be collated in one location.

6. Use persona-based scenarios [Cooper 1999] as framework for reasoning about re-design. A number of persona-based scenarios were developed and

applied to support further analysis of the EAP features and functions. It is recommended that the reported scenarios together with the client analysis and needs analysis reported in this document should be further used to develop more specific scenarios to reason about future re-designs of the system.

5 Conclusion and Lessons Learnt

This paper highlights some of the challenges in the use of technology to provide information to the socially disadvantaged. The work reported here involved the orchestration of nine different user-centred methods to evaluate the fitness for purpose of a technology-based system to provide such people with independent access to government information and services. We developed a socio-demographic profile of the users which was translated in terms of information needs and use, and usage (how used) characteristics. We then evaluated how well the EAP satisfied users' needs and usage requirements. One of the key challenges faced in this study was ethical in nature: it was essential to ensure complete confidentiality of the individual. In practice this meant that, for example, observations made of individuals using the kiosk had to be divorced from any descriptive information that we could use to link those observations to useful categorization data such as ethnic group, age, and gender, as it would require interaction with the user. As such we had to employ techniques to create user profiles which would later be mapped across to usage patterns that were developed from different sources of information. Similarly, we could not perform usability evaluations directly using participants from the target user group. Some lessons we have learnt from this study are reported next.

5.1 Lessons About Methodology

The fragmentation of methods in this study raises the issue of what principles we should employ in the selection of these methods, and how these should be combined:

1. What methods are there for conducting such fit for purpose evaluations? The techniques used in this case study were not novel, but combining them in the manner we did, was different. Each technique provided a different perspective on the problem. The Client-Information Profiles are important for describing the information needed and why it is needed, and therefore the form in which the information is needed. The usability evaluations, e.g. co-discovery evaluation and the cognitive walkthrough provided insights about the difficulties and to investigate how these users constructed their searches and how they articulated their problems. These are important in designing interaction techniques for lowering the human-technology threshold.

2. How do we identify strategies and practical techniques for conducting such fit for purpose evaluations? This case study highlights the increasing need for criteria-based selection of techniques and batteries of techniques yielding complementary information. Much of the investigation was compromised by factors such as time, resources and, significantly, ethical and confidentiality issues. Therefore a number of technique selections were made with the aim of compensating for the incompleteness or following up an issue discovered

by deployment of another technique. Our investigations trawled interface and task-level usability, as well as further quality attributes such as the user-experience attributes of trust and privacy. An understanding of systems' fitness for purpose requires an integrated approach that can identify and characterize social and user-experience issues as well as addressing cognitive ergonomic issues.

3. Can such an involved evaluation be done in the real world? What was done in this case study was probably too involved for industrial use. More work needs to done to find ways for streamlining the process and reducing the effort to produce an assessment of the goodness of fit between the user and their needs with the technology and information delivery mechanism. While a singular method is not yet available, the basic notion is fundamental and should guide future evaluations we conduct.

5.2 Lessons About Fit For Purpose

So, what have we learnt about considering usability in terms of fit for purpose?

1. Yes, apparently good designs can lead to usage failure, as was observed in this case study. The designers had taken great care to address usability, navigation and accessibility guidelines. The system had access to the kind of information these people needed. Yet, the system had difficulty meeting the needs of these people. Good interaction design is about ensuring compatibility between its purpose, the users, the problems they need answers to, and the delivery mechanism. This is the notion of fit for purpose. While encapsulating the principles of user-centred design methods, mechanical notions of usability and accessibility while useful at a surface level, do not usually address the deeper, semantic compatibility requirements of the target users.

2. What does it mean to know who are our users? In this case study, the system was intended for use by the clients of the CAB in an area of social disadvantage. Our analysis showed that even within the small geographical area that this study represented, the characteristics of the user groups were diverse. The common characteristics however were their abilities that result from their socio-economic background — low literacy, poor information seeking skills, and the lack of ability to articulate their problems, and hence define the information they need. Such user characteristics are usually not considered in conventional usability evaluation methods. Yet these characteristics significantly influence what a user can or cannot do with what would otherwise be a usable system. To be useful to designers, these socio-cultural and economic profiles need to be translated into terms that can be used to guide the design of information delivery methods, such as the information needs and literacy framework reported in this paper.

3. If we subscribe to the notion that we should provide answers and not links to links, how and in what form should we present the information — answers — on an interface? Current link-of-links design is intended to reduce the

volume of information that is presented. This should not just mean better menu structures, e.g. the Life Events organizing structure used by some councils, or meta-data definition such as the work on APLAWS [Priest 2004], but the provision of answers that users are seeking for. Assumptions made by systems developers — educated, computer literate — cannot be easily transferred to systems used by socially disadvantaged. We should not underestimate the barriers to accessible information for people who have limited skills in information seeking.

Acknowledgements

We would like to thank Ms Helen Kelavey, Manager Barnet CAB, Mr Andrew Enever, IT Manager, Barnet CAB, and other CAB and PCT staff for their support in this project. The reported work was commissioned by the Barnet CAB as an end of project assessment for HM Treasury's Invest to Save Programme.

References

Bishop, A. P. [1999], Making Digital Libraries Go: Comparing Use Across Genres, *in* N. Rowe & E. A. Fox (eds.), *Proceedings of the Fourth ACM Conference on Digital Libraries (DL'99)*, ACM Press, pp.94–103.

Blandford, A., Keith, S., Connell, I. & Edwards, H. [2004], Analytical Usability Evaluation for Digital Libraries: A Case Study, *in* H. Chen, H. Wactlar, C. chih Chen, E.-P. Lim & M. Christel (eds.), *Proceedings of the 4th ACM/IEEE-CS Joint Conference on Digital Libraries (JCDL'04)*, ACM Press, pp.27–36.

Carroll, J., Koenemann-Belliveau, J., Rosson, M. & Singley, M. [1993], 'Critical Incidents and Critical Threads in Usability Evaluation, *in* J. Alty, D. Diaper & S. Guest (eds.), *People and Computers VIII (Proceedings of HCI'93)*, Cambridge University Press, pp.279–92.

Cooper, A. [1999], *The Inmates are Running the Asylum: Why High-tech Products Drive us Crazy and How to Restore the Sanity,*, Sams Technical Publishing.

Hvannberg, E. & Law, E. [2003], Classification of Usability Problems (CUP) Scheme, *in* M. Rauterberg, M. Menozzi & J. Weeson (eds.), *Human–Computer Interaction — INTERACT '03: Proceedings of the Ninth IFIP Conference on Human–Computer Interaction*, IOS Press, pp.655–63.

Keenan, S., Hartson, R., Kafura, D. & Schulman, R. [1999], The Usability Problem Taxonomy: A Framework for Classification and Analysis, *Empirical Software Engineering* 4(1), 71–104.

Keith, S. & Wong, B. L. W. [2004], Fit for Purpose: Accessibility of On-line Public Service Information through the Barnet CAB Electronic Advice Project, Technical Report IDC-001-04, Middlesex University. Report prepared for the Service Manager, Barnet CAB, Middlesex University Contract No. MUVL-6505.

Keith, S., Springett, M. & Wong, W. [2005], Purpose and Context: Selecting Multiple Methods for Evaluating a Pilot Public Information Terminal, *in* P. D. Bust & P. T. McCabe (eds.), *Contemporary Ergonomics 2005: Proceedings of the Annual Conference of the Ergonomics Society*, Taylor & Francis, pp.175–9.

Kemp, J. A. M. & van Gelderen, T. [1996], Co-discovery Exploration:ă An Informal Method for the Iterative Design of Consumer Products, *in* P. W. Jordan, B. Thomas, B. A. Weerdmeester & I. L. McClelland (eds.), *Usability Evaluation in Industry*, Taylor & Francis, pp.139–46.

Nielsen, J. [1994], Heuristic Evaluation, *in* J. Nielsen & R. L. Mack (eds.), *Usability Inspection Methods*, John Wiley & Sons, pp.25–62.

Priest, J. [2004], Local Authority Websites National Project: Information Architecture in the APLAWS+ Templates, http://www.aplaws.org.uk/project/standards.php (retrieved 2004-12-07). Office of the Deputy Prime Minister APLAWS Pathfinder Project.

Springett, M. [1992], The Utility of User Actions Models for Direct Manipulation design, *in* J. Larson & C. Unger (eds.), *Engineering for Human–Computer Interaction: Proceedings of the IFIP TC2/WG2.7 Working Conference on Engineering for Human–Computer Interaction*, North-Holland, pp.102–15.

Thompson, J. [2000], Social Inclusion, http://www.niace.org.uk/information/Briefing_sheets/Socialexclusionmar00.html (retrieved 2004-12-07).

Wharton, C., Rieman, J., Lewis, C. & Polson, P. [1994], The Cognitive Walkthrough Method: A Practitioners Guide, *in* J. Nielsen & R. L. Mack (eds.), *Usability Inspection Methods*, John Wiley & Sons, pp.105–40.

A Visuo-Biometric Authentication Mechanism for Older Users

Karen Renaud

Department of Computing Science, University of Glasgow, Glasgow G12 8RZ, UK

Email: *karen@dcs.gla.ac.uk*

The Web is an invaluable resource for users of all ages, but it especially offers facilities which can make a huge difference to the lives of elderly users, many of whom have to contend with limited mobility and frequent illness. Whereas there is some understanding of the issues that pertain to designing websites for this group of users, the issue of specialized Web authentication has not received much attention. Web authentication is often treated as a one-size-fits-all problem with ubiquitous use of the password, and indeed authentication is seldom tailored to the needs of either the site or the target users. Sites are seldom subjected to a risk analysis before an authentication mechanism is chosen. This paper proposes a technique for matching the risk levels of a website to the security rating of an authentication mechanism and presents an authentication mechanism that is tailored to the needs of elderly users for protecting sites with a low risk rating. Usage data from a field test of this mechanism is reported, which show that the mechanism is indeed feasible and meets older users' needs.

Keywords: authentication, risk, security, elderly users, visual, biometrics.

1 Introduction

The Web has come of age, and offers immeasurable enrichment to many people's lives. The special group of interest to this paper is older users who no longer need to be excluded from things like shopping, social interchange and banking when they or their friends are house-bound due to ill health or long-term infirmity. The Web offers access to a variety of these kinds of facilities and more besides. Much attention has been paid to designing websites for the aged [Hawthorn 2003], but one of the biggest obstacles still remaining is the issue of user authentication, which often requires that the user remember a password, something that becomes more and more difficult with age and presents an oft-insurmountable obstacle.

A popular and reliable authentication mechanism is the biometric — either physiological or behavioural. However, the former has limitations related to secure biometric capture at enrolment in an uncontrolled environment such as the Web, and many users also have concerns related to privacy [Braghin 2000; Berghel 2000] and the impossibility of replacement should it be leaked. Furthermore, recording the most popular biometric, the fingerprint, is notoriously fraught with difficulty for older users [Garfinkel 2002]. Behavioural biometrics have some potential but are often difficult to measure in a Web environment without specialized software being installed on the user's machine, something that many Web administrators are reluctant to require of their users.

Web users are thus usually authenticated by means of a knowledge-based mechanism — either a password on its own or accompanied by a token such as a smart card — implementing a stronger two-factor authentication. Smart cards work admirably and can be tailored for the use of older users [Gill 2004], but they can also be mislaid or stolen. They are currently fairly costly to issue so their use will probably be restricted to high risk sites. In knowledge-based authentication the user carries the burden of proof — having to remember a personal identification number (PIN) or password. This is a particular problem for users with short-term memory limitations, which is often the case in older users.

The direct consequence of this is that Web users are almost ubiquitously authenticated by a password and eventually they find that they have far too many passwords to remember. Since passwords rely on uncued exact recall, it becomes more and more difficult to keep track. Some schemes have been proposed which can accommodate less than perfect recall [Ellison et al. 2000] but these require special software, and are not widely used on the Web.

Passwords are no picnic for the system administrator either. The first problem is to decide whether to issue or request passwords. System-specified passwords present memorability difficulties resulting in frequent requests for replacement passwords. Reports of between a third [Walker 2001] and a half [Doran 1999] of help-desk calls being related to passwords emphasize the size of this problem. Passwords *can* be automatically replaced by means of email, but this is seldom encrypted, and thus easy for a determined hacker to intercept. The more memorable self-selected passwords tend also to be too predictable, which impacts security. System administrators have various strategies in dealing with the "password problem" [Dhamija & Perrig 2000]: carry out proactive password checking when the password is specified by the user to ensure that a strong password is chosen; impose a forced-renewal policy so that leaked passwords eventually age; allow a limited number of tries before locking an account; run a password cracking program regularly to identify weak passwords; or offer training and education to users to increase security awareness.

The latter has very limited success in a Web environment [Friedman et al. 2002], and the other mechanisms are essentially technical solutions to a human problem. Apart from the *human* (both client and administrator) problems, we need to consider the strength of the authentication mechanism. Passwords have the potential to be very strong — with an unlimited number of possibilities. In reality people usually make use of a word in their own language: limiting the possibilities to 10^6 in a language like English. Since most websites have a policy of 3-tries-lockout these odds are probably large enough to protect most Web content. However, in some cases the password is too strong to protect fairly innocuous Web content. Maintaining security is not a simple one-size-fits-all problem [Starren et al. 2001]. Developers should consider using a site-content-tailored authentication mechanism so that low-risk websites can be protected by a mechanism which does not have the memorability drawbacks of the password.

This paper will present a visuo-biometric mechanism which has been tailored specifically toward the needs of older users. Section 2 will consider factors which should be considered in determining the risk level for a particular website. Section 3 will discuss the target user group. Section 4 will introduce the visuo-biometric mechanism and Section 5 reports on the results of a field test of the mechanism, called *Handwing*. Section 6 concludes.

2 Risk

In determining the risk associated with a website we have to take cognisance of the information and functionality that needs to be protected. The stronger the authentication mechanism the more expensive it will be, and an analysis of the risks will help ensure that the level of security maintained by the chosen authentication mechanism matches the perceived risks. What we need to consider, in terms of risk, is the nature of the threats, why they are worth considering, who we should guard against, and how to do it [Damle 2002]. Performing a full risk analysis of a Web site is a complex process [Schreider 2003] and is done in order to formulate the overall security policy and techniques to counteract perceived threats for the entire website. A simplified risk analysis is proposed here solely for the purpose of choosing a suitable authentication mechanism.

The first step in this analysis is a consideration of the website content. websites can hold the following kinds of data [IASEP 2000]:

Sensitive: The integrity of this information is paramount, such as financial transactions.

Confidential: Personal information such as hospital patient records.

Private: Information intended for use within a certain setting, such as school or church records.

Public: Any information that cannot be classified as any of the above. For this kind of information no authentication mechanism would be required.

Any website that offers access to confidential or sensitive information should be considered to be a high risk website and will require user authentication. There are two issues to granting access: identification and authentication. Sometimes it is necessary to identify users only for personalization purposes, or merely to keep track of site usage, and it is not necessary to confirm this identification with an

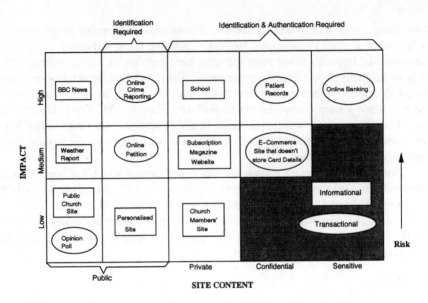

Figure 1: Website category examples.

---

authentication step. Many websites erroneously use authentication instead of pure identification when there are far less heavyweight mechanisms available or when only identification is necessary, such as, perhaps, for the use of public-information websites.

If we decide that an authentication mechanism *is* warranted, the next step considers the functionality of the website. Websites are essentially either informational, providing one-way communication, or two-way transactional. Transactional websites could involve the transfer of funds, setting up contracts with financial or legal liability or involving information protected by law [Leonard 2003] and obviously pose greater risk than informational sites. Informational websites may require less secure authentication mechanisms than transactional websites, simply because of the extended functionality offered by transactional websites, but this depends on the classification of information content.

The risk assessment also needs to consider the impact of an intrusion which takes account of the potential loss should an intruder gain access. Factors to be considered here are [Miller 2000]:

- The cost of recreating the information should an intruder modify or delete it.

- The value of the information to the website owners. What would the liability to the organization be if it leaked out?

- The impact if the information was unobtainable to legitimate users?

- The exclusivity of the information: consider how much someone might be prepared to pay for it.

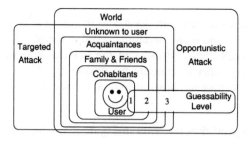

Figure 2: Rating guessability of a key.

Level	Group	Web Content	Security Required
3	World	Public	Lowest
	Unknown to User		↓
	Acquaintances		↓
2	Family & Friends	Private	↓
	Cohabitants		↓
1	User Only	Sensitive & Confidential	Highest

Table 1: User groups.

- The impact on the organization if the website were unavailable. This could range from a lack of confidence and possible abandonment by site users to minor inconvenience at the lowest end of the scale.

We should classify the site as either low, medium or high impact based on these considerations. The higher the impact the stronger the required authentication mechanism. These steps should help us to classify the website as one of the categories shown in Figure 1 listed in increasing order of risk.

Having carried out the risk analysis, we need to choose an authentication mechanism that offers a matching level of security. The security of a knowledge-based authentication mechanism is often judged based purely on the guessability of the key determined in terms of the theoretical size of the dictionary. This is a somewhat impoverished approach, however, because it does not take account of things such as shoulder-surfing or the possibility of users sharing or recording their authentication key or choosing a weak key. A more comprehensive way to assess the security of a knowledge-based authentication mechanism is required. We have to consider the extent of the threat. Attacks are essentially either *targeted* or *opportunistic*. Opportunistic attacks can take place either by someone happening to observe entry of the key or discovering the recorded key. These attacks are unrelated to the size of the dictionary: brute force attacks, the success of which is related to the size of the dictionary, are unlikely to succeed against 3-try-lockout mechanisms. *Targeted* attacks involve either social engineering or research. Research-based attacks are far more likely to succeed in this environment, and these are related more to the type of access the intruder has to the user rather than the size of the dictionary. Three dimensions are therefore needed to adequately reflect the strength of a mechanism: *guessability* to measure the likelihood of success of research-based attacks, *observability* to measure the possibility of an opportunistic attack, and *recordability* to reflect the possibility of a social engineering or opportunistic attack:

Guessability: This considers the level in Figure 2 at which an attack is likely to succeed. Various levels of access to the user can be considered, under the premise that people closest to the user know her best. These levels can be aligned to the Web content classification from the previous section, as shown in Table 1.

This does not imply that members of the group should be given the user's key or be given access to the information in the website without the user's knowledge, it means that the fact that members of this group are likely to guess the key is an acceptable risk for the particular site's content.

Observability: This denotes the extent to which the authentication key lends itself to observation.

Recordability: This denotes the ease with which a user can record or share a key.

We need to rate the authentication mechanisms under consideration in terms of the security dimensions, and ensure that the authentication mechanism meets the needs of the particular system. Consider the password: if a user is asked to produce a password he or she often makes use of a familiar name or place, since that is likely to be remembered. Users often use birthdates or names of family members. Anyone with a detailed knowledge of the user, such as a family member, has a good chance of being able to guess these passwords. As we move further from the user, a potential intruder will not know the user as well, and is less likely to be able to guess the password but can perhaps discover the password by doing some research. Thus the password's guessability can reasonably be assigned to Level 2, observability is low and recordability is high.

It is very important also to consider the needs of users in choosing an authentication mechanism. The next section will consider the special needs of older users before Section 4 presents the visuo-biometric mechanism.

3   Older Users — The Target User Group

In an ageing world [Engardio & Matlack 2005], we need to ensure that older Web users are not disadvantaged or marginalized by Web authentication mechanisms, since they can derive great benefit from the information and facilities available via the Web. There is no such thing as a typical older user — they vary in terms of disability, dexterity, cognitive ability and motivation to use the Web. However, many do have particular disabilities or limitations that need to be considered when an authentication mechanism is chosen. There are basically two problems which have to be addressed: *accessibility* and *memorability*.

We need to ensure that websites are accessible to all users, in essence, that are not disadvantaged by cognitive, physical or sensory disabilities. This entails consideration of the following factors [Renaud 2004]:

Inclusivity:

Memory: Knowledge-based mechanisms rely exclusively on recall memory, a skill which is particularly problematic for people with short-term memory limitations. [Akatsu & Miki 2004; BBC 2003] — often the case for older users. This problem needs to be given serious consideration.

Mobility: Older users may have coordination problems caused by tremors or arthritis so websites should not require users to point too precisely with the mouse [Chisnell & Redish 2005].

Vision: Older users may have failing vision which means that any Web-oriented authentication mechanism should not require them to observe very fine details on the screen [Chisnell & Redish 2005]. They like large print and less content on pages [Chisnell et al. 2004].

Convenience: Two factors need to be considered here:

Time: Previous studies have shown that users become annoyed when an authentication mechanism is too time-consuming [Renaud & De Angeli 2004]. Thus most websites have to walk a fine line between inconvenience and security. Older users, however, tend to be less impatient [Trostel & Taylor 2001] and do not want to be hurried [Chisnell et al. 2004]. Thus the time-consuming nature of a mechanism is less of a problem for older users.

Geographic distribution of users: A very important aspect to consider in the use of any mechanism that requires the controlled collection of the authentication key, as opposed to uncontrolled collection over the Web, is that the potential users should all be within easy travelling distance.

Special Requirements: Some older users have a limited understanding of computers and the Web and any special software or hardware that needs to be installed, or technical expertise required, will be a barrier to the use of the website.

Many of the accessibility problems can be addressed by giving due consideration to the target group throughout the authentication mechanism design and implementation process. The memorability problem, however, is inherent in most knowledge-based mechanisms, and another approach is required. The issue of memorability will be examined in the next section.

4 Improving Memorability

The main problem with the use of knowledge-based mechanisms, such as passwords, is that they are not memorable. Users react to this by either choosing predictable passwords or writing them down, which makes them less secure. The traditional way of jogging a person's memory is by the use of cues but it is very difficult for the password entry mechanism to offer cues without an intruder making use of these cues to break into the site.

In providing an alternative, therefore, we need to ensure that the key is more memorable than passwords, but, in order to perform as an effective authentication key it also has to be unpredictable. There are three ways to alleviate the memorability problems: either use an authentication mechanism that relies on another type of memory, or provide cues, or both.

Fortunately there *are* other types of memory that can be exploited which tend not to depend as much on short-term memory. One example of of this is memory for pictures with images richer in detail being more memorable (e.g. photographs are more memorable than a line drawings). Under experimental conditions memory for pictures shows little or no age-related decline [Park et al. 1986]. De Angeli et al. have explored the use of pictorial passwords and have achieved good results [De Angeli et al. 2002]. This is a particularly good option for use on the Web because all browsers can display images without extra software or hardware.

The use of cues also needs to be investigated. Even an interface that requires users to recognize an authentication key, rather than recall it, provides no cues other than the authentication key itself. The user and the intruder are faced with the same pictures — and the legitimate user gets no help from the interface to jog his or her memory.

The provision of cues is a tricky one. If the interface provides too many cues an intruder may be able to use these cues to gain access to the system. One therefore has to try to provide cues that will make sense only to the legitimate user. Weinshall [2004] proposes an ingenious scheme whereby a cue is provided by a slight change in the image being displayed which the user has been trained to observe. The theory is that an imposter's change-blindness will prevent him or her from seeing the slight changes and thus the cue will only be observed by the rightful user. Unfortunately the changes to the images have to be fairly slight in order to go unobserved by an impostor and thus this scheme will not work very well for users with failing sight, as is often the case with older users.

One of the oldest biometrics — handwriting — offers unexpected potential for provision of cues to the legitimate user that may not be helpful to an intruder. Educated humans learn to write at a young age, moving from numerals to block capitals to manuscript to cursive writing. People recognize their own handwriting, but this recognition is a far more complex process than mere picture recognition. Heckman et al. [2001] carried out experiments with stroke and dementia patients and concluded that handwriting recognition was a special skill which was independent of verbal and lexical tasks. Longcamp et al. [2003] argue that we recognize our own handwriting not just visually but also because it is related to the learnt process of writing the letters and numerals, something referred to as "kinesthetic facilitation" [Seki et al. 1995], which is combined with the visual control process [Zimmer 1982].

Longcamp et al. [2003] report a study by Bartomoleo et al. [2002] which found that patients with alexia[1] who could no longer recognize letters visually could be assisted in recognizing letters when they traced the letters with their fingers. Longcamp et al. believe that a multimodal letter representation is built up which assists recognition because the writing motor processes in the brain were activated when people passively observed letters.

There is some difference between the individuality of letters and numbers, with letters being far more distinctive and recognizable to people other than the author. Different digits have varying degrees of individuality [Srihari et al. 2003]. For example, it is almost impossible to attribute a written digit "1" to anyone whereas a "2" is far more distinctive and variable. Hence a sequence of digits is harder for another person to attribute to the writer than a written word. If we wish to limit the strength of the provided cues we should use digits rather than words. However, we need to ensure that sufficient digits are displayed to give the legitimate users sufficient cues to recognize their own handwriting.

The flip side of provision of a cue of this apparent strength to the legitimate user is the usefulness of this cue to intruders. If we consider users working from the centre outwards in Figure 2 it is possible for users up to the level of *acquaintance* to recognize another person's handwriting. Hence it is necessary to pair any authentication technique that makes use of handwriting recognition with some other kind of recognition in order to strengthen the mechanism and to bring the guessability closer to the user in Figure 2. A biometric which is not as popular as handwriting is line drawings or doodles. This is something which even family members of the user may not easily recognize. However, it too provides cues to the legitimate user, related to the contribution of the user's previous action-planning structures which support recognition [Knoblich & Prinz 2001].

The use of handwriting recognition in authentication should thus be paired with something like recognition of a doodle to strengthen the mechanism. The level of cues provided by handwriting disqualifies their use in systems requiring strong authentication. However, their use for a low-risk website is justified by the increased memorability.

The mechanism presented in the next section is referred to as visuo-biometric because it relies on a graphical password (visuo) and a behavioural biometric (handwriting and drawing).

5 Handwing: Visuo-Biometric Authentication

The Handwing mechanism was developed to test the idea of using handwriting recognition as a cue in recognition-based graphical authentication mechanisms. A members-only website for a church was developed, and Handwing was used to control access to the site. The church members are predominantly over 60, and members were not keen to make use of yet another password mechanism to protect the site since many of the members felt that they had enough passwords and PINs to remember. Their details were collected on a form as shown in Figure 3. Individual

---

[1] Letter-by-letter reading.

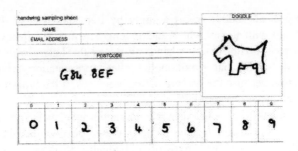

Figure 3: Biometric collection.

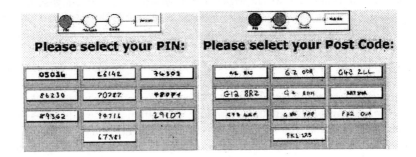

Figure 4: Handwriting stages of Handwing.

numerals, doodles and written postal codes were extracted so that they could be used by the authentication mechanism.

5.1 Risk Assessment

The site risk assessment results were as follows:

Content & Type: The site is transactional and holds *private* data which does require identification and authentication.

Impact: There is little cost related to recreating the information and although the Web content has value to the church members it was felt that it did not have any market value. There was little impact if the website were unavailable. The worst that could occur is a level of inconvenience since members are unlikely to leave the church because the website is not functioning. Hence the impact of intrusion is *low*.

Thus although the site needed identification and authentication, a relatively weak authentication mechanism is required since the impact is low.

5.2 Authentication Procedure

Users were identified by means of their email address, and the welcome page allowed users to request that their password be renewed should they experience difficulties

Figure 5: The Doodle Stage.

accessing the system. Once they were identified they were authenticated by means of a 3-stage process:

1. The first screen presented the user with a selection of 10 PIN numbers, each written in a different handwriting, as shown on the left in Figure 4. The user is assisted in choosing the correct PIN by recognition of his or her own handwritten digits.

2. Once the user chose one of the options the next page displayed 10 postal codes, each in the handwriting of a different user, as shown on the right in Figure 4. The user chooses his or her own postal code.

3. The final screen displayed 12 hand-drawn doodles — one of which belonged to the user, as shown in Figure 5. The user chooses his or her own doodle and is allowed to enter the site.

5.3 Security Assessment

In terms of the security assessment proposed in Section 2, Handwing demonstrated the following characteristics:

Guessability: To break into this system via recognition of the PIN a recognition of the user's handwriting is necessary. Since people communicate almost exclusively either electronically or with typewritten letters these days only people fairly close to the user will ever see his or her handwriting, and rarely at that. Hence a cohabitant or family member is likely to be able to recognize the handwriting, and friends and colleagues may also be able to do this but it is unlikely that anyone outside this circle will be able to recognize handwritten numerals. The resulting guessability level of 2 matches the *private* content-rating of the website.

Observability: The system has high observability, since the keys are displayed on the screen.

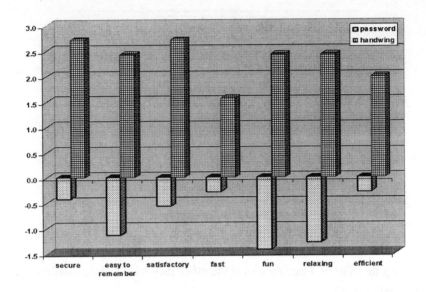

Figure 6: User feedback.

Recordability: The PIN and Postal Code are relatively easy to record but the doodle is more difficult to describe. The system was seeded with over 200 different hand-drawn doodles and many are similar. (Most of the doodles are either faces or stick figures.) This poses no problems to the doodle author, though, as people have been observed unerringly homing in on their own doodle in the presence of very similar doodles.

Hence this mechanism was classified as maintaining *low security*, which matched the risk rating of the website.

5.4   Evaluation and Experience

The website has been running for 9 months. In that time there have been 137 accesses by the twenty users (11 female and 9 male), of whom two thirds are over 50. The majority of the users (18) only use computers for emailing and Web surfing. The website usage is not equally distributed over all users — 9 users account for 90% of the Web site accesses. However, the other users, even with relatively infrequent use, are almost universally able to authenticate without difficulty. In 9 months only one authentication attempt failed. This was due to incorrect selection of the doodle, and since the user's doodle was very different from the selected doodle it appears that the user merely made a mistake in clicking on the incorrect doodle and was not confused by similarity between doodles. This impression is confirmed by the fact that the user was authenticated successfully a minute later.

5.5 Usability Assessment

The intention with this authentication mechanism was to design a mechanism that would cater for the needs of older users. Usability was assessed as follows:

- The three traditional dimensions of usability (from the ISO 9241 standard):

  Effectiveness: Users were able, with only one exception, to gain access to the website at the first attempt. The one exception gained access at the second attempt. Thus in terms of effectiveness the mechanism is extremely usable.

  Efficiency: The time-consuming use of multiple screens to authenticate was not an issue for this group of users and did not affect the usability of the mechanism.

  Satisfaction: User opinions were gathered by means of a questionnaire addressing a range of usability and security dimensions. The ratings were averaged and differences in averages between passwords and Handwing are shown in Figure 6. A statistical analysis was not performed since only a third of the site users responded to the questionnaire. The surveys were submitted in the form of questionnaires instead of electronically since that usually results in a better response [Mavis & Brocato 1998], but since the site is a very low usage site — which makes it ideal for testing memorability of authentication keys — many of the users did not respond.

- The inclusivity issues for the specific target user group:

  Memorability: Handwing relies on recognition memory rather than recall memory to cater for infrequent access and memory limitations and offers strong cues to the user on different levels.

  Mobility: Large clickable areas to accommodate limited mobility;

  Vision: Large screen display to accommodate failing sight;

  Special Requirements: No special software or hardware required.

  Geographic Distribution: All users live within a 10km radius and congregate regularly so biometric collection is feasible.

The Handwing mechanism meets all the requirements, both in terms of the ISO standard and the needs of the target user group.

6 Conclusion

This paper proposes a Web authentication mechanism which can be used to safeguard low-risk sites. It is particularly suitable for users with short-term memory loss. Although such users can make use of passwords quite successfully if they employ some strategy for remembering the password, such as writing it down, passwords are simply too strong to protect some websites. The Handwing mechanism is weaker, more memorable and infinitely more usable.

The usage statistics gathered from logging and questionnaires show that the mechanism meets the needs of the particular user group far better than a traditional password would. The Handwing mechanism is only a prototype, but it does demonstrate the considerable potential of less stringent, more memorable, authentication mechanisms for low-risk websites.

There is much scope for future work. This experiment has demonstrated the feasibility of the use of handwritten numerals as a cue. One of the strengths of this mechanism is the difficulty of transferring this knowledge to other users, and there are many other skills at which humans are adept which could be used to authenticate users far more reliably than knowledge-based mechanisms. The website is still functioning but a section has now been added for the youth group, and the resulting usage data should offer some insights as to their experiences with the mechanism.

Acknowledgements

I acknowledge the work of Scott Porter on the Handwing mechanism, and attribute the nomenclature of the mechanism to him.

References

Akatsu, H. & Miki, H. [2004], Usability Research for the Elderly People, *Oki Technical Review* **71**(3).

Bartomoleo, P., Bachoud-Lévi, A.-C., Chokron, S. & Degos, J.-D. [2002], Visually and Motor-based Knowledge of Letters: Evidence from a Pure Alexic Patient, *Neurosychologica* **40**(8), 1363–71.

BBC [2003], Clue to Old Age Memory Loss. http://news.bbc.co.uk/2/hi/health/3040203.stm.

Berghel, H. [2000], Identity Theft, Social Security Numbers, and the Web, *Communications of the ACM* **43**(2), 17–21.

Braghin, C. [2000], Biometric Authentication. Available at http://citeseer.ist.psu.edu/436492.html (last accessed 2005-04-13).

Chisnell, D. & Redish, J. [2005], Who is the Older Adult in Your Audience?, *intercom* . http://www.stc.org/intercom/PDFs/2005/200501_10.pdf (last accessed 2005-04-13).

Chisnell, D., Lee, A. & Redish, J. [2004], Design Web Sites for Older Users: Comparing AARP's Studies to Earlier Findings. http://www.aarp.org/olderwiserwired/oww-features/Articles/a2004-03-03-comparison-studies.html (last accessed 2005-04-13).

Damle, P. [2002], Social Engineering: A Tip of the Iceberg, *Information Systems Control Journal* **2**. http://www.isaca.org/Template.cfm?Section=Archives&CONTENTID=17032&TEMPLATE=/ContentManagement/ContentDisplay.cfm.

De Angeli, A., Coutts, M., Coventry, L. & Johnson, G. I. [2002], VIP: A Visual Approach to User Authentication, *in* S. Levialdi (ed.), *Proceedings of the Conference on Advanced Visual Interface (AVI2002)*, ACM Press, pp.316–23.

Dhamija, R. & Perrig, A. [2000], Déjà vu: A User Study Using Images for Authentication, *in Proceedings of 9th USENIX Security Symposium*, The USENIX Association, Denver, Colorado, pp.45–58. http://www.usenix.org/events/sec2000/full_papers/dhamija/dhamija.pdf.

Doran, G. D. [1999], Touchy Subject Biometric Technology: Is It Time for Your Computer to Get to Know You?, http://www.entrepreneur.com/Magazines/Copy_of_MA_SegArticle/0,4453,230131,00.html. Entrepreneur magazine.

Ellison, C., Hall, C., Milbert, R. & Schneier, B. [2000], Protecting Secret Keys with Personal Entropy, *Future Generation Computer Systems* **16**, 311–8.

Engardio, P. & Matlack, C. [2005], Global Aging. Business Week, JANUARY 31, http://www.businessweek.com/magazine/content/05_05/b3918011.htm.

Friedman, B., Hurley, D., Howe, D. C., Nissenbaum, H. & Felten, E. [2002], Users' Conceptions of Risks and Harms on the Web: A Comparative Study, *in* D. Wixon (ed.), *Proceedings of SIGCHI Conference on Human Factors in Computing Systems: Changing our World, Changing Ourselves (CHI'02)*, CHI Letters **4**(1), ACM Press, pp.614–615.

Garfinkel, S. [2002], Biometrics Slouches Toward the Mainstream. CSO Online. http://www.csoonline.com/read/090402/machine.html.

Gill, J. [2004], Design of Smart Card Systems to Meet the Needs of Disabled and Elderly Persons. Tiresias.org Scientific and Technological Reports. http://www.tiresias.org/reports/ecart.htm.

Hawthorn, D. [2003], How universal is good design for older users?, *in CUU '03: Proceedings of the 2003 conference on Universal Usability*, ACM Press, pp.38–45.

Heckman, J. G., Lang, C. J. & Neundorfer, B. [2001], Recognition of Familiar Handwriting in Stroke and Dementia, *Neurology* **57**(11), 2128–31.

IASEP [2000], Data Security Protocol for Education, http://iasep.soe.purdue.edu/Protocol/home_page.htm. Center for Information Assurance and Security and the Indiana Assessment System of Education Proficiencies. Purdue Research Foundation.

Knoblich, G. & Prinz, W. [2001], Recognition of self-generated actions from kinematic displays of drawing, *Journal of Experimental Psychology: Human Perception and Performance* **27**(2), 456–65.

Leonard, K. [2003], The Importance of Being Secure: The ROI of Web Security, *Information Systems Control Journal* **5**. http://www.isaca.org/Template.cfm?Section=Archives&CONTENTID=16729&TEMPLATE=/ContentManagement/ContentDisplay.cfm.

Longcamp, M., Anton, J. L., Roth, M. & Velay, J. L. [2003], Visual Presentation of Single Letters Activates a Premotor Area Involved in Writing, *Neuroimage* **19**(4), 1492–500.

Mavis, B. E. & Brocato, J. J. [1998], Postal Surveys versus Electronic Mail Surveys. The Tortoise and the Hare Revisited, *Evaluation & The Health Professions* **21**(3), 395–408.

Miller, J. C. [2000], Risk Assessment for your Web Site, http://www.irmi.com/irmicom/expert/articles/2000/schoenfeld09.aspx. IRMI.com. International Risk Management Institute.

Park, D. C., Puglisi, J. T. & Smith, A. D. [1986], Memory for pictures: Does an age-related decline exist?, *Journal of Psychology and Aging* **1**(1), 11–7.

Renaud, K. & De Angeli, A. [2004], My Password is Here! An Investigation into Visuospatial Authentication Mechanisms, *Interacting with Computers* **16**(6), 1017–41.

Renaud, K. V. [2004], Quantification of Authentication Mechanisms — A Usability Perspective, *Journal of Web Engineering* **3**(2), 95–123.

Schreider, T. [2003], Risk Assessment Tools: A Primer, *Information Systems Control Journal* **2**. http://www.isaca.org/TemplateRedirect.cfm?template=/ContentManagement/ContentDisplay.cfm&ContentID=16222.

Seki, K., Yajima, M. & Sugishita, M. [1995], The Efficacy of Kinesthetic Reading Treatment for Pure Alexia, *Neuropsychologica* **33**(5), 595–609.

Srihari, S. N., Tomai, C., Lee, S. & Zhang, B. [2003], Individuality of Numerals, *in* A. Antonacopoulos (ed.), *Proceedings of the Seventh IEEE International Conference on Document Analysis and Recognition*, IEEE Computer Society Press, Edinburgh, Scotland, pp. 1096–100.

Starren, J., Sengupta, S., Hripcsak, G., Ring, G., Klerer, R. & Shea, S. [2001], Making Grandma's Data Secure: A Security Architecture for Home Telemedicine, *in* S. Bakken (ed.), *Proceedings of the AMIA Symposium*, AMIA, pp. 657–61.

Trostel, P. A. & Taylor, G. A. [2001], Theory of Time Preference, *Economic Inquiry* **39**(3), 379–95.

Walker, T. [2001], Fighting Security Breaches and Cyberattacks with Two-factor Authentication Technology, *Information Systems Control Journal* **2**. http://www.isaca.org/TemplateRedirect.cfm?template=/ContentManagement/ContentDisplay.cfm&ContentID=17187.

Weinshall, D. [2004], Secure Authentication Schemes suitable for an Associative Memory, Technical Report TR 2004-30, Hebrew University, Leibniz Center for Research in Computer Science.

Zimmer, A. [1982], Do We See What Makes Our Script Characteristic — Or Do We Only Feel It? Modes of Sensory Control in Handwriting, *Psychological Research* **44**(2).

C — HCI in the Greater Cultural Context

A Computer Science HCI Course

Beryl Plimmer

Department of Computer Science, University of Auckland,
Private Bag 92019, Auckland, New Zealand

Tel: *+64 9373 7599*

Email: *beryl@cs.auckland.ac.nz*

Can a computer science student learn to be a designer and a psychologist as well as a computer scientist? Unlikely, but they can learn to appreciate what other disciplines offer HCI. The need for computer science students to understand the big picture, that HCI is multidisciplinary in nature, has been recognized for many years. Yet successfully integrating HCI into a computer science degree is still difficult. Our thesis is that an appropriately structured course can take advantage of the existing knowledge of students for each to learn more than they otherwise would, and experience the contributions other disciplines make to HCI. This paper presents the theoretical background for this thesis and our experiences with delivering the course in a New Zealand University. In this course, by carefully defining the project requirements, the students experienced designing and prototyping a program where psychology, design and computer science contributed to the software creation process.

Keywords: HCI education, Computer Science education, student group projects.

1 Introduction

Human Computer Interaction (HCI) skills are increasingly important for computing professionals. There is no doubt that an ever-increasing percentage of program code is devoted to providing a simple and effective user interface. At the same time many of the algorithmic techniques yesteryears' students needed to master are provided by the operating system or programming language.

Computer scientists are not expected to be HCI specialists [Douglas et al. 2002]. However they do need to have a good understanding of HCI principles and appreciate the roles that others, with different expertise, can play in the design process. According to Lethbridge [2000] HCI/user interface design skills are ranked second (to negotiation) in the list of skill gaps for software professionals. This can be attributed to the rapid change in the nature of interfaces and the cross disciplinary nature of HCI. The challenge for computer science educators and students is to first accept the importance of HCI and then to learn to work with people with different backgrounds to design and deploy better computer interfaces [Douglas et al. 2002].

There are suggestions that HCI should be integrated across the curriculum in Software Engineering degrees [Phillips & Kemp 1996], and that a more cross disciplinary approach is necessary [Milewski 2004]. Other institutions have developed degrees or diplomas specifically in HCI, however, New Zealand is a small country; there is not sufficient demand to justify an HCI qualification.

This course is situated in a computer science department that has diverse interests. Yet, most of the students find employment as commercial programmers where HCI knowledge is useful. Our approach is pragmatic; by carefully structuring the course it can include the basic theories behind HCI and, via a project, give students the experience of designing and building software where HCI fundamentals are at the heart of the process.

The structure of the remainder of this paper is as follows: the next section provides a background from both HCI and educational psychology. HCI, as a discipline, is discussed alongside its penetration into the New Zealand software development industry. This section also provides a brief précis of relevant educational psychology and a description of the student demographics. These ideas are then pulled together to suggest a teaching and learning strategy. Section three explains the plan, linking the elements of the learning experience to educational and HCI theories. Section four describes the implementation giving examples of the student work. The evaluation and discussion in section five includes survey results and comments from the students and faculty.

2 Background

Planning a HCI course requires consideration of the desired learning outcomes and the underlying educational psychology. This section looks briefly at HCI and the real-world application of HCI as a basis for desirable learning outcomes. Educational psychology and the attributes of typical computer science major students provide a background for the pedagogy. These disparate ideas are then brought together to suggest a teaching and learning approach for this computer science, HCI course.

2.1 HCI as a Discipline

HCI is truly a multidisciplinary field drawing on many different strands of research. The three main contributing areas are design, psychology and computer science. From design HCI draws the creative inspiration and knowledge of what is pleasing to humans. Psychology provides knowledge of human physical and mental capabilities. Lastly computer science provides the technology to build the interactive environment.

Human computer interaction is a very recent area of research. Early computers were operated by specialists who were trained in the specific requirements of the system. Now computers are everyday tools, with interfaces integrated into everyday objects. Advances in hardware and artificial intelligence are continually pushing the boundaries of what is possible.

2.2 The Real World

We are preparing students to enter the New Zealand workforce as computer science graduates. The reality in New Zealand, as it is in many other places [Greenburg 1996], is that HCI and interaction design are not widely recognized as an important part of software development. There are about 10 people practicing as fulltime HCI/usability professionals in the entire country [Mankelow 2004]. New Zealand industry is characterized by many small organizations (< 5 staff) and very few organizations with more than 50 IT development staff [Ministry of Economic Development 2004]. Greenburg [1996] pointed out in his article that in many workplaces there would be little or no knowledge of HCI and usability. This is likely to be the position many of our graduates find themselves in.

In addition best practice for designing and testing interfaces involves ongoing contact with real users. User-centred design assumes that users take part in the early discovery phases of design and usability testing. The reality of software development is that real users are often not available [Greenburg 1996]. A result of this is that a common complaint about current interfaces is that the computer scientist has designed it for himself [Turban 2003]. It is often suggested that the computer interaction experience is absolutely fine if you are a 20 to 30 year old male, but for the rest of the population computers are incomprehensible.

Yet, the demands of real world systems make it increasingly important for interfaces to be well designed and well engineered. Computers are experiencing an ongoing change of audience [Turban 2003] and computer interfaces are frequently ubiquitous and imbedded. In most instances we must assume that the user will have no training, and no access to a manual or on-line help. Therefore the interaction must be intuitive for the user.

One of the goals for this course is to prepare the students for the local workplace. A place where knowledge of HCI and usability are often minimal, where there may be no access to real users, but the software must be such that it is usable by the target audience without instruction.

2.3 Education

Our approach in the design of this course is not unique. We have drawn on well defined educational psychology principles. First, the ideas espoused by Vygostsky [1978] that people learn more, and perhaps more effectively, from their peers than they do from the teacher. Second, constructivism and the learning cycle, that people learn most by learning about the theory, doing and then reflecting on what they have done [Kolb 1984]. This is similar to activity theory that Nardi [1996] advocates for use in HCI. Last, group projects provide a wide range of benefits for students [Koppelman et al. 2000], however group work also presents some challenges for teachers, particularly in how to fairly assess the individual.

2.4   Course

This project is a major part of a third year computer science 'Introduction to HCI' course. The course is run over fourteen weeks, twelve teaching weeks with a two week break in the middle. There are three one hour lectures a week and each student attends one two hour laboratory a week. The majority of the 100 students in the course are CS majors, in a traditional three year under-graduate Bachelor of Science degree. The requirement for the major is eight CS papers at least four of which must be at third year. This is the only undergraduate CS course the department offers that has HCI or interface design as a part of its learning outcomes. However, we are situated in a large university (30,000 students) and the BSc structure is such that students can, and do, select courses from a wide range of disciplines including fine arts, psychology and media studies. More than half the students are studying towards either a 'double major' or 'con-joint' degree. A double major is a degree with majors in two science disciplines such as computer science and mathematics, physics or psychology. A con-joint is two degrees; BSc/BCom is a popular choice for CS students. Many of the students are in their final semester of study.

The demographics for the most resent offering of the course were: gender, 70% male, 30% female; ethnicity, 40% Chinese, 26% Pakeha (New Zealanders of European descent), 10% other Asian, 11% other, 8% Indian, 5% Maori; age, median 23, 4% of the students over 30. There are two main groups of Asian students, international students and new immigrants. The official languages in New Zealand are English and Maori; all instruction in the department is in English and foreign students must meet English proficiency levels. The mix of cultures in the class adds a enjoyable diversity of prior experience including different social norms and school systems.

2.5   Teaching Approaches

Bringing together the diverse roots of HCI, the local industry and our student population we have indeed a very large landscape in which to situate the course! One HCI course can but introduce the principles and make the students aware of the wider issues in HCI. The lectures deliver the basic theoretical principles and the laboratories and project enrich the course with practise. Based on Vygostsky's [1978] principles we hypothesize that the students can learn more from each other about design, a subject that is difficult to teach in a computer science course, and psychology than we have time to 'teach'.

The project runs for the first eight weeks of the course (six teaching and two break). The overall goal for the project to encourage the students to think deeply about the interface and interaction design, and also to appreciate the roles of design and psychology in HCI. It draws on the individual strengths of the group members in design and psychology to add to the learning experience.

3   Plan

In order to achieve the goals a great deal of thought was put into the project scope and requirements. We considered which parts of the project would be fully defined and in which parts the students would have latitude to explore. The learning plan includes timeline, scenario, information sources, group formation and assessment plan.

3.1 Scenario

The scenario needs to be quite specific to allow the students to focus and limit the size of the project. The problem must specify a user or users quite different from the 'average' class member so that the students can be in no doubt that they are not the primary audience for the software. Also, if the interaction is restricted to a non-standard subset of a normal PC the students are obliged to think of different ways standard functionality can be achieved. Finally the topic needed to be such that it provides design opportunities, some challenges for the geeks in the class and be achievable in the eight week timeframe.

3.2 Resources

We wanted the students to research the requirements from secondary sources as this exposes them to the wide variety of information that is available. This reflects the reality that many software development companies do not involve users in the development process. Another practical reason for not using real people, other than class members, is that using people imposes a quite onerous ethical approval process on us. We, certainly, did not want to use class members, as they can not represent a naïve user.

A choice left to the students is the implementation environment. The prototype could be built using any programming language available on the university network. The network computers are standard PCs running Microsoft Windows XP and languages available include Java, C++, Visual Studio .Net C# and VB.

3.3 Assessment

There are two assessment deadlines, one three weeks into the project and another at the end of the project. At the first date the background research, user requirements and a non-functional prototype must be presented and handed in. This is timed so that the students complete this phase before doing the programming. The presentation encourages them to formalize their ideas and lets each group see what the other groups are planning. They may review their designs after the presentation. The second hand-in and presentation is of the prototype software and also a short report on the experience. The background research, user requirements and non-functional prototype will be checked for completeness and a reasonable design. The prototype will be reviewed against Nielsen's [1994] usability heuristics.

Assessment is often problematic with group projects; it is difficult to judge each individual's effort verses the team effort. However, the computer science department has a policy of minimizing the course work's contribution to the final grade and retesting course work in controlled assessments (test and exam). Accordingly the entire project contributed 8% to each student's total grade. Clearly this does not represent the effort required for the projects. Test and exam questions directly related to the project contributed further 20%. This assessment approach means that the project can be considered more a formative than summative: neither the students nor teachers need be overly concerned about how much each individual receives for the project as opposed to the group score.

3.4 Integration with Theory

A number of elements of the project were directly linked to the theory portion of the course. The use of personas and interface storyboards and Wizard-of-Oz techniques are explained in the theory part of the course and expected to be used in the project. The theory also considers human physical capabilities such as vision, and cognitive capabilities such as problem solving strategies. There was a clear expectation that the user will be able to use the software without help or instruction, therefore the students must design within expected abilities. The theory also discusses where HCI fits into the software development life-cycle and which techniques are suitable at which stages.

4 Implementation

In this section we describe in detail the implementation of this project into the introduction to HCI course offered in the second semester 2004 (July–November). The assignment specification was given to the class in the first lecture.

4.1 Scenario

The problem was to design and build a drawing package for a specific six year-old child. According to the scenario the child, Lindsay is disabled and can only interact with the computer using an eye-gaze device (the students emulated this with mouse clicks). Lindsay wants to be able to draw pictures like his/her classmates but drawing with normal drawing software is too slow. Lindsay's teacher saw an article on some software that let the user put together a picture from pre-existing bits (see http://www.mrpicassohead.com/) but feels the software is inappropriate for a six year old. The project is to design and prototype a drawing program specifically for Lindsay that he/she can operate alone.

The gender of Lindsay was determined by the makeup of the group (see below). Lindsay was the opposite gender to the majority of the group. Given the demographics of the class most groups were developing for a girl. If the group was evenly balanced, male and female, they could choose the gender of 'their Lindsay'. In this case the gender had to be specified with the group registration.

4.2 Resources

We provided a number of resources on children's drawing developmental stages from the library and Internet [e.g. Druin et al. 1997; Golomb 2004]. We did not make any provision, or actively encourage the students to talk with children. As described above it is quite common to rely on secondary data for user needs and we wanted to make the students aware of how much research there is readily available. And, a practical consideration, the university has very strict ethical processes to work with children. Of course many of the students have young family members that they could relate this problem to or know primary school teachers with whom they could discuss the domain.

Students were required to find out about eye-gaze products from the Internet and selected a particular product that their Lindsay hypothetically used. While they could use any programming language available on the university network some felt a bit daunted by the prototyping task. We provided a two hour tutorial on the Microsoft Visual Studio .Net Tablet SDK ink classes that offer a set of easy-to-use ink capture and manipulation methods. This allayed their fears about implementation difficulties.

4.3   Group Formation

The students formed their own groups with the following restrictions and recommendations. Group size was set at four; however groups of three or five were acceptable when necessary to balance numbers. The class split into approximately thirds for the laboratory sessions, all the members of a group had to be in the same laboratory session. We recommended that each group had at least: one person with art/design skills (any highschool course counted), one person with some knowledge of psychology or educational psychology (any undergraduate course), and one 'A' programmer.

In the tutorials there was time for group formation. To get to know each other and each others' skills each member of the class wrote him/herself a name label and added to it a red dot if they knew about design, a blue dot if they knew about psychology or educational psychology and a grade in the range A–C of their programming ability.

We were a little nervous as to whether enough students would have skills in psychology and design. About 30 students had some knowledge of psychology or educational psychology and about 35 students had design skills. The students then had time to chat and form provisional groups. It was left to them to ensure they had an appropriate mix of skills. The provisional groups work together on a small lab exercise (on Fitts' law) this gave them an opportunity to get to know each other better before the groups were finalized. A couple of groups formed around existing friendships, rather than skills. If they didn't have the skills within the group their work did suffer. We did not interfere as we felt that this was a part of the learning process.

By the following week everyone had to notify the course administrator of their group. We gave some suggestions on the ways that they divide the work such as research into requirements, interface design, functional requirements and programming. They were not required to account for the division of work but were reminded that it would all be in the examination. Students could appeal to us if there were group problems. While we are certain that some people did more work than others, no one came to us and complained about their group.

4.4   Research and Non-functional Prototypes

Most of the groups did a very thorough job of researching into children's drawing and eye-gaze interaction. In week three the groups presented their requirements and non-functional prototypes. We were delighted with what they created.

From their research the groups discovered that six year-old children are generally in the schematic drawing stage. At this stage children are drawing pictures to convey a story. They have fixed presentations of objects but this may be varied to emphasize an import feature, for example they may have a standard representation of the family dog, but if the picture is about the dog eating the family dinner the dog's mouth may be much larger than normal. Spatial awareness is developing so objects are set in relative adjacency, but all sit on the same base-line, a 'horizon' that typically runs across the picture. Size is relative to importance rather than a representation of reality.

They also were required to find out about eye-gaze interaction. There are some clear indications as to what is possible with this type of interaction that they were expected to identify. However, for the next stage of the project, the development of the prototype they emulated eye-gaze with mouse-only interaction.

They were encouraged to develop a low-fidelity prototype of the interface first, but could present either a low or high-fidelity design. Figures 1 & 2 show two of the sketches that one group produced. The first sketch gives the general layout of the form in drawing mode and briefly describes the function of each of the buttons in a list down the right-hand side. They produced similar sketches for: save, make stamp, make colour and picture gallery. Figure 2 shows a colour mock-up of the interface where flaps are folded over the different areas so that the prototype can be used as a storyboard. This group used the mock-up as a prop for a use-case based presentation where they described the process of Lindsay making and saving a picture.

Figures 3 & 4 show a different group's high-fidelity design. This group were very creative with their design. The rocket shown on the left of Figure 3 and in Figure 4 'lauched' as the program started-up. Once in position the door would open, the astronaut come out and introduce himself (their Lindsay was a boy) to Lindsay as the help agent (using text-to-speech) who could be called on at anytime by clicking the icons on the rocket door.

Another unique feature of this group's design were the drawing tools and colour icons shown at the bottom of Figure 3. Their plan was to change the colour icons and colours for each different type of tool. Their argument was that different tools had different colour ranges and different drawing effects. For example the crayons are bright colours that laid down thick solid ink while the felts are lighter colours that produced slightly transparent ink. This group implemented both of these features in their functional prototype.

With the gender mix of the class, most of the target applications were for a female Lindsay. Two of the all male groups made rather telling, and amusing, comments about their design for Lindsay. One said that their window surround was 'yucky pink' and they had lots of 'pretty' colours in the palette because girls like colours like this! Another group said that they had real colours like blue and red and then a few girlie colours like pink.

The examples shown are typical of most of the project designs. However, there were three groups who had simply not got into the problem/design space. Having this early presentation meant it was very clear to these groups that they were off track. One of these groups completely overhauled their design and created a good prototype. Almost all the groups decided to change their specification or interface in some way as a result of their peers' questions or seeing other groups' presentations. We encouraged them to do whatever revisions they deemed useful and they could submit a revised design with their prototype.

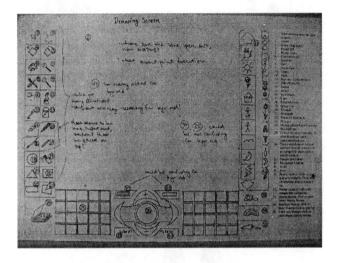

Figure 1: Sketch showing functional elements.

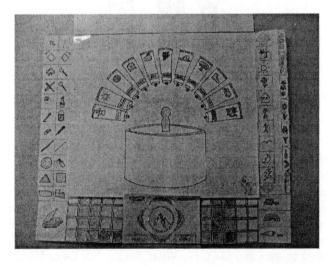

Figure 2: Interactive low-fidelity prototype with flaps that show changes in interface depending on tool or state.

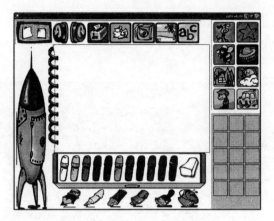

Figure 3: High-fidelity interface design.

Figure 4: Detailed images of rocket astronaut and icons for design in Figure 3.

4.5 Prototypes

The most frequent question we had to answer in the first couple of weeks was "what language do we *have* to use for the prototype?" Many of them were quite concerned by the answer which was "anything that is available on the university network". We see this as an indication of the computer science centricity of many of the students.

The main teaching language in the department is Java. Most of students had also completed courses that use C++, Visual Studio .Net C# or Visual Studio .Net VB. The ease of implementing in Visual Studio .Net with the ink SDK meant that most groups used this for their prototype. There were three projects written in Java and one in C++.

We stressed that they were creating a prototype. Given the three/four week timeframe we were not looking for a complete or robust piece of software, rather a prototype that could be used to demonstrate the design and interaction principles. They were, however, expected to write clear, readable code.

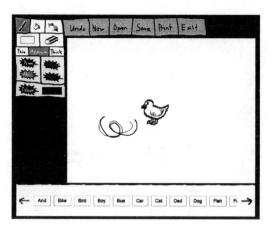

Figure 5: Duck stamp, freehand ink and word vocabulary.

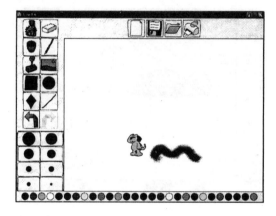

Figure 6: Animated stamp, varied width pen and colour palette.

All of the prototypes had basic functionality to facilitate drawing, erasing, new picture, print, save, load etc. There was a wide range of other features that groups provided derived from their research into children's drawing. Screen shots of four groups interfaces are shown in Figures 5–8. A number of groups provided 'stamps'. Figure 5 shows a duck stamp while Figure 6 shows a little dog; the dog (and all this group's stamps) is an animated GIF: the dog hops up and down. The group that created the prototype shown in Figure 7 allowed Lindsay to save portions of his/her own pictures as stamps, the most recent of which are shown on a clipboard on the right of the screen. The final prototype shown here (Figure 8) allowed the user to construct a creature by selecting a body, head, eyes etc., this screen shot shows the 'mouths' that could be added to the creature on the picture.

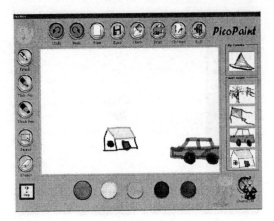

Figure 7: Collection of Lindsay's previous objects shown on left. These can be 'stamped' onto a new picture.

Figure 8: Background and creature created from body parts — nose/mouth options shown at left.

The prototype shown in Figure 5, and a number of other groups, added a vocabulary list and an on-screen keyboard. Some went to considerable trouble to discover a suitable list of words and considered different keyboard arrangements. A number of groups provided a set of backgrounds, Figure 8 shows a typical background.

4.6 Presentations

After the mid-semester break (two weeks) a show-and-tell session was held in one of the labs. Each group was required to have their prototype running on a computer. We invited a few local industry people to the session too. Each group had one person looking after their demonstration and answering questions. Everybody else was encouraged to circulate and try out the prototypes.

Twenty-six prototypes and 100+ people meant that this session took on a festive air. The students and industry people really enjoyed looking at all the different solutions to the same problem.

4.7 Marking

Marking was undertaken for both parts of the project after the final hand-in. The first part of the project, delivered in week 3 was worth 50% of the marks. This 50% was split between user needs ½, interface specification ¼, and presentation ¼. The user needs were evaluated against what we would have expected them to find out about six year olds' drawing skills and eye-gaze interaction, and the reasonableness of the persona and design.

For the second part of the project, ¾ of the marks were for the prototype and ¼ for the review. The prototype was evaluated against Nielsen's usability heuristics [Nielsen 1994] with an additional item for the project's special case, which was Lindsay's special needs. A small portion of the marks were allocated for professional looking code and innovation. In the project review the group was expected to reflect on the project and the process, describing what they did well, what they could have done better and features they were particularly proud of. In this section we looked for a thoughtful approach.

5 Evaluation and Discussion

Our goal with this project was to give students the opportunity to work on a software development project where HCI was the focus. To this end we deliberately set a scenario that constrained the interaction and the target user could not be construed as being themselves. This made them research into the likely needs of the user and develop a persona. The timetable for deliverables was such that they needed to complete the non-functional design before they started to program.

The group work gave the students that had skills in psychology and/or design the opportunity to draw on those skills. It transpired that several of the students in the class were doing a double major degree in Computer Science and Psychology. One particular student in this category said in week three of the course 'now I know where my two majors fit together'. She has gone on to get a work with one of the only HCI consultancy firms in New Zealand.

We were a pleasantly surprised at the number of students who had excellent skills in graphic design. Several of these students made comments that they had chosen computer science as a career over design because there were more jobs in computer science. One student demonstrated a real flare for designing icons. She, through one of the other class members, has a contract to design icons for a local company that develops applications for mobile phones. We hypothesize that she can do this so well because she has a deep understanding of the function a particular button accesses and she is an excellent designer.

There were, of course, students in the class who did not have skills in either psychology or design. However they have had the opportunity to work in a team where the contributions of these other disciplines were vital to the project's success. Some commented that this experience has given them a better concept of the resources that are freely available about different types of users and that there are people other than information technology specialists who can make a significant contribution to a software project.

Of the 26 projects all but two demonstrated that the students had well understood the brief. The software was clearly targeted at six year-old drawing skills and they had thought carefully about the interaction so that a keyboard was not required. For example, most groups simplified file persistence so that the user would not have to understand or interact with the operating system's file systems. The remaining two groups presented rather poor imitations of a standard paint program. We hope that by seeing what other groups produced they may realize the possibilities.

Many commented that the presentations (in Weeks 3 and 8) were inspiring. This was the first time that they had seen so many diverse approaches to the same problem. They remarked that this reinforced the theory of producing multiple ideas.

We conducted standard student surveys during the class. Overall the class rated well above average. Many students commented that this was the first group project they had done in computer science and that they enjoyed the group work. Others remarked that they were in their final semester of study and that the experience had made them rethink their approach to programming.

This was the first offering of an HCI course at this university. Some of the hard-core computer science students were surprised that the course de-emphasized programming. A couple commented that they did not think that it was computer science at all. We are prepared to live with that view and suspect that they may give a different answer after they have been working for a couple of years.

6   Conclusions and Future Work

This paper describes why and how we designed a project into a computer science course that drew on the students' existing knowledge of design and psychology. The project that we prescribed required them to learn about user requirements and constraints from the psychology literature and a novel interaction device. They were then required to design a creative interface for a user that we deliberately made very different from them. The targeted user together with the limited interaction required them to carefully reconsider standard interaction such as file save/load.

The prototypes that the groups created were inventive and demonstrated attention to HCI principles. Their comments showed that they had gained as much as we had hope from the experience. They enjoyed working together and having the opportunity to be creative.

We considered using the same project as a case-study for usability testing in the second-half of the course. Because this was the first offering of the course we decided to separate the two parts and use a different project for usability testing. However given the success of this project, next time we are planning to set a project with similar constraints and extend its use into the usability testing part of the course.

References

Douglas, S., Tremaine, M., Leventhal, L. & Wills, C. [2002], Incorporating Human–Computer Interaction into the Undergraduate Computer Science Curriculum, *in* J. Gersting,

H. M. Walker & S. Grissom (eds.), *Proceedings of the 33rd SIGCSE Technical Symposium on Computer Science Education*, ACM Press, pp.211–2.

Druin, A., Stewart, J., Proft, D., Bederson, B. & Hollan, J. [1997], Kidpad: A Design Collaboration between Children, Technologists and Educators, *in* S. Pemberton (ed.), *Proceedings of the SIGCHI Conference on Human Factors in Computing Systems (CHI'97)*, ACM Press, pp.463–70.

Golomb, C. [2004], *The Child's Creation of a Pictorial World*, second edition, Lawrence Erlbaum Associates.

Greenburg, S. [1996], Teaching Human–Computer Interaction to Programmers, *Interactions* 3(4), 62–76.

Kolb, D. [1984], *Experiential Learning: Experiences as the Source of Learning and Development*, Prentice–Hall.

Koppelman, H., van Dijk, E. M. A. G., van der Mast, C. P. A. G. & van der Veer, G. C. [2000], Team Projects in Distance Education: A Case in HCI Design, *in* J. Tarhio, S. Fincher & D. Joyce (eds.), *Proceedings of the 5th Annual SIGCSE/SIGCUE ITiCSE Conference on Innovation and Technology in Computer Science Education*, ACM Press, pp.97–100.

Lethbridge, T. C. [2000], What Knowledge Is Important to the Software Professional?, *IEEE Computer* 33(5), 44–50.

Mankelow, T. [2004], Usability in New Zealand, http://www.optimalusability.com/downloads/presentations/UPA-07Sep2004.pdf (last accessed 2005-02).

Milewski, A. E. [2004], Software Engineers and HCI Practioners Learning to Work Together: A Preliminary Look at Expectations, *in* T. B. Horton & A. E. K. Sobel (eds.), *Proceedings of the 17th Conference on Software Engineering Education and Training (CSEET'04)*, IEEE Computer Society Press, pp.45–9.

Ministry of Economic Development [2004], SMEs in New Zealand: Structure and Dynamics — 2004, http://www.med.govt.nz/irdev/ind_dev/smes/2004/index.html (last accessed 2005-02).

Nardi, B. A. (ed.) [1996], *Context and Consciousness: Activity Theory and Human–Computer Interaction*, MIT Press.

Nielsen, J. [1994], Enhancing the Power of Usability Heuristics, *in* B. Adelson, S. Dumais & J. Olson (eds.), *Proceedings of the SIGCHI Conference on Human Factors in Computing Systems: Celebrating Interdependence (CHI'94)*, ACM Press, pp.152–8.

Phillips, C. & Kemp, E. [1996], Towards the Integration of Software Engineering and HCI Education: A Cross-disciplinary Approach, *in* J. Grundy & M. Apperley (eds.), *Proceedings of OzCHI'96 The Sixth Australian Conference on Computer–Human Interaction*, IEEE Computer Society Press, pp.145–50.

Turban, R. [2003], Approaches to Implementing and Teaching Human–Computer Interaction, *in International Conference on Information Technology: Computers and Communications (ITCC'03)*, IEEE Computer Society Press, pp.81–85.

Vygostsky, L. S. [1978], *Mind in Society: The Development of Higher Psychological Processes*, Harvard University Press.

Use and Usefulness of HCI Methods: Results from an Exploratory Study among Nordic HCI Practitioners

Ida Bark[†‡], Asbjørn Følstad[†] & Jan Gulliksen[‡]

[†] *SINTEF, Forskningsv. 1, 0314 Oslo, Norway*
Email: *asbjorn.folstad@sintef.no*

[‡] *Uppsala University, Box 337, SE-751 05 Uppsala, Sweden*
Email: *Jan.Gulliksen@hci.uu.se*

As an HCI practitioner, it would be of great value to know which methods other HCI practitioners find most useful in different project phases. Also it would be interesting to know whether the type of ICT projects has any effects on HCI practitioners' perception of the usefulness of the methods. This paper presents results from an exploratory survey of HCI practitioners in the Nordic countries conducted in the fall of 2004. 179 of the respondents were usability professionals or UI designers with two or more years of experience. The survey results give insights with regard to whether or not HCI practitioners are included in those project phases regarded as most important. Also it describes which HCI methods that are used in different project phases, and how useful different HCI methods are perceived to be. The study complements existing HCI practitioner survey investigations by an explicit allocation of the HCI methods under consideration to concrete project phases, and by including analyses of group differences between practitioners working with different kinds of development projects.

Keywords: usability, user-centred design methods, prototyping, evaluation, professionals, survey.

1 Previous Research

1.1 Studies of HCI Work Practice

Several previous studies have explored the nature of HCI work practice. Industrial integration of user-centred design was investigated by Venturi & Troost [2004]. They report that the most frequently used methods were interviews, high and low fidelity prototyping, expert evaluation, 'quick and dirty' usability test and observation of real usage.

Similar results were found in a Swedish survey on the usability professional [Gulliksen et al. 2004], where the highest rated methods typically are comparatively informal, concerned with design issues, and involve users. The study also noted critical success factors for usability work, e.g. usability as a part of the project plan from the start, and acceptance from software developers. Twelve key principles have been proposed to help adopt user-centred systems design throughout the system life cycle [Gulliksen et al. 2003].

Rosenbaum et al. [2000] used survey results to produce a toolkit for the usability community; to enable practitioners to learn from the experiences of others in similar situations.

A survey study done by Vredenburg et al. [2002] in 2000 concerning user-centred design practice conclude that informal and less structured methods tend to be used more widely than more formal and structured methods. Some of the methods ranked highest on importance (e.g. field studies and user requirements analysis) were not the most frequently used, probably due to cost-benefit considerations.

1.2 Evaluating HCI Methods and Work Practice

One of the earliest approaches to evaluate HCI methods and work practices was the 'cost-justifying usability', see for example Bias & Mayhew [1994], Karat [1997] and Mantei & Teorey [1988]. According to the cost-justifying approach, the costs and benefits of adding usability engineering to the software development project can be calculated — and used when trying to 'sell in' HCI activities to a reluctant project manager or customer. However, cost-benefit ratios at times indicate almost ridiculously high return on investments, for example Nielsen & Gilutz [2003], and there is little precision with regard to which usability methods that are used. Therefore it may be difficult to utilize literature on cost-justification as support for choosing between different HCI methods.

A more 'reductionist' approach of evaluating HCI methods has been proposed, for example Gray & Saltzman [1998]; Law & Hvannberg [2002]; Law & Hvannberg [2004], according to which HCI methods are evaluated according to their reliability, thoroughness, and validity in addition to design change effectiveness and cost-effectiveness. Also, downstream utility, the utilization of the results from HCI methods in the overall development process, is suggested as a possible evaluation criterion [Andre 2000; Hartson et al. 2001]. The reductionist approach has been criticized by, for example, Wixon [2003] for not being sufficiently oriented towards evaluating HCI methods as part of a development process.

A different approach may be to ask the HCI practitioners themselves, which methods they use in different contexts and how useful they find the different methods.

This may be called an 'ask-the-expert'-approach and includes, for example, the previously presented survey studies of Gulliksen et al. [2004] and Vredenburg et al. [2002].

2 Research Questions

The main research questions of the present study included:

1. Which HCI methods are perceived to be the most useful by HCI practitioners? Answers to this question may help other practitioners to settle method decisions, or may even inspire practitioners to start using new methods.

2. To what extent different HCI methods are used by HCI practitioners? Knowing both perceived usefulness and actual use may help us to say something about HCI-practitioners level of freedom in development projects.

3. Are HCI practitioners 'optimally' involved in development projects? On a general level this issue is addressed with regard to whether HCI practitioners are involved in the project phases they regard to be most crucial. This is important, given that it traditionally seems to have been a mismatch between the HCI ambition of being involved from the very beginning of development projects and the actual involvement of HCI practitioners on later project phases only. On a more detailed level, it is interesting to find out whether HCI practitioners actually use the HCI methods that are perceived to be the most useful. It is assumed that if HCI practitioners are not optimally involved in development projects, this will be visible in a lack of match between how much methods are used and their perceived usefulness.

3 Method

To enable data collection that may be representative of a certain population of HCI practitioners, it was decided to conduct a questionnaire survey. The population was restricted to include mostly usability practitioners from the Nordic countries.

3.1 Participants

The object of investigation is the population of HCI practitioners. The precise extent of this population is unknown, thus a random selection of participants is difficult to achieve. To be able to reach a reasonably representative selection of such a population, convenience sampling from HCI conferences and HCI organization mailing lists were chosen as a suitable vehicle to reach a fair number of participants. Participants who reported:

1. that their role in projects was usually 'Usability professional' and/or 'UI designer'; and

2. had two year or more user-centred work experience, were included in the survey analysis (n = 179).

The other participants were filtered out, and not included in the analyses of the present paper. The main focus of the survey was the Nordic population of HCI practitioners. However, a minor number of other nationalities were included in the final sample.

3.2   Recruitment

The survey was distributed at three HCI conferences: Yggdrasil'04 (Lillehammer, Norway), NordiCHI'04 (Tampere, Finland), and STIMDI'04 (Gothenburg, Sweden). Yggdrasil is a Norwegian industrially oriented HCI and user documentation conference. NordiCHI is a more academically oriented HCI conference. STIMDI is equally valid for industry and academia. The survey was also distributed as a Web-survey, with invitations sent via e-mail to colleges of the participants in the conference survey distribution, and to the mailing lists of the following HCI organizations: STIMDI (Sweden), Danish SIGCHI.dk, and Icelandic SIGCHI.is. As incentive, the participants were offered to be part of a raffle with two Apple iPod mini as prizes. The participants were also offered information with regard to the survey results through the project home page.

3.3   Material

The questionnaire included 27 items.   It was distributed as pen-and-paper questionnaires at the conferences, and as a Web-based questionnaire to the other participants.   The questionnaire items were developed on basis of a pre-study including eight semi-structured interviews with HCI practitioners, and piloted on a small number of HCI practitioners.

3.4   Analysis

Since the study was conducted as an exploratory investigation, no statistical hypothesis testing was conducted. Descriptive data analyses were conducted for all variables. Analyses of differences between groups or relationships between variables were conducted as visual inspections of graphical representation of descriptive analyses. To illustrate magnitude of relationship between some of the variables, bivariate rank correlation analyses were conducted using Spearman's rho.

3.5   Description of the Development Process in the Survey

In the pre-study interviews, the participants clearly expressed that they preferred to discuss HCI methods as belonging to the project's start, mid, or late phases, rather than according to a project phase description of, for example, ISO [1999]. We therefore chose to describe the HCI methods included in the questionnaire as belonging to one or more of three different phases:

Start phase — planning of the project, analysis and specification.

Mid phase — design-input activities, implementation and early evaluation.

End phase — evaluation of the late and final versions of the system.

	Start Phase	Mid Phase	Mid Phase and End Phase
	Planning, analysis and specification	Design input	Evaluation
Questionnaire surveys	✗		✗
Interviews	✗		✗
Field studies	✗		
Workshops	✗		
Personas	✗		
Scenarios	✗		
Use cases	✗		
Focus groups	✗	✗	
Task analysis	✗		
Rapid prototyping		✗	
Advanced prototyping		✗	
User tests		✗	✗
Design patterns		✗	
Card sorting		✗	
Storyboarding		✗	
Guidelines		✗	
Heuristic evaluation			✗
Cognitive walkthrough			✗
Expert evaluation			✗
Evaluation workshop			✗

Table 1: HCI methods included in the survey, with associated purpose and project phase.

3.6 HCI Methods Included in the Survey

The methods included in the survey were selected on basis of Maguire [2001], Usabilitynet (http://www.usabilitynet.org), and the pre-study interviews with practitioners. The methods are presented in Table 1, where it is indicated which purposes and project phases the different methods are allocated to in the questionnaire. Which methods are placed in which phases is a combination of what the literature says, results from the interviews and questionnaire piloting, and the subjective opinion of the authors.

The methods were only described by name in the survey, which may be considered a methodological weakness. However, it was assumed that the HCI community has a fairly consolidated understanding of the different methods. (Possible exceptions from this may be the methods of focus groups and workshops, which, from the authors' experience, may be interpreted somewhat differently among different HCI practitioners). It should also be noted that the different methods allocated to the same purpose may be complementary in nature. For example, field studies and use-cases are complementary in the sense that field studies is a data collection methods whereas use-cases is a method to systematize data (maybe collected through field studies).

4 Results

A total 277 responses were received. Only participants that answered that their project role usually was 'Usability professional' and/or 'UI designer', and that their user-centred working experience was more than two years, were considered. All results presented below are from this sample of 179 responses.

Respondents of the sample were inspected with regard to the variation in their responses on all 5-point scale variables in the questionnaire. Respondents with an inter-variable variation close to zero (sd < 0.3) were not included in further analyses.

4.1 Respondents' Profile

The participants were asked which project role(s) they usually hold. (Multiple responses possible.) In the selected sample population (n = 179) 78% answered 'Usability professional' and 66% answered 'UI designer'. In addition reported 18% project manager, 11% software developer, and 13% 'other'. The user-centred work experience among the participants was between 2 and 35 years, with a median value of 5 years. 53% of the participants reported to be in-house experts, 48% consultants, 19% researchers and 3% 'other'. (Multiple responses possible.)

The respondents were, with a few exceptions, divided among the Nordic countries. 33% from Sweden, 27% from Finland, 23% from Norway, 12% from Denmark, 2% from Iceland and 4% from other countries. (The amount of participants from each Nordic country corresponding fairly similarly with the number of inhabitants of each country; only Denmark somewhat underrepresented).

The respondents were asked what kind of systems they usually worked on. (Multiple responses possible). 67% answered Web-based applications, 45% business applications, 41% mobile ICT, 22% forms and documentation, 15% big complex systems, and 23% other types of systems.

4.2 Which HCI Methods are Perceived to be Most Useful

The participants were asked to rank the usefulness of a number of HCI methods applied in the different phases of the development process. The score 1 represented 'Not at all useful' and 5 represented 'Very useful'.

Start phase. The methods to be rated on usefulness in the start phase of projects were Surveys, Interviews, Field studies, Workshops, Personas, Scenarios, Use cases, Focus groups, and Task analysis. The three methods given the highest mean rating were Field studies (mean = 4.3; sd = 0.9); Interviews (4.2; 0.8) and Scenarios (4.0; 0.9). The three lowest rated methods were, from the bottom, Focus groups (mean = 3.3; sd = 1.2), Surveys (3.4; 1.0) and Personas (3.5; 1.0).

Mid phase. The methods to be rated on usefulness in the mid phase were Rapid prototyping, Advanced prototyping, User tests, Card sorting, Storyboarding, Guidelines, Heuristic evaluation, Focus groups, Design patterns, Cognitive walkthrough, Expert evaluation, and Evaluation workshop. The three methods given the highest mean rating were User tests (mean = 4,6; sd = 0.6), Rapid prototyping (4.5; 0.7) and Expert evaluation (4.0; 0.9). The three lowest rated

	All	Web based appl. (n=111)	Busi- ness appl. (n=75)	Big complex systems (n=26)	Mobile ICT (n=59)	Forms docu- ment (n=38)
User tests	4.6 (0.7)	4.6 (0.6)	4.6 (0.6)	4.4 (0.9)	4.6 (0.6)	4.5 (0.7)
Rapid prototyping	4.5 (0.7)	4.5 (0.7)	4.6 (0.6)	4.6 (0.6)	4.5 (0.5)	4.4 (0.8)
Expert evaluation	4.0 (0.8)	4.1 (0.8)	4.1 (0.8)	4.0 (0.7)	4.0 (0.9)	4.3 (0.7)
Advanced prototyping	3.7 (1.0)	3.8 (1.0)	3.8 (1.1)	3.9 (0.8)	3.9 (1.0)	3.6 (1.2)
Heuristic evaluation	3.7 (0.9)	3.8 (0.9)	3.8 (0.9)	3.6 (1.0)	3.7 (0.8)	3.8 (0.9)
Evaluation workshop	3.5 (1.0)	3.6 (1.0)	3.5 (1.1)	3.2 (0.9)	3.5 (1.1)	3.6 (1.1)
Story-boarding	3.5 (1.0)	3.5 (1.0)	3.6 (1.1)	3.9 (0.9)	3.7 (1.1)	3.5 (1.1)
Cognitive walkthrough	3.5 (1.0)	3.5 (1.0)	3.5 (1.1)	3.3 (1.0)	3.5 (1.0)	3.5 (1.1)
Guidelines	3.3 (0.9)	3.4 (0.9)	3.3 (1.1)	3.0 (0.8)	3.3 (1.0)	3.5 (0.9)
Card sorting	3.2 (1.1)	3.5 (1.1)	3.2 (1.2)	3.1 (0.9)	3.0 (0.9)	3.3 (1.1)
Design patterns	3.1 (0.9)	3.2 (0.9)	3.1 (1.0)	3.0 (0.7)	2.9 (0.9)	3.1 (1.0)
Focus groups	3.0 (1.1)	3.1 (1.1)	2.9 (1.0)	2.8 (0.9)	3.0 (1.0)	2.8 (1.0)

Table 2: Mean and standard deviations of HCI method usefulness ratings in the mid phase; across groups of practitioners working with different kinds of systems.

methods were, from the bottom, Focus groups (mean = 2.9; sd = 1.1), Design patterns (3.2; 0.9) and Card sorting (3.2; 1.1).

End phase. The methods to be rated on usefulness in the end phase were User tests, Heuristic evaluation, Expert evaluation, Surveys, Evaluation workshop, Interviews, and Cognitive walkthrough. The three methods that were given the highest mean rating were User tests (mean = 4.5; sd = 0.8), Expert evaluation (3.9; 1.0) and Heuristic evaluation (3.7; 1.0). The three lowest rated methods were, from the bottom, Surveys (mean = 3.0; sd = 1.0), Cognitive walkthrough (3.3; 1.2) and Evaluation workshop (3.5; 1.1).

The distributions for all variables reported in this section were uni-modal, except for the distribution of perceived usefulness of focus groups in the start phase which peaked at two values (2 and 4).

4.3   Perceived Usefulness Across Different Project Types

There was fairly little difference between practitioners working with different kinds of systems, with regard to how useful they perceive the different HCI methods to be. As an example, Table 2 presents mean usefulness ratings of the methods allocated to the mid phase, for the different groups of practitioners.

The degree of similarity in scoring patterns between the groups may be illustrated by bivariate rank correlation analyses between the groups using Spearman's rho, where the rank order of each group's mean scores was the input to the analyses. Bivariate correlation of this rank order was conducted for all ten pairs of groups. The correlation coefficients indicated high similarities in scoring patterns between the groups; the lowest correlation between any two groups was found between 'Big complex systems' and 'Forms and documentation' with $r_s = 0.88$.

4.4 Degree of HCI Methods Use by HCI Practitioners

The participants were asked to report if they actually used the different HCI methods in the different phases of the development process. In the questionnaire the participants were asked to report whether they used the different methods 'yes, sometimes', 'yes, often', or 'no, not at all'. When analysing the data, differentiating between 'yes, sometimes' and 'yes, often' was not judged to provide much added insight, only complexity in reporting. Thus the results are presented as belonging to the categories 'yes' or 'no'.

Start phase. The methods reported to be most used by the participants in the start phase of projects were Interviews (92%), Scenarios (89%), and Use cases (89%). The methods reported to be least used were Focus groups (64%), Personas (65%) and Surveys (70%).

Mid phase. The methods reported to be most used by the participants in the mid phase were User tests and Rapid prototyping (both 95%), and Expert evaluation (93%). The methods reported to be least used were Card sorting (43%), Design patterns (48%), and Focus groups (53%).

End phase. The methods reported to be most used by the participants in the end phase were User tests (97%), Expert evaluation (88%), and Heuristic evaluation (75%). The methods reported to be least used were Cognitive walkthrough (47%), Evaluation workshop (52%), and Surveys (53%).

4.5 Reported Use of Methods Across Project Types

With regard to reported use across different development projects, there were only minor differences between practitioners working with different kinds of systems. Most differences were found with regard to practitioners working with big complex systems and forms and documentation. As an example of this, Table 3 presents the reported usage for the methods allocated to the mid phase across practitioners working with different kinds of systems.

Bivariate rank correlation analyses between the groups were conducted using Spearman's rho, where the rank order of each group's percentage of reported use of each method was the input to the analyses. The bivariate rank correlation analysis was conducted for all ten pairs of groups. The correlation coefficients indicated high similarities between the groups; the lowest rank correlation between any pair of groups was found between 'Big complex systems' and 'Forms and documentation' with $r_s = 0.80$.

4.6 HCI Practitioners Involved in Crucial Project Phases?

The participants were asked at which point in the development process they believed it is most crucial for HCI practitioners to be involved. 76% answered the start phase, 23% the mid phase and 1% the end phase (only one choice allowed). The participants were also asked at what point in the development process they usually were involved

	All	Web based appl. (n=111)	Busi- ness appl. (n=75)	Big complex systems (n=26)	Mobile ICT (n=59)	Forms docu- ment (n=38)
User tests	95%	97%	97%	84%	96%	97%
Expert evaluation	96%	97%	97%	100%	96%	100%
Rapid prototyping	92%	92%	94%	91%	91%	85%
Heuristic evaluation	82%	84%	85%	92%	92%	81%
Advanced prototyping	74%	74%	71%	92%	78%	63%
Guidelines	73%	76%	80%	73%	79%	79%
Cognitive walkthrough	62%	63%	71%	63%	73%	62%
Evaluation workshop	58%	57%	60%	52%	57%	69%
Storyboarding	56%	60%	62%	71%	62%	61%
Focus groups	53%	55%	52%	50%	61%	47%
Design patterns	47%	55%	54%	52%	38%	47%
Card sorting	43%	53%	47%	50%	38%	53%

Table 3: Percentage of respondents that reported to use the different HCI methods in the mid phase; across groups of practitioners working with different kinds of systems.

the most. 30% answered the start phase, 38% the mid phase, and 17% the end phase. 15% answered 'not applicable'.

Combined, the results from the two questions above shows that the great majority of the participants reported that the start phase is the most crucial to be involved in. 93% of those most involved in the start phase, along with 70% of those most involved in the mid phase and 67% of those most involved in the end phase, reported that they see the start phase as most crucial. In comparison only 30% of those most involved in the mid phase, together with 7% of those most involved in the start phase and 29% of those most involved in the end phase, reported that they see the mid phase is the most crucial phase. And only 4% of those actually most involved in the end phase report that they see this as the most crucial phase.

4.7 HCI Practitioners Using the Most Useful Methods?

The participants' responses on which methods they actually use were compared with their responses on which methods they perceive to be the most useful. The comparison was conducted by:

1. sorting the methods according to mean perceived usefulness; and

2. sorting the methods according to reported usage of the methods.

Deviations between the two diagrams indicate methods that are used more or less than their perceived usefulness should account for. Pair wise bar diagrams for the three project phases are presented in Figures 1–3 leading to the following observations:

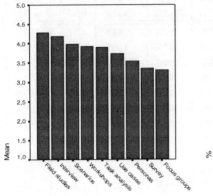

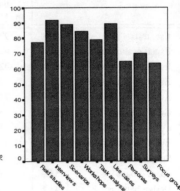

(a) Mean rating of usefulness of methods used.

(b) Usage of methods.

Figure 1: The start phase.

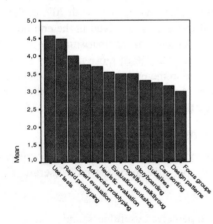

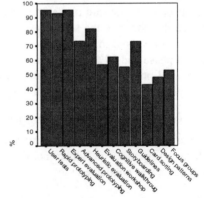

(a) Mean rating of usefulness of methods used.

(b) Usage of methods.

Figure 2: The mid phase.

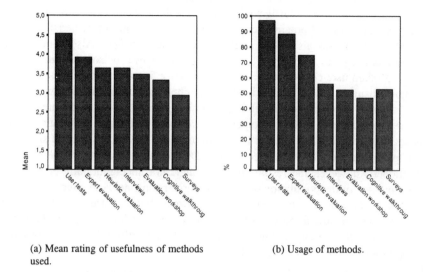

(a) Mean rating of usefulness of methods used.

(b) Usage of methods.

Figure 3: The end phase.

Start phase (See Figure 1) The magnitude of the difference between actual use and perceived usefulness of the methods in the start phase may be illustrated by using Spearman's rho to calculate their rank correlation coefficient, with regard to the rank order of the different methods. $r_s = 0.72$ ($p = 0.03$). Field studies seem to be used less than their perceived usefulness should indicate. Use cases seem to be used more than their perceived usefulness indicate.

Mid phase (See Figure 2) Rank correlation coefficient calculated by Spearman's rho: $r_s = 0.90$ ($p = 0.00$). In the mid phase expert evaluation, heuristic evaluation, guidelines, and focus groups seem to be used more than these methods perceived usefulness should indicate. Advanced prototyping, evaluation workshops and card sorting may seem to be used somewhat less than their perceived usefulness seem to indicate.

End phase (See Figure 3) Rank correlation coefficient calculated by Spearman's rho: $r_s = 0.96$ ($p = 0.00$). In the end phase it mostly seems like the methods perceived as the most useful are also the most used, and vice versa. But surveys and interviews are reported to be used a little more than the methods perceived usefulness may indicate.

5 Discussion

The results presented provide insights in HCI work practices, and opinions building on similar work practices, on basis of a sample of 179 HCI practitioners. The participants were sampled by convenience, not by randomized sampling techniques, because the precise population of HCI practitioners is not known. However, the participants' profiles agree fairly well with at least the authors' intuitions with regard to the population of HCI practitioners at large. The participants described themselves as usability professionals (78%) and/or UI designers (66%). Also some of the participants report to hold a project manager role (18%), or software developers (11%). Median user-centred work experiences were 5 years, half in-house experts, and half consultants. 20% reported to be researchers, indicating that this group were not too heavily represented even though the questionnaires were distributed at HCI conferences. The bulk of the participants worked with Web-based applications, with business applications, and mobile ICT as runners up. There was a good spread of participants between the Nordic countries. Due to the main focus on Nordic HCI practitioners, however, the results may of course not unconditionally be taken as representative for the population of HCI practitioners outside these countries.

The discussion of the results' implications, with regard to the research questions, will be structured according to the four research questions of the paper. Following this the validity and generalizability of the results will be discussed, and possible future work will be suggested.

5.1   Which HCI Methods are Perceived Most Useful?

Knowledge on which methods are perceived most useful by other HCI practitioners is interesting information for practitioners choosing methods in their own work practice. The results indicate that in the start phase of projects field studies, interviews, use of scenarios, workshops and task analysis were among the methods rated most useful, whereas focus groups, surveys and personas were rated the least useful. It is interesting to note the difference in perceived usefulness for methods that mainly are meant for data collection, e.g. field studies, interviews, surveys and focus groups. Field studies and interviews were rated highest, surveys and focus groups were rated lowest. A reason for the low rating of focus groups may be the inherent weakness of the method that the discussions of the group may be biased due to, for example, group dynamics to such a degree that the results are not sufficiently reliable. The weakness of the survey method may be that the information gathered may be regarded as too shallow to work properly as input to a project. In field studies and interviews, methods that are often combined, the HCI practitioner may gain a deeper and more unbiased understanding of the relevant needs and requirements for the project.

The two methods of the mid phase perceived to be most useful, represented no surprise: User tests and rapid prototyping. These are strongly advocated methods throughout the HCI literature, and they have not been the target of negative critiques in more recent literature like e.g. heuristic evaluation. It was however a bit surprising that in spite of a steady trickle of negative studies with regard to the reliability and validity of heuristic evaluation, see for example Law & Hvannberg [2004], this method still is rated higher for usefulness than, for example, cognitive walkthrough. The reason for this may be that the method is cheap and easily applicable, and that the individual HCI practitioner may feel that the quality of the results from heuristic evaluations may be high enough provided that the evaluator has sufficient expertise. It may also be noted that the methods of guidelines and design patterns are rated among the lowest on usefulness in this phase. This may seem a bit odd, given that one of the more important design inputs for any practitioner would be good design examples and principles of the past. The reason for these methods low rating may indicate that the existing body of design patterns and guidelines does not serve the purpose for HCI practitioners. As in the start phase, focus groups are rated lowest with regard to usefulness. This may be due to the common knowledge on this method's weaknesses even though they apply more to focus groups for evaluation purposes rather than focus groups for the purpose of design input.

In the end phase none of the other methods even comes close to the usefulness rating given to user tests. It seems to be beyond discussion that this method is perceived as the most useful method by HCI practitioners both in the mid and end phases of development projects. Expert evaluation was rated second highest, probably due to the low-cost and versatile nature of this method. As in the mid phase, heuristic evaluation rates quite high on usefulness, despite the fact that this method has received severe criticism in later years. Cognitive walkthrough rates surprisingly low on perceived usefulness, given that this is a low-cost task oriented method. Perhaps its low usefulness is due to the method's cumbersome evaluation procedure, sometimes making cognitive walkthroughs uninspiring and drawn out. The method rating lowest on usefulness is surveys, which is somewhat surprising given the convenience and ease with which a survey evaluation may be carried out. Practitioners not being able to gain sufficiently detailed feedback using surveys may cause low rating. But it may indicate that subjective feedback on user satisfaction (traditionally being a main focus of evaluation surveys) is not regarded as interesting as objective feedback on user problems.

Interestingly enough there was fairly little difference between practitioners working with different kinds of systems, and how useful they perceived different HCI methods. Even though the systems the participants worked with were as different as mobile ICT, Web-based applications and big complex systems. One conclusion may be that HCI practitioners tend to look to the mainstream HCI tradition with regard to their personal evaluation of different methods rather than the methods usefulness in their daily work.

5.2 To What Degree are Different HCI Methods Used?

In order to investigate whether HCI practitioners actually use the methods they find most useful, it was necessary to investigate how much different HCI methods are used. In the start phase the methods that most practitioners were using include interviews, scenarios, use cases and workshops. All of these are used by more than 80% of the participants. Personas and focus groups seem to be the two least used methods. Use cases has a high frequency of use, probably as a description format that is complementary to other methods like, for example, interviews and scenarios, and may also be regarded an important vehicle to communicate requirements and specifications to other system developers. The low frequency of use for personas may be due to that the method is fairly new compared to other methods.

In the mid phase the most used methods are user tests, rapid prototyping and expert evaluations, followed by heuristic evaluation, advanced prototyping and guidelines. In the end phase user tests, expert evaluations, and heuristic evaluation are the most used methods. Not terribly surprising but again some surprise may be expressed with regard to the frequency of use of heuristic evaluations. Also for frequency of use, as for perceived uɔɔfulness, there were surprisingly small differences between practitioners working with different kinds of systems. This finding is not at all according to the intuitions of the authors, given the great differences in both development process and process requirements for projects belonging to mobile ICT, big complex systems, Web-based applications and business applications. One bleak conclusion may be that HCI practitioners perceive all systems like nails, for which the ultimate hammer is user tests. This tentative conclusion would be interesting for future research.

5.3 *Are HCI Practitioners Optimally Involved in Projects?*

To find out whether HCI practitioners find themselves involved in development projects in the best possible manner, this research question will be discussed from two perspectives:

1. whether HCI practitioners seem to be involved in the most crucial project phases; and

2. whether HCI practitioners are using the HCI methods perceived to be the most useful.

When looking at the relationship between participants' reported views on which project phase is most crucial to be involved in, and participants' reports on which phase they are most involved in, the picture is familiar to similar investigations. Almost all practitioners most involved in the project start phase (30% of the total number of participants) also report that this is the most crucial phase to be involved in. It may be assumed that these participants find themselves to be right on target with regard to the timing of project involvement. This also goes for the one fourth of the participants claiming both that the mid phase was most crucial and also to be most involved in this phase. On the other hand, about 70% of the participants most heavily involved in the mid phase of project reported that the start phase was the most crucial. And almost all practitioners reporting to be most involved in the end phase reported that earlier project phases are more crucial. This means that many HCI practitioners find themselves most involved in later phases than the most important to be involved in. It seems that the HCI community is still abundant with practitioners feeling that they get involved to late in projects.

The issue of HCI practitioners' influence and freedom in projects may be gauged by the match between the perceived usefulness of methods and their frequency of use. From the comparative analysis conducted on the results on perceived usefulness and reported use of HCI methods it may be noted that in the end phase there is an almost perfect match between the methods most frequently used and the methods perceived to be most useful. This may indicate that in this phase, the HCI practitioners are given relatively great degrees of freedom and influence. This is in line with the finding that HCI practitioners find that they are involved a little later in the project than they would really like to have been.

In the mid phase, several methods are more used than their usefulness scores should indicate. This goes in particular for expert evaluations, heuristic evaluations, and guidelines, and to a certain degree focus groups. This finding may indicate that other forces than the best judgement of the HCI practitioners are at play in the mid phase of projects, even with regard to the choice of HCI methods. The reason for the popularity of expert evaluations and heuristic evaluations may be that they are extremely low-cost methods, and may be easily fitted to a tight project cost and timeframe. With regard to guidelines and focus groups, these may be methods required by other persons than the HCI practitioner.

As for the start phase, the comparatively low rank correlation between actual use and usefulness of the methods may indicate that this is the phase where the HCI practitioners seem to be least in control with regard to a free choice of methods. One method that is a lot less used than one should assume on basis of the reported usefulness of the method, is field studies. This probably is due to the cost demanding nature of this method. Field studies may be something that HCI practitioners know are useful, but that not all practitioners are allowed to use because of e.g. budget and time constraints. But cost and time may not be the only factors affecting HCI work in the start phase. Use cases are somewhat more used than their perceived usefulness may account for. This probably is due to the need for using use cases as a description format to communicate findings with others in the development project.

5.4 Validity and Generalizability

The validity of the present study greatly depends on the quality of the questionnaire and whether the sample of participants is representative of the HCI community at large. The questionnaire was developed on basis of a series of HCI practitioners, interviews and adjusted based on early piloting. Also the face validity of the items of the questionnaires was quite high, in that the questions explicitly focused on the information sought. (The intentions of the items were not hidden from the participants as may be the case in other questionnaires.) These factors should contribute to a confidence in the quality of the questionnaire.

With regard to the sample, the procedure for sampling was a convenience sample. This sampling method was chosen since the exact extent of the population of HCI practitioners is not known. This is an obvious weakness of the study. However, the participants' profiles were quite in line with the authors' intuitions with regard to the characteristics of the HCI population at large. Hopefully the participants' profile is as convincing to the readers of this paper as well. The sample of participants is mainly from the Nordic countries why the conclusions may not be generalized to the HCI population at large. However, many of the findings presented in the present paper are in line with results from other surveys, for example Vredenburg et al. [2002]. Depending on whether a HCI community may be seen as sufficiently similar to the participants' profile of this survey, some conclusions in this paper may be applicable also outside the Nordic countries.

6 Future Work

There are several interesting themes in the present investigation that may be continued future work. One interesting finding is that HCI practitioners working with very different kinds of systems seem to rate HCI methods similarly on usefulness, and to a certain extent also frequency of use. This is surprising, and future comparative studies may provide insights into whether this finding holds true, and if so, what may be the cause for this.

Also, it would be interesting to explore the issue of perceived usefulness of HCI methods as seen from the perspective of other actors in development projects. In particular whether the usefulness ratings from HCI practitioners match the usefulness ratings of project leaders employing HCI practitioners in their projects.

References

Andre, T. S. [2000], Determining the Effectiveness of the Usability Problem Inspector: A Theory-based Model and Tool for Finding Usability Problems, PhD thesis, Virginia Polytechnic Institute and State University.

Bias, R. G. & Mayhew, D. J. (eds.) [1994], *Cost-Justifying Usability*, Academic Press.

Gray, W. D. & Saltzman, M. C. [1998], Damaged Merchandise? A Review of Experiments that Compare Usability Evaluation Methods, *Human–Computer Interaction* 13(3), 203–61.

Gulliksen, J., Boive, I., Persson, J., Hektor, A. & Herulf, L. [2004], Making a Difference — A Survey of the Usability Profession in Sweden, in A. Hyrskykari (ed.), *Proceedings of Third Nordic Conference on Human–Computer Interation (NordiCHI'04)*, ACM Press, pp.207–15.

Gulliksen, J., Göransson, B., Boivie, I., Blomkvist, S., Persson, J. & Cajander, Å. [2003], Key Principles for User-centred Systems Design, *Behaviour & Information Technology* 22(6), 397–409. In special section "Designing IT for Healthy Work".

Hartson, H. R., Andre, T. S. & Williges, R. C. [2001], Ultimate Criterion for UEM effectiveness — Finding Real Usability Problems, *International Journal of Human–Computer Interaction* 13(4), 373–410.

ISO [1999], ISO 13407 International Standard. Human-centred Design Processes for Interactive Systems. International Organization for Standardization, Genève, Switzerland.

Karat, C. [1997], Cost-Justifying Usability Engineering in the Software Life Cycle, in M. Helander, T. K. Landauer & P. V. Prabhu (eds.), *Handbook of Human–Computer Interaction*, second edition, North-Holland, pp.767–78.

Law, E. L.-C. & Hvannberg, E. T. [2002], Complementarity and Convergence of Heuristic Evaluation and Usability Test: A Case Study of Universal Brokerage Platform, in O. W. Bertelsen, S. Bødker & K. Kuuti (eds.), *Proceedings of NordiCHI 2002*, ACM Press, pp.71–80.

Law, E. L.-C. & Hvannberg, E. T. [2004], Analysis of Strategies for Improving and Estimating the Effectiveness of Heuristic Evaluation, in A. Hyrskykari (ed.), *Proceedings of Third Nordic Conference on Human–Computer Interation (NordiCHI'04)*, ACM Press, pp.241–50.

Maguire, M. [2001], Methods to Support Human-Centered Design, *International Journal of Human–Computer Studies* **56**(4), 587–634.

Mantei, M. M. & Teorey, T. J. [1988], Cost/Benefit Analysis for Incorporating Human Factors in the Software Lifecycle, *Communications of the ACM* **31**(4), 428–39.

Nielsen, J. & Gilutz, S. [2003], *Usability Return on Investment*, Nielsen Norman Group.

Rosenbaum, S., Rohn, J. A. & Humburg, J. [2000], A Toolkit for Strategic Usability: Results from Workshops, Panels, and Surveys, *in* T. Turner & G. Szwillus (eds.), *Proceedings of the SIGCHI Conference on Human Factors in Computing Systems (CHI'00), CHI Letters* **2**(1), ACM Press, pp.337–44.

Venturi, G. & Troost, J. [2004], Survey on the UCD Integration in the Industry, *in* A. Hyrskykari (ed.), *Proceedings of Third Nordic Conference on Human–Computer Interation (NordiCHI'04)*, ACM Press, pp.449–452.

Vredenburg, K., Mao, J., Smith, P. W. & Carey, T. [2002], A Survey of User-centered Design Practice, *in* D. Wixon (ed.), *Proceedings of SIGCHI Conference on Human Factors in Computing Systems: Changing our World, Changing Ourselves (CHI'02), CHI Letters* **4**(1), ACM Press, pp.471–8.

Wixon, D. [2003], Evaluating Usability Methods, *Interactions* **10**(4), 29–34.

Building Usability in India: Reflections from the Indo-European Systems Usability Partnership

Andy Smith[†], Jan Gulliksen[‡] & Liam Bannon[§]

[†] *Institute for IT, Thames Valley University, Wellington Street, Slough SL1 1YG, UK*
Tel: *+44 1753 697565*
Email: *andy.smith@tvu.ac.uk*

[‡] *Department for Information Technology / HCI, Uppsala University, Box 377, SE-751 05 Uppsala, Sweden*
Tel: *+46 18 471 2849*
Email: *jan.gulliksen@hci.uu.se*

[§] *Interaction Design Centre, Department of Computer Science and Information Systems, University of Limerick, Limerick, Ireland*
Tel: *+353 61 202632*
Email: *liam.bannon@ul.ie*

In this paper, we address the big picture of developing HCI in a global context. We focus on India and reflect on the activities of the Indo-European Systems Usability Partnership, an EU funded project linking the British HCI Group with the Computer Society of India and supported by three European universities. We focus on the themes of interaction design and user centred systems design and their place in the Indian context. We conclude with our views of what is needed next for HCI in India and on global HCI from an Asian perspective.

Keywords: IESUP, interaction design, rUCSD, off-shoring, HCI education.

1   Introduction

Starting in October 2002 the British HCI Group / British Computer Society (BCS) joined in partnership with the Computer Society of India (CSI) and three European Universities to collaborate in issues relating to the design of usable interactive IT systems that support people in their everyday and working lives.

Support from the European Commission's ASIA IT&C Programme provided funding for the Indo-European Systems Usability Partnership (IESUP), a two-year project, to support links between key experts in usability and HCI throughout Europe and their counterparts in India. By working together in developing usability and human-computer interaction throughout India, we the partners within IESUP, focused on four main themes:

1. HCI in University Curriculum.

2. User Centred Systems Design.

3. Interaction Design.

4. Culture and HCI.

Activities within the project included seminars and workshops in India, visits from India's growing HCI community to Europe, together with virtual communities and other methods of larger scale communication.

Overall we sought to support the integration of HCI and usability into both Indian IT education programmes, and software development projects, mirroring that which occurs in Europe and the USA.

We started with fairly small scale activities, often arranging seminars in Indian Universities attempting to engage both with university computing academics and industry based IT practitioners in Indian industry. In the early stages we were happy to engage with an audience size only just making double figures. By the end of the project we witnessed a significant growth in the interest given to HCI within India, not least through a small but developing HCI community. The project culminated in December 2004 with IESUP arranging IHCI2004, India's first international conference on HCI. IHCI2004 attracted over 180 delegates from across India and with additional industry and IFIP sponsorship enjoyed speakers from five continents.

In this paper we reflect on our experiences within IESUP. The paper will focus on our perceptions of the problems and opportunities for HCI in India, and establish some key issues to be addressed to support HCI in India, a country which will figure increasingly prominently on the global IT scene in the years to come.

2   HCI in India

At the start of the IESUP project we were aware that in comparison with developed nations India's status as an information society was at an early stage. However the information revolution in India is now clearly coming of age, encouraged by the declining cost of information and communication technologies world-wide, and the increased availability of high-quality and low-cost technology-enabled products and services in the country.

When we started IESUP we were aware that in May 1998, the Prime Minister of India formed a National Taskforce on Information Technology and Software Development in order to formulate a long term national IT policy. The main objective was to help India emerge as an *'IT software superpower'*. Although the industry has been growing fast the penetration of IT within the whole Indian society is still very low.

According to NASSCOM [2002] — National Association of Software and Services Companies — a key strength of the Indian IT industry is a *'focus on a high value, software off-shoring model'* However, this strength is balanced by key weaknesses such as a low presence in the global packaged software market. At the start of IESUP we believed that India would not be able to claim IT superpower status without key developments, and that usability / HCI would have to play a key role. High levels of usability are critical to the quality of software products in a global market. Although the HCI community in India is growing it is still very small and far below what will be needed to integrate usability into the development process to any significant degree. Jakob Nielsen [2002] picked up these ideas in an Alertbox early in the project and, somewhat exaggeratedly perhaps, calculated that India would need to train 400,000 usability professionals by 2008.

2.1 A Strange Digital Divide

The 'skill base and proficiency' of the Indian IT industry provides a very interesting contrast compared to the information and communication needs of Indian society. On the one hand there are about 340,000 Indians employed by the Indian IT industry, including both hardware and software [NASSCOM 1999]. These are in addition another 180,000 people of Indian origin, now working in the US alone (March 2000).

Indian IT industry is considered to be the third most significant foreign exchange earner in the country. On the other hand India has an extreme paucity of IT products and services in the Indian market (and perhaps a big hidden opportunity). There are only 4.5 computers per 1000 people in India, 32 telephones and 3.5 cell phones [Bomsel & Ruet 2001].

While English is understood by less than 5% of the population, operating systems with Indian language support were launched only as late as 2000 and still have only a minuscule installed base. English continues to be the predominant language used even in products such as cell phones and ATMs. How can a country with such a large IT industry harbour such a strange digital divide? Two reasons can be attributed to this divide in India — the off-shoring / outsourcing based business model of the Indian IT industry and the location of HCI research and education within Indian academia.

2.2 The Problems of Off-shoring

In the past two decades, the Indian IT industry has relied on providing quality software services in a cost-effective manner. It has effectively leveraged the huge difference between the labour costs of equivalent skills in India and the developed part of the world. At the lowest end, this required Indian entrepreneurs to market 'skills' to international companies on 'costs plus time basis'. At the highest end, companies get outsourced projects — partly to be executed off-shore in India. The larger the off-shore component, the higher is the profitability. Usually the Indian IT company deals with an IT group within the outsourcing organization. The highest end Indian IT companies have developed excellent software engineering processes to manage such projects effectively — the largest number of 'CMM level 5' companies are from India [NASSCOM 1999].

From the perspective of designing human-computer interaction, this had terrible consequences. By this very nature of their business, a problem typically reached a group within an Indian IT company well after it had been identified and earmarked as 'one that needs solving' and clear enough for outsourcing. Usually (though not always) user requirements were already specified. At times, even the design requirements were ready before an Indian company got involved. This effectively transferred the responsibility of many HCI and usability issues in the first part of the project to the client.

At the end of the development life cycle, the product was developed and evaluated for quality against requirements by the Indian IT company and sent back for 'acceptance testing' to the client. Formal usability evaluations were rarely done until recently. Informal usability evaluations, if at all, were usually carried out as part of acceptance tests and were managed as 'upgrades' or 'change requests' as they were deviations from the original requirements. Trends in the last three years already show changes to this pattern. Many of the top Indian IT companies have started incubating usability groups. Others have started hiring professional interaction designers on freelance basis for critical projects. There seem to be two reasons for this change.

Hopefully assisted by the work of IESUP, awareness about usability and HCI design has increased, not only among the Indian IT companies, but also among their international clients. Along with technical skills, clients now demand to see (though not routinely yet) proven capabilities towards usability and HCI design. Secondly, there is a growing need for Indian companies to move up the value chain — from proven provider of quality skills at highly competitive prices to providers of well-managed outsourced projects to providers of end-to-end solutions.

2.3 HCI Education and Research: The Link with Interaction Design

One strength of the Indian IT community as a whole is a strong educational orientation that produces high-class engineering graduates skilled in computer science. Currently however, very few universities address HCI in their curricula. As we go on to explore, where HCI does exist, it is from within the design area rather than computing / information systems.

In many ways the fact that HCI in Indian academia is rooted in the discipline of design matched well with the themes of the project and the specific personnel involved. One of the themes of IESUP has been the field of Interaction Design — a new arena for teaching, research and development in the HCI field. This topic is emerging as one of the most active areas of HCI in North America and Europe in the past few years, bringing the traditional strengths of the design field — in industrial design, product design, graphic design, and material design — into the HCI field, which had been dominated by people from the human, social and engineering sciences.

Given that the general field of HCI in India is still in its infancy (indeed, part of the rationale for the IESUP effort was to promote HCI and usability in the IT industry and in academia) what was the rationale for including a 'leading-edge' area such as Interaction Design in the IESUP program? This was included on the basis that future IT markets might not simply reproduce existing large industrial markets for large information systems. Rather, consumer electronics, games, personal productivity tools, etc. could become large markets, and in these areas, the boundary between aspects of (industrial) design, usability and software development becomes blurred. Also, given that there was a fledgling interest in HCI in design schools in India, this could be developed further.

While in most parts of the developed world, HCI has become a mainstream activity with HCI courses being offered as an integral part of standard computing curricula, in India, it is still in its infancy. Although developments in field of ergonomics (both in the industry and in academia) highlighted the importance of human-machine interaction in the late 70s (especially with respect to issues of display and control devices), it was the growth of the IT industry in India in the early 90s that has brought HCI to a more prominent position.

Only a few Institutes / Universities in India offer courses in HCI (just one or two basic courses, not full programs), so the IT industry initially struggled to find skilled individuals with HCI expertise for their projects. Graduates with a design background who were already working in the area of usability and user interface design quickly filled this void. The multidisciplinary approach of design education in India — with training in 'problem solving' and 'identifying unmet needs' in addition to 'creativity' and 'artistic expression' has helped design graduates to constantly explore new avenues, including areas of HCI such as usability and more recently, interaction design. The growing demand for HCI professionals in the IT industry has encouraged many people from design backgrounds to 'cross over' into the HCI field, and today the Indian HCI community is dominated by people from design backgrounds.

Recent development in HCI education in India (with the National Institute for Design in Ahmedabad offering a full-time program in HCI and courses being offered by Indian Institute of Technology (IIT) Mumbai and IIT Guwahati) is a welcome and timely step towards the future of computing in India, as it coincides with the emergence of 'interaction design' — signifying a fundamental change in approach to understanding the field of computing. With 'interaction design' advocating 'desirability' and 'user experience' rather than simply the more traditional concerns about 'usability', the potential role of design in computing is coming to the fore. HCI professionals in India, with their background in design, have the potential to play a significant role in this emerging field.

3 Extending the Off-shoring Model: Remote UCSD

An increasing proportion of software development is now moving to low-pay countries to manage the increasing competition in contract software development.

Whilst the dominance of off-shoring / outsourcing has significantly constrained the development of HCI in India, it does lead to a significant research and development issue. How do we integrate sound user centred systems design (UCSD) principles into an outsourcing development approach? Again we were fortunate to have identified UCSD early on in the project and to have project partners actively engaged in the field.

User-Centred Systems Design (UCSD) is an approach to systems development that focuses on the need to develop usable systems and to focus on the users throughout the entire development project. UCSD is all about making the user and their needs the focus of the design process; on the basis that this is the way to build usable systems. We believe that there are further opportunities for the Indian IT-industry to offer competitive advantage in a global market.

Importantly however, for many of India's off-shoring projects the end-user is remote from the development team. But this may not mean that UCSD is impossible. IESUP has enabled us to begin the process of exploring how the concept of 'remote UCSD' could enhance both the range and quality of India's off-shoring IT services. Specifically we are interested in the following issues:

- How to develop systems with an active user focus when the users are thousands of miles away?

- How to organize and distribute usability expertise given the offshore conditions?

- What are the concerns and critical issues for integrating UCSD in offshore development?

3.1 UCSD — Problems in Europe

Even in Europe, usability is still not receiving the attention that it deserves to produce the required impact to software development in practice. Constantly when arguing for usability activities and UCSD in organizations usability professionals come across all sorts of dangerous assumptions about what it is, and scepticism about its benefits and feasibility. We have found the following client responses to be typical:

- Usability increases cost and development time.

- Usability is a subjective quality, everyone has their own opinion about it.

- Specific usability activities are not needed as long as you follow the development process e.g. RUP.

- The most usable system can be defined by a requirements specification.

- Context of use is not essential.

- Style Guides gives the answer to all design problems.

- Usability is about testing.

- There is no such thing as a usable system, it's all about deployment.

- It's better to adapt users to the system than the system to users.

- Engineering the system excludes usability activities.

At the outset of IESUP it was clear to us that not only was the awareness level of HCI and usability in India much less that that in Europe but that these dangerous assumption in Europe were replicated in a much larger way. Of course as HCI professionals we would see usability testing as only one element within a full life-cycle approach user centred design, but it was clear that even at this level there was a great confusion (indeed perceived equivalence) between usability testing and 'acceptance' testing.

3.2 An Agenda for Research and Development

Applying UCSD requires proximity and active engagement of the users [Gulliksen et al. 2003]. One of the challenges of the future is that a large part of the software development will take place at a large distance from the users and without financial opportunities to make developers and users meet. Current efforts in India to address HCI and usability issues in offshore development have been undertaken by some Indian companies such as Cognizant [Henry 2003] and Human Factors International [Shaffer 2004]. Although we believe these efforts are a good start, it is evident that India has a long way to go before HCI and usability is institutionalized within the Indian offshore development process. Essentially we need to develop new methods, tools, processes and roles to address the problem of the distance between users and developers into account

In order to structure a discussion on, and establish an agenda for research and development to address UCSD in the off-shoring model we have utilized Göransson et al.'s [2003] user-centred process framework as provided in Figure 1. We believe that the following are issues of importance relating to the process framework.

3.2.1 Vision

How do we communicate the business objectives to the offshore development team? We know that a shared, mutual understanding of the overall business objectives and visions are important but we know less about how to communicate this in an efficient way.

How can we make the offshore development team understand the business objectives? Communicating the business objectives is one thing but actually giving the offshore team an understanding of this is a lot more difficult.

How can we plan for UCSD? We know that the project plan is the means for getting any response for UCSD activities, so therefore all activities that can be undertaken to facilitate usability activities and split responsibilities is of utmost importance.

3.2.2 Analyse

How do we communicate the richness in the context of use? The users' context of using the system is heavily influenced by the culture, both the organizational culture as well as the essence of the culture of the nation in which the product is meant to be used. We must develop new ways of communicating the richness of the context of use to the offshore development team. Can we make any use of user profiles? Are

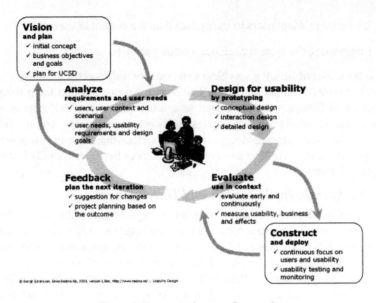

Figure 1: User-centred process framework.

actual users or archetypes the best and most economical way of arriving at a proper analysis of the use situation?

In what ways can we actually facilitate 'meeting users'? We know that meeting real users is essential to actually make a commitment to UCSD. But do we really need to meet the users physically or can we make use of any type of simulations of users?

3.2.3 Design for Usability

Should the design happen with or without users' active participation? Many argue that users should not be involved in the design of their own systems. This is because users are often conservative and work against innovation. But our experience is contrary to this. Users are the people that inevitably know the use situation the best and should therefore be involved to communicate this, often tacit, knowledge. To be able to overcome the conservative factors we might want to work with a specifically selected sample of users and also we need to provide the users with insights into the potential of the new technology.

What tools and techniques would work best for this type of development; lo-fi, high-fi? Low-fidelity techniques such as paper prototyping and cheap mock-ups often serves a better purpose than more advanced tools, simply because user's expectation is that prototypes produced by advanced tools gives you more of a feeling that the design is almost finalized.

How should the design be represented? Users need concrete design representations to predict their future use of the system and developers need more formal specifications. This constitutes a gigantic translation problem between these two very different notations of the design. This problem is not only a problem of offshore development but also a problem of all types of development.

How can we communicate design artefacts? It is said that a picture says more than a thousand words. But, still images do not communicate very well how the developers have intended that the system should be used. We therefore need to develop new notations to accompany these artefacts in order for them to be understood in the intended way. Indian industry has a lot of design knowledge. But when, and how, this knowledge should be used to make the best possible use of it is still unsolved.

3.2.4 Evaluate

How can we recreate the context of use in an offshore setting? We know that the context of use is important for UCSD and since it is not always economically feasible to evaluate the systems in the work setting the questions then becomes how we can mimic these situations in the offshore setting.

The best evaluations are the ones performed with representative users. How can we then recruit users that are representative given the offshore condition? Is it at all possible?

Is it possible to monitor users at a distance? We know that direct contact with users is of utmost importance so therefore we need to investigate ways of putting offshore developers in remote contact with on-site users and provide means for effective, as well as social, contacts between these different groups. This becomes even more difficult given that we have differences in time, cultural differences, etc. Could we make any use of live displays of users or recorded versions of their use? Recorded use situations also have the benefit that you can rewind and re-analyse what actually happened.

Should we use participative methods or more expert-based methods? Expert-based assessments have received a lot of critique lately and do not provide the rich picture of the quality of the system as a user-based assessment does. But, to be able to do this we need to develop ways of performing user-based evaluations remotely.

What are the requirements on the documentation? We know that often a lot of documentation is produced in projects that serve no or little purpose for the developers. Does this change in an offshore condition or will the offshore condition actually make the documentation more needed? Do we need to develop new forms or structures for the documentation?

3.2.5 Feedback

How do we update the specifications? Many of the formative evaluations that are performed during the development project do not result in any changes. We believe that this is because there is usually no specific process for taking care of the evaluation results that have been acquired. We need to decide in what way our response to the evaluation actually should result in any updates to the requirement specifications or whether new negotiations in the contracts are required.

Often evaluations are good at reporting usability problems, but not at proposing any new solution suggestions. The methods used should encourage participants to actually document the potential new ideas of designs that occur during the evaluations, even if this is not included in the methods. One important part of the evaluation is to prioritize and make trade-offs between which problems to actually take care of in the subsequent process. But, there are very few methods of making these decisions, often resulting in only the easy problems to solve being fixed.

The feedback process involves a decision making process in which the actions called upon by the evaluation is decided. Who makes these decisions and who participates in the process? What type of decisions should be made? In many evaluation meetings the documentation of the decisions made is rarely made. As a consequence, whether or not a usability problem is fixed or not is left to chance. Therefore a process for documenting the decisions made must be in place.

In what way do we provide stakeholder feedback? To maintain everybody's confidence in the process we need to communicate back both positive and negative results to the people involved in the process.

What are the implications for project planning and resource allocation? Time and resources must be allocated for the feedback process. Ensuring feedback generates an important extra step in the whole process.

3.2.6 Construct

What is the level of specification details to make good use for the offshore development team? To what extent do the developers need formal descriptions of the design? Model-driven development has received increasing attention lately, and it is tempting to propose such approaches given the offshore conditions. But how do we incorporate usability aspects into such approaches given that they are applied as a standard operating procedure in the project and involved organizations?

Can we make use of a prototype-driven design process? We know that prototyping facilitates user collaboration — but to what extent do prototypes control the rest of the development?

What are the effects of this on the business agreement? How do we handle change management? New methods need to be specified for offshore conditions.

What are the opportunities for incremental deliveries? We know that incremental development with iterative design in each increment is one of the success factors for UCSD, but to what extent can incremental development work in an offshore development project? Can we avoid a waterfall process? Do we have any possibilities whatsoever to iterate?

3.2.7 Cultural Differences in Remote UCSD

Compounding the problems of implementing a UCSD process within a remote context are the additional complexities brought about by cultural differences across a global development environment. Although IT researchers and practitioners have long been aware of the challenges of the global market, there are still many unsolved problems concerning the extent to which culture may affect the development process. Effective strategies that address cultural issues in both the *product* and the *process* of development are now often are critical to systems success.

In relation to the *product* of development, cultural differences in signs, meanings, actions, conventions, norms or values, etc., raise new research issues ranging from technical usability to methodological and ethical issues of culture in information systems. In relation to the *process* of development, cultural differences can affect both the manner in which developers and users are able to collaborate in

UCSD. They can also affect the manner in which users are able to act as subjects in evaluation studies.

In relation to UCSD although most Western software developers would support the underlying concepts and assumptions, these have been derived from USA / Northern European cultures. It is inevitable that those tools and techniques which involve users the most would be those very techniques which were most sensitive to cultural issues and the most susceptible to misinterpretations which could have serious impact on the quality of communication between designers and users. Research into contact between different cultural groups has long recognized the scope for conflict and misunderstandings. Small differences between groups are often exaggerated and distorted to provide a mutually negative image or stereotype based on 'us' and 'them' differentiation. Bochner [1988] showed harmonious relations arise when both parties share a super-ordinate goal — a goal that both groups want to attain and neither can attain if they compete.

3.2.8 Towards a Process Model for rUCSD

Smith et al. [2004] propose a process model for development that addresses cross-cultural issues in design. We are currently seeking to embark on research activities designed to answer questions as identified above with the aim of developing a similar process model for remote user centred systems design (rUCSD). It seems that at the outset there are two very different ways of approaching the problem:

1. Moving towards more model-based development processes in which the on-site team and the offshore team works separately and communicates through formal specifications. Known problems in this approach include the lack of understanding of the documentation among the various stakeholders, the inability to capture all aspects in formal specifications, the increasing need to get a first hand understanding of the context of use and direct contact between developers and users.

2. Increasing the technologies for remote collaboration and developing processes and project organizations to meet these new challenges. This would involve refining video methods to communicate the user's situation and the context of use to developers at a distance and providing opportunities for developers to monitor their systems in use over distance using CSCW systems.

The model itself will need to integrate current practice in UCSD, address the agenda for research discussed above, and recognize the challenges involved in cross-cultural collaborations.

4 India: Where Next for HCI?

In India our discipline has a long way to go, but the design schools that have already taken the initiative in this field and are poised to play a leading role. Education and research is going to be the key for further development in this area. The following issues, in our opinion, are crucial for the growth of HCI in India.

4.1 Ownership and Institutionalization

Essentially IESUP has been preaching the institutionalizing of HCI in India —
supporting national institutions such as the Computer Society of India (India's
representative on IFIP) to take ownership of the discipline. The EU Asia ITC
programme, IFIP and the British Computer Society have been instrumental in
enabling us to make some small contribution here. However we suggest that further
assistance is necessary to facilitate partnership between Indian and European HCI
practitioners, especially those working in academia where funding levels do not
support engagement in the international HCI community at anywhere near the level
experienced by those in Europe.

4.2 Education and Skills Development

Currently, India is struggling with shortage of skilled HCI professionals. Most of
the people working in HCI are self-taught, are working with the IT industry, and
hence cannot spare enough time for education. Short term/long term training of
people already involved in HCI education is immediately required. More educational
institutes in India need to offer courses in HCI. (This raises the problem of the
shortage of skilled professionals who can perform this task.) The curriculum for such
programs needs to be discussed. It is important for the future of interaction design in
India that all concerned arrive at a common understanding of approaches towards
education and research in this field. We suggest that efforts be made to ensure
that HCI be included within the computing curricula of engineering and computing
courses. All computing students should at least be aware of the topic, and know what
they don't know in this area. More specialized courses should also be developed in
particular areas. These could be offered both in computing and in design colleges.

4.3 Localizing Methods to the Indian Context

If HCI is to grow in India it needs to be rooted in the needs of the country. Not only
does this involve the nature of the IT industry itself (the off-shoring nature) but it
also relates to cultural differences between Indian and Western users and developers.
Both of these issues require the localization of methods, the first in relation to the
collaborative (Indian / Western) development of process models for rUCSD and the
second in relation to adapting established HCI tools and techniques to the specific
cultural context.

  The most striking example here is that of user based testing / evaluation
techniques. These are often based upon the concepts of cooperative evaluation
[Carroll & Mack 1984] or contextual inquiry [Beyer & Holtzblatt 1998] and are
embodied in a variety of methods such as thinking-aloud protocols and DUCE [Smith
& Dunckley 2002]. The methods aim to gain meaningful information about the
user's work by empowering the users in direct conversation with the designer on
equal terms. Usability professionals trying to undertake such techniques in Asian
cultures often find that users have particular difficulty [Yeo 2000, 2001]. Users vary
in their ability and willingness to articulate their thoughts to the evaluator depending
on both their individual personality and cultural background.

  As one example of the need for methods localization, within IESUP we were
told by practising usability engineers with experience of both Indian and Western

development projects that the design of task scenarios must be much richer for effective use of verbal protocols with Indian users. With the changing demographics of global computer access and usage we predict that there is much to be gained both nationally and internationally to explore in greater depth the optimum approach to HCI methods in India and neighbouring countries.

5 The Big Picture: Global HCI from the Asian Perspective

Our work in IESUP should be seen in the context of the growth of HCI in other developing countries. In recent years the global HCI community has facilitated communication and collaboration between key Western experts and those in developing countries (e.g. CHI2004 Development Consortium) such as South Africa, Russia and China and Eastern European countries. In addition collaboration is required with more developed (both in HCI and wider terms) Asia countries such as Singapore. Collaboration at this level is not only necessary to address the IT development agenda discussed in this paper but also the wider issues relating to our communities contribution to the elimination of the digital divide.

In the very recent years, there has been a visible momentum within India towards building a national agenda for addressing the issues concerning user demographics, and the emerging information society. India faces monumental social challenges and is hampered by bureaucracy, political strife and the legacies of a controlled economy. Yet the nation is endowed with so many highly trained, ICT workers that many believe technology will launch India into the developed world.

In the emerging Indian information society 'design for all' is the conscious and systematic effort to apply principles, methods and tools, in order to develop information technology and communications products and services which are accessible and usable by all citizens.

Within IESUP we were impressed by a range of innovative human-computer solutions being developed to support the needs of the urban and rural poor across India, only a few of which have received publication in Western / international publications. We believe that western HCI professionals have much to learn from the Indian experience in relation to the development of usable artifact within the increasingly global information society.

Acknowledgements

We wish to thank the EC Asia ITC programme for part financing the IESUP Project. We would also like to acknowledge the underpinning contributions of Kaushik Ghosh, Anirudha Joshi and Parag Deshpande in producing this paper. We would also like to acknowledge the contribution of these and so many others in India, most notably Sanjay Prasad and Iqbal Ahmed in helping make IESUP such a success.

References

Beyer, H. & Holtzblatt, K. [1998], *Contextual Design: Defining Customer-centered Systems*, Morgan-Kaufmann.

Bochner, S. [1988], *Cultures In Contact*, Pergamon Press.

Bomsel, O. & Ruet, J. [2001], Digital India — Report on the Indian IT industry, http://www.cerna.ensmp.fr/Documents/DigitalIndia-MainFindings.pdf (last accessed 2005-02-03). CERNA, Centre d'economie industrielle.

Carroll, J. M. & Mack, R. L. [1984], Learning to Use a Word Processor: By Doing, By Thinking and By Knowing, *in* J. C. Tomas & M. L. Schneider (eds.), *Human Factors in Computer Systems*, Ablex, pp.13–51.

Gulliksen, J., Göransson, B., Boivie, I., Blomkvist, S., Persson, J. & Cajander, Å. [2003], Key Principles for User-centred Systems Design, *Behaviour & Information Technology* 22(6), 397–409. In special section "Designing IT for Healthy Work".

Göransson, B., Gulliksen, J. & Boivie, I. [2003], The Usability Design Process - Integrating User-Centered Systems Design in the Software Development Process, *Software Process: Improvement and Practice* 8(2), 111–31.

Henry, P. [2003], Advancing UCD While Facing Challenges Working from Offshore, *Interactions* 10(2), 38–47.

NASSCOM [1999], NASSCOM-McKinsey Report 2002, Technical Report, National Association of Software and Service Companies.

NASSCOM [2002], Indian IT Industry, http://www.nasscom.org/Download/ITIndustry.pdf (retrieved 2002-03-05).

Nielsen, J. [2002], Offshore usability, http://www.useit.com/altertbox/20020916.html (retrieved 2002-10-10). Alertbox, September 2002.

Shaffer, E. [2004], *Institutionalization of Usability. A Step by Step Guide*, Pearson Education.

Smith, A., Dunckley, L., French, T., Minocha, S. & Chang, Y. [2004], A Process Model for Developing Usable Cross-cultural Websites, *Interacting with Computers* 16(1), 63–91.

Smith, A. & Dunckley, L. [2002], Early Prototype Evaluation and Redesign: Structuring the Design Space through Contextual Techniques, *Interacting with Computers* 16(6), 821–43.

Yeo, A. [2000], Usability Evaluation in Malaysia, *in* K. Y. Lim (ed.), *Proceedings of the 4th Asia–Pacific Conference on Computer–Human Interaction (APCHI 2000) and 6th SE Asian Ergonomics Society Conference (Asean Ergonomics 2000)*, Elsevier, pp.275–80.

Yeo, A. W. [2001], Global-software Development Lifecycle: An Exploratory Study, *in* J. A. Jacko, A. Sears, M. Beaudouin-Lafon & R. J. K. Jacob (eds.), *Proceedings of SIGCHI Conference on Human Factors in Computing Systems (CHI'01)*, *CHI Letters* 3(1), ACM Press, pp.104–11.

Visualizing the Evolution of HCI

Chaomei Chen, Gulshan Panjwani, Jason Proctor, Kenneth Allendoerfer, Jasna Kuljis[†], Serge Aluker, David Sturtz & Mirjana Vukovic

College of Information Science and Technology, Drexel University, Philadelphia, PA 19104–2875, USA

Tel: *+1 215 895 6627*

Fax: *+1 215 895 2494*

Email: *chaomei.chen@cis.drexel.edu*

URL: *http://www.pages.drexel.edu/~cc345*

[†] *School of Information Systems, Computing and Mathematics, Brunel University, Uxbridge, Middlesex UB8 3PH, UK*

A study of the evolution of the HCI community is described based on information extracted from leading HCI journals. The study includes a traditional author co-citation analysis and a progressive domain visualization of a co-authorship network of 3,620 authors and a 1,038-node hybrid network of topical terms and cited articles. Emerging trends and prominent patterns of these networks are identified and compared with an existing survey of the field. The study contributes to the understanding of HCI at a macroscopic level as well as to the improvement of methodological implications.

Keywords: HCI and other communities, social network analysis, author co-citation analysis, co-citation networks.

1 Introduction

Human-Computer Interaction (HCI) is an interdisciplinary field. It takes years to educate and train an HCI expert and even longer to develop a thorough understanding of the subject matter as a whole and a visionary grasp of the past, present, and future of challenging issues and important directions. In many scientific fields, knowledge advances so fast that scientists must rely on comprehensive surveys and literature reviews to update their mental big picture of the field [Price 1965].

The literature of published articles in a field of study is a valuable resource for the scientific community. Scientists document and archive their work in their publications. Furthermore, scientists often make significant connections that may not previously have been conceivable, from connections within a field to connections across different disciplines. When scientists make references to earlier contributions, their behaviour can be seen as an endorsement of the significance of underlying issues. When a domain expert is preparing a subject matter review, the literature has an invaluable role to play. The expert would typically conduct thorough searches for relevant articles that were ever published on the subject. Then the expert would digest a large amount of articles; hundreds of articles would not be uncommon. The expert would augment her own view of the subject with details from these articles and develop themes that can tie the pieces together. Such surveys tend to cite more than 100 articles. The process is time consuming and subject to the biases of individual experts. By the time it is done, it may need substantial update. Finally, such surveys may not exist at all simply because no one commits to the daunting task.

Comprehensive surveys of scientific literature compiled by experts are indispensable to the growth of the scientific community. For example, such surveys tend to identify trends and make predictions. In this article, we describe an approach that is still being iteratively developed to facilitate both experts and novices to form a big picture of their field based on visual exploration of the literature.

The goal of our approach is to enable domain experts to quickly narrow down thousands of articles on a given subject to a small number of high-quality articles. These high-quality articles, along with emerging patterns of how they are perceived by fellow researchers in the field, are used to form a concise representation of the field. Our vision is that such approaches will largely simplify the time-consuming task of locating important articles in the literature. Furthermore, we expect that, because the automated process can be repeated easily, one would be able to take a snapshot of an evolving field more frequently. The big pictures produced by such an approach are expected to provide scientists and practitioners insights into how a scientific community communicates. The work has its own implications for HCI. The design of the visualization component and associated task analysis all pose new challenges to HCI.

The focus of this article is on the extent to which the approach can reveal significant structures and trends in the HCI literature. Five high-impact-factor HCI journals were identified as the input sources. All articles published in these journals were used to generate a co-authorship network and a hybrid network of topic terms and cited articles. The networks were visualized and analysed to identify interesting patterns and emergent trends. John Carroll's survey of HCI was used as our gold standard to interpret the resultant visualizations [Carroll 1997, 2001].

The rest of the article is organized as follows: first, we describe the method to be used; second, we describe the data and details of modelling and visualization;

third, we explain prominent structures, patterns, and trends found in the visualized networks; and fourth, we compare Carroll's survey with the resultant networks.

2 Methods

The study has three components:

1. A traditional author co-citation analysis.

2. A progressive knowledge domain visualization study.

3. A comparison with the comprehensive survey of the evolution of HCI [Carroll 1997, 2001].

2.1 A Traditional Author Co-citation Analysis (ACA)

We followed the standard bibliometric procedure described in White & McCain [1998]. We asked a group of HCI experts to identify the most relevant HCI journals from a list of candidate journals. The following 10 journals were chosen for the author co-citation analysis:

1. Behaviour & Information Technology.

2. Human–Computer Interaction.

3. IEEE Transaction on Systems, Man & Cybernetics.

4. International Journal of Man–Machine Studies.

5. Perception and Psychophysics.

6. Interacting with Computers.

7. User Modelling and User-adapted Interaction.

8. International Journal of Human–Computer Interaction.

9. Interfaces.

10. International Journal of Human–Computer Studies.

The 60 most-cited authors in the 10 journals were identified using the science citation database SciSearch. Next, the search was extended to all journals indexed in SciSearch to obtain the co-citation counts among the 60 authors. The 60 most-cited authors in the expanded search were used in the subsequent analysis. Traditionally, the number of authors is arbitrarily selected, although this process tends to become substantially time consuming with large numbers of authors. The search led to a 60-by-60 author co-citation matrix. A multidimensional scaling (MDS) solution was derived to represent the co-citation relationships between these authors.

Journal	Range	Articles
Human-Computer Interaction (HCI)	1994–2004	139
International Journal of Human-Computer Studies (IJHCS) — formerly International Journal of Man–Machine Studies (IJMMS)	1980–2004	1651
International Journal on Human-Computer Interaction (IJHCI)	1994–2004	232
Interacting with Computers (IwC)	1992–1999	254
	2002–2004	
User Modelling and User-Adapted Interaction (UM)	2001–2004	33
Total	1980–2004	2309

Table 1: Six HCI journals used in the knowledge domain visualization.

2.2 Progressive Knowledge Domain Visualization

The second part of the study is a progressive, knowledge-domain visualization of co-authorship relationships and article-term relationships [Chen 2004, in press]. Prominent patterns and emerging trends in a co-authorship network and a hybrid network of topical terms and cited articles were identified and discussed.

Six HCI journals of high impact factor were identified using the Journal Citation Report (JCR). Bibliographic records of articles in these journals were retrieved from the Web of Science (See Table 1).

The six HCI journals consisted of 2,309 articles. A co-authorship network was generated first. To qualify for the network, an author must have had at least one cited article in at least one year during the period between 1980 and 2004.

The second task was to generate a hybrid network that could represent emergent trends as well as prominent patterns concerning the big picture of HCI. The network was constructed based on fast-growing topical terms and co-cited articles. A subset of topical terms used in the titles, abstracts, and keyword lists of the 2,309 articles were selected by a burst detection algorithm [Kleinberg 2002], such that topical terms associated with a sharp increase in popularity were selected to represent emergent trends [Chen 2004, in press]. Articles cited by the 2,309 articles were selected if their citation counts exceeded citation thresholds varying across the 1980–2004 range. The entire range was divided into 25 time slices. Each time slice corresponded to one year. Since the general volume of the literature increases over time, an incremental threshold scheme was used, such that low threshold levels were used in the earlier time slices and high threshold levels were used in more recent time slices. Within each time slice, an associative network was constructed with two types of nodes: topical terms and cited articles. The two node types led to three link types:

1. Term-term.

2. Article-article.

3. Term-article.

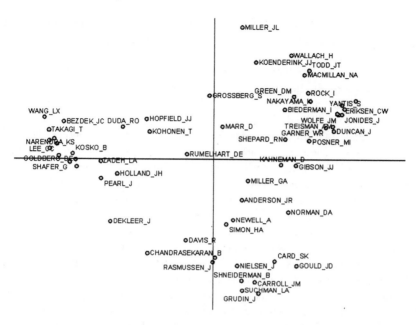

Figure 1: A multidimensional scaling solution of the 60 authors based on their co-citation relationships. Three clusters: left, upper right, and lower right.

The term-term links were between co-occurring terms, i.e. if two terms were found in the same article published in an HCI journal, for example, the term *website* and the term *evaluation* were found in the same article. The article-article links were between two articles that were cited together by articles in the five HCI journals. The term-article links were between a term *t* and an article *a*, such that the term *t* was in an article that cited article *a*. The time series of networks from all time slices were merged into a network that represents the entire period of time.

The resultant networks were visualized to reveal the citation and co-citation structure of the HCI literature. The entire procedure was automated [Chen in press]. Network visualizations were enhanced by highlighting high centrality nodes, which are regarded as playing salient roles in the global topological structure of a network. Emerging trends and prominent patterns in these networks were shown as timed links progressing from one time slice to another.

3 Results

3.1 Author Co-Citation Analysis

The multidimensional scaling (MDS) solution of the 60 authors' co-citation image suggests three groups of authors: the left, the upper right and the lower right ones (See Figure 1). The meaning of each grouping was identified by additional searches. A domain expert is expected to recognize a substantial number of the authors, whereas it could mean very little to a newcomer to a domain, which is one of the major inadequacies of the traditional ACA approach. The following interpretations were offered by three of the authors of this article, based on their own knowledge and additional searches.

Authors in the left half of the map are known for their work in Artificial Intelligence, especially fuzzy logic and fuzzy systems. Zadeh, just below the X axis, is best known for the idea of fuzziness. This group also includes names such as Kohonen, Duda, Pearl, and Shafer.

The upper right group includes Posner, near the X axis, Garner, Treisman, Duncan, Yantis. These names are usually associated with research on attention, visual attention, and visual search. Some were interested in neurograph, some in computer vision based on human cognitive models. Garner and Gibson, slightly below the X axis, were associated with writings on perception in the 1950s. On the X axis, near to Gibson, Kahneman was interested in decision making and uncertainty. Further to the south, there is Miller, the principle investigator of the WordNet project. Below Miller, Anderson was associated with cognition and learning. Gibson, Miller, Kahneman, and Anderson are prominent figures in cognitive psychology and cognitive science. Rumelhart, near to the origin in the upper left quadrant, is a founder of connectionism. It makes sense to see Kohonen nearby.

The lower right group includes Newell, Simon, Norman, Card, Nielsen, Gould, Shneiderman, Carroll, Suchman, and Grudin. Newell and Simon were famous for their work in artificial intelligence and fundamental cognitive science.

In summary, the MDS provides a loosely defined structure based on author co-citation profiles. Interpretations are primarily subjective because little information is directly available from the map. The following findings, produced by progressive knowledge-domain visualization, provide explicit and additional information concerning the time and nature of various groupings. The findings were obtained from a substantially larger sample of articles.

3.2   Co-authorship Network

A co-authorship network of 3,620 authors was generated for the period of 1980–2004. An author must be cited at least once in any of the time slices to be included in the network. The network contains a total of 5,401 co-authorship links. All links were preserved in the visualization of the network.

The 3,620-author co-authorship network can be seen as a social network. The largest component of a network and the longest path in such networks tend to reveal some interesting insights into the underlying phenomenon. The largest component of the 3,620-author network contains slightly more than 400 authors, which is more than 10% of the size of the entire network. The largest component consists of two branches and a dense cluster of 120 authors. One of the branches forms the longest path. A visualization of the co-authorship network is shown in Figure 2. The size of a circle denotes the number of articles that a given author published in the 5 HCI journals. The colour of a link shows the first time the two connected authors published an article together. The colours of an author show the number of articles the author published over time. The time-coloured rings progress inside out.

The largest co-authorship chain is highlighted in Figure 3. The path starts with Sutcliffe_A from the left and ends with the dense cluster of authors in the

Figure 2: The co-authorship network of 3,620 authors, including 5,401 co-authorship links (1980–2004). The image at the lower left corner shows the snapshot of an earlier stage of the layout process. The finalized layout is shown in the larger image. The largest component of the network is essentially in the upper left quadrant. The dense cluster of 120 authors is located in the centre.

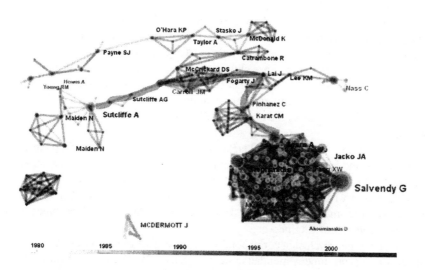

Figure 3: The largest component contains approximately 400 authors among the total of 3,620 authors. Salvendy, Stephanidis, and Jacko are prominent members of the 120-author cluster.

lower middle. There are a number of small clusters along the path. The following discussions will focus on the key points on the main path. Starting with Sutcliffe, the path includes Carroll, Fogarty, Lai, Pinhanez, Karat, and Sears as its key elements. The path is connected to the dense cluster via Sears. Within the dense cluster, Salvendy, Stephanidis, and Jacko are prominent cluster members in terms the size of their nodes. Some name labels in the image were added by hand for improved readability. The software, called *CiteSpace*[1], also produced visualization images in full colour.

To illustrate the type of information one can find from such visualizations, we traverse the path from Sutcliffe to Sears and to the 120-author cluster. For each co-authorship link on the main path, we located articles in the dataset as evidence. Authors off the main path will not be discussed in this article.

The first co-authorship link between Sutcliffe_AG and Carroll_JM was due to a 1999 article in IJHCS [Sutcliffe & Carroll 1999]. Sutcliffe_AG was in City University, England and Carroll_JM was in Virginia Tech, USA. The article describes reusable claims as a repository of HCI knowledge.

Carroll_JM and Fogarty_J are linked in the map because of a 2001 article in IJHCS on MOOsburg [Carroll et al. 2001]. All the authors were with Virginia Tech. The co-authorship link between Fogarty_J and Lai_J was because of a 2004 article in IJHCS [Fogarty et al. 2004]. Instead of Virginia Tech, Fogarty's more recent affiliation became Carnegie Mellon University. Lai_J's affiliation on this article was also Carnegie Mellon University. It is interesting to note that the third author was from IBM TJ Watson Research Center. The co-authorship link between Lai_J and Pinhanez_C led to a 2002 article [Lai et al. 2002]. Lai's affiliation on this article was IBM TJ Watson Research Center.

Pinhanez_C and Karat_CM are connected by a 2002 IJHCS article [Karat et al. 2002]; IBM TJ Watson was their affiliation. The connection between Karat_CM and Sears_A was established by a 2003 article in HCI [Sears et al. 2003].

Sears_A belongs to the dense cluster of authors. An interesting question would be what brings these authors together? In this article, we address some simple questions. Who are the prominent authors in this cluster? What articles did they co-author in the dataset? Does the cluster imply an emergent trend or even a paradigm shift in HCI?

A 20-author IJHCI article [Jacko et al. 2002], including Stephanidis_C, Salvendy_G, and Sears_A, in part explains the multiple connections. Stephanidis_C introduced the concept of 'User Interfaces for All' in 1995. Salvendy_G is the founding editor of the *International Journal on Human-Computer Interaction and Human Factors and Ergonomics in Manufacturing*. He is also a member of the National Academy of Engineering.

Does the dense cluster correspond to an emergent trend? Given the research interests of its prominent members, such as Salvendy_G and Stephanidis_C, we conjecture that the cluster might be related to *ubiquitous computing or user interfaces for all*. To verify this conjecture, we examine a hybrid network of cited articles and abruptly rising topical terms. We expect to find the presence of *ubiquitous computing or user interfaces for all* in the hybrid network.

---

[1]CiteSpace is available at http://cluster.cis.drexel.edu/~cchen/citespace

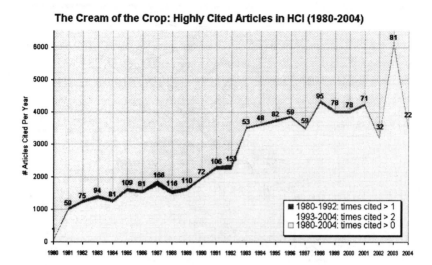

Figure 4: A total of 1,038 unique articles at the top layer are featured in the visualization, including 2,759 associative links.

3.3 Emerging Trends and Prominent Patterns

A 1,038-node hybrid network of topical terms and cited articles was visualized (See Figure 4 and Figure 5). The network contains two types of nodes: terms and articles. A link between a term and an article indicates that the term was found to be cited in the article. A link between two articles denotes a co-citation link; in other words, the two articles were cited together by other articles.

The process was configured as follows. The 25-year time span was divided into 25 time slices from 1980 through 2004. Three sets of thresholds were chosen for the first, the middle, and the last slices; and threshold levels for the remaining slices were obtained by linear interpolation. The three sets of thresholds were (2, 2, 20), (3, 2, 30), and (3, 3, 40), where the first number in a group is a citation threshold level, the second number is a co-citation threshold, and the third is a co-citation coefficient. For example, if (2, 2, 20) is assigned to a slice, it means that within the slice, an article needs to be cited at least twice, co-cited with at least two other articles, and its normalized co-citation coefficient is 0.20 or greater. It took 25 seconds to produce the visualization of the network of 1,038 nodes and 2,759 links.

Figure 5 shows a grey-scale version of the visualization. The legend bar on the top of the figure shows the time-coded grey-scale levels from 1980 through 2004. Therefore, lighter lines in the image were made earlier than darker lines. Similarly, lighter rings denote earlier citations than darker rings. In other words, recent patterns and emerging trends should be represented by darker shades.

Three types of information in the image are of particular interest:

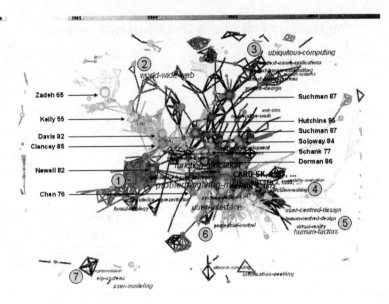

Figure 5: Seven areas of interest in a hybrid term-and-article network (Nodes = 1,038, Links = 2,759). Hubs are shown with purple rings, including three most prominent articles at the centre, Card et al. [1983], Newell & Simon [1972], and Nielsen [1993].

1. Topical terms.

2. Hub articles.

3. Areas.

Some of the topical terms are shown in Figure 5. Given that all selected topical terms demonstrated sharp increases in their popularity, they can be seen as tokens of emerging trends. Because they are directly connected to the cited articles in the network, topical terms provide direct evidence for us to interpret the nature of a link and even that of a cluster.

Hub articles were those with high centrality. They are shown as a circle with an extra purple ring and a label such as (0.14), which is the value of its centrality. Fifteen such articles are marked in the figure. For example, [Zadeh 1965] denotes a 1965 article by Zadeh. The citations of the articles and their centrality are summarized in Table 2.

The third type of information is areas identified by circled numbers (1–7) in the Figure. These numbers identify areas of a trend in the past or an emerging trend. The nature of such an area can be characterized by corresponding topical terms and hub articles.

Seven areas of interest are marked in Figure 5. Each area is identified in connection with a number of topical terms and prominent articles. The seven areas are:

# Citation	Centrality	Author	Year
144	0.38	Card SK	1983
91	0.22	Newell A	1972
72	0.02	Nielsen J	1993
44	0.06	Suchman L	1987
40	0.19	Suchman LA	1987
40	0.07	Norman DA	1986
35	0.11	Zadeh LA	1965
34	0.12	Newell A	1982
33	0.14	Kelly GA	1955
33	0.12	Schank RC	1977
31	0.22	Clancey WJ	1985
30	0.09	Hutchins E	1995
28	0.11	Davis R	1982
25	0.05	Soloway E	1984
22	0.06	Chen PPS	1976

Table 2: The 15 marked hub articles in the hybrid network.

1. Knowledge representation and problem solving methods.

2. The World Wide Web.

3. Ubiquitous computing and context-aware computing.

4. Usability evaluation.

5. User-centred design.

6. Perceptual control.

7. Enterprise resource planning.

The core of HCI, at the centre of the network, is featured by three overwhelmingly prominent articles: Card et al. [1983], Newell & Simon [1972], and Nielsen [1993]. The citations to these three were so high that we did not attempt to specify the nature of such references. We conjecture instead that the three masterpieces formed the cornerstones of HCI. By examining other emerging trends, we expect to improve our understanding of the roots of HCI.

1. Knowledge representation and problem solving methods. The hub article in this area includes [Newell 1982], [Clancey 1985], and [Davis & Lenat 1982]. Moving upwards, we found a branch stretching to the upper left corner, containing [Zadeh 1965], and [Kelly 1955].

2. The World Wide Web. The topical word world-wide-web in this area points to [Bush 1945] and [Berners-Lee et al. 1994]. Earlier hypertext articles are also concentrated in this area, including [Conklin 1987] and [Halasz 1988].

3. Ubiquitous computing and context aware computing. This area is highlighted by terms such as ubiquitous-computing, context-aware-systems, context-aware-computing, and context-aware-applications. This area includes [Dey et al. 2001] and [Dourish 2001]. This area appears to be rooted in the main HCI continent via a hub article [Suchman 1987]. There is another entry for the same book, nearer to the centre of the structure. The connection between situated actions and context aware computing appears to be evident. [Hutchins 1995] is another hub article, which should be also important to ubiquitous computing. An earlier footprint in the adjacent area was made by group support systems. A lighter grey area is partially covered by the context-aware-systems term. Its colour is lighter than the ubiquitous computing area, suggesting that it was an earlier trend in the evolution of HCI. Articles here include [Short et al. 1976], [Bly et al. 1993], [Keisler et al. 1984], and [Nunamaker et al. 1991].

4. Usability evaluation. [Cohen 1960] and [Nielsen & Mack 1994] are the highly cited members of this area. The area is connected to the core of HCI via [Gray & Salzman 1998], which turns out to be a review of experiments that compare usability evaluation methods.

5. User centred design. This area is characterized by terms such as user-cantered-design, human-centred-design, human-factors, and virtual-reality. Articles in this area include [Card et al. 1978], [Shneiderman 1998], [Cuff 1980], [Gaines 1981], and a 1992 edition of Shneiderman's *Designing User Interfaces*. [Gaines 1981] also has a centrality of 0.08. An interesting observation is the frequent British spelling of the word 'centred', which suggests that there was a trend of articles being published by British HCI researchers.

6. Perceptual control. This is a relatively small area compared with the others. It is interesting because it is connected to the primarily light grey area of the core HCI. Cited articles in this area include [Powers 1978] and [Engel & Haakma 1993]. [Taylor 1988] appears to be a main connection between this area and the core HCI; the article was about layered protocols for computer-human dialogue.

7. Enterprise resource planning. This area is currently isolated from the largest component of the HCI network. [Davenport 1998] and [Sumner 1999] are included in this area.

The hybrid network reveals a rich body of information concerning the evolution of HCI. Ubiquitous computing, rooted in situated actions and context aware computing, is indeed shown as an emerging trend, which echoes the dense cluster of 120 highly collaborating HCI authors we found in the co-authorship network of HCI. The findings of the three networks, namely a traditional author co-citation network of 60 authors, a co-authorship network of 3,620 authors, and a hybrid network of 1,038 topical terms and cited articles, are discussed with reference to a leading HCI expert's account of the evolution of HCI [Carroll 1997].

4 Discussions

Carroll identified four roots of HCI [Carroll 2001] and suggested that the evolution of HCI can be seen as being driven by a grand challenge of bringing them together. The four roots were identified as follows:

1. Prototyping and iterative development from software engineering.

2. Software psychology and human factors of computing systems.

3. User interface software from computer graphics.

4. Models, theories, and frameworks from cognitive science.

To verify and evaluate the viability of our methods, we need to address the extent to which one can identify the four roots in the visualizations of the HCI literature. The present study only used a limited part of the HCI literature, namely only from 10 journals in author co-citation analysis and 5 journals in the second part of the study. Publications in the ACM SIGCHI conference series are currently not included. We are planning to expand the coverage of the data in further studies in the near future. In the following discussions, we should bear this limitation in mind. On the other hand, the data we used in this study ranges from 1980 through 2004, whereas Carroll's review was published in 1997 [Carroll 1997] and updated in 2001 [Carroll 2001]; we expect that we may see some emerging trends that were not covered in the 2001 update. [Carroll 1997] cited 136 references, 43 of which were also found in the hybrid network in this study. The mean of citations across the 1,038-node network is 7.96 (standard deviation of 8.75). In contrast, the mean of citations of articles in both the network and Carroll's reference list is 20.7 (standard deviation of 25.4). At least for the topics common to both Carroll's review and our network, articles picked by Carroll tend to have 2 or 3 times more citations. This interesting finding shows the indispensable value of comprehensive surveys conducted by leading experts.

The Carroll review identified that user-centred system development was a framework that was intended to integrate the two foci of methods and software in the broader context of the first root. In earlier sections, we identified user-centred design as one of the seven areas in the hybrid network.

The closest connection was found with the 4th root — Models, Theories, and Frameworks. The prominent example given by Carroll in his review is the GOMS model for analysing routine human-computer interactions. Carroll cited [Card et al. 1983], which is shown as the most highly cited article in the hybrid network. With reference to Carroll's review, the core HCI identified in our visualization appears to be the foundations of HCI in terms of models, theories, and frameworks.

The trend of universal access is relatively easy to notice because of the prominent dense cluster in the co-authorship network. The unusually large number of co-authoring clusters tends to be a sign of a large movement involving many people. Co-authorship network visualization, especially analysing the largest component and the longest paths, appears to be an effective and interesting way to learn the structure of invisible colleges in a field. The two articles, [Stephanidis et al. 1998] and [Stephanidis et al. 1999], can be identified as the white papers of the universal access movement.

The primary strength of this approach is the provision of a tool that enables a wide variety of users to explore the dynamics of their domain literature. The tool can largely reduce the complexity of literature survey tasks by identifying potentially important articles from a vast body of publications. The tool also provides researchers with an alternative perspective so that they can cross reference issues identified in literature surveys conducted in traditional methods and those identified in the knowledge-domain visualization approach.

This approach is quantitative in nature. It has limitations and weaknesses. For example, what is visualized is determined by what input is provided to the system. To an extent, the views of domain experts are already reflected in the visualized patterns because they represent an abstraction of the latent, collective, and accumulative citing patterns. On the other hand, the selection of journals based on journal citation impact ratings may lead to a visualization that could considerably differ from a visualization based on a different source, for example, articles published in HCI conference proceedings as we mentioned earlier. As one reviewer pointed out, long-term interests in the literature may not be sufficiently reflected in the visualizations because of the emphasis on burst terms, although long-term interests could be represented by clusters of cited articles.

Domain analysis typically raises issues beyond the knowledge domain *per se*. One researcher may be particularly pleased and willing to accept the validity of a given visualization because his/her work is prominently featured. In contrast, one may be reluctant to do so if the visualization is considerably different from his/her mental model. Users should bear these factors in mind when using such visualizations. We recommend a hybrid methodology that combines quantitative and qualitative perspectives [Hjorland & Albrechtsen 1995].

5 Conclusions

In conclusion, the study has enabled us to compare the big pictures of HCI as it is delineated by different methods. Co-authorship networks and hybrid networks of topical terms and co-cited articles are a valuable tool for both experienced domain experts and relatively inexperienced newcomers. For domain experts, the tool can reduce the burden of locating various potentially relevant articles and help select high quality publications from the much larger pool of published articles. Because the method is much less expensive compared to a conventional expert review, it can be operated repeatedly and periodically. For newcomers to a field, the method can provide a guided tour of the landmarks of a field.

In terms of future work, it would be valuable to compile a comprehensive dataset of the HCI literature. Our next goal is to investigate quantitative approaches to the identification of patterns and emerging trends that may not yet form a prominent profile. This is a significant technical challenge as we acknowledge the fact that visualizations generated by the current method tend to be overwhelmed by a few high-profile articles, whereas low-profile ones tend to be underrepresented or undetected. A potential contribution to the field of HCI as a whole is to improve the understanding and recognition of HCI to a wider public and to people who know little about the field of HCI.

HCI is such an interdisciplinary, ubiquitous, and evolving field that it is vital to maintain a big picture of its growth. The examples, as shown in this study, invite new perspectives of HCI so that one can develop more usable and useful tools.

References

Berners-Lee, T., Cailliau, R., Luotonen, A., Nielsen, H. F. & Secret, A. [1994], The World-Wide Web, *Communications of the ACM* **37**(8), 76–82.

Bly, S., Harrison, S. R. & Irwin, S. [1993], Media Spaces: Bringing People Together in a Video, Audio and Computing Environment, *Communications of the ACM* **36**(1), 28–47.

Bush, V. [1945], As We May Think, *Atlantic Monthly* **176**(1), 101–8.

Card, S. K., English, W. K. & Burr, B. J. [1978], Evaluation of Mouse, Rate-controlled Isometric Joystick, Step-keys and Text Keys for Text Selection on a CRT, *Ergonomics* **21**(8), 601–13.

Card, S. K., Moran, T. P. & Newell, A. [1983], *The Psychology of Human–Computer Interaction*, Lawrence Erlbaum Associates.

Carroll, J. M. [1997], Human–Computer Interaction: Psychology as a Science of Design, *International Journal of Human–Computer Studies* **46**(4), 501–22.

Carroll, J. M. [2001], The Evolution of Human–Computer Interaction, http://www.awprofessional.com/articles/article.asp?p=24103 (retrieved 2004-10-02).

Carroll, J. M., Rosson, M. B., Isenhour, P., Ganoe, C., Dunlap, D., Fogarty, J., Schafer, W. & van Metre, C. [2001], Designing our Town: MOOsburg, *International Journal of Human–Computer Studies* **54**(3), 725–51.

Chen, C. [2004], Searching for Intellectual Turning Points: Progressive Knowledge Domain Visualization, *Proceedings of the National Academy of Sciences* **101**(Suppl.1), 5303–10.

Chen, C. [in press], CiteSpace II: Detecting and Visualizing Emerging Trends and Transient Patterns in Scientific Literature, *Journal of the American Society for Information Science and Technology* .

Clancey, W. J. [1985], Heuristic Classification, *Artificial Intelligence* **27**(3), 289–350.

Cohen, J. [1960], A Coefficient of Agreement for Nominal Scales, *Edicational and Psychological Measurement* **20**(1), 37–46.

Conklin, J. [1987], Hypertext: An Introduction and Survey, *IEEE Computer* **20**(9), 17–41.

Cuff, R. N. [1980], On Casual Users, *International Journal of Man–Machine Studies* **12**(2), 163–87.

Davenport, T. H. [1998], Putting the Enterprise into the Enterprise System, *Harvard Business Review* **76**(4), 121–31.

Davis, R. & Lenat, D. B. [1982], *Knowledge-based Systems in Artificial Intelligence: Two Case Studies*, McGraw-Hill.

Dey, A. K., Salber, D. & Abowd, G. D. [2001], A Conceptual Framework and a Toolkit for Supporting the Rapid Prototyping of Context-aware Applications, *Human–Computer Interaction* **16**(2-4), 97–166.

Dourish, P. [2001], Seeking a Foundation for Context-aware Computing, *Human–Computer Interaction* **16**(2-4), 229.

Engel, F. L. & Haakma, R. [1993], Expectations and Feedback in User–System Communication, *International Journal of Man–Machine Studies* **39**(3), 427–52.

Fogarty, J., Lai, J. & Christensen, J. [2004], Presence vs. Availability: The Design and Evaluation of a Context-aware Communication Client, *International Journal of Human–Computer Studies* **61**(3), 299–317.

Gaines, B. R. [1981], The Technology of Interaction-dialogue Programming Rules, *International Journal of Man–Machine Studies* **14**(1), 133–50.

Gray, W. D. & Salzman, M. C. [1998], Damaged Merchandise? A Review of Experiments that Compare Usabilty Evaluation Methods, *Human–Computer Interaction* **13**(3), 203–61.

Halasz, F. [1988], Reflections on NoteCards: Seven Issues for the Next Generation of Hypermedia Systems, *Communications of the ACM* **31**(7), 836–52.

Hjorland, B. & Albrechtsen, H. [1995], Toward a New Horizon in Information Science: Domain Analysis, *Journal of the American Society for Information Science* **46**(6), 400–25.

Hutchins, E. [1995], *Cognition in the Wild*, MIT Press.

Jacko, J., Salvendy, G., Sainfort, F., Emery, V., Akoumianakis, D., Duffy, V., Ellison, J., Gant, D., Gill, Z., Ji, Y., Jones, P., Karsh, B., Karshmer, A., Lazar, J., Peacock, B., Resnick, M., Sears, A., Smith, M., Stephanidis, C. & Ziegler, J. [2002], Intranets and Organizational Learning: A Research and Development Agenda, *International Journal of Human–Computer Interaction* **14**(1), 93–130.

Karat, C. M., Karat, J., Vergo, J., Pinhanez, C., Riecken, D. & Cofino, T. [2002], That's Entertainment! Designing Streaming, Multimedia Web Experiences, *International Journal of Human–Computer Interaction* **14**(3-4), 369–84.

Keisler, S., Siegal, J. & McGuire, T. W. [1984], Social Psychological Aspects of Computer Mediated Communication, *American Psychologist* **39**(10), 1123–34.

Kelly, G. A. [1955], *The Psychology of Personal Constructs*, Norton Publishing.

Kleinberg, J. [2002], Bursty and Hierarchical Structure in Streams, *in* D. Hand, D. Keim & R. Ng (eds.), *Proceedings of the eighth ACM SIGKDD International Conference on Knowledge Discovery and Data Mining*, ACM Press, pp.91–101.

Lai, J., Levas, A., Chou, P., Pinhanez, C. & Viveros, M. [2002], BlueSpace: Personalizing Workspace through Awareness and Adaptability, *International Journal of Human–Computer Studies* **57**(5), 415–28.

Newell, A. [1982], The Knowledge Level, *Artificial Intelligence* **18**(1), 87–127.

Newell, A. & Simon, H. A. [1972], *Human Problem Solving*, Prentice–Hall.

Nielsen, J. [1993], *Usability Engineering*, Academic Press.

Nielsen, J. & Mack, R. L. (eds.) [1994], *Usability Inspection Methods*, John Wiley & Sons.

Nunamaker, J. F., Dennis, A. R., Valacich, J. S., Vogel, D. R. & George, J. F. [1991], Electronic Meeting Systems to Support Group Work, *Communications of the ACM* **34**(7), 40–61.

Powers, W. T. [1978], Quantitative Analysis of Purposive Systems: Some Spadework at the Foundations of Scientific Psychology, *Psychological Review* **85**(5), 417–35.

Price, D. D. [1965], Networks of Scientific Papers, *Science* **149**(3683), 510–5.

Sears, A., Feng, J. J., Oseitutu, K. & Karat, C. M. [2003], Hands-free, Speech-based Navigation During Dictation: Difficulties, Consequences and Solutions, *Human–Computer Interaction* **18**(3), 229–57.

Shneiderman, B. [1998], *Designing the User Interface: Strategies for Effective Human–Computer Interaction*, third edition, Addison–Wesley.

Short, J. A., Williams, E. & Christie, B. [1976], *The Social Psychology of Telecommunications*, John Wiley & Sons.

Stephanidis, C., Salvendy, G., Akoumianakis, D., Arnold, A., Bevan, N., Dardailler, D., Emiliani, P. L., Iakovidis, I., Jenkins, P., Karshmer, A., Korn, P., Marcus, A., Murphy, H., Oppermann, C., Stary, C., Tamura, H., Tscheligi, M., Ueda, H., Weber, G. & Ziegler, J. [1999], Toward an Information Society for All: HCI Challenges and R&D Recommendations, *International Journal of Human–Computer Interaction* **11**(1), 1–28.

Stephanidis, C., Salvendy, G., Akoumianakis, D., Bevan, N., Brewer, J., Emiliani, P. L., Galetsas, A., Haataja, S., Iakovidis, I., Jacko, J., Jenkins, P., Karshmer, A., Korn, P., Marcus, A., Murphy, H., Stary, C., Vanderheiden, G., Weber, G. & Ziegler, J. [1998], Toward an Information Society for All: An International R&D Agenda, *International Journal of Human–Computer Interaction* **10**(2), 107–34.

Suchman, L. A. [1987], *Plans and Situated Actions — The Problem of Human–Machine Communication*, Cambridge University Press.

Sumner, M. [1999], Critical Success Factors in Enterprise-wide Information Management Projects, *in* W. D. Haseman & D. L. Nazareth (eds.), *Proceedings of the 1999 Americas Conference on Information Systems (AMCIS 99)*, Association for Information Systems, pp.232–4.

Sutcliffe, A. G. & Carroll, J. M. [1999], Designing Claims for Reuse in Interactive Systems Design, *International Journal of Human–Computer Interaction* **50**(3), 213–42.

Taylor, M. M. [1988], Layered Protocols for Computer–Human Dialogue I: Principles, *International Journal of Man–Machine Studies* **28**(2-3), 175–218.

White, H. D. & McCain, K. W. [1998], Visualizing a Discipline: An Author Cocitation Analysis of Information Science, 1972–1995, *Journal of the American Society for Information Science* **49**(4), 327–56.

Zadeh, L. A. [1965], Fuzzy Sets, *Information Control* **8**(3), 338–53.

"I thought it was terrible and everyone else loved it" — A New Perspective for Effective Recommender System Design

Philip Bonhard & M Angela Sasse

Department of Computer Science, University College London, Gower Street, London WC1E 6BT, UK

Tel: *+44 20 7679 0353*

Email: *{p.bonhard, a.sasse}@cs.ucl.ac.uk*

Recommender Systems have been developed to help people make choices, for instance when deciding what books to buy or movies to see. Research to date has focused on developing algorithms to improve the predictive accuracy of recommender systems. This paper presents an HCI approach to recommender systems design, based on the strategies people employ when seeking advice in taste domains from various sources. The results from a qualitative study with 44 participants show that participants have different requirements for different choice domains. In taste domains, the relationship between the advice seeker and recommender is extremely important, so ways of indicating social closeness and taste overlap are required. Recommender systems must establish a connection between the advice seeker and recommenders through explanation interfaces and communication functions.

Keywords: recommender systems, advice seeking, social networking, decision making.

1 Introduction

"The new millennium is an age of information abundance." [Terveen & Hill 2001]. This statement sums up the problem that people these days are often faced with when making decisions about what film to see, which book or CD to buy, or which restaurant to choose for a romantic dinner. The above choices are examples of choices in taste domains, where no objective right or wrong exists; whether it was right for the advice seeker can only be determined by herself, after she has 'consumed' the recommended item.

When faced with overwhelming choice or lacking knowledge or expertise, people seek advice from their peers. Recommender systems aim to assist and augment this naturally social process [Resnick & Varian 1997] in expanding the network of sources of potentially useful advice, by drawing on the data contained in a large user database. However, merely providing data is not making a recommendation — the user still has to examine the data and judge its validity and appropriateness. Because the data is often presented as item information or simple rating predictions (such as '3-stars') without any explanations or justifications, the user struggles to convert it to *meaningful* information for the purpose of making a choice, and this is a problem that an effective recommender system should be solving rather than creating.

In this paper, we first present an introduction to recommender systems, followed by an overview of the psychology literature on advice seeking. We then provide a brief analysis of the background, which sets out the motivation for this research. This is followed by a description of the study in which we conducted semi structured interviews and focus groups on the topic of recommendations and applied Grounded Theory [Strauss & Corbin 1998] to extract key themes from them. We then present our findings on how people seek advice and recommendations in taste domains, and infer guidelines for effective recommender system design. The aim is to improve decision-making task performance by making it easier for users to judge whether a recommendation is well-founded and trustworthy.

2   Background

Recommender systems have been deployed in various e-commerce contexts, such as book or music shopping like Amazon (www.amazon.com), general rating sites such as www.ratingzone.com, and specific rating sites such as *MovieLens* (http://movielens.umn.edu). All of these recommender systems take some form of information about the user's preferences as input, which are established through either implicit or explicit procedures. *Amazon*, for example, uses both. Implicit information is collected on the user's search and shopping history. Explicit information is collected through specific ratings and customer written reviews. Other sites such as *RatingZone* and *MovieLens* use just explicit provision of preferences through rating specific items (i.e. movies, books, CDs).

Recommender systems aggregate the information received and redirect it to the appropriate recipients. Depending on the recommendation strategies or algorithms employed, users are presented with options based on their personal preference profiles identified through ratings, keywords, usage history, content analysis, item to item or user to user correlation, to name just a few. A common technique is Collaborative Filtering (CF) where recommendations are based on taste overlap among users.

2.1   *Collaborative Filter Recommender Systems*

While many strategies for computing recommendations have been explored, such as item-based collaborative filtering [Sarwar et al. 2001], Bayesian networks [Breese et al. 1998] and factor analysis [Canny 2002], collaborative filtering has emerged as one of the dominant ones because it is not bound to a particular item domain. Recommendations are generated for a given user by comparing her existing ratings to those of all other users in the database. In doing so, a neighbourhood of similar users is established, and based on that rating predictions are computed for items that the user has not yet rated, but her closest neighbours have.

The assumption behind this strategy is that if User A and B have rated several items in a similar fashion, chances are that they have a taste overlap. Thus items that B has rated highly but which A has not yet acquired might be of interest to A. Even though these systems have been developed with the aim of supporting users in their decision-making there are no user studies to establish what exactly their requirements are, and few HCI evaluations of the systems already exist.

2.2 Evaluating Recommender Systems

Recommender systems research to date has predominantly focused on designing algorithms for more effective and efficient computation of rating predictions. The former aims to increase the precision of predicting ratings. This is tested through existing rating data sets, where part of the rating set is deleted, and the prediction results from algorithms are compared against the real ratings. Prediction efficiency is concerned with the computational cost in terms of time and resources for calculating these predictions.

HCI approaches to recommender systems research have been limited to examining existing recommender systems in order to establish interaction design guidelines [Herlocker et al. 2000; Swearingen & Sinha 2001, 2002].

Swearingen & Sinha [2001, 2002] examined how advice from recommender systems is perceived, especially compared to advice from friends. They found that users preferred recommendations from their friends, although some appreciated the system's ability to provide serendipitous recommendations that broadened their horizons. They identified two factors as fundamentally important in the overall usefulness of a recommender system: *familiar recommendations* and *system transparency*. Familiar recommendations can come in different forms: *items previously consumed*, or *items that are related to known items* (i.e. books by the same author). Familiar items can generate trust in the system, but it can also make the recommendations seem too simplistic. As for *transparency*, understanding the inference leading to a recommendation (and agreeing with it) not only increases trust in the recommendation, and the system providing it, but also makes the user more likely to follow the recommendation.

Using a similar approach, Herlocker et al. [2000] conducted an extensive study examining what effect explanations for collaborative filtering results have on the user's perception of the system. In testing different explanation interfaces, they found that explanations are important to users, because their own reasoning does not match the inference mechanism of the system. Users were less likely to trust recommendations when they did not understand *why* certain items were recommended to them. Herlocker et al. [2000] suggest that a rating histogram of the user's closest neighbours is the most effective way of explaining the results of collaborative filtering.

These two studies took an evaluation approach to improving recommender systems, where a recommender system has already been built. In our view, however, the user requirements for recommender systems have not been specified. Rather than continue the current cycle of deploying a matching algorithm and see how users respond, we take a step back and examine existing literature on advice seeking and decision making strategies, to identify what support users seek during these activities. We also conducted a user study to examine in more depth what makes people trust a recommendation and more likely to follow it.

2.3   Trust Research and Recommender Systems

Previous HCI studies on recommender systems aimed to increase user trust in these systems by helping users understand how its inference is derived. Related HCI research in recent years has investigated trust in e-commerce systems [Riegelsberger et al. 2005], social networking, virtual communities and recommender systems [Massa & Avesani 2004; O'Donovan & Smyth 2005]. Each of these aims to address different aspects of the concept of trust depending on the definition applied.

Massa & Avesani [2004] addressed the problem of data sparseness in collaborative filtering: in a huge database, on average two users are unlikely to have rated the same items in a similar fashion. Thus it will be difficult to calculate their similarity, which in turn reduces the size of a user's recommendation neighbourhood. To overcome this problem, Massa & Avesani [2004] use trust data where users explicitly state that they trust specific recommenders. They create a trust graph based on the degree of connectedness of users, using the distance in terms of arcs between two users on this graph as a measure of trust. This transitive trust graph is then used to increase the number of comparable users.

O'Donovan & Smyth [2005] takes a different approach by using past rating reliability to generate trust values that increase or decrease the weight on predictions of neighbouring users. They divide trust into two possible categories, *profile level* and *item level* trust. On the *profile level* they compare all common existing ratings of an advice seeker and a recommender, and examine whether the recommender would have been able to predict the correct ratings for a given advice seeker. The percentage of correct predictions across all common items is their profile-level trust value. *Item-level* trust is more fine grained which and only measures the percentages of recommendations for one item that were correct.

Each of these approaches addresses a different challenge for collaborative filtering (CF) algorithms. Whereas the Massa & Avesani [2004] approach can be used to overcome a technical problem in order to quicker generate recommendations, O'Donovan & Smyth [2005] mainly aims to increase accuracy (precision) of such a CF algorithm. However, both approaches address a particular technical problem without considering the user's perspective on trust.

Riegelsberger et al. [2005] developed a trust model for interactions between two actors in a situation of uncertainty and risk, such as an exchange of goods, information or advice. A *trustor* engages with a *trustee* in an exchange in which both can realize some gain. The two actors have a direct impact on each other, in the sense that the trustor chooses to engage in the exchange with the trustee, who in turn can choose to fulfil her promise or defect. The model divides means of signalling trustworthiness into *symbols* and *symptoms*, both of which the technology involved can transmit. *Symbols* can be e-commerce trust seals or a professionally looking website. *Symptoms*, on the other hand, cannot be specifically created; rather they are a by-product of trust worthy actions. In the context of recommender systems, a recommender who repeatedly gives good advice to an individual shows symptoms of trustworthiness. Someone who has given good advice to others may become a symbol of trustworthiness.

Briggs et al. [2002] identified trust warranting factors for online advice. They concluded that three factors were paramount for users to perceive information as trustworthy, *source credibility, advice personalization* and *predictability*. *Source credibility* refers to the overall impression of a site, *personalization* to whether the information is tailored to the users needs, and *predictability* to whether information presented reflects the user's knowledge, prior experience with this and other sites. However, Briggs et al. actually examine information seeking, rather than advice seeking and which elements of a site design make the information appear trustworthy.

In recommender systems research, there has been a significant lack of considering established decision making and advice seeking research. For recommender systems to support address users' needs in this domain, however, the requirements of the user's task need to be considered. The next section gives a brief overview of the relevant psychological literature on this issue, and identifies the support requirements which can be inferred from it.

2.4 Decision Making and Advice Seeking

The main purpose of recommender systems is to aid its users in their decision making by presenting a reduced set of options in the form of advice or recommendations. To understand how people normally deal with advice from other sources it is instructive to examine the decision making and advice seeking literature in psychology.

2.5 Advice Seeking

The advice seeking literature has predominantly focused on objective domains where advice can be classified as right or wrong [Harvey & Fischer 1997; Yaniv 2004b,a; Yaniv & Kleinberger 2000]. Generally, advice seeking is seen as a problem of weighting different information sources to come to a final conclusion. One of the key questions is how decision makers arrive at their weightings. The classic approach to this problem argues that "decision makers are exquisitely rational beings in solving judgement and choice problems" [Payne et al. 1998]. Studies have shown that advice seekers tend to place a greater weight on their own opinion than that of the adviser (*egocentric discounting*) [Yaniv & Kleinberger 2000]. The assumption is that advice seekers can assess what they know and the strength of their opinions, which they are not able to do for the opinions of others. Related to that is that the confidence in one's opinion depends on how much evidence can be retrieved that supports it [Yaniv 2004b]. Harvey & Fischer [1997] found that, when advice is given, there is basic shift in opinion, no matter what the level of expertise of the advice seekers. When advisers are believed to be more knowledgeable than the advice seekers, they add this component to the basic shift. Only when advice seekers believe they have acquired sufficient expertise does this expert bias have less effect.

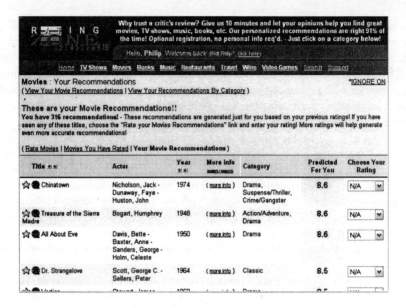

Figure 1: De-contextualized recommendations.

Whereas the benefit of combining opinions in matters of fact is both demonstrable and understood theoretically, the same is not true for matters of taste [Yaniv 2004b]. Simple aggregation of opinions in matters of taste raises conceptual difficulties as people are entitled to different opinions on movies, music or restaurants. Yaniv argues that the most promising strategy to examine these factors in matters of taste would be in considering the *personal match* between advice seeker and recommender, assuming that the greater the similarity between them, the greater the impact and benefit of advice received [Yaniv 2004b]. This strategy is more like a "decision making short cut" or heuristic that simplifies the decision making process [Gigerenzer 2004]. The argument is therefore not to find optimal solutions, but rather using heuristics that simply find good solutions.

2.6 Social Embedding of Recommendations

Researchers have pointed out that recommendations have to be considered in the social context in which they are delivered [Perugini et al. 2004]. Most current recommender systems, however, do not display or consider this social context. Further, they operate in the rational tradition, which assumes that the world can be described objectively and that optimal solutions to problems can be deduced from these objective descriptions [Lueg 1997]. Consequently, recommendations from such systems are de-contextualized thus ignoring the *situatedness* of a recommendation. Figure 1 gives an example of such a de-contextualized recommendation.

The user is shown a list of films with data, without any further explanation or justification.

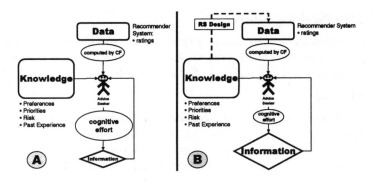

Figure 2: User cognitive effort of judging recommendation data.

Another example is Amazon's recommendation feature, which makes recommendations based on all previous purchases and search behaviour. If the user buys a children's book for a child of a friend or relative twice a year, the system will continue to recommend items from that domain even though the user only has no interest in them. The system does not consider the context that the user is shopping in and thus ends up making inappropriate recommendations.

Understanding the social embedding of a recommendation can be key to generate more useful, trustworthy and understandable recommendations.

3 Analysis

The review of advice seeking and decision-making the literature raises many conceptual challenges. The classic recommender system approach has been to develop algorithms that are capable of predicting user ratings more accurately based on an assumed taste overlap among users. Once the data has been matched with the right user, she would be able to draw appropriate use from it. From a user perspective, data presented becomes information once it is coupled with her knowledge about the system, her own taste, preferences and constraints.

Currently, the user therefore has a significant cognitive effort to expend before the data from the recommender system actually becomes useful information to her. Recommender systems are designed on the premise that users are interested in recommendations from like-minded people. However, simply providing data on what others have chosen does not help the user evaluate their appropriateness for the specific decision to be made (Figure 2A). Figure 2 illustrates this mismatch.

Matching recommender system design with people's actual advice seeking and decision making strategies would not only significantly reduce the user's cognitive effort in judging the information presented, but also increase the information value to the user (Figure 2B). Effective recommender systems have to be modelled around the advice seeking and decision making processes that users employ in the real world. A clearer understanding of the decision processes people engage in when seeking and evaluating recommendations is needed, which is what motivated the study described in the next section.

4 Advice Seeking Study

Since recommender systems aim to give advice in taste domains, we decided to investigate how people choose what books or CDs to buy, which films to see, in which restaurant to eat or even how to find a reliable dentist.

4.1 Method

Twelve semi-structured interviews were conducted with eight male and four female participants, with an age range from 21 to 46, including university students as well as professionals. The aim was elicit concepts and priorities that are important to decision makers when seeking advice, which would then guide the subsequent focus groups.

Five focus groups were conducted and with a total of 32 participants, evenly divided between males and females. The age range was between 19 and 35, including university students as well as professionals.

At the beginning of the focus groups, in order to familiarize participants with the each other and the subject at hand, participants were asked to interview one another about the last time they had to make a decision about shopping or going out, which possibly involved seeking a recommendation or advice from someone or somewhere. After that they would report on their interviewees' findings. This helped eliciting participants' decision making and recommendation seeking strategies in an anecdotal context, which was a lot easier for them to relate to than an abstract concept. The rest of the focus group tended to be more free flowing and only steered into the appropriate direction by the moderator with the following guiding questions (not necessarily in that order):

- Do you remember a good or bad experience when someone recommended a film / restaurant / book etc. to you?

- Who do you consult for advice, who not, and why? — friends / family / colleagues/ magazines / newspapers / Internet / other

- What about reviews in newspapers and magazines (e.g. TimeOut), and consumer magazines (like PC User, Cinema)

- Do you look at seller reputations on eBay, Amazon — Do you trust them? Are they convincing?

- Are there any situations where you only make a decision after taking advice, or doing research? Why?

- If you are new to a city and you are looking for a dentist or hairdresser, plumber, doctor etc. who do you ask? Why?

4.2 Results

To analyse the data and model the advice seeking strategies and processes people employ, we drew on an established approach from social psychology called *Grounded Theory* [Strauss & Corbin 1998]. With Grounded Theory, the model

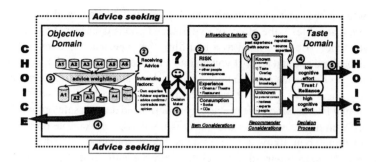

Figure 3: A model of advice seeking in objective and taste domains.

emerges from the data rather than formulating a model and running a study to prove it. This approach has been successfully employed in HCI research to unpick user perceptions and decision making in previously ill-understood areas such as privacy in multimedia environments [Adams & Sasse 2001], compliance with security policies [Weirich & Sasse 2001] and consumer trust in e-commerce systems [Riegelsberger & Sasse 2001].

The core concepts identified will first be presented individually, and then put together in a model of the advice seeking. The model is summarized in Figure 3.

4.2.1   Domains of Interest

Participants clearly differentiated between *objective* and *taste* domains. *Objective item domains* items are characterized by measurable and comparable specifications. These are perceived as being neutral to different ideas of taste. Items that fall into this category are things like electronic goods, computer hardware and software and cars. The perception is that, even though expert reviews of these might differ in some details, a consistent picture emerges that gives the decision maker information base from which to make her own judgement. Thus expert reviews from reputable sources are seen to be a valuable baseline for making further judgements.

Items in *taste domains* are seen as far harder to find advice on. Here one item can be rated differently by two recommenders, and both can justify their ratings. Examples for such items are music, books, films and restaurants.

4.2.2   Item Considerations — Risk

Regardless of the item domain, a key consideration is the potential risk and the consequences in making a choice. At its most basic and common level, one of the first considerations is a *financial* one ("It also comes down to the value of the thing."). Participants generally said the financial risk was involved in a particular choice, the more detailed and careful their research would be before coming to a decision.

Participants differentiated between goods, which are bought and consumed like books or CDs and goods, which are linked to an experience and thus carry a higher opportunity cost, like restaurant and cinema visits. Whereas consumed goods can often be returned and thus the damage of any potential bad choice is limited ("... they recommended the Streets. So I went to a record shop and bought it and I thought it was awful, it was just unlistenable. So I went straight back and got something much more listenable."), the effect of experienced goods is harder if not impossible to change. Once you have been to a bad film, the experience is over and there is nothing to be done about it ("... if you go into a movie and you hated it, you feel kind of deflated. So I'd wanna trust someone more who was recommending me films."). Thus, if the choice involved an experience like watching a film, the consensus was that consulting friends who have previously experienced it was a safe option. Further, this risk is even higher when another party is involved, for example on a date ("... there's one thing about liking a restaurant and taking somebody else there.").

So people adapt their advice seeking with the nature of the good since the associated risk and opportunity cost is higher for experienced goods. Advisers who are seen as trustworthy are therefore sought with this type of experience, namely known recommenders and or those with a good track record.

Linked to experienced items are *services*. We asked participants how they chose specific services (hairdressers, plumbers, lawyers, doctors) and found that people tend to seek advice from friends even though these were not experts in any of the fields they were making recommendations for. Advice seekers here do not aim to get reliable information about the quality of service provided. The results are seen in a binary fashion, either it was good/OK or these friends would not recommend the service in the first place. The motivation for consulting friends for recommendations in these domains is *reassurance*. Especially when completely lacking information ("new in town"), participants sought advice rather than randomly choosing a service without any knowledge about it ("... looking for a doctor or a lawyer, you know that when you get recommended one ... Even getting the knowledge makes you feel a bit more secure than no knowledge at all.").

In addition to that, the experience associated with the service has a major impact on the choice ("... even though they're doing a professional job, I go back to the dentist that I like ... I still feel that the whole experience is, perhaps it's even not that enjoyable, but the experience is good."). Thus decision makers want to not only avoid a bad result from a particular service, but they want to feel good about it as well, both in the sense of having the security of a prior recommendation and afterwards about the whole experience as such.

4.2.3 Recommender Considerations — Known vs. Unknown

Across all interviews and focus groups, the relationship with the recommender is seen to be extremely important when seeking advice in taste domains. While it might seem common sense that people would consult their friends for recommendations for CDs or films, participants clearly pointed out that the relation to the recommender alone is not sufficient. In addition to knowing the recommender, one of two important conditions has to be fulfilled before an advice seeker will trust a recommender. Either:

- the advice seeker knows that the recommender has similar or the same tastes (*taste overlap*); or

- both advice seeker and recommender have sufficient *mutual knowledge* about each others' tastes, so that even with taste differences, the recommender will be able to predict what the advice seeker will like ("... because if somebody knows you well, they know what you like and if you know them well and you've been friends for ten years, clearly for 10 years you've had some sort of compatibility. So you trust them ...").

Knowing the recommender also plays a crucial role in trusting *serendipitous recommendations*. Participants said they are much more willing to explore items they had not considered to match their tastes, if the recommendation came from a close friend ("... a friend, who I really feel that we are on the same intellectual sort of thinking. So, we do sort of put ideas to the other, to try and explore different things.").

Even in taste domains, people consider advice from (personally) unknown sources such as reviews, critiques, experts and strangers lacking any alternatives (e.g. hotel concierge). Nonetheless, participants often expressed their disagreement with the sources of such reviews. Thus these sources become less valuable to the decision maker, as these review are seen to be heavily dependent on the taste of that particular reviewer, which might not match that of the decision maker ("When I read a review, it's someone's view, if I read it, I appreciate it, but it doesn't mean that I trust it.").

Although reviews were seen as aiming to address a broader population and thus more neutral, participants are quite wary about trusting them because in taste domains the reviewer is expressing a personal opinion ("[it's] more or less an opinion of a person on a movie or a book."). Nonetheless participants did say that on occasion if they agree with a particular reviewer they are likely to consider him in the future ("You can guess whether their tastes actually match yours and if it does you keep going until they start getting it wrong.").

Participants noted that they often like to consult sources with aggregated opinions, simply to get a general overview of the popularity of an item ("If more people say it's good and less people say it's bad then I'll go to it."). Such measures are seen as a tentative indicator of quality, although no guarantee for a good recommendation because it is not personalized in any way. Respondents reported on experiences where the popular consensus was that an item was great, and they felt they were the only ones disagreeing ("I thought it was terrible and everyone else loved it.").

4.2.4 Decision Process — Trust and Reliance

Past experience, source reputation and *expertise* have a significant impact on the final judgement of a recommendation, both from a known or unknown source. They tend to increase or decrease the level of *trust* in, or *reliance* on, any given advice. In this context, we define *trust* as faith in a known adviser in a first time context, whereas *reliance* is based on past experience. *Past experience* simply means once advice seekers have received good recommendations, they tend to stick with a particular recommender. *Reputation* and *expertise* of a recommender can both increase the trust in a first-time encounter. Equally, even if they have not received any advice from a particular adviser in the past, but know that this source is either very knowledgeable or is known to give good advice, this can increase trust in a first time encounter.

Recommendation explanations:	
Nearest neighbour explanations	Explanations based on real people are easier to judge for users.
Social & communicative functions:	
Communication facilities	Users should be able to communicate among one another. Not only user to user, but also user to recommender communication should be encouraged.
Social network display	Social network functionality should be supported.
People matching	Users should be matched according to collaborative filtering as well as other criteria to encourage communication.
Discussion boards	Users should be able to exchange ideas about rated items.

Table 1: Recommender system design guidelines.

Many people take guidance from their own past experience instead of making a new choice every time. Participants reported that they to stick to restaurants they have been to and enjoyed before, watch films by the same directors and read books by the same authors ("Now I just stick to one or two things. I have a good experience and I don't change after that.").

Overall, when the recommender is known, and especially if advice seekers have had past experience with her, then the decision process requires less of a cognitive effort because trust and reliance have a greater impact. When the source is unknown the cognitive effort is larger because the advice seeker still has to judge the validity and appropriateness of the recommendation. This effort is reduced over time with future encounters.

4.3 Discussion — Advice Seeking & Recommender Systems

Considering recommender systems from an HCI perspective offers a new approach for their design. The aim is to reduce the user's cognitive effort in judging the relevance of given recommendations, improve confidence when following recommendations, and increase likelihood of satisfaction when acting on those recommendations.

Everyday advice seeking contains inherently social elements that are not supported in current recommender systems, which might explain users' limited uptake and general dissatisfaction with these. Our study supports findings from previous HCI evaluations of recommender systems, but also takes a step further in explaining problems found by these.

4.3.1 Design Recommendations

Recommender system designers should consider the following two important points, *recommendation explanations* and *social, communicative functions*. Both of these are interrelated because the recommendations can encourage the communication among users — as summarized in Table 1.

For *recommendation explanations* designers need to consider the users' need for system transparency as a trust-building necessity. As shown above, people consult trusted sources for advice, where trust is established through past experience, taste overlap and mutual knowledge. Recommender systems can support this by bridging the gap between advice seeker and recommender. Explanations should therefore be based on the nearest neighbours and selected profiles explicitly included in the explanations. That way, users are more aware that recommendations are based on people and thus the relationship between the advice seeker and recommender strengthened.

Users should be able to communicate with one another in order to question or discuss certain opinions, as they would in the real world. Further they should be able to specify explicitly trusted sources and these would carry greater weight in the recommendation process. Users should be able to specify their social networks and view those of others, and differentiate between friends and recommenders. For the system this could be useful data, which could improve the recommendation process. Users should be matched not only according to a simple ratings overlap, but also by interests specified in their profiles. Users would therefore not only gain from the system as a source of information, but also as communication tool. This way the relationship between the advice seeker and the recommender can become a focal point in the recommender system.

Recommender systems can therefore become more than a simple source of data. Depending on the user's preferences a recommender system can become communication tool that allows users not only to receive recommendation information from it, but also exchange ideas about related items and communicate with like-minded users.

5   Conclusion and Future Work

Advice seeking in taste domains is an area that requires further research. This paper has presented results from a qualitative study that provides insight on the advice seeking strategies in these domains. We showed that the relationship between advice seeker and recommender plays a central role in determining how a recommendation is judged. Within this two concepts are important, either both of them having a taste overlap, thus they will like the same items; or mutual knowledge that can enable the recommender to give advice that does not correspond to his own tastes, but the advice seeker might like. Recommendation explanations focusing on the recommender profiles rather than merely presenting data should make it easier for the user to judge their appropriateness and validity. Coupled with communication features recommender systems can become more than a source of recommendation data.

We are currently implementing a restaurant recommender system that incorporates these functions. The system will provide a world test-bed for in-vivo experiments on use and uptake of recommendations, user confidence and satisfaction.

References

Adams, A. & Sasse, M. A. [2001], Privacy in Multimedia Communications: Protecting Users, Not Just Data, *in* A. Blandford, J. Vanderdonckt & P. Gray (eds.), *People and Computers XV: Interaction without Frontiers (Joint Proceedings of HCI2001 and IHM2001)*, Springer-Verlag, pp.49–64.

Breese, J. S., Heckerman, D. & Kadie, C. [1998], Empirical Analysis of Predictive Algorithms for Collaborative Filtering, *in* G. F. Cooper & S. Moral (eds.), *Proceedings of the 14th Conference on Uncertainty in Artificial Intelligence (UAI-98)*, Morgan-Kaufmann, pp.43–52.

Briggs, P., de Angelo, A., Burford, B. & Lynch, P. [2002], Trust in Online Advice, *Social Science Computing Review* **20**(3), 321–32.

Canny, J. F. [2002], Collaborative Filtering with Privacy via Factor Analysis, *in* M. Beaulieu, R. Baeza-Yates, S. H. Myaeng & K. Järvelin (eds.), *Proceedings of the 25th Annual International ACM SIGIR Conference on Research and Development in Information Retrieval (SIGIR'02)*, ACM Press, pp.238–45.

Gigerenzer, G. [2004], Fast and Frugal Heuristics: The Tools of Bounded Rationality, *in* N. Harvey & D. Koehler (eds.), *Handbook of Judgment and Decision Making*, Blackwell, pp.62–88.

Harvey, N. & Fischer, I. [1997], Taking Advice: Accepting Help, Improving Judgement, and Sharing Responsibility, *Organizational Behavior and Human Decision Processes* **70**(2), 117–33.

Herlocker, J. L., Konstan, J. A., Borchers, A. & Riedl, J. [2000], Explaining Collaborative Filtering Recommendations, *in* W. Kellogg & S. Whittaker (eds.), *Proceedings of 2000 ACM Conference on Computer Supported Cooperative Work (CSCW'00)*, *CHI Letters* **2**(3), ACM Press, pp.241–50.

Lueg, C. [1997], Social Filtering and Social Reality, *in* L. Kovács (ed.), *Proceedings of the 5th DELOS Workshop on Filtering and Collaborative Filtering*, European Research Consortium for Informatics and Mathematics (ERCIM), pp.73–77.

Massa, P. & Avesani, P. [2004], Trust-aware Collaborative Filtering for Recommender Systems, *in* R. Meersman & Z. Tari (eds.), *On the Move to Meaningful Internet Systems 2004: CoopIS, DOA, and ODBASE: Proceedings of OTM Confederated International Conferences, CoopIS, DOA and ODBASE 2004*, Vol. 3290 of *Lecture Notes in Computer Science*, Springer, pp.492–508.

O'Donovan, J. & Smyth, B. [2005], Trust in Recommender Systems, *in* J. Herlocker (ed.), *Proceedings of the 10th ACM International Conference on Intelligent User Interface (IUI 2005)*, ACM Press, pp.167–74.

Payne, J. W., Bettman, J. R. & Luce, M. F. [1998], Behavioural Decision Research: An Overview, *in* M. H. Birnbaum (ed.), *Measurement, Judgement and Decision Making*, Academic Press, pp.303–59.

Perugini, S., Goncalves, M. A. & Fox, E. A. [2004], A Connection Centric Survey of Recommender System Research, *Journal of Intelligent Information Systems* **23**(1), 107–43.

Resnick, P. & Varian, H. R. [1997], Recommender Systems, *Communications of the ACM* **40**(3), 56–8.

Riegelsberger, J. & Sasse, M. A. [2001], Trustbuilders and Trustbusters: The Role of Trust Cues in Interfaces to E-commerce Applications, *in* B. Schmid, K. Stanoevska-Slabeva & V. Tschammer (eds.), *Towards the E-Society: Proceedings of the 1st IFIP Conference on E-commerce, E-business, and E-government*, Kluwer, pp.17–30.

Riegelsberger, J., Sasse, M. A. & McCarthy, J. D. [2005], Do People Trust Their Eyes More Than Their Ears? Media Bias While Seeking Expert Advice, *in* G. van der Veer & C. Gale (eds.), *CHI'05 Extended Abstracts of the Conference on Human Factors in Computing Systems*, ACM Press, pp.1745–8.

Sarwar, B. M., Karypis, G., Konstan, J. A. & Reidl, J. [2001], Item-based Collaborative Filtering Recommendation Algorithms, *in* V. Y. Shen, N. Saito, M. R. Lyu & M. E. Zurko (eds.), *Proceedings of the Tenth International World Wide Web Conference (WWW10)*, ACM Press, pp.285–95. See also http://www10.org/.

Strauss, A. & Corbin, J. [1998], *Basics of Qualitative Research — Techniques and Procedures for Developing Grounded Theory*, second edition, Sage Publications.

Swearingen, K. & Sinha, R. [2001], Beyond Algorithms: An HCI Perspective on Recommender Systems, *in* J. Herlocker (ed.), *Proceedings of the ACM SIGIR 2001 Workshop on Recommender Systems*, ACM Press, pp.24–33.

Swearingen, K. & Sinha, R. [2002], Interaction Design for Recommender Systems, http://www.rashmisinha.com/articles/musicDIS.pdf (last accessed 2005-06-27).

Terveen, L. & Hill, W. [2001], Beyond Recommender Systems: Helping People Help Each Other, *in* J. M. Carroll (ed.), *Human–Computer Interaction in the New Millenium*, Addison–Wesley, pp.487–509.

Weirich, D. & Sasse, M. A. [2001], Pretty Good Persuasion: A First Step Towards Effective Password Security for the Real World, *in* B. Timmerman & D. Kienzle (eds.), *Proceedings of the New Security Paradigms Workshop 2001*, ACM Press, pp.137–43.

Yaniv, I. [2004a], The Benefit of Additional Opinions, *Current Directions in Psychological Science* **13**(2), 75–8.

Yaniv, I. [2004b], Receiving Other Peoples' Advice: Influence and Benefit, *Organizational Behavior and Human Decision Processes* **93**(1), 1–13.

Yaniv, I. & Kleinberger, E. [2000], Advice Taking in Decision Making: Egocentric Discounting and Reputation Formation, *Organizational Behavior and Human Decision Processes* **83**(2), 260–81.

Rich Media, Poor Judgement? A Study of Media Effects on Users' Trust in Expertise

Jens Riegelsberger, M Angela Sasse & John D McCarthy

University College London, Department of Computer Science, Gower Street, London WC1E 6BT, UK

Tel: *+44 20 7679 0351*

Fax: *+44 20 7387 1397*

Email: *{jriegels, a.sasse, j.mccarthy}@cs.ucl.ac.uk*

URL: *www.cs.ucl.ac.uk/staff/jriegels*

In this paper, we investigate how interpersonal cues of expertise affect trust in different media representations. Based on a review of previous research, richer representations could lead either to a *positive media bias* (P1) or *increased sensitivity for cues of expertise* (P2). In a laboratory study, we presented 160 participants with two advisors — one represented by *text-only*; the other represented by one of four alternate formats: *video, audio, avatar*, or *photo+text*. Unknown to the participants, one was an *expert* (i.e. trained) and the other was a *non-expert* (i.e. untrained). We observed participants' *advice seeking* and *advice uptake* to infer their *sensitivity to correct advice* in a situation of financial risk. We found that most participants preferred seeking advice from the *expert*, but we also found a tendency for seeking *audio* and in particular *video* advice. Users' self-reports indicate that they believed that *video* in particular would give them the most detailed insight into expertise. Data for *advice uptake*, however, showed that all media representation, including *text-only*, resulted in good *sensitivity* to correct advice.

Keywords: trust, expertise, video, avatar, audio, photo, CMC, CSCW.

1 Introduction

As technology-mediated interaction gradually replaces face-to-face interaction in many areas of life, trust becomes a central concern for providers of online services [Corritore et al. 2003]. In this context, many researchers investigate how to maintain or increase levels of trust. However, it is also crucial to ensure that users are able to place trust correctly (i.e. are able to discriminate between trustworthy and less trustworthy actors). Experiencing the consequences of misplaced trust can undermine future willingness to interact with online services and technologies. To date, research investigating the correctness of trust decisions mainly focused on deceptive behaviour, see for example Horn et al. [2002]. However, in many everyday situations, questions of trust do not arise from the risk of wilful deception, but because one is uncertain about the other's expertise [Deutsch 1958]. An individual might mean well, but lack the expertise to be truly helpful. Investigating these issues, we focus on cues of expertise, a thus far under-researched constituent of trustworthiness.

Due to bandwidth constraints, online services used to be limited to providing most users with text communication or simple webpages containing photos. However, wide availability of broadband access now allows services to be delivered in richer formats, such as audio or video. In addition, avatars (animated human-like characters) now promise social presence [Short et al. 1976] at a level similar to that provided by video — albeit at a lower cost in terms of production and bandwidth. The four *rich media formats* we examine in this paper are *video, avatar, audio*, and *photo+text*. As a baseline measure for comparisons we include a *text-only* condition. We are particularly interested in how different representations affect users' *sensitivity to cues of expertise*, i.e. the degree to which they can identify correct and incorrect advice. We are investigating whether richer representations result in either a media bias (1) or increased sensitivity for cues of expertise (2). Bias occurs when advice is preferred due to its media format, irrespective of its expertise.

After an overview of online trust research (Section 2), we introduce our predictions and methodological approach (Section 3). Then we present and discuss the results of an experimental study that was conducted to test our predictions (Section 4 and 5). We close with conclusions for researchers and practitioners (Section 6).

2 Background

2.1 *Trust and Interpersonal Cues*

Trust has been defined as a willingness to be vulnerable, based on positive expectations [Corritore et al. 2003]. This implies that trust is required in the presence of *risk* and *uncertainty* [Corritore et al. 2003; Giddens 1990; Deutsch 1958]. Uncertainty arises from the fact that the trustor cannot directly observe the trustee's *ability* (e.g. expertise) and *motivation* (e.g. desire to deceive), but needs to infer those from cues [Bacharach & Gambetta 2001]. *Interpersonal cues* can play an important role in the perception of trustworthiness in face-to-face situations, because they give information about an individual's background (e.g. education, provenance), but also about intrinsic states such as sincerity and confidence [Whittaker & O'Conaill 1997; Zuckerman et al. 1981]. Interpersonal cues include visual cues (e.g. appearance, facial expressions) and audio cues (para-verbal: e.g. pitch [Hinton 1993]).

If interactions are mediated, some interpersonal cues are lost. Text chat, for instance, removes all visual and audio cues. Intrinsic states and personal background can only be inferred from vocabulary and phrasing. In the view of media richness models [Rice 1992], text chat is considered to result in low social presence and is thus seen as a poor channel. In the discussion on trust, it is often implicitly assumed that a poor channel will result in lower trust, as many of the interpersonal cues that are crucial for building trust are not present [Giddens 1990; Handy 1995]. Visual interpersonal cues (e.g. smiles), which are suppressed by text or audio representations, have been identified as particularly powerful in evoking immediate affective responses [Winston et al. 2002].

However, there is also evidence that trust cannot be linked unequivocally to a one-dimensional model of media richness. In the presence of cues for untrustworthiness (e.g. nervousness), a rich channel is unlikely to result in a high level of trust compared to one that suppresses such cues. Walther [1996] found that narrow-bandwidth channels can also result in over-reliance on the few cues available, and thus may lead to unwarranted high levels of trust.

Two predictions regarding the effect of media richness on trust are therefore possible: richer representations may result in (P1) *positive media bias* (i.e. more trust) because they increase social presence or they may result in (P2) *better discrimination* between trustworthy and less trustworthy actors as they convey more information.

2.2 Evidence for Media Bias (P1) and Discrimination (P2)

We briefly review trust research that specifically addressed video, audio, avatars, and photos with a view to P1 and P2.

Video. In social dilemma studies, video resulted in the highest levels of cooperation when compared to audio and text-only communications [Bos et al. 2002; Olson et al. 2002], thus providing some evidence for P1. In a study on interpersonal cues of uncertainty, Swerts et al. [2004], however, found that users' ability to discriminate was lowest for video-only, higher for audio-only and highest for video+audio, thus supporting P2. Investigating the detection of deception in video, Horn et al. [2002] found that slight visual spatial degradation reduced participants' ability to discriminate; giving further support to P2. However, severe degradation of the visual channel resulted in better discrimination. Horn et al. [2002] hypothesized that this effect may result from a reduced bias in the absence of recognizable visual cues. Such an effect would provide support for P1 and suggest that visual cues in particular introduce a positive bias.

Avatars. Virtual humans (avatars and embodied agents) are sometimes presented as simple means to enrich user experience and build trust. They can be easily produced with off-the-shelf tools from an audio stream. However, they can

Advisor 1	Video	Avatar	Audio	Photo+Text
Advisor 2	Text-only	Text-only	Text-only	Text-only
Advisor 1 is the expert	20	20	20	20
Advisor 2 is the expert	20	20	20	20

Table 1: Eight between-subject conditions used in the study.

prompt mixed reactions from users depending on implementation, context, and user characteristics [Fogg 2003]. In a study that varied agent implementation and expertise (albeit not the interpersonal cues given off) van Mulken et al. [1999] found a strong effect of expertise on perceived trustworthiness but only a marginally positive effect for the embodied representation.

Audio. In line with media richness models, audio-only communication in social dilemma studies resulted in levels of cooperation that were lower than those for video, but higher than those found for text-only communications (P1) [Bos et al. 2002; Olson et al. 2002]. Even synthetic speech was found to reduce uncooperative behaviour compared to text chat. Davis et al. [2002] attribute this finding to the social presence afforded by synthetic voice. Swerts et al. [2004] on the other hand found that audio-only allowed better discrimination than video-only, suggesting that audio cues in particular give insight into certainty (P2).

Photos. Photos do not give additional cues with individual advice compared to text-only representations (P2), but they are widely used with the aim to increase social presence and trust. Previous studies found that they can bias users' trust in websites (P1) [Fogg 2003].

None of the studies above induced risk to measure trust and at the same time systematically investigated P1 and P2 across different media representations. Hence, to specifically address these predictions, we designed a study that contrasted expertise and media richness. We modelled our experimental study on a user–advisor relationship, a widely used research paradigm in social psychology [Yaniv & Kleinberger 2000], and gave participants *expert* and *non-expert* advisors, one of them *text-only* and the other in one of the *rich media* representations (see Section 3.1). The study was framed as a general knowledge quiz, similar to the well-known TV show *'Who Wants to Be a Millionaire?'*

3 Method

3.1 Participants and Design

160 participants took part in the study. The median age was 23.75 (sd = 3.30) and the sample was balanced for gender (49% female). The study had a 4 media (*type of rich media representation*) × 2 expertise (*rich media advisor is expert vs. rich media advisor is non-expert*) design, resulting in 8 between-subject conditions with 20 participants each (Table 1).

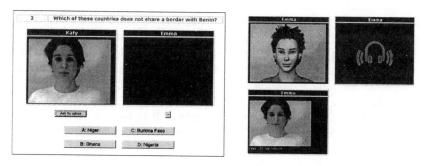

Figure 1: Experimental system (left, *video* advisor selected) and *avatar, audio, photo+text* representations.

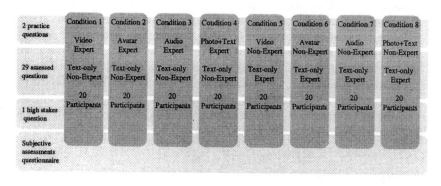

Figure 2: Overview on the experimental procedure and design.

In each between-subject condition, two advisors were available (Figure 1) — one represented as *text-only,* and the other in one of the *rich media representations*. The rich media representations were *video, avatar, audio*, and *photo+text*. Depending on the factor *expertise*, either the *text-only* or the *rich media* advisor gave expert advice, while the other gave non-expert advice. The order of the questions and answer options (A-D) was randomized; the position (left, right) and names (Katy, Emma) of the advisors were counterbalanced.

Prior to starting the assessed part of the experiment, participants completed two training rounds that consisted of easy questions. For these, both advisors gave identical and correct advice. Then participants answered 30 assessed questions, including a final high-stakes question (see Section 3.3). Finally, they were presented with the post-experimental questionnaire eliciting their subjective assessment of the advisors (see Figure 2).

3.2 Questions

To minimize effects of participants' prior knowledge, difficult general knowledge questions were used in the quiz study. To choose the 30 most difficult questions out of a pool of 50, an online pre-study was performed with 80 pre-testers who did not take part in the main part of the study. The most difficult question was defined as the one where the two most often picked answers had the smallest difference in their frequency of being chosen. Examples of questions that were included are *'Who coined the term Philosophical Hermeneutics?'* and *'Who won the Turner Prize in 1984?'* For the 30 questions that were included in the main study, the mean probability for giving a correct answer was 0.31 (sd = 0.11), based on the pre-test results. This value is only marginally above chance (0.25), indicating that very difficult questions had been picked.

3.3 Independent Variables

Expertise. The *non-expert* and *expert* advisors were created by recording advice from the same individual before and after training, respectively. Hence, the *expert* and *non-expert* advisors only differed in the ratio of correct to incorrect advice and in their cues to confidence about the answers. As each participant only had access to one rich media representation of the advisor, they were unaware that both advisors were in fact the same individual recorded at different levels of *expertise*. In the interest of ecological validity, the phrasing of the advice was not prescribed. Based on experience with a pilot study, 6 incorrect (and less confident) pieces of advice from the untrained recording were added to the *expert* so she did not seem artificially perfect. The proportion of correct (i.e. confident) advice was 0.80 for the *expert* and 0.36 for the *non-expert*.

Media Representation. All media representations were created from the same video clips ranging from 1s to 8s in length. The original clips were used for the *video* representation. The *avatar* was created with a commercially available animation tool (V1 by DA Group — http://www.dagroupplc.com) directly from the audio stream without any manual scripting of nonverbal behaviour. The tool synchronized lip movements and added cues of liveliness (e.g. blinks). *Video* and *avatar* were streamed with Windows Media Encoder (350Kb s^{-1}, 320×240). Audio was encoded with 48kHz, 16bit, mono. *Photo+text* included a facial photo of the advisor, otherwise it was identical to the *text-only* representation; for both text appeared dynamically with a delay of 107ms per letter to ensure that all representations had equal playing time.

Risk. Participants' pay was linked to the number of correctly answered questions and thus to their ability to identify the *expert* advisor from interpersonal cues, as the quiz questions were extremely difficult. Pay varied between £8 and £15. A final high-stakes question (worth an additional £3) was included.

3.4 Dependent Variables

3.4.1 Advice Seeking

On each question, participants could chose to ask only one advisor, or not ask for advice at all. Seeking advice from one advisor in preference over the other could thus be interpreted as trust in that advisor, as receiving poor advice carried the risk

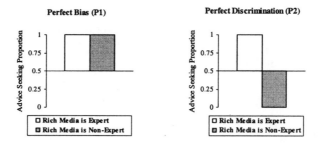

Figure 3: Illustration of predictions P1 and P2 for advice seeking.

of missing out better advice and therefore reduced participation pay. The measure *advice seeking* was defined as the proportion of one advisor being asked out of the total number of times advice was sought by a participant. As each participant had two advisors, but could only choose one of them for advice on each question, the following relationships hold: *expert advice seeking = 1 – non-expert advice seeking* and *rich media advice seeking = 1 – text-only advice seeking*.

Figure 3 illustrates P1 and P2 for the measure advice seeking. In the hypothetical case of total bias (P1), we would expect participants to always seek rich media advice, irrespective of expertise. In the case of perfect discrimination (P2), participants would always prefer expert advice.

3.4.2 Advice Uptake

The second measure taken from participants' behaviour was their *advice uptake*, i.e. whether they followed advice they had received from a particular advisor. Again, following advice can be seen as a trusting behaviour, as incorrect answers lead to a lower participation pay. The measure *advice uptake* was defined as the proportion of pieces of advice from one advisor that are followed relative to the total number of times that advisor was asked. While *advice seeking* contrasted P1 and P2 (see Section 3.4.1) within one measure, *advice uptake* gave individual measures for each advisor. Applying the predictions to *advice uptake*, P1 (media bias), would lead to a higher *advice uptake* for rich media representations, whereas P2 (better discrimination) would lead to a greater effect of expertise on *advice uptake* in richer representations (i.e. an interaction effect between *expertise* and *media representation*).

3.4.3 Sensitivity

To investigate participants' discriminative ability (P2) in different media representations further, their *sensitivity* to correct advice was calculated from the *advice uptake* measure. This measure takes in account the correctness of the advice received (Table 2).

Participants had to assess the correctness of a piece of advice from the interpersonal cues they perceived. This can be understood in terms of a sender and receiver model: the advisor's media representation determined the types and number

	Correct Advice	Incorrect Advice
Follow	Well-placed Trust	Misplaced Trust *(Gullibility Error)*
Not Follow	No Trust *(Incredulity Error)*	No Trust *(Justified)*

Table 2: Correctness of trust decisions (adapted from Fogg [2003]).

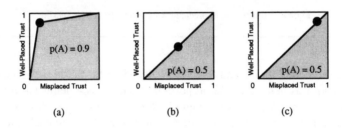

(a)   (b)   (c)

Figure 4: Illustration of $p(A)$.

of cues transmitted. Employing a signal detection paradigm [Thurstone 1927], *sensitivity to correct advice* is a measure of the Receiver Operating Characteristics (ROC). The *sensitivity* measure adopted is $p(A)$, a non-parametric variant of d' [McNicol 1972]. $p(A)$ is the area under a ROC-curve (Figure 4), which is defined by the proportion well-placed trust and misplaced trust (Table 2).

Three examples are illustrated: in Figure 4a the participant almost always follows correct advice and almost never follows incorrect advice. In this case the area under the curve, $p(A)$, approaches 1.0 — the participant has a high sensitivity. In Figure 4b the user decides randomly whether to follow advice whether it is correct or not. In this case, the area under the curve $p(A) = 0.5$, indicating that they cannot detect correct advice (low sensitivity). In the final example, the participant has a tendency to follow any advice given. In this case, $p(A) = 0.5$, as there is no evidence of sensitivity to correct advice. This measure is thus independent from individuals' response biases. Applied to P2, the measure *sensitivity* predicts that richer media result in higher sensitivity scores. P1 predicts no effect on *sensitivity*.

3.4.4 Auxiliary Measures

As auxiliary measures, participants' self-reports were recorded. For each question, each participant was asked to rate his or her *confidence* in the answer they had given. In addition, participants' subjective assessment of the two advisors was elicited after they had completed the study. Agreement with the statements was elicited on 7-point Likert scales with the anchors 1 ('Strongly disagree') — 7 ('Strongly agree'). In a final open-ended question participants were asked to state the reasons for their advisor choice.

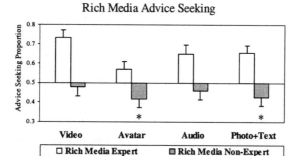

Figure 5: Seeking advice from the rich media advisor. Stars (*) indicate results for one-sided *t*-tests (H: seeking < 0.5; *p* < 0.05).

4   Results

On average, participants sought advice on 26 out of 30 rounds (87%). Only 51 participants (32%) sought advice in every round, even though there was no cost associated with seeking advice. One participant (in the *audio expert* advisor condition) did not ask for advice at all. Participants spent on average 23s on each question. If they asked for advice, they did so on average 13s after the question had been displayed, indicating that they first formed their own opinion before asking an advisor.

4.1   Advice Seeking

Figure 5 shows a main effect for *expertise* on participants' likelihood for seeking advice ($F_{1,154} = 51.56$, $p < 0.001$). This shows that the experts were chosen much more often than non-experts for all types of representation. There is also some indication for a between-subjects effect of the type of *rich media* representation ($F_{3,154} = 2.50$, $p = 0.062$). This indicates that the type of *rich media advisor* that was paired with the *text-only* advisor affected how participants decided between the two.

   To conduct a within-subject test for bias (P1, Figure 3) and discrimination (P2, Figure 3), we investigated *rich media non-expert* advice seeking (grey bars in Figure 5). As discussed in Section 3.4.1, a value <0.5 would provide evidence for discrimination, a value >0.5 would be a sign of bias outweighing discrimination. Figure 5 shows *non-expert avatar* and *photo+text advice seeking* significantly below 0.5 ($t_{19} = 2.00$, $p < 0.05$ and $t_{19} = 1.76$, $p < 0.05$, respectively). No such effect is present for *video* and *audio*, indicating that a media bias towards *audio* and *video* is interfering with users' ability to discriminate. In other words, users are *seeking* advice from *video* and *audio* representations equally often, even though they are *non-experts*.

   Further evidence for a preference for *seeking video* and *audio* is given by the finding that for *video* and *audio expert* advice was chosen more often than *text-only expert* advice (*video*: $t_{38} = 3.60$, $p < 0.001$, *audio*: $t_{37} = 1.69$, $p < 0.05$, both

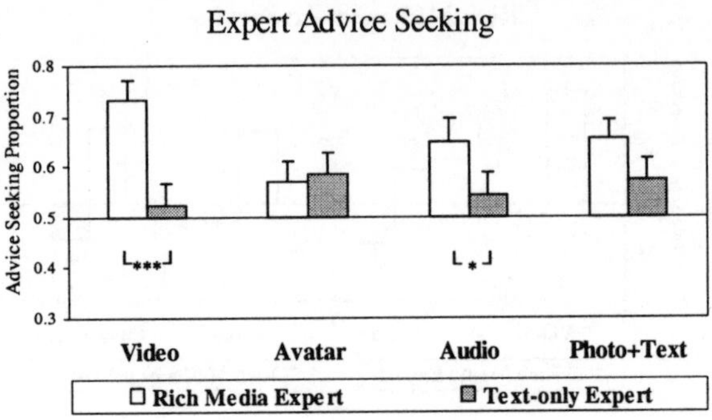

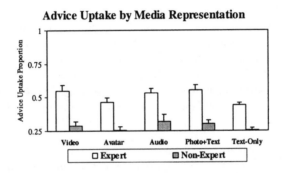

Figure 6: Advice seeking for the expert advisor. Stars indicate significant differences between rich media and text-only expert (*** p < 0.001; * p < 0.05).

Figure 7: Advice uptake by media representation and expertise (plotted against 0.25 which would be random uptake in the presence of 4 answer options, see Section 3.1).

one-sided; see Figure 6). This effect was not present for the *avatar* and *photo+text* representations. *Avatar expert* advice was sought less often than advice from the other rich media *experts* combined ($t_{77} = 2.45$, $p < 0.05$).

4.2 Advice Uptake

As stated in Section 3.4.2, a media bias (P1) in *advice uptake* is present if one media representation leads to a higher proportion of uptake than another. Figure 7 shows *advice uptake* for all media and expertise conditions. In addition, it includes aggregate data for the *text-only* advisor, which was present with each of the other media representations (see Section 3.1). In line with the findings for *advice seeking*, the data for *advice uptake* shows a strong effect for *expertise* ($F_{1,146} = 85.40$, $p < 0.001$). In contrast to the findings for *advice seeking*, a between-subject analysis yields no indication of an impact of media representation ($F_{3,147} = 1.86$, ns.).

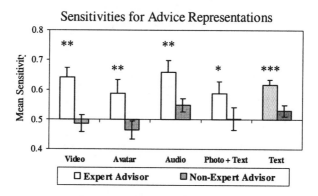

Figure 8: Sensitivities in experimental conditions. Stars (*) indicate results for one-sided *t*-tests (H: sensitivity > 0.5; all text-only advisors collapsed into one bar).

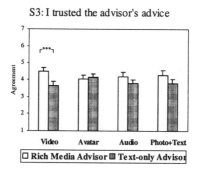

Figure 9: Self-report for trust in the advisors (S3). Stars indicate significant differences between rich media and text-only advisor (*** p < 0.001).

4.3 Sensitivity

The *sensitivity* measure gives values between 0 and 1. A value ≤0.5 means that a participant could not differentiate correct from incorrect advice. The *sensitivity* for advice delivered in the different media representations are shown in Figure 8. For each media representation, we tested, whether the *sensitivity* was greater than 0.5, i.e. whether participants were able to discriminate between correct (confident) and incorrect (less confident) advice (Table 2). When the *rich media advisor* was an *expert*, participants were sensitive to the differences between correct and incorrect advice. Interestingly, when the *text-only advisor* was the *expert* (and thus paired with any *rich media non-expert advisor*, see Section 3.1), it also resulted in a *sensitivity* score higher than 0.5. There was no *sensitivity* for advice given by the *non-expert*.

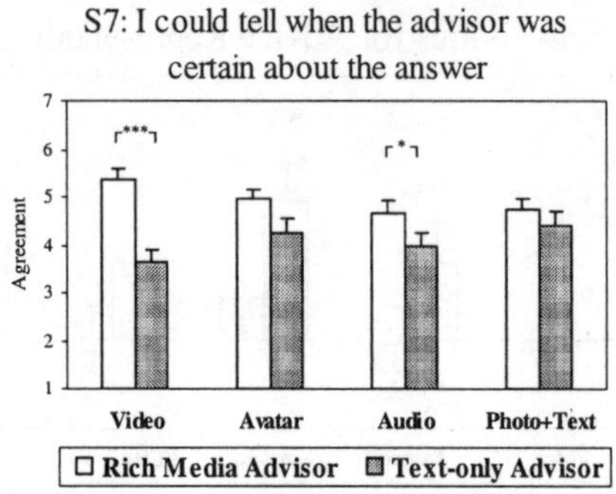

S7: I could tell when the advisor was
certain about the answer

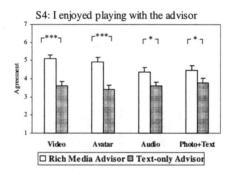

Figure 10: Self-report for ability to infer advisor certainty (S7). Stars indicate significant differences between rich media and text-only advisor (*** p < 0.001; * p < 0.05).

S4: I enjoyed playing with the advisor

Figure 11: Self-report of enjoyment of playing with an advisor (S4). Stars indicate significant differences between rich media and text-only advisor (*** p < 0.001; * p < 0.05).

4.4 Auxiliary Measures

While the focus of this research is on behavioural measures, participants' self-reports were also analysed as auxiliary measures. Getting advice from an *expert* resulted in higher self-reported confidence with an answer ($F_{1,154} = 11.76$, $p < 0.001$), but there was no effect of *media representation* on self-reported confidence. We analysed the post-experimental assessments of the advisors by comparing each participant's rating of the *text-only* advisor to that of the *rich* media advisor, irrespective of the *expertise* of each advisor. Significant differences in assessment between *text-only* and *rich* media advisor are thus indicators of media bias on one statement for one specific *rich* media representation (P1). Notable bias was found for *video*, which was trusted (S3, Figure 9) more, and rated as being better suited for assessing certainty (S7, Figure 10) than *text-only*, irrespective of *expertise*. No such bias was found on these statements for *avatar* and *photo+text* representations. All *rich* media representations resulted in higher ratings of enjoyment (S4, Figure 11).

5   Discussion

5.1   Video

When the *non-expert* was represented in *video*, preference for choosing *video* almost matched the preference for choosing *expert text-only* advice. Hence, in many cases users' preference for receiving *video* advice lead them to disregard better *text-only* advice. This preference for video is particularly problematic, as *video* did not result in a higher *sensitivity* for correct advice than *text-only* advice. This finding opposes prediction P2 — that rich media leads to better discrimination. Participants' own post-experimental assessments, however, appear to support P2: they rated their ability to infer certainty (S7) higher for *video* than for *text-only*. One participant expressed this in her reply to the open-ended question:

> "Since I could see Katie speak and look at her expressions while she answered, I could guess with more confidence when she was correct and thus I chose Katie more number of times."

This disparity between self-reports and actual performance corroborates a similar finding by Horn et al. [2002] in a study on deception detection over video channels. In that study participants had over-estimated their own ability in detecting lies over video. Horn et al. [2002], in the same study, also found that a severe degradation of the visual channel led to an increase in participants' ability in detecting lies. They hypothesized that the visual identification induces a 'truth bias' that may lead individuals to commit gullibility errors (Table 2). There is no clear indication in the behavioural data of our study for such an effect of the visual channel in particular. However, participants' self-reports suggest a bias resulting from *video* that was *not* present for other rich media representations. Irrespective of the advisor *expertise*, participants stated that they trusted the *video* advisor more than the *text-only* advisor (S3). This effect was only found for *video*, i.e. only in the presence of real dynamic visual interpersonal cues.

In summary, participants were able to identify expert advice in the *video* representations, but the data suggest that the additional cues received in *video* compared to *text-only* did not increase their *sensitivity* to correct advice (P2); rather, there is some evidence (in *advice seeking* and in the self-reports) that participants had a tendency to trust *video* (P1), which interfered with their ability to detect *expertise*.

5.2   Audio

Similar to *video*, the preference for seeking *non-expert audio* advice almost matched the preference for *expert* advice, which indicates that the tendency for seeking *audio* advice interfered with participants' preference for *expert* advice (P1). Participants over-estimated their ability to detect certainty (S7) in *audio*, as they did for *video*. However, unlike for *video*, participants did not state that they trusted the *audio* advisor more than the *text-only* advisor (S3). *Expert audio* advice resulted in a good *sensitivity* to correct advice, but it was not significantly better than the *sensitivity* in the *text-only* or any other media representation (P2). In summary, there is some behavioural evidence for interference from a preference for *audio* representations on users' ability to discriminate, but on users' self-reports less bias was detected for *audio* than for *video*.

5.3   Avatar

The *avatar* did not result in a positive bias. To the contrary, *avatar expert* advice was less often sought than other types of *rich media expert* advice. The subjective assessments corroborate the notion of a negative bias resulting from the *avatar*: participants did not think it had been easier to assess the *avatar's* certainty relative to the *text-only* advisor's (S7). For the *audio* advisor, which provided the same audio cues, but not the synthetic visual ones, they considered themselves able to do so. In the words of one participant:

> "Katy didn't seem real so I stopped picking her for advice."

Clearly, these findings cannot necessarily be generalized to other avatar representations or contexts of use. Previous studies showed strong differences in reactions to animated characters due to relatively small differences in behaviour, appearance, or context of use. Nonetheless, the findings indicate that using an avatar created with off-the-shelf tools from the audio stream may not be advisable for building trust at this stage. If the *avatar* and all the visual interpersonal cues given off had been carefully scripted, the *avatar* advisor might have appeared to be more trustworthy. Finally, it was found that the *avatar* was perceived as more enjoyable (S4) than the *text-only* advisor. Our data thus suggest that this representation may be effectively used in e.g. an entertainment context.

5.4   Photo+Text

The *photo+text* advisor offered the fewest additional interpersonal cues relative to the *text-only* advisor. The static visual cues given in a photo did not carry any information about expertise or confidence of individual pieces of advice. Hence, this representation could not be expected to increase participants' ability to discriminate between advisors based on their *expertise* (P2). Only a bias (P1) arising from the presence of static interpersonal cues, could be expected. No such bias was found on any of the measures, but the *photo* did result in higher ratings for enjoyment (S4) compared to *text-only*. This suggests that photos can be used to prompt positive reactions and make interactions more engaging.

5.5   Media Bias (P1) and Discrimination (P2)

Averaging across all rich media representations there was strong evidence for a preference for seeking *expert* advice and some evidence of media bias (P1). Users' ability to discriminate between *expert* and *non-expert* was good, independent of the media representation (P2).

Investigating the rich media representations individually, it was found that the preference for seeking *expert* advice was almost matched by a preference for seeking advice in *video* and *audio* representations. However, this effect was not so strong as to supersede preference for *expert* advice. Nonetheless, it led to participants receiving less trustworthy advice than they otherwise would have. In other words, their preference for *video* and *audio* led them to disregard good advice that was given as *text-only*.

Participants' self-reports show that they preferred to seek *video* and *audio* advice, because they thought these representations allowed them to make better trust assessments of individual pieces of advice: they considered their ability to infer advisor certainty in *video* and *audio* representations as higher than in *text-only* (S7). However, there is also evidence for media bias (P1) in participants' self-reports: for *audio* and *video* participants stated that they trusted the rich media advisor more than the *text-only* advisor (S3).

Whereas effects on *advice seeking* behaviour and users' self-reports are important, one could argue that the real test for media bias is whether someone acts on advice. Hence, we also investigated *advice uptake*. While there was an effect of advisor *expertise* on advice uptake, no effect of media representation, i.e. no media bias was found (P1). This result is reassuring as it shows that users' trust, measured by *advice uptake*, cannot be easily swayed by choice of media representation. On the other hand, the lack of effect of media representation also showed that the richer representations *video* and *audio*, which participants evidently — based on their *advice seeking* behaviour and self-reports — considered to give more insight into trustworthiness, did not allow an improved discrimination between trustworthy and less trustworthy pieces of advice. This conclusion is also supported by the results of the *sensitivity* measure, which did not investigate participants' ability to detect the expert, but their *sensitivity* to the correctness of individual pieces of advice. There was no significant difference in *sensitivity* to correct advice between all the *rich* media representations and *text-only*. The good performance at detecting the correctness of *expert* advice in all media representation suggests that most information was conveyed in lexical cues and that little extra information could be gained by the other interpersonal cues (para-verbal and visual cues) that were conveyed in the *rich* media representations. Hence, while participants thought that *audio* and *video* offer them superior *sensitivity*, no such effect was found.

6   Conclusions

This study investigated whether richer representations result in either a positive media bias (P1) or increased sensitivity for cues of expertise (P2) compared to *text-only* representations. We analysed participants' *advice seeking* and their *sensitivity* to correct advice in a situation of limited advice and financial risk. We found that participants mainly *sought advice* from the expert advisor, irrespective of the media representation (P2). However, we found no *sensitivity* for correct advice when the advisor was a *non-expert*. This indicates that participants could not identify subtle differences between low levels of confidence in any media representation. For *expert* advice, participants showed higher *sensitivity* in all representations, including *text-only*. This finding questions classic media richness models that predicted that text-only communication suppresses cues that are essential for trust assessments.

Results for participants' advice seeking suggest that a bias (P1) for *audio* and in particular *video* representations can interfere with users' ability to discriminate effectively. The interference was caused by users' belief in the superiority of these media for trust assessments, which mirrored classic media richness models. This belief led them to choose *audio* or *video* over *text-only* even at the cost of missing out on *expert* advice. This preference could have negative consequences for users. Consider, for instance, a user browsing a health advice site and focusing exclusively on video advice — and thereby missing our on potentially better text advice. For designers, who wish to ensure high levels of trust, video is the best representation, followed by audio.

The *avatar* was not found to have a positive effect on trust. Creating an avatar from an audio stream without careful scripting may not be an advisable strategy for building trust with the current state of art of avatar development. However, the avatar, and even just a simple photo led to higher ratings of friendliness and enjoyment than text-only. So, if the design goal is engagement rather than inducing trust, our data suggests that these representations can be effective.

In this study we introduced a measure from signal detection theory, $p(A)$, to assess participants' ability to place trust correctly. As it is an easily calculated measure that captures both, (1) correctly placed trust and (2) correctly withheld trust, it can be employed in future studies, which seek to manipulate trustworthiness to assess the correctness of trust decisions. Since we found disparities between participants' self-reports and their actual behaviour, our results also provide further support for measuring trust by observing decision-making under risk, rather than only relying on self-reports. In Riegelsberger et al. [2005] we report an analysis of the effect of the level of financial risk on users' trusting behaviour.

Whilst this study exclusively looked at cues for expertise in the context of a general knowledge quiz, future studies could usefully employ a similar paradigm to research media effects for cues of motivation (e.g. wilful deception) in different trust-requiring situations.

Acknowledgements

We would like to thank Cyril Scott and Laurence Hepburn at DA Group (http://www.dagroupplc.com) for the V1 animation tool, as well as Maia Garau, Philip Bonhard, Hendrik Knoche, Alan Johnston, Clare Harries (UCL), Sascha Mahlke (TU Berlin), Richard Boardman (Google), and Konstantinos Chorianopoulos (Imperial College London). We would further like to thank the anonymous reviewers for their helpful comments.

References

Bacharach, M. & Gambetta, D. [2001], Trust in Signs, *in* K. S. Cook (ed.), *Trust in Society*, Russell Sage Foundation Publications, pp.148–84.

Bos, N., Olson, J. S., Olson, G. M., Wright, Z. & Gergle, D. [2002], Rich Media Helps Trust Development, *in* D. Wixon (ed.), *Proceedings of SIGCHI Conference on Human Factors in Computing Systems: Changing our World, Changing Ourselves (CHI'02), CHI Letters* **4**(1), ACM Press, pp.135–40.

Corritore, C. L., Kracher, B. & Wiedenbeck, S. [2003], On-line Trust: Concepts, Evolving Themes, A Model, *International Journal of Human–Computer Studies* **58**(6), 737–58.

Davis, J. P., Farnham, S. D. & Jensen, C. [2002], Decreasing Online 'bad' Behavior, *in* L. Terveen & D. Wixon (eds.), *CHI'02 Extended Abstracts of the Conference on Human Factors in Computing Systems*, ACM Press, pp.718–9.

Deutsch, M. [1958], Trust and Suspicion, *Journal of Conflict Resolution* **2**(4), 265–79.

Fogg, B. J. [2003], *Persuasive Technology*, Morgan-Kaufmann.

Giddens, A. [1990], *The Consequences of Modernity*, Stanford University Press.

Handy, C. [1995], Trust and the Virtual Organization, *Harvard Business Review* **73**(3), 40–50.

Hinton, P. R. (ed.) [1993], *The Psychology of Interpersonal Perception*, Routledge.

Horn, D. B., Olson, J. S., & Karasik, L. [2002], The Effects of Spatial and Temporal Video Distortion on Lie Detection Performance, *in* L. Terveen & D. Wixon (eds.), *CHI'02 Extended Abstracts of the Conference on Human Factors in Computing Systems*, ACM Press, pp.716–8.

McNicol, D. A. [1972], *A Primer of Signal Detection Theory*, Allen and Unwin.

Olson, J. S., Zheng, J., Bos, N., Olson, G. M., & Veinott, E. [2002], Trust without Touch: Jumpstarting Long-distance Trust with Initial Social Activities, *in* D. Wixon (ed.), *Proceedings of SIGCHI Conference on Human Factors in Computing Systems: Changing our World, Changing Ourselves (CHI'02)*, *CHI Letters* **4**(1), ACM Press, pp.141–6.

Rice, R. E. [1992], Task Analyzability, Use of New Medium and Effectiveness: A Multi-site Exploration of Media Richness, *Organization Science* **3**(4), 475–400.

Riegelsberger, J., Sasse, M. A. & McCarthy, J. D. [2005], Do People Trust Their Eyes More Than Their Ears? Media Bias While Seeking Expert Advice, *in* G. van der Veer & C. Gale (eds.), *CHI'05 Extended Abstracts of the Conference on Human Factors in Computing Systems*, ACM Press, pp.1745–8.

Short, J. A., Williams, E. & Christie, B. [1976], *The Social Psychology of Telecommunications*, John Wiley & Sons.

Swerts, M., Krahmer, E., Barkhuysen, P. & van de Laar, L. [2004], Audiovisual Cues to Uncertainty, Paper presented at the ISCA Workshop on Error Handling in Spoken Dialogue Systems. http://fdlwww.kub.nl/ krahmer/Pubs%5Cerror.pdf (last accessed 2005-06-02).

Thurstone, L. L. [1927], Law of Comparative Judgement, *Psychological Review* **34**, 273–86.

van Mulken, S., Andre, E. & Müller, J. [1999], An Empirical Study on the Trustworthiness of Life-like Interface Agents, *in* H.-J. Bullinger & J. Zieger (eds.), *Proceedings of the 8th International Conference on Human–Computer Interaction (HCI International '99)*, Vol. 2, Lawrence Erlbaum Associates, pp.152–6.

Walther, J. B. [1996], Computer-mediated Communication: Impersonal, Interpersonal and Hyperpersonal Interaction, *Communication Research* **23**(1), 3–43.

Whittaker, S. & O'Conaill, B. [1997], The Role of Vision in Face-to-Face and Mediated Communication, *in* K. E. Finn, A. J. Sellen & S. B. Wilbur (eds.), *Video-mediated Communication*, Lawrence Erlbaum Associates, pp.23–49.

Winston, J. S., Strange, B., O'Doherty, J. & Dolan, R. J. [2002], Automatic and Intentional Brain Responses during Evaluation of Trustworthiness of Faces, *Nature Neuroscience* 5(3), 277–83.

Yaniv, I. & Kleinberger, E. [2000], Advice Taking in Decision Making: Egocentric Discounting and Reputation Formation, *Organizational Behavior and Human Decision Processes* 83(2), 260–81.

Zuckerman, M., de Paulo, B. M. & Rosenthal, R. [1981], Verbal and Nonverbal Communication of Deception, *Advances in Experimental Social Psychology* 14, 1–59.

Cultural Representations in Web Design: Differences in Emotions and Values

Claire Dormann

Human Oriented Technology Lab, Carleton University
1125 Colonel By Drive, Ottawa, Ontario K1S 5A7, Canada
Tel: *+1 613 530 2600 ext 6027*
Email: *cdormann@connect.carleton.ca*

Understanding cultural characteristics of websites is becoming increasingly important in a global context. Hofstede's theories are proposed as a framework for studying cultural differences in websites. An exploratory study based on Hofstede's Masculine–Feminine (MAS) dimension was conducted. We wanted to investigate differences in emotional expressions and values between homepages from countries with different MAS orientations. As emotion is an important aspect of Web design and subject to cultural differences, we wanted to see if users did perceive emotion variations between those homepages. Results from the study emphasize differences between sites belonging to the two MAS poles, both for values and emotions and, in particular, that different types of emotions were identified in relation to homepages.

Keywords: Web design, homepages, cultural differences, Hofstede, cultural dimensions, emotions, values.

1 Introduction

Understanding cultural characteristics of websites is becoming increasingly important not only for modelling information but also for making sites appealing. Embedding relevant values and creating the appropriate emotional context can facilitate comprehension and acceptance of information, and support joy of use. Emotion seems to be a key factor in making appealing and engaging websites [Jennings 2000]. Members of different culture groups interpret information and emotions differently because they apply different sets of values [Tung & Quaddus 2002].

In order to be effective, designers must understand and be aware of the cultural priorities and of the value system of viewers. Thus, we should identify factors that are relevant and sensitive to cultural differences.

Marcus & West Gould [2000] proposed that Hofstede's model could be used to identify and study cultural variations between websites. Hofstede [1997] recognized differences in values between cultures and demonstrated that cultures vary along consistent fundamental dimensions. Besides, emotions, like values, are also culturally dependant. Thus emotions might also vary within these cultural dimensions. As in Web design, little attention has been paid to cultural differences in values and especially in emotions, it was decided to conduct an exploratory study based on Hofstede's theory. The objectives of this paper are to explore differences in emotional expressions and values between homepages varying in a cultural dimension.

In this paper, Hofstede's approach to cultural differences is presented, and then the relation between culture and emotion is highlighted. This paper more specifically focuses on the masculine and feminine (MAS) dimension. The exploratory study is introduced, and results are then presented and discussed. We first discuss value differences found between MAS homepages. Then we consider emotional assessment through quantitative and qualitative data. We then present our conclusions and highlight areas for further study. We hope that knowledge gathered during this study will raise awareness of the importance of cultural differences in emotions, and be useful to Web designers.

2   Culture, Value and Emotion

In this section, we first highlight the role of cultural differences in representations. Then Hofstede's theory is briefly presented regarding cultural dimensions and values. We more particularly focus on the feminine-masculine dimension. Last, we refer to cultural differences in emotions.

2.1   *Cultural Differences in Representations*

The basis of cultural differences can be considered to reside in representations used in the applications and the meaning conveyed by these representations [Bourges-Waldegg & Scrivener 1998]. Interface elements affected by culture like colour, symbols, or sound tend to be problematic because their meanings are not correctly understood and they are interpreted differently by users. Moreover Smith et al. [2004] advocate that site elements should match the expectations of the local culture. Besides sounds and language cues, these elements acting as cultural attractors include visual elements that form the 'look and feel' of websites. Pictures, by communicating values and emotions, are especially important as cultural attractors because visual representations can have different emotional weights in different cultures. In this study, we are more particularly interested in 'cultural attractors' instantiated by visual representations.

2.2   *Cultural Dimension*

Hofstede describes cultures as the collective programming of the mind distinguishing members of one group or category of people from another. Cultural value orientations represent the basic and core beliefs of a culture. Definitions of values are numerous. Christiansen & Hansen [2001] see values as representing motivations. Values can serve as standards that guide our choices, beliefs, attitudes and actions. They can influence preferences and choices for products.

According to Hofstede, a culture varies along different dimensions: power distance, collectivism-individualism, uncertainty avoidance, long and short-term orientation and masculinity-femininity.

To limit the scope of our study, we selected one of Hofstede's dimensions (masculinity-femininity). Masculinity pertains to societies in which social gender roles are clearly distinct, men are supposed to be assertive, tough, and focused on material success whereas women are supposed to be tender and caring for others. Femininity pertains to societies in which social gender roles overlap. Both men and women can, for example, be tender. Femininity-masculinity is instantiated in several cultural values. Masculine cultures promote values such as ambition and competition, while feminine cultures promote values such as good relationships, or quality of life.

In Web design, we assumed that differences in value orientations between sites with opposite MAS orientations can be identified, and that feminine values are expressed more in sites from feminine countries and similarly masculine values in sites from masculine countries.

2.3   Emotion and Cultural Dimension

The idea that emotions are tied to culture has received considerable attention from researchers. Kitayama & Markus [1994] argue that culture and emotion are inextricably linked: cultural experiences shape one's emotional experiences. Cultural variations in the component of emotions included display rules, antecedent events (i.e. what external event cause an emotion) and non-verbal communication [Mesquita 2002]. Besides, emotion differences have also been identified between feminine and masculine cultures. Cultural femininity correlates strongly with higher emotional intensity [Basabe et al. 2002]. Moreover more affluent feminine cultures show higher pleasantness of emotional experiences. Moreover, an important consequence of cultural values of feminine countries is the perceived obligation to provide emotional support.

Aeker [1998], for example, identifies differences in emotional impact of advertisements for different culture orientations. Emphasizing emotional differences is thus pertinent for Web design. As there also exist cultural differences in emotions, contrasts in emotional expressions within homepages should be investigated. It can be expected that, as with values, emotions can be differentiated between sites from different MAS countries and that emotions play a more important role in feminine sites. Han & Shavitt [1996] suggested in relation with the individualism and collectivism dimension that advertisements consistent with the underlying cultural orientation of a specific country are more persuasive. Similarly, webpages which are more congruent with values and emotional orientations of viewers should be more positively evaluated.

3   Investigating Emotions and Values

In order to find out the extent and types of cultural values and emotion orientations expressed in pages from MAS countries we carried out an exploratory study based on Hofstede's theory. We decide to restrict our study to one domain, university homepages.

3.1   Choosing Values

We wanted to find out which values differentiate masculine and feminine countries. Although many cultural studies use Hofstede as a framework, we did not find any consistent definitions or instantiations of values, especially regarding the masculine and feminine dimension. A list of values for each pole of the MAS dimension was established by extracting values from Hofstede's writing and his description of key differences between feminine and masculine societies.

We selected values that we believed were the most pertinent for our domain. The list of values consists of six feminine and six masculine values. The feminine values are caring for others, equal opportunity, good relationships, quality of life, personal development, and tenderness. The masculine values are ambition, authority, competition, high performance, study hard, and toughness. During the analysis of websites, tradition seemed an important factor in university sites. Since tradition might have a bearing on differentiation between sites from different MAS countries, tradition was added to the list of values.

3.2   Emotions Rating

We wanted to initiate an investigation into this aspect of Web design, as emotions seem to be an important marker of cultural differences. It was decided to limit the inquiry to a small number of emotions through a rating scheme and gather further information through qualitative data. Studies of facial expressions of emotions have consistently yielded pleasure and level of arousal as at least two of basic dimensions of emotions. These two dimensions are primary and they typically account for more variance in emotional judgements [Mehrabian & Russell 1977]. We selected four basic emotions: aesthetic, boring, interesting, unpleasant, related to pleasure and arousal, as a general emotional measure for Web design. We added four specific emotions connected to the MAS dimension that could differentiate masculine and feminine sites in our domain: modest, challenge, pride and aggressive.

3.3   Selecting Homepages

The role of visual representations is believed to be especially important as a cultural attractor. To focus on this aspect, homepages from different MAS countries were selected and given in their original language (also different from languages used by participants in the study, none of whom spoke Italian, Danish or Swedish). It was hoped in this way to focus the participants' attention away from the textual information to the visual component. Nevertheless, some of the page keywords (e.g. link words) were understandable (e.g. universitat is close enough to university).

We restricted our investigation to one domain: university homepages. It is thought that values might be more homogeneous inside a specific domain [Hong & Chiu 2001]. Hofstede rated 53 countries on indices for each cultural dimension normalizing values (usually) of 0 to 100 and ranking them on their value rating. A

University	URL	
Universita degli studi di Brescia	www.unibs.it	M
Universita degli studi di Cagliari	www.unica.it	M
Universita degli studi Sannio	www.unisannio.it	M
Universita de l'Insubria	www3.unisubria.it/unisubria/home.html	M
Roskilde Universitetcenter	www.ruc.dk	F
Vaxjo universiteit	www.vxu.se	F
Karlstads universitet	www.kau.se	F
Lulea tekniska universitet	www.luth.se	F

Table 1: Selected homepages.

high value implies a strongly masculine culture and a low value a strongly feminine culture. Moreover, rank 1 is the most masculine country and 53 the most feminine. Homepages were selected from Italy as an example of a very masculine country (score rank 4/5 and MAS score 95) and two Scandinavian countries, Denmark and Sweden, as examples of feminine countries (Sweden score rank 53 and MAS score 5, Denmark score rank 50 MAS score 16), according to Hofstede's [1997] ratings. We looked at all universities in both Scandinavian countries (as smaller in term of population they have fewer universities). As for Italy, a random selection of university homepages was made. To choose pages representative for each country we eliminated first a small number of the most extreme designs. We labelled as extreme designs pages that were very different from the norms of that country. Pages were then chosen on a random basis. The four homepages from masculine countries (M) and four homepages for feminine countries (F) can be seen in Table 1.

3.4 The Exploratory Study

Participants consisted of a sample of 18 students from The Netherlands, 9 males and 9 females from a pool of undergraduates. Participants were paid. It has to be noted that the Netherlands is a feminine country (i.e. score rank 51 and MAS score 14). Each webpage was printed on a sheet and given to participants; we alternated feminine pages with masculine pages. After viewing each page, participants performed tasks as follows. They were first asked to write down their impressions and reactions to the page. Next, participants had to rate emotions and values. Participants rated their emotional impressions of a homepage for each of the eight emotions on a five-point scale (1 none, to 5 very). Then participants had to evaluate a homepage and rate each value on a five point scale considering to what extent the value was present in the homepage (i.e. 1 value is not present, and 5 strongly present). To conclude the session, whenever possible we conducted a short interview with participants and asked them to sort homepages by order of preference.

4 Results

The goal of this study is to investigate differences in value and emotion orientations between homepages from masculine and feminine countries. The results for values

	F	P-value	Aver.F	Aver.M
Caring for other	9.86	0.0035	2.46	1.76
Good Relationship	7.44	0.01	2.86	2.22
Equal opportunity	3.07	0.09	2.49	2.03
Tenderness	8.91	0.005	2.67	2.06
Personal development	5.12	0.03	2.94	2.34
Quality of life	21.29	<0.000	3.16	2.16

(a) Feminine values

	F	P-value	Aver.F	Aver.M
Ambition	0.19	0.67	2.9	3
Competition	8.91	0.005	2.15	2.58
Authority	10.27	0.003	1.8	2.6
Study Hard	1.25	0.27	2.18	2.43
Toughness	11.7	0.002	1.72	2.38
High Performance	0.003	0.95	2.22	2.24
Tradition	72.75	<0.000	1.6	3.21

(b) Masculine values

Table 2: Average and ANOVA for feminine and masculine values.

are first presented. For emotions, the quantitative then the qualitative data are discussed. Directions for future studies are then further highlighted.

4.1 Values in Homepages from MAS Countries

We expected feminine values to have a higher rating in homepages from feminine countries and masculine values to have a higher rating in homepages from masculine countries.

In accordance with Marcus & West Gould [2000], results show that MAS values are indeed represented in websites. Our results confirm our expectation with regard to feminine values: all participants did rate higher all feminine values in feminine homepages, these in accordance with Hofstede (see Table 2a). In Table 2a, the averages for each feminine value are given for the four pages from Feminine countries (Aver.F) and for the four pages from Masculine pages (Aver.M). In order to compare differences between homepages from masculine and feminine countries, we performed an ANOVA analysis for each value.

From the masculine values, only toughness, competition and authority make a significant difference between homepages (see Table 2b). Thus in what we regarded as masculine values, our expectations are only confirmed for three of the values rated higher in homepages from masculine countries. Tradition [p < 0.000] is also significantly different between MAS homepages. The value tradition has higher ratings in masculine homepages than in feminine ones (see Table 2b).

	F	P-value		Aver.F	Aver.M
Aesthetic	4.36	0.04	Aesthetic	3.36	2.84
Unpleasant	6.8	0.01	Unpleasant	1.46	1.92
Exciting	0.09	0.76	Exciting	2.84	2.77
Boring	14.63	<0.000	Boring	1.58	2.36
Challenging	1.85	0.18	Challenging	2.83	2.49
Aggressive	4.64	0.04	Aggressive	1.60	2.01
Modest	0.19	0.66	Modest	2.60	2.50
Pride	3.46	0.07	Pride	2.89	3.27

(a) ANOVA   (b) Means

Table 3: ANOVA and mean on emotions.

In our study, we only evaluated for a limited number of values, thus other masculine values might better characterize masculine sites. In regard to the masculine values of study hard, ambition, and high performance, they were rated in the same way in masculine and feminine sites. It has been shown that countries are not uniformly homogeneous on Hofstede's dimension. Chinese as a cultural group have a moderately high degree of collectivism yet they sometimes show an individualistic orientation in some domains [Hong & Chiu 2001]. Our particular domain, universities, could prove more masculine orientated or exhibit traits normally associated with the masculine pole.

The technology, or Web design 'know-how', could also have influenced the results. The design tradition pertaining to websites, where performance is an important value, could have influenced ratings on sites of both poles of the MAS dimension. As remarked by Nakakoji [1996] reflecting on software design, system functionality is often unconsciously affected by the underlying traditions of the system designer culture.

4.2 Emotions

In this section we highlight the importance of emotions as cultural markers by discussing findings related to the quantitative and qualitative data. The qualitative data is discussed in connection to Osgood's work on cross-cultural affective meaning and stress differences in emotion.

4.2.1 Emotion Rating

Emotions as values were seen as an important vector of cultural variations. It was thought that participants would rate emotions accordingly to MAS orientations (e.g. modest belonging to the feminine pole should be higher in feminine sites and aggressive, challenging and pride belonging to the masculine pole should be higher in masculine pages).

In order to compare differences between homepages from masculine and feminine countries, we performed an ANOVA analysis for each emotion. We did find small significant differences between feminine and masculine pages for aesthetics, unpleasant, and as well as for aggressive and pride for the MAS dimension (see Tables 3a & b). In particular, there was a highly significant difference for boring between pages from countries with different MAS orientations. The masculine pages were rated higher for boring, unpleasant, pride and aggressive while the feminine pages were rated higher for aesthetic (see Table 3b). However no significant differences were found for exciting, modest and challenge.

What is striking here is that negative emotions (especially boring) were attributed with designs that did not match the cultural orientations of the Dutch participants while aesthetics was viewed more strongly in feminine sites. This is congruent with findings from computer studies and consumer behaviour. It has been shown that American retailers who ignore cultural differences and show a lack of sensitivity to local culture incur substantial losses [de Mooij & Hofstede 2002] Sites whose attributes closely match the cultural perceptions of users are more likely to engage them; they provide lower level of consumer dissonance [Simon 2001]. Thus an emotional fit seems to be needed between sites and participants, and this could prove a crucial aspect of Web design.

4.2.2   Qualitative Data

In our study, we asked participants to describe their first impressions and reactions about each page. We asked this because we wanted to learn a little more about design aspects, and which aspects were more noticed.

We performed an initial analysis of participants' answers. We found that answers related to three areas of Web designs: graphical design, informational and emotional design. The graphical aspect is mostly related to the utilization of images and colour, although we also found some reference to typography and layout. The informational aspect is related to links, amount of information, and organization of sites.

In the participants' answers we found a few answers directly describing participants' feelings, some examples are "I feel warmly welcome to go studying there", "It gives me a relaxed feeling", and "Makes me feel that I want to see the building at least". However, participants used a lot of emotional terms in their answers. We found more than sixty terms related to emotion in the qualitative data. Subsequently, an exhaustive list of all emotion terms with their frequencies was made so that the emotional data could be analysed in more depth, and that homepages could be compared.

4.2.3   Emotional Design

Before analysing in-depth the emotional words, some general remarks seem appropriate. We found only one instantiation for most of the terms, although a few terms are more frequently used (see Figure 1). Most of the terms are positive emotional terms; there are fewer negative emotional words. A second distinction can be made between negative and positive emotional words. The negative terms tend to refer to a more intense form of emotion, examples are *difficult, disturbing*, or *messy*. By contrast most of positive terms are situated in the more neutral part of the emotional spectrum: examples are *nice, friendly, quiet*, or *pleasant*.

Looking at emotional terms more closely suggested that they relate to different aspects of emotions, or rather different categories of emotions. Pouivet [2000]

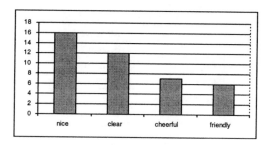

Figure 1: Emotion frequencies.

contrasted aesthetic and cognitive emotions, stressing the relation between aesthetic pleasure and cognition. In our study, terms such as beautiful and harmonious relates to a more aesthetic dimension of emotion while intuitive and difficult pertain to the cognitive dimension of emotion. Moreover emotional terms like friendly seem to indicate a more social aspect of emotion. In order to find if we could establish further emotional differences between designs from MAS countries, it was decided to refine the analysis of these key words.

4.2.4 Affective Qualifiers

Our analysis of emotional terms is related to Osgood's classification of affect metaphors. From the established list of emotional key terms, we develop a taxonomy to include all terms found in our study. Based on this classification, we evaluate differences between designs belonging to sites from the two sides of the MAS dimension.

Emotion knowledge is often organized into a two or three-dimensional structure, with positive-negative valence, activity or arousal, and potency or dominance. Complementary approaches include the development of emotional lexicons ranging from 200 to 3000 terms [Shaver et al. 2001]. By contrast emotional evaluations focus on a small range of emotions reflecting the aim of each study [Chaudhuri & Buck 1995].

In view of the lack of an integrated framework, it was decided to follow Osgood's classification on metaphors of affect [Osgood et al. 1975]. Their research on cross-cultural universals of affective meaning, seemed a suitable starting point to analyse cultural emotional differences. While developing a classification of semantic terms for affective meaning within the evaluation dimension, Osgood et al. identified differences in affective structure factors as related to: social interaction (e.g. likeable), emotional reactions (e.g. happy), aesthetic-sensory experiences (e.g. beautiful) and abstract qualities (e.g. helpful). As our initial analysis observed distinctions similar to Osgood, we based our final analysis on their findings.

As there was no exhaustive list of emotional terms for these categories, we decided to develop a complete taxonomy to cover all terms contained in participants' answers. The list of emotional terms was given to four judges. First a short explanation of the problem and aims of the taxonomy was given. Then each judge

Social interaction	Emotional reaction	Aesthetic-sensory	Abstract quality
Caring	Boring	Attractive	Accurate
Cheerful	Calm	Beautiful	Balance
Friendly	Chaotic	Harmonious	Basic
Traditional	Cold	Horrible	Clear
Trust	Curious	Nice	Dense

Table 4: Affective qualifiers.

was given Osgood's classification and examples. Judges were asked to classify emotional terms into the four categories (i.e. social interaction, emotional reaction, aesthetic-sensory, and abstract quality). Each affective term could be placed into one category only.

As a result, a few of the terms were rejected as not qualifying as affective terms. An agreement was reached for 40 out 66 terms (for three out of four judges). Final agreement was obtained through discussion. Any term that was not agreed upon at that point was discarded. Subsequently, all terms included in the taxonomy were coded as belonging to social interaction (SI), emotional reaction (ER), aesthetic sensory (AS), or abstract quality (AQ). Some examples for each category are given in Table 4. We found a smaller number of affective qualifiers for social interaction compared to other categories (in terms of affective words).

Based on this taxonomy, we compared the homepages from the different MAS countries. We found a small significant effect for emotional reaction (ANOVA, $F = 3.11$, $p = 0.085$) and for aesthetic-sensory ($F = 3.21$) and ($p = 0.08$) between feminine and masculine sites. The participants describe their impressions of homepages more in terms of emotional reaction (average 1.77) or aesthetic-sensory (average 1.89) in the feminine pages than in the masculine pages (ER, average 0.83 and AS, average 1.11). No effect was found for social interaction and abstract quality; these categories were represented in the same way in masculine and feminine homepages.

The results are congruent with Marcus & West Gould [2000] who presumed that aesthetics was a feature distinguishing feminine and masculine pages. As was discussed, feminine cultures tend to express more positive emotions. Our results indicate that emotion might indeed be a more significant factor in feminine websites. However, based on our findings on values, we would have expected also a difference in the social interaction category, but such was not the case. We should refine the role of emotions for the MAS dimension for examples for different types of participants. More generally, the proposed taxonomy could serve as the basis for comparing and designing websites, as different types of emotions might be suited to different cultures or specific sub-cultures.

4.3 Emotion and Cultural Differences

Emotion is an important factor that differentiates feminine and masculine sites. We have suggested that creating an emotional fit between sites is needed. Cultural factors such as emotions, making viewers more or less receptive to Web designs, must be taken into account when designing and comparing sites effectiveness across borders. This is especially relevant for sites where cultural differences are expected to be an important element of an audience or a site domain.

Emotional differences should be further studied in relation with other cultural dimensions. It could be valuable to pursue complementary studies between Hofstede dimensions and emotions, such as for uncertainty avoidance (UAI) or with the collective-individualist dimension. The collective-individualist dimension refers to priority given to the group or the individual; UAI defines the extent to which people feel threatened by an ambiguous situation. Cultures with strong uncertainty avoidance are more emotional while the reverse applies for cultures with weak uncertainty avoidance [Basabe et al. 2002]. In particular, high UAI cultures experience more negative emotions such as fear, anger and sadness. Thus, uncertainty avoidance might enhance or inhibit the need for emotional expressions in websites. Moreover, users from high UAI cultures could experience stronger emotional reactions to usability problems.

In collective culture, emotions tended to be grounded in relationships. These cultures foster emotions that maintain group cohesion and promote harmony as well as empathy. Emotions in these cultures are based on social rather than on inner feelings as in individualistic cultures [Mesquita 2002]. Thus it can be expected that designs from collective cultures will display and generate more social emotions than sites from individualistic cultures.

We believe that exploring the relation between culture and emotion is particularly relevant in connection to appeal. Kim et al. [2003] showed that design factors can be closely connected to the evocation of specific emotions in webpages. We should indeed explore further the role of emotions as cultural attractors.

In websites such as the university domain and electronic shops, the portrayal of people is widespread. Human beings are experts at interpreting facial expressions and body language and consequently they are profoundly susceptible to emotions, moods and actions of others. Empathy with persuasive messages and personas may enhance consumer self image, and express consumer values [Caudle 1990]. Culture influences the expression and recognition of emotions, as well as when emotions are displayed. We believed that human representation is particularly sensitive to cultural differences. Although no formal analysis was undertaken on the university homepages from MAS countries, it was noted that representations of people seem more numerous in feminine countries and that in Sweden women seem to figure more prominently on homepages. Thus cultural differences on Hofstede's dimensions could influence the representations and utilizations of people: their presence or absence, grouping (individual vs. family), gender, perspective and facial expressions, etc.

In some domains, such as retailing, creating the appropriate emotional experience for specific cultural groups could be a key design strategy. Diverse types of appeal, rational vs. emotional or even different emotional genres, might be more appropriate for different cultures. Thus, we could further explore the appropriateness of the emotional mix in functions of different cultures and audiences.

van Slyke et al. [2002] and Simon [2001] stress differences between genders, which impacted the perception of websites. We should investigate in more depth especially, in connection with emotions, what is within a single country or culture, and the extent of gender differences. After all, the stereotype that females are more emotional tends to be pervasive across many countries. In the MAS dimension, men and women's values are expected to be more different in masculine countries, thus a gender effect might also be expected for emotions [Hofstede 1998].

4.4 Limitations

There were several limitations with this study which need to be discussed. There are limitations with the number of homepages included in the sample, and the number of participants. We have only studied a specific domain, and as we have discussed, results could have been swayed by the domain investigated. We should thus extend this study to other domains. Moreover, the cultural orientation of participants (i.e. students) was derived from Hofstede national ratings, thus it is possible that this specific group could have been different from the national norm. Thus future studies should include a larger socio-demographic group and, we might also want to check the value system of participants.

A restricted number of values were evaluated in this study, values which were deemed as more relevant to the university domain. Thus other values could be salient in this domain or dimension. Further studies are needed to develop and validate the construct of values in the MAS dimension, in particular for Web design. We have discussed the possible influence of technology on results; similarly national policies such as 'equal opportunity rights' might also have affected results. When studying cultural differences, we might want to identify characteristics of specific domains that would mediate national culture orientations.

We need to revise and extend emotional rating scales, to evaluate more consistently for emotion differences in relation with a cultural dimension. In particular, we need to look further at the emotion construct. To develop appropriate rating scales for the investigation of cultural differences in emotions might be more complex than anticipated. There might not be a coherent view of what is considered an emotion (e.g. pride). Moreover, different cultures could use the same term differently [Kitayama to appear]. Although we can speak of an aesthetic emotion, cultural differences in aesthetics could be studied separately.

More importantly, we have only carried out this study with participants of a feminine country, thus we should replicate the study with participants from a masculine country. Further experimental studies are needed to investigate emotional cultural differences in Web design.

5 Conclusion

This paper suggests that the understanding of cultural variations is important when designing websites. We have presented an exploratory study related to Hofstede's cultural theories. Within our specific framework, we have shown that there were differences between masculine and feminine sites and that in practice users did perceive cultural differences between websites as described by Hofstede. We observed in accordance with Hofstede's theories that feminine values were more strongly expressed in sites coming from feminine oriented cultures.

We have considered emotion as subject to cultural variations and emphasize differences between the two poles of the MAS dimension. Based on our qualitative analysis, we have proposed a taxonomy distinguishing between different affective factors that could help in contrasting emotional aspects of diverse websites. We think that this taxonomy could also be useful for carrying out emotion evaluations.

Our findings have some relevance for the localization and internationalization debates. We discuss issues that might need to be taken in consideration during localization. The creation of a single universally appealing global site might not be feasible given differences between cultures and users. However, during internationalization, and when a single site is wanted, an awareness of these issues is important especially to minimize negative implications of designs (e.g. emotional impact) for each of the cultures considered.

Future research issues were discussed in relation with emotions. An important issue is related to finding suitable methods for the investigation of cultural differences in emotion research to insure that the same phenomena is measured consistently across cultures.

We suggested studying emotional differences within the diverse cultural dimensions, and for gender differences. We could for example investigate different types of emotional appeals and their effects across cultures. It could also be interesting to look into the relation between human representations, values, and emotions (e.g. such as trust).

We could also extend our investigation from homepages to websites, as we think that cultural differences can also have some bearing on information architecture. In this way we could also evaluate cultural differences for usability. It has been shown that culture influences the relation between pleasant and unpleasant emotions, thus we could explore the influences of cultures on user satisfaction [Schimmack et al. 2002]. We believe that the relation between emotional and cultural differences is a promising area for future research in Web design.

Acknowledgement

A special thanks to Mari Carmen Puerta Melguizo, and Johan Hoorn for helping me with the affective taxonomy and especially Chisalita Cristina for her general support and contribution. This worked was partly carried out with a fellowship from Cognos.

References

Aeker, J. [1998], Individualist versus Collectivist Cultures: How Ego versus Other-focus Emotional Appeal Affect Persuasion, *Asia Pacific Advances in Consumer Research* **3**, 56–66.

Basabe, N., Paez, D. & Valencia, J. [2002], Cultural Dimensions, Socio-Economic Development, Climate and Emotional Hedonic Level, *Cognition and Emotion* **16**(1), 103–25.

Bourges-Waldegg, P. & Scrivener, S. [1998], Meaning as the Central Issue in Cross-Cultural HCI Design, *Interacting with Computers* **9**(3), 287–309.

Caudle, F. [1990], Communication and Arousal of Emotion: Some Implications of Facial Expression Research for Magazine Advertisements, *in* S. Agres, J. Edell & T. Dubtsky (eds.), *Emotion in Advertising*, Quorum Books, pp.127–59.

Chaudhuri, A. & Buck, R. [1995], Affect, Reason and Persuasion, *Human Communications Research* 12(3), 422–40.

Christiansen, C. & Hansen, F. [2001], The Use of Social Psychological and Applied Value Research for the Measurement of Cultural Differences Among Consumers, *Asia Pacific Advances in Consumer Research* 4, 5–22.

de Mooij, M. & Hofstede, G. [2002], Convergence and Divergence in Consumer Behavior: Implications for International Retailing, *Journal of Retailing* 78(1), 61–9.

Han, S. & Shavitt, S. [1996], Persuasion and Culture: Advertising Appeals in Individualistic and Collectivistic Societies, *in* L. A. P. . S. E. Taylor (ed.), *Sociocultural Perspectives in Social Psychology*, Prentice–Hall, pp.217–40.

Hofstede, G. [1997], *Cultures and Organisations Software of the Mind*, McGraw-Hill.

Hofstede, G. [1998], Identifying Organizational Subcultures: an Empirical Approach, *Journal of Management Studies* 35(1), 1–12.

Hong, Y.-y. & Chiu, C.-y. [2001], Toward a Paradigm Shift: From Cross-cultural Differences in Social Cognition to Social–Cognitive Mediation of Cultural Differences, *Social Cognition* 19(3), 181–96.

Jennings, M. [2000], Theory and Models for Creating Engaging and Immersive Ecommerce Web Sites, *in* J. Prasad & W. Nance (eds.), *Proceedings of the ACM SIGCPR Conference on Computer Personnel Research (SIGCPR'00)*, ACM Press, pp.77–85.

Kim, J., Lee, J. & Choi, D. [2003], Designing Emotionally Evocative Homepages: an Empirical Study of the Quantitative Relations between Design Factors and Emotional Dimensions, *International Journal of Human–Computer Studies* 59(6), 899–940.

Kitayama, S. [to appear], Culture and Emotions, *in* N. Smelser & P. Balte (eds.), *International Encyclopedia of the Social Sciences*, Elsevier Science.

Kitayama, S. & Markus, H. R. [1994], An Introduction to Cultural Psychology and Emotional Research, *in* S. Kitayama & H. R. Markus (eds.), *Emotion and Culture: Empirical Studies of Mutual Influence*, American Psychological Association, pp.37–57.

Marcus, A. & West Gould, E. [2000], Crosscurrent Cultural Dimensions and Global Web User-Interface Design, *Interactions* 2(4), 32–46.

Mehrabian, A. & Russell, J. A. [1977], Evidence for a Three-Factor Theory of Emotions, *Journal of Research in Personality* 11(2), 273–94.

Mesquita, B. [2002], Culture and Emotions: Different Approaches to the Question, *in* T. Mayne & G. Bonanno (eds.), *Emotion: Current Issues and Future directions*, Guilford Press, pp.214–45.

Nakakoji, K. [1996], Beyond Language Translation: Crossing the Cultural Divide, *IEEE Software* 15(2), 42–6.

Osgood, C., May, H. & Miron, M. [1975], *Cross-Cultural Universals of Affective Meaning*, University of Illinois Press.

Pouivet, R. [2000], On the Cognitive Functioning of Aesthetic Emotions, *Leonardo* **33**(1), 49–53.

Schimmack, U., Shigehiro, O. & Diener, E. [2002], Cultural Influences on the Relation between Pleasant Emotions and Unpleasant Emotions: Asian Dialectic Philosophies or Individualism-Collectivism?, *Cognition and Emotion* **16**(6), 705–19.

Shaver, P., Schwartz, J. D., Kirson, J. & O'Connor, C. [2001], Emotion Knowledge: Further Exploration of a Prototype Approach, *in* W. G. Parrott (ed.), *Emotions in Social Psychology: Essential Readings*, Psychology Press, pp.27–69.

Simon, S. [2001], The Impact of Culture and Gender on Web Sites: An Empirical Study, *The Database for Advances in Information Systems* **32**(1), 18–37.

Smith, A., Dunckley, L., French, T., Minocha, S. & Chang, Y. [2004], A Process Model for Developing Usable Cross-cultural Websites, *Interacting with Computers* **16**(1), 63–91.

Tung, L. & Quaddus, M. [2002], Cultural Differences Explaining the Differences in Results in GSS: Implications for the Next Decade, *Decision Support Systems* **33**(2), 177–9.

van Slyke, C., Comunale, C. L. & Belanger, F. [2002], Gender Differences in Perceptions of Web-based Shopping, *Communications of the ACM* **45**(8), 82–6.

Interaction Design for Countries with a Traditional Culture: A Comparative Study of Income Levels and Cultural Values

Georg Strøm

*DIKU, University of Copenhagen, Universitetsparken 1,
DK-2100 Copenhagen O, Denmark*
Email: *georg@diku.dk*

It is often necessary to take differences in cultural values and ways of thinking into account when doing interaction design for use in other countries. This paper presents an empirical study of cultural differences between a low-income traditional country and a high-income developed country, and how these differences are reflected in design decisions made in the two countries. The study identifies differences in design decisions and possible consequences of them. The results indicate that the attitudes to reliability are the same in the two countries. The study identifies differences between the two countries as regards attitudes to privacy and honesty and describes how they can be taken into account when doing interaction design for use in other low-income countries.

Keywords: culture, values, international design, privacy, reliability, trust, Hofstede.

1 Introduction

Computers and software are not only used in the developed part of the world, they are essential for companies and public authorities in less developed countries, information processing is increasingly out-sourced to such countries, and they represent some of the fastest growing markets for mobile phones and telecommunication services.

Users of the Latin alphabet and users of the Chinese alphabet have different visual preferences [Prabhu & Harel 1999], and symbols that are acceptable in one culture may be offensive in another [Mullett & Sano 1995]. It is today generally agreed that such differences shall be taken into account in order to ensure that interfaces are usable and acceptable for local users. However, it may also be necessary to take into account that the cultural background of users affects how they operate and interact with an interface. Their goals and how they try to accomplish them are influenced both by their personal values and by the social context in which they live and work.

In this study I will investigate whether there are differences in personal values and ways of thinking that should be taken into account when doing interaction design for use in a less developed or low-income country, even in the case where the alphabet and other visible cultural characteristics are the same as in Europe or the United States.

A number of different methods have been used to determine cultural differences. Foucault et al. [2004] determine cultural differences through mediated immersion, where they surround themselves with artefacts describing another culture, and they do so-called concept explorations where members of the target culture comment on possible interface designs. However, such methods tend to focus on the appearance of an interface, not on how users interact with them.

Hofstede [2001] has investigated cultural variations on five different parameters, and Marcus et al. [2003] have deducted a number of cultural preferences of relevance for interface design from his parameters. Ford & Gelderblom [2003] have also used Hofstede as a basis when investigating how users with different cultures interact with an interface. However, Hofstede's parameters describe how people interact with each other, not how they interact with interfaces or physical objects, making it difficult to use his categories to predict how users will interact with an interface.

Singh & Kotzé [2003] measure cultural values of interest for interaction design directly by asking to what extent their participants agree with a number of statements. However, Nisbett [2003] notes that this method may underestimate cultural differences when the statements are interpreted differently by participants with different backgrounds. It is possible to overcome some of these cultural differences in the interpretations of questions by focusing on people's behaviour as Hall [1959] does in his classic anthropological study of how time and space are used in different cultures.

In this study I will use similar methods to determine differences in cultural values between Denmark and Philippines. The majority in Philippines are Christian, the Latin alphabet is used, the grammar and part of the vocabulary of the national language, Tagalog, are derived from Spanish, a European language, and the school system and the culture in general are strongly influenced by European and American values and cultural symbols. This means that many visible cultural characteristics are the same in Denmark and Philippines. However, the differences in cultural values span a large part of the possible global variation, as it is described by Hofstede [2001] and World Values Survey [Inglehart 1997; World Values Survey 2005], another major study of differences in cultural values. See Table 1.

2 Method

This study was done in three stages:

Philippines	Denmark
Low income (1,080 USD GNI/capita)	High income (33,750 USD GNI/capita)
Traditional	Secular-rational (post-modern)
Masculine — survival values	Feminine — well-being values
Large power distance — inequality and privileges are considered normal.	Small power distance — equality is seen as ideal.
Collectivistic	Individualistic
Medium uncertainty avoidance	Low uncertainty avoidance — people accept ambiguity and new challenges

Table 1: Comparison between incomes and cultural values in Philippines and Denmark. The GNI/capita is now replacing the GNP/capita (The difference between the two figures is minimal). [Hofstede 2001; Inglehart 1997; World Bank Group 2005; World Values Survey 2005].

1. Identification of possible cultural differences through participant-observation.

2. Verification of the observed differences through a questionnaire.

3. Investigation through a questionnaire of how cultural differences were reflected in software design.

2.1 Identification of Possible Cultural Differences

In 2003 I stayed 9 weeks in Polanco, near Dipolog, in the Southern Philippines. My stay made it possible to use participant-observation, i.e.: " ... spending a great deal of time with and participating in the everyday life of the natives" [Nardi 1997]. My wife is Filipino, we stayed in the municipality where she had grown up, and I knew the area from earlier visits. We had rented an apartment, and my everyday activities were similar to those of a local citizen who had returned home after having worked abroad. I went into Dipolog to buy things for the household; I visited family, had dealings with the municipality, went to the local college to arrange for one of my wife's cousins whose studies we supported, and I talked with our neighbour who was a teacher and with other people in the city. People were in general eager to talk, which meant that it was easy to get information, and that I talked with a large number of people.

I did not plan to do particular activities in order to investigate specific cultural differences (that would have biased the investigation towards differences I in advance had expected to find). However, because of my professional background my observations inevitably tended to focus on the use of computers, the Internet, mobile phones and other electronic appliances.

I collected a number of incidents where people in the area appeared to act in ways that were definitely different from how they acted in Denmark. Based on the incidents I identified three cultural characteristics that I believed were relevant for interaction design and with apparent substantial differences between Philippines and Denmark. While doing that I kept a diary to support my memory.

2.2 Verification of the Observed Differences

Based on the participant-observation I designed a questionnaire. As recommended by Dray & Mrazek [1996], I worked with a local assistant (a young computer science graduate in my wife's family) who reviewed the questionnaire. It described eighteen specific situations and five possible emotional reactions, and each participant was asked to select the reaction that best fitted how he or she felt about each situation. The possible reactions were:

1. It is okay, it is the way it should be.

2. It makes no difference for me.

3. I don't like it, but it isn't important.

4. It irritates me.

5. It makes me angry.

The following are three examples of situations that respondents were asked about their reactions to:

1st situation: You have sent a text message with a personal joke to a friend. The joke is about a person you both know. You later find out that your friend has forwarded the message to at least six of your mutual friends.

3rd situation: You use an Internet café, and you know the people who runs it. One day you find out that they can see what sites you visit and that they sometimes read e-mails send from the cafe.

5th situation: The phone company has published on the Internet, phone numbers of all of their subscribers with full names, age and job information.

All situations described use of mobile phones, the Internet or computers in settings that could be understood by both Danish and Philippine students. (In particular the use of mobile phones had grown rapidly in the area since 2000 when I made a study of the introduction of them [Strøm 2002].)

My local assistant helped me to recruit the Filipino participants in the study (among students she knew in the city). The questionnaire was filled out during interviews with fourteen Filipino participants, thirteen students and one recent graduate, and after my return to Denmark by nineteen Danish students. All participants had a good understanding of English so it was possible to use the same English language questionnaire in both countries. There were about 40% male students in each group. The median age of the Danish students were 22 and of the Philippine students 19. (This partly reflects that it is possible to enrol in college after ten years of school in Philippines, whereas twelve years are required in Denmark).

2.3 Investigation of How Differences were Reflected in Software Design

I designed a questionnaire with eight questions about specific decisions that could be made when designing or setting up a computer system and with five possible outcomes for each decision. The decisions described in the questionnaire were of the type where an optimal technical solution cannot be found, so the answers only could be based on the opinions of the respondents, and the decisions were designed to be understandable by computer science students in Denmark and Philippines.

The following is an example of a design decision and possible choices (for reference the decisions are numbered in this paper from 21 to 28):

21st decision: You are setting up a computer to be used by a group of students in college. In addition to reports and course assignments, you can expect that the computer will be used for writing job applications and personal letters. How much will you do to prevent that other users of the computer, students or teachers, can read personal information belonging to one student?

1. It shall only be possible for students to store their materials in one open area on the computer. Anything stored in the open area is visible for and accessible to all users of the computer.

2. Each student can store his or her material in a personal folder. However, there is no protection of the contents of the folders. Other users may open a personal folder and read what is stored in it.

3. It shall be possible for students either to store their material in a personal folder without any protection, or to log on using a password and then store their personal materials in a special area. It may be possible for other users to download tools from the Internet and use them to break into such an area.

4. It shall only be possible for students to store their material on the computer in a special area, which require that they log on using a password. It may be possible for other users to download tools from the Internet and use them to break into such an area.

5. It shall not be possible for students to store any materials on the computer. They can only store material on a personal diskette that they take with them after having used the computer.

The questionnaire was answered by twenty Philippine computer science students and by sixteen Danish Computer Science students (It was sent to Philippines and distributed and collected by my local assistant). The median study experience for the Philippine participants were four years, whereas it was three years for the Danish participants. Seven out of eight Danish participants were male, in contrast to only about one out of three of the Philippine participants (this reflects the gender distributions of computer science students in the two countries).

3 Results

Based on my participant-observation I selected three topics for further study:

Privacy: Because the required level shall be taken into account when deciding how and to what extent privacy shall be protected in a computer system.

Reliability: Because the reliability of a system always is a compromise between costs and the level that is required by users and different stakeholders.

Honesty: Because it shall be taken into account when deciding how and to what extent protection against misuse and fraud shall be built into a system.

I selected these topics because they might influence the use of computer systems, and because I observed a number of incidents where peoples' reactions indicated substantial differences in values between Denmark and Philippines. However, it is likely that there are other important differences that I did not notice during my participant-observations.

3.1 Privacy

The participant-observation indicated that privacy was taken much less seriously in Philippines than in Denmark. Some examples:

- At a Danish university student grades are not even displayed on a bulletin board. In contrast, Philippine newspapers published lists of students with their grades, even for those who barely had passed the exam.

- In Philippines, social and health information for each family is posted on a board in the middle of the barangay (village), whereas such information in Denmark only is available for public employees who need it.

- In Denmark, people normally do not tell the PIN-code to their ATM-cards, even to family members or close friends. In Philippines, a woman who did not know me asked for asked for my assistance when using an ATM-machine and told me her PIN-code, in such a manner that people who stood around us could hear it.

The replies to three of the six questions in the questionnaire indicate that privacy was taken significantly more seriously in Denmark than in Philippines. See Table 2. It is in particular interesting that none of the female Philippine students who replied objected to having their name (showing their gender) and age published together with their phone number if they owned a mobile phone. (The replies that did not indicate any differences in the attitude to privacy are probably influenced by other cultural differences: Question 1 and 2 by honesty being taken more seriously in Philippines than in Denmark, question 4 by a larger power distance, which leads to more distrust of authorities in Philippines compared to Denmark [Hofstede 2001].)

However, the investigation of design decisions shows only a significant difference on one of the three privacy questions, question 21, and in that case the Philippine protection of privacy is on a higher level and more cumbersome than indicated in the Danish replies. See Table 3.

	Situation ↓	Phil.	DK	Exp. from observations
1	Friend passes on personal joke about someone you both know.	2.6	3.3	Phil < DK
2	Friend borrows your phone and copies stored number w/o permission.	4.5	4.3	Phil < DK
3	People running Internet cafe you use read customers' e-mails.	**3.1**	**4.5**	Phil < DK
4	Your boss can get copies of e-mails you send or receive.	4.0	3.5	Phil < DK
5	Publication of phone numbers, with full name, age and occupation.	**1.5**	**3.5**	Phil < DK
6	Phone company store text messages and police has access to them.	**2.6**	**3.5**	Phil < DK

Table 2: Privacy results from questionnaire. One is the most positive emotional reaction; five is the most negative. Statistically significant differences ($p < 0.05$ tested in normal distribution) are highlighted. The column at the right shows the results that were expected based on the participant observation.

	Situation ↓	Phil.	DK	Exp. from ident cultural char.
21	Protection of private files in school computer (privacy)	**4.6**	**3.7**	Phil < DK
22	Protection of e-mails privacy in company (privacy)	3.5	3.1	No diff.
23	Protection of SMS messages (privacy)	3.2	3.4	Phil < DK
24	Protection against computer crashes (reliability)	3.7	3.8	No diff.
25	Indication of unreliable results (reliability)	3.7	3.6	No diff.
26	Requirements for back-up of computer files (reliability)	**3.4**	**4.1**	No diff.
27	Prevention of fraud in group running net-café (honesty)	4.4	4.0	DK < Phil
28	Prevention of fraud with bookkeeping (honesty)	3.0	3.0	Phil < DK

Table 3: Results of investigation of design decisions. One is the reply where least precautions are taken; five is the one where most precautions are taken. Statistically significant differences ($p < 0.05$ tested in normal dist.) are highlighted.

Situation ↓		Phil.	DK	Exp. from observations
7	New mobile phone breaks down.	3.8	4.1	Phil < DK
8	Shop says a repair takes three days.	**1.9**	**3.1**	DK < Phil
9	Phone turns itself off regularly.	3.4	3.9	Phil < DK
10	Shop tells that problem can be solved by putting tape around the phone.	3.5	3.8	Phil < DK
11	Phone has to be sent to manufacturer's shop for repair.	3.1	2.9	DK < Phil
12	Low-cost phone company breaks off one out of three calls.	3.6	4.2	Phil < DK

Table 4: Reliability results from questionnaire. One is the most positive emotional reaction; five is the most negative. Statistically significant differences ($p < 0.05$ tested in normal dist.) are highlighted. (The numbering is continued from Table 2.)

The reply to question 21 is similar to what I observed in a Philippine College. It was impossible for students to store any private files in the college's computer system. They had to keep them on personal floppy disks. In contrast, I observed how users of a Philippine net-cafe stored private files on the hard-disks of the computers, even though it was possible for anyone who used the same computer to read the files. In comparison, at a Danish university it is possible for students either to store files in a private password protected area or in another area where others can read them.

3.2   Reliability

The participant-observation indicates that repairs of electronic equipment were more frequent and acceptable in Philippines than in Denmark.

In Philippines electronic equipment fails fairly often. The available equipment is often of a lower quality than in Denmark, and it is used for longer periods of time in an environment that is more dusty and humid. There were a considerable number of repair shops and shops selling electronic spare parts. In Denmark, electronic equipment is frequently discarded before it breaks down, and when something breaks down, it is often discarded, without trying to find out whether it can be repaired.

In Philippines, it appears that the main concern is to have a working piece of electronic equipment. If a piece of equipment can be repaired, it will be repaired, even if the repair degrades the look of it. In Denmark, electronic equipment that has been repaired is often regarded as being damaged, even if it can be used without problems, and repairs that in any manner degrade the look of a piece of electronic equipment are in general not accepted.

However, five out of six replies to the questionnaire show no significant differences in the attitude towards reliability. See Table 4. This indicates that Filipinos want the same reliability as Danes. (I had expected that questions 8 and 11 showed that Filipinos were less patient than Danes waiting for repairs because of the large number of shops that did repairs while the customer waited. However, it appears that the more relaxed attitude to time in Philippines compared to in Denmark was decisive.)

	Situation ↓	Phil.	DK	Exp. from observations
13	Friend uses phone without permission for prolonged period.	**3.9**	**2.8**	DK < Phil
14	Friend uses phone for international call without permission.	**4.6**	**3.8**	DK < Phil
15	Friend makes calls from faulty payphone that does not charge.	2.9	2.3	Phil < DK
16	Friend makes long international calls from faulty non-charging payphone.	3.1	2.4	Phil < DK
17	One-hour phone card runs out after forty five minutes.	**2.8**	**4.5**	Phil < DK
18	Phone company charges for call customer believe she did not make.	**3.2**	**4.1**	Phil < DK

Table 5: Honesty results from questionnaire. One is the most positive emotional reaction; five is the most negative. Statistically significant differences ($p < 0.05$ tested in normal dist.) are highlighted. (The numbering is continued from Table 4.)

The investigation of design decisions shows only a significant difference on one of the three reliability questions, question 26, where the reply indicates that a substantially less reliable back-up solution would be selected in Philippines compared to Denmark. See Table 3.

3.3 *Honesty*

On a personal level and in daily transactions Filipinos appeared to take more care to be honest than people in Denmark. They frequently stressed the importance of honesty, something that is not done naturally in Denmark. I was visibly wealthy compared to the local level, and expected that some would try to take advantage of it. However, I experienced that shopkeepers took time to explain the actual prices and to ensure that I did not pay more.

I saw how persons working in shops took time to note down every sale with the amount in a small notebook, and had the impression that they took time to demonstrate they were honest. Net-cafés had systems that registered the time each user had used a computer, but that was only a convenience for the cashier. It was only large department stores that had an automatic registration of each payment as it is customary in Denmark.

Filipinos frequently complained about the dishonesty of public officials, and corruption of public officials and politicians appeared to be a serious problem [Chua 1999; Hofstede 2001], whereas Denmark is reported as one of the countries in the world with least corruption [Hofstede 2001]. It should be noted that I had a number of satisfactory dealings with public officials in the area where I stayed, and that none of them demanded or suggested any sort of payments.

The replies to the questionnaire indicate honesty at a personal level was considered significantly more important in Philippines than in Denmark (questions 13 and 14 in Table 5). The replies indicate that Filipinos more often than

Danes expect that large companies are dishonest (questions 17 and 18 in Table 5), and that Filipinos believe people shall be honest towards large companies, even though the companies may be dishonest (questions 15 and 16 in Table 5). (This was not expected. However, it may be explained by taking into account that Philippines is a country with a large power distance where it to some extent is accepted that power is abused [Hofstede 2001], and that Filipinos therefore accept that they are supposed to be honest even though large companies are not.)

The investigation of design decisions shows no significant differences on any of the honesty questions. Computer science students in Philippines choose the same level of protection against misuse and fraud as computer science students in Denmark.

3.4   Costs and Economy are Crucial for Design

The replies and observations about reliability and levels of privacy required in systems are contradictory. Even though privacy is considered less important in Philippines compared to Denmark, Filipino students in general selected a design solution that was more restrictive and cumbersome than the one selected by Danish students, and even though it appears that people in Philippines want the same level of reliability as people in Denmark, computer science students in one case selected a substantially less reliable solution. However, the results can be explained when costs are taken into account. In the cases where one solution appeared to be less costly than another, Philippine students tended to choose the simplest or least costly solution.

4   Discussion

It is necessary to take into account that Philippines has large regional and income differences. The study was done within a middle class population in a provincial area, and the results may for instance not be valid for an upper-class population in the capital (Manila).

Participant-observation can capture more new aspects of a culture than structured interviews or questionnaires, but it is more difficult to determine how reliable the results are. The observer can only capture a small amount of his or her experiences, and in most circumstances it is impossible to determine what has been left out, whether the observations are biased by what the observer expected to see, or because he or she misinterprets some events.

I have therefore verified the results of the participant-observation through questionnaires. Both in Philippines and in Denmark these were answered by students. My observations indicate that their values in both countries probably are the same as for other people with the same age and social background, whereas older people might give different answers. Singh & Kotzé's [2003] results indicate that the detected differences between Denmark and Philippines might have been larger if the respondents had been older. It is also likely that computer scientists with some years of work experience would make different design decisions than the participating computer science students, and it is not possible to determine how their work experience might influence their replies.

In the present study both questionnaires were answered by homogeneous groups of students with similar experience in Denmark and Philippines, such that valid comparisons are possible.

The first questionnaire asked how the respondents would feel about different situations. The interpretation of such questions are less culturally dependent than questions about values in general, but they may give false indications of differences in cultural values if the respondents from one culture in general react stronger than those from another. However, an analysis of the results shows that the ranges of reactions are similar in Denmark and in Philippines, confirming that the detected differences are valid.

Eight out of eighteen questions about reactions in different situations showed significant differences ($p < 0.05$). With such a number of results there is a substantial risk that one or more of them are generated by chance, even if they separately are statistically significant. However, a test shows a >90% probability that none of the significant differences ($p < 0.05$) are generated by chance.

Seven of the eight significant results confirm the results of the participant observation.

Replies to seven of the questions that do not confirm the results of the participant observation were influenced by other cultural differences than those the questions were supposed to measure, and the remaining four cases where the replies do not confirm the results of the participant-observation can be attributed to the observations not taking sufficiently into account that the actions might have been determined by external circumstances more than by cultural values. This means that all differences between the participant-observation and the first questionnaire can be accounted for, and it demonstrates the need of combining participant-observations and questionnaires or interviews.

Danish computer science students have comparatively more access to computers and computer magazines. This might have made them more aware of possible problems and their consequences and led to generally higher values in their answers. However, averages of the responses from computer science students are almost identical in Denmark and in Philippines (Total averages of all replies to design questions: Phil = 3.4, DK = 3.3), indicating that these differences did not affect the results.

5 Relations between Income Levels and Cultural Characteristics

It is possible that the income level of a particular culture is sufficient to determine a number of cultural characteristics that shall be taken into account when a system or an interface is adapted for use in another culture.

Inglehart [1997] describes how there is a high level of constraint between the different cultural attributes; he describes how high income societies are rational-secular and well-being oriented, whereas low-income societies are traditional or survival oriented. Hofstede [2001] describes how a low income-level is correlated with a large power distance and collectivistic and masculine values. See Table 6. (Which fits the cultural differences between Denmark and Philippines. See Table 1.)

The cultural differences identified in this study appear to be closely related to income levels. In a low-income society where several people live together in the

Parameters	Correlation with GNP/Capita
Large power distance — inequality and privileges are considered normal.	−0.64
Individualism vs. collectivism	0.84
Masculinity vs. femininity values (survival vs. well-being values)	0.51
Uncertainty avoidance — people avoid ambiguity and new challenges	−0.28

Table 6: Correlations between Hofstede's [2001] parameters and GNP/Capita.

same room, children learn to live with almost no privacy. It is also likely that privacy only is expected in an affluent society with individualism and well-being values. When computer students in the Philippines consistently choose cheaper solutions than Danish students, even though the same level of reliability was required, it is likely because the equipment compared to local income levels was about five times more expensive. In a low-income society where many people live together personal honesty is important, whereas corruption and a large power distance both are correlated with low income levels [Hofstede 2001], and lead to the distrust of large organizations that is indicated by the study.

Hofstede's parameters and the results of World Values Survey suggest a number of additional relations between income levels and how people interact with an interface or a system. Denmark is a rational secular society. In such a society it is considered important to have imagination, to feel responsible and to be tolerant. [Inglehart 1997]. In contrast, Philippines is a traditional society [World Values Survey 2005]. In such a society it is considered important to work hard and to respect authorities [Inglehart 1997]. However, I have not made any observations that conclusively indicate how these differences affect how users interact with computers or other equipment.

There is a correlation between low incomes and Hofstede's [2001] masculine values (similar to what is called survival values in World Values Survey [Hofstede 2001]), and people with such values tend to trust science and technology [Inglehart 1997]. This may make it less likely that they will anticipate and prevent problems. Hofstede [2001] also finds a strong correlation between low incomes and a large power distance, and anecdotal evidence suggests that users in a community with a large power distance will tend to wait for instructions and keep problems hidden from their superiors. Hofstede [2001] discusses a number of studies that find correlations between higher airline accident rates, a large power distance and masculine values. However, he finds that the higher accident rates can be explained as consequences of fewer resources in low-income countries for maintaining planes, training crews and managing airports. It appears that masculine values and a large power distance do not affect the accident rate. The results of my own observations in Denmark and Philippines are inconclusive.

Hofstede [2001] shows that there is a weak correlation between uncertainty avoidance and low incomes. This is the only parameter where Denmark and

Philippines are similar: None of the countries have a high level of uncertainty avoidance. See Table 1. Hofstede [2001] describes that a culture with high uncertainty avoidance is less innovative and more resistant to change. It is possible that a high level of uncertainty avoidance makes it less likely that people will adopt new technology and learn to use it by trying to do something and seeing what happens. However, I have not found any conclusive information that supports such a relationship. All these possible relations between income levels and interactions with interfaces may be subjects of further studies.

6 Conclusion

In an affluent society the protection of private information is considered valuable in itself. Systems that take the customary level of privacy in an affluent society into account will therefore to some extent also protect against misuse of the information for instance for identity theft or fraud. The results indicate that is not the case in a traditional or a low-income society. In addition, when the protection of private information is considered less important, it is less natural for users to comply with rules to protect it.

When discussing specifications for systems for use in low income countries, it is therefore in particular necessary to explore how stored private information can be misused, and how misuse shall be prevented. (Given that the risk of phone harassment has been discussed in Philippine medias, it is interesting that all female Philippine students who answered the questionnaire accepted that age and full names of subscribers were published.).

An access control based on the use of personal passwords may be inadequate in a traditional society. When privacy is not normal, it may even be considered a little odd to insist that a password cannot be shared. It may therefore be necessary to use ID cards or biometrics instead of passwords for access control.

The results indicate that breaches of trust in a traditional society are considered more serious than breaches of privacy. In many cases it is therefore likely that users will not object to private information being spread as long as they are clearly informed about how it is spread and to whom.

In an individualistic society where privacy is considered important it makes sense to adapt the information to each individual user. In contrast, in a traditional and more collectivistic society it may be advantageous to use systems where the same information is shared within a group. For instance such that some social information about each household is available for all families in a community, or such that persons working on a project in a company not only can see their own tasks and work-hours, but also the work-hours and tasks of all other persons working on the project.

The results indicate that system designers in low-income countries tend to choose the cheapest or most easily available solutions, even though the operating conditions because of dust, humidity and less reliable power supplies often are more demanding than in a high-income country, and even though the same level of reliability is required.

This must be taken into account when specifying a system for use in a low-income country. It is necessary to quantify the level of reliability that is required, and to discuss how it shall be accomplished. At the same time it is necessary to reduce the costs of both hardware and all materials used when operating a computer system (CD's may for instance be so expensive compared to the local price level that it is unrealistic to expect that they are used for back-ups).

In a high-income country a closer integration is normally worthwhile because it provides a more efficient workflow. In a low-income country it may be worthwhile to compartmentalize a system such that a fault only affects part of it.

It is possible to increase the reliability by ensuring that the computers only are used in rooms with a stable temperature and with reduced levels of dust and humidity. When the equipment costs are high compared to salaries it is also worthwhile to introduce preventive maintenance that increases the reliability of the equipment, and it is possible to reduce the problems caused by less reliable equipment by improving the procedures and interfaces used for maintaining a system such that it can be repaired faster. In essence, it is worthwhile to introduce interactions with the equipment that are similar to those that were common in the developed countries fifty years ago when computers were more costly and less reliable.

The results indicate that people in a traditional low-income country expect that large companies and probably also public authorities are dishonest. It may therefore be both beneficial and necessary for them to make their systems transparent to demonstrate that they act honestly towards the users (that may for instance be necessary for a Web-based service to calculate personal taxes).

The present study shows that people in a traditional country express that they want a high level of honesty, and that they are aware of the amount of fraud and corruption in their society. This means that it is possible openly to discuss the risk of misuse of computer systems and how to design interactions that makes it more difficult.

In contrast, when people in a traditional society tend to expect a higher level of honesty on a personal level, they may be less suspicious and less likely to object when someone deviate from procedures that are set up to prevent misuse and fraud. At the same time, it appears that honesty on a non-personal or organizational level is smaller than in a high-income country, such that there is a considerable risk of fraud or other dishonest behaviour.

It is common that cashiers in Philippine department stores work in pairs, such that a single cashier cannot let a friend leave the shop with goods that only are partly paid. A similar system may be used for some software systems, such that some operations only are possible when two users work in unison.

According to the available information, corruption is a widespread problem in Philippines as in other low-income countries. It may therefore be worthwhile to design systems and interactions that restrict information and enforce decision processes that make corruption more difficult.

It is also necessary to ensure that misuse and fraud is not possible because the designers of a system in a low-income country have chosen the cheapest and easiest available solution. Otherwise, it is for instance conceivable that out-sourced customer information including complete credit card details are kept on a standard PC that are used by a number of people without any access control.

It appears that it often is advantageous to take differences in attitudes towards privacy, reliability and honesty into account when designing systems for use in low-income countries. In contrast, my observations indicate that people often are tolerant and culturally flexible. They tend to accept software and electronic equipment almost no matter what cultural values they embody if they feel that the interaction with it gives them a more satisfying experience of their daily life. Two well-known examples are mobile phones and the Internet: Both are designed so they fit and encourage a small power distance, individualism and self-expression. However, because of the advantages they offer, they are without modifications accepted in cultures with large power distances, collectivism and survival-oriented values.

Acknowledgements

Thanks to Arlene Y.Cinco, Polanco, Philippines, for her assistance in the Philippine part of the study, to the participants for their time and to Kasper Hornbæk, University of Copenhagen, for his comments to the paper and to the reviewers for their comments.

References

Chua, Y. T. [1999], *Robbed — An Investigation of Corruption in Philippine Education*, Philippine Center for Investigative Journalism.

Dray, S. & Mrazek, D. [1996], A Day in the Life: Studying Context across Cultures, *in* E. M. del Galdo & J. Nielsen (eds.), *International User Interfaces*, John Wiley & Sons, pp.242–55.

Ford, G. & Gelderblom, J. H. [2003], The Effects of Culture on Performance Achieved through the Use of Human–Computer Interaction, *in* J. Eloff, A. Engelbrecht, P. Kotzé & M. Eloff (eds.), *Proceedings of the 2003 Annual Research Conference of the South African Institute of Computer Scientists and Information Technologists on Enablement through Technology (SAICSIT'03)*, ACM Press, pp.218–30.

Foucault, B., Russell, R. S. & Bell, G. [2004], Techniques for Researching and Designing Global Products in an Unstable World: A Case Study, *in* E. Dykstra-Erickson & M. Tscheligi (eds.), *CHI'04 Extended Abstracts of the Conference on Human Factors in Computing Systems*, ACM Press, pp.1481–4.

Hall, E. T. [1959], *The Silent Language*, Doubleday.

Hofstede, G. [2001], *Culture's Consequences*, second edition, Sage Publications.

Inglehart, R. [1997], *Modernization and Postmodernization — Cultural, Economic and Political Change in 43 Societies*, Princeton University Press.

Marcus, A., Baumgartner, V.-J. & Chen, E. [2003], User Interface Design and Culture, *in* C. Stephanidis & J. Jacko (eds.), *Human–Computer Interaction, Theory and Practice. Proceedings of Human–Computer Interaction International 2003*, Vol. 2, Lawrence Erlbaum Associates, pp.153–157.

Mullett, K. & Sano, D. [1995], *Designing Visual Interfaces*, SunSoft Press.

Nardi, B. A. [1997], The Use of Ethnographic Methods in Design and Evaluation, *in* M. Helander, T. K. Landauer & P. V. Prabhu (eds.), *Handbook of Human–Computer Interaction*, second edition, North-Holland, pp.361–6.

Nisbett, R. E. [2003], *The Geography of Thought*, Nicholas Brealey Publishing.

Prabhu, G. & Harel, D. [1999], GUI Design Preference Validation for Japan and China — A Case for KANSEI Engineering, *in* H.-J. Bullinger & J. Zieger (eds.), *Proceedings of the 8th International Conference on Human–Computer Interaction (HCI International '99)*, Lawrence Erlbaum Associates, pp.521–5.

Singh, S. & Kotzé, P. [2003], The Socio-political Culture of Users, *in* M. Rauterberg, M. Menozzi & J. Weeson (eds.), *Human–Computer Interaction — INTERACT '03: Proceedings of the Ninth IFIP Conference on Human–Computer Interaction*, IOS Press, pp.900–3.

Strøm, G. [2002], The Telephone Comes to a Filipino Village, *in* J. E. Katz & M. Aakhus (eds.), *Perpetual Contact: Mobile Communication, Private Talk, Public Performance*, Cambridge University Press, pp.274–83.

World Bank Group [2005], GNI Per Capita 2003, http://www.worldbank.org/data/quickreference/quickref.html (last accessed 2005-02).

World Values Survey [2005], Value Map (The Inglehart Map), http://www.worldvaluessurvey.org/images/feature_pics/valuemap.gif (last accessed 2005-02).

Researching Culture and Usability — A Conceptual Model of Usability

Gabrielle Ford[†] & Paula Kotzé[‡]

[†] *School of Information Systems and Technology, University of Kwa-Zulu Natal, King George V Avenue, Durban, South Africa*

Email: *fordg1@ukzn.ac.za*

[‡] *School of Computing, University of South Africa, PO Box 392, UNISA 0003, South Africa*

Email: *kotzep@unisa.ac.za*

An experiment conducted to determine the effects of subjective culture on the usability of computerized systems did not provide sufficient evidence that any of the tested cultural dimensions affected the usability of the product. Analysis indicated that the differences in scores could have been attributed to variables other than those tested and controlled for. This indicated a need to build a more detailed conceptual model of usability before empirical research of this nature can be effectively carried out. Additional variables influencing usability and strategies for controlling for these variables under experimental conditions were identified and validated. The valid variables were incorporated into a conceptual model of usability for use in future research endeavours. This paper presents this conceptual model as well as strategies to control the variables.

Keywords: culture, usability, context of use, cultural dimensions.

1 Introduction

This paper reports on a research project [Ford 2005] at the Universities of South Africa and Kwa-Zulu Natal. The primary objective of this research was to design a conceptual model of usability that can be used to effectively research the relationship between subjective culture and usability. This objective arose as a result of the initial problem identified for this research, which was to establish empirical evidence that

Category	Variable	Validity
Variables relating to subjective culture	Cultural dimension strengths	To be considered
	Cultural dimension interplays	To be considered
	Relative impact of cultural dimensions on usability	To be considered
	Other subjective cultural dimensions	To be considered
Variables relating to the interface	Partial representation of cultural dimensions	Accepted
	Usability principles, heuristics and guidelines	Accepted but only those relevant to the context of use
	Relative impact of components	To be considered
	Nature of the cultural dimensions	To be considered
Variables relating to user acceptance	Information technology (IT) role, educational level, prior similar experience, organizational support, tool functionality, facilitating conditions	Accepted but only those relevant to the context of use
Variables relating to speed of performance	Hardware platforms	Accepted
	Level of Internet traffic	Accepted
	Navigational decisions	Accepted
	Number and length of bodies of text	Accepted
Variables relating to objective culture	Nationality and ethnicity	Accepted

Table 1: Validity of variables proposed to have influenced the experiment.

subjective culture affects usability. Inconclusive results of an experiment designed to measure the effects of Hofstede's [2001] cultural dimensions on accuracy, speed and satisfaction, led to the identification of variables that could have influenced the results. It became evident that the existing context of use frameworks are lacking in major aspects that could make their application invalid in multi-cultural environments. Therefore it was necessary first to identify the variables that should be taken into account when conducting research on culture and usability so that they can be controlled for when carrying out an experiment of this nature. The existing context of use frameworks were then synthesized and extended into a proposed conceptual model of usability that incorporates these variables, which include new aspects concerning culture. The background to the proposed model is presented in Section 2 of this paper and the model in Section 3. Section 4 comments on strategies for controlling the variables when researching the effects of culture on usability. Section 5 concludes by highlighting the contribution of this research and topics for further research.

2 Background to the Model

We began our research by reviewing the existing body of knowledge surrounding the effects of *subjective culture* on usability, including the concepts of performance, usability and culture, and the arguments for and against the importance of culture in human-computer interaction (HCI). We argued that culture influences communication, and as an interactive system is dependent on communication, culture is important in the development of such system's interface. We reviewed approaches to culturalization, and proposed that subjective and objective cultural

Conceptual model of usability	User Context	User characteristics
		User knowledge
	Task Context	Task characteristics
		Task execution
	Environment Context	Organizational environment
		Technical environment
		Physical Environment

Table 2: Overview of conceptual model of usability.

concepts be incorporated into the design of interfaces. In attempting to identify the most appropriate cultural models to be used as a basis for subjective cultural design guidelines, we found that cultural dimension models, and in particular Hofstede's model of culture, influences usability from the perspectives of reducing the cognitive load, user acceptance, objective usability and context of use [Ford et al. 2005]. We then conducted an experiment (a usability test) [Ford & Gelderblom 2003; Ford 2005], in order to obtain conclusive empirical evidence of the effects of subjective culture on usability. The inconclusive results of the experiment led us to identify five additional categories of variables that could have influenced the results, those relating to:

1. subjective culture;

2. the interface;

3. user acceptance;

4. speed of performance; and

5. objective culture.

(As reflected in Table 1.) The validity of the variables in these categories was then investigated by doing an in-depth literature study, resulting in our acceptance of the variables relating to user acceptance, speed of performance and objective culture. Of the four variables identified relating to the interface, only the partial representation of cultural dimensions and usability principles, guidelines and heuristics were accepted. The other two variables and the four variables relating to subjective culture could not be empirically established as valid, but there was sufficient theoretical evidence not to reject them either. The impact of the variables on experimental design, and on the results of prior research, was also addressed. Finally, all the variables identified were synthesized into the conceptual model of usability as presented in Section 3. Where possible, strategies for controlling for the variables when carrying out experimental research were also proposed (Section 4).

3 Conceptual Model of Usability

The objective of this section is to present a unified set of distinct variables, through a proposed conceptual model of usability, that should be considered when doing research into culture and usability. In line with past frameworks to present various contexts of use, we format the model into three contexts with variables that relate to:

1. user characteristics;

2. task characteristics; and

3. the environment.

An overview of the conceptual model of usability is presented in Table 2 (all the figures should be read as hierarchies from left to right). The contexts of use proposed by Bevan & Macleod [1994], Kirakowski & Cierlik [1999], together with the performance determinants proposed by Mayhew [1992] form the broad basis for the user, task and environment contexts. The *additional variables* identified as a result of our research (indicated as bold italic entries in Tables 3–9) are incorporated into the model, and we discuss these additional variables and the contexts in more detail in the sections to follow.

3.1   The User Context

3.1.1   User Characteristics

The variables included in the user characteristics category have been grouped into the classes of culture, physical characteristics and psychological characteristics. As illustrated in Table 3, additional variables were identified in terms of user acceptance, objective cultural variables and subjective cultural variables:

Culture: Our research identified this to be a valid class of variables for inclusion into the model. The culture class is divided into the two sub-classes of objective culture and subjective culture:

Subjective culture relates to the psychological features of a culture, including assumptions, values, feelings, beliefs and patterns of thinking [Hoft 1996], and can be measured using various cultural dimensions, such as those proposed by Hofstede [2001], Victor [1992], Hall [1959] and Trompenaars [1993]. *The strengths of the cultural dimensions* relates to the variation in strength of each side of each dimension displayed by different users [Hofstede 2001]. The *interplays between dimensions* takes into consideration that one cultural dimension could override the impact of the other cultural dimensions on the interaction, particularly if the user displays a substantially high level of strength for that dimension. *The relative impact on usability* refers to the possibility that the different cultural dimensions may have a stronger or weaker impact on usability [Smith & Chang 2003; Ford & Kotzé 2005].

Objective culture in contrast, is visible and tangible as it is represented in terms of the institutions and artefacts of the culture. *Nationality* is defined as the status of belonging to a particular nation by birth or naturalization [Wordnet 2003], while *ethnicity* is defined as "of peoples from other cultures" [Hartley 2002, p.83] or heritage. *Economic systems,*

Use Characteristics	Culture	Subjective	Strengths	
			Interplays	
			Relative Impact	
		Objective	Nationality and ethnicity	Economic system
				Social customs
				Political structures
				Arts, crafts and literature
			Religion	
			Social class	
	Physical	Age		
		Gender		
		Capabilities and limitations	Handedness	
			Colour blindness	
			Other	
	Psychological	Cognitive ability	Cognitive style	
			Verbal fluency	
			Visual acuity	
			Digit span is STM	
		Motivation	Perceived enjoyment	
			Professional status	
		Attitude	Self-efficacy	General self-efficacy
				Computer self-efficacy
				Computer anxiety
			Relative importance of measures	
			User preferences	
			Computer playfulness	
			Ease of finding	
			Ease of understanding	
			Information quality	

Table 3: User characteristic variables.

social customs, political structures and arts, crafts and literature are seen to be dependent on the nationality and ethnicity of the users. *Religion* and *social class* were also identified as variables relating to objective culture.

Physical characteristics: All the variables included in this class were previously identified in the existing literature and thus not discussed further.

Psychological characteristics: Previously proposed contexts of use and performance determinants identified cognitive ability, motivation and attitude, as psychological characteristics related to user context. We expanded on these to include additional variables:

Cognitive ability is defined as the ability of users to process information, make decisions and solve problems. Cognitive ability is partly dependent on the users' cognitive styles, verbal fluency, visual ability and digit span in short-term memory (STM) [Choong & Salvendy 1998].

Cognitive styles refer to the way in which people approach problem solving tasks. Different cognitive styles require different levels of detail of information, e.g. users with a receptive cognitive style will find interfaces that only provide summarized information, to be less usable than those providing detailed information. *Verbal fluency* relates to the users' ability to express and understand ideas using language. *Visual abilities* refer to the ability of the users to discriminate between visual patterns. Interfaces that predominantly make use of pictorial icons, rather than text, may be considered less usable by users who have low visual abilities. *Digit span* in STM relates to the amount of data that can be held in the user's STM. The amount of information that the interface requires the user to remember will hence influence the usability of the interface, particularly if the users' digit span in STM is smaller than the average of the population.

Attitude relates to the attitudes of the users to their jobs and tasks, to a specific software product, to IT in general, and to the organization that employs the users. Attitudes can be positive, negative or neutral [Mayhew 1992]. *Self-efficacy* influences attitude [Baron & Byrne 2000]. *Computer anxiety, computer self-efficacy* and *system self-efficacy* are similar in nature, as they all relate to the users' confidence in their ability to use and succeed with technology [Brown 2002; Venkatesh 2000], and are therefore seen as dimensions of self-efficacy. The *relative importance of usability measures* relates to the significance that users attach to the usability measures of speed, accuracy and satisfaction [Evers & Day 1997], and is seen as an attitudinal issue. *User preferences* relate to attitudes in terms of likes and dislikes [Evers & Day 1997]. *Computer playfulness* refers to the degree of cognitive spontaneity during interactions [Venkatesh 2000]. *Ease of finding* refers to how easy it is to navigate between interface elements and influences attitudes by impacting on the perceived ease of use of a system, while *ease of understanding* refers to the comprehensibility of the content of the interface [Brown 2002]. *Information quality* refers to the completeness, accuracy, timeliness, and relevance of information [Lederer et al. 2000].

Motivation can be internal, related to work performance in terms of the need for competence and self-determination, or external to the actual performance of work [Hoft 1996]. *Perceived enjoyment* is the extent to which using a computer is seen as enjoyable by the users [Venkatesh 2000]. *Professional status* is defined as the extent to which using the system will enhance the user's professional status as perceived by the user's peers [Succi & Walter 1999] and relates to external motivation.

3.1.2 User Knowledge

User knowledge variables are grouped into four classes:

1. system knowledge,

2. organization knowledge,

User knowledge	System	System Experience	Application experience	Product experience
				Tool experience
			Use of other systems	
			Frequency of use	
			IT role	
	Organization	Job category	Task Experience	
	Education	Training		
		Qualifications		
	Linguistic ability	Native language		
		Reading language		

Table 4: User knowledge variables.

---

3. education, and

4. linguistic ability,

which are different to those used in the existing contexts of use and set of performance determinants. However, as illustrated in Table 4, the majority of the variables included in the user knowledge category were identified in previously proposed contexts of use and performance determinants. Two additional variables, namely tool experience and IT role, were identified from the set of user acceptance variables:

IT role refers to the level of system expertise in terms of whether the user is a novice or expert user. This is related to *system experience* which refers to knowledge of the particular language or mode of interaction used in a system.

Tool experience relates to the user's abilities to use tools appropriate to performing tasks [Dishaw & Strong 1999], including computer-based tools such as spreadsheets, or non-computer based tools such as calculators. Since application experience refers to experience with products of the same genre, e.g. accounting packages, tool experience is a dimension of it.

3.2 The Task Context

3.2.1 Task Characteristics

The classes related to task characteristics are job category, risk, demands and linkages. As illustrated in Table 5, three additional variables were identified as a result of our research:

The number of navigational decisions (identified from the user acceptance variables) relates to the number of decisions a user has to make in terms of the links to follow to find the required information.

The number and length of bodies of text (identified from speed of performance variables) refer to the text that needs to be read in order to find the required

Task characteristics	Job category	Task goal	Task breakdown
			Task output
			User role
		Task duration	*Navigational decisions*
			Number and length of bodies of text
		Task criticality	Task importance
		Discretion	
	Risk	Errors	
		Side effects	Physical
			Psychological
			Information
	Demands	Physical	
		Mental	
		Task-technology fit	
	Linkages	Linked tasks	
		Autonomy	

Table 5: User characteristic variables.

Task Execution	Dependencies	Information
		Events
		Technology
		Other tools
	Flexibility	System use
		Task postponement
		Pacing
		Structure
	Frequency of task	Frequency of events

Table 6: Task execution variables.

information. If the task is performed using technology, then the number of navigational decisions and the number and length of bodies of text will naturally influence the duration of the task [Forer & Ford 2003].

Task-technology fit is the match between user task needs and the available functionality of the IT [Dishaw & Strong 1999]. Mental and physical demands on the users will be increased if the technology does not support the task.

3.2.2   Task Execution

Task execution relates to the variables that affect the way in which the task is carried out, and is therefore seen to comprise of the classes of dependencies, flexibility and frequency of the task, as illustrated in Table 6. Although the classes that we have grouped the variables into are a little different, all of the variables included in this

Organizational environment	Organizational structure	Management	
		Communication	
	Organizational culture	Performance monitoring	
		Performance feedback	
		Work autonomy	
		Interruptions	
		Hours of work	
		Single / multi user environment	
		Organizational support	Assistance available

Table 7: Task execution variables.

category were also identified in the contexts of use and performance determinants, and the variables are therefore not discussed further.

3.3 The Environment Context

The environment context is divided into the sub-contexts of organizational, technical and physical environments. This is in contrast with the four environments of organizational, technical, physical and social, proposed by Kirakowski & Cierlik [1999]. We have included the variables allocated to the social environment into the organizational environment and the technical environment as they are actually directly related to these environments, and not an environment on their own.

3.3.1 The Organizational Environment

As illustrated in Table 7, the variables related to the organization environment have been grouped into two categories: organizational structure and organizational culture. Only one additional variable, *organizational support*, defined as encouragement by top management and allocation of adequate resources [Davis 1989], was identified as a result of our research. Assistance available (social environment) and facilitating conditions (user acceptance variables) both relating to the availability of assistance for users, were identified as a duplication of each other, and is therefore incorporated as a dimension of organizational support.

3.3.2 The Technical Environment

As illustrated in Table 8, the variables related to the technical environment have been grouped into two categories: functionality and specifications. Five additional variables affecting computer-based interfaces were identified and included as dimensions of the general usability of the software class:

Partial representation of cultural dimensions refers to the possibility that the components of a given interface do not accommodate the same side of a given cultural dimension [Forer & Ford 2003], which will increase the effects on usability of the nature of the cultural dimensions and its relative impact.

Nature of the cultural dimensions takes cognisance of the possibility that accommodating one side of four of the cultural dimensions proposed by Hofstede [2001] into the design of the interface is likely to produce a

Technical environment	Functionality	Main application area					
		Major functions					
	Specifications	Computer-based	Stand-alone / networked	Hardware	Hardware platforms		
				Software	General usability	*Partial representation of cultural dimensions*	
						Nature of the cultural dimension	
						Principles and heuristics	
						Relative impact of components	
						Level of Internet traffic	
		Non computer-based	Materials				
			Office equipment				
			Protective clothing and equipment				

Table 8: Technical environment sub-categories and classes.

---

generally more usable interface than accommodating for the opposite side of the same dimensions [Ford & Kotzé 2005].

Usability principles and heuristics although inherently flawed because they do not take the context of use into consideration, are valid in at least some cultural and other user contexts [Hall et al. 2003]. Consequently interfaces that accommodate principles and heuristics relevant to the specific context of use will increase usability.

Relative impact of components refers to the possibility that interface components could influence usability to various degrees [Forer & Ford 2003].

Level of Internet traffic (if applicable) relates to the number of users accessing the Internet at any particular time, influencing the speed of interaction. For users that value speed of performance, this variable can substantially influence the user's perceived usability of the interface.

3.3.3   The Physical Environment

No new variables relating to the physical environment were identified as a result of our research. All of the variables included in the model correspond to those used by Kirakowski & Cierlik [1999]. Analysis of the variables suggests that the variables be categorized into workplace conditions, workplace safety and workplace design, as reflected in Table 9.

This concludes our discussion of the variables related to the user, task and environment contexts. We now turn our attention to using these variables in empirical research projects.

Physical environment	Workplace conditions	Location	
		Auditory	
		Visual	Lighting
		Thermal	
		Instability	
		Atmospheric	
	Workplace safety	Health Hazards	
	Workplace safety	Furniture and equipment	
		Space	
		Posture	

Table 9: Physical environment sub-categories and classes.

4   Strategies for Controlling for the Variables

In this section, we propose strategies for controlling for the variables included in the usability model when doing experimental research related to culture. We discuss the variables in terms of their relevance to the components of an experimental research design, namely:

1. the selection of test subjects;

2. the identification of test interfaces;

3. the identification of the test environment; and

4. setting of test tasks.

The usability model proposed in Section 3 incorporates all the variables that have been identified from our research that influence usability in general. We note, however, that not all of the variables identified as valid are valid in all contexts of use. When designing an experiment in the form of a usability test, the variables that need to be controlled for are dependent on the context within which the product is expected to be used [Honold 2000; Bevan & Macleod 1994; Duncker 2002] Thus the model should not be seen as a static tool that is generically appropriate for all contexts. Rather, it should be used as a guideline that requires interpretation within specific contexts, in order to be able to extract the variables that are appropriate to the intended context within which the product is to be used.

4.1   Selection of Test Subjects

As illustrated by the number and complexity of the variables included in the user context of the usability model, humans are complex entities, comprising numerous character traits that are also sometimes interdependent. Whilst it is not possible to identify and control for every possible trait that could influence performance, the basic strategy proposed is to ensure that test subjects are homogeneous in all of the variables, other than the variable being tested. We expand on this basic strategy for some of the more important variables below.

Subjective culture: Test subjects should differ only in the subjective cultural dimension that is being tested, e.g. when testing the influence of power distance on usability, the cultural profile of the test subjects should differ only in terms of the power distance dimension. The strength of each dimension within the users' cultural profile should be similar. If Hofstede's cultural dimensions are used as a basis for the experiment, a validated and reliable tool for determining the cultural profile and the strengths of each dimension of test subjects is Hofstede's [2001] Value Survey Model (VSM). The VSM was developed to determine the cultural profile of users within a work context Should test users be students or the context be other than work, the VSM will need to be adapted and tested prior to use. If more than one cultural dimension is being tested at the same time, Taguchi orthogonal arrays provide a useful tool for reducing the number of experiments that need to be carried out (the use of this tool is discussed in detail by Smith & Chang [2003]). In addition, the relative impact of the cultural dimensions can be established and controlled for by performing the point-biserial coefficient statistic on the results.

Other user characteristics: Objective culture, physical and psychological characteristics also need to be controlled for. Questionnaires, similar to the one used in our experiment [Ford 2005], can be used to identify test subjects that are homogeneous in terms of these variables. Controlling for the nationality and ethnicity variable will also result in controlling for cognitive abilities [Choong & Salvendy 1998] and the relative importance of usability measures, user preferences [Evers & Day 1997], computer playfulness [Venkatesh 2000], and ease of finding and understanding [Brown 2002]. All other variables related to the test subjects' psychological and physical characteristics will need to be controlled for separately, as they are not related to nationality.

User knowledge: As with the user characteristics variables, the variables relating to user knowledge are best controlled for through the use of a questionnaire to identify homogeneous test subjects. To better control for the knowledge variables, it will be necessary to identify the users' prior experiences with applications or websites that belong to the same genre as the test interfaces, and to ensure that the same mental models and functionality is available on these interfaces.

4.2 Identification of Test Interfaces

The variables that need to be controlled for include the user context variables and the variables that influence the general usability of the interface. User context variables can be controlled for in the test interfaces by ensuring that the components of the test interfaces are homogeneous, and compatible to the objective and subjective culture, physical characteristics, and the psychological characteristics of the test subjects. The general usability of the interface should be controlled for by ensuring that partial representation, principles and heuristics and the relative impact of components are controlled for. Strategies for controlling for these variables are discussed next:

Subjective culture: Like test subjects, test interfaces should differ only in the subjective cultural dimension that is being tested. Care should be taken to ensure that each interface component renders the same cultural dimension side in the same strength, thus controlling for the cultural dimension strengths, cultural dimension interplays, the relative impact of cultural dimensions and interface components on usability, and partial representation of the cultural dimensions. If entirely suitable interfaces cannot be found, and test interfaces cannot be developed for whatever reason, it will be necessary to develop test tasks that do not require access to the components that do not display the relevant sides of each dimension.

Objective culture: Test interfaces should be consistent to the test subjects' objective cultural dimensions. This will require ensuring that the language and content used in the interface are appropriate to the test subjects' nationality and ethnicity, religion and social class.

Physical characteristics: Age and gender can be controlled for by choosing interfaces incorporating applicable content, and handedness by ensuring that the input and output devices used on all test interfaces are of the same type. Colour-blindness should be controlled for by selecting interfaces not using colour combinations that cause difficulty for colour-blind users.

Psychological characteristics: Only the cognitive ability variables and some of the attitude variables are relevant to the test interfaces. It is important to ensure that if more than one interface is used in the experiment, all interfaces are homogeneous in terms of the cognitive styles, use of text and pictorial icons, and the amount of information that the test subjects are required to remember. This will control for the cognitive abilities, as well as some of the user preferences of the test subjects. To avoid unforeseen differences in user attitude, all test interfaces should be homogeneous in terms of information quality, ease of finding and understanding, and the amount of computer playfulness incorporated into their design. In terms of user preferences, the number of and type of colours, type of menus and sounds used in all the interfaces need to be homogeneous. Input and output devices will already be controlled for by controlling for handedness.

The relative impact of interface components on usability and **partial representation of the cultural dimensions** will already be controlled for by controlling for the subjective cultural dimensions.

The test interfaces should be homogeneous in terms of the **usability principles, heuristics and guidelines** that have been accommodated into their design. Only those principles, guidelines and heuristics are relevant to the test subjects' cultural profiles need to be controlled for. This will require that the test interfaces are evaluated prior to their use. In addition, the evaluators used to assess the interfaces should be homogeneous in terms of their subjective and objective culture, which should also match the cultural profiles of the test subjects. This will control for the possibility of the evaluators' cultural profile distorting the evaluation of the general usability of the test interfaces.

4.3 Identification of Test Environment

To ensure that the test environment is homogeneous in terms of general usability, it will be necessary to ensure that the technical environments used for testing are equivalent in terms of the hardware platforms used, as well as the level of Internet traffic (if applicable) experienced at the time of completing the task.

4.4 Setting Test Tasks

The variables that should be taken into consideration when setting test tasks include those applicable to the user context, the technical environment and the task context. Specific controlling strategies for the relevant variables are proposed next.

User context variables: Test tasks should be appropriate to the test subjects' subjective culture, physical and psychological characteristics and user knowledge. Subjective culture influences the type of tasks that test subjects would want to perform, e.g. high power distant users would not want to send an email to their superiors. Therefore, test tasks should be identified that are representative of the tasks that the test subjects would want to, or normally do, perform, while omitting redundant and offensive tasks. In terms of user knowledge, it is important to ensure that all the test tasks are homogeneous in terms of the knowledge and experience required by the test subjects to perform the tasks, e.g. setting test tasks that require domain knowledge of, say, library systems and airline bookings would result in different performance levels between test subjects with and without such knowledge. The best way to control for variations within the test subjects would be to use the information obtained from the users to identify the task domains that all test subjects are either familiar or unfamiliar with. In addition, it is important that the test tasks are appropriate to the test subjects' age and gender, e.g. setting a task where test subjects are required to identify the 2004 F1 Grand Prix winner may increase the possibility of reduced performance by most female test users due to lack of interest, low motivation levels or lack of domain knowledge.

Technical environment variables: Technical environment variables that are relevant to the test tasks include the functionality as well as some of the specification variables. Test tasks should be representative of the main application area and major functions that the test interfaces were developed for, e.g. if an e-commerce website is being used as a test interface, then tasks relating to e-commerce functions should be identified. Test tasks should control for any non-computer based equipment that is normally used to complete the tasks under real conditions. This can be done by selecting test tasks that require the test subjects to make use of any materials, office equipment or protective clothing and equipment in order to complete the tasks. In addition, the test tasks should require that the same components of the interfaces are used between tasks, to further control for the relative impact of the interface components on usability.

Task context: It is necessary to ensure that the time taken to complete the test tasks is attributable to the variables being tested, rather than inherent differences in the tasks. Therefore, variables that influence the duration of the test tasks need to be controlled for. This requires homogeneous test tasks in terms of the navigational decisions, and the number and length of bodies of text that are required in order to complete the tasks, e.g. test subjects should be able to complete the test tasks by reading two bodies of text of similar lengths, navigating through five pages and making four navigational decisions.

5 Conclusion

In this paper we have presented our proposed conceptual model of usability. The model, which synthesizes our research and the results of numerous other works in this field of study, comprises of the three contexts of the user, the task and the environment. We have also proposed strategies for controlling for these variables. The conceptual model of usability is seen to be unique and useful to both academics and practitioners in the field of HCI. From the practitioner perspective, the model can be used to establish design goals appropriate to the specific context of use of a particular product, which in turn contributes a more cost-effective approach to designing global software products. From an academic perspective, the model provides a more holistic view of the issues that influence usability, which can be used as a basis for structuring tertiary coursework in the HCI field of study. Finally, the conceptual model of usability contributes to the existing body of knowledge by providing a stepping stone in the long-term effort of fully defining the effects of cultural diversity on HCI. Although this research contributes to the problem of cultural diversity in HCI, it does not provide a complete solution, and also raises issues that require further research. The model proposed should provide researchers with a more effective tool for continued research into the complex issue of usability, and in particular, into the issue of cultural diversity in HCI. Research is currently in progress to determine the validity of the model.

Acknowledgement

The work reported upon in this article is largely based on research for a master's degree completed at the University of South Africa [Ford 2005]. The research was partly funded by a grant from the National Research Foundation GUN:2050310.

References

Baron, R. & Byrne, D. [2000], *Social Psychology*, ninth edition, Allyn and Bacon Publishers.

Bevan, N. & Macleod, M. [1994], Usability Measurement in Context, *Behaviour & Information Technology* **13**(1-2), 132–45.

Brown, A. [2002], Individual and Technological Factors Affecting Perceived Ease of Use of Web-based Learning Technologies in a Developing Country, *The Electronic Journal on Information Systems in Developing Countries* **9**(5), 1–15. http://www.ejisdc.org/ (retrieved 2004-02-24).

Choong, Y. & Salvendy, G. [1998], Designs of Icons for Use by Chinese in Mainland China, *Interacting with Computers* **9**(4), 417–30.

Davis, F. D. [1989], Perceived Usefulness, Perceived Ease of Use and User Acceptance of Information Technology, *MIS Quarterly* **13**(3), 319–40.

Dishaw, M. & Strong, D. [1999], Extending the Technology Acceptance Model with Task Technology Fit Constructs, *Information and Management* **36**(1), 9–21.

Duncker, E. [2002], Cross-cultural Usability of the Library Metaphor, *in* W. Hersh & G. Marchionini (eds.), *Proceedings of the 2nd ACM/IEEE-CS Joint Conference on Digital Libraries (JCDL'02)*, ACM Press, pp.223–30.

Evers, V. & Day, D. [1997], The Role of Culture in Interface Acceptance, *in* S. Howard, J. Hammond & G. K. Lindgaard (eds.), *Human–Computer Interaction — INTERACT '97: Proceedings of the Sixth IFIP Conference on Human–Computer Interaction*, Chapman & Hall, pp.260–7.

Ford, G. [2005], Researching the Effects of Culture on Usability, Master's thesis, University of South Africa.

Ford, G. & Gelderblom, J. H. [2003], The Effects of Culture on Performance Achieved through the Use of Human–Computer Interaction, *in* J. Eloff, A. Engelbrecht, P. Kotzé & M. Eloff (eds.), *Proceedings of the 2003 Annual Research Conference of the South African Institute of Computer Scientists and Information Technologists on Enablement through Technology (SAICSIT'03)*, ACM Press, pp.218–30.

Ford, G. & Kotzé, P. [2005], Designing Usable Interfaces with Cultural Dimensions, *in* M. F. Costabile & F. Paternò (eds.), *Human–Computer Interaction — INTERACT '05: Proceedings of the Tenth IFIP Conference on Human–Computer Interaction*, Vol. 3585 of *Lecture Notes in Computer Science*, Springer.

Ford, G., Kotzé, P. & Marcus, A. [2005], Cultural Dimension Models: Who is Stereotyping Whom?, *in* N. Aykin (ed.), *Proceedings of the 11th International Conference on Human–Computer Interaction (HCI International 2005)*, Lawrence Erlbaum Associates.

Forer, D. & Ford, G. [2003], User Performance and User Interface Design: Usability Heuristics versus Cultural Dimensions, *in* J. Mende & I. Sanders (eds.), *Proceedings of the South African Computer Lecturer's Association 2003 Conference*, University of Witwatersrand.

Hall, E. T. [1959], *The Silent Language*, Doubleday.

Hall, P., Lawson, C. & Minocha, S. [2003], Design Patterns as a Guide to the Cultural Localisation of Software, *in* V. Evers, K. Röse, P. Honold, J. Coronado & D. L. Day (eds.), *Proceedings of the 5th Annual International Workshop on Internationalisation of Products and Systems (IWIPS 2003)*, Product & Systems Internationalisation, Inc., pp.79–88.

Hartley, J. [2002], *Communication, Cultural and Media Studies: The Key Concepts*, Routledge.

Hofstede, G. [2001], *Culture's Consequences*, second edition, Sage Publications.

Hoft, N. L. [1996], Developing a Cultural Model, *in* E. M. del Galdo & J. Nielsen (eds.), *International User Interfaces*, John Wiley & Sons, pp.74–87.

Honold, P. [2000], Culture and Context: An Empirical Study for the Development of a Framework for the Elicitation of Cultural Influence in Product Usage, *International Journal of Human–Computer Interaction* **12**(3 & 4), 327–45.

Kirakowski, J. & Cierlik, B. [1999], Context of Use: Introductory Notes, ftp://ftp.ucc.ie/hfrg/baseline/CoU20.rtf (retrieved 2004-09).

Lederer, A., Maupin, D., Sena, M. & Zhuang, Y. [2000], The Technology Acceptance Model and the World Wide Web, *Decision Support Systems* **29**(3), 269–82.

Mayhew, D. J. [1992], *Principles and Guidelines in Software and User Interface Design*, Prentice–Hall.

Smith, A. & Chang, Y. [2003], Quantifying Hofstede and Developing Cultural Fingerprints for Website Acceptability, *in* V. Evers, K. Röse, P. Honold, J. Coronado & D. L. Day (eds.), *Proceedings of the 5th Annual International Workshop on Internationalisation of Products and Systems (IWIPS 2003)*, Product & Systems Internationalisation, Inc., pp.89–104.

Succi, M. J. & Walter, Z. D. [1999], Theory of User Acceptance of Information Technologies: An Examination of Health Professionals, *in Proceedings of the 32nd Hawaii International Conference on System Sciences*, IEEE Computer Society Press. http://csdl.computer.org/comp/proceedings/hicss/1999/0001/04/0001toc.htm (retrieved 2004-09).

Trompenaars, F. [1993], *Riding the Waves of Cultur*, Nicholas Brealey Publishing.

Venkatesh, V. [2000], Determinants of Perceived Ease of Use: Integrating Control, Intrinsic Motivation and Emotion into the Technology Acceptance Model, *Information Science Research* **11**(4), 342–65.

Victor, D. [1992], *International Business Communications*, Harper Collins.

Wordnet [2003], Wordnet 2.0, http://dictionary.reference.com/search?q=nation (retrieved 2004-10-11). Princeton University.

I — HCI Down at the Interface

Distinguishing Vibrotactile Effects with Tactile Mouse and Trackball

Jukka Raisamo, Roope Raisamo & Katri Kosonen

Tampere Unit for Computer–Human Interaction, Department of Computer Sciences, FIN-33014 University of Tampere, Finland
Email: *{jr,rr,katri}@cs.uta.fi*

Vibration is used for drawing users' attention to notifications in electronic devices, such as mobile phones. However, it has not been studied how much information vibrotactile effects are capable of conveying. To begin this work we studied the detection thresholds for differences in frequency and magnitude of vibration with a mouse and a trackball in the frequency range from 10 to 40Hz. Twelve participants completed 30 trials with both devices. The task in each trial was to sort five effects in a descending order based on either their magnitude (16 trials) or frequency (14 trials). The results showed that magnitude was easier to distinguish than frequency. Moreover, the participants distinguished the differences between the effects better with the mouse than with the trackball.

Keywords: vibrotactile feedback, effect discrimination, haptics, tactile mouse, tactile trackball.

1 Introduction

Visual and auditory modalities are commonly used in various desktop user interfaces while knowledge on other modalities and their applicability is just emerging. We believe that the haptic modality involving the sense of touch can help to create more natural and informative interfaces. This has been utilized, for example, in designing interfaces for visually impaired users [e.g. Patomäki et al. 2004].

The term haptic refers to the sense of touch and relates to virtually all the information a human perceives via physical contact. Touch is a cutaneous sense, meaning that tactile information is perceived via skin. The glabrous (hairless) skin found in palms and fingertips is especially sensitive because it has the finest resolution of the receptive fields of tactile mechanoreceptors conveying the stimuli to the brain [Goldstein 1999, pp.416-8].

Goldstein [1999, pp.423-4] describes that touch can be used for active exploration and for passive sensing. Active touching and exploring is efficient in identifying the physical properties of objects while passive sensing is better in identifying the fine surface details [Goldstein 1999, pp.423-4]. Lederman & Klatzky [1993] explain that this is why we tend to use different ways of touching depending on what information we are looking for, both intentionally and unintentionally.

In the user interfaces haptic feedback is often used in two ways. The first is to imitate the physical laws and objects of the real world. The second is to give the user contextual information about the events and actions of a system. In the first case, the feedback has a crucial role and thus its quality has to correspond to the sensations familiar from the real world. The devices and models needed for the second case are much simpler. This makes haptic feedback a realistic option for enhancing human-computer interaction in the desktop environment.

Haptic interfaces are intrinsically bi-directional, since touching always involves haptic feedback. In desktop applications, touch can be utilized to provide an additional input and output channel. A major problem with the haptic devices is that most of them are either special research prototypes or their prices are too high for an average computer user. However, there are also low-cost tactile feedback devices are available. Most of them use the TouchSense technology developed by Immersion Corporation (http://www.immersion.com) to provide vibrotactile feedback for the user. Raisamo et al. [2004] suggest that even though the quality of the feedback of these devices is far from that of the more sophisticated devices, they can still be used to add extra value to the current user interfaces.

As using vibrating alerts in mobile phones and pagers has become a common practice, it can be assumed that the use of the tactile modality will grow fast in the near future; both as supportive information channel providing better accessibility for people with special needs and as enriching the mobile contents for all users. This emergence is more than expected because the tactile modality has several interesting characteristics: it is always ready to receive information, it attracts one's attention effectively, and it is private.

Thus, it is not a surprise that tactile feedback has recently been applied to areas that are present in our everyday life. Research has been done, for example, to add vibrotactile feedback to strengthen meaning and expression in instant messaging [Rovers & van Essen 2004], to reduce drivers' navigational workload in automobiles [van Erp & van Veen 2001], as well as to enhance the interaction in hand-held mobile devices [O'Modhrain 2004]. In these application areas the contribution of vibrotactile feedback varies but it still brings a new dimension compared to current interfaces.

As a part of this progress, Brewster & Brown [2004] introduced a new interaction paradigm called tactile icon, or Tacton. Tactons are defined as "efficient language to represent concepts at the user interface. Tactons encode information by manipulating the parameters of cutaneous perception" [Brewster & Brown 2004]. As tactile feedback is being applied to new application areas there is room for research on various domains. There are some recent studies on detection thresholds for subtle haptic effects with more advanced haptic devices [Dosher et al. 2001]. Although there are some general guidelines available for using vibrotactile feedback in various domains [ETSI 2002; van Erp 2002], there is still no clear picture how its various parameters are perceived by the user. This kind of basic research is especially essential when looking for the best way to use low-quality feedback devices in user interfaces.

In this paper, we describe an experiment that was conducted to find out how well different feedback magnitudes and frequencies can be distinguished with two tactile feedback devices, a mouse and a trackball. The main contribution of this study is to provide basic knowledge of the effect of magnitude and frequency in distinguishing vibrotactile effects that can be used in various domains.

2　Previous Work

When using a mouse in a standard graphical user interface, for example, the act of picking up and dragging an icon is moderately intuitive and is associated with the real-life action of physically moving objects. The standard computer mouse, however, only provides passive haptic feedback; we obtain both visual and kinaesthetic information about the movement and position of the mouse. Furthermore, the button clicks can be perceived as tactile and auditory feedback and dragging causes a light feel of passive force feedback. However, these outputs are more or less sporadic and cannot be directly controlled by the application.

Even though touch input devices, such as different kinds of touchscreens, tablets and touchpads, have been available for years, haptic feedback devices are not widely spread. Some promising results have been achieved with various prototypes of tactile mice in single interaction events, for example in target selection [Akamatsu et al. 1995; Göbel et al. 1995] and movement times [Akamatsu & MacKenzie 1996]. In addition to previous ones, Hughes & Forrest [1996] have conducted a study on the use of touch in the perceptualization of data. However, the use of tactile feedback in more complex and realistic interaction tasks has not been widely studied, neither has the detection of tactile effect properties on existing low-cost tactile devices.

The studies mentioned above show that tactile devices can be used effectively at least in basic interaction tasks with visual feedback. Because of the low quality of the tactile feedback that these devices produce, they are at their best in providing an additional feedback channel that can be used, for example, to inform the user of events and to indicate the states of ongoing processes. However, the tactile channel has potential for much more than giving simple one-bit information. Tactile feedback similar to what we tested has previously been used in a relatively small role to support visual feedback [Raisamo et al. 2004].

The vibrotactile feedback devices used in this study, the Logitech iFeel mouse (see http://www.logitech.com) and the Kensington Orbit3D trackball (see http://www.kensington.com), are based on the TouchSense technology developed by Immersion Corporation. Both the devices are inexpensive and they have a small motor inside them to produce the vibrations. Earlier work done with the iFeel mouse suggested that some users find both the feel and the sound of the tactile mouse rather unpleasant [Raisamo et al. 2004]. This evokes the question of adequate but comfortable detection thresholds for the frequency and magnitude to be able to take the full advantage of such low-frequency tactile feedback devices.

Figure 1: The Logitech iFeel mouse (left), a DC motor inside the devices (middle) and the Kensington Technologies Orbit3D trackball (right).

Some research concerning the tactile threshold has been done but most of it relates to either direct skin contact or high quality haptic devices. Thus, these results cannot directly be applied to the devices used in this study. For example, for frequency, a minimum detection threshold of 20 percent has been suggested by van Erp [2002]. Van Erp also states that the minimum threshold is not enough if there is a need to code more than a simple message and that there is major individual differences in perceiving stimulus intensity.

3   Experiment

The experiment was carried out in a usability laboratory. The participants wore hearing protectors during the test to mute most of the noise caused by the vibrating devices. Before the session, the participants were asked to fill in a questionnaire on their background and previous experience in using tactile and force feedback devices. During the test, the participants evaluated their subjective performance individually for each task and marked it on the paper. At the end, they filled in a questionnaire about their opinions on the devices and they were briefly interviewed to get more detailed comments. The program saved experimental data for empirical analysis.

3.1   Participants

Twelve volunteered participants, eight students and four employees of the Department of Computer Sciences participated in the experiment. Five of them were female and seven were male, and their age was between 21 and 33 years (mean 25.5, SD = 3.1). All participants were experienced computer and mouse users, but only two of them had used a trackball before. Five of the participants had previously tried the tactile mouse, but none of them had tried the tactile trackball. None of the participants used either of the tested devices on the regular basis and only three of them were frequent users of game controllers that provide vibrotactile feedback.

3.2   Apparatus

The tactile feedback devices used in the experiment are shown in Figure 1 (Logitech iFeel Mouse on the left and the Kensington Orbit3D trackball on the right). The vibrotactile feedback of the devices is generated with a small electrical partial-rotation direct current (DC) motor (Figure 1, in the middle). A similar type of motor

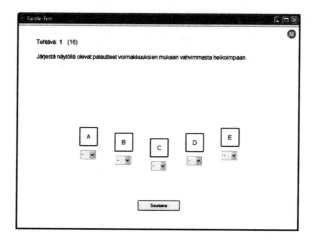

Figure 2: A snapshot of the application used in the experiment.

is linked to the body of both the devices with a nylon cam that can only rotate a few degrees per rotation cycle. The frequency of the vibration is based on the speed the cam completes a cycle, and the magnitude on the angle of rotation.

A Java application (Figure 2) with the Immersion TouchSense SDK for Java was used in the experiment to provide the tactile effects. The application presented the participants arranging tasks that had five similar rectangles called *tactile objects* shown on the screen. The application provided vibrotactile feedback when the mouse was moved over them. The feedback lasted as long as the mouse cursor was kept over the object. The objects were placed on the screen in a curve so that also the furthermost objects would be easier to compare (see Figure 2). There was a combo box under each tactile object to assign indexes for the objects.

3.3 Tasks

The participants were asked to arrange the feedback in a descending order based on the property being varied. The participant needed to select an appropriate index (1..5) from the combo box for each tactile object where one meant the effect with the highest magnitude or frequency and five the effect with the smallest. By default all the effects were given an empty index and at least one object had to be indexed before the participant could proceed to the next task. Also, each index could be assigned for only one tactile object.

Each participant ran the test twice, once with both devices. In the test, the participants were given two rounds of tasks that contained sixteen (magnitude) or fourteen (frequency) quintets of tactile objects (as in Figure 2). All the tactile objects had one constant property, the frequency (25Hz) or the magnitude (8000, in scale 0..10000), but the other property varied according to the designed pattern. The constant values for both magnitude and frequency were decided on the basis of a pilot test conducted to roughly estimate the limits of the devices.

Threshold category (%)	Number of tactile quintets (magnitude)	Number of tactile quintets (frequency)
10	3	4
15	3	3
20	3	2
25	2	2
30	2	2
40	2	1
50	1	

Table 1: The distribution of detection threshold categories used in the experiment.

In the magnitude round, the effect magnitude was varied from 2000 to 10000 units (in scale 0..10000) with a constant frequency of 25Hz. The detection threshold categories for this round were 10, 15, 20, 25, 30, 40, and 50 percent, meaning the difference in the intensity between two consecutive effects. In the frequency round, the frequencies of the effects varied from 10 to 40Hz with a constant magnitude of 8000 units. The detection threshold categories for the frequency round were 10, 15, 20, 25, 30, and 40 percent, respectively. The tasks in both rounds were designed to cover the whole range within each detection threshold category. In practice, this means that the categories with lower threshold have more tasks to cover the range than categories with the higher ones. For magnitude tasks the number of categories varied from 3 to 1 and for frequency tasks from 4 to 1. More detailed data on the distribution of threshold categories can be found in Table 1.

The order of the devices and the rounds was counter-balanced between participants. The order of the tasks inside rounds and the order of the tactile objects inside each task were randomized within a test to avoid learning effects. Also, the threshold categories had no effect to the order of the tasks but were used only in the analysis of the results. Average task completion times, number of touches, touch durations, and number of right answers were calculated from all tasks separately. The right answers were counted per object so that in one task there could be a maximum of five of those.

4 Results

A repeated measures ANOVA between the means calculated for the detection threshold categories revealed significant main effects in the magnitude tasks for threshold ($F_{1,6} = 24.86$, $p < 0.001$) as well as in the frequency tasks ($F_{1,5} = 3.90$, $p < 0.05$). There were also significant effects for device in the magnitude tasks ($F_{1,6} = 55.49$, $p < 0.001$) and in the frequency tasks ($F_{1,5} = 4.96$, $p < 0.05$). Figure 3 shows the average number of right answers for both task types with the mouse and the trackball as a function of detection threshold category.

Results of a paired samples t-test for the number of right answers showed that the mouse was significantly more accurate in distinguishing both the magnitude ($t_6 = 8.5$, $p < 0.001$) and the frequency ($t_5 = 4.0$, $p < 0.05$) of the effects. Furthermore,

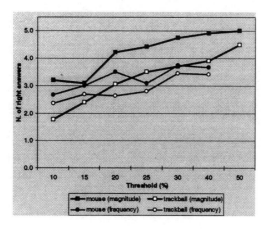

Figure 3: The average number of right answers per input device among the detection threshold categories for magnitude and frequency.

Threshold Category (%)	MM	TM	MF	TF
10	3.19	1.78	2.67	2.35
15	3.08	2.39	3.00	2.69
20	4.22	3.06	3.50	2.63
25	4.42	3.50	3.08	2.79
30	4.75	3.71	3.75	3.46
40	4.92	3.92	3.67	3.42
50	5.00	4.50		

Table 2: Average number of right answers (out of five) per detection threshold category with mouse and trackball.

the magnitude was distinguished significantly more accurately than the frequency with the mouse ($t_{11} = 3.6$, $p < 0.01$) but not with the trackball ($p = 0.10$). The average number of right answers for each condition, mouse with magnitude (MM), trackball with magnitude (TM), mouse with frequency (MF), and trackball with frequency (TF), can be seen in Table 2.

The task completion times were significantly lower with the mouse than with the trackball in the magnitude tasks ($t_6 = 16.0$, $p < 0.001$) as well as frequency tasks ($t_5 = 6.0$, $p < 0.01$). The task completion times for both rounds and devices among the threshold categories can be seen in Figure 4.

Furthermore, the participants spent less time to touch the tactile objects with the mouse in the magnitude tasks compared with the trackball ($t_6 = 2.5$, $p < 0.05$) but in the frequency tasks the objects were touched faster with the trackball ($t_5 = 4.3$, $p < 0.01$). Figure 5 illustrates the average time spent over the objects per task for both rounds and devices among the detection threshold categories.

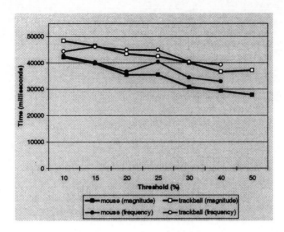

Figure 4: The average task completion times among the detection threshold categories for mouse and trackball.

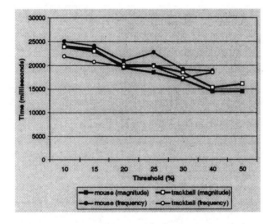

Figure 5: The average time spent touching the objects per task among the detection threshold categories for mouse and trackball.

Meaning the average number of times the cursor was moved over the tactile objects per task, with the trackball the participants had significantly less touches in the frequency tasks ($t_5 = 2.7$, $p < 0.05$). In the magnitude tasks such an effect was not found ($p = 0.10$). In general, it is also evident that the participants needed less touches to complete the tasks with the higher threshold categories than with the lower ones. The average number of touches per task for both rounds and devices among the detection threshold categories can be seen in Figure 6.

Based on the subjective ratings the test participants felt that they succeeded equally well with both the devices in the frequency tasks. Instead, in the magnitude

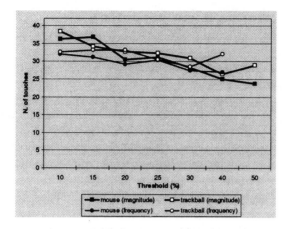

Figure 6: The average number of touches per task among the detection threshold categories for mouse and trackball.

tasks the success with the mouse was estimated somewhat higher than with the trackball. The correlations between the subjective ratings and the corresponding right answers were 0.75 for the mouse and 0.72 for the trackball in the magnitude tasks, and 0.55 and 0.80 in the frequency tasks, respectively. An interesting finding is that the participants were not only able to perceive the frequency faster and with less touches with the trackball but also that they were able to judge their performance relatively well in that case.

5 Discussion

Our study takes a first step to find out the general capabilities of using the vibrotactile devices in desktop environment. Thus the results are applicable, for example, in designing Tactons [Brewster & Brown 2004]. The study focused on two basic properties of vibration, the magnitude and the frequency, that were varied independently. We covered only low frequencies (10–40Hz) while the magnitude was constrained by limits set by the devices. Considering the devices used in the study, our interest was to find out if there were any differences between them in the users' ability to detect different properties of the effects.

Our results show that the magnitude is significantly more important factor in distinguishing vibrotactile effects than the frequency with the tested devices. Furthermore, the results suggest that the device has a remarkable effect in users' ability to distinguish the effects. However, generalizing these results would require a more extensive study with a variety of different devices. Also, the temporal aspects of vibration as well as the effect of composing effects with several dynamic parameters remain to be solved in later studies.

Concerning the detection threshold categories, the results show that in magnitude tasks the detection threshold between the adjacent effects should be at least 20 percent with the mouse to gain 80 percent of right answers. However, with the trackball respective amount of right answers was obtained with no less than 50 percent detection threshold. Here the device differences were proven especially remarkable.

In respect to detection threshold categories in the frequency tasks, there were not as great differences between the devices. However, more interesting was the fact that there was practically no difference between the 30 and 40 percent threshold categories that both gained a peak average of about 75 percent of right answers for the mouse and about 70 percent for the trackball. Furthermore, with the 20 percent threshold the corresponding percentage was 70 for the mouse but only 53 for the trackball. Surprisingly, in the 25 percent threshold category the percentage of right answers for the mouse was lower than in the 20 percent category.

Our results seem not directly to support the minimum detection threshold of 20 percent for frequency given by van Erp [2002]. Here the main reason is most probably in the test setup as our experiment had quite practical setup with low resolution vibrotactile devices and relatively demanding tasks requiring the participants to distinguish the mutual differences of five objects at time. Nevertheless, based on our results it seems that the 20 percent threshold is enough to distinguish 50 percent of the objects right within all conditions — in some cases this accuracy may be enough but in more demanding tasks it is definitely not satisfactory.

Although this study suggests magnitude to be a dominant property over frequency these two properties seem to have a connection to perception of effects. This is supported by, for example, van Erp [2002] who says that changing the frequency also leads to change in the perceived magnitude. Moreover, Brewster & Brown [2004] have stated that with vibrotactile transducers changing magnitude of an effect also causes a change in the perception of frequency. These factors may be one reason why the magnitude was distinguished better among the participants than the frequency while also the method the studied devices produce the vibration may favour the magnitude. However, the interaction between these two parameters should be studied more in the future.

We are aware that giving the participants a better opportunity to learn the feedback of the devices would probably have affected the results as presented by Imai et al. [2003]. Also, in this study we were only interested in the frequencies between 10 and 40Hz. However, based on the psychophysical studies, the range of the practical vibrotactile frequency response of human skin is from 10 to roughly 500Hz [Goldstein 1999, p.411], and it is most sensitive around 250Hz [van Erp 2002]. Thus, in the case of higher frequencies or broader frequency range the results would likely be different as the different types of tactile receptors are sensitive for different frequency ranges [Goldstein 1999]. However, based on our pilot tests the devices used in this study seem not to support frequencies over 333Hz.

The dynamic range of DC motors typical in consumer devices such as those used in this study is quite limited for adequate expression. Therefore, for example a small acoustic speaker could be more suitable for this kind of devices because of its better resolution of response to represent subtle changes in signal. For example, Hughes & Forrest [1996] have ended up with this solution in their design of tactile mouse.

Our method of using hearing protectors may have affected the results as it is not common that users would wear them in the real world. However, in this experiment we wanted the participants to concentrate more on perceiving the vibration of the devices by minimizing the sound cues. The decision was made on the basis of the pilot studies as well as previous studies on the effect of haptic and sound correlations [Peeva et al. 2004].

6 Conclusions and Future Work

We reported an experiment aimed to find out how the detection threshold affects the user's ability to distinguish vibrotactile effects. The results indicate that the detection threshold has an effect on distinguishing the vibrotactile effects especially on low threshold values. Furthermore, the results show that the user performance depends greatly on both the device and the property that is being evaluated. The mouse was better in both magnitude and frequency tasks compared to the trackball. In general, the magnitude was easier to distinguish than the frequency with the corresponding detection threshold values.

It is evident that the results of this study are somewhat dependent on the devices used. It is also obvious that the quality of the feedback of these devices is far from that of the more sophisticated ones. However, our results can be used as the basis for designing more detailed signal language for the devices using a similar kind of technology, such as mobile phones, beepers and computer input devices. In the future, we are going to study the detection thresholds covering a wider range of frequencies and also pay more attention on the interaction effect of magnitude and frequency.

Acknowledgements

We thank all the people who participated in the experiment and our colleagues for giving their valuable comments. This research was funded by the Academy of Finland (grants 104805 and 105555).

References

Akamatsu, M. & MacKenzie, S. [1996], Movement Characteristics using a Mouse with Tactile and Force Feedback, *International Journal of Human–Computer Studies* 45(4), 483–93.

Akamatsu, M., MacKenzie, S. & Hasbrouq, T. [1995], A Comparison of Tactile, Auditory and Visual Feedback in a Pointing Task using a Mouse-type Device, *Ergonomics* 38(4), 816–27.

Brewster, S. A. & Brown, L. M. [2004], Non-Visual Information Display Using Tactons, *in* E. Dykstra-Erickson & M. Tscheligi (eds.), *CHI'04 Extended Abstracts of the Conference on Human Factors in Computing Systems*, ACM Press, pp.787–8.

Dosher, J., Lee, G. & Hannaford, B. [2001], Detection Thresholds for Small Haptic Effects, *in* M. L. McLaughlin, J. P. Hespanha & G. S. Sukhatme (eds.), *Touch in Virtual Environments*, Pearson Education, Chapter 12, pp.205–16.

ETSI [2002], Human Factors: Guidelines on the Multimodality of Icons, Symbols and Pictograms, Technical Report ETSI EG 202 048 v 1.1.1 (2002-08), European Telecommunications Standards Institute. Available via http://www.etsi.org (last accessed 2005-04-28).

Goldstein, E. B. [1999], *Sensation & Perception*, fifth edition, Brooks/Cole Publishing Company.

Göbel, M., Luczak, H., Springer, J., Hedicke, V. & Rötting, M. [1995], Tactile Feedback Applied to Computer Mice, *International Journal of Human–Computer Interaction* **7**(1), 1–24.

Hughes, R. G. & Forrest, A. R. [1996], Perceptualisation using a Tactile Mouse, *in* R. Yagel & G. M. Nielson (eds.), *Proceedings of the 7th IEEE Visualization Conference (VIS'96)*, IEEE Computer Society Press, pp.182–6.

Imai, T., Kamping, S., Breitenstein, C., Pantev, C., Lütkenhöner, B. & Knecht, S. [2003], Learning of Tactile Frequency Discrimination in Humans, *Human Brain Mapping* **18**(4), 260–71.

Lederman, S. J. & Klatzky, R. L. [1993], Extracting Object Properties through Haptic Exploration, *Acta Psychologica* **84**(1), 29–40.

O'Modhrain, S. [2004], Touch and Go — Designing Haptic Feedback for a Hand-held Mobile Device, *BT Technical Journal* **22**(4), 139–45.

Patomäki, S., Raisamo, R., Salo, J., Pasto, V. & Hippula, A. [2004], Experiences on Haptic Interfaces for Visually Impaired Young Children, *in Proceedings of the 6th International Conference on Multimodal Interfaces (ICMI'04)*, ACM Press, pp.281–8.

Peeva, D., Baird, B., Izmirli, O. & Blevins, D. [2004], Haptics and Sound Correlations: Pitch, Loudness and Texture, *in* E. Banissi, K. Börner, C. Chen, M. Dastbaz, G. Clapworthy, A. Faiola, E. Izquierdo, C. Maple, J. Roberts, C. Moore, A. Ursyn & J. J. Zhang (eds.), *Proceedings of the Eight International Conference on Information Visualization (IV'04)*, IEEE Computer Society Press, pp.659–64.

Raisamo, J., Raisamo, R. & Kangas, K. [2004], Interactive Graph Manipulation Tools Enhanced with Low-frequency Tactile and Force Feedback, *in* M. Buss & M. Fritschi (eds.), *Proceedings of EuroHaptics 2004*, Technische Universität München, pp.407–12.

Rovers, A. F. & van Essen, H. A. [2004], HIM: A Framework for Haptic Instant Messaging, *in* E. Dykstra-Erickson & M. Tscheligi (eds.), *CHI'04 Extended Abstracts of the Conference on Human Factors in Computing Systems*, ACM Press, pp.1313–6.

van Erp, J. B. F. [2002], Guidelines for the Use of Vibro-tactile Displays in Human–Computer Interaction, *in* S. A. Wall, B. Riedel, A. Crossan & M. R. McGee (eds.), *Proceedings of EuroHaptics 2002*, EuroHaptics, pp.18–22. Papers published online, see http://www.eurohaptics.vision.ee.ethz.ch/2002.shtml.

van Erp, J. B. F. & van Veen, H. A. H. C. [2001], Vibro-Tactile Information Presentation in Automobiles, *in* C. Baber, M. Faint, S. A. Wall & A. M. Wing (eds.), *Proceedings of EuroHaptics 2001*, EuroHaptics, pp.99–104. Papers published online, see http://www.eurohaptics.vision.ee.ethz.ch/2001.shtml.

HyperGrid — Accessing Complex Information Spaces

Hans-Christian Jetter, Jens Gerken, Werner König, Christian Grün & Harald Reiterer

Department of Computer & Information Science, Workgroup HCI, University of Konstanz, 78457 Konstanz, Germany

Email: *{Hans-Christian.Jetter, Jens.Gerken, Werner.Koenig, Christian.Gruen, Harald.Reiterer}@uni-konstanz.de*

URL: *http://hci.uni-konstanz.de*

In this paper, we describe a new interaction and visualization concept for non-expert users to easily access complex heterogeneous information spaces. The HyperGrid combines well-known table visualizations with zoomable user interface concepts to provide a two-dimensional grid as an access tool to multi-dimensional and relational data. It allows the presentation of attributes of multiple data types, various modalities and various levels of detail in a compact and consistent visual structure. Our concept is illustrated by a use-case based on our experiences and evaluations from preceding projects in the field of visual information seeking systems.

Keywords: HyperGrid, visualization, zoomable user interfaces, interaction techniques, heterogeneous information space, multi-dimensional data, information retrieval, evaluation.

1 Motivation

Many everyday tasks in our life are centred around decision-making based on accessing, sorting, comparing and relating multi-dimensional data. Imagine a salesman has to decide for one of several suggested flight connections at his local travel agent. To choose a connection which suits his requirements he needs to focus on multiple dependent variables simultaneously (e.g. travel time, number of necessary changes, ticket price). A highly efficient way to perform such comparisons is collecting and structuring information in a table with the individual candidates in rows and the individual properties (or attributes) in columns. The orientation and sorting direction of the table allow a quick insight into similarities and differences among the candidates and reasonably increase the efficiency of decision-making.

Using information technology requires a large number of decisions based on multi-dimensional data as well: Everyday we decide for or against documents or websites found by search engines or we select media objects like images or songs from large catalogues. These decisions are normally based on the given metadata sets for each candidate or object. In most cases this metadata is textual (e.g. name, URL), numeric (e.g. file size, date), and in some cases visual (e.g. thumbnails). As data formats and display sizes are well-defined, a traditional table with the metadata for each candidate displayed in the columns of the candidate's row can be used for visualization. The possibility to arbitrarily rearrange rows, columns or sorting orders has made the table to be a simple but very popular visual structure — even for navigation tasks in hierarchical data. Accordingly tables are not only used in classical spreadsheet or business applications but also as interfaces for presenting, selecting and manipulating file system or email objects (e.g. in Microsoft Windows Explorer or Outlook). In our preceding projects INSYDER and INVISIP evaluations of table-based visualizations [Gerken 2004] have shown that tables are never inferior and for certain tasks superior to lists in effectiveness and efficiency. Furthermore we have recently concluded a summative usability study with a non-expert user group (n = 24) to compare the Web interface of the search engine for the library of the University of Konstanz (KOALA) with our table-based information seeking system MedioVis. It revealed significant ($p < 0.01$) superiority in efficiency, appeal [Hassenzahl et al. 2003] and SUS scores [Brooke 1996]. However, loosely structured lists seem to remain the dominant design for the presentation of search results, document collections or other content on the Web.

The handling of metadata and content will become even more demanding for non-expert users regarding the future of Web applications: The information spaces of future e-commerce sites will constantly grow in quantity, dimensionality and in the heterogeneity of the contained data. In future search engines thumbnails, Flash animations or photographs of products will function as 'teasers' to attract visitors and customers. Video-on-demand systems will not only contain posters or textual metadata, but a collection of video trailers, interviews, and other background information about featured films to advertise for buying access rights. Digital libraries or museums will increasingly contain complete scans from valuable historical originals (e.g. scrolls, books, maps), thus providing access to digitized full-text as well as catalogue metadata.

Regarding the growing challenge of handling content of this complexity, it is doubtful whether traditional list or table concepts can succeed on the long-run. Therefore it has been our focus during the development of the HyperGrid to create a strongly user-oriented interface to complex heterogeneous metadata and content at different levels of detail whilst remaining in a clearly structured and oriented visual environment. In the following we will introduce the key concepts of the HyperGrid and illustrate them in a use-case-scenario.

2 The HyperGrid Concept

The name 'HyperGrid' is derived from the two key concepts on which our design is based on: 'Hyper' stands for the ability to present interlinked hypertext or hypermedia content with different modalities, 'Grid' stands for the two-dimensional orthogonal structure which is used for the interactive visualization. Although many aspects of the HyperGrid might remind of traditional tables at a first glance, the semantic structure of the grid and the role of the contained data cells differ fundamentally as we will outline in the following.

2.1 Cells, Columns and Rows in the HyperGrid

In our use-case and evaluations we used the HyperGrid to access a subset of the Internet Movie Database IMDb which is freely accessible under http://www.imdb.com. This online relational database is constantly growing and contains about 6.3 millions individual film or television credits and offers information ranging from the full cast of a film over the actors biographies and photos to user comments and reviews. Accordingly a film can have a remarkable number of attributes or metadata to describe it: the title of the film, actors, directors, producers, sound technicians, year of filming or length in minutes, long texts such as the plot or reviews, film posters or even video trailers.

Problems with table-based visualizations arise when the amount of attributes respectively columns exceeds the number that can be displayed simultaneously. The user is forced to either navigate horizontally through multiple pages or to reconfigure the selection of visible columns to reflect his current need of information. Problems even intensify when the information space to access is represented in a relational data model with great variances in the information density. Joining all tables and relations into one large table with numerous columns to 'flatten' the information space will scatter data and leave gaps with no values assigned in between. For navigating such a large and sparsely filled table the user has to continuously keep an eye on his current position and orientation within the table and constantly recall his individual need of information. There is an immanent danger of getting lost in 'table-space', a phenomena which is commonly known to Microsoft Excel-users working with large sheets. Furthermore special attributes of little importance for the average user can gain equally prominent positions within the table as those essential for the majority.

Like in traditional tables the cells of one row of the HyperGrid all belong to one individual data object or candidate. However, the columns are not assigned to single attributes but to groups of attributes with semantic proximity. Each of these groups or clusters of attributes represent one aspect of interest. The introduction of these higher-ranking aspects of interest is necessary to pre-process the amount of information for the user, who otherwise would face large unusable tables with dozens of columns. The assignment of attributes to columns is discussed in detail in Section 2.3.

For our use-case we assigned the individual films to the data rows. Each film is characterized by three aspects of interest, which were assigned to the first three columns of the grid: 'Film' representing information about the film itself, 'Content' representing information about the plot or genre and 'People Involved' containing

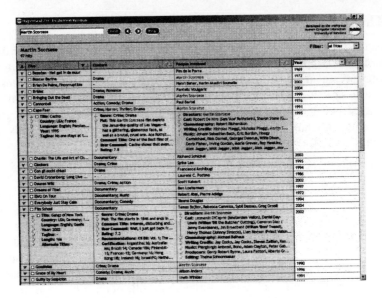

Figure 1: HyperGrid with film data from the IMDb.

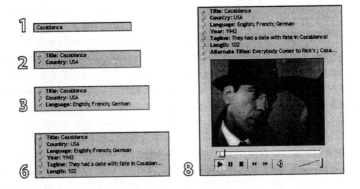

Figure 2: Levels of detail with increasing DOI.

directors, authors, cast, producers, etc. Figure 1 shows a screenshot of the fully functional HyperGrid from our test environment, showing those films from the IMDb which were retrieved by a simple keyword search.

As multiple attributes appear in one column the HyperGrid cells are not only static containers for one value. We regard every cell as one possible starting point for the exploration of the information space with the row defining the object of interest (the film) and the column defining the aspect of interest (e.g. 'People Involved'). The third parameter controlled by the user is the degree of interest (DOI) [Rao & Card 1994].

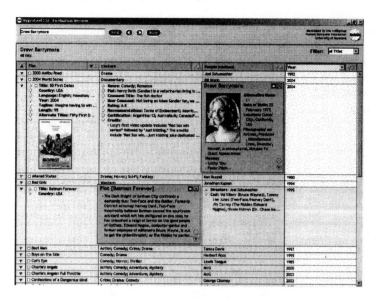

Figure 3: Overlaying browser windows on top of the HyperGrid.

In the HyperGrid the DOI is directly mapped to the level of detail and the size of visible information. Increasing the DOI leads to a growth of the cell size and more and more detailed attributes are fetched from the depth of information space and are presented on the HyperGrid's surface. Reducing the DOI leads to a reduction of the cell size and thus to a reduction of visible attributes. Therefore controlling the DOI allows smooth changes between abstract metadata, rich multimedia metadata, or full text in the cell (see Figure 2). We refer to this mechanism as zooming.

Our interpretation of the HyperGrid cell as dynamic window is taken a step forward by including hypertext or hypermedia data. As mentioned above the IMDb contains not only films but also persons as data objects. All entities of the database (e.g. actor, film, etc.) are carrying 1-to-n or n-to-n relationships among themselves. A film data set contains a list of actors; an actor data set contains a list of films.

The traditional way to provide such relational data on the Web is to offer individual webpages for each entity. However, changing between them leads to a loss of the visual context and a change of layout or even modalities.

Since in our scenario films are the central object of interest there is no consistent way to integrate person-related biographies or filmographies directly into the rows. One solution would be to switch the whole interface from a film-related to a new person-related grid, if requested by the user. However this would lead to a complete loss of the context from which the information was requested. For this reason we prefer the concept of transforming grid cells into small browser windows to allow the user excursions into other objects of interest. This concept combines the browsing of conventional hyperlink structures with table-based visualization: Every object from the information space which carries additional information — but is not the central object of interest — is represented via a classical hyperlink within the cells. For example, if a user has the need to get more information about an actor from a HyperGrid displaying films, he can click on the actor's name as hyperlink. Instead of switching to a new person-related table, a browser-like window is opened in front of the corresponding cell (see Figure 3).

Unlike standard Web browsers the browser window in the grid is integrated directly in the link's context. Neighbouring cells, selected objects or sort orders remain preserved. If more space for the window is necessary, its size can be gradually enlarged up to a size filling the complete grid area. Therefore we reduce the changes of modalities and the danger to get 'lost in hyperspace'.

Additionally the overlaying browser windows can be used to fully display attributes which are especially space-consuming like long texts, lists or video-trailers. Since some attributes need to be truncated in the cell because of space limitations, the user can open an overlaying window by clicking on the '...' or an arrow icon behind the shortened content (see Figure 3, plot 'Batman Forever').

2.2 Visual Information Seeking with the HyperGrid

In the following we will discuss the HyperGrid against the background of Shneiderman's 'Visual Information Seeking Mantra' [Shneiderman 1996]. Through leaving out subtle distinctions Shneiderman identifies two diametrically opposed kinds of information need: 'Known-item search' and 'Browsing'. In our understanding the first assumes that the user has a specific information need which he expresses for example by entering precise keywords in a search engine or navigating to specific nodes in an information hierarchy. Browsing-oriented access to information spaces assumes the contrary: The user has only a vague and less specific information need which he can hardly express in keywords or by systematic navigation. While browsing the information space the user gradually refines his information need by deciding for or against information he is confronted with. To support user goals reaching from known-item search to browsing, Shneiderman identifies seven tasks in his 'task by data type taxonomy': Overview, zoom, filter, details-on-demand, relate, history, and extract. Based on this framework we will discuss how the HyperGrid succeeds in providing task-oriented functionality to support the user in reaching his individual goals.

2.2.1 Overview

Whether the HyperGrid displays a whole catalogue of thousands of items or just dozens of results from a search query is a question of the application domain. Our intention was to develop the HyperGrid as a generic visualization which works independently from previous information retrieval. Figure 4 shows the initial state of the HyperGrid offering an overview of search results retrieved with 'Martin Scorsese' specified as keyword. However the table content could also be an entire film collection catalogue without previous searching.

The HyperGrid does not offer a graphical overview based on scatter plots [Ahlberg & Shneiderman 1994a] or distortion techniques from the TableLens [Rao & Card 1994]. This decision is based on experiences from our previous projects in the field of visual information seeking systems. There are only very few quantitative attributes in our use-case, which significantly reduces the benefit of mapping data

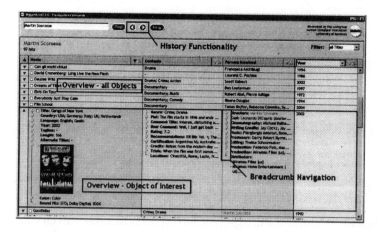

Figure 4: HyperGrid Overview.

to visual variables like position of a data point or the length of bars. Regarding our project VisMeB [Klein et al. 2003] we have observed that purely visual overview techniques often lead to a small conformity with user expectations. During our user tests these problems lead to a complete ignorance of the users towards the integrated TableLens concepts [Gerken 2004]. This observation led to the decision to reduce overview in the HyperGrid to the initial appearance of a table, without distortion effects or bar representations of quantitative data.

Although a table is a rather traditional visual structure it incorporates high conformity with user expectations with the advantages tables have compared to loosely structured result lists common in Web-based applications. As a non-expert access tool the HyperGrid does not strain the user with unexpected visual structures in an initial state. However advanced techniques like scatter plots can be offered optionally outside the grid and can be coupled with the HyperGrid with brushing and linking techniques as realized in our MedioVis (see Section 1) system.

Furthermore we provide an overview of a single object of interest. This function is realized via the small arrow icon in the very first column on the left. By clicking the user can expand a row to the maximum size and request an overview of all attributes that are available for an object of interest at any time (see Figure 4, film 'Gangs of New York'). He can then choose the attribute of interest directly without having to navigate through the whole information space by zooming into cells.

2.2.2 Zoom

Figure 2 illustrates how zooming techniques allow increasing the level of detail within a cell while preserving the user's sense of position and context. Zooming interaction is provided by simple mouse clicks as suggested by Shneiderman [1996]. Unlike conventional zooming the HyperGrid allows selective zooming into one of multiple dimensions: By clicking into an individual cell the user expresses a higher DOI for an individual aspect of interest of an individual object.

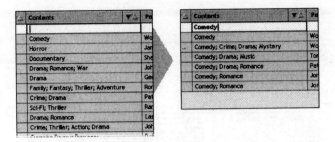

Figure 5: The table filter with one criterion for the 'Content' column.

Since a table structure does not allow completely independent cell sizes (vertical and horizontal size of a row or column is always defined by the cell with maximum size in this particular row or column) unintended growth of neighbouring cells during zooming has also to be addressed. Our concept is to compensate such an unintended growth of cell size by automatically filling the resulting space with information. If a user has chosen one aspect of interest and starts to zoom into one cell, he has implicitly expressed an interest into the whole object as well. Thus we carefully increase the level of detail in the neighbouring cells to enable the user to gradually get an overview of the whole information available and reveal other potentially interesting attributes.

2.2.3   Filter

Possible filter techniques are strongly dependent from the application domain and available data types. Trying to provide a generic concept, the standard HyperGrid contains only very simple filter functionality. In Figure 4 a drop down box is situated in the top right corner of the screen with three possible selections for the display mode: 'all titles', 'selected titles', and 'zoomed titles'. As proposed by Shneiderman [1996] this drop down box allows the user to control the contents of the display and to filter out uninteresting objects. In a first step the user defines a sub-set of all interesting objects by selecting or zooming into them. In a second step a filtered display is activated by the user, selecting the desired display mode from the drop down box.

Leaving the generic concept of the HyperGrid allows more powerful but domain-specific filter techniques: Apart from dynamic queries like in FilmFinder as proposed by Ahlberg & Shneiderman [1994a] we suggest the table filter inspired by Microsoft Excel's auto filter function. The table filter reduces the displayed objects in the table to the sub-set which corresponds to the filter criteria specified in the top row of the table (see Figure 5). For each column a value can be entered into the top row which defines the keywords that must be contained in the attributes of the corresponding aspect of interest. If the keyword is not found, the object is filtered out. Only those objects are displayed which fulfil all criteria in each column simultaneously (AND-relation). This way the amount of information displayed can be reduced to the user's information need very efficiently without new search queries or database accesses.

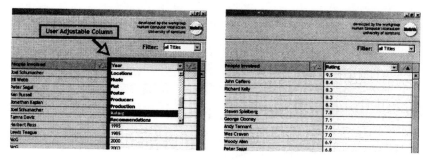

Figure 6: The user adjustable column.

2.2.4 Details-on-demand

As illustrated in Section 2.1 the hyperlink concept and the overlaying browser windows allow easy access to details which cannot be integrated consistently into the table cells (see Figure 3). Offering the functionality of a small browser application, each browser window can be used as a starting point of browsing-oriented excursions into the information space or connected information resources from the World Wide Web. Similar to the zooming in Section 2.2.2 the user's sense of position and context is preserved.

2.2.5 Relate

Based on the user's selection of one or several quantitative or categorical attributes as sorting criteria, table-based visualizations allow quick and systematic comparisons between several objects of interest. To further support this functionality, we included an additional user-adjustable column into the HyperGrid. This column is visually separated from the other columns and contains only one attribute which is selected by the user from the variety of attributes contained in the aspects of interest (see Figure 6). As a result relating, comparing, and sorting values of an attribute that is hidden deep inside the information space can be achieved easily without navigating the aspects of interest at high levels of detail.

In a future version the hyperlinks described in Section 2.1 could also be used to analyse relationships among objects of interest by using them as input for query refinement or dynamic queries. Hyperlinks to objects of interest that are contained in the HyperGrid could also be used to jump to particular positions in the grid or to expand or select related rows.

2.2.6 History

History functionality is integrated into the HyperGrid on two levels: On a first level each interaction step that changed the face of the HyperGrid (e.g. zooming in or out, expanding or collapsing a row, opening a browser window) is stored in a browsing history. Users are offered an undo-function by clicking forward / backward buttons as known from Web browsers (see Figure 4). This very simple implementation of history is motivated by our observations from early user testing, where many users had the strong tendency to move the mouse pointer to the top left corner of the screen,

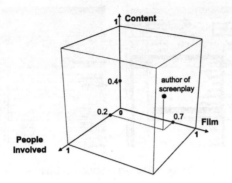

Figure 7: An attribute in the attribute space.

obviously searching for a button to undo changes or returning to previous states of the HyperGrid. In some cases such functionality was explicitly requested by the users referring to popular interfaces like Microsoft Internet or Windows Explorer.

On a second level a visualization of the history of information growth is integrated into each cell. Since it is difficult to communicate the outcome of the zooming interaction step in advance, the information growth within a cell must be transparent for the user. Otherwise the user might get the feeling of losing the ability to control the DOI. For this reason the amount and kind of information added with zooming is illustrated with a vertical breadcrumb navigation within each cell (see Figure 4). Similar to breadcrumb navigation used on the World Wide Web (e.g. to visualize the progress of the checkout process in online e-commerce shops), the user has the possibility to navigate back to an attribute by clicking on the breadcrumb and to retrace his path through information space.

2.2.7 Extract

As the HyperGrid shall be introduced as a generic visualization and interaction concept, it is not possible to discuss the extraction of data for later use in general terms. It is necessary to relate to specific application domains to illustrate the possibilities the HyperGrid can offer in future applications. One typical example is the application of the HyperGrid in digital libraries. Here the current selection of objects of interest from the grid could be saved to a portable medium, printed out or sent by e-mail like it is possible in MedioVis. Advanced systems can manage multiple collections per user or allow the exchange of collections among them for collaborative work.

2.3   The Attribute Space

To illustrate the concept how attributes can be assigned to aspects of interest (respectively columns) we have introduced the attribute space, which lays a simple mathematical foundation for structuring data in the HyperGrid and offers possibilities for future work concerning an optimized or user-adaptive information presentation and assignment.

According to our IMDb use case we want to assign each attribute of a film to one of the three aspects of interest mentioned above ('Film', 'Content' and 'People Involved'). In the attribute space every aspect of interest is equivalent to a dimension (see Figure 7). Attributes are equivalent to points in attribute space, but are limited to positive Cartesian coordinates between 0.0 and 1.0. In our example the attribute space is therefore 3-dimensional and contains a cloud of points limited to a cube of edge length 1.0 in positive direction of Cartesian space.

The location of the attributes in the attribute space is defined by one or multiple experts by assigning a semantic distance to each attribute for every aspect of interest. Assigning 0.0 as location for an attribute on an axis means a very close relation to this aspect of interest (respectively a small distance to the origin). A 1.0 means there is practically no semantic proximity of this attribute to the aspect of interest. For example an attribute containing 'author of screenplay' is very closely related to the third dimension 'Persons Involved', however it has also reasonable influence on the second dimension 'Content'. Regarding the first dimension 'Film' authors are normally less interesting than actors or directors. Accordingly an expert could assign the location (0.7, 0.4, 0.2) to the attribute 'author of screenplay'. Without any doubt this is a subjective assessment which might vary between experts with different mental models and needs of information. However this weighed assignment of attributes to aspects of interest allows various strategies how to project attribute space onto the HyperGrid columns or to cluster or join attributes of small semantic distance.

At this early stage we were already able to achieve reasonable results by merging the assessment of two members of our workgroup who were supported by a researcher in the field of media science. The merging was simply done by calculating the average position for each attribute and assigning the attribute exclusively to the aspect of interest it was most related to.

In future more intelligent strategies and dynamic adaptation during usage could improve user satisfaction with data structuring in the HyperGrid. Using our DROID logging technology [Jetter 2003] we are able to collect information about the popularity of attributes and number and duration of visits. Like suggested in the representation matrix of Rüger et al. [1996] such information could be used to optimize attribute space on the basis of simple statistical mathematics, without complex user modelling or inferences on user-behaviour.

3 User Testing and Redesign

As mentioned before our intention behind the HyperGrid is to offer an intuitive interaction and visualization concept for non-expert users. Therefore development has been accompanied from the scratch by intensive use of inspection methods to verify the concepts at all stages of implementation. However user testing is essential to measure how far these efforts were successful. Since the maturity of our theoretical concepts and their implementation in our Java prototype had not then reached a stage to measure effectiveness and efficiency and compare them with existing systems, we were focussed on identifying fundamental problems in our concept and therefore conducted a formative evaluation. Nevertheless our HyperGrid Java implementation was already fully functional.

3.1 Test Setting

We tested a group of five non-expert users with strong differences concerning computer literacy with the above mentioned IMDb use-case. The test was carried out in our usability lab with one test person per session. Our test-design was a mixture of several qualitative methods to increase the validity of the outcomes: observing user's behaviour and comments during an unguided exploration phase, 'thinking aloud' user testing with realistic tasks, and a concluding semi-structured interview. Two questionnaires, AttrakDiff [Hassenzahl et al. 2003] (see also http://www.attrakdiff.de) and Software Usability Scale (SUS) [Brooke 1996] were included to measure additional quantitative data. Because of the small size of the test group complex statistical analysis was not regarded as reasonable.

3.2 Test Results

3.2.1 Usability Problems & Redesign Approaches

We could identify two central usability problems. First users felt that the content of a cell changed rather randomly during zooming and was hardly predictable. This problem occurred because of the layout and truncation algorithm which failed to provide a consistent layout within the cell while simultaneously guaranteeing a steady increase of cell size during zooming. As a consequence further effort must be put into the improvement of the algorithm. The second problem originated from too many interaction possibilities that were offered in each single cell. Users could zoom in, zoom out, click on the breadcrumb arrows to zoom in/out entirely, click on a breadcrumb or attribute name to focus one attribute, and last but not least click on hyperlinks to see additional information on a person or an attribute in a browser window. Whereas this variety of options might be suitable for experienced users, it seems not adequate for non-experts.

Since our focus lies especially on ease-of-learning, we will now aim at reducing the amount of different interaction elements. Therefore we have to rethink the breadcrumb navigation. Its initial idea was to visually structure the information growth during zooming in order to improve comprehensibility for the user. However it remains questionable if it succeeded in this task. Furthermore the interaction possibilities were mainly redundant. We will therefore evaluate ways to replace the breadcrumb navigation completely which will reduce interaction possibilities within a cell to zooming and hyperlinks (e.g. person names for biographies or attribute names for full view of attributes).

3.2.2 Approved Concepts

Besides the above mentioned conceptual flaws the fundamental concepts of the HyperGrid were approved:

1. All users seemed to comprehend the mechanism of zooming into and out of cells and could clearly relate cell content to the table context.

2. Controlling the DOI by mouse clicks was no challenge: The affordance generated by changing the shape of the mouse pointer over the cell appeared to be sufficient.

3. The HyperLink concept to integrate additional information in separate browser windows seemed to fit the users' needs very well. Users comments varied from 'nice to have' to 'really cool' and users enjoyed the intuitive interaction.

4. The user adjustable column was considered as extremely helpful to compare several movies with one specific attribute.

5. The sorting functionality was discovered by all users thanks to larger and more meaningful sort buttons in the column header.

6. The filter functionality to show only selected or zoomed rows was understood and adopted. Especially in large result sets, our subjects made frequent use of it. Nevertheless we will integrate a superior filter concept directly within the table visualization as mentioned in Section 2.2.3.

Finally the two questionnaires AttrakDiff and SUS underlined the overall positive feedback: Although users ran into some usability problems, the questionnaire results suggest that users liked the HyperGrid in terms of functionality (SUS) and hedonic quality (AttrakDiff). While the small sample size doesn't allow an in-depth interpretation of the exact results, they are listed below for the sake of completeness: The SUS scored with a 71 on the 0–100 scale, which we regard as an acceptable value for a system still under development. Average AttrakDiff scores (scale 1.0 to 7.0) lie at 4.9 for pragmatic quality, at 5.2 for hedonic quality (identity), at 5.4 for hedonic quality (stimulation), and at 5.3 for appeal. Hedonic quality and appeal seem therefore already very satisfying.

4   Related Work

The extension of traditional tables by using distortion techniques was introduced by the TableLens [Rao & Card 1994] and was further developed by Spenke et al. [1996] and Bederson et al. [2004]. TableLens and Bederson's DateLens are focussed on distortion and semantic zooming and are the foundation of the HyperGrid's concept of combining zoomable user interfaces [Raskin 2000] with grid structures, semantic zooming and browsing (see Sections 2.1 and 2.2.1).

In our preceding projects INSYDER and INVISIP we have extended traditional tables to control the level of detail of displayed metadata for entire tables or single rows [Reiterer et al. 2000; Mann 2002; Göbel et al. 2002].

The assignment of multiple attributes to 'aspects of interest' at different degrees of interest is based on the representation matrix introduced by Rüger et al. [1996] which lays the foundation for the attribute space (see Section 2.3).

The HyperGrid's novelty lies in merging concepts of TableLens and DateLens with a cell-oriented semantic zooming to gradually reveal complex heterogeneous metadata attributes and content of different modalities according to the 'attribute space' model. Furthermore it allows browsing-oriented excursions into the information space or connected information resources from the World Wide Web.

5   Conclusion and Outlook

In the past various technologies have been introduced to access complex information spaces and support decision-making by visualizing multi-dimensional data. For example Attribute Explorer [Tweedie et al. 1994], InfoZoom [Spenke et al. 1996], hyperbolic trees [Lamping & Rao 1994] or scatter plots [Ahlberg & Shneiderman 1994b] can largely simplify decisions by exploiting the human visual processing to reduce the cognitive load of many tasks.

However these technologies are seldom found in standard applications or large e-commerce websites to this day. It seems that the loosely structured list-based presentations on websites and the traditional table widget in desktop applications remain dominant because they have a small or irrelevant learning threshold and a great conformity with user expectations.

We are convinced that the usability of information systems could be largely improved by replacing poorly structured hypertext or list-based presentation of multi-dimensional data by the HyperGrid.

Based on the concept of the Granularity Table [Klein et al. 2002] that reduces cognitive overload by smooth transitions between focus and context and integrating data of different modalities in one data row the HyperGrid takes a step forward: the user can express his individual degree of interest into every table cell by a zoom-like interaction. Furthermore the HyperGrid does not lack the ability to deal with non-quantitative, non-categorical or non-textual metadata (e.g. images, video and sound clips) and can handle hyperlinks between different data objects enhancing the application domain from flat data tables to relational databases. The HyperGrid's close relation to well-known table concepts improves the ease-of-learning by the great conformity with user expectations. The apparent structure, orientation and the possibility of comparing and relating data should sustain a superior ease-of-use.

We are convinced that a matured design of the HyperGrid ready for deployment opens new perspectives for information presentation on websites and the design of information seeking systems. Introducing a standard component like the HyperGrid to access complex information spaces (regardless whether it is flight connections, Wikis, e-commerce or digital library catalogues) could improve efficiency and the consistency of websites with user expectations.

Furthermore the HyperGrid could be extended to additionally offer user interface components. These components could be placed as interactive objects in the depth of information space like normal textual attributes, video trailers or graphics. This way it would be possible to use the grid structure to integrate text fields or sliders for user comments or ratings into digital libraries or to implement e-commerce processes (e.g. ordering a product or requesting support) directly into catalogues.

References

Ahlberg, C. & Shneiderman, B. [1994a], Visual Information Seeking: Tight Coupling of Dynamic Query Filters with Starfield Displays, *in* B. Adelson, S. Dumais & J. Olson (eds.), *Proceedings of the SIGCHI Conference on Human Factors in Computing Systems: Celebrating Interdependence (CHI'94)*, ACM Press, pp.313–7.

Ahlberg, C. & Shneiderman, B. [1994b], Visual Information Seeking using the Filmfinder, *in* C. Plaisant (ed.), *Conference Companion of the CHI'94 Conference on Human Factors in Computing Systems*, ACM Press, p.433.

Bederson, B. B., Clamage, A. D., Czerwinski, M. P. & Robertson, G. R. [2004], DateLens: A Fisheye Calendar Interface for PDAs, *ACM Transactions on Computer–Human Interaction* **11**(1), 90–119.

Brooke, J. [1996], SUS: A Quick and Dirty Usability Scale, *in* P. W. Jordan, B. Thomas, B. A. Weerdmeester & I. L. McClelland (eds.), *Usability Evaluation in Industry*, Taylor & Francis.

Gerken, J. [2004], Evaluation of a Metadatabrowser — Listview vs. Leveltable, Bachelor-Thesis, University of Konstanz.

Göbel, S., Haist, J., Reiterer, H. & Müller, F. [2002], INVISIP: Usage of Information Visualization Techniques to Access Geospatial Data Archives, *in* A. Hameurlain, R. Cicchetti & R. Traunmüller (eds.), *Database and Expert Systems Applications: Proceedings of the 13th International Conference (DEXA 2002)*, Vol. 2453 of *Lecture Notes in Computer Science*, Springer-Verlag, pp.371–80.

Hassenzahl, M., Burmester, M. & Koller, F. [2003], AttrakDiff: Ein Fragebogen zur Messung wahrgenommener hedonischer und pragmatischer Qualität, *in* J. Ziegler & G. Szwillus (eds.), *Mensch & Computer 2003: Interaktion in Bewegung*, B G Teubner, pp.187–96.

Jetter, H.-J. [2003], Usability Evaluation im Rahmen von INVISIP, Bachelor-Thesis, University of Konstanz.

Klein, P., Müller, F., Reiterer, H. & Eibl, M. [2002], Visual Information Retrieval with the SuperTable + Scatterplot, *in* E. Banissi (ed.), *Proceedings of the Sixth International Conference on Information Visualization (IV'02)*, IEEE Computer Society Press, pp.70–5.

Klein, P., Müller, F., Reiterer, H. & Limbach, T. [2003], Metadata Visualization with VisMeB, *in* E. Banissi, K. Borner, C. Chen, G. Clapworthy, C. Maple, A. Lobben, C. Moore, J. Roberts, A. Ursyn & J. Zhang (eds.), *Proceedings of the Seventh International Conference on Information Visualization (IV'03)*, IEEE Computer Society Press, pp.600–5.

Lamping, J. & Rao, R. [1994], Laying Out and Visualizing Large Trees using a Hyperbolic Space, *in* P. Szekely (ed.), *Proceedings of the 7th Annual ACM Symposium on User Interface Software and Technology, UIST'94*, ACM Press, pp.13–4.

Mann, T. [2002], Visualization of Search Results from the WWW, PhD thesis, University of Konstanz.

Rao, R. & Card, S. K. [1994], The Table Lens: Merging Graphical and Symbolic Representations in an Interactive Focus and Context Visualization for Tabular Information, *in* B. Adelson, S. Dumais & J. Olson (eds.), *Proceedings of the SIGCHI Conference on Human Factors in Computing Systems: Celebrating Interdependence (CHI'94)*, ACM Press, pp.318–22.

Raskin, J. [2000], *The Humane Interface: New Directions for Designing Interactive Systems*, Addison–Wesley.

Reiterer, H., Mußler, G., Mann, T. & Handschuh, S. [2000], INSYDER — An Information Assistant for Business Intelligence, *in* N. Belkin, P. Ingwersen & M.-K. Leong (eds.), *Proceedings of the 23rd Annual International ACM SIGIR Conference on Research and Development in Information Retrieval (SIGIR'00)*, ACM Press, pp.112–9.

Rüger, M., Preim, B. & Ritter, A. [1996], Zoom Navigation: Exploring Large Information and Application Spaces, *in* T. Catarci, M. F. Costabile, S. Levialdi & G. Santucci (eds.), *Proceedings of the Conference on Advanced Visual Interface (AVI'96)*, ACM Press, pp.40–8.

Shneiderman, B. [1996], The Eyes Have It: A Task by Data-type Taxonomy for Information Visualizations, *in Proceedings of the 1996 IEEE Symposium on Visual Languages (VL'96)*, IEEE Computer Society Press, pp.336–43.

Spenke, M., Beilken, C. & Berlage, T. [1996], FOCUS: The Interactive Table for Product Comparison and Selection, *in* D. Kurlander, M. Brown & R. Rao (eds.), *Proceedings of the 9th Annual ACM Symposium on User Interface Software and Technology, UIST'96*, ACM Press, pp.41–50.

Tweedie, L. A., Spence, B., Williams, D. & Bhogal, R. [1994], The Attribute Explorer. Video presentation at CHI'94.

Mixed Interaction Space — Expanding the Interaction Space with Mobile Devices

Thomas Riisgaard Hansen, Eva Eriksson & Andreas Lykke-Olesen[†]

Centre for Pervasive Healthcare & Centre for Interactive Spaces, ISIS Katrinebjerg, Department of Computer Science, University of Aarhus, Denmark

Email: *{thomasr, evae}@daimi.au.dk*

[†] *Department of Design, Aarhus School of Architecture, Denmark*

Email: *alo@interactivespaces.net*

Mobile phones are mainly interacted with through buttons, thumbwheels or pens. However, mobile devices are not just terminals into a virtual world; they are objects in a physical world. The concept of Mixed Interaction Space (MIXIS) expands the interaction with mobile phone into the physical world [Hansen et al. 2005]. MIXIS uses the camera in mobile devices to track a fixed-point and thereby establishes a 3 dimensional interaction space wherein the position and rotation of the phone can be tracked. In this paper we demonstrate that MIXIS opens up for new flexible ways of interacting with mobile devices. We present a set of novel, flexible applications built with MIXIS and we show that MIXIS is a feasible way of interacting with mobile devices by evaluating a MIXIS application against a traditional mobile interface. Finally, we discuss some design issues with MIXIS.

Keywords: mixed interaction space, mixed reality, mobile HCI, zoomable interfaces, mobile computing, spatial aware displays, drawable interfaces, gesture interaction.

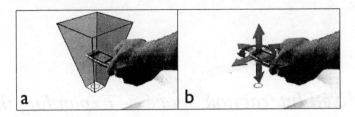

Figure 1: (a) Diagram of the Mixed Interaction Space. (b) Diagram of gestures for interaction.

1   Introduction

Mobile devices such as mobile phones and PDA's have been adopted into our daily life. Researchers at Nokia have observed that an important factor contributing to this is the personalization of the device, not just the communication possibilities [Vänänen-Vaino-Mattila & Ruuska 2000]. In constant use the mobile device becomes a personal object to such extent that it intensifies the user's feeling of being inseparable from this unique thing. Still, the mobile devices are more and more becoming a personal computer in both functionality and interaction. The most common interaction is through buttons, thumbwheel or pen, and through something that can be characterized as a downscaling of the classic WIMP interface. The mapping of navigation and functionality to buttons, wheels and icons is not flexible and with low degrees of customization. The standard technique to view a large picture or map is scrolling by repeatedly press a button, roll a thumbwheel or drag a pen, and it is impossible to combine the manoeuvre with zoom, since the user has to divert the attention switching button to change function.

Designing for small mobile devices involves the classical problems of limited screen space, mapping functionality to small multifunctional buttons and traditionally a 2D interface. These problems can be reduced by expanding the interaction space outside the limits of the screen and the physical frames, and by using natural body gestures, the interface combine the digital and the physical world in a new 3D interaction space. By transforming the interface of the device into a 3D object it becomes a space belonging to the real world instead of the digital, and therefore reduces the cognitive load on the user.

1.1   The Concept of Mixed Interaction Space

In this paper we present a set of applications that expand the classical interface and interaction of the mobile device, to create a more natural interaction with a mixed reality interface. The applications are built on mixed interaction space [Hansen et al. 2005], and demonstrate a new way to interact with digital information by using the existing camera of a mobile device to extract location and rotation of the device. Independent of the applications, the concept is to expand the interface of the mobile device outside the display by using the space between the front of the camera and a fixed-point, as illustrated in Figure 1a. The space becomes the interaction space for gesture recognition. Moving the phone in the interaction space can be mapped to actions in the graphical user interface shown in the display or an action on a nearby device or display.

To interact with the system the user only need one hand for the mobile device, and then use the natural gestures of the body to address the system. Depending on the application the device can be seen as having one to four degrees of freedom [Beaudouin-Lafon 2000]. Figure 1b displays how a four degree of freedom device can be generated by tracking the position and rotation of the device.

The size of the interaction space sets the borders both for the gesture recognition input and for the augmented interface, and is dependent on the size of the circle symbol representing the fixed-point and its distance from the viewpoint of the camera. A larger symbol spans a larger interaction space and therefore the gestures can be coarser. The fact that there is no fixed size opens up for the possibility to have small mixed interaction spaces, where the user have to use fine motor coordination or large spaces that requires the user to use larger movement.

The symbol can be anything as long as the camera can detect it. In the implemented concept a circle is used, it can be drawn or be a part of a decoration of some type and it can consist of different colours. Choosing simple symbols and using tolerant detection algorithms opens up for the possibility of drawable interfaces. The symbol can also be associated with a unique id, and combined with some type of generic protocol to send information, the concept can be used for controlling pervasive devices in the environment.

Even though the interaction is based upon natural body gestures, the concept does not require external sensor technology or specialized hardware. The concept can be implemented on standard mobile phones or PDA's equipped with a camera.

The applications presented in this paper are built upon the principles of direct manipulation [Shneiderman 1998], the actions are rapid, incremental and reversible and whose effect on the object is visible immediately. The users are able to act through gesturing and the display feedback or device functionality occurs immediately which convey the sense of causality.

In this paper we will demonstrate that MIXIS is a new and flexible concept for interacting with mobile devices that combines some of the properties of tangible interfaces with traditional mobile device interaction. We will argue for the novelty and flexibility of the concept by presenting four applications build with the concept. We have discussed several of the applications at small workshops, and we have made a formal evaluation of one of the applications to investigate and demonstrate that MIXIS is also a feasible way of interacting with mobile devices. Finally, we will discuss mapping and identity; two central aspects of MIXIS.

2 Related Work

Beaudouin-Lafon [2004] claims that it is becoming more important to focus on designing interaction rather than interfaces. Inspired by that, we argue that our applications are new compared to related work because they:

1. support a high degree of mobility in the sense that it is not depending on any external tracking hardware;

2. are highly flexible because a wide set of different applications can be built by using the mixed interaction space in different ways; and

3. provide a natural mapping between gestures and the interface since we are able to get quite precise information about the position of the mobile device in 4 dimensions.

2.1 New Interaction Techniques for Mobile Devices

Several projects have explored different new interaction techniques for mobile devices [Fitzmaurice et al. 1993; Yee 2003; Patridge et al. 2002; Fällman et al. 2004; Masui et al. 2004]. Fitzmaurice et al. [1993] uses a 6D input device to navigate in a virtual world, Yee [2003] uses special hardware from Sony to track a PDA and interact with different applications using 3 dimensions and Patridge et al. [2002] have equipped a small portable device with tilt sensors for text entries. These systems use specialized tracking hardware that limits the mobility [Fitzmaurice et al. 1993; Yee 2003; Masui et al. 2004] or tracks the device in just two dimensions [Fällman et al. 2004; Yee 2003; Masui et al. 2004], constraining the flexibility of the systems.

Accelerometers, can interact with an application by using tilting, rotation and movement of the device as input. The clear advantage of this interaction technique is its independence of the surroundings why it supports mobility very well. It supports new ways of interacting with applications e.g. scrolling in applications by tilting the device [Harrison et al. 1998].

2.2 Using Cameras with Mobile Systems

Other projects have experimented with using the camera on mobile devices for tracking and augmenting reality [Rekimoto & Ayatsuka 2000; Rohs 2004; SemaCode Corporation 2005; OP3 2005]. Several of these projects aim at augmenting reality by using bar codes in the environment to impose a 3D digital image on reality [Rekimoto & Ayatsuka 2000] and do not focus on the interaction. SemaCode Corporation [2005] is focusing on how to bridge the gap between digital and physical material. OP3 [2005] and Rohs [2004] focus on the interaction, but both systems rely on tracking two dimensional barcode and not on drawable symbols.

Interaction techniques that use integrated cameras strongly resemble interactions that can be designed with accelerometers. The movement, rotation and tilting of the device, can partly be extracted from running optical flow algorithms on the camera images. However, the camera images can provide more information than the movement, tilting or rotation vector. It can be used to identify a fixed point, and it can calculate its relative rotation, tilting and position according to this point.

2.3 Physical Interfaces

MIXIS is related to tangible user interfaces (TUI) in the sense that both interaction techniques try to bridge the physical with the digital [Ishii & Ullmer 1997]. TUIs focus on hiding the computer and having the interaction mainly in the physical world. This opens up for highly intuitive interfaces, but TUIs are not that suitable for more advanced interfaces with much functionality, because each object or function in the program would have to be associated with a physical representation. MIXIS uses a combination of the physical and digital world. Most of the interaction possibilities are presented in the digital world, but to guide the interaction and to build shortcuts in the navigation a fixed-point is used in the real world.

3 Applications

3.1 Implementation

Based on the conceptual discussion we designed and implemented a component to track the position and rotation of a mobile device within the mixed interaction space and identify a symbol drawn in the centre of the circle. Thereafter four applications based on the concept were implemented.

One of our main design goal was to build a system that everyone could use anywhere without having to acquire any new kind of hardware. Using the camera of mobile devices to track a fixed point fulfilled our requirements.

A circle is chosen as fixed-point in our prototype implementation of MIXIS, and it is appropriated for several reasons:

1. It is a symbol most people recognize and are able to draw.

2. There exists a lightweight algorithm for finding a circle in a picture.

3. The radius of the circle provides information about the distance between the camera and the circle.

4. The circle is suitable as a frame for different icons.

To detect the circle, we implemented the Randomized Hough Circle Detection Algorithm as described by Xu et al. [1990] on the phone. The main reason for choosing the randomized version is that it is lightweight and much faster than the Non-Randomized Hough Algorithm [Kälviäinen et al. 1995]. We optimized the algorithm for the specific use by e.g. looking for only one circle in the picture.

The system is implemented in C++ for Symbian OS 7.0s on a Nokia 7610 mobile phone. To keep the interaction fluent and to reduce the memory used, we capture video in a resolution of 160x120 pixels in most of the prototype applications. In some of the applications where an instant response from the program was not required we used 320×240 pixels.

In the current implementation a black circle on a mainly non-black surface is tracked. The circle does not have to be perfect, the algorithm easily recognizes a hand drawn circle and the algorithm is also able to find the circle in different light conditions, which makes it more robust for use in different environments. Figure 2 demonstrates how the applications use the generic component.

3.2 Applications

We have implemented four applications that use the mixed interaction space concept. To test the feasibility of the concept we carried out a formal evaluation of one of the applications and a set of workshops discussing some of the other applications. The conclusions from the evaluation are presented in the next section.

Example Application

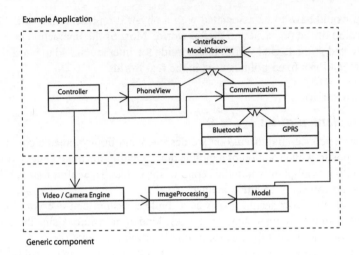

Generic component

Figure 2: Diagram of the system and how the applications use the generic component. Depending on what application, the communication model is used to communicate with external devices.

3.2.1　*ImageZoomViewer*

The first application allows the user to pan and zoom simultaneously on a picture by moving the phone in the mixed interaction space, see Figure 1c. When moving the phone closer to or further away from the circle the application zoom in and out on the image. Moving the phone to the left — right or up — down makes the application pan the image in the direction the phone moved.

We have worked with a basic scenario; navigation on a map. Maps are normally too large to fit on the screen of a mobile device and users need both an overview of the entire map and details like street names. In Figure 3c we demonstrate the use of the ImageZoomViewer for browsing a subway map, here using a printed circle placed on a wall. The arrow points at the visual cue displayed on top of the map that indicated what kind of interaction the user was performing. In the picture the visual cue on the display shows that the user has placed the physical circle slightly to the right of the centre of the camera view why the visible area of the map is panning slowly to the left. The applications resembles the application implemented by Yee [2003] and Fällman et al. [2004], but in our application no specialized tracking equipment is used and we were able to both pan and zoom at the same time.

3.2.2　*LayeredPieMenu*

In the application called LayeredPieMenus MIXIS is investigated and used to navigate a menu structure. The interaction space can contain numerous menus organized as pie menus [Callahen et al. 1988] on top of each other. When the camera recognizes the circle a pie menu appears and augments the circle on the display. The pie menu consists of up to eight function segments that surround an info text explaining which menu is at hand. The functions in each menu can be selected

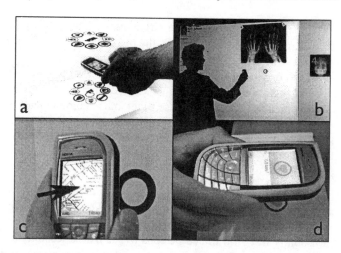

Figure 3: MIXIS applications (a) Diagram of the LayeredPieMenu application. (b) DROZO in use on a wall display. (c) ImageZoomViewer in use. (d) DrawME, "Call Andy?" "no" — left, "yes" — right.

by panning the phone towards the specific segments and back to the centre. By making a simple gesture towards the circle and back again the next menu is selected and moving the phone away from the circle and back again selects the previous menu. The diagram in Figure 3a demonstrates the principle of the LayeredPieMenu application where virtual pie menus are stacked on top of each other.

3.2.3   DrawME

In the DrawME application the device is, besides from recognizing the clean circle, also able to distinguish between a set of hand drawn symbols within the circle. Like in Landay & Myers [2001] DrawME opens up for the idea of drawable interfaces where the user is able to draw shortcuts, to applications in the real world e.g. on paper, whiteboards and walls. In a sense the user add another layer or functionality to disposable doodling. When the user draws a circle containing a specific symbol the camera recognizes the input and performs the function mapped to the specific symbol. The algorithm stores a set of masks of known symbols and finds the best match between the symbol in the centre of the circle and the known masks. At the moment the mask is hard-coded to the different symbols, but we are working on a user interface for creating and mapping new symbols. In DrawME we mapped different symbols to the single function of calling a certain contact from the address book illustrated in Figure 3d. To either confirm or reject calling the contact appearing on the display the user pan towards the yes and no icons displayed on the phone interface.

3.2.4   DROZO

The application Drag, Rotate and Zoom (DROZO) focus on how the mobile device can be used to interact with pervasive devices in the surroundings equipped with an interactive circle. The commands are sent through a generic protocol, see Figure 2.

We enhanced the application by putting a circle underneath an x-ray picture on a large wall display, allowing the user to drag the picture around on the screen using the mobile device. The user is able to zoom in and out on the picture by moving the device closer to or away from the display, and to rotate the picture by rotating the phone. In our first prototype we used GPRS to communicate between the wall and the phone, but in the new version we use Bluetooth to communicate between the device and the screen. To be able to rotate the picture we added a small mark to the circle that allowed us to detect rotation as illustrated in Figure 3b.

4   Evaluation

Our main purpose of introducing the MIXIS concept is not to argue that this is necessary a faster way to interact with mobile devices: Our main purpose is to show an alternative and more flexible interaction concept. With the ImageZoomViwer we performed a usability test with fifteen persons to see if it is feasible to use MIXIS as an interaction technique. We have had some preliminary experiences with some of the other applications at a workshop where we invited a group of users and their children to test some of the applications. However, in this paper we will focus mainly on the usability test of ImageZoomViewer.

4.1   Usability Test of ImageZoomViewer

We wanted to investigate if users were able to use our interface as efficient as the traditional interface offered by mobile devices, to use the result as guidelines for further development. Therefore a usability study was conducted, comparing the ImageZoomViewer application to a standard application for picture viewing from Nokia. An even more important aspect was to test if MIXIS was perceived as a fun complement to traditional interaction techniques. The participants were 15 in total, and they had various degrees of experience from mobile devices, spanning from not owning one to software developers for mobile phones. None of them had ever before seen or used gesture interaction for mobile devices.

The test was performed in a quiet conference room, a Nokia 7610 mobile phone was used, and there was a drawn circle on a white paper on the table. The two tasks were designed to test map viewing, a typical use case for mobile devices, including shifting degrees of zoom for overview and detail. For each of the two tasks, a conventional Nokia interface for image viewing using buttons was compared to the ImageZoomViewer application. Each participant did both tasks using both interfaces, where half of the participants started out with the conventional interface and half with the new interface and then switched for the second task. Before starting instructions were given in both techniques and both interfaces were practised on a dummy data set for a few minutes before proceeding with timing tasks. For each task a new data set was used, to reduce learning effects. The order in which the different data sets were used changed for half of the test group.

4.1.1   Task 1

First application: Given a subway map, locate the blue line and follow it from the most southern end station to the most northern end station of that line. Read the names of the end stations out loud.

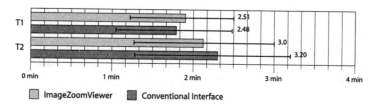

Figure 4: Experimental data from the usability test where ImageZoomViewer was tested against a conventional Nokia interface for viewing pictures. The bars represent the time to complete two tasks (T1 and T2) for each interface.

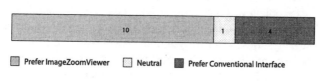

Figure 5: Subjective preferences from the usability test.

Second application: Locate the green line and follow it from the most southern to the most northern station. Read the names of the end stations out loud.

4.1.2 Task 2

Second application: Given a second subway map, locate a station in the centre of the map and tell out loud the colour of all the lines that stop there. Follow one of those lines to the two end stations and tell the name of those.

First application: Go to a different centre station and tell what lines stop there. Follow one of those lines to its both end stations, and tell the names of the end stations out loud.

4.2 Result of Usability Test with ImageZoomViewer

Independent of what data set or interface, the user error rates were not significant, and there was no difference between the two data sets for each task. After the test was over, the participants were asked which application they preferred. The majority of the test persons, 80%, strongly preferred ImageZoomViewer for map viewing. Figures 4 & 5 present a summary of the experimental data.

The conventional interface was 6% faster then ImageZoomViewer in the first test, but in the second test the ImageZoomViewer was 9% faster, as illustrated in Figure 4. These results show that gesture interaction with ImageZoomViewer is a quicker method the second time, concluding that with some practice the concept is actually a more effective navigational technique.

During the user tests, it became obvious that the distance between the camera on the mobile device and the circle on the object was very relevant. The female test persons were a bit shorter in height, and the positioning of a circle on the table made the phone end up closer to the face leading to that the interaction was not natural to the same extent as for the men. It was a lack in our test that the test persons were not asked to test different positions of both the circle and of themselves, to find the most comfortable and effective distance.

The most positive comments were about the direct connection between the physical movement and the interface, and also the possibility to pan and zoom simultaneously. The overall experience was that it was intuitive, fun and effective.

The most frequent complaint concerned the refresh rate and the sensitiveness of the system. This problem was due to the size of the circle: we should have chosen a larger circle, since enlarging the circle also enlarges the span of the interaction space and therefore the gestures. The ImageZoomViewer was due to the sensitiveness considered a bit less precise than the conventional interface. In some cases there were comments about the small size of the letters, which was a problem due to the quality of the picture we had chosen.

5   Discussion

The main outputs from the tracking component are the location and rotation of the device in relation to the fixed-point and in some cases information about the symbol inside the circle. Applications can use this information in a number of ways to interact with the device. This flexibility open up for the creation of a wide variety of different types of applications as shown above. We found two aspects relevant in describing the characteristics of the different application. The first was how the movement of the phone in the mixed interaction space was mapped to the application and the second was if the tracked fixed-point was associated with an identity or ID. Below we will thoroughly discuss these two aspects.

5.1   *Mapping Applications to the Mixed Interaction Space*

Basically two different types of mapping were found present in the applications we explored, natural and semantic mapping.

5.1.1   *Natural Mapping*

In the first type of applications we tried to make a tight coupling between the physical movement and the application, trying to accomplish natural mapping introduced by Norman [2002, p.23]. One example of this is in the ImageZoomViewer application, where moving the device to the left, right, up or down makes the application pan the image. Moving the phone closer or further away from the circle the application zoom in and out. Another example is the DROZO application that uses the rotation of the phone to rotate the current picture.

To further discuss mapping we need to introduce a distinction between absolute and relative mapping. In absolute mapping there exists a one to one mapping between a specific position in the mixed interaction space and the application. e.g. each time the phone is in a specific position in the space the application will scroll

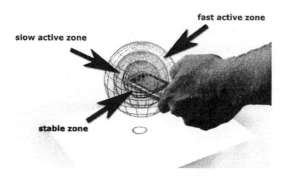

Figure 6: Diagram of the stable zone in relation to the drawn circle.

and zoom to the same position. The project suggested by Yee [2003] uses what we call absolute mapping.

Relative mapping maps a specific position in the space to a movement vector instead of a position. Keeping the device in the centre of the mixed interaction space resembles the movement vector null, which we call the stable zone illustrated in Figure 6. If the device is moved outside the stable zone the position of the device is mapped to a movement vector in the application. e.g. moving the device to the left of the stable zone would be mapped to keep scrolling to the left until the device is moved back into the stable zone. The further away the device is moved from the stable zone the faster the application scrolls. The project suggested by Fällman et al. [2004] uses relative mapping.

We explored both relative and absolute mapping in e.g. the ImageZoomViewer application. With absolute mapping moving the phone towards the circle results in a zoomed in picture, moving the phone to the left edge of the space moves the focus to the left edge of the picture and so on. One of the problems with absolute mapping is that the Mixed Interaction space has the form of an inverted pyramid (see Figure 1a), meaning that, if the device is close to the fixed-point, the x, y plane is smaller than when the device is far from the fixed-point. This property makes mixed interaction space unsuitable for absolute mapping or at least absolute mapping on all three axes. It is still possible to use absolute mapping for instance for zooming and then use relative mapping for panning. We found two other problems with absolute mapping. The image captured by the camera has to have similar size as the picture being watched; otherwise a small movement with the device will make the picture jump several pixels. Secondly, because the mechanism for determining the exact position and radius of the circle is not always exact, the picture becomes more vivid than with relative mapping.

Relative mapping is best suited in our applications. As an example, using a circle with a diameter about 2.5cm made a stable zone approximately 10cm above the circle as illustrated in Figure 6. When the device is within this zone the picture is fixed and when moving the phone forward towards the circle or away from the circle the picture is zoomed in or out with a speed relative to the distance from the stable zone. The same applies for panning. The disadvantage with relative mapping is that it does not provide the same spatial awareness as absolute mapping about the position on the picture. Relative mapping is used in the evaluated applications.

5.1.2   Semantic Mapping

The second type of mapping we use is what we call semantic mapping. With semantic mapping moving the phone in a specific direction does not necessarily map to the application moving in the same direction. With semantic mapping a metaphor is used to bridge between the physical movement and the action on the device. For instance moving the phone to the left might correspond to the action play media file and not to move left. This kind of mapping resembles the mapping used in gesture based application where performing a gesture is mapped to a specific function and not the same movement in the interface.

A characteristic of semantic mapping is that it is discrete; the space is divided into different zones that can be mapped to activate different functions. e.g. in the LayeredPieMenu moving the phone down towards the fixed-point and into the stable zone is mapped to the function 'go to the next menu'. The semantic mapping between the gesture in the interaction space and the application can be arbitrary which also results in problems with purely gesture based interfaces. How are the gestures the system recognizes visualized and how are these gestures mapped to the different applications? With LayeredPieMenu we use the display of the mobile device to guide the user. By graphically visualize the different menu items in the display the user was helped figuring out e.g. that making a gesture to the left would activate the function displayed to the left on the screen.

5.2   Mixed Interaction Space with or without Identity

One of the main strengths we found of Mixed Interaction Space in comparison to other systems [Rohs 2004; SemaCode Corporation 2005; OP3 2005] is that the system also works with simple symbols e.g. a circle drawn by hand. We found, that a set of very different applications could be designed by giving the circle different types of identity. We made a distinction between interfaces needing solely a simple circle to function (simple fixed-point interfaces), interfaces that uses a simple fixed-point with an associated icon drawn by hand (drawable interfaces) and interfaces that need to associate a unique ID with the fixed-point (identity interfaces).

5.2.1   Simple Fixed-Point Interfaces

The simple circle interface proved to be the most flexible. A simple interface just needs to have the software to recognize a circle to work. The circle could be drawn with a pen, but we also explored how to use different things as a marker like special finger rings or a black watch. The ImageZoomViewer and the LayeredPieMenu are examples of simple interfaces.

5.2.2   Drawable Interfaces

The main characteristic of drawable interfaces is that the system is can recognize different symbols drawn by hand within the circle and provide a set of different mixed interaction spaces on top of each circle, as illustrated in DrawME. Landay & Myers [2001] present an application recognizing the widget in a hand drawn interface. We wish to pursue the possibility with drawable interfaces but, in contrast to Landay & Myers, in our system the drawing is the actual interface.

Instead of squeezing a lot of functionality into a single device, drawable interfaces are able to customize the interface with only the functions required in the given situation. The drawn symbols can be seen as physical shortcuts into the digital world and resemble TUIs that also try to distribute the controls to the real world. One of the problems with TUIs as pointed out by Greenberg & Boyle [2002] is that you have to carry a lot of special tangible objects with you if you want to use these interfaces in a mobile setting. Greenberg & Boyle [2002] propose using easily customizable tangible objects, but still you have to use a set of tangible objects. With drawable interfaces all you need is a drawable surface and a pen, and after use the interface can be wiped out or thrown away.

Another advantage with drawable interfaces is that each circle can be associated with a 4D mixed interaction space with the interaction possibilities demonstrated in, for example, ImageZoomViewer. Furthermore this application can be combined with the LayeredPieMenu concept as a fast physical shortcut to certain predefined functions in the phone, for example, the four most called persons, send/receive mail and so on.

The number of symbols the system recognizes and tracks is dependent on the software, the hardware and the context. Sometimes it is difficult for the application to recognize a colour because the colour seen by the camera depends on the quality of the camera, the lightning, the pen used to draw the colour, and the surface. Therefore a small set of different colours are best suited for drawing the symbols. The same restriction applies for symbols. Because the symbols are hand drawn and not computer generated to symbols never looks exactly the same. Choosing a set of symbols that does not resemble each other works best with drawable applications.

Drawable interfaces opens up for a whole new area of customization and personalization of the interface of the mobile device, which is one important factor contributing to the success of mobile devices. The user is able to adjust the device to recognize new and personal symbols, to make it even more 'intelligent' and unique, since the user becomes the interface designer. In the workshop with DrawME, the participants strongly welcomed this possibility to customization, both because it is fun and that it provides the ability to personalize their device. The workshop also taught us the importance of having the user in total control of the mapping, and not have automatic mapping of any kind. We consider that it should be fun to interact with technology, and especially with the mobile and personal devices. Schneiderman [2004] highlights this aspect with a recent question:

> Did anyone notice that fun is part of *fun*ctionality?.

5.2.3 Identity Interfaces

In the final type of interfaces the fixed-point is associated with a specific identity or unique ID. The identity can be read by printing a barcode in the circle [SemaCode Corporation 2005], providing the identity by using short range Bluetooth (see for example Blip Systems, http://www.blipsystems.com/) or by RFID tags [Want et al. 1999]. The corresponding mixed interaction space can then be stored in the device, transmitted through for instance Bluetooth or downloaded from the Internet. We used identity interfaces in the DROZO application.

Identity interfaces are especially suitable for interacting with external devices or as shortcuts to specific places on the Internet. Using MIXIS to interact through identity interfaces can be seen as a possible method to interact with the 'invisible computer'. When computers get smaller, embedded or even invisible it is becoming more difficult for the user to know how to interact with them. A circle on a wall can be used as a visual cue, signalling the existence of a hidden MIXIS interface and can at the same time be used as fixed point for the interaction space. In this way, the context can be used to reduce interface complexity.

6 Conclusion

The main contribution of this paper has been to introduce Mixed Interaction Space, a concept that investigate and demonstrate that the interaction with mobile devices is not something that has to be limited to the screen and buttons on the phone. By using the camera of a mobile device we are able to combine the phones abilities with the physical environment and introduce a new interaction concept.

In this paper the main focus has been to introduce MIXIS and demonstrate some novel applications with the concept. The applications use the camera in the mobile device to track a fixed point and thereby establish a 3 dimensional interaction-space wherein the position and rotation of the device is calculated. The first application, ImageZoomViewer, allows the user to pan and zoom simultaneously on a picture by moving the phone in the mixed interaction space. In the application called LayeredPieMenu the mixed interaction space is used to navigate a layered menu structure. In the DrawME application the device is able to distinguish between a set of hand drawn symbols within the circle. The application Drag, Rotate and Zoom (DROZO) focus on how the mobile device can be used to interact with pervasive devices in the surroundings equipped with an interactive circle.

Mapping and identity, two central issues with MIXIS have been discussed and some relevant distinctions and design challenges have been pointed out. However, mapping and identity are just two aspects of MIXIS and we can see several other possibilities in combining tangible interfaces and mobile phones. Because the mobile phone is a highly personal device most people have we are, for example, currently looking into how to use the concept to design multi-user applications and so far MIXIS seems to have some interesting properties in this domain.

Acknowledgements

The work has been supported by funding from Centre for Interactive Spaces and Centre for Pervasive Healthcare under ISIS Katrinebjerg at the University of Aarhus. We would like to thank people at Centre for Interactive Spaces and Centre for Pervasive Healthcare, especially Kaj Grønbæk and Jakob Bardram.

References

Beaudouin-Lafon, M. [2000], Instrumental Interaction: An Interaction Model for Designing Post-WIMP Interfaces, *in* T. Turner & G. Szwillus (eds.), *Proceedings of the SIGCHI*

Conference on Human Factors in Computing Systems (CHI'00), *CHI Letters* **2**(1), ACM Press, pp.446–53.

Beaudouin-Lafon, M. [2004], Designing Interaction Not Interfaces, *in* M. F. Costabile (ed.), *Proceedings of the Conference on Advanced Visual Interface (AVI2004)*, ACM Press, pp.15–22.

Callahen, J., Hopkins, D., Weiser, M. & Shneiderman, B. [1988], An Empirical Comparison of Pie vs. Linear Menus, *in* J. J. O'Hare (ed.), *Proceedings of the SIGCHI Conference on Human Factors in Computing Systems (CHI'88)*, ACM Press, pp.95–100.

Fitzmaurice, G. W., Zhai, S. & Chignell, M. H. [1993], Virtual Reality for Palmtop Computers, *ACM Transactions on Office Information Systems* **11**(3), 197–218.

Fällman, D., Lund, A. & Wiberg, M. [2004], Scrollpad: Tangible Scrolling with Mobile Devices, *in* M. Shepherd (ed.), *Proceedings of the 37th Hawaii International Conference on System Sciences (HICSS-37)*, IEEE Computer Society Press, pp.286–91.

Greenberg, S. & Boyle, M. [2002], Customizable Physical Interfaces for Interacting with Conventional Applications, *in* M. Beaudouin-Lafon (ed.), *Proceedings of the 15th Annual ACM Symposium on User Interface Software and Technology, UIST'02*, *CHI Letters* **4**(2), ACM Press, pp.31–40.

Hansen, T. R., Eriksson, E. & Lykke-Olesen, A. [2005], Mixed Interaction Space — Designing for Camera Based Interaction with Mobile Devices, *in* G. van der Veer & C. Gale (eds.), *CHI'05 Extended Abstracts of the Conference on Human Factors in Computing Systems*, ACM Press, pp.1933–6.

Harrison, B. L., Fishkin, K. P., Gujar, A., Mochon, C. & Want, R. [1998], Squeeze Me, Hold Me, Tilt Me! An Exploration of Manipulative User Interfaces, *in* M. E. Atwood, C.-M. Karat, A. Lund, J. Coutaz & J. Karat (eds.), *Proceedings of the SIGCHI Conference on Human Factors in Computing Systems (CHI'98)*, ACM Press, pp.17–24.

Ishii, H. & Ullmer, B. [1997], Tangible Bits: Towards Seamless Interfaces Between People, Bits and Atoms, *in* S. Pemberton (ed.), *Proceedings of the SIGCHI Conference on Human Factors in Computing Systems (CHI'97)*, ACM Press, pp.234–41.

Kälviäinen, H., Hirvonen, P., Xu, L. & Oja, E. [1995], Probabilistic and Non-probabilistic Hough Transforms: Overview and Comparisons, *Image and Vision Computing* **13**(4), 239–52.

Landay, J. & Myers, B. [2001], Sketching Interfaces: Toward More Human Interface Design, *IEEE Computer* **34**(3), 56–64.

Masui, T., Tsukada, K. & Siio, I. [2004], MouseField: A Simple and Versatile Input Device for Ubiquitous Computing, *in* N. Davies, E. Mynatt & I. Siio (eds.), *UbiComp 2004: Ubiquitous Computing (Proceedings of the Sixth International Conference on Ubiquitous Computing)*, Vol. 3205 of *Lecture Notes in Computer Science*, Springer, pp.319–28.

Norman, D. [2002], *The Design of Everyday Things*, Basic Books.

OP3 [2005], ShotCodes, http://www.op3.com/en/technology.

Patridge, K., Chatterjee, S., Sazawal, V., Borriello, G. & Want, R. [2002], TiltType: Accelerometer-supported Text Entry for Very Small Devices, *in* M. Beaudouin-Lafon (ed.), *Proceedings of the 15th Annual ACM Symposium on User Interface Software and Technology, UIST'02, CHI Letters* **4**(2), ACM Press, pp.201–4.

Rekimoto, J. & Ayatsuka, Y. [2000], CyberCode: Designing Augmented Reality Environments with Visual Tags, *in* W. E. Mackay (ed.), *Proceedings of DARE 2000 on Designing Augmented Reality Environments*, ACM Press, pp.1–10.

Rohs, M. [2004], Real-world Interaction with Camera Phones, *in* H. Tokuda & H. Murakami (eds.), *Proceedings of the 2nd International Symposium on Ubiquitous Computing Systems (UCS 2004)*, Information Processing Society of Japan (IPSJ), pp.39–48.

Schneiderman, B. [2004], Designing for Fun: How Can We Design User Interfaces To Be More Fun?, *Interactions* **11**(5), 48–50.

SemaCode Corporation [2005], Sem@Code, http://semacode.org/ (last accessed 2005-05-15).

Shneiderman, B. [1998], *Designing the User Interface: Strategies for Effective Human–Computer Interaction*, third edition, Addison–Wesley.

Vänänen-Vaino-Mattila, K. & Ruuska, S. [2000], Designing Mobile Phones and Communicators for Consumers' Needs At Nokia, *in* E. Bergman (ed.), *Information Appliances and Beyond; Interaction Design for Consumer Products*, Morgan-Kaufmann, pp.169–204.

Want, R., Fishkin, K. P., Gujar, A. & Harrison, B. L. [1999], Bridging Physical and Virtual Worlds with Electronic Tags, *in* M. G. Williams & M. W. Altom (eds.), *Proceedings of the SIGCHI Conference on Human Factors in Computing Systems: The CHI is the Limit (CHI'99)*, ACM Press, pp.370–7.

Xu, L., Oja, E. & Kultanen, P. [1990], A New Curve Detection Method: Randomized Hough Transform (RHT), *Pattern Recognition Letters* **11**(5), 331–8.

Yee, K.-P. [2003], Peephole Displays: Pen Interaction on Spatially Aware Handheld Computers, *in* V. Bellotti, T. Erickson, G. Cockton & P. Korhonen (eds.), *Proceedings of SIGCHI Conference on Human Factors in Computing Systems (CHI'03), CHI Letters* **5**(1), ACM Press, pp.1–8.

Static/Animated Diagrams and their Effect on Students Perceptions of Conceptual Understanding in Computer Aided Learning (CAL) Environments

Ruqiyabi Naz Awan & Brett Stevens

University of Portsmouth, Department of Information Systems and Computer Applications, Burnaby Terrace, Burnaby Road, Portsmouth PO1 3AE, UK

Tel: *+44 23 9284 6418, +44 23 9284 6403*

Fax: *+44 23 9284 6402*

Email: *Naz.Awan@port.ac.uk, Brett.Stevens@port.ac.uk*

This study investigated the affect of static/animated diagrams on conceptual understanding. Conceptual understanding was defined as the objective accuracy of reported test answers and confidence estimates for perceived understanding. Subjects were asked to view either a static or animated diagram of a toilet flushing and refilling and were later asked to answer three questions and provide confidence estimates of their performance for each question. There was no significant difference between the two conditions for two test questions, the final test question found significantly higher scores for the static condition. Confident estimates reported by users were however affected by the diagrammatic display. Those in the animated condition consistently overestimated their test performance whilst those in the static condition consistently underestimated. These results suggest that the use of animated/static diagrams in educational environments should be treated with caution and that measures of confidence estimates may provide an insight into subjects' perceptions of their own conceptual learning in a CAL environment.

Keywords: diagrams, animation, educational multimedia, instructional design, CAL.

1   Introduction

There has been a trend in recent years for multimedia learning applications to feature illustrated diagrams as a central means of instruction.   An overriding assumption in the design and development of instructional materials for computer aided learning (CAL) environments has been that the explicit depiction of motion somehow stimulates viewers attention, provides learning interest and in some way benefits the learning process [Rieber 1995].

In contrast static diagrams of dynamic processes require the viewer to mentally infer motion in a 'piecemeal manner' [Hegarty 1992, p.1085] [Hegarty 2000, p.196] and the serial nature of this task leaves individuals unable to mentally animate all the parts of the diagram; due to the constraints of working memory [Hegarty 2000]. This line of reasoning suggests that if static diagrams of dynamic processes are difficult due to the increase in working memory load, then the visual explicitness of motion inherent in an animation reduces the amount of cognitive effort needed to understand a diagram and should facilitate understanding of a dynamic process more so than static representations [Bauer-Morrison et al. 2000; Park & Gittelman 1992].

Although numerous studies have been conducted that have sought to compare static and animated diagrams and their impact on the learning process, the results generated by these studies have been mixed, the inconsistency in results being attributed to a number of methodological problems and variance across studies [Park 1998].   It has for these reasons been difficult to challenge the pervading assumption that animation enables greater learning gains. One means of assessing this assumption does however arise from the observation that different static diagrams of the same information 'can activate completely different processes' and different levels of conceptual understanding [Zhang & Norman 1994, p.118]. Therefore in order to evaluate the purported learning gains of animation, different diagrams (Static, Animation) of the same problem have been compared to see what type of affect the mode of presentation has on learner's conceptual understanding [Jones & Scaife 2000; Park 1998; Park & Gittelman 1992].

The common theme throughout the majority of studies seeking to evaluate conceptual understanding has centred upon viewers demonstrating they have understood the diagram by performing various tasks that seek to assess how much information has been retained and/or their ability to transfer and use newly learnt information in a similar problem domain.

Although a beneficial means of analysis, this information does not provide an adequate reflection of how much information the viewers themselves believe to have understood from the diagram. It has long been acknowledged that an individual's beliefs shape attitudes that in turn affect behaviour; 'self efficacy' as it is termed refers to a belief in "one's capability of performing a specific task" [Bandura 1986, p.391]. The central tenets of this theory contest that "people's level of motivation, affective states and actions are more based on what they believe than on what is objectively true" [Bandura 1997, p.2]. It could therefore be argued that conceptual understanding of computer-based diagrams might be better evaluated in terms of how accurately viewers estimate their own understanding of the viewed diagram. Thus far in the field of 'diagrammatic learning materials' research the impact of the mode of diagrammatic display (Static, Animated) in relation to individual's subjective interpretations of their understanding has been largely ignored.

In a qualitative study conducted by Jones & Scaife [2000, p.240] student's remarks and comments were analysed while they worked with either static or animated diagrams. The results of this study revealed that animation increased the complexity of offered explanations, prevented learners from paying appropriate attention to information and appeared to generate artificially high levels of reported confidence in terms of how much information students felt they had understood. If illustrated diagrams are being used as a central means of instruction it would be better to avoid the 'artificially high levels of confidence' that encouraged individuals to believe that they had completely understood the diagrams when in reality they had not. In order to investigate the use of illustrated diagram as a central means of instruction in CAL environments, this paper evaluates learner's behaviour by assessing:

- The *objective accuracy* of learners' conceptual understanding; as measured by the amount of information accurately retained from the display as well as the transfer of knowledge to solve problems in similar problem domains.

- Learners *own estimates* of their conceptual understanding for how accurate they *believe* their answer to be.

The purpose of this study was therefore to investigate these measures in relation to learning from Static/Animated diagrams in Computer Aided Learning (CAL) Environments.

2   Method

2.1   Subjects

Forty subjects participated in this study. Subjects were aged 18–28 and were full time University students (Animated Condition M = 20.5 years old; Static Condition M = 20.3 years old). Subjects were primarily recruited from the Faculty of Technology although other faculties were approached (Animated Condition = 19 Undergraduate Technology students, 1 Post Graduate Arts student; Static Condition = 18 Undergraduate Technology students, 2 Post Graduate Arts students). More males participated in this study than females however both sexes were equally represented in both conditions (Animated Condition = 17 Males, 3 Females; Static Condition = 16 Males, 4 Females). Due to the method of assessment involving written tasks only subjects that classified themselves as 'Native English Speakers' and as 'Not suffering from Dyslexia' were allowed to participate in this study.

2.2   Materials

Subjects could not be presented with a diagram that required specific knowledge of appropriate diagram reading protocols e.g. circuits, weather maps, biological systems. A diagrammatic representation of a cross section internal view of 'a toilet' depicting the flushing and refilling process was therefore chosen. The toilet represents a mechanical household object that has a mechanical process of no more than 10 distinct steps and requires no specific diagram reading knowledge.

The animated condition had a diagram of a toilet that required the learner to 'click' in order to activate the flushing and refilling sequence and could be viewed as many times as the learners wished during the timed exercise. The static condition featured two diagrams (each the same size as the diagram featured in the animated condition) that appeared on the screen at the same time, one was of a toilet at the start position and had a series of arrows from which the toilet flushing process could be inferred, the second diagram was of the flushed toilet with a series of arrows from which the refilling process could be inferred. Both diagrams were labelled (1, 2) in order to aid the learner identify the diagram viewing order. Both the animated and static diagrams were developed and presented to users as short computer based tutorial.

2.3   Apparatus

The diagrams were developed using Macromedia Flash and were viewed within a webpage. A timer was built into the application and ran for the duration of the tutorial (10 minutes). The tutorial was hosted on a Web server and accessed via Internet Explorer Version 6.0

Subjects viewed the tutorial on desktop computers. The tutorial was viewed using 18″ Iiyama LCD flat screen monitors. Paper based post CAL questions were administered to subjects.

2.4   Procedure

Upon arrival subjects were randomly assigned to either the static or animated condition. Subjects were presented with a consent form and a personal details form that also asked how much actual experience they had fixing and repairing household/appliances and machines. Upon completing the paperwork the subjects' attention was directed to the computer and an 'Instructions page'. The experimenter read out the instructions that explicitly stated that the learning objective was 'to gain a full understanding of the diagram and system represented by the diagram on the following page'; subjects were asked if they had any questions before moving onto the tutorial.

Once the application had run its ten minutes subjects were asked to view the www.bbc.co.uk website for ten minutes. At the end of the ten minutes subjects closed the Internet connection. Subjects were then presented with instructions to complete a task that required them to answer three questions that would be presented individually and that answers must be written; sketching or drawing the diagrammatic display was not permissible. Additionally on each question page they were required to rate how confident they were that their given answer was correct on a scale of 0%–100%. Subjects had twenty minutes within which to complete all three questions:

Q1. Please write down an explanation of how a toilet works, your explanation must detail the processes involved in a toilet flushing and refilling. Pretend you are writing for someone that doesn't know much about toilets.

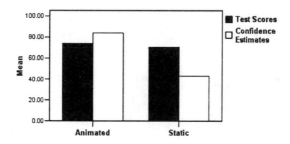

Figure 1: Question 1 (Retention of Process): Mean test scores and confidence estimates.

Q2. You try to flush your toilet but nothing happens. What could have gone wrong? Please state as many possible explanations as you can think of for this scenario.

Q3. Below is the diagram of the toilet you viewed in the tutorial, label all the parts.

3 Results

All subjects were asked to rate the amount of actual experience they have for fixing/repairing household appliances and machines. A one-way ANOVA was performed and found no significant differences between the two groups ($F_{1,38} = 1.48$, $p = 0.23$).

For Question 1 (Retention of Process) subjects' answers were analysed against a coding framework. This assessed the *sequence of processes* not whether subjects had correctly identified the names of individual components/parts.

A *t*-test (related) analysed the apparent discrepancy in subjects' question one test scores and corresponding confidence estimates (See Figure 1). A significant difference in the discrepancy in test scores and confidence estimate was found for the animated ($t_{19} = -2.07$, $p < 0.05$) and static condition ($t_{19} = 8.29$, $p < 0.001$). Moreover a significant positive correlation was found for both the animated ($r_{20} = 0.51$, $p < 0.01$) and static condition ($r_{20} = 0.78$, $p < 0.001$).

An analysis of variance (ANOVA) assessed whether there was a significant difference in subjects' test scores and confidence estimates between conditions. No significant difference for test scores was found ($F_{1,38} = 0.22$, $p = 0.63$), there was however a significant difference found for confidence estimates ($F_{1,38} = 38.71$, $p < 0.001$).

For Question 2 (Transfer of Knowledge), the coder was not concerned with whether the component parts had been identified correctly but that subjects' provided logically feasible explanation(s) of what may have caused the malfunction.

A *t*-test (related) analysed the apparent discrepancy in some subjects' question two test scores and corresponding confidence estimates (See Figure 2). A significant difference in the discrepancy in test scores and confidence estimate was found for the animated condition ($t_{19} = -4.78$, $p < 0.001$), in contrast no significant difference was found for the static condition ($t_{19} = -0.78$, $p = 0.44$). A significant positive correlation for subjects' test answers and corresponding confidence estimates was

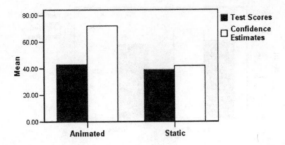

Figure 2: Question 2 (Transfer of Knowledge) Mean test scores and confidence estimates.

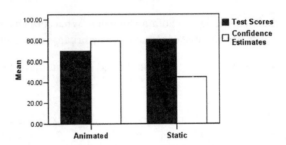

Figure 3: Question 3 (Label the Diagram/Retention of Part Names) Mean test scores and confidence estimates.

found for the static condition ($r_{20} = 0.63$, $p < 0.01$) but not for the animated condition ($r_{20} = 0.15$, $p = 0.51$).

An analysis of variance (ANOVA) assessed whether there was a significant difference in subjects' test scores and confidence estimates between conditions. No significant difference for test scores was found ($F_{1,38} = 0.36$, $p = 0.55$), although a significant difference for subjects confidence estimates was noted ($F_{1,38} = 23.36$, $p < 0.001$).

For Question 3 (Label the Diagram/Retention of Part Names) subjects' answers were checked against the list of the labels used to label the toilet in the CAL tutorial.

A t-test (related) analysed the apparent discrepancy in subjects' question three test scores and corresponding confidence estimates (See Figure 3). A significant difference in the discrepancy in test scores and confidence estimate was found for both the animated ($t_{19} = -2.70$, $p < 0.01$) and static condition ($t_{19} = 9.65$, $p < 0.001$). A significant positive correlation was also found for both the animated ($r_{20} = 0.46$, $p < 0.04$) and static condition ($r_{20} = 0.47$, $p < 0.03$).

An analysis of variance (ANOVA) assessed whether there was a significant difference in subjects' test scores and confidence estimates between conditions. A significant difference for test scores ($F_{1,38} = 4.60$, $p < 0.38$), and confidence estimates ($F_{1,38} = 52.62$, $p < 0.001$) was found.

4 Discussion

Results revealed that subjects in the static condition were able to retain and report as much back to Question One (Retention of Process) as the animated condition. Their performance on Question Two (Transfer of Knowledge) revealed that they were able to generate as many explanations concerning the noted toilet malfunction as the animated condition. Furthermore, they were better able to retain and report the static elements of the display (Question Three — Retention of Part Names) when compared to those in the animated condition. These results suggest that retention of information for dynamic processes is not 'better' retained for future recall or transfer if it is animated and that animating a diagram may result in individuals paying less attention to the static elements of display (Retention of Part Names).

The effect of animation upon subjects' task performance has generated numerous possible explanations, such as the suggestion that due to the speed and visual complexity of information presented in animation viewers experience cognitive overload as they are unable to attend to and process all incoming information [Lowe 2003] this results in them either not attending to or 'missing out' key aspects of the display [Reimann 2003].

Another striking finding was that the diagrammatic display significantly affected subjects' beliefs concerning how much of the material they believed they had accurately understood. On all three questions those in the animated conditions were found to overestimate their test performance whereas those in the static conditions were found to underestimate. This suggests that the mode of presentation for diagrammatic content affects how content is perceived by the viewer. The explicit depiction of motion shown in animation has been argued to present information in a way that is 'visually explicit'; less inferencing is therefore required by the viewer and hence affords a perception of the learning material as being easier to understand [Jones & Scaife 2000]. This view does not however credit the viewer as an active participant in the learning process and presents a 'black box' view of the psychological mechanisms that underlie diagrammatic reasoning [Scaife & Rogers 1996].

Generative learning [Wittrock 1974, 1990; Peper & Mayer 1978, 1986] suggests that the act of learning requires the activation of a variety of skills by the learner ranging from their ability to create, deconstruct, extrapolate, organize, structure, analyse and hypothesis about incoming and stored information and further that in order to successfully execute these skills requires 'mental effort' [Salomon 1983, 1984]. From this perspective, a diagram affects viewers' perceptions of how easy/difficult it is to understand in terms of their existing knowledge and how that task difficulty is affected by the format in which the content is presented.

A long standing concern regarding the use of computers in education has been that computers may 'cognitively de-skill' students by displacing skills that traditionally required 'mental effort and exercise' [Salomon et al. 1991]. Content difficulty has been found to be an important variable that affects how learners perceive and interact with learning materials. A study conducted by Salomon [1984] into the effects of learning from TV and print, revealed that students perceived learning from TV to be easier than learning from print. These students were also found to hold higher self efficacy about learning from TV and consequently were found to invest less mental effort. In contrast print was considered a more 'difficult' medium to learn from and was therefore perceived to require more mental effort. If the explicit motion inherent in animation caused viewers to believe that the diagrammatic content was therefore 'easier' to learn, we would expect viewers to exert less mental effort and hold higher self efficacy for learning from this medium. The issued confidence estimates may therefore be more than a measure of subjects perceived test performance but may also be a measure of their self efficacy for learning from the presented medium.

It is difficult to conclusively comment on the specific reasons for the noted differences observed between the conditions (Static, Animated) and subjects test performance and confidence estimates. This study has however highlighted that the use of diagrams as a central means of instruction in CAL environments should be treated with caution. The results generated by this study suggest that animation may result in learners feeling they have fully comprehended presented material when in reality they have not. Whereas static diagrams in contrast appear to result in learners underestimating how much of the diagram they have actually understood. Although these issues require further research in order to better understand the impact of Static/Animated diagrams in CAL environments, this study has demonstrated that for future studies it may be beneficial to include measures that assess learner's conceptual understanding both in terms of their objective accuracy and confidence estimates.

References

Bandura, A. [1986], *Social Foundations of thought and action: A Social Cognitive Theory*, Prentice–Hall.

Bandura, A. [1997], *Self Efficacy: The Exercise of Control*, Freeman.

Bauer-Morrison, J. B., Tversky, B. & Betrancourst, M. [2000], Animation: Does it Facilitate Learning, *International Journal of Human–Computer Studies* 57(4), 279–315.

Hegarty, M. [1992], Mental Animation: Inferring Motion from Static Diagrams of Mechanical Systems, *Journal of Experimental Psychology: Learning, Memory and Cognition* 18(5), 1084–102.

Hegarty, M. [2000], Capacity Limits in Diagrammatic Reasoning, *in* M. Anderson, P. Cheng & V. Haarslev (eds.), *Theory and Application of Diagrams, First International Conference, Diagrams 2000*, Vol. 1889 of *Lecture Notes in Artifical Intelligence*, Springer-Verlag, pp.194–206.

Jones, S. & Scaife, M. [2000], Animated Diagrams: An Investigation into the Cognitive Effects of using Animation to Illustrate Dynamic Processes, *in* M. Anderson, P. Cheng & V. Haarslev (eds.), *Theory and Application of Diagrams, First International Conference, Diagrams 2000*, Vol. 1889 of *Lecture Notes in Artifical Intelligence*, Springer-Verlag, pp.231–44.

Lowe, R. K. [2003], Animation and Learning: Selective Processing of Information in Dynamic Graphics, *Learning and Instruction* 13(2), 157–76.

Park, O. [1998], Visual Displays and Contextual Presentations in Computer Based Instruction, *Educational Technology, Research & Development* **46**(3), 37–50.

Park, O. & Gittelman, S. [1992], Selective Use of Animation and Feedback in Computer Based Instruction, *Educational Technology, Research & Development* **40**(4), 27–38.

Peper, R. J. & Mayer, R. E. [1978], Note Taking as a Generative Activity, *Journal of Experimental Psychology* **70**(4), 514–22.

Peper, R. J. & Mayer, R. E. [1986], Generative Effects of Note Taking during Science Lectures, *Journal of Experimental Psychology* **78**(1), 34–8.

Reimann, P. [2003], Commentary: Multimedia Learning: Beyond Modality, *Learning and Instruction* **13**(2), 245–52.

Rieber, L. P. [1995], A Historical Review of Visualisation in Human Cognition, *Educational Technology, Research & Development* **43**(1), 44–6.

Salomon, G. [1983], The Differential Investment of Mental Effort in Learning from Different Sources, *Educational Psychologist* **18**(1), 42–50.

Salomon, G. [1984], Television is 'Easy' and Print is 'Tough': The Differential Investment of Mental Effort in Learning as a Function of Perceptions and Attribution, *Journal of Educational Psychology* **76**(4), 647–58.

Salomon, G., Perkins, D. & Globerson, T. [1991], Partners in Cognition: Extending Human Intelligence with Intelligent Technologies, *Educational Research* **20**(3), 2–9.

Scaife, M. & Rogers, Y. [1996], External Cognition: How do Graphical Representations Work?, *International Journal of Human–Computer Studies* **45**(2), 185–213.

Wittrock, M. C. [1974], Learning as a Generative Process, *Educational Psychologist* **11**(2), 87–95.

Wittrock, M. C. [1990], Generative Processes of Comprehension, *Educational Psychologist* **24**(4), 345–76.

Zhang, J. & Norman, D. A. [1994], Representations in Distribution Cognitive Tasks, *Cognitive Science* **18**(1), 87–122.

Media Co-authoring Practices in Responsive Physical Environments

Carlo Jacucci, Helen Pain & John Lee

Institute for Communicating and Collaborative Systems, Human Communication Research Centre, University of Edinburgh, 2 Buccleuch Place, Edinburgh EH8 9LW, UK

Email: *c.iacucci@ed.ac.uk, helen@inf.ed.ac.uk, J.Lee@ed.ac.uk*

This paper describes an approach to devising co-authoring practices of digital media in physical environments. The discussion draws from a design case addressing media literacy, and focuses on the problem of devising new forms of authoring practices enabled by interactive features in the environment. The design is approached as a collaborative effort to create new practices and address both formal aspects and the nature of participation. The issues discussed include the design of physical objects, the interactive features, as well as the rules, conventions and procedures imposed or favoured in the design sessions. The aim of this paper is to contribute to an understanding of the design problem in the large, by reviewing and adopting concepts from recent literature.

Keywords: tangible interfaces, CSCW, learning, media literacy, media studies.

1 Introduction

Current developments of tangible interfaces can lead to new ways of experiencing and exploring digital media in spatial arrangements. A research goal relating to the HCI tradition is to account for how the architecture of these responsive environments can shape and be shaped to the life of people. This paper will rely on descriptions of how pupils in a primary school have creatively coped with designers' instructions in participatory design sessions in order to make sense of the use of augmented objects to co-author media genres. If we consider a broader picture, the different production traditions that exist within Education, Interaction Design, Film and Broadcast Media can nourish the innovation of novel ways to produce and access the media with a wide variety of 'languages', authoring styles or genres. These forms of expression

(a)   (b)   (c)

Figure 1: Contrasting with the example of conventional graphical interfaces to video editing (a), Figures (b) and (c) show parts of the environment we describe below. It enables participants to handle objects in the physical environment in order to collaboratively define compositions of visual and time-based representations. Accordingly, 'authoring' practices acquire quite a different nature than with graphical interfaces, with respect to collaboration, emergence of media genres, and media consumption. Nevertheless, we can organize the physical environment in order to favour people's access to the same type of media languages, such as the language of news media, commercial trailers or documentaries.

are increasingly being combined together. However, each one of them calls for specific interpretive skills, media, audiences, social purposes. At the same time, the growing body of research addressing the 'augmentation' of physical environments with sensing and interactive technology introduces a number of concepts to drive design through an understanding of human experience [e.g. Stanton et al. 2001; Ciolfi & Bannon 2002; Marshall et al. 2003; Binder et al. 2004].

The analytic attention in recent studies on technology design towards the practical accomplishment of organized practices, and the ways in which formalisms, both social and technical feature in day-to-day conduct [Heath & Luff 2000, p.11], in our case motivates a careful attention to pupils' embodied practices to inform design. As Heath and Luff note in a study concerning collaborative media authoring in professional settings, if research separates systems, both technical and human, from social action, "we are unable to recover just how tools and artefacts and the 'rest of the furniture' of modern organization is constituted in and through the activities of the participants themselves." [Heath & Luff 2000, p.7] In our case, the intent to study social action is driven by a constructivist pedagogical interest, shared with most studies on the design of augmented environments in educational settings. As in some of these studies, we aim to devise learning experiences in which learners build their own understanding of the task (Figure 1). Participants must be supported in order to rely upon what they already know, and expand their current skills and understanding by constructing new knowledge in ways which make sense to them. This task needs to be approached by favouring perpetual exchanges of thought and different kinds of experimental interaction [Vygotsky 1978; Marshall et al. 2003].

2   Background and Related Research

Recent accounts of designing digitally augmented environments in educational settings or public spaces, such as museums, as in Ciolfi & Bannon [2002] and

Ferris et al. [2004], point to relevant conditions for 'shaping' experiences and applying tangible interfaces. Concerning our understanding of how these media and tools can invite people to interact and explore, technologically augmented environments should provide clues, triggers or adequate affordances to make visible which actions the visitors are allowed to perform [Ferris et al. 2004]. Moreover, they should support: "different layers of activity in a way that successive surprises and discoveries are encouraged" [Ferris et al. 2004]. Such designing goals are then intimately related to understanding the nature of these sorts of human activities.

As an instance of designed artefacts, Sokoler & Edeholt [2002] have addressed the use of tangible 'videocards' augmented with interactive features via RFID tags, to enable new participatory design practices. The videocards approach that they describe redefines aspects of video remote control for how their augmented objects (in that case, videocards) embed means for control of video playback in novel ways. As argued in Iacucci et al. [2003], if similar kinds of video cards are used to enable authoring practices in spatial arrangements, then describing peoples' joint work for expressing and interpreting leads to new ways of defining the simple terms of media authoring. In particular we need to address the specific ways in which users articulate their work in 'media authoring' in 'spatial arrangements'.

2.1 Media Authoring in Spatial Arrangements

Mackay & Pagani [1994] proposed solutions to combine the power of paper video storyboards with the full capabilities of video editing software. The system they describe, Video Mosaic, uses an augmented reality approach to extend the static information that appears on paper and provide it with active temporal dimension. One point of interest lies in transposing some of the editing in the physical space, while keeping doing some of the activities in a digital interface. A point of interest is in discussing how such an hybrid system enables users to commit more flexibly to partial results. Relevantly to this point, Mackay & Pagani note that "Current tools tend to concentrate on the production of a final version, rather than on supporting the user in the development and exploration of ideas" Mackay & Pagani [1994, p.168]. In order to apply such terms as 'sketch', 'version', 'editing', 'partial result', 'production', or 'exploration' in a way that is sensitive to human practices, we need to examine what kind of 'authoring' practices are performed by users in a setting.

2.2 Conceptualizing Tangibles and Sensible Interfaces

As recent literature has shown, tangibles can work as 'ready-to-hand' or as 'present-at-hand' thereby favouring different ways of exploring, rationalizing, objectifying and abstracting [Chalmers 2001]. Marshall et al. [2003] furthered the discussion pointing to differences in the way users can attend to the tangibles in a present-to-hand manner, and use two classes of tangible systems: expressive and exploratory. *Expressive* features of the system embody aspects of the user's actions with the system or embody some of the learner's behaviour either digital or physical. And when users attend to the tangible as present-to-hand they can focus on an external representation of their own activity. *Exploratory* features do not embody the user's activity. When attending to this type of tangible as present-at-hand, the user will be more likely to focus on the way the system works, thereby exploring a model decided by someone else. Rogers & Muller [2004] argue for a distinction between activities that can be modelled as dialogues with machines and more open ended exploratory activities. Given these differences, augmenting physical objects can serve to enable, to complement or support.

3 A Case Study

The case study described in the following is a series of collaborative authoring practices that we devised with groups of pupils in a primary school.   Pupils collaborated through a tangible interface to rearrange, produce and modify temporal media in order to create different genres of video presentations, from documentaries to news and advertisement. By manipulating digitally augmented physical objects they selected, edited and produced multimedia material through a series of collaborative tasks of reading, scripting, interpreting, annotating, editing, video-shooting, and composing visual and temporal recordings. The audiovisual material, broadly concerned history, and included pictures, video, texts and music from a variety of sources: educational documentaries from schools' and TV archives, interviews with historians, a storyteller, teachers and other pupils. At the end of the activities, pupils displayed and presented to the school the final products of the practices, and aimed at being integrated with traditional learning resources.

The media and tools had only in part been designed in advance. They were developed further in collaboration with pupils and teachers. The description we give below aims to explain how they enabled creative practices in which media 'access', 'deconstruction' and 'authoring' acquired specific forms.

3.1 Goals of the Activities with the Pupils

The goal of these practices was to provide pupils with the necessary skills and resources in order to 'access', 'deconstruct' and 'author' some genres of media compositions through which the subjects taught can be represented. An underlying assumption of our approach is that abilities to critically *read* media texts cannot be addressed fully without favouring also the acquisition of *expressive* abilities of *authoring* with the same sort of media texts. In this sense, we aimed to turn the knowledge of media languages that pupils acquire in their daily life into a resource. Responsive physical environments provide new opportunities to apply such a resource to critical reading and composition of documentaries, trailers, interviews, adverts, reviews and other broadcast or narrowcast media genres.

3.2 Overview of the Activities

Three groups of four pupils were engaged in selecting, editing, composing and producing video material in order to create a set of crafted products such as: interactive installations displaying a three dimensional visual representation of the content of the documentaries, a set of short documentaries in digital video, and a series of trailers of the documentaries. Hence, at the end of the participatory design sessions, interactive installations constituted at the same time final products and shared representations of ongoing collaborations. They could be explored by accessing visual and temporal recordings in digital format through the interactive facilities embedded in the physical objects. All final edited products, such as

(a)   (b)

Figure 2: Triggering the projection of an episode by scanning an object in conjunction with a location or with other objects.

documentaries and their trailers were produced in different alternative versions, suggesting different points of view and highlighting different themes. The whole set of practical tasks addressed the deconstruction of the language of documentaries and other common media 'languages' [Bell 1991]. All activities were preceded by introductory examples and tutorial sessions in order to train pupils on how to read and modify some instances of genres of media texts. In these training sessions we addressed different types of TV news, documentaries and interviews. Pupils were provided with instructions and resources through which they could operate simple editing and compositions with the physical objects.

3.3   Setting the Field

The setting devised in our study enables some simple forms of physical manipulation and rearrangement of temporal recordings. Video episodes are mostly represented as cards and are displayed on screens or projections by scanning barcodes attached to them. Through the activities, each card is set to represent an 'abstraction' of different possible versions of a given video episode. A variety of objects, including paper, are augmented with digital links, via barcodes and can be set to represent digital editing features. We articulated the setting into a *construction kit* provided with conventions, procedures, conceptual and notational constructs, in such a way to suggest operations of composition and interpretation, as outlined in Figure 2.

3.3.1   Material and Initial Design

The videos are in part taken from several broadcast media sources. The videos were chunked in segments and elaborated in alternative versions with annotations, sounds, voice-overs, titles and sometimes partially arranged in montage sequences. Other physical objects employed and augmented in the environment to make compositions were mouldable plastic, Lego bricks and hard-paper signs. Digital representations were displayed both by screens and projections. In a preliminary phase, prior the start of the design sessions with pupils, pupils were trained in basic skills on critically reading and re-editing interviews. Also video interviews were shot among pupils, teachers, and a storyteller, in such a way that the overall multimedia material had 'absorbed' representation from the cultural context of the school in which the project was taking place.

3.3.2 Instructing Open-Ended Tasks

As part of the participatory design approach of this study, the instructions given to pupils aimed at describing open-ended tasks. However, participants to the project need not to be disorientated and must focus to some extent on the same kind of resources and activities. When working in a primary school this issue becomes critical. The instructions and the rules we defined aimed at the same time at constraining and inspiring pupils' tasks. The overall task was instructed as a film-making exercise, in which *"each group of pupils will build an interactive installation. This will be done by selecting, annotating and putting together the objects provided."*.

3.3.3 Initial Organization: Categories, Rules and Procedures

Conducting participatory design of such environments poses a trade off between letting free or constrain the activities. Participants need some freedom to be creative and explore new applications, but at the same time we need to constrain their tasks in order to both support and inspire them. A priority in our study is to encourage cooperation, in order for participants to reach a shared understanding of the tasks. We incrementally defined types of activities to which each group could orient their attention to. We also had to organize time and resources in order to enable different groups to work at the same time.

The environment inevitably favours some ways of transforming instructions into procedures, a major question is how the creation of interactive installations is defined and enabled in the first place. Installations were set to address a theme. They were defined as spaces that visitors could explore by following paths with a barcode scanner, thereby triggering the projection of sequences of digital representations. Installations were defined as displaying paths that not only visitors could follow, but that had actually to be made into finished documentaries.

Such rules and such an organization entail the following 'design abstractions' and categorizations:

1. A finished interactive installation has a form provided with some *unity*, it contains one or more start points, and displays paths that can be explored by a visitor.

2. Such paths are sequential organizations of the elements (also referred to as the 'syntagmatic structure'), and can be of different forms (e.g. rhetoric, associational, categorical). The only requirement is that the exploration of paths suggests editings that *develop* the theme.

3. The *elements* that get organized in sequences (also referred to as the 'paradigmatic structure') are varied and can be modified with some freedom, provided that they bear a relation with the digital representation to which they link.

4. There are no constraints on the type of *relation* between the physically accessible features of an object and the digital representation it triggers. Such

a relation can be a resemblance (iconic), a matter of convention (symbolic), or an index set even unintentionally or by common sense.

5. Such *relations* and the other terms mentioned in the previous points are the scope of instructions and questioning in addressing spectators' *expectations, closure, openness*, and *critical reading* of the media texts produced in the tasks.

3.4   Methodology

The goal of the design effort was to devise new forms of cultural practices. The methods we applied draw from practical approaches of visual and performing arts, and practices of media production, such as advertisement and news.

3.4.1   Imposing constraints

In order to foster creativity and participation in the design process we relied on some of the possible virtuous effects of imposing constraints to action [Iacucci et al. 2002]. The limits posed by the media and tools employed in the setting need to be identified and formulated into directions that make constraints more effective as resources for creativity. The goal of such an approach is to direct the design sessions as a series of creative activities in which participants are helped in their imaginative effort. In this case, pupils participated to design primarily by creatively interpreting and making sense of our instructions and displaying a shared understanding of what they were doing. It is by inspecting how they put together the different elements in the work setting (representations, tools, rules, procedures, conventions) that we can describe what practices emerged, in terms of their skilled behaviour and its outcomes. Before getting to the stage were pupils operated with the tools, and either made sense of our instructions or discarded them, we had introduced and trained parts of the tasks. We had presented the tools, and trained the pupils with examples. We applied an approach to devising media which focuses on the benefit they provide to creativity and expression not only as enablers but also for their constraining functions. Table 1 shows a few examples of simple constraints.

3.4.2   Supporting the Evolution of Smaller and Digressive Tasks

Important design interventions were aimed at facilitating and identifying subtasks. This influenced the ways participants could be trained and supported. In most tasks a central problem is to find a shared definition of the content of temporal representations. Participants are motivated to make choices concerning relevance and points of view. Subtasks that could be identified include: indicating alternative ways of segmenting a set of video episodes made accessible through a set of objects; operations of video alteration and modulation, such as titling, shortening, adding voiceovers; sub-tasks of composition, e.g. establish rhetorical functions or relationships between episodes; subtasks creating procedures for comparison, such as identifying salient verbal features in the episodes and visualizing spoken words, finding different episodes to introduce a videoed statement; shortening a given sequence of video episode by a half; creating alternative trailers.

Examples of constraints to the compositions' paradigm			
Media constraint	Reformulation	Limited outcome	Creative solutions observed
Cards display a picture (chosen by the designer) from their video episode	Compose a collage using the static pictures	The features manipulated by pupils are static. They contrast with the time-based content	Branching structures suggest video sequences. Rhetorical figures link spatial to temporal aspects: small place to scan trailers (timely short)
Changes to the editing of video can be indicated only by verbal annotations	Instruct the editor by annotating objects	Suggestions about changes to dynamic aspects become encrypted and not easily shareable	The composition format (or genre), embodies editing aspects: e.g. using spatial predominance (tower) to suggest features redundancy in the edited sequence

Examples of constraints to the compositions' syntagm			
Media constraint	Reformulation	Limited outcome	Creative solutions observed
Barcodes need to be pointed at to be scanned; scanning is easier if the barcode is near the picture	Display pictures openly	Sequences of static pictures in compositions become predominant structures	The one-sided nature of the cards is exploited to create architecture types that invite to explore physically, turning around and move: as in town, or museum formats
Scanning different objects with the same barcode reader triggers projections on the same screen	Identify possible paths to explore the installation with beginning and an end	Exploring an installation by acting with a scanner became the screening of an improvized film	New conventions for shaping some genres as graphs in the space: multiple points of entry and multiple points of exit, but linked by paths inducing sequences

Table 1: Dealing with media constraints to direct selection and composition.

3.4.3   Rhetorical Figures for the Responsive Environment

The digital augmentation of physical objects can enable intuitive ways of accessing digital media through physical actions. These can be researched by finding rhetorical figures to link physical actions to events in the digital environment. For example, scanning a smaller card triggers a shorter version; scanning a card and the barcode on the window triggers an edited version giving a specific interpretation (view) associated to that window.

3.5   Observations from Instances of Work of Composing

3.5.1   The 'Composed' 'Installations'

At the end of the sessions installations had become the places containing links to finished films. But, at the same time, represented incomplete alternatives and the discarded versions of those films. As a result, the whole practice became geared around the 'composition' of interactive 'installations', which became shared representations to both access and construct media texts. They became repositories of partly conventionalized information to which all composing practices were oriented. In this sense, they became privileged places where exploration of the texts and the negotiations about its 'meaning' or 'purpose' could take place. As we explain below, the use of installations developed, beyond limited spaces, towards integrating them into broader environments, such as the room or the building.

The resulting environment aims to be more than an informational tool. It became an artistic medium allowing for constructive practices. It doesn't have the objective and the capacity to create the same empathy and emotion as films or theatre productions, and is less perfect in its achievement. There are no detailed scripts, no rehearsals, and no retakes, but only the construction of a *workable* multimedia structure. The following sections will address what 'workable' can mean in the scope of providing people with media 'access'.

3.5.2   Attributing Meaning to Physical Patterns

One aspect of pupils' compositions concerns the ways they put physical objects together in order to create architectural patterns. We favoured the evolution and negotiation of the architectural features within each group. By doing so we became involved in the discovery and definition of a language to make sense of such collaborations. After our engagement in tutoring such practices we can describe the 'architecture' of the compositions in terms of the following features. In reviewing these terms we chose to adopt a language from the architecture of 'packaging' [Fawcett-Tang & Mason 2004], in order to stress the role these compositions have in packaging representations. The various dimension of packaging media texts created different 'formats'. They realized a method for both organizing and exploring either physical or digital elements and representations. Three examples are:

1. The 'museum' format, in which the video-cards and objects divided the space into different thematic areas, and had an entrance and an exit, applying common metaphors from the architecture of museums.

2. The 'town' format, in which the space was organized into streets and avenues, and included the use of architectures enabling interactions such as towers, doors, and backyards.

3. The 'geometric or abstract' format, applying abstract geometrical shapes as circle, radial, or the square, which displays and exploits the architecture of 'opposite sides'.

Different formats favoured different forms of organizing and exploring the digital representation through the physical environment. The museum format favoured an encyclopedic style; the town format favoured a geographical style, in which exploring can be associated with travelling and arriving; the geometric/abstract favoured an argumentative style, in which the lack of rhetorical figures calls for connectives of argumentation: 'therefore', 'but', 'for example', 'and'.

As argued below, we see the creation of such formats as one aspect of the creation of 'genres' for authoring and participation. More practically, these formats facilitated a next step: the integration of installations in wider environments. In

(a)   (b)

Figure 3: Elements get composed together in such a way to invite, by their spatial arrangements and verbal and visual inscriptions, the evocation of multimedia objects. The initial environment is characterized by a certain openness of interpretation for what constitutes the relationship between spatial and temporal features. For example, spatial adjacency or contiguity can potentially suggest possible temporal editings. We address the ways in which participants overcame such an openness and created local conventions.

fact, the rhetorical figures and architectural experimentations could, in a later stage, leave the table and be adapted to the wider environment. Dimensions of exploration through spatial montage were discovered by pupils who created *parallelisms* with the environment of everyday life. These were of two types:

1. Framing multimedia features *into* the daily environment.

2. Embedding features in the dedicated installation *from* the daily environment.

As examples of (1), rooms acquired *themes*, and opposed windows, being associated with different episodes, alternative *views*. As examples of (2), exploring town shapes generated branching film architectures or sub-narratives, thematic areas, or architectural spaces built as towers and 'gardens'.

3.5.3 Framing: Reconciling Time and Space

A possible drawback in this dimension of pupils' explorations is that the act of *framing* temporal recordings in the physical installation was at times subordinated to the structural constraints of the architectural compositions. For example, two walls can be made out of video cards and built facing each other. They will display two sequences of cards (linking to as many video episodes). Other than simply suggesting two different sequences, they will suggest binary oppositions between cards that end up being physically facing each other. In this case, the spatial framing of the video episodes becomes subordinated to the oppositions in the architecture which is put in place. And such structural features are not related a priori with the media content. We can call this feature of spatial compositions its *geometrical closure*: every time that an architectural shape is started, geometrical constraints appear. Such constraints often have pragmatic consequences on the interpretation of the installation. For example, building a curve limits an inner space, building in height causes predominance, using apposite sides imposes movement from side to side for visual exploration. In order to achieve coherence and unity in the framing of the multimedia content, these constraints need to be explicitly interpreted and conventionalized.

3.5.4 History of Emerged 'Genres' in the Setting

Some design solutions resulted from carrying out the tasks with pupils and included the following features. These solutions developed as conventions. They had initially been adopted by a small group and at a later stage had become universally accepted and implemented.

1. Different ways for physical objects to represent abstraction of digital videos or images: there are zones of the space that represent the modulation of videos according to a principle attached to each zone (e.g. the zone of the shortened versions, the zone of the titled versions, the zone of the perspective according to the Jacobites). Hence, the same video-card, which always *evokes* the same video episode, in different zones evokes different versions of that same episode.

2. Changeable properties of the digital representations were made consistent with changeable physical properties of the objects triggering their access: with double sided video-cards the video episodes on opposite sides of the object represent opposite thematic or rhetoric aspects; object's weight is increased in accordance to the difficulty perceived in reading the digital representation contents.

3. Associations of objects and their digital content: scanning a couple of video-cards syntheses their rhetorical relationship in the context of the composition in which they are scanned. For example, two objects representing two video episodes of contrasting historical accounts will be synthesized as a very short editing displaying the inconsistency between the two accounts.

3.5.5 Handling Versions

While the tasks were carried out, certain aspects of compositions' form, and in particular, variations, motifs, and parallelisms became increasingly encoded 'under the physical surface' of the physical compositions. For example, as soon as the convention of abstracting video episode versions was introduced — thereby permitting to use the same physical object to represent different versions of the same video episode — the physical compositions started to become more and more abstract representations of the same digital compositions. In other words, physical compositions became representations of the different possible ways of editing the documentary that uses those multimedia objects in the sequences displayed physically.

3.5.6 Reconciling the Digital and the Physical Worlds

We are interested in binding a formal analysis of the environment to an understanding of the forms of participation that are enabled in it. To this end, we look at the ways pupils accommodated differently mediated ways of authoring. For example, we can

(a)   (b)

Figure 4: Sequences from an area of a physical composition of multimedia objects, which represents different possible alternatives of editing a same documentary.

see how the ways discursive structures get articulated in collages depended on what the physical tools and objects suggest one can 'do' with them.

In the case of a short film created from the installation in Figure 4, the sequence was taken from an easily explorable area of the collage: a linear sequence. The projection of a similar short film can be triggered by scanning those elements in sequence. But in the digital version some of the contextualizing features of the collage are lost. Hence, in the final product pupils were encouraged to introduce some rhetorical features that accommodate for this loss. Formal features of the environment which are present in the digital and in the physical domain call for participation of pupils in negotiating how representations should cross the boundaries between digital and physical media. When *instantiating* a film from a collage, pupils move the representation of a sequence of episodes from the physical installation into another medium: the linear sequence in a digitally edited video. Physical-digital couplings in this case of film authoring create dissonances between the intended structure in the physical collage, and the actual digital film that is produced as an end of the practice.

4 Discussion

From the case presented above we draw considerations on ways to direct design sessions in this setting and on the outcomes. We will approach the discussion by applying some terms which we gather by describing the practices. We intend to apply descriptions of the forms of exploration and expression we observed in order to inquiry on what such terms as 'authoring' or 'genre' can mean in our context. This will in turn provide us with guidelines to understand how aspects of form link to the nature of 'participation'. A treatment of the two themes — directing the practices and studying their outcomes — should reflect their mutual dependency. In fact, as we described in the case study, the sorts of practices we observed are somehow specific to the way design sessions were *directed*. Such form of directorship is what we propose here as an element of the design methodology. Designing responsive physical environments, to enable and support media co-authoring, poses a set of alternatives for designers. Alternatives concern ways of imposing constraints with media, tools, rules and conventions — in order to facilitate participants' creative work — and ways of applying notions of genres and authorship as generative principles — to envision new authoring and interpreting practices. The scope of the following discussion is to bind the design approach and its 'outcomes' in a unified account addressing both 'form' and 'participation' in our setting.

4.1 Authoring: Exploration and Expression

A major aim of the practices around the installations is to provide participants with the skills and the knowledge they need to reach beyond the act of *reading* intended as a sole interpretation of an original media text. Such an aim can be addressed by allowing for forms of explorations that stress the alternatives of editing and framing. When done relying on the spatial and responsive features of the physical environment, these operations acquire particular forms. They can enable practices that open a variety of composed media to inquiries and engage users into exploring the effects of their alterations. In the case of spatial arrangements of multimedia material, we need to review the role of *temporal editing*, and consider structures of a broader nature. Here we can make some considerations on the ways in which participants enriched and recombined the material that was presented in the original version. The design of the physical objects and of their responsiveness, along with rules and conventions permitted cooperative inquiries into the surrounding reality. These could be accomplished through rapid manipulations of the environment. The 'authoring' nature of those cooperative inquiries that can be discussed for how they qualify as *explorations* of the environment. In doing this, we take the meaning of exploration as in reviewed in Section 2. Exploration and digressive actions took participants out of the reading of original forms — as the plot or arguments of broadcast media — and lead them to deconstructing the working of those forms. Artistic practices with tangible objects included copying, modulating, re-framing, segmenting, and performing the presentation of installations. In our study these actions suggested design principles for supporting pupils in acting as critics and as designers. A principle can be drawn from the activities that can be described as *recycling*. Some explorations of the setting aimed to rearrange and compose outcomes of past productions. This involved adapting the resources available in order to accomplish new *functions*. In pupils' work, recycling became a process of finding any kind of *unity* by modifying media texts through a play with modulation and alteration. In particular, the augmented physical objects enabled the institution of specific *motifs* and forms of recycling.

4.2 Cultivating the Emergence of 'Genres'

As Frow postulates, referring to the general practice of creating intertextual links in several forms in the literary and visual arts:

> What is relevant to intertextual interpretation is not, in itself, the identification of a particular intertextual source but the more general discursive structure (genre, discursive formation, ideology) to which it belongs. [Frow 1990, p.46]

These forms are defined by such features as *repetition* and *motif* and far as they provide some unity, because unity in the composition is what frames peoples' reading. The creation of such genres can be postulated to be motivated and dictated by the constraints in cooperation. A similar problem relating to the nature of 'genres' has already been considered in film studies. In fact, if we take common definitions of *genre*, they bind artistic aspects to production and marketing issues, as in Gledhill's [2000] definition of genre as a 'conceptual space' in which:

> issues of texts and aesthetics ... intersect with those of industry and institution, history and society, culture and audience. [Gledhill 2000, p.221]

Other definitions also describe different genres in terms of their collective significance. Some critics suggested abandoning the term 'genre' itself in favour of such terms as repetition, seriality, cycle, trend and mode. The main concern in the type of setting we address here is that defining and recognizing genres has implications on the working of pupils' collaborations in production, spectatorship and criticism. To those who participate as authors it gives stylistic guidelines. It also provides those who review the work of others with tactical means of evaluating a composition's achievements in terms of the ways it affords particular effects by extending, challenging or reinterpreting particular features of a genre [Bordwell & Thompson 2004]. By establishing features of unity and continuity, conventionalized genres guide participants in activities of composition and criticism as they can be used as: acomposition paradigm providing a model for rearranging stylistic elements, a set of rules and expectations for spectators to organize their reading, or a critical framework for reviewers.

4.3   Media in Space: Form and Participation

The setting addressed above enables forms of exploration and expression that are constrained, supported or motivated by the alternatives available to 'reconcile' physical and digital aspects. Investigating the motives and the quality of such 'reconciliation' can provide us with a ground for understanding how matters of form relate to the nature of participation. In the history of media we know of different established production practices that aim to create forms in our physical environment that change our behaviour and motivate proactive responses. In the design of visual and tangible advertisement, for example, the design of contents and their medium is driven by a general principle according to which their design should 'create new needs', for example Berger [1977]. These needs are often researched either by putting constraints to our perception of space or representations, or by creating conflicting representations or enigmas, calling for attention and for reconciliation. Similar principles hold in our setting, but they allow for different sorts participation. Digital representations such as pictures, video sequences and sounds needed to be 'evoked' through physical actions. The digital environment needed to be 'evoked' by acting on the physical, contrasting with the ever-visible and ever-accessible physical pictures, surfaces and other features. Moreover, digital representations could be 'condensed' into physical ones, in the sense that they were lined to static displays while they were actually distributed on a timeline. Accordingly, in their designing tasks pupils were led to investigate the effects of triggering, meeting, and evaluating the expectations of people. This is exemplified by how participants handled 'versions' of media texts. Physical compositions acquired the abstracting function of standing for different versions of the same media texts. This came at the expense of having to re-balance the role of physical details compared to wider structural properties. In fact, by looking at a physical composition, pupils could better understand that once an editing sequence is given — i.e. physical objects are displayed in a spatial arrangement — a lot of editing details still need to be fixed in order to have a film which sorts a desired outcome.

5 Conclusion

This paper has described an approach to integrating responsive and digital features into physical environments in order to enable collaborative authoring practices. Such applications can open media genres to inquiries and engage users into exploring the effects of their alterations by acting on a physical setting. As a critical issue in directing open-ended tasks, the introduction of conventions and procedures, and their influence on the creative use of resources, has been discussed. In particular, we have argued for an open treatment and exploitation of the constraints imposed by media to physical action, and their reformulation as directives in such a way that they can become resources for creativity in the practices. We have addressed the need to understand the virtuous role of constraints in instructing and directing participants activities in design. In our specific case, this effort concurred to favouring the emergence of composition 'genres'. Such effort can be inscribed into a wider struggle in the study of aesthetics and the experience of art, in which for every new field there is the need to find ways of linking structural analyses of form to the nature of participation.

Acknowledgements

Thanks to Judy Robertson for her precious support in the work in the school, thanks to the pupils and the staff at the Blackhall Primary School in Edinburgh, and thanks to Giulio Jacucci for providing the software.

References

Bell, A. [1991], *The Language of News Media*, Blackwell.

Berger, J. [1977], *Ways of Seeing*, Penguin.

Binder, T., de Michelis, G., Gervautz, M., Iacucci, G., Matkovic, K., Psik, T. & Wagner, I. [2004], Supporting Configurability in a Tangibly Augmented Environment for Design Students, *Personal and Ubiquitous Computing* **8**(5), 310–25. Special Issue on Tangible Intrfaces in Perspective.

Bordwell, D. & Thompson, K. [2004], *Film Art: An Introduction*, McGraw-Hill.

Chalmers, M. [2001], Book Review of Dourish [2001], *Computer Supported Cooperative Work* **14**(1), 69–77.

Ciolfi, L. & Bannon, L. [2002], Designing Interactive Museum Exhibits: Enhancing Visitor Curiosity through Augmented Artefacts, *in* S. Bagnara, S. Pozzi, A. Rizzo & P. Wright (eds.), *Proceedings of the Eleventh European Conference on Cognitive Ergonomics (ECCE11)*, European Association of Cognitive Ergonomics (EACE).

Dourish, P. [2001], *Where the Action Is: The Foundations of Embodied Interaction*, MIT Press.

Fawcett-Tang, R. & Mason, D. [2004], *Experimental Formats and Packaging*, RotoVision.

Ferris, K., Bannon, L., Ciolfi, L., Gallagher, P., Hall, T. & Lennon, M. [2004], Shaping Experiences in the Hunt Museum: A Design Case Study, *in* D. Gruen & I. McAra-McWilliams (eds.), *Proceedings of the Symposium on Designing Interactive Systems: Processes, Practices, Methods and Techniques (DIS'04)*, ACM Press, pp.205–14.

Frow, J. [1990], Intertextuality and Ontology, *in* J. Still & M. Worton (eds.), *Intertextuality: Theories and Practices*, Manchester University Press, pp.45–55.

Gledhill, C. [2000], Rethinking Genre, *in* C. Gledhill & L. Williams (eds.), *Reinventing Film Studies*, Arnold Publishers, pp.221–43.

Heath, C. & Luff, P. [2000], *Technology in Action*, Cambridge University Press.

Iacucci, C., Pain, H. & Lee, J. [2003], Collaborative Authoring Practices with Video Episodes: Designing for Accountability of Learners' Methods in Re-using Video Material, *in* B. Wasson, S. Ludvigsen & U. Hoppe (eds.), *Designing for Change in Networked Learning Environments: Proceedings of the International Conference on Computer Support for Collaborative Learning*, Kluwer Academic Publishers, pp.239–48.

Iacucci, G., Iacucci, C. & Kuutti, K. [2002], Imagining and Experiencing in Design: The Role of Performances, *in* O. W. Bertelsen, S. Bødker & K. Kuuti (eds.), *Proceedings of NordiCHI 2002*, ACM Press, pp.167–76.

Mackay, W. & Pagani, D. [1994], Video Mosaic:äLaying Out Time in a Physical Space, *in* J. J. Garcia-Luna (ed.), *Proceedings of the Second ACM International Conference on Multimedia (Multimedia'94)*, ACM Press, pp.165–72.

Marshall, P., Price, S. & Rogers, Y. [2003], Conceptualising Tangibles to Support Learning, *in* S. MacFarlane, T. Nicol, J. Read & L. Snape (eds.), *Proceedings of Interaction Design and Children*, ACM Press, pp.101–10.

Rogers, Y. & Muller, H. [2004], A Framework for Designing Sensor-based Interactions to Promote Exploration and Reflection, *International Journal of Human–Computer Studies* . In press. Available at http://www.slis.indiana.edu/faculty/yrogers/papers/Rogers_Muller_accepted.pdf (last accessed 2005-06-13).

Sokoler, T. & Edeholt, H. [2002], Physically Embodied Video Snippets Supporting Collaborative Exploration of Video Material during Design Sessions, *in* O. W. Bertelsen, S. Bødker & K. Kuuti (eds.), *Proceedings of NordiCHI 2002*, ACM Press, pp.139–48.

Stanton, D., Bayon, V., Neale, H., Benford, S., Cobb, S., Ingram, R., O'Malley, C., Ghali, A., Wilson, J. & Pridmore, T. [2001], Classroom Collaboration in the Design of Tangible Interfaces for Storytelling, *in* J. A. Jacko, A. Sears, M. Beaudouin-Lafon & R. J. K. Jacob (eds.), *Proceedings of SIGCHI Conference on Human Factors in Computing Systems (CHI'01)*, *CHI Letters* 3(1), ACM Press, pp.482–9.

Vygotsky, L. S. [1978], *Mind In Society: The Development of Higher Psychological Processes*, Harvard University Press. Edited by Michael Cole, Vera John-Steiner, Sylvia Scribner, Ellen Souberman.

Cognitive Model Working Alongside the User

Ion Juvina & Herre van Oostendorp

Center for Content and Knowledge Engineering, Institute of Information and Computing Sciences, Utrecht University, 14 Padualaan, 3584CH Utrecht, The Netherlands
Email: *{ion,herre}@cs.uu.nl*

A computational cognitive model of Web navigation is proposed. The model was used to generate navigation support and this support was offered to users in real time during their navigation sessions. The consequences of providing model-generated navigation support were experimentally investigated. Two experiments are presented. In the first experiment navigation support was offered in the auditory modality and it had a positive effect on users task performance, especially for users with low spatial abilities. In the second experiment navigation support was offered in the visual modality and it was well received, users navigated in a more structured way, perceived the system as more usable, and themselves as less disoriented. Men took more advantage from being provided with navigation support than women. Finally, some aspects regarding the validity of the proposed model and its practical relevance are discussed.

Keywords: cognitive modelling, Web navigation, navigation support, individual differences.

1 Introduction

Several attempts to model cognitive processes involved in Web navigation are based on the assessed semantic relevance of screen objects to users' goals (information scent) [Kitajima et al. 2000; Pirolli & Fu 2003]. In a previous study we found out that not only semantic but also spatial processes are employed in Web navigation tasks [Juvina & van Oostendorp 2004]. Based on this and also on other findings [Chen 2000; Howes et al. 2002; Wen 2003], we assume that assessing relevance of a particular screen object to the user's goal depends not only on user's knowledge about that particular screen object but also on the contexts of a navigation session, i.e. what has been done up to that moment, where the current position is represented in the information space, how close to the target the user perceives herself etc. In this paper, we argue for considering 'path adequacy', that is the relevance of a navigation path to the user's goal, beside 'information scent', in modelling Web navigation. This would be a first step in modelling the role of contextual information in selecting specific navigation actions.

The next section introduces the model of Web navigation that we propose and discusses its practical relevance. Then two studies are described, which attempted at validating the model and examining its practical relevance. In the end, results of these studies are commented and further developments of the model are suggested.

2 A Cognitive Model of Web Navigation

There are various approaches in cognitive modelling of Web navigation behaviour. Pirolli & Fu [2003] developed SNIF-ACT (Scent-based Navigation and Information Foraging in the ACT architecture), a computational cognitive model that simulates users performing Web tasks. Their model predicts navigational choices, i.e. where to go next and when to stop (leave the website) based on the concept of information scent (IS). IS is calculated as a mutual relevance between the user's goal and link texts based on word occurrences and co-occurrences in the Internet. Kitajima et al. [2000] introduced CoLiDeS — a *C*omprehension-based *Li*nked model of *De*liberate *S*earch. CoLiDeS measures relatedness of a particular screen object to user's goal (information scent) based on three factors: semantic similarity, frequency and literal matching. Semantic similarity is calculated based on co-occurrences between words and documents with the aid of an algorithm called Latent Semantic Analysis (LSA). Miller & Remington [2004] model the common situation in which link labels are not fully descriptive for their targets or users are not knowledgeable enough to accurately assess the relevance of link descriptions to their goals. Their model, called MESA (Method for Evaluating Site Architectures), does not give an account for how link relevancies are assessed, but takes them as input. It rather focuses on effectiveness of various link selection strategies, given various link relevancies and site structures.

2.1 CoLiDeS+

We have made few amendments to an existing cognitive model of Web navigation, namely CoLiDeS [Kitajima et al. 2000], and we have conducted a series of studies to refine the model and check its validity. The altered model has been labelled CoLiDeS+, to indicate that it is a working version, shares the main assumptions with the original CoLiDeS, and is intended to eventually be an augmented model.

CoLiDeS compares user's goal with link texts on webpages using Latent Semantic Analysis and selects the link that best matches the user's goal. The selected link is clicked on and the process of judging link relevance (information scent) and selecting a link is repeated until the user's goal is attained or the user gives up. CoLiDeS+ brings in the concept of 'path adequacy' as a complement to the concept of 'information scent'. Path adequacy is the semantic similarity between a navigation path and a user's goal. A navigation path is a succession of links that have been selected prior to a particular moment in a navigation session. A high similarity means that the path is likely to lead toward the targeted item. Previous research found significant positive correlations between *path adequacy, spatial ability* and *task success*, respectively [Juvina & van Oostendorp 2004]. By including the user's navigation path in the model we aimed to making the model accountable (at least to some extent) for users spatial cognition involved in Web navigation. Therefore, in CoLiDeS+ selecting a link on a specific webpage is a function of *goal* description, *link* description and *path* description.

CoLiDeS models mainly the ideal situation of forward linear navigation; backtracking steps are considered erratic actions. When no particular object on the current page sufficiently matches user's goal, an impasse is said to have occurred. Solutions to impasses are only described and not computationally modelled by Kitajima et al. [2000]. However, backtracking and impasses seem to be natural in Web navigation and rather frequent [Cockburn & McKenzie 2001; Wen 2003]. Therefore they need to be modelled within the same framework as forward linear navigation. Miller & Remington [2004] propose navigation strategies to deal with ambiguity of link labels or with users' errors in judging link relevance.

CoLiDeS+ tries to incorporate navigation strategies. First, it tries to prevent impasses by checking at each step for latent impasses based on path adequacy. A latent impasse occurs when path adequacy does not increase after selecting a link and it is a possible reason to switch the path. It is called latent because it only signals a possible path switch and it causes considering concurrent paths. If a concurrent path with a better adequacy is found, the current path is switched toward the concurrent one. If impasses still occur, CoLiDeS+ reacts with a strategy that we called 'next best' and it is at some extent similar with the opportunistic strategy of Miller & Remington [2004]. 'Next best' means that not only the link with the highest similarity to user's goal is considered but also links with lower similarities provided that they contribute to an increase in path adequacy. And eventually the options of backtracking one or more pages or going to index pages are available.

A short description of the algorithm used by CoLiDeS+, presented below, shows how task execution is simulated and how the concept of path adequacy is considered in addition to link relevance (see also Figure 1):

- A task description is taken as input and assumed to be equivalent to user's goal.

- A webpage is attended to, parsed in several areas, and a particular area is focused on (e.g. a menu).

- Menu entries are comprehended (based on how semantically similar to the user's goal they are) and one entry (the one that is most relevant to the user's goal) is selected and acted on (e.g. clicked on).

- A new page is attended to and if the target information cannot be found, the cycle is reinitialized.

- The selected element is retained in a memory structure that maintains user's navigation paths.

- Starting with the second cycle, a navigation path is available to be taken into consideration when screen objects are checked for their goal relevance. A

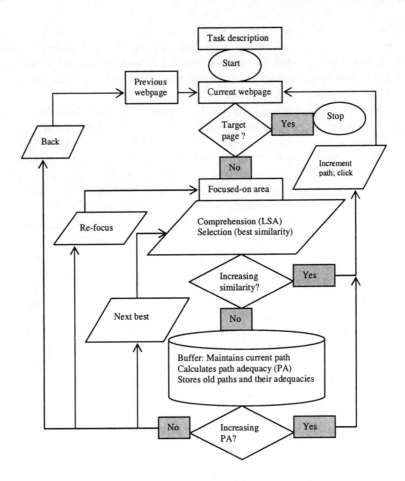

Figure 1: A simplified diagram of the algorithm that implements the CoLiDeS+ model.

metric called *path adequacy* is calculated as a semantic similarity between a path and user's goal. Selections of screen objects to be acted on are made if they contribute to an increase in path adequacy.

- Otherwise an impasse is declared and dealt with by considering 'next best' options, changing the focused-on area and backtracking.

- If the focused-on area happens to be a search engine, keywords are generated by the LSA *nearest neighbours* module (terms that are semantically most similar to user's goal), and the engine's results page is treated as any other webpage.

- The algorithm stops when the current page contains the target information.

2.1.1 Practical Relevance

Before presenting the two experiments aimed at validating the model, a short introduction to the practical relevance of the model for the field of Human Computer Interaction is necessary, since the experiments are testing both theoretical and practical aspects of the model.

CoLiDeS has been used to identify and repair Web usability problems [Blackmon et al. 2003]. With the amendments proposed here and with future improvements, such a model could be used in supporting navigating users more actively and in real time. A cognitive model could be running few steps ahead and prompt the user with a reduced number of options that are likely to be relevant for the task at hand. For some categories of users suggesting relevant actions to users could be essential for a satisfactory Web experience. For example, blind users access the Web by the aid of 'screen readers' — tools that read out loud the Web content and options. Since using the Web naturally involves revisits to certain pages [Cockburn & McKenzie 2001], blind users would have to repeatedly listen to large amounts of menu options or contents. Therefore, tools are needed to assist users in selecting the relevant information. One of the solutions proposed by di Blas et al. [2004] is to bring in linguistic models, and we propose cognitive models to be brought in. A cognitively plausible process model of Web navigation would be appropriate to generate navigation support in such cases since it preserves the users' experience. In contrast, providing users with direct access to particular information based on literal matching as in the case of search engines may be efficient but not necessarily satisfactory.

3 Experiments

Two experiments have been conducted one after another in order to investigate the model's validity and practical relevance. In the first experiment it was expected that offering model-generated navigation support in an auditory modality will improve users performance and will compensate for users deficits in spatial abilities. In the second experiment the navigation support was offered in a visual modality and more dependent measures were considered such as user perceptions and user actions.

3.1 First Experiment

It was hypothesized that CoLiDeS+ would be able to simulate real users navigation behaviour and the navigation support generated based on simulations would have a positive influence on users navigation behaviour and task performance. This positive influence was expected to be bigger for users with a deficit of spatial ability, since CoLiDeS+ took over the job of representing a complex information structure and remembering past selections.

Six realistic Web tasks were built based on the collection of cases gathered by Morrison et al. [2000] and indications of Kitajima et al. [2000] related to size and elaboration of task descriptions. Each task had an associated website. The following is an example of task:

> You want to buy a new car but you don't have enough money. The
> Internet has made getting a loan much easier because it provides you

with the resources you need to find the right loan, the approval process is quicker, there is less documentation that needs to be filled out, and you can do it in the privacy of your own home. You want to shop around for an auto loan lender, find an attractive interest rate, and find out how much your monthly payment will be. Also you wonder what will happen if you become unable to make your payments due to various conditions (sickness, etc.).

Given facts: You cannot afford to pay more than 180 pounds per month for more than 48 months.

Use http://www.alliance-leicester.co.uk/to:

- Calculate how much you can loan.
- Calculate how much your monthly payment will be.
- Look for one way to handle situations when you cannot pay.

The six tasks were simulated with CoLiDeS+ prior to the actual navigation sessions. The results of simulations were successful paths, i.e. successions of links leading to the target pages, and 'dead-ends', i.e. pages that are not linked with target pages, making it necessary for the user to backtrack. Based on these results of the simulations, two types of suggestions were generated: link suggestions — when a link contained in a successful path was visible on the screen, the user received the suggestion *Click on* <link label>; path switch suggestions — when a 'dead-end' page was downloaded, the user got the suggestion *Go back*.

Participants (students, sufficient Web experience, non-domain and non-Internet experts) were randomly assigned to two conditions: a control condition in which 15 participants had to perform as many of the six tasks as possible in 45 minutes, and a 'support' condition in which 14 participants did the same while receiving the generated navigation support (suggestions). These participants were instructed in advance that suggestions were generated by a robot, they were meant to help with task execution, and they were not mandatory: participants could follow them or not at their discretion. Suggestions were provided in the auditory modality. This way of delivering navigation support was selected since it can be implemented in combination with screen readers for improving the Web access of visually impaired users.

Solutions to tasks were reported on paper by the participants and evaluated afterwards for correctness. The average duration of tasks per participant was calculated by dividing the total navigation time (45 minutes) to the number of tasks attempted. An overall estimate of task performance was calculated by dividing the total correctness score to the average duration of tasks. The natural logarithm of this ratio was taken to correct for a skewed distribution. Participants' spatial ability was tested with a mental rotation task [Juvina & van Oostendorp 2004]. Navigation actions of participants were automatically recorded with a Web logging software (Scone).

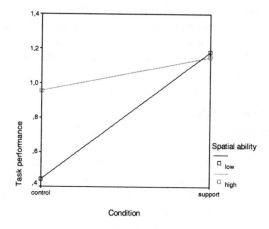

Figure 2: The effect of providing navigation support on task performance for users with low and high spatial ability.

3.1.1 Results of the First Experiment

The first outcome was that CoLiDeS+ was able to generate successful paths and 'dead ends'. However, the way it navigated the websites was not as straight and forward as suggested by Kitajima et al. [2000]. It made extensive use of 'next best' trials, refocusing, and backtracking. The number of steps to solutions was even higher than the actual users took. In general, the model took different decisions than the actual users did, but, due to the mechanisms of solving impasses, the correct paths and dead-ends were correctly identified. The main explanation for the differences between the model and the actual users is the weakness of the LSA technique. The 'general reading' semantic space available at http://lsa.colorado.edu was used. These results show that LSA is limited as a tool to model user's relevance assessments. However this limitation exists for users as well. This is why contextual information and navigation strategies to deal with impasses are needed.

Providing navigation support made a significant difference in users' navigation behaviour and task performance. The number of navigation steps was lower in the support condition than in the control condition ($t_{27} = 3.86$, $p = 0.001$). It took an average of 30 steps to execute a task in the control condition and only 19 steps in the support condition. The average duration of tasks was shorter in the support condition than in the control condition ($t_{27} = 2.16$, $p = 0.039$). It took an average of 10.26 minutes to complete a task in the support condition and 12.49 minutes in the control condition. Task performance was significantly higher in the support condition (mean = 1.16) than in the control condition (mean = 0.68) ($t_{27} = 2.16$, $p = 0.04$).

As expected, the correlation between spatial ability and task performance was significant for the control condition ($r_{13} = 0.64$, $p = 0.01$) and not significant for the support condition ($r_{12} = 0.15$, $p = 0.60$). Participants were divided in two groups with high and low spatial abilities (the median of test scores was taken as a cutting point). The difference in task performance induced by navigation support was checked separately for low and high spatial ability participants. Results are depicted in Figure 2. One can see that the difference induced by the navigation support is bigger for participants with low spatial ability ($t_{12} = 2.27$, $p = 0.044$) than for participants with high spatial ability ($t_{12} = 0.73$, $p = 0.48$).

3.2 Second Experiment

During the first experiment it was noticed that providing suggestions in the auditory modality was perceived as rather disturbing for users natural navigation behaviour. Therefore, we decided to offer suggestions in the visual modality and to investigate also subjective consequences of providing navigation support. In addition, we were interested in examining further the difference made by the provided navigation support in users navigation behaviour.

Navigation support was generated in the same way as in the first experiment. Only link suggestions were offered this time by the means of highlighting. Path switch suggestions ('Go back') were considered too directive and, based on observation from the first experiment, not very helpful.

Tasks, participants and materials had the same characteristics as in the first experiment. This time 32 participants were recruited and randomly assigned to two conditions (navigation support vs. control). Demographics of the sample were similar to the ones of the first experiment.

As dependent variables we considered users perception measures and users navigation behaviour metrics. Users perceptions were measured with a post-navigation questionnaire. The questionnaire contained items referring to perceived usability of the used websites, and users' perceived disorientation [Ahuja & Webster 2001]. The 16 participants in the support condition had to fill in 4 additional items about how they perceived the provided suggestions. These items are: "The suggestions given by the robot were helpful"; "I felt the suggestions were intrusive / annoying"; "I believed I could trust the suggestions given by the robot"; "I felt being manipulated by the given suggestions".

A set of metrics of users navigation behaviour such as: back button usage, the amount of home page visits, compactness [McEneaney 2001], stratum [McEneaney 2001], and average connected distance was used. They are described in Juvina & Herder [to appear]. Here, only their relevant aspects will be discussed in the results section.

3.2.1 Results of the Second Experiment

Suggestions were generally well received. Most of the participants do not perceive suggestions as intrusive, annoying or manipulative; a relatively high number of participants (11) trusted suggestions; but there is no clear evidence that suggestions are perceived as useful.

Participants in the support condition disagreed at a larger extent than participants in the control condition with the following statements: 'It was difficult to find the information I needed on these sites' ($t_{27} = -2.72$, $p = 0.01$), and 'Labels of links and categories confused me' ($t_{27} = -2.83$, $p = 0.008$). Participants receiving suggestions agreed at a larger extent than participants in the control group that 'The

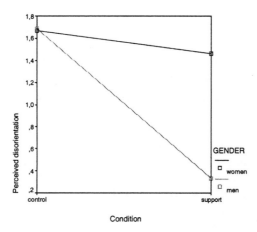

Figure 3: The interaction between gender and support in relation to perceived disorientation.

websites can be used without previous experience' (t_{27} = 2.33, p = 0.027). For all the other items, differences were not significant. Thus, suggestions made finding information look less difficult, using websites less depending on users previous experience, and link labels less confusing.

When looking at aggregated measures of user perceptions — perceived disorientation and perceived usability, the differences between conditions appear to be non significant.

However, there is a marginally significant result: the level of disorientation is lower in the support condition but this difference is significant only at an alpha level of 0.10 (two tailed). And there is a significant interaction between the variable *gender* and the variable *support* in relation to perceived disorientation ($F_{1,28}$ = 5.12, p = 0.032). Thus, men and women subjectively benefit to different extents from being provided with suggestions. When the interaction between gender and support is taken into consideration, the effect of support becomes significant ($F_{1,28}$ = 9.43, p = 0.005). Therefore, it is now clear that there is a significant effect of providing suggestions on perceived disorientation, but only for men (Figure 3).

We checked if link suggestions changed the structure of users navigation behaviour. In the support condition, participants: used the back button less (t_{27} = -2.24, p = 0.03), their navigation paths had a lower compactness (t_{27} = -3.02, p = 0.005) and a higher stratum (t_{27} = 3.42, p = 0.002), i.e. the paths were more linear, and the average connected distance in the navigation path was higher (t_{27} = 2.26, p = 0.031), than in the control group. Thus, link suggestions caused the subjects to navigate in a more linear manner and reduced the amount of backtracking.

4   Conclusions

The technique used by CoLiDeS+ to model user's assessments of relevance (LSA) was rather weak, i.e. it modelled a rather bad assessor. For instance, the similarity between *hotel* and *sleep* (0.24) was lower than the similarity between *hotel* and *wait* (0.34). This is why CoLiDeS+ had to make extensive use (more than actual users) of its mechanisms of preventing and dealing with impasses before finding solutions. These mechanisms were based on path adequacy — a measure of contextual information involved in user navigation.

When CoLiDeS+ simulations were offered as navigation support, users performed the given tasks in fewer steps, faster and with better results. The navigation behaviour became more linear (goal directed), more structured and less redundant. It seems that the offered navigation support prevented users to spend time and cognitive resources with those kinds of navigating actions that are not directly effective but are usually employed in order to accurately represent the information structure (exploring how information nodes are linked and where the relevant information is placed). As other researchers have found [Cockburn & McKenzie 2001; Howes et al. 2002; Wen 2003], real users do engage in seemingly useless navigation actions in order to get acquainted with the context of a particular piece of information, which is eventually useful in judging the value of that particular information. By making use of path adequacy CoLiDeS+ gives an account for this type of behaviour.

The correlation between spatial ability and task performance was once more replicated in this study. It indicates that users' ability to mentally represent and manipulate information spaces is crucial for Web navigation tasks. However, when provided with the kind of navigation support that CoLiDeS+ generated, users' performance did not depend any more on their spatial abilities. Users with low spatial abilities had a higher performance increase due to navigation support than users with high spatial abilities. Since in a previous study [Juvina & van Oostendorp 2004] we found a positive correlation between spatial ability and path adequacy, we decided to include the navigation path in the CoLiDeS model, and we expected the new model to account to some extent for spatial cognition involved in Web navigation. This expectation was confirmed. Users with low spatial abilities are probably less able to represent the information space and remember past selections and this is why they benefit considerably when the cognitive model is doing this job for them. We consider this result to be an additional proof that CoLiDeS+ gives an account not only for the process of assessing relevance of screen objects to users' goals but also for the ability of users to represent and manipulate an information space.

In general, suggesting users with links that are relevant to the task at hand is a well-received navigation support. Users provided with suggestions were expected to perceive websites as more usable and themselves as less disoriented, but this expectation was confirmed only for men. Women seem to profit from suggestions only objectively — their navigation graph becomes more structured, but not subjectively — their perceptions do not improve when receiving suggestions. This result needs further investigation.

A cognitive model running few steps ahead and providing users as they navigate with filtered information relevant to their goals has various possibilities of application. We have suggested the use of such a model together with screen readers for improving the Web experience of visually impaired users. In fact such a model can be used whenever users' cognitive or perceptive limitations interacts with information overload. The model takes over part of the user's burden in representing and processing information. In turn, if such support proves to be effective, it is one type of evidence for the validity of the model.

5 Discussion and Further Developments

CoLiDeS+ is a process model of Web navigation, which describes the step-by-step process by which information presented on the screen is attended to and processed in order to perform various types of Web tasks.

So far in our simulations we have used the whole path from the beginning of the task to the current step. This was justified by the fact that the number of steps to solutions was rather small. However, there are theoretical and empirical reasons for limiting the amount of elements that are active at a particular moment. In text comprehension, it is estimated that one sentence is carried over to the next cycle [Kintsch 1998]. Other approaches limit the total amount of available activation rather that a number of elements. We will try to identify meaningful sub-sequences (equivalents of sentences) in a navigation path based on path switches.

In the current version, all the previously selected text elements are taken into account with an equal weight. Differentiation based on recency or frequency were not considered necessary since paths were rather short and repetition of a link label in a path is a rather rare event. However, an appropriate decay mechanism needs to be implemented if more complex tasks are modelled.

Another point to be addressed in the next version of CoLiDeS+ is the dynamic characteristic of user's memory representation (including the goal representation); in the current version the goal remains unchanged during a navigation session, and this is a questionable assumption. In addition, we will seek a way to input the user goal, instead of relying on the task description as equivalent of the user goal.

References

Ahuja, J. S. & Webster, J. [2001], Perceived Disorientation: An Examination of a New Measure to Assess Web Design Effectiveness, *Interacting with Computers* **14**(1), 15–29.

Blackmon, M. H., Kitajima, M. & Polson, P. G. [2003], Repairing Usability Problems Identified by the Cognitive Walkthrough for the Web, *in* V. Bellotti, T. Erickson, G. Cockton & P. Korhonen (eds.), *Proceedings of SIGCHI Conference on Human Factors in Computing Systems (CHI'03)*, *CHI Letters* **5**(1), ACM Press, pp.497–504.

Chen, C. [2000], Individual Differences in a Spatial-Semantic Virtual Environment, *Journal of the American Society for Information Science* **51**(6), 529–42.

Cockburn, A. & McKenzie, B. [2001], What Do Web Users Do? An Empirical Analysis of Web Use, *International Journal of Human–Computer Studies* **54**(6), 903–22.

di Blas, N., Paolini, P. & Speroni, M. [2004], "Usable Accessibility" to the Web for Blind Users, Paper presented at UI4ALL'04 conference. Not published in the conference proceedings.

Howes, A., Payne, S. J. & Richardson, J. [2002], An Instance-based Model of the Effect of Previous Choices on the Control of Interactive Search, *in* W. Gray & C. Schunn (eds.), *Proceedings of the 24th Meeting of the Cognitive Science Society (CogSci2002)*, Cognitive Science Society, pp.476–81. Proceedings available at http://www.cognitivesciencesociety.org/confproc/gmu02/.

Juvina, I. & Herder, E. [to appear], The Impact of Link Suggestions on User Navigation and User Perception, *in Proceedings of the Tenth International Conference on User Modelling, UM2005*, Springer-Verlag.

Juvina, I. & van Oostendorp, H. [2004], Individual Differences and Behavioral Aspects Involved in Modeling Web Navigation, *in* C. Stary & C. Stephanidis (eds.), *User-Centered Interaction Paradigms for Universal Access in the Information Society: Proceedings of the 8th ERCIM Workshop on User Interfaces for All (UI4ALL'04)*, Vol. 3196 of *Lecture Notes in Computer Science*, Springer, pp.77–95.

Kintsch, W. [1998], *Comprehension: A Paradigm for Cognition*, Cambridge University Press.

Kitajima, M., Blackmon, M. H. & Polson, P. G. [2000], A Comprehension-based Model of Web Navigation and Its Application to Web Usability Analysis, *in* S. McDonald, Y. Waern & G. Cockton (eds.), *People and Computers XIV (Proceedings of HCI'2000)*, Springer-Verlag, pp.357–73.

McEneaney, J. E. [2001], Graphic and Numerical Methods to Assess Navigation in Hypertext, *International Journal of Human–Computer Studies* **55**(5), 761–86.

Miller, C. S. & Remington, R. W. [2004], Modelling Information Navigation: Implications for Information Architecture, *Human–Computer Interaction* **19**(3), 225–71.

Morrison, J. B., Pirolli, P. & Card, S. K. [2000], A Taxonomic Analysis of What World Wide Web Activities Significantly Impact People's Decisions and Actions, UIR Technical report, Xerox PARC.

Pirolli, P. & Fu, W.-T. [2003], SNIF-ACT: A Model of Information Foraging on the World Wide Web, *in* P. Brusilovsky, A. Corbett & F. de Rosis (eds.), *Proceedings of the Ninth International Conference on User Modelling, UM2003*, Vol. 2702 of *Lecture Notes in Artifical Intelligence*, Springer-Verlag, pp.45–54.

Wen, J. [2003], Post-Valued Recall Web Pages: User Disorientation Hits the Big Time, *IT & Society* **1**(3), 184–94.

Revisiting Web Design Guidelines by Exploring Users' Expectations, Preferences and Visual Search Behaviour

Ekaterini Tzanidou, Shailey Minocha, Marian Petre & Andrew Grayson[†]

Department of Computing, The Open University, Walton Hall, Milton Keynes MK7 6AA, UK

Email: *{e.tzanidou, s.minocha, m.petre}@open.ac.uk*

[†] *Division of Psychology, Nottingham Trent University, Burton Street, Nottingham NG1 4BU, UK*

Email: *andy.grayson@ntu.ac.uk*

The majority of existing Web design guidelines have been derived by expert heuristic evaluations, apparently without involving the users themselves. In this paper we report two studies of an on-going research programme in the area of eye tracking in which we are investigating the relationship between the users' expectations, preferences, and visual search behaviour. The first study captures the position of first fixations while the users look for cues of the brand identity and services of the site. The second study examines how quickly users adapt to an unfamiliar design layout during repeated exposures by measuring the position of first fixation, time to target fixation and sequence of fixations (scan path). In both the studies, the eye tracking data is supported by qualitative data from pre- and post-session questions which elicited the users' expectations and preferences about the target Web-link.

Keywords: Web design guidelines, eye tracking, visual search behaviour, homepages, e-commerce, user-adaptation.

1 Introduction

When considering the design of websites for e-commerce, the HCI literature proposes a variety of design guidelines for websites [Nielsen et al. 2001; van Duyne et al. 2003]. In addition, others have suggested that these guidelines have been derived by personal reviews and anecdotes without reporting the involvement of human participants [Ivory et al. 2001].

The homepage is viewed more than any other page on a website and first impressions are important in attracting new users. Nielsen & Tahir propose that:

> The homepage must communicate in a short glance where users are, what your company does and what the users can do at your site. [Nielsen & Tahir 2002]

van Duyne et al. [2003] suggest that the first visit of the homepage is often the site branding which must be initially clear to users. A detailed study has been reported in Nielsen & Tahir [2002] of heuristic evaluations of 50 homepages. Although the guidelines proposed in these studies are straightforward to implement, it has been stated that they could be too general to apply to a particular case, so a wide range of websites are not supported [Beier & Vaughan 2003]. The first study reported in this paper used eye tracking to investigate what users inspect on their first visit to a homepage and how quickly can they establish the brand identity. The study recorded what users looked at first (i.e. position of first fixation) and their initial scanning behaviour. The eye movement data was compared to users' responses to questions about company identity and services during the post-session interviews.

Another set of design guidelines is based on an assumption that visual search behaviour is shaped by expectations, hence they suggest designing user interfaces that conform to conventions. Nielsen et al. underline the importance of maintaining consistency with other websites and webpages:

> All webpages are much the same from the user's perspective, they share interaction techniques, they are downloaded (slowly) from the Internet, and they have relatively similar layouts. Those similarities are in fact good because they allow users a measure of transfer of skill from one site to the next. Users complain bitterly when a site doesn't try to use navigation from the majority of other sites. [Nielsen et al. 2001, p.189]

But how do users learn conventions and develop expectations?

Ehret [2002] suggests that when locations of design elements remain constant, performance improves over exposures as users learn the placements of design elements. This implies that consistency of placement of a design element influences visual search. But a recent eye tracking study by McCarthy et al. [2003] investigated the impact of changing the location of design elements and how users performed when viewing the element in unexpected locations. They found that following conventions with other websites did not matter, as users quickly adapted to unexpected design layouts. So, is it important to follow consistency with other websites?, or is it acceptable to place design elements in non-consistent placements on the user interface? The second study reported in this paper investigated how quickly users adapt to a different location of a design element over repeated exposures. Specifically, it focused on the 'About Us' link on a website.

When users encounter webpages, they are often presented with an overwhelming amount of information, which is a mix of visual and textual design elements clamouring for attention. Thus, understanding the factors that influence the visual search behaviour on the user interface is extremely valuable. Eye tracking has been chosen as the primary evaluation technique for both the studies being reported in this paper. The eye movement data has been supported by outcomes of conventional techniques, such as self-reports of expectations and preferences as elicited from pre- and post-session questions, which enabled a better understanding and interpretation of the outcomes of the two studies.

1.1 Visual Search Behaviour

Theories of visual search, as reported by Horowitz & Wolfe [1998], conclude that visual search relies on accumulating information about the identity of design elements over time. This knowledge enables designers to structure the user interface effectively and influence the user's visual search behaviour. Post-cognitive modelling research, as cited in Horowitz & Wolfe [1998], has demonstrated that people use anticipatory location information to guide visual search, and that visual features sometimes guide the visual search (i.e. expectations and salience) [Hornof & Halverson 2003]. It is primarily through visual search that users locate the content of their Web-based tasks. Despite extensive research into visual search behaviour in disciplines such as psychology, recent research in HCI [Hornof & Halverson 2003] has underlined the importance of developing a unified understanding of users' visual search behaviour. Visual search behaviour on websites is influenced by user's expectations about what is being looked for and where it might be located. Pirolli & Card [1995] talk about the design layout of the display as a bottom-up influence and expectations as a top-down influence. Bottom-up processing refers to the design elements influencing the visual scene itself, such as presentation format, colour, and position, whereas top-down processing refers to the expectations the users develop such as the cognitive processes when viewing a scene. The interactions between top-down and bottom-up influences is identified as Information Scent or Information Foraging [Pirolli & Card 1995]. Unless the design elements such as colour, menu items, graphs (bottom-up) are looked at, there is no 'scent', and therefore, there is no basis for selection.

2 Tracking Eye Movements to Assess Usability

Conventional usability evaluation techniques such as user-observations, think-aloud protocols, questionnaires and interviews focus more on the activities of user performance rather than the understanding of users' cognitive processes [Goldberg et al. 2002]. Therefore, aspects of task performance such as screen navigation, selection of menu items, can be captured but the inferences of cognitive processes are more difficult to explain. Eye tracking studies in cognitive psychology have established that eye movements give an insight into the users' cognitive processes, for example see Just & Carpenter [1976]. Eye movements in reading and information processing have been studied by Rayner & Pollatsek [1994] and concluded that eye-movement data indicates how easy it is to process a display.

The use of eye tracking in HCI is not a new concept, as Jacob & Karn [2003] have illustrated in their review. Fitts [1954] was the first to conduct a systematic eye-tracking study of pilots using cockpit controls and instruments. In recent years eye tracking devices have become more affordable, and the technology has improved, enabling an increasing number of HCI researchers to engage in eye tracking studies [Dix et al. 2003]. In general, eye-movement data is used to support recommendations for how a user interface should be changed, rather than a broad assessment of the interface's usability [Goldberg & Winchansky 2003].

Previous research [Cowen et al. 2002; Goldberg & Kotval 1999; Renshaw et al. 2003] has established that specific design elements influence eye movements in a predictable way, and they demonstrate that eye tracking metrics are sensitive enough to detect them. Eye tracking has been applied in HCI in two ways: as a real-time input device and its use as a usability evaluation technique [Jacob & Karn 2003]. In the studies reported in this paper, eye tracking has been applied for usability evaluation of websites.

2.1 Eye Tracking Studies of Websites

Granka et al. [2004] report that only a small number of studies have been conducted on eye movement behaviour on webpages. Visual preferences of text and images have been explored by two studies [Ellis et al. 1998; Lewenstein et al. 2002]. Ellis et al. [1998] demonstrated that users completed tasks more quickly and easily on text-based screens, although they preferred image-based screens. The Stanford Poynter Project study Lewenstein et al. [2002] examined how users read on-line and off-line news; they found that text was viewed more than images for readers who read on-line news, whereas the opposite occurred for readers who read off-line news.

Two studies, Josephson & Holmes [2002] and Goldberg et al. [2002] , have examined the navigational styles on user interfaces of webpages. Josephson & Holmes [2002] examined users' scan paths on different kind of images widely used on the Internet to test Norton & Stark's scan path theory and identified strong similarities among scan paths, suggesting that different users' eye movements may follow a 'habitually preferred path'. Goldberg et al. [2002] captured navigational styles of users navigating Web portals. They concluded that headers of links are not always viewed before the main body. This research went on to develop specific design recommendations for portals based on the eye-movement data.

The studies discussed above explored navigational styles that the users apply on both off-line and on-line channels but did not investigate the factors that influence the navigation styles. However, recent studies, for example Outing & Ruel [2004] and Pan et al. [2004], aim to understand the factors that influence user's visual-search behaviour.

Pan et al. [2004] investigated some of these factors, such as individual differences, design characteristics of the webpages, the order in which webpages are viewed and different tasks that were given to the users to complete. Gender and viewing order were found to be the key determinants of visual search behaviour.

Men applied different scan paths from women and the order in which the stimuli were presented influenced the scan paths as well.

The Stanford Poynter Project [Outing & Ruel 2004] extended their previous work [Lewenstein et al. 2002] on how users read news websites. They applied a more methodological approach in their latter study. Some of the key points of their latest study [Outing & Ruel 2004] suggest that users navigate more on the upper part of news websites rather than left or right of the page. The size of text was found to be influential in terms of encouraging focused viewing behaviour; smaller text drew more fixations while larger sizes promoted lighter scanning. The users fixated more on headlines with large text rather than headlines with small text.

2.2 Eye Movement-based Metrics and Terminology

In our research programme, Study 1 used the following eye movement-based metrics:

1. Initial gaze: where the participant looked for less than half a second 100 milliseconds (ms) prior to the homepage appearing on the screen.

2. Entry point: the first fixation within 300ms of the display of the homepage. 300ms is the duration of a typical fixation and the typical time in which information extraction occurs [Cowen et al. 2002].

Study 2 used the following eye movement-based metrics:

1. Time to target fixation: the time users need to fixate on the target link gives a basis of performance measurement when a specific search target exists. Since we are in interested how quickly or slowly the target link is fixated the time to target fixation is an indication of user performance. The target link in our study is the 'About Us' link.

2. Location of fixation: the location of fixations is used as an indicator of where users look on a webpage to locate the target link.

3. Initial Gaze: initial gaze measures the user's first gaze during 50ms of the webpage appearing on the screen in order to examine where users expect to find the target link.

4. Entry Point: Entry point measures the user's first fixation within 250ms of the webpage appearing on the screen in order to examine which design elements first draw user's visual attention.

5. Scan path: the sequence of fixations indicates the order in which the user looked at areas on the webpage.

The difference in milliseconds (300ms and 250ms) for the capture of initial gaze and entry point between the two studies is due to different sampling rates of the two eye tracking devices used in the two studies. Similar to what has been proposed by Granka et al. [2004], we used a location grid of 6 equal areas (Figure 1) for the analysis of 'initial gazes' and 'entry points' in the two studies.

Figure 1: Sample location grid to analyse eye-movement data with respect to the location of the design elements.

3 Study 1 — Experiment Design

Study 1 collected four types of data:

1. A background questionnaire (eliciting Internet experience and typical Internet usage).

2. Eye tracking data.

3. Responses to questions regarding user's expectations of brand identity and services on e-commerce home pages.

4. Protocols of post-session interviews eliciting users' perceptions of interacting with home pages of e-commerce websites.

The principal focus in the research design was to explore the relationship between user's scanning behaviour and the ability to identify the brand and services on a home page. Our secondary focus was to capture the relationship between user's previous experiences and, therefore, expectations, with their scanning behaviour.

3.1 Participants

Ten volunteers (5 male and 5 female) with age range of 22–51 from the staff and postgraduate student population of the Open University participated in this study. Eight participants were regular (using the Internet 2–3 times per day) Internet users and 2 were frequent (using the Internet throughout the day as a part of their job) Internet users. None of the participants had viewed the homepages used in the study prior to their participation.

3.2   Stimuli and Equipment

Five e-commerce homepages were selected as stimuli for the first study:

- Walt Disney http://www.disney.com (family entertainment).

- Pet Smart http://www.petsmart.com (retail supplier for pets).

- General Motors http://www.gm.com (corporate automaker).

- Federal Highway Administration http://www.fhwa.dot.gov (US department of transportation).

- Global Sources http://www.globalsources.com (product and trade information for volume buyers).

These 5 sites were chosen from the 50 homepages Nielsen & Tahir [2002] had evaluated as a part of their study. The aim was to compare the design guidelines derived by Nielsen & Tahir [2002] to the outcomes of our eye tracking study. Therefore, the selected homepages were chosen based on the ones that retained the same design layout since Nielsen & Tahir had performed the heuristic evaluations.

Previous research [Loftus 1976] has shown that 15 seconds is sufficient to capture a complete scan path for the first inspection of a display. Therefore, the homepages were presented for 15seconds each. Eye movements were recorded using a SensoriMotoric Instruments (SMI)'s Head-Mounted Eye Tracking Device II (HED-II) at a sample rate of 50Hz [SensoriMotoric Instruments 1999]. An MPEG video file was produced with a moving dot representing the user's eye movements.

3.3   Procedure

After a brief introduction about the study, each participant completed a consent form and a background questionnaire. The eye tracking equipment was then calibrated for the participant. The five selected homepages appeared as a PowerPoint slide show. The order of presentation of the homepages was varied for each participant, in order to reduce possible order effects. The task questions were:

- 'What does this company do?'

- 'What can you do on this site?'

The participant's eye movements were recorded, and the participant's verbal responses and interactions with the webpages were audio- and video-recorded. A post-session, semi-structured interview followed which was also audio-recorded.

3.4   Pre-test Questionnaire

The aim of the pre-test questionnaire was to collect demographic data, and frequency and purpose of Internet usage. In addition, the participants were asked to state three websites they visited often and three websites they were familiar with. The purpose of these questions was to look at those websites and analyse how the users' previous experiences influenced the way they expected to find information related to the task questions in our study. Our analysis showed that in most cases, the websites that the participants had visited regularly or were familiar with had the logo and name of the company either at the top-left corner or in the top-middle of the homepage.

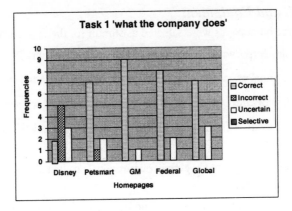

Figure 2: Frequency of responses for Task 1 'What does the company do' across all homepages.

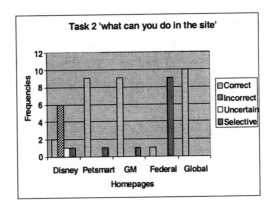

Figure 3: Frequency of responses for Task 2 'What can you do in the site' across all homepages.

3.5 Eye Tracking Session

A common trend was found for the eight users who classified themselves as regular Internet users. Their initial gaze prior to the presentation of the homepage was in the middle of the screen across all homepages whereas the two participants who classified themselves as frequent users looked at the top of the screen. The majority of 'entry points' across homepages were found on the top left and top middle of the page. 60% of 'entry points' fixated on Area A and 40% fixated on Area B of the page (Figure 1 shows Area A and B on a sample webpage).

A coding system was developed to classify the answers given for the task questions. Figure 2 demonstrates the frequency of the type of responses as given for Task 1 across homepages and Figure 3 for Task 2. The GM homepage gathered the highest accurate responses in both task questions indicating that it was easier to

Themes from Post — session Interview	Categories of Responses
Annoying/frustrating design elements.	Too much text; flashy images; images; adverts; introduction page; pop up windows; small fonts.
General preferred design elements.	Simple/clear links; images; sub links to menu items; less text; company's contact details; short description under bold titles; 'About the Company' link; clear structure; easy access to products.
Expectations of homepages.	The name of the company; links to the rest of the site; the company info; large font size of text of company name; title of page; generic information; logo; navigation tool; keywords/phrases.
Perceived position of first look.	Top middle or top left corner of the page; left side of the page.
Perceived first design element to look at.	A peripheral look to confirm it is the site aimed for; the name of the company; links to the rest of the sites.
Perceived factors that influence first fixation.	Information presented on paper documents; natural way of reading; visiting other websites; information presentation of other media (i.e. newspapers).

Table 1: Post-Session responses (users' perceptions) of homepage design.

identify what the company does and what can be done within the site. The Disney homepage gathered the most incorrect answers. The banner of a Visa Disney card on the top of the page caused a great deal of confusion for the users — who confused the site for a place to make an application for a Disney's credit card.

3.6   Post-session Interviews

The post-session interviews consisted of semi-structured questions to allow the participants to elaborate more on their perceptions of homepage-design. We identified themes in this self-report data of the users and developed a catalogue of these themes which detail the characteristics of homepages (Table 1).

It is interesting to see in Table 1 that design elements such as images come under both 'annoying' and preferred' design elements. Users have varying opinions: some prefer to see images of the products they intend to buy and users who dislike images on the homepage as they perceive images as adverts and ignore them.

3.7   Discussion — Study 1

The main aim of Study 1 was to re-examine the existing homepage design guidelines by employing an alternative, user-centred evaluation technique of tracking users' eye movements. This study confirmed the general guideline in Nielsen & Tahir [2002] which is to *'place important information at the top of the page'*. All 'entry point' fixations were at the top left or top middle of the homepage. However, Study 1 data contrasted with guidelines in Nielsen & Tahir [2002] specific to particular homepages, suggesting refinements in the Web design guidelines. These variations are now discussed:

3.7.1 Banner Advertisements

In the homepage study conducted by Nielsen & Tahir [2002] it is suggested that "users tend to ignore anything that looks like a banner ad so it is a poor way of promoting site elements" (p125). Our study suggests that whether or not a banner advert will be ignored depends on its position and presentation format. For example, the banner for credit card on top of Disney page was mistaken for the name of the company, due to its position and size. The 'entry points', responses to questions, and self-reports all confirm this confusion.

3.7.2 Product Images

It is suggested in Nielsen & Tahir [2002, p.241] that Petsmart's (one of the homepages of this study) biggest strength is that it shows examples of the products and content offered on the site. Our study suggests that user's dislike for images on homepages may conflict with the images' advantages in 'drawing the eye'. All participants fixed on product images, even those who disliked and claimed to ignore them. However, those who disliked the use of product-images gave less accurate responses about brand and services. Although this requires further investigation, the use of product images on the homepage could be an obstacle in search efficiency for those users who tend to dislike images.

3.7.3 Design Layout

It is argued in Nielsen & Tahir [2002] that designers should use 'liquid layout' that allows users to adjust the homepage size. For example, the Federal homepage, using a 'liquid layout' that filled the screen, was described *'as well defined and easily recognisable'* (p161), whereas the GM homepage, which had a fixed size and did not fill the (1280 by 1024 pixels) display, was described *'as one that doesn't make clear whom it is trying to serve or what users can do'* (p185). However, completeness of inspection and accuracy of brand and service identification in this study ran contrary to the guideline. Users inspected the fixed-size GM homepage fully, whereas their inspection of the full-screen Federal homepage was incomplete, reaching only half way through the homepage. Further, there were more correct task responses for the GM homepage than for the Federal homepage.

4 Study 2 — Experiment Design

The second study reported in this paper examines how quickly users adapt to an unfamiliar design layout and, in particular, how quickly the users adjust their expectations of where to look for a given target link during repeated exposures to a new design layout. A counterbalanced experiment design was applied varying the ten exposures of webpages to eliminate possible order effects. Ten webpages of e-commerce sites were selected and amended so that they would appear in each of the three different exposure styles. So, for example, each webpage was amended in order to have:

1. The 'About Us' link at the bottom of the page.

2. The 'About Us' link at the top of the page.

Exposures	Description	Purpose
Exposure 1	Did not include the 'About Us' link.	To explore users' expectations of where to find the 'About Us' link before the repeated exposure session.
Exposure 2–7	Six repeated exposures where the 'About Us' link appeared at the bottom of the page.	To examine the effect of consistent design element placement on visual search behaviour.
Exposure 8	The 'About Us' link appeared at the top of the page.	To capture the users' visual reactions when introduced to an alternative design layout after being presented with the repeated exposures in which the 'About Us' link appeared at the bottom of the page.
Exposure 9	The 'About Us' link appeared at the bottom of the page again.	To assess persistence of any affect of repeated exposures on visual search behaviour.
Exposure 10	Did not include the 'About Us' link.	To explore users' expectations where to find the 'About Us' link after the repeated exposure session.

Table 2: Description and purpose of the exposures in the counterbalanced design.

3. No 'About Us' link.

The description of each exposure and purpose is presented in Table 2.
   Study 2 tested two sets of hypotheses:

1. The first set addressed the effect of the consistent placement of the target link (About Us link) for Exposures 2 to 7 and predicted that the placement of the target link at the bottom of the page over six repeated exposures would result in the participants' decrease in the time to target fixation and also change in participant's expectations of where to find the target link.

2. The second set examined the effect of the alternative placement of the target link (About Us link) and predicted that the placement of the target link at the top of the page in Exposure 8 would result in quick adaptation to an unexpected design layout.

Specifically, we anticipated that the two sets of hypotheses will be evidenced by shorter times to target fixation, modifications of scan patterns, change of location of first fixations and self-report of preferences and expectations.

4.1   Participants

Ten volunteers (5 male and 5 female) with age range of 22–56 from the staff and postgraduate student population of the Open University participated in this study. 5 participants were regular (using the Internet 2–3 times per day) Internet users and 5 participants were frequent (using the Internet throughout the day as part of their job) Internet users. None of the participants had viewed the homepages used in the study prior to their participation.

4.2 Stimuli and Equipment

Prior to the selection of the stimuli, a survey was conducted to identify the position of the 'About Us' link on homepages. 50 European and 50 American e-commerce sites were chosen on the basis of their reported sales. 80% of the homepages placed the 'About Us' link on the top of the page as a global navigation link its position in the navigation bar varied on different websites. On the basis of this survey, we concluded that the convention is to place the 'About Us' link at the top of the page. This led to the assumption that Internet users might be used to finding the 'About Us' link on the top of the page or at least expect to find it in that position due to their previous experiences. Therefore, the position of the target link in the repeated exposures session (Exposures 2–7) was on the bottom of the page.

Ten UK e-commerce homepages from a variety of domains were selected as stimuli for this study:

- Cover4students http://www.cover4students.com (campus insurance).

- Hatton Garden Online http://www.hattongardenonline.com (jewellery).

- Diamond Daisy http://www.diamonddaisy.com (jewellery).

- Travelodge http://www.travelodge.co.uk (accommodation).

- Travel Bag http://www.travelbag.co.uk (travel).

- Train Line http://www.thetrainline.com (travel).

- Saga Holidays http://www.sagaholidays.com (holidays).

- Hotel net http://www.hotelnet.co.uk (accommodation).

- Past Times http://www.past-times.co.uk (gifts).

- To Book http://www.tobook.com (accommodation).

The criteria for choosing homepages were that pages should have:

- A design layout that fits within the computer screen (17″ flat screen with a resolution of 1024×768 pixels) without requiring scrolling.

- Either a top- or bottom-page navigational bar where the 'About Us' link could appear.

Eye movements were recorded using an ASL (Applied Science Technologies) 504 eye tracking remote pan-tilt camera [ASL 2004] capturing eye movement data at a sample rate of 60Hz. The presentation of the stimuli was controlled by means of the Gaze Tracker? software and presented on the screen and viewed by the participants from a distance of 55cm from the screen.

4.3 Procedure

The duration of a session including the briefing and calibration process was approximately thirty minutes. The session started by giving an introduction of the eye tracking equipment and the study to the participant. The participant completed a consent form and a background questionnaire. The questionnaire captured age, gender, previous Internet experience, and frequency and purpose of Internet use. The participant was asked the following questions regarding the 'About Us' link:

- Where do you look when you want to find information regarding the company?

- Where do you prefer to find it?

These questions were aimed to collect information about the user's expectations and preferences regarding the placement of the 'About Us' link before the eye-tracking session.

The researcher then calibrated the eye tracking camera for the participant. The participant was asked to look at each webpage and find the 'About Us' link. The participant was asked to say aloud where on the interface they found the 'About Us' link in order to indicate that the task had been completed, so that the researcher could press the 'enter' key on the keyboard for the next page to appear. There was no time limit for the task so as to encourage a natural navigation of the webpage. To avoid the researcher's reaction times influencing the data, the eye movement data were used as a measure of the task completion times. After the eye tracking session, the participants were asked:

- Where would you like to find the 'About Us' link?

- What do you think about the webpages you just saw?

- Was it easy to find the 'About Us' link?

These questions aimed to collect information about the user's perceptions and preferences regarding the 'About Us' link after the repeated exposures session.

4.4 Repeated Exposures Effect

The descriptive statistics of the scores to target fixation across repeated exposures are shown in Table 3. There is a difference between the sum of time to target fixation for the first of the repeated exposures (Exposure 2) *179.10* and the last of the repeated exposures (Exposure 7) *38.7*.

A non-parametric Trend test [Page 1963] was applied to predict if there was a trend of learning where to look when presented with a sequence of six repeated exposures of homepages where the 'About Us' link appears on the bottom of the page. A Page's L analysis [Page 1963] on the ranked scores of time to target fixation for the repeated exposures revealed a significant trend across exposures: $L_{10,6} = 792$, $p < 0.05$. A trend of time to target fixation decreases as the number of exposures increases was found.

The eye tracking measures were supported by the qualitative data as retrieved from the pre- and post-session questions. When the participants were asked before

Exposures	N	Minimum	Maximum	Sum	Mean	Std. Dev.
Exposure 2	10	3.52	38.86	179.10	17.90	11.41
Exposure 3	10	1.44	44.97	120.16	12.01	13.11
Exposure 4	10	0.72	17.98	64.63	6.46	5.65
Exposure 5	10	1.53	31.64	83.26	8.32	9.99
Exposure 6	10	1.20	41.13	122.62	12.26	14.09
Exposure 7	10	0.91	6.80	38.70	3.86	1.61
Exposure 8	10	2.53	16.16	58.48	5.84	3.99
Exposure 9	10	1.80	22.86	91.00	9.09	6.79

Table 3: Descriptive statistics: Time to target fixation for repeated exposures in milliseconds.

the eye tracking session where they expected to find the 'About Us' link they answered *'on top of the page'* or it doesn't matter as long as they can see it. But, when the participants were asked after the eye tracking session where would they like to find the 'About Us' link they answered *'on the bottom of the page'*. In addition to the eye tracking data where a trend of adaptation was found as exposures increased, the modification in answers from the pre- and post-session questions suggests an influence of change in location-preferences of the link.

4.5 Alternative Design Layout Effect

A two-tailed paired t-test was used to establish whether there were significant differences between the time to target fixation before the repeated exposures (About Us link at the bottom of the page) and after repeated exposures (About Us link at top of the page) at the 5% alpha level of confidence. There is evidence that the users found the target link quicker when the 'About Us' link was placed at the top of the page after having seen it on the bottom of the page in the repeated exposures session as $t_9 = 3.35$, $p < 0.05$.

After transforming the raw scores using a two-related samples Wilcoxon test, the distributions between the time to target fixation after the repeated exposures (About Us link at top of the page) and after the alternative exposure (About Us link at bottom of the page again) were compared at the 5% alpha level of confidence. Despite the significance difference found when the About Us link is presented on the top of the page, when it is then presented again at the bottom of the page there is a significant difference as $t_9 = 1.98$, $p < 0.05$.

The results indicate that when placing the target link on the top of the page users find it quicker than when it was placed at the bottom of the page. This might be an effect of their previous experiences which was also indicated in their self-report data. Also, this finding is consistent with the norm captured in our survey regarding the placement of the 'About Us' link on leading e-commerce sites. But when presented with the 'About Us' link at the bottom of the page again after the repeated exposure a second expectation had developed possibly caused by the consistent placement of the 'About Us' link on the bottom of the page over the repeated exposures, indicating that users had adapted to the new design.

4.6   Before and After Repeated Exposures Effect

'Initial gaze' for all participants was always in Areas A or B (i.e. the top left or top middle of the screen — see Figure 1 for the areas) for both Exposures 1 and 10. None of the 'initial gazes' focused on the right side or bottom of the screen (Areas C, D, E and F). This is more of an indication of similar visual search strategies of initial gazes starting from the upper part of the page rather than any indication of user-adaptation across exposures. The very small amount of time (50ms) during which 'initial gazes' where measured might not have allowed the observation of any possible scan path modification. Therefore, the location of the 'entry point' for each participant was measured during the first 250milliseconds of the homepage appearing on the screen to indicate where the participant first fixated. The 'entry points' were not consistent across participants and varied from homepage to homepage. Nevertheless none of the 'entry points' included the right side of the screen (Areas C and F). This might be influenced by the visual attraction of specific design elements rather than just by the consistent placement of the 'About Us' link.

On comparing the users' scan paths in Exposure 1 and Exposure 10, five users where found to have modified their scan patterns from the first to the last exposure. They started their scan paths in the upper area of the screen (Areas A and B) whereas after the repeated exposures session they started their scan paths in the lower part of the screen (Areas D and E) suggesting an indicator of adaptation after finding the 'About Us' link at the bottom of the page. When looking at the profile of these five users we found that they were frequent Internet users (used it throughout the day) suggesting that they were highly skilled users which might explain their quick adaptation to consistent placement of the 'About Us' link.

4.7   Discussion — Study 2

When placing the target link in a consistent position over a series of exposures the results show that users adapt to consistent placement of the target link which improves their visual-search performance. A trend was found of more exposures leading to decreased time-to-target fixation. Eye movement data was supported by self-reports of change in expectations and preferences of where the target link was expected to be found. The results of Study 2 are in sync with the previous research by Ehret [2002] which suggested that users learn the locations of design elements over series of repeated exposures. On the contrary, McCarthy et al. [2003] found no evidence that performance improves when the target link is placed in expected positions. They found that users adapt quickly to unexpected design layouts. In our study, we found that although users adapt to a design (which is not the norm, e.g. 'About us' link at the bottom of the page) over repeated exposures indicated by decreasing time-to-target fixations (see Table 3), when they are exposed to a design which is as per the norm, their visual-search performance is even better. This shows that in spite of the fact that users 'learn' and adapt to designs different from the norm, they still perform better to designs that follow the norms, indicating that the influence of repeated exposures or adaptation is a secondary effect and it does not overrule the effect of the previous experiences.

5   Conclusions and Future Work

This paper reports two studies of an on-going research programme in applying eye tracking to validate and elaborate Web design guidelines. Our aim has been to capture the user's visual search behaviour and to explore the relationship between user's eye-tracking behaviour, expectations, and preferences based on their previous experiences. Both the reported studies follow a common model of research design employing:

1. Background questionnaire.

2. Eye-movement data.

3. Pre- and post-session interviews.

The results of the two studies corroborated existing design guidelines for webpages, but also identified potential refinements.   The first study provided insights of which design elements attract attention and where on the homepage users expect to find specific information about brand identity and website services. The second study found that although more exposures led to decreased time-to-target fixation, indicating that user-adaptation or learning occurred, visual search behaviour is, nevertheless, strongly influenced by previous experiences of visiting other websites.

We have recently conducted three more studies as a part of the next phase in our research programme:

1. The effect of the presence or absence and the size of images on E-travel sites on user's task performance.

2. The presentation format (icon or a textual link) of the key steps in a transaction on an e-commerce site.

3. The optimal combination of text and background colour of e-commerce homepages.

We will be reporting our results from these three studies in the near future.

Acknowledgements

The research in this paper is being supported by an EPSRC Research Studentship. The authors would like to thank the participants and anonymous reviewers.

References

ASL [2004], Model 504, http://www.a-s-l.com/model504.htm (last accessed 2005-04-25). Applied Science Laboratories.

Beier, B. & Vaughan, M. W. [2003], The Bull's-eye: A Framework for Web Application User Interface Design Guidelines, in V. Bellotti, T. Erickson, G. Cockton & P. Korhonen (eds.), Proceedings of SIGCHI Conference on Human Factors in Computing Systems (CHI'03), CHI Letters 5(1), ACM Press, pp.489–96.

Cowen, L., Ball, L. J. & Delin, J. [2002], An Eye-movement Analysis of Web Page Usability, in X. Faulkner, J. Finlay & F. Dètienne (eds.), *People and Computers XVI (Proceedings of HCI'02)*, Springer-Verlag, pp.317–35.

Dix, A., Finlay, J., Abowd, G. D. & Beale, R. [2003], *Human–Computer Interaction*, third edition, Prentice–Hall.

Ehret, B. D. [2002], Learning Where to Look: Location Learning in Graphical User Interfaces, in D. Wixon (ed.), *Proceedings of SIGCHI Conference on Human Factors in Computing Systems: Changing our World, Changing Ourselves (CHI'02)*, *CHI Letters* **4**(1), ACM Press, pp.211–8.

Ellis, S., Candrea, R., Misner, J., Craig, S., Lankford, C. & Hutchinson, T. [1998], Windows to the Soul? What Eye Movements Tell Us about Software Usability, in *Proceedings of the Usability Professionals' Association 7th Annual Conference*, Usability Professionals' Association, pp.151–6.

Fitts, P. M. [1954], The Information Capacity of the Human Motor System in Controlling Amplitude of Movement, *Journal of Experimental Psychology* **47**(6), 381–91.

Goldberg, J. H. & Kotval, X. P. [1999], Computer Interface Evaluation Using Eye Movements: Methods and Constructs, *International Journal of Industrial Ergonomics* **24**(6), 631–45.

Goldberg, J. H. & Winchansky, A. [2003], Eye Tracking in Usability Evaluation, in J. Hyönä, R. Radach & H. Deubel (eds.), *The Mind's Eyes: Cognitive and Applied Aspects of Eye Movements*, Elsevier, pp.493–516.

Goldberg, J. H., Stimson, M. J., Lewenstein, M., Scott, N. & Wichansky, A. M. [2002], Eye Tracking in Web Search Tasks: Design Implications, in A. T. Duchowski, R. Vertegaal & J. W. Senders (eds.), *Proceedings of the Symposium on Eye Tracking Research & Applications (ETRA 2002)*, ACM Press, pp.51–8.

Granka, L., Joachims, T. & Gay, G. [2004], Eye-Tracking Analysis of User Behaviour in WWW Search, in K. Järvelin, J. Allan, P. Bruza & M. Sanderson (eds.), *Proceedings of the 27th Annual International ACM SIGIR Conference on Research and Development in Information Retrieval (SIGIR'04)*, ACM Press, pp.478–9.

Hornof, A. J. & Halverson, T. [2003], Cognitive Strategies and Eye Movements for Searching Hierarchical Computer Displays, in V. Bellotti, T. Erickson, G. Cockton & P. Korhonen (eds.), *Proceedings of SIGCHI Conference on Human Factors in Computing Systems (CHI'03)*, *CHI Letters* **5**(1), ACM Press, pp.249–56.

Horowitz, T. S. & Wolfe, J. M. [1998], Visual Search Has No Memory, *Nature* **357**, 575–7.

Ivory, M. Y., Sinha, R. R. & Hearst, M. A. [2001], Empirically Validated Web Page Design Metrics, in J. A. Jacko, A. Sears, M. Beaudouin-Lafon & R. J. K. Jacob (eds.), *Proceedings of SIGCHI Conference on Human Factors in Computing Systems (CHI'01)*, *CHI Letters* **3**(1), ACM Press, pp.53–60.

Jacob, R. J. K. & Karn, K. S. [2003], Eye Tracking in Human–Computer Interaction and Usability Research: Ready to Deliver the Promises, in J. Hyönä, R. Radach & H. Deubel (eds.), *The Mind's Eyes: Cognitive and Applied Aspects of Eye Movements*, Elsevier, pp.573–605.

Josephson, S. & Holmes, M. E. [2002], Visual Attention to Repeated Internet Images: Testing the Scan Path Theory on the WWW, *in* A. T. Duchowski, R. Vertegaal & J. W. Senders (eds.), *Proceedings of the Symposium on Eye Tracking Research & Applications (ETRA 2002)*, ACM Press, pp.43–51.

Just, M. A. & Carpenter, P. A. [1976], Eye Fixations and Cognitive Processes, *Cognitive Psychology* **8**(4), 441–80.

Lewenstein, M., Edwards, G., Tatr, D. & de Vigal, A. [2002], The Stanford Poynter Project, http://www.poynter.org/eyetrack2000 (last accessed 2005-04-25).

Loftus, G. R. [1976], A Framework for a Theory of Picture Recognition, *in* R. A. Monty & J. W. Senders (eds.), *Eye Movements and Psychological Processes*, John Wiley & Sons, pp.499–513.

McCarthy, J., Sasse, M. A. & Riegelsberger, J. [2003], Could I Have the Menu Please? An Eye Tracking Study of Design Conventions, *in* E. O'Neill, P. Palanque & P. Johnson (eds.), *People and Computers XVII: Designing for Society (Proceedings of HCI'03)*, Springer-Verlag, pp.401–14.

Nielsen, J. & Tahir, M. [2002], *Hompage Usability: 50 Web sites Deconstructed*, New Riders Publishing.

Nielsen, J., Molich, R., Snyder, C. & Farrell, S. [2001], *E-Commerce User Experience*, Nielsen Norman Group.

Outing, S. & Ruel, L. [2004], Eye Track III, http://www.poynterextra.org/eyetrack2004/ (last accessed 2005-04-25).

Page, E. B. [1963], Ordered Hypotheses for Multiple Treatments: A Significance Test for Linear Ranks, *Journal of American Statistical Association* **58**(301), 216–30.

Pan, B., Hembrooke, H., Gay, G., Granka, L., Feusner, M., & Newman, J. [2004], The Determinants of Webpage Viewing Behaviour: An Eye Tracking Study, *in* A. T. Duchowski & R. Vertegaal (eds.), *Proceedings of the Symposium on Eye Tracking Research & Applications (ETRA 2004)*, ACM Press, pp.147–54.

Pirolli, P. & Card, S. K. [1995], Information Foraging in Information Access Environments, *in* I. Katz, R. Mack, L. Marks, M. B. Rosson & J. Nielsen (eds.), *Proceedings of the SIGCHI Conference on Human Factors in Computing Systems (CHI'95)*, ACM Press, pp.51–8.

Rayner, K. & Pollatsek, A. [1994], *The Psychology of Reading*, Lawrence Erlbaum Associates.

Renshaw, J. A., Finlay, J. E., Tyfa, D. & Ward, R. D. [2003], Designing for Visual Influence: An Eye Tracking Study of the Usability of Graphical Management Information, *in* M. Rauterberg, M. Menozzi & J. Weeson (eds.), *Human–Computer Interaction — INTERACT '03: Proceedings of the Ninth IFIP Conference on Human–Computer Interaction*, IOS Press, pp.144–51.

SensoriMotoric Instruments [1999], *iview version 3.0*.

van Duyne, D. K., Landay, J. A. & Hong, J. I. [2003], *The Design of Sites: Patterns, Principles and Processes for Crafting a Customer-centred Web Experience*, Addison-Wesley.

Comparing Automatic and Manual Zooming Methods for Acquiring Off-screen Targets

Joshua Savage[†] & Andy Cockburn[‡]

[†] *LeftClick Ltd., Canterbury Innovation Incubator, PO Box 13761, Christchurch, New Zealand*
Tel: *+64 3 364 2987*
Fax: *+64 3 364 2569*
Email: *Josh.Savage@leftclick.co.nz*

[‡] *Human-Computer Interaction Lab, Department of Computer Science, University of Canterbury, Christchurch, New Zealand*
Email: *andy@cosc.canterbury.ac.nz*

Previous studies indicate that user performance with scrolling can be improved through Speed-Dependent Automatic Zooming (SDAZ), which automatically couples the document's zoom-level with scroll-speed. These studies have compared traditional scrolling techniques (scrollbars and rate-based scrolling) with SDAZ, leaving a potential confound that the efficiency gains are due to zooming rather than the automatic binding of zoom-level with speed. It is therefore possible that decoupling zoom from speed, allowing users separate but concurrent control of each, could further enhance performance. This paper describes an experiment (n = 35) that examines user performance, workload and preference in tasks that involve scroll-based acquisition of off-screen targets using SDAZ and manual zooming. Three different types of document navigation are explored: text documents, 'flat' 2D maps, and a 'globe browser' that allows multi-level zooming of a globe-map of Earth and underlying city views. Results show that automatic zooming not only improves performance but that it does so with substantially less subjective workload and that it is strongly preferred. We also confirm limited previous work using Fitts' Law as a model for off-screen target acquisition and show that it applies even when zooming is employed.

Keywords: speed-dependent automatic zooming, scrolling, zooming, target acquisition, Fitts' Law.

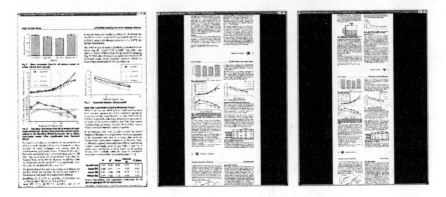

Figure 1: The automatic-zooming test interface with slow, medium and high speed scrolling

1 Introduction

Scrolling is the main interface technique for navigating through documents that are too large to be displayed within a single window. The fundamental importance of scrolling has led contemporary software and hardware vendors to develop a wide range of enhanced scrolling techniques. These include rate-based scrolling (which is activated by dragging the middle mouse button in Windows platforms), semantic scrolling (supported by Microsoft Word through the extension at the bottom of the vertical scrollbar), mouse-wheel scrolling, and isometric input devices such as the IBM TrackPoint. Variable magnification zooming is another commonly supported interface control that is related to scrolling because it changes the proportion of the document visible within each window. The 'Dynamic Zoom' feature of Adobe Reader 6 attempts to exploit the scroll-zoom relationship by allowing concurrent scroll-zoom actions.

When scrolling for target acquisition (such as browsing for a particular heading, picture, or other landmark in a document), it is most efficient to scroll as quickly as possible to the target. But rapid scrolling induces motion-blur [Burr 1980]: the information moves across the screen so quickly that our eyes cannot keep up. Igarashi & Hinckley [2000] proposed 'speed-dependent automatic zooming' (SDAZ) as a method to overcome motion blur. With SDAZ, the zoom-level is automatically adjusted as the scroll-rate increases, allowing rapid document movement at visually manageable pixel movement rates (see Figure 1). The scroll-speed is controlled through normal rate-based scrolling-the further the user drags the middle button, the faster they scroll-but automatic zooming means that the faster they scroll, the 'higher' they fly above the document.

Igarashi & Hinckley's preliminary evaluation indicated that SDAZ allows comparable performance to other scrolling techniques. Our earlier work showed that in text-document and map navigation domains SDAZ can outperform commercial systems using traditional scrollbars and panning [Cockburn & Savage 2003]. More recently we described theoretical and empirical measures for calibrating the relationship between speed and zoom and we eliminated the possibility that our previous results were confounded by rate-based controls outperforming traditional scrollbars [Cockburn et al. 2005]. The evaluation showed that SDAZ outperforms traditional scrollbars, rate-based scrolling, and another variant of automatic zooming based on van Wijk & Nuij's [2004] work on optimal pan-zoom trajectories.

This paper adds three further pieces to a strong argument in favour of commercial deployment of SDAZ. First, it reports the results of an experiment (n = 35) comparing off-screen target acquisition using SDAZ (rate-based scrolling plus automatic zooming) with that of rate-based scrolling plus manual zooming. The central hypothesis is that automatic zooming allows faster target acquisition with lower cognitive effort than manual zooming. Second, it extends the prior evaluations, which focused on text-document scrolling, to other domains with maps and a globe browser. Third, it validates a small set of research on using Fitts' Law as a performance model for off-screen target acquisition [Guiard et al. 2004; Hinckley et al. 2002]. Although Fitts' Law is well known for modelling on-screen target acquisition, we confirm its accuracy for off-screen scroll-based target acquisition, even when zooming is employed.

Further details on background studies are presented in Section 2. Section 3 then describes the three interfaces examined in our evaluation. Section 4 describes the evaluation method, Section 5 presents the results and Sections 6 and 7 discuss implications and conclude.

2   Background

Although SDAZ was introduced to the research community by Igarashi & Hinckley in 2000, a similar concept was first demonstrated in the computer game 'Grand Theft Auto' in 1997. The game gave users a plan view of their car in a city street, which automatically zoomed to show progressively more city blocks on acceleration. The need for zooming in the game is clear: without it, the rate of display change (the speed of pixel movement) can exceed human visual processing limits, inducing 'motion blur'. Zooming-out decreases the rate of pixel movement, allowing higher speeds in the information space without overloading the visual system.

As described in the introduction, there have been three main evaluations of scrolling interfaces that automatically zoom. First, Igarashi & Hinckley's preliminary study with seven participants found no definitive performance differences between SDAZ and normal scrolling. Second, in our prior work, we showed that SDAZ allowed users to complete map and text-document browsing tasks more rapidly than traditional scrollbar navigation in standard commercial systems. This result had a potential confound because the experiment compared rate-controlled scrolling (with automatic zooming) against scrollbar scrolling. To eliminate this potential confound, our recent work compared user performance with normal scrollbars, with rate-based scrolling, and with two versions of automatic zooming: one based on manipulation of a virtual scroll-thumb and the other based on rate-based input. Again, the results favoured the SDAZ behaviour of rate-based input with automatic zooming.

The experiment reported in this paper focuses on the cause of the efficiency improvements of SDAZ. The previous evaluations have shown that automatic zooming allows enhanced performance, but it remains unclear whether automatic zooming is better or worse than manual zooming. It is reasonable to suspect that manual zooming could outperform automatic zooming because it decouples scroll-speed from zoom level, allowing greater independent control of speed and zoom. Furthermore, there is evidence that parallel input of separate controls through bimanual interaction can enhance performance over serial input. Leganchuk et al. [1998] and Casalta et al. [1999] both showed performance benefits for bimanual interaction in rectangle editing tasks. In a domain more closely related to our work, Zhai & Selker [1997] showed that scrolling and pointing tasks are improved by using parallel control separation with a mouse in one hand and a joystick in the other. Finally, Hinckley et al. [1998] describe and theoretically evaluate two-handed interaction for panning, zooming and rotation, but they did not empirically validate their findings.

2.1 Fitts' Law

Fitts' Law [Fitts 1954] accurately models the time taken to acquire on-screen targets in graphical user interfaces across a very wide range of input devices. The 'Shannon formulation' of Fitts' Law [MacKenzie 1992] predicts that cursor movement time MT increases linearly with the Index of Difficulty (ID), which is the logarithm of the distance moved (amplitude, A) over the target width (W): $MT = a + b \times ID$, where $ID = \log_2(A/W + 1)$; also $IP = 1/b$. The constant b, determined through linear regression, provides a useful estimate of hand-eye coordination using the targeting method and its reciprocal gives the 'Index of Performance' (IP), also termed 'bandwidth', measured in units of 'bits per second'.

Although Fitts' Law has been extensively studied for acquisition of on-screen targets, few studies have examined its effectiveness in modelling the acquisition of off-screen targets. Hinckley et al. [2002] examined user performance with a variety of scrolling input devices (but no zooming), showing that Fitts' Law accurately modelled off-screen target acquisition. Guiard et al. [2004] describe two types of pointing involved in multi-scale (zoomable) off-screen target acquisition: *view-pointing* in which the user moves their view until the target is visible; and *cursor-pointing* in which the user moves the cursor over the final target. They theoretically examine the user's movement through pan-zoom space using space-scale diagrams, predict conformance to Fitts' Law, and empirically confirm the theory using bimanual parallel input for pointing (controlled by a stylus-tablet combination) and zooming (a joystick in the non-dominant hand).

3 Experimental Interfaces

We developed three experimental interfaces in C++ using the OpenGL graphics library: a text-document browser (Figure 1), a 'flat' map browser, and a globe map browser (Figure 2). The OpenGL graphics libraries allow rapid frame-rates and smooth animation through graphics hardware acceleration. Scrolling in all interfaces is controlled by rate-control, with the scroll-speed increasing linearly with the distance between the current and mouse-down cursor locations. Like the Microsoft Windows standard, all of our interfaces used the middle-mouse button to control rate-based scrolling. Each interface supported two zooming modes, either manual

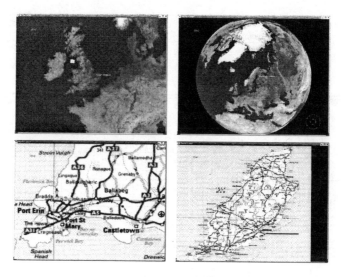

Figure 2: The automatic-zooming globe interface at slow (left) and high (right) speeds in the globe-view (top) and in the city view (bottom).

zooming controlled by the 'a' and 'z' keyboard keys, or automatic zooming in which the zoom-level is bound to the scrolling velocity. The relationship between mouse-displacement and scroll-speed was identical for each of the manual and automatic zooming pairs, as described in the subsections below.

The text-document browser only allows vertical scrolling, with the scrolling velocity controlled purely by vertical displacement of the mouse. The 'flat' map browser allows 2D scrolling in any direction up to the boundary of the map, with the scrolling velocity and direction dependent on the absolute distance between the mouse-down and current cursor locations. The globe browser also allows 2D scrolling in any direction, with the underlying globe rotating under the user's cursor. In addition to the 'global view' of landmasses and oceans, the globe is populated with fifteen city maps that are represented as small coloured rectangles over each city's location in the global view. When the user moves slowly or stops over a city the view rapidly zooms into the underlying map details.

In all interfaces the cursor is warped to the centre of the screen when the user begins scrolling. A red-arrow connects the screen-centre with the current cursor location as the user drags the mouse. The arrow's direction shows the scrolling direction and the arrow's length depicts the scroll-speed.

The automatic zooming interfaces have a 'maximum falling rate' which rapidly animates the transition between zoomed-out and zoomed-in views. Without a maximum fall rate there is a highly disconcerting effect of 'slamming into the document' when the user stops scrolling by releasing the mouse button, or when reversing from rapid scrolling one direction to the other. All automatic zooming interfaces also supported a 'scroll-to-cursor' function, which rapidly brings the document region under the user's cursor to the screen centre when they stop scrolling

	Limits for automatic and manual zooming			Automatic zooming calibration of scroll speeds for various magnification levels						
	Max speed @100%	Min mag. %	Max speed @min mag	100%	75%	60%	50%	45%	25%	12.5%
Text (cm s^{-1})	48	12.5	170	0–48	57	–	67	–	100	118–170
Map (cm s^{-1})	10	12.5	80	0–10	20	–	30	–	40	50–80
Globe view (degrees s^{-1})	15	45	60	0–15	35	–	55	60	–	–
City view (minutes s^{-1})	5	60	25	0–5	–	15–25	–	–	–	–

Table 1: Speed and zoom calibration settings for the three interfaces with manual and automatic zooming.

(by releasing the mouse button). Prior to implementing this function we found that users would often release the mouse button when the zoomed-out target was under their cursor, only to have the target fall outside the viewable region when the view returned to full-zoom. We observed that trial users' eyes typically followed the cursor when scrolling and that they stopped scrolling when the cursor is over the target. The scroll-to-cursor function, therefore, brings the target to the screen centre through rapid animation. Issues associated with this function are discussed in Section 6.

The user's experience with zooming interfaces is strongly influenced by the precise calibration of the system's behaviour. This is particularly true of automatic zooming interfaces. To aid replication of our studies, exact details of the calibration settings for each of the interfaces (both manual and automatic zooming) are provided below and are summarized in Table 1. These values are based on theoretical and empirical analysis described by Savage [2004] and in Cockburn et al. [2005].

3.1 Text-browsing Interface

The text-browsing interface allows vertical document scrolling. Any Postscript or PDF document can be displayed, with the evaluations using a 157 Masters Thesis. On loading a document, each A4 page is converted into a 512×512 Targa Image File. Each page measured a true 21×27cm on the screen when rendered at 100% magnification on the displays used in the experiment.

Automatic and manual zooming both used a one-to-one relationship between vertical mouse displacement (in pixels) and resultant scroll-speed (in cm s^{-1}). Note that scroll-speeds are reported as document scroll-rates, rather than the rate that the pixels move across the screen-for example, at 50% magnification the document scroll-speed is twice the pixel movement rate.

In calibrating the behaviour of manual zooming, we were careful to make decisions that we felt would optimize its use. We were aware that leaving maximum velocities unconstrained at any particular zoom-level would allow pixel movement rates that exceed the capacity of the human smooth-pursuit visual system [Morgan & Benton 1989], yet we wanted to allow users to quickly accelerate to rapid document movement when zoomed out. Through informal experimentation with several trial users we decided to use five discrete zoom levels, activated through successive clicks of the 'a' (zoom in) and 'z' (zoom out) keys, each of which changed the magnification level by 17.5% between maximum and minimum zoom-levels of 100% and 12.5%. To reduce the disorienting effect of excessive scroll-speeds at each zoom-level, we applied maximum scrolling velocities at each zoom-level (in preliminary trials without the velocity caps several users complained of getting lost due to excessive speeds, particularly when 'backing up' after overshooting a target). Table 1 shows the maximum velocities at the 100% and 12.5% magnification levels. Maximum velocities for each of the four discrete magnification levels between 100% and 12.5% were determined by linear interpolation.

Calibration settings for the automatic zooming interface are also shown in Table 1. At speeds below 48cm s^{-1} the document remains at full-zoom, but smooth zooming is applied beyond 48cm s^{-1} through linear interpolation between the values shown. Between 118cm s^{-1} and the maximum speed of 170cm s^{-1}, the minimum zoom-level of 12.5% is applied.

3.2 Map-browsing Interface

The map-browsing interface allows 2D rate-based scrolling over a detailed city map. The underlying map scrolls smoothly in whatever direction the user drags the mouse. The map used in the evaluation was a street map of Christchurch, New Zealand, displayed at 5120×3072 pixels (360×216cm on the screen at 100% magnification).

The mapping between mouse-displacement and scroll-speed was identical for both manual and automatic zooming modes, with a linear relationship of speed (cm s^{-1}) = 0.4×displacement (pixels), up to a maximum displacement of 200 pixels (and consequently 80cm s^{-1}). The maximum map scroll-speed (80cm s^{-1}) is lower than the maximum text document scroll-speed (170cm s^{-1}) because the map continues to fill the display window at low zoom levels, while the text interface does not (Figure 1 shows that at low zoom levels the text window contains large blank regions).

Calibration of the manual zooming interface is similar to that of the document interface, with five discrete key-presses moving between full and minimum zoom levels of 100% and 12.5% respectively. Table 1 shows the maximum scroll-speeds at the full and minimum manual zoom levels. Linear interpolation is used to determine maximum speeds at each discrete intermediate zoom level.

The automatic zooming calibration settings are also shown in Table 1. Linear interpolation is used to allow smooth zooming with changes in scroll-rate.

3.3 Globe-browsing Interface

The globe-browsing interface is the most complex of the three due to its dual-view interaction of globe- and city-views. In the globe view, users can navigate around a globe representation of planet Earth, with rate-based scrolling causing the globe to rotate at an angular velocity proportional to the mouse-drag distance. Horizontal scrolling is unconstrained (the globe can endlessly rotate on its axis), but vertical scrolling is constrained to disallow rotation over the poles, without which the globe can be inverted, causing disorientation. Magnification levels in the globe view range from a minimum of 45%, showing the entire planet in a single window (see Figure 2), to 100%, which shows 20 degrees of arc at the equator in one window-width. The '100%' zoom level for the globe view was arbitrarily selected as the point at which further magnification of the images yields little benefit due to pixelation of the images.

The globe-browsing interface also supports a city view. Fifteen city maps are placed on the surface of the globe at a size of 2×1cm at 100% magnification on the displays used in the experiment. If the user slows or stops movement over one of the city maps, they zoom into a close view of the underlying map. The 'fall' into the city view is automatic when using automatic zooming, but is under explicit user control with manual zooming. Once in the city view, the system behaves similarly to the map interface (Section 3.2), except that dragging off the map 'snaps' back to the globe view with automatic zooming.

The relationship between mouse displacement and scroll-speed is different in the city and globe views. In the globe view there is a two-step relationship, allowing fine-control at slow speed and more coarse control at higher speeds: below 150 pixels displacement, scroll-speed (degrees s^{-1}) = $0.1 \times$ displacement (pixels); between 150 and 250 pixel displacement, scroll-speed = $-52.5 + 0.45 \times$ displacement. In the city view, a linear relationship applies up to a maximum displacement of 200 pixels, with scroll-speed (minutes s^{-1}) = $0.1 \times$ displacement.

With manual zooming there are five discrete zoom levels for the globe-view (between 100% and 45%) and a further five for the city-view (between 100% and 60%). Maximum scroll-speeds for the boundary conditions in both the globe and city views are shown in Table 1. Linear interpolation determines scroll-speeds for each of the intermediate zoom levels.

With automatic zooming, the zoom level is smoothly adapted to scroll-speed. Table 1 shows the relationship between speed and zoom in both the globe and city views. Linear interpolation is used between the values shown.

4   Experimental Details

The experiment is designed to answer two primary questions. First, does SDAZ (rate-based scrolling with automatic zooming) allow faster off-screen target acquisition than rate-based scrolling with manual zooming? Second, do users prefer SDAZ over rate-based scrolling with manual zooming and do they find it less cognitively challenging? We also scrutinize the accuracy of Fitts' Law in modelling user performance in zoom-based off-screen target acquisition.

The participants' tasks involved acquiring a target depicted by a red rectangle that was 2×2cm on the screen when displayed at 100% magnification. The direction to the target was continually cued by a green arrow at the window centre. In the globe interface, the final target was always placed within a city view and the city containing the target was highlighted red in the globe view. To complete the task, the user had to place the target, zoomed to 100%, under a cross in the window-centre and click the left mouse-button. Completing one task caused the next task to be generated, with the green arrow cueing the search direction. All user actions were continually logged by software.

It is important to note that these tasks do not require the user to extract and parse semantic information from the information space-rather, they mechanically 'chase' the red squares in the direction cued by the arrow, using rate-based scrolling plus either manual or automatic zooming. The decision to analyse mechanical interaction with the systems was intentional, as our prior work has already demonstrated that SDAZ better supports tasks that involve information seeking (although it did not investigate manual-zooming).

Thirty-five undergraduate Computer Science students (30 male, 5 female) took part in the experiment. All completed a questionnaire gathering background demographics regarding age, gender, dominant hand, and gaming experience. Training involved first watching a five minute demo of each of the three interfaces (text, map, and globe) in both zooming modes (automatic and manual zooming). They were explicitly instructed to combine scroll and zoom actions when using the manual-zooming interfaces. They were then given a few minutes to experiment with each zoom-type with each interface. Six practice tasks immediately proceeded each block of tasks with each interface and each zooming type. Data from the practice tasks were discarded. The order in which participants were exposed to each interface-type was controlled using a Latin square and order of exposure to automatic and manual zooming was alternated across participants. Both manual and automatic zooming tasks were completed with each interface type (text, map, globe) before proceeding to the next interface type. NASA-TLX worksheets [Hart & Staveland 1988] were administered by software after each block of tasks, with participants using 5-point Likert scales to report various workload measures. On completing all tasks with each interface-type, the participants stated whether they preferred automatic or manual zooming.

4.1 Experimental Design

The experiment is designed as a 2×6 repeated-measures analysis of variance (ANOVA) for factors zooming condition (automatic vs. manual) and distance. The same experimental design is used to analyse data from each of the three interface-types: text, map, and globe. The factor 'distance' determines how far the target is placed from the starting position, as follows for the three interface types:

- Text interface — 5, 10, 15, 20, 25 and 30 pages, where 1 page = 27cm.

- Map interface — 50, 100, 150, 200, 250 and 300cm.

- Globe interface — 4, 8, 16, 32, 64 and 128 degrees.

In the text and map interfaces, three tasks were completed at each distance with each zooming mode. In the globe interface two tasks were completed at each distance with each zooming mode. Therefore, including the six practice tasks, the tasks blocks consisted of 24 tasks with the text and map interfaces and 18 tasks with the globe interface. Two tasks blocks were created for each interface and the order that the blocks were used with each zooming condition was varied across participants.

To prevent extreme outliers, all acquisition times greater than the mean plus three standard deviations were removed from the analysis.

4.2 Apparatus

Participants used identical Athlon 1600+ computers with 256MB of RAM running Red Hat Linux 9.0, with Geforce 2 MX video cards outputting to 19-inch (36×27cm) Compaq monitors at 1280×1024 pixel resolution. Input was provided through three-button Logitech mice with sample rates of 60Hz. The default Red Hat Linux 9.0 control-display gain settings were used: acceleration 2/1 pixels, threshold 4 pixels.

5 Results

Although the participants were able to complete almost all tasks quickly, they sometimes became 'lost' in the information space, overshooting the target and failing to attend to the green arrow directing them toward the target. As planned, we discarded 'outlier' tasks that exceeded the mean by more than three standard deviations. In total, 4.5%, 0.3% and 0.8% of tasks were discarded with the text, map and globe interfaces respectively.

General observation of the participants indicated marked differences between the two zooming conditions, with much higher levels of concentration and physical activity when using manual zooming. These observations are supported by the analysis of NASA-TLX worksheets.

The following subsections present the analysis of variance of task completion times, then the Fitts' Law modelling investigation, followed by the analysis of subjective measures of workload and preference.

5.1 Comparative Performance Analysis

Automatic zooming showed a small but statistically significant performance advantage over manual zooming with both the text and map interfaces (see Figures 3a & b). Mean task times with the automatic and manual conditions for text tasks were 6.8 (standard deviation 2.0) and 7.1 (sd 2.0) seconds respectively ($F_{1,34} = 5.7$, $p < 0.05$) and for map tasks they were 5.6 (sd 1.7) and 6.2 (sd 2.0) seconds ($F_{1,34} = 15.8$, $p < 0.01$). Mean task times for automatic and manual zooming with the globe interface (Figure 3c) were similar at 10.9 (sd 2.2) and 11.1 (sd 2.3), yielding no significant difference ($F_{1,34} = 0.18$, $p = 0.7$).

As expected, there was a strongly reliable main effect for distance for all interfaces, but this simply confirms that tasks get harder as distance increases. More interestingly, while there was no interaction between factors zooming-condition and distance with the text and globe interfaces ($F_{5,170} < 1$ and $F_{5,170} = 1.9$, $p = 0.1$), there was an interaction with the map interface ($F_{5,170} = 5.4$, $p < 0.05$). The cause of the interaction is visible in Figure 3b, which shows that performance with automatic zooming degrades less quickly than manual zooming as distance increases, particularly at high distances.

5.2 Fitts' Law Analysis

In the Fitts' Law analysis we used linear regression to calculate the line of best fit for the relationship between movement time and 'Index of Difficulty' (see Section 2.1).

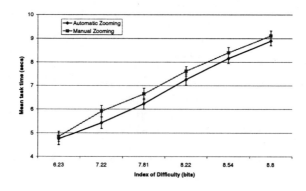

(a) Text interface

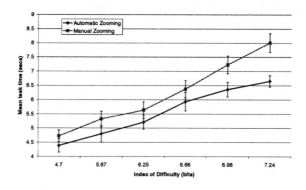

(b) Map interface

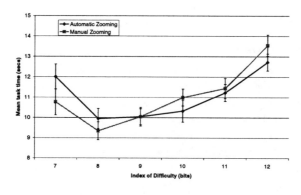

(c) Globe interface

Figure 3: Mean task times for the three interfaces with automatic and manual zooming across various index of difficulty values. Error bars show the mean ± one standard error.

Interface type	Zooming	Line of best fit	R^2	IP
Text	Automatic	MT = 1.62 ID – 5.82	0.92	0.62
	Manual	MT = 1.64 ID – 5.69	0.96	0.61
Map	Automatic	MT = 0.92 ID – 0.21	0.93	1.08
	Manual	MT = 1.23 ID – 1.44	0.82	0.82
Globe	Automatic	MT = 0.22 ID + 8.96	0.13	
(all tasks)	Manual	MT = 0.60 ID + 5.28	0.62	
Globe	Automatic	MT = 0.67 ID + 4.11	0.84	1.49
(7-bit tasks removed)	Manual	MT = 0.98 ID + 1.27	0.93	1.02

Table 2: Fitts' Law regression models for the three interface types with automatic and manual zooming.

Index of Difficulty (ID), is calculated as $ID = \log_2(A/W + 1)$, with W being the target size at 100% zoom (2×2cm or the equivalent number of minutes of arc in the globe-interface) and A being the total distance between the start and target locations at 100% zoom (in cm for text and maps and in minutes of arc for the globe-viewer).

Fitts' Law accurately modelled user performance with both zooming types (automatic and manual) in the text and map interfaces. Table 2 shows the lines of best fit and the R^2 values for each interface-type and zooming condition. The good linear fits (with more than 90% of variance explained by the model) is normal for Fitts' Law pointing studies and Hinckley et al.'s investigation of scrolling to off-screen targets (without zooming) showed R^2 values in excess of 0.8.

Although data for the globe viewer initially suggests poor modelling by Fitts' Law, subsequent analysis reveals a good model ($R^2 > 0.8$) once the shortest distance tasks (4 degrees, or $ID = 7$) are removed. The outlier poor performance with the short distance tasks is probably explained by a training effect from the majority of tasks: with the short-distance tasks, users would almost invariably overshoot their targets, snapping out of the city view and scrolling rapidly in the direction of the guiding arrow before realizing they had overshot the target.

5.3   *Subjective Measures*

The analyses above show a small performance advantage for automatic zooming over manual zooming. The subjective measures, however, reveal a large difference between the zooming conditions, confirming our informal observations that manual zooming demanded substantially more concentration and effort than automatic zooming.

The NASA-TLX worksheets divide workload into six categories: mental demand (concentration), physical demand (manipulation work), temporal demand (pace and time pressure), performance (self-sense of good performance), effort and frustration. Table 3 summarizes the results, measured from five-point Likert-scales, with 'better' interfaces producing lower values (low demands/effort/frustration or good performance). Automatic zooming uniformly received better mean scores, with all but two of the 18 metrics yielding significant differences (Wilcoxon matched-pairs tests). In particular, the high rating for 'Physical demand' with the manual

	Text Interface		Map Interface		Globe Interface	
	AZ	MZ	AZ	MZ	AZ	MZ
Mental Demand	2.3	2.9	2.3	2.9	2.7	3.2
	(1.1)	(1.0)	(1.0)	(1.0)	(1.0)	(0.9)
Physical Demand	2.2	3.7	2.1	3.6	2.6	3.9
	(0.8)	(0.8)	(0.9)	(1.0)	(0.9)	(0.9)
Temporal Demand	2.6	3.3	2.5	2.9	2.6	3.0
	(0.9)	✗ (0.9)	(1.0)	(0.9)	(1.0)	(1.0)
Performance	2.0	2.3	2.0	2.5	2.1	2.6
	(1.1)	(0.9)	(0.9)	(0.9)	(0.9)	(0.8)
Effort	2.6	3.3	2.5	3.1	2.9	3.4
	(0.9)	(0.9)	(1.0)	(1.1)	(0.9)	(0.9)
Frustration	2.3	2.7	2.5	2.8	2.6	3.4
	(1.0)	(1.2)	(1.1)	(1.0)	(1.0)	✗ (0.8)

Table 3: NASA-TLX workload measures for automatic zooming (AZ) and manual zooming (MZ) with the three interfaces. Mean (standard deviation) values shown, with lower values indicating lower workload or better performance. ✗ indicates not significant at $p < 0.05$.

zooming interface (3.7, 3.6 and 3.9 for text, map and globe browsing vs. 2.2, 2.1 and 2.6 with automatic zooming) supports our observations of heavy manipulation burdens arising from parallel bimanual input.

After completing all tasks with both zooming types for each interface type, the participants were asked to state which interface they preferred. In text tasks 27 preferred automatic zooming and 8 preferred manual ($\chi^2 = 9.3$, $p < 0.01$); in map tasks 26 preferred automatic zooming ($\chi^2 = 7.3$, $p < 0.01$); and in globe tasks 23 preferred automatic zooming vs. 12 preferring manual ($\chi^2 = 2.9$, $p < 0.1$).

6   Discussion

The results show that automatic zooming allows faster off-screen target acquisition than manual zooming with less cognitive and manipulation effort. Automatic zooming was also strongly preferred to manual control. Finally, the results confirm that Fitts' Law is a robust model for zooming-based off-screen target acquisition.

In designing the experiment we were careful to avoid experimental bias towards automatic zooming. We knew that by using Computer Science students as participants we were likely to have a high proportion of users who regularly play interactive computer games, which expose users to high rates of screen-based visual flow. We therefore collected background information on their gaming experience and used this to classify participants as 'gamers' or 'non-gamers' depending on whether they played interactive computer games for more than two hours per week. Through this scheme we divided our participant pool in sixteen gamers and seventeen non-gamers (nine of whom did not play games at all). We then compared gamer vs. non-gamer performance with automatic and manual zooming in a 2×2 mixed factors ANOVA. Gamers outperformed non-gamers with the text interface (means of 6.2 vs.

7.5 seconds, $F_{1,33} = 19.5$, $p < 0.01$) and with the map interface (means of 5.2 vs. 6.5, $F_{1,33} = 10.1$, $p < 0.01$), but not with the globe interface (means of 9.8 vs. 12.0, $F_{1,33} < 1$). Importantly, however, there were no significant interactions between gamer-type and zooming type with any of the interfaces, meaning that there is no evidence to support the hypothesis that gamers are better able to exploit automatic zooming than non-gamers. This suggests that the benefits of automatic zooming should be available to a wide group of users.

There is also one reason for suspecting that our experimental method produced artificially favourable results for manual zooming. In order to generate the 'best-case-scenario' of performance with manual zooming we explicitly instructed users to use parallel bimanual controls by simultaneously zooming with the keyboard and scrolling with the mouse. Several commercial interfaces allow this style of interaction, but we suspect that most users overlook the capability because of the higher cognitive and manipulation workloads they demand. If our participants had not used parallel controls for zoom and scroll then their workload assessments for manual zooming would almost certainly improve, but at the cost of worse performance due to serial manipulation of scroll and zoom.

Another obvious experimental concern is that the tasks involved 'chasing a red blob' rather than meaningfully extracting information from the underlying information space. Again, this experimental design decision was intentionally made to better cover the sample-space of our previous and on-going research; while our previous work has focused on realistic information-extraction tasks, this experiment focuses on best-case mechanics of interaction.

Finally, several participants reported an important interaction problem with 'hunting and overshooting' when using automatic zooming. One participant summarized the problem as 'playing ping-pong over the final target'. It seems that the problem was caused by the 'scroll to cursor' function described in Section 3, which brings the portion of the information space under the cursor to the centre of the screen when the user releases the mouse button. While this technique works well at high velocities (that is, when zoomed out), it appears to work poorly when scrolling slowly at full zoom. The participants seemed to naturally adapt to using scroll-to-cursor for approximate view pointing ('focus on the bit around here'), but they did not anticipate the same behaviour when scrolling at full-zoom. As a result, we believe that scroll-to-cursor should be disabled when scrolling at full-zoom.

7 Conclusions

Speed-dependent automatic zooming is an attractive interaction technique that automatically binds a document's zoom level with its scroll-speed. In order to further test the effectiveness of automatic zooming, this paper investigated whether users can benefit from de-coupling the automatic relationship between speed and zoom, allowing users the freedom to explicitly control each property concurrently.

Results of a thirty-five participant study showed that participants completed tasks more quickly with automatic zooming than with manual zooming, that the user's found automatic zooming less demanding and strongly preferable, and that the acquisition of off-screen targets is accurately modelled by Fitts' robust model, even when scrolling is combined with zooming.

There is now substantial evidence that speed-dependent automatic zooming allows users to navigate through documents more quickly and with less effort than traditional document navigation techniques. In our further work we will conduct field studies of how our mature automatic zooming interfaces are used in everyday office work.

References

Burr, D. [1980], Motion Smear, *Nature* **284**(13), 164–5.

Casalta, D., Guiard, Y. & Beaudouin-Lafon, M. [1999], Evaluating Two-handed Input Techniques: Rectangle Editing and Navigation, *in* M. E. Atwood (ed.), *CHI'99 Extended Abstracts of the Conference on Human Factors in Computing Systems*, ACM Press, pp.236–7.

Cockburn, A. & Savage, J. [2003], Comparing Speed-dependent Automatic Zooming with Traditional Scroll, Pan and Zoom Methods, *in* E. O'Neill, P. Palanque & P. Johnson (eds.), *People and Computers XVII: Designing for Society (Proceedings of HCI'03)*, Springer-Verlag, pp.87–102.

Cockburn, A., Savage, J. & Wallace, A. [2005], Tuning and Testing Scrolling Interfaces that Automatically Zoom, *in* G. van der Veer & C. Gale (eds.), *Proceedings of SIGCHI Conference on Human Factors in Computing Systems (CHI'05)*, ACM Press, pp.71–80.

Fitts, P. M. [1954], The Information Capacity of the Human Motor System in Controlling Amplitude of Movement, *Journal of Experimental Psychology* **47**(6), 381–91.

Guiard, Y., Beaudouin-Lafon, M., Bastin, J., Pasveer, D. & Zhai, S. [2004], View Size and Pointing Difficulty in Multi-Scale Navigation, *in* M. F. Costabile (ed.), *Proceedings of the Conference on Advanced Visual Interface (AVI2004)*, ACM Press, pp.117–24.

Hart, S. & Staveland, L. [1988], Development of NASA-TLX (Task Load Index): Results of Empirical and Theoretical Research, *in* P. Hancock & N. Meshkati (eds.), *Human Mental Workload*, North-Holland, pp.139–83.

Hinckley, K., Cutrell, E., Bathiche, S. & Muss, T. [2002], Quantitative Analysis of Scrolling Techniques, *in* D. Wixon (ed.), *Proceedings of SIGCHI Conference on Human Factors in Computing Systems: Changing our World, Changing Ourselves (CHI'02)*, *CHI Letters* **4**(1), ACM Press, pp.65–72.

Hinckley, K., Czerwinski, M. & Sinclair, M. [1998], Interaction and Modeling Techniques for Desktop Two-handed Input, *in* E. Mynatt & R. J. K. Jacob (eds.), *Proceedings of the 11th Annual ACM Symposium on User Interface Software and Technology, UIST'98*, ACM Press, pp.49–58.

Igarashi, T. & Hinckley, K. [2000], Speed-dependent Automatic Zooming for Browsing Large Documents, *in* M. Ackerman & K. Edwards (eds.), *Proceedings of the 13th Annual ACM Symposium on User Interface Software and Technology, UIST'00*, *CHI Letters* **2**(2), ACM Press, pp.139–48.

Leganchuk, A., Zhai, S. & Buxton, W. [1998], Manual and Cognitive Benefits of Two-handed Input: An Experimantal Study, *ACM Transactions on Computer–Human Interaction* **5**(4), 326–59.

MacKenzie, I. A. [1992], Movement Time Prediction in Human–Computer Interfaces, *in* N. Jaffe (ed.), *Proceedings of Graphics Interface '92*, Canadian Information Processing Society, pp.140–50.

Morgan, M. & Benton, S. [1989], Motion-deblurring in Human Vision, *Nature* **340**(6232), 385–6.

Savage, J. [2004], The Calibration and Evaluation of Speed-Dependent Automatic Zooming Interfaces, Master's thesis, University of Canterbury, Christchurch, New Zealand.

van Wijk, J. & Nuij, W. [2004], A Model for Smooth Viewing and Navigation of Large 2D Information Spaces, *IEEE Transactions on Visualization and Computer Graphics* **10**(4), 447–58.

Zhai, S. Smith, B. A. & Selker, T. [1997], Improving Browsing Performances: A Study of Four Input Devices for Scrolling and Pointing Tasks, *in* S. Howard, J. Hammond & G. K. Lindgaard (eds.), *Human–Computer Interaction — INTERACT '97: Proceedings of the Sixth IFIP Conference on Human–Computer Interaction*, Chapman & Hall, pp.286–92.

Forward and Backward Speech Skimming with the Elastic Audio Slider

Wolfgang Hürst, Tobias Lauer, Cédric Bürfent & Georg Götz

Institute of Computer Science, University of Freiburg,
Georges-Köhler-Allee 051, D-79110 Freiburg, Germany
Email: *{huerst,lauer,buerfent,ggoetz}@informatik.uni-freiburg.de*

In pursuit of the goal to make recorded speech as easy to skim as printed text, a variety of methods and user interfaces have been suggested in the literature, involving time-compressed audio, speech segmentation and recognition, etc. We propose a new user interface, the elastic audio slider, which makes navigation in speech documents similar to video navigation or text scrolling. The approach supports navigation at variable speed in both forward and backward direction while providing immediate intelligible audio feedback during the user's interactions. A user study was conducted to prove the usefulness of backward replay of speech for tasks such as topic classification. In addition, we show that the proposed interface offers the opportunity to combine the advantages of existing approaches within a single, easy-to-use UI component that complements and enhances the common user interfaces known from standard audio player software.

Keywords: speech skimming, elastic interfaces, audio slider, time-scaled audio, backward speech replay.

1 Introduction

In order to cope with the growing amount of digital audio available today, interaction techniques and interface designs are needed which make speech signals as easy to skim and navigate as textual documents. While research in this area dates back to (at least) the early 1990s (see for example Arons [1994]) common media players have only recently started to integrate techniques such as time-compressed replay in order to enable easier, interactive audio skimming. In addition, user interface designs are often still based on the well-known but insufficient tape recorder metaphor or on

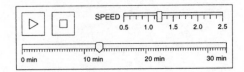

Figure 1: Exemplary illustration of a standard audio player interface design with start/stop buttons, speed controller (top right) and audio progress bar (bottom).

simple modifications of replay speed. Most standard interfaces feature, if at all, some sort of speed controller and an audio progress bar in combination with a slider interface for random access (cf. Figure 1). The slider on the progress bar can be used to set (or re-set) replay to any position within the file, e.g. in order to re-listen to some specific information. Modification of replay speed (*time-scaled replay*) using techniques such as SOLA [Roucos & Wilgus 1985] can be useful, e.g. to quickly skim over areas of minor interest or to locate specific parts with high relevance for some particular information need. Studies have shown that people are still able to understand the content of a speech recording (*intelligibility*) if it is replayed with up to 1.8 times the normal replay speed [He & Gupta 2001], and that they are able to classify the overall topic (*comprehension*) at replay speeds as high as 2.5 to 3 times normal replay [Arons 1997]. Slower than normal replay rates can be useful, e.g. if the speech recording is not in the user's native language [Amir et al. 2000].

While the interface design illustrated in Figure 1 improves audio skimming, there are a lot of situations where it is not comfortable or flexible enough and lacks usability. For example, assume a user wants to skim a longer radio news show recording in order to find some particular stock quotes or the latest soccer results. One reasonable search and interaction strategy for this task might be as follows: First, increase the replay rate to 2.5 times normal speed in order to skim the data and roughly identify the area of interest (e.g. the part of the news show containing business news or sports coverage, respectively). Once the overall topic has been found, decrease replay speed to 1.8 in order to find the data of interest (e.g. reports from the stock market or soccer games, respectively). If the searched position is found, audio replay is re-set to the beginning of the corresponding segment and replay speed must be reduced to normal replay again (or even slower, e.g. if it is necessary to listen to this part carefully or to take notes while listening). While such a search strategy can be performed with the interface illustrated in Figure 1, its design is clearly not optimal in terms of usability. First, the involved interactions require continuous changes between different interface elements: The speed controller is used to increase replay speed to 2.5, then to decrease it to 1.8. Then the slider is used to re-set replay to the beginning of the segment, before the speed controller is used again to decrease replay speed to normal replay (cf. Figure 2A). Secondly, re-setting audio replay to the beginning of a particular segment is not easy because users generally do not know the exact position and audio replay is normally muted while the slider thumb is being dragged. In general, moving back to re-listen to a particular part of an audio file is an essential task users often want or need to perform

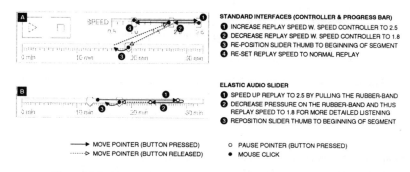

STANDARD INTERFACES (CONTROLLER & PROGRESS BAR)
❶ INCREASE REPLAY SPEED W. SPEED CONTROLLER TO 2.5
❷ DECREASE REPLAY SPEED W. SPEED CONTROLLER TO 1.8
❸ RE-POSITION SLIDER THUMB TO BEGINNING OF SEGMENT
❹ RE-SET REPLAY SPEED TO NORMAL REPLAY

ELASTIC AUDIO SLIDER
❶ SPEED UP REPLAY TO 2.5 BY PULLING THE RUBBER-BAND
❷ DECREASE PRESSURE ON THE RUBBER-BAND AND THUS
   REPLAY SPEED TO 1.8 FOR MORE DETAILED LISTENING
❸ REPOSITION SLIDER THUMB TO BEGINNING OF SEGMENT

⟶ MOVE POINTER (BUTTON PRESSED)   ○ PAUSE POINTER (BUTTON PRESSED)
⤏ MOVE POINTER (BUTTON RELEASED)   ● MOUSE CLICK

Figure 2: A typical example for interaction using different interface designs.

when skimming speech recordings because in many situations you only know that you found the correct position once you have already passed it. Especially if a file is replayed at higher speed, the need to re-set replay to a particular position after a point of interest was identified is very likely. However, few audio interfaces pay tribute to this demand.

It should be noted that the example just given oversimplifies the general course of interactions when skimming speech files in search for information. Normally, we can expect much more interaction to take place — e.g. repeated re-positioning of the slider thumb might be necessary in order to find the correct target position, as described above. In addition, if the topic has not been classified correctly in the first place, it may be necessary to speed up and slow down replay again. In the worst case, the user will end up switching several times between the speed controller and the progress bar, continuously re-setting replay speed and re-positioning the slider thumb until the target position has been found. Therefore, we can not and will not draw general conclusions from this simple example, but just use it in the following in order to illustrate the advantages and limitations of the different user interface approaches described. The goal of this paper is to introduce a new interface and interaction design for interactive audio skimming which is particularly useful for searching and navigating speech documents. The approach builds on our previous work which is summarized in Section 2 together with a general discussion of audio skimming. Section 3 describes how this approach can be extended to improve speech skimming, in particular when trying to move backwards in order to re-listen to some previously heard parts of a file. Section 4 reviews related works and puts them in relationship to our approach. Section 5 concludes the paper with a short summary and an outlook on future work.

2   Time-Scaled Forward Replay for Speech Skimming

Both speech and text have a linear dimension defined by the sequence of words spoken or written, respectively. However, speech is linear in time while text is arranged in a spatial dimension (i.e. left to right, top to bottom). This is the main reason why text is much easier to skim than a speech signal. Layout and meta-

Figure 3: Visualization of the elastic audio slider. The distance between the mouse pointer and the slider thumb (i.e. the 'force' on the 'rubber band') determines the replay speed.

information such as headlines, paragraphs, font styles (bold, italic, etc.), punctuation, etc., serve as visual cues which help the user in scanning the content. Comparable meta-information exists in speech: Speakers use intonation to make a point, pause before introducing a new topic, etc. In case of text, the speed at which the static visual information is processed and absorbed is under full control of the user (e.g. depending on how fast or slow the user's eyes move over the text), while in case of audio, this speed basically depends on the source of the sound signal. Not surprisingly, many approaches for audio skimming aim at making up for the time restriction implied in the audio signal by enabling the user to modify the replay speed, that is, by transferring the control over the replay speed from the system to the user. In addition, signal processing algorithms can be used to automatically extract *acoustic cues* similar to the visual cues from text. Advanced interface designs for audio skimming make use of these cues in order to facilitate navigation in the file. Several such interfaces have been introduced in the past which we will refer to in Section 4 where we relate them to our work.

The approach presented here is based on the intuitive assumption that a time-based progress bar or slider seems to be a good and natural choice for quick and easy navigation in an audio file since speech is linear in time. However, when a user is dragging the slider thumb along the time-line, audio feedback is generally muted or normal replay continues and is not re-set until the mouse button is released, that is, there is a lack of immediate feedback during the interaction. The reason for this is grounded in the nature of these signals. Digital speech (and digital audio in general) consists of a continuous sequence of individual *samples* which, if played in the correct order, make up the sounds representing the words and phrases. Therefore, just playing individual samples corresponding to certain positions on the progress bar while the slider thumb is being dragged would result in unintelligible audio feedback.

Generally there are two approaches in order to deal with this problem. One is to give up the strict synchronicity between the slider thumb position and the document progress and to always play a certain amount of successive samples (i.e. an intelligible piece of audio). Once the current audio snippet is finished, replay is set to the position of the thumb at that time and the next audio segment is played. The other approach is to restrict users in their options to move the thumb in such a way that intelligible audio feedback can be provided. Our initial tests with the first approach showed that it works quite well for rough topic classification of the whole document but might be problematic when searching for more detailed, specific information due to the resulting loss of synchronization between audio feedback and slider movements.

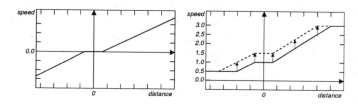

Figure 4: Left: distance-to-speed mapping in the elastic slider for visual scrolling. Right: redefined mapping for the elastic audio slider. The dashed line shows the modified mapping after the default speed was set to 1.5 times the normal speed.

The approach proposed here is based on the second idea, i.e. restricting the possibilities of the user to move the thumb (and therefore to navigate the file) in a way which still permits intelligible audio feedback. It is based on the concept of *elastic interfaces*, introduced by Masui et al. [1995] for visual data browsing of static data such as text or images. In this approach, the thumb of a slider or a scrollbar is not dragged directly but follows the mouse pointer along an imaginary 'rubber-band' tied between the mouse pointer and the thumb. The greater the distance between the two (i.e. the harder the band is stretched) the faster the thumb will move (see Figure 3). When it gets closer to the mouse pointer (e.g. because the user has stopped dragging), it will slow down as the 'force of the rubber-band' decreases, and eventually stop when it arrives at the pointer position.

Technically, the distance between the slider thumb and the mouse pointer is mapped to a speed value at which the document progress is displayed (see Figure 4, left). Thus, while sliders and scrollbars are interfaces for position-based navigation (since the slider position corresponds to a document position), they can be used for speed-based scrolling with the elastic interfaces approach. Masui et al. [1995] describe the usage of this concept for navigation of static, time-independent data, such as text or images. Hürst et al. [2004a] showed the viability and usefulness of the approach for dynamic visual documents such as video.

One interesting characteristic of an elastic slider is that the thumb movement is always 'smooth' in the sense that there are no sudden jumps. This is because the slider positions are not manipulated directly by the user but only implicitly via the speed changes resulting from the distance to the mouse pointer. This property makes it possible to use the concept of elastic interfaces in order to create a slider for audio navigation with immediate acoustic feedback while the thumb is being pulled along the time-line. However, transferring the concept from visual data to the audio domain requires some substantial modifications and considerations regarding both the actual realization and the resulting usability [Hürst et al. 2004b,c]. In the following, we summarize the final approach taken by us.

When transferring a concept for visual navigation to the audio domain, a first issue which should be considered is that the default output value (i.e. when the user is not dragging the slider) should not be paused audio (in analogy to a static frame in the visual domain) but replay at normal speed. Secondly, the range of possible speedup factors has to be restricted to values that make sense for time-scale modified speech. For example, it does not make sense to allow a replay rate of more than 3 times the normal speed, nor is it useful to play speech slower than half the normal rate. These constraints lead to a redefined mapping function which is shown in the right image of Figure 4.

The resulting interface (cf. Figure 2B) is used as follows: the slider thumb can still be grabbed directly and dragged as usual for quick navigation without acoustic feedback. The new functionality is evoked by pressing and holding down the mouse button on the slider bar anywhere next to the thumb (but not on it). A visualization of the elastic band between the thumb and the mouse pointer is shown, together with a label displaying the current speed (see Figure 3). Dragging to the right increases the speed, while moving to the left slows down replay, depending on the tension of the rubber-band. A neutral area around the slider thumb represents replay at normal speed. If the mouse pointer is dragged to the left of this area, playback is slowed down below the normal rate. Releasing the mouse button is equivalent to 'letting go' of the elastic band and reverts replay to normal speed instantly. The interface also features a standard speed controller interface element allowing users to set the replay speed to a preferred value. If it is adjusted to a speed faster or slower than normal, the elastic slider adapts to that value in the sense that it uses this speed as its new default value and speeds up or slows down from there, as illustrated in Figure 4 (dashed line). For a detailed description about individual design decisions together with a heuristic study leading to the final implementation of such an *elastic audio slider*, we refer to [Hürst et al. 2004c]. Transferring a successful method for visual data skimming to the acoustic domain might not be reasonable in terms of usability. Therefore, a usability study with the proposed interface design and a group of twelve test users was conducted, showing the feasibility and usefulness of the proposed approach [Hürst et al. 2004b].

Looking at our introductory example of searching for a specific news message in a recorded news show, the situation is much easier with the new interface in terms of usability. All interactions needed to find the target position can now be done using one single interface element, the elastic audio slider (cf. Figure 2B): Speedup to a high replay rate (for rough classification) can be done by dragging the elastic slider to the far right. If the overall topic is found, the speed can be reduced to a value allowing more detailed comprehension by moving the pointer closer to the slider thumb. Replay can be reset to the preferred rate by simply releasing the mouse button. Some test users in the evaluation explicitly noticed that being able to return to the default speed by just releasing the mouse button while skimming a file at higher speed is a very useful and convenient feature. In order to go back to the beginning of the paragraph after the relevant part has been found, users can grab the slider thumb and drag it back in exactly the same way as they would do with the standard interface. No switching from one UI component (the speed slider) to the other (the progress slider) is necessary because the elastic audio slider integrates speed-based and position-based audio navigation into a single UI component. Although the resulting interaction seems much easier and more fluid, the problem that a user has to re-set the slider thumb to an unknown position without any acoustic feedback still remains. This drawback is accompanied by an additional disadvantage, the *scaling problem*, see for example Hürst et al. [2004a]. In long documents, short backward (and forward) steps are often impossible to accomplish with a slider since even a very small distance (e.g. one pixel) on the slider bar corresponds to a large portion of the document. In order to resolve these problems and provide feedback for navigation in both directions, some sort of backward audio replay might be useful. This issue is addressed in the next section.

3   Backward Audio for Speech Skimming

Skimming and searching usually involves navigating through a document in both directions. For example, when scanning printed text in order to find some specific information, the layout may help find the respective paragraph, but in order to locate a particular sentence, users generally have to go back and forth within the actual text. In non-static visual documents such as video, fast-forward and backward is often used for search. A slider or scrollbar mapping the document length to the length of the slider bar allows navigation in both directions with full control over the speed if the screen display is updated in real time. It seems helpful and desirable to be able to do the same when searching and skimming recorded speech. In order to provide such a feature for both scrolling directions, some way of 'intelligible backward replay' needs to be realized.

3.1   *Approaches to Intelligible Backward Replay*

As has been stated in Section 2, audio is stretched over time and a certain continuity of the signal is necessary in order to obtain intelligible feedback. This is different from video, which — beside the temporal dimension — has a spatial distribution of information. Thus, playing a video sequence backwards frame by frame still allows viewers to extract information from it, while doing the same with audio, i.e. playing samples in reverse direction, results in meaningless sound. Even though this method may help in detecting pauses and distinguishing speech from non-speech, the only way to provide any kind of intelligible audio feedback when going backwards in a document is to preserve the original direction and continuity of the signal over at least a short period of time. This means that small snippets of audio must be played in forward direction, containing a segment of the speech long enough to make sense to the listener. (In text scanning, too, readers do not go backwards letter by letter or word by word, but use 'units' consisting of several words that are read at a time.) Following this approach, continuous backward replay can be realized as a sequence of audio segments played normally (i.e. in forward direction), but in reverse order of their occurrence in the document.

Several approaches to speech skimming have used this method in order to establish intelligible backward audio. Some systems, for example Arons [1997], try to partition the signal into meaningful segments consisting of words or phrases, which involves employing specialized algorithms. Others use fixed-length segments throughout the document, accepting fragmented speech within and between these segments. For example, Kim [2002] and Schmandt et al. [2002] use a fixed length of 4 seconds. Interestingly, none of the known systems providing this type of backward replay report on any empirical basis for their specific choice of the segment length, although this is a critical parameter: on the one hand, segments must be long enough to contain some complete words or phrases in order to ensure intelligibility; on the other hand, they should be as short as possible for a fine granularity of the backward steps. Furthermore, no more than anecdotal evidence is given as to how useful this kind of backward speech actually is, i.e. how well users perform in search or classification tasks.

3.2   User Study

In order to address some of these open questions, an empirical evaluation was conducted with the following twofold goal: the first objective was to test the overall suitability and usefulness of backward speech replay for the task of topic classification and thus to confirm the intuitive arguments claiming that backward replay of audio can be useful for search. The second one was to determine suitable values for some of the parameters involved. An approach with fixed-size segments was chosen, rather than using adaptive segment lengths resulting from partitioning the signal according to parts of speech. The two main parameters affecting the resulting signal in this approach are the duration s_l of each segment and the jump width s_j determining how much of the signal is skipped in each backward leap from the end of the segment just played to the beginning of the next segment to be played. Time-saving backward replay can be realized by increasing s_j to a value higher than $2s_l$. In this case, parts of the signal are omitted. (Conversely, if $s_j < 2s_l$, segments would overlap and some parts would be played twice.) The other straightforward way to allow faster backward replay is audio time-compression, in which case the speedup factor is the main parameter.

The study described in the following is a follow-up to an earlier evaluation presented in Hürst et al. [2005], where preliminary results are reported. The data discussed here is based on a larger number of participants, which is why the results are more reliable and an additional, more detailed analysis of the data could be carried out. 30 users, aged 16 to 61 (average 32.2), participated in this evaluation. Twelve of them were female, 18 male. 16 of the test subjects were students, the other 14 came from different professional backgrounds. No one had any previous experience with backward speech. The overall duration of the evaluation was 20 to 30 minutes per user.

The study was subdivided into three experiments, A, B, and C, which all had the same structure but tested different parameters. In experiment A, the independent variable was the segment duration s_l, while the jump width s_j was always set to be $2s_l$. The speech data consisted of news clips of 8 to 10 seconds in length, which were extracted from radio news messages. Each experiment contained two tests. First, users were asked to listen to the same audio clip several times with different values for s_l (in ascending order). In the test, the segment lengths 0.25, 0.5, 0.75, 1, 1.5, 2, 2.5, and 3 seconds were evaluated. Users listened to the backward clip with the particular segment length, and had to rate this specific value on a 5-point scale ranging from 'far too small' to 'far too large'. The participants could listen only once to each version and then had to give their judgement. Later changes on the judgements were possible, but no re-listening was permitted. Different speech files were assigned to different users, but each participant was given the same file for all parameter values during this test. The goal of this test was to identify a threshold value for the segment length at which replay would generally be agreed to be intelligible.

The second test of experiment A evaluated the same range of values for s_l, but now the goal was to see how users performed at the task of classifying the topic and contents of the different news clips. In this part, the values were given in random order. Participants listened to a news clip played backwards and then had to classify the contents based on a given list of topics. 20 different clips were extracted from 10 news messages about sports (3 about soccer, 3 about car racing, 2 about cycling, and 2 about other sports). The participants got a different clip for each value of the segment length. The mapping of clips to parameter values was equally distributed among the users. Participants were allowed to listen to each file only once and had to answer the questions immediately. No re-listening or later modification of the judgements was permitted in this test. Two detail levels for classification were offered: Users had the option to relate the clip to the actual news message it was extracted from (e.g. 'Lance Armstrong wins at Tour de France'), to select the overall topic (e.g. 'cycling'), or to give no classification if they were not able to classify the clip at all. In addition, they were asked to give the same subjective rating as in the first test.

Experiments B and C both tested some form of accelerated backward replay. Experiment B provided faster backward skimming through the omission of segments, as described above. Here, the jump width s_j (determining the amount of omitted material) was the parameter to be evaluated. Based on initial testing, the segment length s_l was fixed to 2 seconds for this test. Again, the participants performed two tests set up similarly as in experiment A. In this case the test started with the 'best' value, i.e. $s_j = 2$, $s_l = 4$ seconds (where no parts of the signals were omitted). Values for the jump width s_j increased in the first test (4, 4.5, 5, 5.5, 6 and 6.5 seconds), and were randomly ordered in the second one. User ratings were again done on a 5-point scale, this time ranging from 'very good' to 'very bad'. Experiment C provided an alternative way of faster backward skimming, using time-compressed audio replay. Hence, the speedup factor was the independent variable, with the following values being tested: 1, 1.25, 1.5, 1.75, 2 and 2.25 times normal replay speed. These values were chosen in order to achieve the same overall time savings as in experiment B, and the two experiments were set up in the exact same way. Again, a fixed segment length $s_l = 2$ seconds was used. In order to exclude possible learning effects resulting from the order of these two experiments, 50% of the participants started with experiment B, the others with experiment C.

Throughout the study, users were encouraged to make verbal comments. After completing the three experiments, the test subjects were interviewed and had to answer a short questionnaire. Although some users were rather sceptical about backward replay before the test, afterwards 80% agreed that it is a useful feature for speech skimming, and 29 out of 30 users thought backward audio could be a useful enhancement for skimming and searching audio-visual documents, e.g. video browsing. When asked about faster backward speech, 63% preferred time-

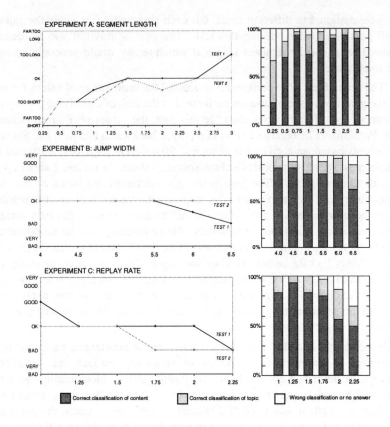

Figure 5: Results of the classification tasks in the three experiments.

compression, while 23% favoured the omission of segments. These preferences did not have any measurable influence on the classification task, where all users performed equally well.

The results of the subjective user judgements (median of all participants) for both tests of each experiment are illustrated in Figure 5 (left column). When comparing the outcomes of the two tests of each experiment, it is important to keep in mind that in the second tests the order of the parameter values was randomized to eliminate learning effects. Moreover, the users did not just listen to the file but had to solve an actual task. Therefore, the subjective judgements were expected to correspond to the users' perceived success in the task and thus be less regular than in the first tests, an assumption that is confirmed by the data. The rather large deviations found in the subjective user judgements were somewhat surprising. A closer look at the data showed that judgements varied both within one document between different users and between documents for a single user. This indicates that subjective perception of backward speech highly depends on the user as well as on the actual document.

The results of the second test of each experiment are illustrated in Figure 5 (right column). Users performed unexpectedly well in the classification task; even parameter values considered critical yielded predominantly correct results. For example, at a jump width of 6 seconds (i.e. 2 seconds of every 4-second block were omitted), 80% of the users were still able to identify the corresponding news message and another 17% were able to at least classify the overall topic. Performance with time-compressed audio decreased more obviously with higher values, but even at the highest rate of 2.25 times normal speed, half of the users were able to identify the corresponding news message. Thus, the most important finding is that the type of backward speech examined here does preserve enough intelligibility for users to classify the overall topic and, in a lot of cases, details of the contents. This is strong evidence that a proper integration of backward replay will enhance an audio skimming interface.

Considering the individual parameters, no clear trends or thresholds could be identified, except for the obvious findings that shorter segments, larger jump widths, and faster replay lead to a decrease in comprehension. This decrease is gradual for all three parameters; there is no sudden drop in intelligibility at any point. In the case of segment length, this finding did not match our expectation that a clear lower threshold value could be identified. However, it became apparent that rather short segments are sufficient for classification. Even at the lowest value of 250 ms (subjectively rated as 'far too short' by almost all participants), more than half of the users were still able to identify the overall topic correctly. Regarding faster backward skimming, the variant which omitted parts of the signal showed a slightly better performance than the version using time-compressed audio, although 63% of the users expressed a preference for the latter.

3.3   Backward Skimming with the Elastic Audio Slider

Considering the high classification performance and the positive user feedback, it makes sense to integrate this approach for backward replay into the elastic interface described in Section 2 and to provide audio feedback during scrolling in either direction. The findings of the study also suggest that either of the tested methods for faster backward replay could be used for implementing backward speech with interactively adjustable skimming speed.

The original interface prototype did not support backward skimming in its 'elastic' function: when the mouse was dragged to the left of the slider thumb, replay was slowed down below the default speed (with the elastic band acting as a 'brake') rather than reverted. This behaviour is useful for close listening (e.g. if the speech document is not in the user's native tongue) and still conforms to the rubber-band imagery. However, it may be counter-intuitive to users who want to navigate backwards while using the elastic slider.

This function can be replaced with our method to play audio backwards in the following way: when a user drags the mouse pointer to the left of the slider thumb, audio is set to backward replay, with the time-compression rate depending on the distance to between pointer and thumb just as in the forward scrolling scenario. The distance-to-speed mapping of the interface needs to be modified as illustrated in Figure 6 (left). The disadvantage in this approach is the complete loss of the option

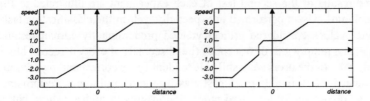

Figure 6: Redefined distance-to speed mappings. Left: backward replay replacing slower than normal speed. Right: backward replay plus slower than normal speed.

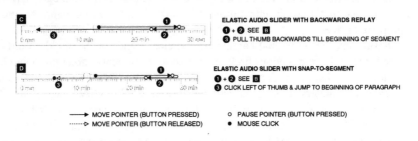

Figure 7: Example for navigation with (C) backwards audio and (D) snap-to-segment.

to scroll at a rate slower than the default speed. In order to preserve this function, we implemented a third variant including both time-stretched replay and backward replay. This, again, required a redefinition of the distance-to-speed mapping, which is shown in Figure 6 (right). Scrolling to the right still works as usual. When dragging to the left, replay first slows down until half the normal rate. If the user drags the mouse further to the left, backward replay is activated, starting with a low speed, which increases with the distance. First tests confirmed that this last approach seems to be the most useful one. The possible problem that the sudden change of replay direction might confuse the users was not confirmed, since an additional colouring of the backward region of the slider bar serves as an indicator and the label displaying the current speedup rate shows a negative number when scrolling backwards in the document. However, some more testing is required in order to establish the best parameter settings, particularly those for faster backward skimming, which could be realized in either of the methods mentioned above, or even by a combination of the two.

Backward speech replay further enhances the interface and facilitates skimming and search. In our example, once the user has detected the desired news message and wants to listen to it from the beginning, it is possible to navigate backwards while getting immediate audio feedback by simply dragging the elastic slider to the left (cf. Figure 7C). That way, the user is less likely to miss the beginning of the message and be forced to re-position the slider several times, as is often the case when no audio feedback is given.

4 Discussion

Throughout this paper we have used a simple but realistic type of interaction from a typical search task as an example to motivate our approach and to illustrate its advantages. Specific issues and individual parts of the proposed interface have been evaluated in separate studies in order to support our intuitive arguments, to show the feasibility of the overall approach, and to optimize its parameter settings. The example and the different evaluations showed that the elastic audio slider offers advantages in particular situations, especially when skimming a speech file in search for information. However, we do not claim that it is superior to other techniques in *all* situations and under all circumstances. Instead, we argue that it complements existing methods and thus a combination of approaches should be used in practice. In this section, we review related works on speech skimming and argue if and how it can be combined with the elastic audio slider interface.

As noted before, one additional approach to speech skimming is to locate acoustic cues in the sound signal in order to emulate the visual cues found in text documents. Such cues can be used to create a segmentation into sentences or phrases [Stifelman et al. 2001]. With this, advanced, more 'intelligent' navigation of a file can be supported using, e.g. simple interface elements, such as clickable 'jump to next / previous segment' icons [Arons 1997]. Such a segment-based navigation is particularly useful for search since it provides easy navigation in both directions.

Other approaches, including the one presented in this paper, enable faster replay of the speech signal in order to make up for the missing ability of the ear to 'skim over sound' in the same way as the eyes can quickly scan printed text. Such time-scaled replay can be offered to the user via simple controller-like interfaces (cf. Figure 1) or via more advanced approaches such as the elastic audio slider introduced in the previous sections. One of the main advantages of the latter is the ability to continuously move backwards in a file while still getting audio feedback. This type of backward skimming can have advantages compared to the segment-based backward jumps described before. Assume a situation where a user hears some stock quotes while skimming a file at high velocity. Instead of re-listening to the whole sentence or even the whole paragraph from the beginning, the user might just want to go back a few seconds to replay the respective numbers but not the whole sentence or even paragraph from its very beginning. On the other hand, there are situations where jumps to the beginning of the previous segment might be more suitable (e.g. if the user is not just interested in the actual stock quotes but also in some background information and therefore wants to listen to the whole paragraph). Hence, the ultimate question is how to integrate all these varieties of options and techniques into the user interface in the most beneficial way.

Maybe the most extensive and historically interesting work on user interface design for speech skimming is the SpeechSkimmer [Arons 1994, 1997]. The SpeechSkimmer incorporates time as well as content compression techniques by enabling replay modification in two dimensions, which is reflected in the layout of the interface. For content compression, parts of the speech signal are identified as less relevant based on automatic identification of pauses and intonation. Those parts are skipped during replay in order to increase replay speed. In the horizontal dimension of the interface, users can choose between different, discrete browsing levels where more or less parts of the speech signal are removed. Both forward and backward replay are supported. Within each level, replay speed can be adjusted continuously by moving a mark in the vertical dimension. Moving up or down this indication mark increases or decreases replay speed, respectively. Additional interface elements are provided, such as bookmark-based navigation along a time-line or buttons to jump to the previous or next segment. Segmentation is done, again, based on automatic pause detection and intonation analysis. When skimming a file a higher speed, one feature turned out to be particular useful: A 'jump & play' button allows a user to go back to the beginning of the current segment and to continue replay at normal replay speed. Therefore, the SpeechSkimmer interface design incorporates three different concepts for speech skimming: content-compression in the horizontal dimension, speed-modification in the vertical dimension, and navigation by jumping to distinguished positions (personal bookmarks, segment borders, etc.) using a time-line and an additional button field. One consequence of this richness of functions is the rather extensive layout of the SpeechSkimmer interface, making it difficult to integrate it into existing software implementations such as media players. (In fact, Arons [1997] suggests the use of a special hardware component developed specifically for the SpeechSkimmer.)

Content-compressed replay is a very good feature for quick classification of the overall content of a file or to find larger parts of one topic, but not necessarily for a detailed search for particular information, a situation in which the elastic audio slider unfolds its full strength. Modification of replay speed in the SpeechSkimmer is done in a similar way as with the controller interface element illustrated in Figure 1 (but with a different orientation, i.e. vertically instead of horizontally) which again, is useful and sufficient in many situations but lacks flexibility and power in others, as has already been argued in the previous sections. Segment-based navigation can complement the elastic slider in a useful and reasonable way, which is why we suggest the following extension to our interface, where segment-based navigation can be done with the elastic slider by clicking at random positions on the progress bar. The two common implementations for mouse clicks at a random position of the progress bar are *snap-to-tick* and *snap-to-click*. Snap-to-click sets the slider thumb (and thus, the document position) to the position of the mouse pointer. With snap-to-tick, the slider thumb jumps to the closest tick on the slider scale in the direction of the mouse pointer. The ticks are equidistant marks on the (linear) scale and, in the case of audio documents, usually represent units of time. However, if a segmentation of the audio file in meaningful units is available or can be calculated from the signal it is possible to use segment borders instead of ticks and thus to implement a *snap-to-segment* functionality: Here, the thumb jumps to the beginning of the previous or following segment depending if the pointer is left or right of the current thumb position, respectively, a behaviour that Stifelman et al. [2001] refer to as 'audio snap-to-grid'.

This feature allows users to skim a file with the elastic slider as outlined in the preceding sections or through a segment-based navigation by clicking continuously at random positions of the slider bar. Switching between both modes can easily be done, since both interaction types are integrated in one single interface. Based on the good results from Arons [1997] with the 'jump & play' button, we suggest that replay after a click should fall back to the user's pre-selected default speed. Which kind of segmentation is the best to use mainly depends on the data and the expected usage. For example, for highly structured data (such as news shows), a content-based segmentation might be useful (such as single news messages), while in case of single speaker files, pauses or the beginning of individual phrases and sentences can be a better choice.

Reconsidering the example used to illustrated and motivate the elastic audio slider, the situation becomes as follows: A user can quickly skim forward at a rather high speed, reduce replay speed in order to listen more carefully to the content, and then, once a part of particular interest is identified, go back using backwards skimming (cf. Figure 7C) or jump back to the beginning of, e.g. the respective news show message (cf. Figure 7D), depending on his aim to either just re-listen to the stock quotes or to the whole news message, respectively. The important issue here is that all these functionalities are integrated smoothly into the overall interface design, thus offering much more possibilities to the user while at the same time avoiding to overload the interface with additional interface elements and complicated interaction concepts. In fact, the basic design of the proposed interface is no different from the current, established layout of common audio and media players as illustrated in Figure 1, and aside from the snap-to-segment behaviour, all standard interactions offered by the original interface can still be used in the same way as before. Thus the elastic audio slider does not replace but complement common approaches in a reasonable and beneficial way.

5   Summary and Future Work

In the preceding sections we described a new interface design for interactive skimming of speech recordings. First, our previous work in this area was reviewed, describing its advantages, and identifying its limitations. Then, we presented an evaluation showing that backward replay of speech signals realized in a suitable fashion preserves enough of the intelligibility of the signal to be usable for speech skimming and we described how it can be integrated in the elastic audio slider interface. Finally, we related our work to other approaches and proposed an extension of the elastic slider which can further improve its usability.

Our first focus for future work is therefore the implementation and evaluation of the proposed extension of the interface. Other areas for further research include the question of how content compression can be integrated in a reasonable way. While we argued that content compression is not suitable when searching for detailed, particular information, Arons' work showed that it can be very useful for rough topic identification. Thus, it should be considered in the interface design, e.g. by an option to automatically eliminate or shorten longer pauses in the speech signal. In addition, the combination with approaches should be evaluated where not just meta-information and characteristics of the acoustic signal are presented in the interface but the actual content of the speech file, e.g. by generating a transcript of the spoken words using automatic speech recognition. Related work showed that this is offers great benefits if the ASR system produces transcripts of high word accuracy [Stark et al. 2000], but can even be useful when the transcripts are laden with errors [Vemuri et al. 2004]. Maybe the most interesting area for future research is the combination of our interface for acoustic skimming with visual data browsing, e.g. TV news show recordings where important information might be located in the acoustic signal as well as in the visual stream.

In addition to these extensions of the current interface design, its further evaluation in different scenarios is one of our key interests. The evaluations presented in this paper and the ones cited from our previous work proved the feasibility and usefulness of the approach. However, it will be very interesting to see how the elastic audio slider is used in actual, real-world scenarios. One area we are particularly interested in is to evaluate the interface with students who use lecture recordings for learning, e.g. when preparing for exams. We believe that the advanced navigation functionality and interactivity provided by the system will greatly improve the overall user experience and usability in this scenario.

References

Amir, A., Ponceleon, D., Blanchard, B., Petkovic, D., Srinivasan, S. & Cohen, G. [2000], Using Audio Time Scale Modification for Video Browsing, *in* R. H. Sprague, Jr. (ed.), *Proceedings of the 33rd Hawaii International Conference on System Sciences (HICSS-33)*, IEEE Computer Society Press, p.3046.

Arons, B. [1994], Interactively Skimming Speech, PhD thesis, MIT Media Lab.

Arons, B. [1997], SpeechSkimmer: A System for Interactively Skimming Recorded Speech, *ACM Transactions on Computer–Human Interaction* **4**(2), 3–38.

He, L. & Gupta, A. [2001], Exploring Benefits of Non-linear Time Compression, *in* N. D. Georganas & R. Popescu-Zeletin (eds.), *Proceedings of the Ninth ACM International Conference on Multimedia (Multimedia'01)*, ACM Press, pp.382–96.

Hürst, W., Götz, G. & Lauer, T. [2004a], New Methods for Visual Information Seeking through Video Browsing, *in* E. Banissi, K. Börner, C. Chen, M. Dastbaz, G. Clapworthy, A. Faiola, E. Izquierdo, C. Maple, J. Roberts, C. Moore, A. Ursyn & J. J. Zhang (eds.), *Proceedings of the Eight International Conference on Information Visualization (IV'04)*, IEEE Computer Society Press, pp.450–55.

Hürst, W., Lauer, T. & Bürfent, C. [2005], Playing Speech Backwards for Classification Tasks, *in Proceedings of IEEE International Conference on Multimedia & Expo (ICME'05)*, IEEE Computer Society Press. In press.

Hürst, W., Lauer, T. & Götz, G. [2004b], An Elastic Audio Slider for Interactive Speech Skimming, *in* A. Hyrskykari (ed.), *Proceedings of Third Nordic Conference on Human–Computer Interation (NordiCHI'04)*, ACM Press, pp.277–80.

Hürst, W., Lauer, T. & Götz, G. [2004c], Interactive Manipulation of Replay Speed While Listening to Speech Recordings, *in* D. Li, H. Schulzrinne & N. Dimitrova (eds.), *Proceedings of the Twelfth ACM International Conference on Multimedia (Multimedia'04)*, ACM Press, pp.488–91.

Kim, J. S. [2002], TattleTrail: An Archiving Voice Chat System for Mobile Users over Internet Protocol, Master's thesis, MIT.

Masui, T., Kashiwagi, K. & Borden IV, G. R. [1995], Elastic Graphical Interfaces for Precise Data Manipulation, *in* J. Miller, I. Katz, R. Mack & L. Marks (eds.), *Conference Companion of the CHI'95 Conference on Human Factors in Computing Systems*, ACM Press, pp.143–4.

Roucos, S. & Wilgus, A. [1985], High Quality Time-scale Modification for Speech, *in Proceedings of the IEEE International Conference on Acoustics, Speech, and Signal Processing (ICASSP'85)*, Vol. 2, IEEECSP, pp.493–6.

Schmandt, C., Kim, J. S., Lee, K., Vallejo, G. & Ackerman, M. [2002], Mediated Voice Communication via Mobile IP, *in* M. Beaudouin-Lafon (ed.), *Proceedings of the 15th Annual ACM Symposium on User Interface Software and Technology, UIST'02, CHI Letters* **4**(2), ACM Press, pp.141–50.

Stark, L., Whittaker, S. & Hirschberg, J. [2000], ASR Satisficing: The Effects of ASR Accuracy on Speech Retrieval, *in* B. Z. Yuan, T. Y. Huang & X. F. Tang (eds.), *Proceedings of the 6th International Conference of Spoken Language Processing (ICSLP2000/Interspeech 2000)*, China Military Friendship Publishers, pp.1069–72.

Stifelman, L., Arons, B. & Schmandt, C. [2001], The Audio Notebook. Paper and Pen Interaction with Structured Speech, *in* J. A. Jacko, A. Sears, M. Beaudouin-Lafon & R. J. K. Jacob (eds.), *Proceedings of SIGCHI Conference on Human Factors in Computing Systems (CHI'01)*, *CHI Letters* **3**(1), ACM Press, pp.182–9.

Vemuri, S., DeCamp, P., Vender, W. & Schmandt, C. [2004], Improving Speech Playback Using Time-Compression and Speech Recognition, *in* E. Dykstra-Erickson & M. Tscheligi (eds.), *Proceedings of SIGCHI Conference on Human Factors in Computing Systems (CHI'04)*, ACM Press, pp.295–302.

Design Patterns for Auditory Displays

C Frauenberger[†‡§], T Stockman[†], V Putz[§] & R Höldrich[§]

[†] *Department of Computer Science, Queen Mary University of London, Mile End Road, London E1 4NS, UK*

Email: *frauenberger@dcs.qmul.ac.uk, tonys@dcs.qmul.ac.uk*

URL: *http://www.dcs.qmul.ac.uk*

[‡] *Signal Processing and Speech Communication Laboratory, Graz University of Technology, Inffeldgasse 12, A-8010 Graz, Austria*

URL: *http://spsc.tugraz.at*

[§] *Institute of Electronic Music and Acoustics, University of Music and Dramatic Arts Graz, Inffeldgasse 10/3, A-8010 Graz, Austria*

Email: *v.putz@gmx.at, hoeldrich@iem.at*

URL: *http://iem.at*

This paper proposes the use of patterns in the design process for auditory displays and /or interfaces realized in other modalities. We introduce a meta-domain in which user interfaces can be designed using these patterns without determining their means of realization. The mode-independent description of such interfaces can then be used to create the real interface maintaining the strengths of the different interaction channels. While this work is focused on how this approach can be applied on auditory displays, we keep in mind that the approach shall be applicable on other interaction modalities equally. The development of a set of mode independent interaction patterns is shown along with descriptions of their representations in the auditory domain. A real world application was chosen to evaluate the approach; Microsoft Explorer was analysed, described through the mode independent interaction patterns

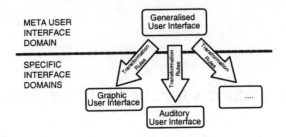

Figure 1: The meta domain as common ground for different representations of a user interface.

and transformed into the auditory domain making extensive use of 3D audio rendering techniques. The result, a file manager created in a virtual audio environment, was evaluated with sighted persons as well as visually impaired and blind participants showing the feasibility and usability of the approach.

Keywords: auditory displays, design patterns, virtual audio environments, assitive technology.

1 Introduction

The auditory mode in human-computer interaction is increasingly recognized as a strong and reliable channel of communication. However, the field is still very experimental, lacking widely accepted design principles and little is known about what makes good auditory displays. This paper proposes an approach towards establishing such design principles and guidelines for the auditory domain by adapting well known design methods from GUIs to other modalities. Doing so, however, we keep in mind that human senses are significantly different and interaction and information processing follows different rules — *"Many people get their auditory representations wrong because they think visually"* (anonymous paper reviewer). Therefore, we approach this problem field by introducing a common ground for user interfaces realized in different modalities: a mode-independent description of user interfaces that would determine the functionality without their means of realization. In such a meta-domain designers can use well known concepts like design patterns while their realization can maintain the particular strengths of each interaction channel. Figure 1 illustrates the approach.

We aim at developing design patterns that can be used to create user interfaces in the meta-domain and at providing tools and guidelines to create the real interfaces in the auditory domain. Although our work is focused on the audio mode, we develop concepts keeping in mind that they shall be usable with every other interaction channel equally. The design of multi-modal interface may also benefit from this approach, because it allows to split a user interface between modalities according to user interaction tasks.

The following sections describe in detail the motivation behind the approach and the state-of-the-art in auditory design and HCI design. Subsequently, section 2 describes the approach of using mode independent interaction patterns for the design of user interfaces, showing the way the patterns were developed and describing an example with an auditory realization of a pattern. Section 3 describes the evaluations conducted using this design method including the details of the test design, the evaluation and the analysis. Finally, we conclude this paper and state ideas for future work.

1.1 Motivation

Audio has been part of user interfaces since the very early days of computers and sounds were first deployed to indicate errors or warnings while processing a request. It was straight forward that sound is an appropriate way to alert users and the simple beeps used in such interfaces were about the same technical level as the graphical output at that time. Since then, the development of graphical user interfaces has been substantial, greatly outstripping the development effort and understanding of auditory interfaces. Currently audio is radically under used in human-computer interfaces, being still predominantly used to signal the occurrence of an error, or to draw the user's attention to the occurrence of a specific event. Sound remains largely unused as a fully integrated element of multimedia interfaces, and is little used in support of mainstream task performance.

The most important reasons to change this in the context of modern user interface design can be summarized by [Kramer 1994; Frauenberger et al. 2004a]:

- Increased complexity of tasks.

- Miniaturization of devices.

- Mobility of the user.

- Naturalness of interfaces.

- Accessibility for disabled users.

Many requirements for an improved user interface resulting from the points above can be achieved by auditory displays, whether sound is being used as an element of a multimedia interface or on its own as a single medium. To prevent user interfaces from being overloaded due to the complexity of tasks, multi-modal approaches can be utilized to exploit human sensory capabilities to their optimum. Auditory displays can be designed as virtual or augmented reality and do not require much physical space. Sound is also highly portable and integrable in mobile devices. Since audio is an important part of our every-day environment, the integration of audio clearly improves the naturalness in human-computer interaction. Finally, visually impaired users rely on non-visual modes to interact with the increasing number of information technologies integrated in our lives.

Past research has shown that audio is capable of contributing much more than beeps to user interfaces. There are, however, significant problems in understanding human methods of acoustic communication and how complex tasks in human-computer interaction can be rendered in the auditory domain. Many prototypes have been developed and evaluated and very satisfying solutions were created for specific problem statements. But as audio displays become more widespread, user interface designers must be provided with robust, but customizable patterns and design principles.

1.2 State of the Art

The increasing computational power available for digital signal processing made increasingly complex simulations of acoustical environments possible. The term *Virtual Audio Environment* describes the simulation of acoustical scenes with sound reproduction techniques. The goal is to create natural environments which are customizable and controllable in real time, very much as visual virtual environments were developed [Lokki 2002]. Acoustical rendering of objects (sound sources), the environment and the listener can be realized using a number of different techniques like Ambisonics [Bamford 1995], Wave Field Synthesis [Verheijen 1998] or Vector Based Amplitude Panning [Pulkki 1997]. These techniques were just recently utilized to realize auditory displays[Strauss et al. 2003; Frauenberger et al. 2004b].

While these techniques may provide accurate acoustical rendering there are still many questions about the human capability of auditory perception. A problem still subject of investigation is sound source segregation in virtual environments when rendering sound sources concurrently [McGookin & Brewster 2003], another one is providing robust orientation cues for navigation [Gröhn et al. 2003]. Further challenges result from complex psychoacoustic effects like informational masking which are not fully understood in the context of auditory displays [Oh & Lufti 1999].

A variety of auditory displays were developed for specific problem domains (e.g. [Kobayashi & Schmandt 1997; Schmandt 1998; Walker et al. 2001]) and some efforts were taken towards a structured approach to more generic solutions. Early proposals include the *Mercator* project, the first framework targeting customary Unix desktops [Edwards et al. 1993; Mynatt 1995]. Another proposal was *Y-Windows* also following the idea of building alternative, audio rendering engines (servers) for existing clients requesting their user interface representation [Kaltenbrunner 2002]. However, both approaches implied that graphical concepts were translated into the auditory domain and had therefore their limitations. A first attempt to break up with this and introducing a mode independent meta-domain was made in [Frauenberger et al. 2004a] and subsequently led to the proposal stated by this paper.

Attempts to use common HCI engineering methods in the design of auditory displays include the investigation of audio metaphors [Mynatt & Edwards 1995] and other structural approaches to include sound into human-computer interaction (Earcons [Blattner et al. 1989; Brewster 1994]). Recently, the proposal of using patterns in sonification highlights the advantages of such methods in re-usable designs [Barrass 2003; Adcock & Barrass 2004].

However, auditory representations of user interfaces are in need of profound heuristics to assess user satisfaction similar to those in the graphical domain [Nielsen 1993]. Examples of where work is needed to identify heuristics to guide the process of auditory display design include minimizing the problems incurred due to the transient nature of sound, quantifying how the effectiveness of interactions can be improved through learning and providing guidelines for how sound can best be integrated with other media [Kramer et al. 2005]. The design pattern approach is one of the most widespread and popular techniques for user interface design in the graphical domain[van Welie & Trætteberg 2000; Trætteberg 2000] and we believe that it is also suitable for the task given. The subsequent section will elaborate on the use of this technique in the context of mode-independent design.

2 Interaction Patterns

The concept of interaction patterns is well known in user interface design, but is very much focused on graphical interfaces and there are very different approaches to it available. Despite the fact that patterns are often created from the perspective of the programmer or designer, they also tend to be very specific to a certain problem domain. A more generalized approach that aimed at user-centred pattern design led to a set of patterns addressing the most common user requirements[van Welie & Trætteberg 2000]. These patterns are task-related and address different types of user requirements (e.g. the need to be able to locate specific commands and to find out how to activate them), based upon the most fundamental usability principles [Norman 1988]:

Availability: The required parts of the application need to be available at the right time and should imply correct usage. Availability[1] concerns the mapping between intended actions of the user and the operations actually required.

Affordances provide strong clues to the operation of things (e.g. knobs are for turning, buttons for pushing). When affordances are effectively used within an interface, the user knows what to do with no further instruction needed.

Constraints minimize the number of possible actions and give additional information about the correct usage of the interface elements.

Natural mapping: If the relationship between the controlling elements of an application and their results are natural for the user, it simplifies the learning of the application and assists recall. Natural mapping depends on physical analogies and cultural standards and is therefore subjective to different user groups.

Conceptual models: By interacting with an application, the user builds up a conceptual model of it. If this model is equivalent to the task model of the application, it allows the user to predict the effects of his actions.

Feedback: Information about the result of his actions is sent back to the user and enables immediate control of the input.

In order to re-formulate the chosen set of patterns from [van Welie & Trætteberg 2000] we slightly changed the terminology used: The *representation medium* means

---

[1]The term availability was chosen to replace visibility to avoid visual associations.

the domain or the combination of the domains in which the user interface will be realized. Within this representation medium there are *representation areas* defined which provide the boundary for *objects* of the user interface. These objects may result from one or more *interaction patterns* transformed into the representation medium.

2.1 Structure

While developing the patterns, we recognized that certain tasks or parts of patterns recurred in other patterns too. This led to the concept of atoms and contextual attributes; similar to a vocabulary for instantiating designs. A set of atoms was developed from which patterns may draw when addressing a particular set of user requirements. This also implies consistent representation of similar elementary units throughout the whole interface although atoms are not sufficient to solve any interaction problem. The name indicates that this level should be the smallest piece in any pattern to avoid over exaggerating modularity.

In order Not to end with a totally unrelated patchwork of small pieces of a user interface, each atom provides contextual attributes. These attributes need to be set by the parent pattern in order to indicate their context. In the graphical domain this would, for example, mean that certain elements like buttons or text fields are *in the same window* sharing the same frame and background colour. The following contextual attributes were identified for our set of atoms:

Similarity: Atoms in the same pattern share properties like timbre, rhythm or type of voice in their acoustical representation.

Proximity: Atoms in the same pattern are grouped together based on the available dimensions of the representation area (space or pitch ranges).

Homogeneity: The same types of atoms should be placed adjacently in a pattern on the basis of the available dimensions of the representation area (space or pitch ranges).

It is important to state that not only the patterns and the atoms undergo the transformation process in order to form a real user interface, but also the contextual attributes must be mapped into the different representation media. Their realization in the auditory domain will differ considerably from the visual domain.

2.2 The Patterns

Each pattern consists of a description of the related *user-problem*, a listing of further *conditions* which must be fulfilled to solve the problem, a possible *solution* for the problem and a listing of the *attributes* which must be mapped. Figure 2 shows how those descriptions were made (example taken from [Putz 2004]).

Similar descriptions were made for all patterns from [van Welie & Trætteberg 2000] (Command area, Wizard, Contextual menus, Mode cursor, Setting attributes, Link in the real world, List browser, Continuous filter, Preview, Navigating categories, Container navigation, Unambiguous format, Focus / Selection, Grouping layout, Progress, Hinting, Message / Warning, Shield, Preferences, Favourites).

Command Area	
Problem	**The user needs to know where to find the possible commands and how to activate them.**
Conditions	• Immediate access to all available functions increases interaction speed but consumes a large amount of the available representation area. • The main working area should be kept as large as possible. • Concurrent representation of many objects increases the cognitive load. • Some functions are used more often then other functions. • Some functions need additional parameters to be set by the user before they can be executed.
Solutions	**Put the shortcuts to the possible commands in a specific recognisable area** A part of the representation area is reserved for shortcuts to the functions of the application. This area should be distinguishable from other working areas because of contextual attributes. If the number of shortcuts is large, they should be conceptually grouped. The command area can be subdivided to give access to a group of commands. The command area and the included shortcuts should be accessible as direct as possible, especially frequently used shortcuts. Feedback information about the availability of the shortcuts can be given. The number of represented functions should not be too large to limit the necessary representational area and the cognitive load.
Attributes	• Atoms for the representation of the shortcuts (Links, Triggering Elements, Selections). • Separation of groups, when conceptual grouping is required
Graphical Example: Command Area of MATLAB 6.5	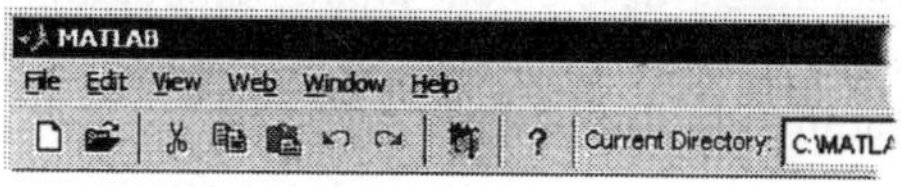

Figure 2: An example of a pattern description.

Besides the example of a visual realization given in the description, auditory representations were developed for the patterns needed in the prototype.

To illustrate such an auditory representation, the *Command Area* pattern is used. It is addressed to solve the following interaction problem: The user needs to know where to find the possible commands and how to activate them. When solving this problem, several further conditions have to be taken into account:

1. Immediate access to all available functions of the application increases interaction speed but consumes a large amount of the available representation area.

2. The amount of the remaining representational media space for the main working area should be kept as large as possible.

3. Concurrent representation of many objects increases the cognitive load.

4. Some functions are used more often then other functions.

Menu headers

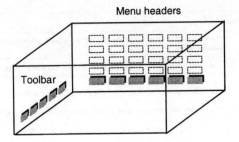

Figure 3: The layout of the auditory representation of the Command Array pattern.

5. Some functions need additional parameters to be set by the user before they can be executed.

The solution describes the creation of a recognizable area in the representation medium which contains shortcuts to important functions of the applications and a menu. The shortcuts exploit affordances to indicate the usage and use metaphors (natural mapping) to save representation space. Atoms used by the pattern are the link atom and the triggering element atom. The atoms will be connected to the pattern by similarity attributes and triggering elements will be grouped together, if necessary, in meaningful sub-groups (e.g. for a menu).

Transforming this interaction pattern to the auditory domain was performed for our evaluation test described in Section 3. The two main parts — the menu headers and the toolbar — are situated alongside two different walls of the virtual room as shown in Figure 3.

The triggering elements of the toolbar are presented with short rhythmic patterns (Earcons). The toolbar elements are connected by proximity and homogeneity with regard to space and similarity with regard to the sound design. The menu headers are presented as combination of speech and instrumental sound presented concurrently. The name of each menu item is spoken accompanied by an unobtrusive sound with rising pitch, starting with lowest pitch at the first header item and increasing in pitch while moving towards the last one. The menu headers are connected by proximity and homogeneity with regard to space and pitch and by similarity with regard to the compound sound design (speech and instrumental tone). The sub menu items belonging to the menu headers are placed above the headers within the virtual room also providing compound sounds.

3   Evaluation

For evaluation purposes a real world application was chosen and analysed. Its user interface was described through the mode independent interaction patterns and then transformed to the auditory domain. As one of the key applications on a computer desktop a file manager was chosen — the Microsoft Windows Explorer.

File	Edit	View	Favourites	?
New Folder	Undo	Statusbar	www.iem.at	Information
Delete	Cut	List	www.orf.at	Support
Rename	Copy	Details	www.google.com	
Properties	Paste	Sort		
Close	Select All	Change To		
		Reload		

Figure 4: Implemented functions of the auditory Explorer version.

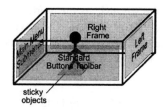

Figure 5: The virtual audio environment for the explorer.

3.1 Prototype Design

For testing, the complexity of the application was reduced, rarely used functions were not implemented. The remaining menu structure is shown in Figure 4. It still covers the basic functionality of a file manager.

From the standard buttons toolbar, five shortcuts were implemented: Undo, Delete, Cut, Copy, Paste. Through the context menu the functions Cut, Copy, Delete, Rename and Properties were available.

The functions described of the Explorer application was analysed and interaction patterns were identified. The *Container Navigation* pattern was used to describe the two main frames of the Explorer. For the folder tree in the left frame the *tree structure* atom was used and the *list* atom described the right content frame. The *Command Area* pattern described the menu structure and the tool bar area. Finally, the *Contextual Menu* pattern solved the availability of the context menu and the *Message* pattern was used for all pop-up windows at their occurrence. Figure 5 shows the basic layout of the virtual audio environment into which the patterns were transformed.

The container navigation pattern was transformed into the auditory domain as two different areas in the virtual environment, the walls to the front and to the right. The list at the front wall was stretching out to the top using speech for the name of the items with different voices to indicate the type (folder or file). The tree structure was laid out on a grid on the wall to the right with the left-bottom corner being the root and the right-top corner the last hierarchical level. Unfolding and folding a node in the tree was also implemented. In both areas the user was able to select items and get a context menu. The contextual pattern was realized as sticky objects following the user wherever she moves. The content of the contextual menu pattern was again solved by triggering elements. The same concept was used to realize pop-up windows — sticky objects remaining to the front of the user, but with different background sound. The menu and toolbar was realized as shown in the example described above.

All sounds were audible when the user moved into their range. This means that there was silence in the starting position, but moving towards a wall meant that one could hear the 5 menu items at once at different levels depending on the distance.

Interaction with the prototype was done by joystick and keyboard. To avoid confusion while navigating through the virtual environment no relative movements are supported. Bringing the joystick to the starting position means moving to the centre of the room facing the front wall. Moving up, along the z-axis, in the environment was implemented using the throttle handle of the joystick. The localization of different sound sources was improved by using a head tracker.

3.2 Implementation

The prototype was implemented using Pure Data (PD) by Miller Puckette and the binaural Ambsonics library extension for PD developed at the Institute of Electronic Music and Acoustics Graz [Noisternig et al. 2003b,a]. This extension allows the simulation of virtual audio environments with binaural Ambisonics of 3rd order and room acoustics including reflections and late reverberation. Multiple sound sources may be placed in such an environment and will be rendered efficiently for headphones in real time allowing interaction with joysticks, head-trackers or other feedback devices.

The content of the hard disk was faked in order to keep complexity low and not to introduce additional problems for the prototype interacting with the operating system.

3.3 Test Design

The test was performed by a group of 15 test participants divided into two groups. Group S were seven students of the Graz University of Technology and one person already holding a masters degree. All of them were between 20 and 27 years old and had good experience with computers and Windows. Group B consisted of four persons who are totally blind and three persons with visual disabilities. The use of visual screens was only feasible for them using additional magnification software. Six participants in Group B hold the ECDL (European Computer Driving License) and use a computer in their work being very experienced with Windows software. One member had little experience with computers, but was attending the course for receiving the ECDL. In average Group B was a little older.

After instruction, the participants got 15minutes of training time with the application, participants were given a list of 7 tasks to perform. The tasks involved finding out how many files are in a specific folder, finding the size of files, copying, moving and creating files or folders.

Throughout the test, different types of data were collected. On the one hand, the hierarchic structure of files and folders after the test is stored in a text file. Apart from that, two further lists report the whole test sequence, one list containing the movement of the joystick within the virtual room (x,y,z-coordinates, rotation around

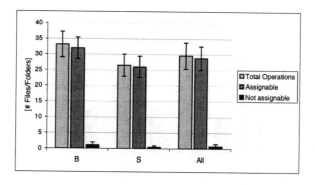

Figure 6: Number of file/folder handling operations

the z-axis) in a resolution of 50ms, the other list reporting any action performed by the participants with a time index, so that both lists can be combined. With these two lists, the whole test performance of the participants can be reproduced and visualized. The list of reported events can also be used to compute the quantity of different events. Apart from that, the whole performance of the participants was attended by the test administrator via headphones who additionally took notes.

After the test, the participants had to answer two questionnaires. One concerning the individual background of the participants, the other trying to catch the subjective impression of the participants after the test.

3.4 Analysis

The three-dimensional layout of the virtual room with the different meanings of the four surrounding walls and the two-staged movement (ground-plane movement towards the walls, vertical movement for selection) proved to be sufficient to host the elements of a real-world application. On the ground floor, at least 20 items (5 on each wall) can be placed, not to mention the potential with regard to vertical placement. The thematic grouping of elements on the different walls was easy to memorize for the test users. The usability of the mappings of particular interaction patterns is different. While the menu structure was easy to use for most test participants, the representation of the folder hierarchy is in need for improvement: Hardly any test user had a clear overview of the file and folder structure. According to the participants the static grid layout was confusing because they lost track of the absolute position while navigating through the tree structure. This was fostered by the fact that hardly anyone could re-construct the file structure correctly after the test.

Remarkable is the percentage of user operations on items which are not related to the task, which were performed by mistake. Figure 6 shows that Group B (the blind user group) required slightly more file handling operations to fulfil the tasks than Group S (normal sighted user group). Hardly any file or folder was selected by mistake, the percentage of selected files that can be assigned to one of the tasks lies between 97% and 98% for all groups. The same was observed with menu selections.

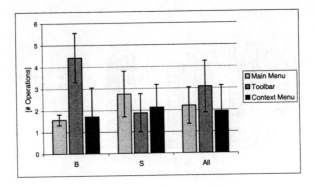

Figure 7: Usage of different menus

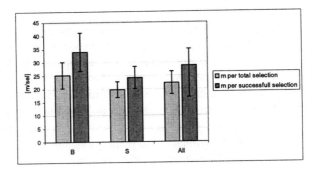

Figure 8: Covered distance per selection

Group B needed slightly more menu operations, but no single user chose a menu item not related to the task he was performing.

Throughout the whole test, the participants were free to choose how to fulfil the tasks: With the aid of the main menu, the standard buttons toolbar or the context menu. Figure 7 shows, which option was preferred by the two groups. Group B had a clear preference for the toolbar, whilst Group S had a slight preference for the main menu. The usage of the context menu is similar for the group averages. The standard deviation is high for all values.

The virtual distance covered by the participants for one successful selection of an item shows that it lies within the dimension of the virtual room (10m x 14m and 12m high = 26m diagonal). Again it is slightly more for Group B, but also lies within the standard deviation (Figure 8). These measures are comparable with mouse movements in graphical interfaces although no comparable data was collected for the graphical Explorer application.

In general, the subjective questionnaire showed that the users liked the system and felt comfortable to solve the problems given. The sound design was chosen to be as non-obtrusive as possible and the silent centre position was appreciated.

The main goal of the application was to have equal usability for blind and sighted users. With regard to the main performance measurements (total test time, necessary file/folder handling operations, necessary menu handling operations, working speed and the percentage of correct results), the two groups of users have reached similar results, although there is a high standard deviation for some values.

4 Conclusions

This paper proposed a set of mode independent interaction patterns for designing user interfaces in different interaction domains. The approach was chosen to overcome the difficulties of translating existing user interfaces into other domains like GUIs into auditory displays. The idea behind the patterns and their structure were explained followed by an evaluation of a real world application. The existing graphical user interface of this application was analysed, described through the proposed set of interaction patterns and transformed into the auditory domain.

The evaluation showed that the approach is feasible and promising for establishing design principles for auditory displays. Both groups of test participants, blind and normal sighted persons, were able to use the application with equal efficiency. All participants reported that they felt comfortable and could imagine to work with a similar system in their real working environments.

Problems remained with some of the representations where either sound design or the idea of representation was weak. However, having the user interface built from patterns and atoms, it is possible to isolate the problems and improve the transformation of the single item instead of re-designing the whole interface.

Future work needs to look closer into the mechanisms of acoustic communication considering psychoacoustics, learning effects, mental load and cross modal interactions. The patterns need to be revised and improved in their acoustical representation and more flexible frameworks must be developed in order to ease the integration of auditory displays into customary computing systems.

5 Acknowledgements

We would like to thank all who volunteered to participate in the evaluation. Especially the people from the ISIS group (Integration, Service, Information and Schooling) in Graz / Austria for the close collaboration and for giving us an idea about the needs the visually impaired have when it comes to computers. ISIS is a project run by BFI (Berufsförderungsinstitut) Styria.

Support by the SonEnvir (http://sonenvir.at) project sponsored by the Zukunftsfonds Steiermark is gratefully acknowledged.

References

Adcock, M. & Barrass, S. [2004], Cultivating Design Patterns for Auditory Displays, *in* S. Barrass & P. Vickers (eds.), *Proceedings of the International Conference on Auditory Display (ICAD'04)*, International Community for Auditory Displays. Proceedings will be online via http://www.icad.org/.

Bamford, J. S. [1995], An Analysis of Ambisonic Sound Systems of First and Second Order, Master's thesis, University of Waterloo. http://audiolab.uwaterloo.ca/~jeffb/thesis/thesis.html.

Barrass, S. [2003], Sonification Design Patterns, *in* E. Brazil & B. Shinn-Cunningham (eds.), *Proceedings of the International Conference on Auditory Display (ICAD'03)*, Boston University Publications for International Community for Auditory Displays, pp.170–5. http://www.icad.org/websiteV2.0/Conferences/ICAD2003/paper/42 Barrass.pdf.

Blattner, M. M., Sumikawa, D. A. & Greenberg, R. M. [1989], Earcons and Icons: Their Structure and Common Design Principles, *Human–Computer Interaction* **4**(1), 11–44.

Brewster, S. A. [1994], Providing a Structured Method for Integrating Non-speech Audio into Human–Computer Interfaces, PhD thesis, University of York, England, UK.

Edwards, W. K., Mynatt, E. D. & Rodriguez, T. [1993], The Mercator Project: A Nonvisual Interface to the X Window System, *The X Resource* **7**(summer).

Frauenberger, C., Höldrich, R. & de Campo, A. [2004a], A Generic, Semantically Based Design Approach for Spatial Auditory Computer Displays, *in* S. Barrass & P. Vickers (eds.), *Proceedings of the International Conference on Auditory Display (ICAD'04)*, International Community for Auditory Displays. Proceedings will be online via http://www.icad.org/.

Frauenberger, C., Putz, V. & Höldrich, R. [2004b], Spatial Auditory Displays — A Study on the Use of Virtual Audio Environments as Interfaces for Users with Visual Disabilities, *in* G. Evangelista (ed.), *Proceedings of the Seventh International Conference on Digital Audio Effects (DAFx04)*, Universita degli Studi di Napoli Federico II, pp.384–9.

Gröhn, M., Lokki, T. & Takala, T. [2003], Comparison of Auditory, Visual and Audio-Visual Navigation in a 3D Space, *in* E. Brazil & B. Shinn-Cunningham (eds.), *Proceedings of the International Conference on Auditory Display (ICAD'03)*, Boston University Publications for International Community for Auditory Displays, pp.200–3. http://www.icad.org/websiteV2.0/Conferences/ICAD2003/paper/49 Grohn.pdf.

Kaltenbrunner, M. [2002], Y-Windows: Proposal for a Standard AUI Environment, *in* R. Nakatsy & H. Kawahara (eds.), *Proceedings of the International Conference on Auditory Display (ICAD'02)*, Advanced Telecommunications Research Institute (ATR) for International Community for Auditory Displays, pp.154–8. http://www.icad.org/websiteV2.0/Conferences/ICAD2002/proceedings/74_Kaltenbrunner.pdf.

Kobayashi, M. & Schmandt, C. [1997], Dynamic Soundscape: Mapping Time to Space for Audio Browsing, *in* S. Pemberton (ed.), *Proceedings of the SIGCHI Conference on Human Factors in Computing Systems (CHI'97)*, ACM Press, pp.194–201.

Kramer, G. (ed.) [1994], *Auditory Display: Sonification, Audification, and Auditory Interfaces*, Vol. 18 of *Santa Fe Institute Studies in the Sciences of Complexity*, Addison–Wesley.

Kramer, G., Walker, B., Bonebright, T., Cook, P., Flowers, J., Miner, N. & Neuhoff, J. [2005], Sonification Report: Status of the Field and Research Agenda, http://www.icad.org/websiteV2.0/References/nsf.html.

Lokki, T. [2002], Creating Interactive Virtual Auditory Environments, *IEEE Computer Graphics and Applications, special issue "Virtual Worlds, Real Sounds* 22(4), 49–57. Electronic publication http://www.computer.org/cga/.

McGookin, D. K. & Brewster, S. [2003], An Investigation into the Identification of Concurrently Presented Earcons, *in* E. Brazil & B. Shinn-Cunningham (eds.), *Proceedings of the International Conference on Auditory Display (ICAD'03)*, Boston University Publications for International Community for Auditory Displays, pp.42–6. http://www.icad.org/websiteV2.0/Conferences/ICAD2003/paper/10 McGookin.pdf.

Mynatt, E. [1995], Transforming Graphical Interfaces into Auditory Interfaces, PhD thesis, Georgia Institute of Technology.

Mynatt, E. D. & Edwards, W. K. [1995], Metaphors for Nonvisual Computing, *in* W. K. Edwards (ed.), *Extraordinary Human–Computer Interaction*, Cambridge University Press, pp.201–20.

Nielsen, J. [1993], *Usability Engineering*, Academic Press.

Noisternig, M., Höldrich, R., Musil, T. & Sontacchi, A. [2003a], A 3D Ambisonic based Binaural Sound Reproduction System, *in Proceedings of the AES 24th International Conference: Multichannel Audio, The New Reality*, Audio Engineering Society.

Noisternig, M., Musil, T., Sontacchi, A. & Höldrich, R. [2003b], 3D Binaural Sound Reproduction using a Virtual Ambisonic Approach, *in Proceedings of the 2003 IEEE International Symposium on Virtual Environments, Human–Computer Interfaces and Measurement Systems (VECIMS'03)*, IEEE Publications, pp.174–8.

Norman, D. A. [1988], *The Psychology of Everyday Things*, Basic Books.

Oh, E. L. & Lufti, R. A. [1999], Informational Masking by Everyday Sounds, *Journal of the Acoustical Society of America* 6(106), 3521–8.

Pulkki, V. [1997], Virtual Sound Source Positioning Using Vector Base Amplitude Panning, *Journal of the Audio Engineering Society* 45(6), 456–66.

Putz, V. [2004], Spatial Auditory User Interfaces, Master's thesis, Institute of Electronic Music and Acoustics, University of Music and Dramatic Arts Graz. http://iem.at/projekte/dsp/spatial/dp_putz.

Schmandt, C. [1998], Audio Hallway: A Virtual Acoustic Environment for Browsing, *in* M. E. Atwood, C.-M. Karat, A. Lund, J. Coutaz & J. Karat (eds.), *Proceedings of the SIGCHI Conference on Human Factors in Computing Systems (CHI'98)*, ACM Press, pp.163–70.

Strauss, M., Höldrich, R. & Sontacchi, A. [2003], A Spatial Audio Interface for Desktop Applications, *in Proceedings of the AES 24th International Conference: Multichannel Audio, The New Reality*, Audio Engineering Society.

Trætteberg, H. [2000], Model Based Design Patterns, Unpublished position paper given at CHI'00.

van Welie, M. & Trætteberg, H. [2000], Interaction Patterns in User Interfaces, *in Proceedings of the Pattern Languages of Programs Conference (PLoP2000)*, number wucs-00-29 *in* "Washington University Technical Report", Washington University. http://jerry.cs.uiuc.edu/~plop/plop2k/proceedings/Welie/Welie.pdf.

Verheijen, E. [1998], Sound Reproduction by Wave Field Synthesis, PhD thesis, TU Delft.

Walker, A., Brewster, S. & McGookin, S. A. [2001], Diary in the Sky: A Spatial Audio Display for a Mobile Calendar, *in* A. Blandford, J. Vanderdonckt & P. Gray (eds.), *People and Computers XV: Interaction without Frontiers (Joint Proceedings of HCI2001 and IHM2001)*, Springer-Verlag, pp.531–40.

Closing Keynote of HCI2005: The Bigger Picture

Grand Challenges in HCI: the Quest for Theory-led Design

Alistair Sutcliffe

Centre for HCI Design, School of Informatics, University of Manchester, PO Box 88, Manchester, UK

Tel: *+44 161 200 3315*

Email: *ags@manchester.ac.uk*

A grand challenge of theory-led design is proposed for HCI. The history and state of the art in HCI theory and knowledge is reviewed, expanding on Long & Dowell's conception of HCI. A new approach to bridging from theory to design practice is proposed that uses generic task models as a means of locating theory-based design advice. Theory-based knowledge is also transferred to design as bridging models and as critical cognitive aspects which are applied to task models. Design of specific applications uses theory-based knowledge via mappings to generic task models and by the application of bridging models. The approach is illustrated by a case study investigation of the design issues in notifier systems and explained with a design scenario of hospital patient monitoring.

Keywords: theory, cognitive models, claims, bridging representations.

1 Introduction

Grand challenges have been much in vogue in the computer science community [UKCRC 2005]; however, the computational emphasis in the grand challenges competition has sidelined HCI to a lip-service role in Memories for Life challenge. Fred Brooks [2003], however, was more enlightened and cites design of effective user interfaces as one of three major challenges for the 21st century. The HCI community should not be depressed by this outcome; instead, I argue it should propose more ambitious and wider ranging grand challenges of its own, and in doing so demonstrate that it has a broader ambition than computer science. In this paper I will propose and expound the challenge of Theory-led Design.

The development and application of theory is a sign of intellectual respect in most scientific or engineering disciplines, and HCI should be no exception. Long &

Dowell's conception of HCI as craft, science and engineering urged systematic development of principles, laws and guidelines derived from theory [Long & Dowell 1989; Dowell & Long 1998]. Barnard and colleagues in the AMODEUS project represent the most concerted effort to translate theory into design practice over several years. The cognitive theory of Interacting Cognitive Sub-Systems [Teasdale & Barnard 1993], in combination with more formal system modelling was proposed as a toolbox for designers [Barnard et al. 2000]. In restricted case studies, these models could be demonstrated to 'cohabit', i.e. applications of each model analysed different views on the same problem [Harrison & Barnard 1993]. However, a key problem has been how to translate knowledge in psychological theory into a form that is usable by designers. The task artefact theory has been proposed as a means of developing HCI knowledge [Carroll & Rosson 1992], using claims to express fragments for theory-based knowledge with contextual references to design problems, artefacts and scenarios [Sutcliffe 2000; Sutcliffe & Carroll 1999]. While claims continue to make modest progress [Carroll 2000; Sutcliffe et al. 2003], they have not as yet become widespread as a bridging representation between theory and design practice. The state of the art for HCI advice still remains as principles [Sutcliffe 2003; Dix et al. 2003], or golden rules [Shneiderman & Plaisant 2004] and the legion of, one suspects, under-used ISO guidelines [ISO 1997, 1998, 2000]. More recently HCI patterns have proliferated [Borchers 2001; Van Welie 2005], often without any validation. While patterns can express knowledge in a more contextualized manner, unless they are composed into a pattern language [Alexander et al. 1977], they can present incompatible, inconsistent and fragmentary pieces of HCI knowledge. The standardization process of developing an HCI pattern language has been slow to emerge and one can question whether it would be necessary since patterns duplicate much knowledge already present in better regulated sets of guidelines.

Some may consider development of exemplar artefacts as a more productive way to advance HCI. However, I believe that without theory, HCI will be doomed to the invention of stimulating yet ephemeral artefacts [e.g. Ishii et al. 2001] without generating generalized long-term knowledge. The thesis in this paper is to urge the HCI community to adopt the Science of Design [NSF 2004] and thereby become more than a sub-discipline of computer science. Instead, HCI can become the Science of User-Centred Technological Design. In the remainder of this paper, I will review the role of theory and HCI knowledge, and then propose an innovative approach based on a new role for familiar task models. This will be followed by application of the approach to investigate a particular area of attentive user interfaces, with a brief discussion to conclude the paper.

2   Theories and HCI Knowledge

HCI is not short of cognitive theories to apply to design; see for example ACT-R, [Anderson & Lebiere 1998], EPIC [Kieras & Meyer 1997] and LICAI [Kitajima & Polson 1997]. However, theories of cognition have proved difficult to apply in practice. They can be used to motivate experiments and demonstrate interesting and useful design phenomena, for example Hornoff's work on optimizing menu layout

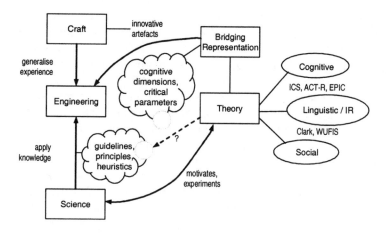

Figure 1: Long & Dowell's conception of HCI, revisited.

for efficient search, and eyetracking studies that demonstrate that banner adverts are not attended to or remembered but do impose subliminal cognitive cost [Burke et al. 2004]. This work uses EPIC as its theoretical lens. GOMS is the prime exemplar of applicable theory [John & Kieras 1995], and continues to be the focus of many studies although evidence of its effective use in industry is hard to find. A cut-down version of LICAI has been successfully developed in combination with an information searching algorithm (latent semantic indexing) in the CoLiDes systems that can predict design flaws in website navigation and link cues given a model of the user's search goals [Blackmon et al. 2003].

The quest for bridging models from theory to design was pursued with some vigour, first via design rationale, providing the glue to synthesize contributions from different modelling approaches [Bellotti et al. 1995], and more convincingly by developing Cognitive Task Models to analyse task sequences and diagnose potential design problems indicated by reasoning with the ICS cognitive architecture [Barnard et al. 2000]. Barnard, in his 1998 plenary address to this conference, proposed 'syndetic theory' and a blending of several theoretical influences that could be applied to design problems at different levels of granularity — micro and macro theory. Unfortunately, application of this approach to scaled-up industrial design problems has never been demonstrated.

Interest in theoretical approaches has continued in cut-down approaches such as the Resource Theory that proposes an event modelling view incorporating cognitive issues such as working memory and selective attention [Wright et al. 2000]. Interactors [Dix & Mancini 1998] provided an interesting approach for encapsulating HCI knowledge in what are essentially 'abstract interaction types' (cf. ADTs) as specifications or code for generic interactive functions, e.g. multi-level undo. More specialized approaches, such as Information Foraging Theory, continue to motivate research in information retrieval [Pirolli & Card 1999], while

Activity Theory [Nardi 1996] has been much in vogue as an analytic framework for ethnographic-style studies of CSCW and CMC systems. Although theory is being used, its prime role seems to be an indirect influence on design via analytic frameworks or general conceptual influences. For instance, it is difficult to extract prescriptive design advice from the concepts of conflict, activity level, artefacts and zone of proximal development in Activity Theory even though some have attempted to derive heuristics from such opaque theory [Bertelsen & Bødker 2003]. The range of applicable theory has been demonstrated by interest in theories of emotion [e.g. Ortony et al. 1988], as an inspiration to frame design questions [Norman 2004], and more directly as an embedded cognitive model to drive the emotional response that embodies conversational agents [Cassell et al. 1999]. So theory is far from dead, but the pathway for theory application in design research is fragmented, and more critically to design practice, is unclear. The status quo is summarized in Figure 1. The influence of theory-based research on design is tending to be recruited via the scientific route in Long & Dowell's framework, i.e. theory motivates experiments or case studies, the results of which provide design guidelines.

So is there a consensus of what has been achieved so far? In the majority of HCI text books, for example [Dix et al. 2003; Preece et al. 2002; Shneiderman & Plaisant 2004], theory is present as the Model Human Processor [Card et al. 1983], and as a bridging model in Norman's [1986] action cycle. What is missing is the meta-level guidance on how to exploit and develop theory in the design process: the grand challenge of theory-led design.

We need to return to the debate on bridging from theory to design. Some promising directions have emerged in cognitive dimensions [Green & Petre 1996] which propose principles for the design and evaluation initially of notations but more recently of interactive systems. Object system models [Connell et al. 2003] attempt to apply cognitive dimensions within design contexts for particular problems, while critical parameters focus attention on key cognitive requirements for interactive systems [Newman et al. 2000]. The important direction, I believe, is to focus on typical classes of problems which are common in HCI, understand the cognitive and social implications of those problem classes and then apply the appropriate theories to solving them. HCI needs to investigate tasks more deeply in order to understand the psychological implications of certain classes of problem. Take monitoring tasks as a specific example. Monitoring tasks are known to be error prone and people find it difficult to concentrate over long periods of time. The types of errors people make and their problem-solving strategies can be predicted using several theories [Norman 1988; Rasmussen 1986; Hollnagel 1998]. Human error theory predicts that interruptions and time pressures produce frequency and recency gambling pathologies resulting in sub-optimal problem-solving strategies [Reason 1990].

Monitoring tasks involve a perceptual process of recognizing significant events, cognitive processes of interpreting events, and domain knowledge to evaluate the significance of events in context. Norman's [1986] cycle of action can be reversed to set these issues in an interaction context; i.e. once a significant event has been recognized, interpreted, and evaluated one has to plan, specify and execute the appropriate response. The critical cognitive aspects of monitoring tasks are

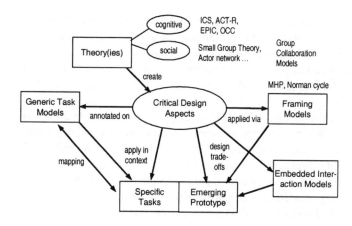

Figure 2: Process map of theory-led design.

selective attention and recognition of events, reasoning with domain knowledge to interpret the events and then planning appropriate responses. To develop effective support systems the designer has to understand the problem, isolate the critical cognitive aspects, then use the appropriate theories or experimental evidence to find appropriate solutions. This approach is summarized in Figure 2.

By linking theory to generic task models and bridging representations — be they cognitive dimensions, claims or critical parameters — a library of HCI knowledge can be built which enables effective reuse. Generic task models [Sutcliffe 2002] can play a key role by providing an access point from task analysis to reusable knowledge. If specific tasks could be mapped to generalized tasks, and if the latter are associated with theoretical, sound design advice, then designers will have advice placed in the context of their current problem. They still have to specialize the advice and reason about trade-offs but this is an advance on ploughing through libraries of design guidelines or patterns. However, generic task models need to be associated with 'critical aspects' to place theory in its application context. I have used the aspect oriented programming analogy since it illustrates the problem. Theory provides knowledge that is applicable in many parts of a design, i.e. cross-cutting concerns. The problem is to define the theory treatment for the aspect and when to apply it at 'point cuts' in the design. Linking critical aspects to generic task models indicates the point cuts, but defining the treatment is not so simple. This requires reasoning about trade-offs using bridging models. There is no silver bullet for producing high quality designs; however, theory-led design can make the bullet easier to aim. In the following section I will put this approach to the test with an exploration of design for notifier user interfaces, which support monitoring tasks.

3 Application of Theory-led Design

To illustrate how we should apply theory in HCI, I will investigate a current research area as a 'gedanken experiment'. Notifiers, attentional user interfaces or dual task displays have attracted considerable attention over recent years [Horvitz et al. 2003; McCrickard et al. 2003]. This research is motivated by a general user need, i.e. to enhance support for multitasking and to monitor information such as stock markets or the weather, while performing another primary task. The research problem is best encapsulated by a scenario. Marilyn, a senior staff nurse, is in charge of a chronic care ward and has to keep an eye on her patients during the night shift. The patients are automatically given medication via drips for management of chronic and post-operative conditions, e.g. pain relievers, anti-coagulants, etc. The patients' heart and respiratory rates and blood pressure are automatically monitored and displayed on a screen in Marilyn's office. She has to monitor patients' condition and adjust the rate of medication if the measured parameters depart from the expected treatment plan. More urgent alerts must be triggered if the patients experience distress which could be picked up by heart ECG sensors or an emergency call button which can be activated by patients. If all is quiet Marilyn is expected to catch up on the day's paper work to complete duty rosters, treatment records, etc.

Several approaches have been taken to this problem and many systems have been implemented which provide background monitoring displays as information tickers [Maglio & Campbell 2000], ambient wallpaper [Stasko et al. 2004] and radar metaphors to communicate the status of monitored information to the user [McCrickard & Chewar 2003]. However, these designs are based on intuition and give no guarantee of their effectiveness. Horvitz et al. [2003] have taken a more principled approach by proposing a cost of interruption measure expressed as the cost of diverting from the primary task compared with the benefit from the information gained from the monitoring tasks. This enables reasoning about when to interrupt using Bayesian networks with user defined valuation of the task activity, cost of interruption and environmental measures. Chewar et al. [2004] have elaborated this idea with a conceptual framework composed of three dimensions: Interruption, Reaction and Comprehension, that draws attention to the cognitive parameters of the problem, namely, when and how to alert the user to draw their attention away from the primary task, how to communicate information relevant to the secondary task and how to promote comprehension of such information. While these approaches are better than craft-level design, they do not constitute a theory-based approach.

To examine the problem in a more principled manner we have to understand the problem from a psychological viewpoint, and this is the first impact of theory: the ability to conceptualize interaction problems. The first part of the problem is alerting the users to relevant information for the secondary task. This poses the system initiative question. Should the monitored information be accessible to the user all the time, and hence possibly distracting from the primary task, or should it only be made available when the system decides it is critical for the user's interests? The second issue is how to ensure the user has seen or heard the critical information and responded to it. The third part of the problem is to support the user's transition from the primary task to the secondary task.

When to alert requires a model of the user's task, the user and the context. This is part of a user modelling grand challenge since acquiring a model of the user and their context requires solving the difficult problem of inferring complex states from

Cognitive Aspect	Problem	Environmental issues	Design Solutions
Perceptual issues	Stimulus salience for reliable response	Number of events, distractions, salience	Use audio, speech, animation
Selective Attention	Competitive demands of primary task and monitoring	Distractions, event frequency	Plan interleaving of task activity, alerts, aid memoirs
Reasoning level	Skill based errors — slips and lapses	Time limits, motivation, fatigue	Add reminders, layers of alerts with increasing salience
Working memory	Large number of monitored events/objects	Interruptions	External memory — information available on demand
Mental Model	Maintaining model of the domain	Complexity of domain	External memory-displays mirror domain, abstract views

Table 1: Cognitive task audit: Monitor and Evaluate tasks.

low-level data streams. I shall finesse this challenge and return to my main theme. Task analysis is the conventional HCI approach to understanding the user's domain [Diaper 2002; Johnson 1992]. While a goal model and procedural sequences can give us breakpoints where intervention should be more appropriate it doesn't go far enough. The cognitive demands of the primary task will influence when the user interface should signal an alert. The role of theory is to provide a cognitive audit so we can understand the critical aspects of a particular task and plan appropriate action. An example of the cognitive task audit is illustrated in Table 1. In the hospital patient monitoring scenario, working memory has to cope with keeping track of several patients while selective attention will be distributed between the several patient monitoring devices and the foreground tasks of updating drug registers and patient records. Reasoning will be rule-based using the nurse's training, but knowledge intensive judgement [Rasmussen 1986] will have to be applied when the unexpected happens.

A cognitive task audit requires application of general psychological knowledge to the task in question. While this does utilize theoretical knowledge, it does so only second hand via education. The designer has to know the theory in order to apply it in a cognitive task analysis. However, if a set of generic task models could be developed and annotated with cognitive aspects, then theoretical knowledge could be reused by non-HCI expert designers. A taxonomy of generic tasks exists [Sutcliffe 2002]; however, the process of mapping from specific task to these generic models, annotating them with cognitive properties and then applying such knowledge are open research questions.

Three tasks involved in the notifier problem are illustrated in Figure 3, showing the critical cognitive aspects. For recognition the salience and modality of the stimulus is important. This is set against environmental obstacles such as complexity of the environment and competing, similar stimuli. Precise design advice depends on knowledge of perceptual psychology [e.g. Ware 2000] which can not be encapsulated

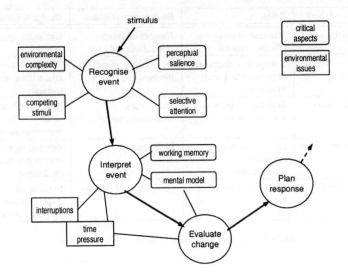

Figure 3: Monitor, Interpret and Evaluate generic tasks annotated with critical aspects and environment issues.

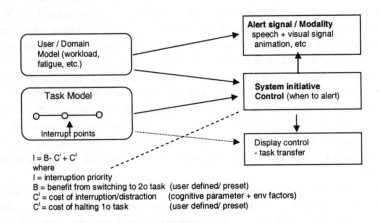

Figure 4: Components in the Embedded Interaction Model for system initiative control.

in simple models, although design principles for choice of media and modalities provide some guidance [Sutcliffe 2003]. These need to be combined knowledge critical aspects such as selective attention to understand possible problems arising from competing stimuli on the same modality, and the effect of distractions on the monitoring task. In the Interpret and Evaluate tasks the critical aspects point to the need to reduce working memory burden by supplying appropriate information for understanding the event within a display appropriate to the user's task and context.

Attention Resource Theory [Wickens 2002] can provide an appropriate framework for analysing the selective attention and when to intervene problem. This provides the basis for specifying an embedded cognitive model which predicts when to intervene, given a task model and monitored inputs of the user's activity. This embedded interaction model (see Figure 4) could be configured to other notifier systems, thereby contributing another conduit by which theory can influence design via reusable computational models that embed theory for solving interaction problems.

Knowledge of the salience of perceptual stimuli and how the stimulus properties affect attentional executive processing are necessary to design the alerting stimuli. Such knowledge is only partially formulated even in cognitive theory such as EPIC [Kieras & Meyer 1997] and experimental derived knowledge [Ware 2000], so the designer will have to use several sources to understand how the salience of stimuli interacts with users' knowledge and motivation in perceptual mechanism. This points to a need for new theoretical development. However, sufficient knowledge already exists to suggest a design solution for the appropriate alerting stimulus and modality. In our scenario, the alert will depend on the criticality of the information. If the monitored parameters stray out of a normal range but into a non-critical zone then a low-level stimulus will be used (e.g. colour change in the information display); whereas if parameters stray into a critical zone then more salient alerts, such as voice or sound coupled with visual highlighting, or animated displays, are required. Note that this design adaptation will also be driven by the embedded interaction model.

Applying theory also helps understanding how to manage the transition from the primary to a secondary task, although once again the task has a critical intermediary role. Marilyn has to monitor several stimuli, interpret the measurements and then decide on appropriate adjusting action. However, when an emergency occurs she has to rapidly interpret the event, diagnose the problem and take remedial action. In both cases her training will prepare her for the correct response. However, the patient-monitoring task is close to a skill and requires little reasoning; in contrast, responding to an emergency requires more conscious rule- and knowledge-based reasoning (Rasmussen, 1986). Diagnosis places different cognitive demands and hence requires information displays localizing the problem, while suggesting possible causes and remedial actions

The storyboard design that might be prompted by the application of theory-led design is illustrated in Figure 5.

The user's foreground task occupies most of the screen, as windows with Word and Excel that Marilyn uses for updating her records, writing reports and planning rosters. The monitor is placed on continuous display on the side of the screen, since change in the background monitored system is gradual so Marilyn can sample a patient's state on demand. A current and recent past display enables her to glance at the display and see if the state of any patient has changed in the recent time period. The display maps to rooms occupied by individual patients on the ward, with colour coding used for change in parameters: from green within normal range to red signalling a dangerous digression. Dangerous changes trigger an audio alarm and highlight the patient's location. The audio alarm uses canned speech messages

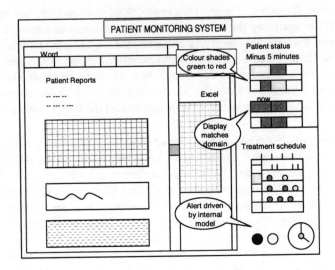

Figure 5: Storyboard design for the patient monitoring system.

which can be tailored to reinforce the message. Below the 'room map' display a time line gives the sequence of visits to check on condition, changes to medication, and reminders when periodic checks are due.

The above design decisions were motivated by several critical aspects. Use of a continuous display monitor was motivated by the periodic nature of the monitoring task and the cognitive aspect on reducing working memory burden. When to use an explicit alert used the embedded model to calculate the trade-off between the criticality of the event and the cost of interrupting the foreground task. Third was how to alert the user to change; a variety of strategies were indicated linking the strength of the stimulus to the criticality of the event. This used media design principles as well as knowledge of language theory and selective attention. The final design issue is how to make the transition between the foreground and background tasks. System actions are tuned to the criticality of the monitoring task. For low-level alerts the foreground task is automatically saved but no further action is taken apart from displaying more information on the critical patients. For critical alarms the work is saved, the Word and Excel windows are closed, and patient information is displayed with appropriate treatment suggestions for the individual concerned. In this case the system has made the transfer from supporting documentation to a diagnosis task.

4 Conclusions

This exercise in theory-led design proposed a solution via three complementary strands for applying theory to design: internalized knowledge of simplified psychological theory, reuse of knowledge located via mapping generic tasks applicable to the problem, and design of reusable embedded interaction models. It will always be difficult to separate the relative contribution to a design solution from internalized and tacitly applied theory, reusable knowledge, external guidance and advice. To an extent I argue for both as a necessary prerequisite for good design. My quest is to provide different pathways by which knowledge from theory can be applied to the design process. This is where I believe generic tasks and critical aspects can play their role, first as a retrieval mechanism and secondly as a method of structuring HCI to teach it in the first place.

It is germane to reflect whether this approach is really new. For example, application of Ecological Interface Design [Vicente 1999] could have led to the same metaphor domain representation of the patient monitor interface, although this method would not have provided advice on cognitive aspects of media selection. Claims and the task artefact cycle provide a similar access path to theory-based knowledge, which I have proposed as a precursor to this approach [Sutcliffe 2000]. In an extended schema [Sutcliffe & Carroll 1999] claims have been linked to generic task models and organized in taxonomies. Claims could therefore provide design advice for specific critical aspects. The critical aspects are not dissimilar to cognitive dimensions, and provide summaries of cognitive knowledge linked to a particular design concern [Green & Petre 1996]. Generic task models, embedded cognitive models and critical aspects supplement those views, but bring theory-based knowledge closer to the designer by providing a more direct mapping to tasks and design problems.

The example used in this paper has inevitably biased the focus towards cognitive theory and single user systems. The impact of social theory and critical aspects for collaborative systems has hardly been researched. For example are there critical aspects of shared identity, mutual awareness, collective motivation, the glue of social relationship as factors that influence the success of groups? So far we have but a few heuristics to use, although a more well formed theory, such as Small Groups as Complex Adaptive Systems [Arrow et al. 2000; Sutcliffe 2005] could provide more insight into theory-led design for collaborative systems.

In conclusion, theory will continue to play a vital role in design, not only in HCI but in the wider context of technology design, as computers become part of everyday products. The quest to translate theory into usable knowledge for design is still underway, and in this paper I have argued for a multi-path route via reuse of knowledge in the head and theory embedded in computation models, as well as localizing knowledge in a task context. This grand challenge has a wide-ranging scope as a general theoretical approach to design not only of computing related and computer embedded artefacts but to all designs that involve human interaction or use. HCI could transform itself into the Science of Design by rising to this challenge.

References

Alexander, C., Ishikawa, S., Silverstein, M., Jacobson, M., Fiksdahl-King, I. & Angel, S. [1977], *A Pattern Language: Towns, Buildings, Construction*, Oxford University Press.

Anderson, J. R. & Lebiere, C. [1998], *Representing Cognitive Activity in Complex Tasks*, Lawrence Erlbaum Associates.

Arrow, H., McGrath, J. E. & Berdahl, J. L. [2000], *Small Groups as Complex Systems: Formation, Coordination, Development and Adaptation*, Sage Publications.

Barnard, P., May, J., D, D. & Duce, D. [2000], Systems, Interactions and Macrotheory, *ACM Transactions on Computer–Human Interaction* **7**(2), 222–62.

Bellotti, V., Buckingham Shum, S., MacLean, A. & Hammond, N. [1995], Multidisciplinary Modelling in HCI Design: In Theory and in Practice, *in* I. Katz, R. Mack, L. Marks, M. B. Rosson & J. Nielsen (eds.), *Proceedings of the SIGCHI Conference on Human Factors in Computing Systems (CHI'95)*, ACM Press, pp.146–53.

Bertelsen, O. W. & Bødker, S. [2003], Activity Theory, *in* J. M. Carroll (ed.), *HCI Models, Theories and Frameworks: Toward a Multidisciplinary Science*, Morgan-Kaufmann, pp.291–324.

Blackmon, M. H., Kitajima, M. & Polson, P. G. [2003], Repairing Usability Problems Identified by the Cognitive Walkthrough for the Web, *in* V. Bellotti, T. Erickson, G. Cockton & P. Korhonen (eds.), *Proceedings of SIGCHI Conference on Human Factors in Computing Systems (CHI'03)*, *CHI Letters* **5**(1), ACM Press, pp.497–504.

Borchers, J. [2001], *A Pattern Approach to Interaction Design*, John Wiley & Sons.

Brooks, F. P. [2003], Three Grand Challenges for Half Century Old Computer Science, *Journal of the ACM* **50**(10), 25–6.

Burke, M., Gorman, N., Nilsen, E. & Hornof, A. [2004], Banner Ads Hinder Visual Search and Are Forgotten, *in* E. Dykstra-Erickson & M. Tscheligi (eds.), *CHI'04 Extended Abstracts of the Conference on Human Factors in Computing Systems*, ACM Press, pp.1139–42.

Card, S. K., Moran, T. P. & Newell, A. [1983], *The Psychology of Human–Computer Interaction*, Lawrence Erlbaum Associates.

Carroll, J. M. [2000], *Making Use: Scenario-based Design of Human–Computer Interactions*, MIT Press.

Carroll, J. M. & Rosson, M. B. [1992], Getting Around the Task–Artefact Framework: How to Make Claims and Design by Scenario, *ACM Transactions on Office Information Systems* **10**(2), 181–212.

Cassell, J., Bickmore, J., Billinghurst, M., Campbell, L., Chang, K., Vilhjalmsson, H. & Yan, H. [1999], Embodiment in Conversational Interfaces: REA, *in* M. G. Williams & M. W. Altom (eds.), *Proceedings of the SIGCHI Conference on Human Factors in Computing Systems: The CHI is the Limit (CHI'99)*, ACM Press, pp.520–7.

Chewar, C. M., McCrickard, D. S. & Sutcliffe, A. G. [2004], Unpacking Critical Parameters for Interface Design: Evaluating Notification Systems with the IRC, *in* D. Gruen & I. McAra-McWilliams (eds.), *Proceedings of the Symposium on Designing Interactive Systems: Processes, Practices, Methods and Techniques (DIS'04)*, ACM Press, pp.279–88.

Connell, I., Green, T. R. G. & Blandford, A. [2003], Ontological Sketch Models: Highlighting User-system Misfits, *in* E. O'Neill, P. Palanque & P. Johnson (eds.), *People and Computers XVII: Designing for Society (Proceedings of HCI'03)*, Springer-Verlag, pp.163–78.

Diaper, D. [2002], Tasks, Scenarios and Thought, *Interacting with Computers* **15**(4), 629–38.

Dix, A., Finlay, J., Abowd, G. D. & Beale, R. [2003], *Human–Computer Interaction*, third edition, Prentice–Hall.

Dix, A. & Mancini, R. [1998], Specifying History and Back Tracking Mechanisms, *in Formal Methods in Human–Computer Interaction*, Formal Approaches to Computing and Information Technology, Springer-Verlag, Chapter 1, pp.1–23.

Dowell, J. & Long, J. B. [1998], Conception of the Cognitive Engineering Design Problem, *Ergonomics* **41**(2), 126–39.

Green, T. R. G. & Petre, M. [1996], Usability Analysis of Visual Programming Environments: A 'Cognitive Dimensions' Framework, *Journal of Visual Languages and Computing* **7**(2), 131–74.

Harrison, M. D. & Barnard, P. J. [1993], On Defining the Requirements for Interaction, *in* S. Fickas & A. Finkelstein (eds.), *Proceedings of the IEEE International Symposium on Requirements Engineering (RE'93)*, IEEE Computer Society Press, pp.50–5.

Hollnagel, E. [1998], *Cognitive Reliability and Error Analysis Method (CREAM)*, Elsevier.

Horvitz, E., Kadie, C. M., Paek, T. & Hovel, D. [2003], Models of Attention in Computing and Communications: From Principles to Application, *Communications of the ACM* **46**(3), 52–9.

Ishii, H., Mazalek, A. & Lee, J. [2001], Bottles as a Minimal Interface to Access Digital Information, *in* J. A. Jacko & A. Sears (eds.), *CHI'01 Extended Abstracts of the Conference on Human Factors in Computing Systems*, ACM Press, pp.187–8.

ISO [1997], ISO 9241 International Standard. Ergonomic Requirements for Office Systems with Visual Display Terminals (VDTs). International Organization for Standardization, Genève, Switzerland.

ISO [1998], ISO 14915 International Standard. Multimedia User Interface Design Software Ergonomic Requirements — Part 1: Introduction and Framework. International Organization for Standardization, Genève, Switzerland.

ISO [2000], ISO 14915 International Standard. Multimedia User Interface Design Software Ergonomic Requirements — Part 3: Media Combination and Selection. International Organization for Standardization, Genève, Switzerland.

John, B. E. & Kieras, R. E. [1995], The GOMS Family of User Interface Analysis Techniques: Comparison and Contrast, *ACM Transactions on Computer–Human Interaction* **3**(4), 320–51.

Johnson, P. [1992], *Human–Computer Interaction: Psychology, Task Analysis and Software Engineering*, McGraw-Hill.

Kieras, D. E. & Meyer, D. E. [1997], An Overview of the EPIC Architecture for Cognition and Performance with Application to Human–Computer Interaction, *Human–Computer Interaction* **12**(4), 391–438.

Kitajima, M. & Polson, P. G. [1997], A Comprehension-based Model of Exploration, *Human–Computer Interaction* **12**(4), 345–89.

Long, J. & Dowell, J. [1989], Conceptions of the Discipline of HCI: Craft, Applied Science and Engineering, *in* A. Sutcliffe & L. Macaulay (eds.), *People and Computers V (Proceedings of HCI'89)*, Cambridge University Press, pp.9–34.

Maglio, P. P. & Campbell, C. S. [2000], Trade-offs in Displaying Peripheral Information, *in* T. Turner & G. Szwillus (eds.), *Proceedings of the SIGCHI Conference on Human Factors in Computing Systems (CHI'00)*, *CHI Letters* **2**(1), ACM Press, pp.241–8.

McCrickard, D. S., Catrambone, R., Chewar, C. M. & Stasko, J. T. [2003], Establishing Tradeoffs that Leverage Attention for Utility: Empirically Evaluating Information Display in Notification Systems, *International Journal of Human–Computer Studies* **58**(5), 547–82.

McCrickard, D. S. & Chewar, C. M. [2003], Attuning Notification Design to User Goals and Attention Costs, *Communications of the ACM* **46**(3), 67–72.

Nardi, B. A. (ed.) [1996], *Context and Consciousness: Activity Theory and Human–Computer Interaction*, MIT Press.

Newman, W. M., Taylor, A. S., Dance, C. R. & Taylor, S. A. [2000], Performance Targets, Model and Innovation in Design of Interactive Systems, *in* D. Boyarski & W. A. Kellogg (eds.), *Proceedings of the Symposium on Designing Interactive Systems: Processes, Practices, Methods and Techniques (DIS2000)*, ACM Press, pp.381–7.

Norman, D. A. [1986], Cognitive Engineering, *in* D. A. Norman & S. W. Draper (eds.), *User Centered System Design: New Perspectives on Human–Computer Interaction*, Lawrence Erlbaum Associates, pp.31–62.

Norman, D. A. [1988], *The Psychology of Everyday Things*, Basic Books.

Norman, D. A. [2004], *Emotional Design: Why We Love (or Hate) Everyday Things*, Basic Books.

NSF [2004], Science of Design, http://www.nsf.gov/funding/pgm_summ.jsp?pims_id=12766 (last accessed 2005-04-26). National Science Foundation: Directorate for Computer & Information Science & Engineering.

Ortony, A., Clore, G. L. & Collins, A. [1988], *The Cognitive Structure of Emotions*, Cambridge University Press.

Pirolli, P. & Card, S. [1999], Information Foraging, *Psychological Review* **106**(4), 643–75.

Preece, J., Rogers, Y. & Sharp, H. (eds.) [2002], *Interaction Design: Beyond Human–Computer Interaction*, John Wiley & Sons.

Rasmussen, J. [1986], *Information Processing and Human–Machine Interaction: An Approach to Cognitive Engineering*, North-Holland.

Reason, J. [1990], *Human Error*, Cambridge University Press.

Shneiderman, B. & Plaisant, C. [2004], *Designing the User Interface: Strategies for Effective Interaction*, fourth edition, Addison–Wesley.

Stasko, J., Miller, T., Pousman, Z., Plaue, C. & Ullah, O. [2004], Personalized Peripheral Information Awareness through Information Art, *in* N. Davies, E. Mynatt & I. Siio (eds.), *UbiComp 2004: Ubiquitous Computing (Proceedings of the Sixth International Conference on Ubiquitous Computing)*, Vol. 3205 of *Lecture Notes in Computer Science*, Springer, pp.18–35.

Sutcliffe, A. G. [2000], On the Effective Use and Reuse of HCI Knowledge, *ACM Transactions on Computer–Human Interaction* **7**(2), 197–221.

Sutcliffe, A. G. [2002], *The Domain Theory: Patterns for Knowledge and Software Reuse*, Lawrence Erlbaum Associates.

Sutcliffe, A. G. [2003], *Multimedia and Virtual Reality: Designing Multisensory User Interfaces*, Lawrence Erlbaum Associates.

Sutcliffe, A. G. [2005], Extending Small Group Theory for Analysing Complex Systems, *in* C. W. Johnson (ed.), *Proceedings of the Workshop on Complexity in Design and Engineering*, Department of Computer Science, University of Glasgow, pp.139–48. GIST Report 2005-1.

Sutcliffe, A. G., Fickas, S., Sohlberg, M. M. & Ehlhardt, L. A. [2003], Investigating the Usability of Assistive User Interfaces, *Interacting with Computers* **15**(4), 577–601.

Sutcliffe, A. G. & Carroll, J. M. [1999], Designing Claims for Reuse in Interactive Systems Design, *International Journal of Human–Computer Interaction* **50**(3), 213–42.

Teasdale, J. D. & Barnard, P. J. [1993], *Affect, Cognition and Change: Re-modelling Depressive Thought*, Lawrence Erlbaum Associates.

UKCRC [2005], Grand Challenges for Computing Research, http://www.ukcrc.org.uk/grand_challenges/index.cfm (last accessed 2005-04-26). UK Computing Research Committee.

Van Welie, M. [2005], Patterns in Interaction Design: Web Design Patterns, http://www.welie.com/patterns (last accessed 2005-04-26).

Vicente, K. J. [1999], *Cognitive Work Analysis: Towards Safe, Productive and Healthy Computer-based Work*, Lawrence Erlbaum Associates.

Ware, C. [2000], *Information Visualization: Perception for Design*, Morgan-Kaufmann.

Wickens, C. [2002], Multiple Resources and Performance Prediction, *Theoretical Issues in Ergonomics Science* **3**(2), 150–77.

Wright, P. C., Fields, R. E. & Harrison, M. D. [2000], Analysing Human–Computer Interaction as Distributed Cognition: The Resources Model, *Human–Computer Interaction* **15**(1), 1–41.

Author Index

Keyword Index